Caledonian Wagons
and
Non-Passenger Coaching Stock

Frontispiece
A scene inside Aberdeen goods shed. On the left-hand track are two outside framed Diagram 67 10-ton goods vans. In the distance, the two trumpet ventilators suggest a Diagram 1 meat van. On the middle track are two drop-side goods wagons, which, Caledonian-owned, are to Diagram 15. The open goods wagons bearing a number which looks like 796 or 798 is a GNSR 10-ton open goods wagon. It may have a door on the left-hand side only. This was a common arrangement on the GNSR. Standing on the right-hand track are two flush-sided Diagram 67 vans, separated by a horizontally-boarded van to Diagram 3. The Diagram 67 van further away from the photographer has a roof door. Behind it is a pre-diagram book 6-ton CR van.

Caledonian Wagons
and
Non-Passenger Coaching Stock

Mike Williams

Lightmoor Press & the Caledonian Railway Association

Contents

Chapter 1: Introduction and Sources of Information
- 1.1: Introduction 7
- 1.2: Sources of Information – The Caledonian Railway 9
- 1.3: Sources of Information – Outside Contractors 13
- 1.4: Sources of Information – The Technical and Enthusiast's Press 15

Chapter 2: The Growth and Development of the Wagon Fleet
- 2.1: Commercial Influences and Infrastructure 17
- 2.2: Types of Wagon and Numbers in Service 29
- 2.3: Technical Development – Historical Overview 33
- 2.4: Running Gear 35
- 2.5: Brakes 39
- 2.6: Buffers and Drawgear 41

Chapter 3: Wagon Livery and Numbering
- 3.1: Livery 47
- 3.2: Letter and Number Styles 51
- 3.3: Location of Letters and Painted Numbers 59
- 3.4: Cast Number and Builder's Plates 67
- 3.5: Allocation of Numbers 69

Chapter 4: Non-Passenger Coaching Stock Livery and Numbering
- 4.1: The NPCS Livery 73
- 4.2: NPCS in Passenger Livery 77
- 4.3: Lettering and Numerals 79
- 4.4: Allocation of Numbers 81

Chapter 5: General Mineral Wagons
- 5.1: Introduction 83
- 5.2: The Early 'Bogies' 85
- 5.3: Four-Wheeled Wagon Development 1883-1899 89
- 5.4: Bogie Mineral Wagons 93
- 5.5: Four-Wheeled Wagon Development Post 1900 99

Chapter 6: Specialised Mineral Wagons
- 6.1: Hopper Wagons 107
- 6.2: Coke 111
- 6.3: Pig Iron Wagons 113

Chapter 7: Private Traders' Wagons
- 7.1: Wagons Owned by Private Traders 117
- 7.2: Thirled Wagons 121
- 7.3: Tank Wagons 123

Chapter 8: Steel, Timber and Stone Wagons
- 8.1: Four- and Six-Wheeled Rail and Tube Wagons 125
- 8.2: Timber and Swivel Wagons 131
- 8.3: Twin Wagons 137
- 8.4: Stone Wagons 141

Chapter 9: Ordinary Goods Wagons and Vans
- 9.1: Open Goods 143
- 9.2: Covered Goods 151
- 9.3: Empty Barrel Trucks 163
- 9.4: Road Vans 165

Chapter 10: Perishable Goods
- 10.1: Meat Vans 167
- 10.2: Fish, Fruit and Milk 173

Chapter 11: Livestock Wagons
- 11.1: Cattle ... 183
- 11.2: Sheep and Other Livestock ... 191
- 11.3: Horses ... 193

Chapter 12: Carriage and Scenery Trucks
- 12.1: Open Carriage Trucks ... 199
- 12.2: Covered Carriage Trucks ... 203
- 12.3: Scenery Trucks ... 207

Chapter 13: Special Class Wagons – The Trollies
- 13.1: Introduction and Pre-Diagram Book Designs ... 209
- 13.2: Trollies with 18/20-foot Wells ... 211
- 13.3: Trollies with 25-foot Wells ... 213
- 13.4: Trollies with 35/40-foot Wells ... 215

Chapter 14: Other Special Class Bogie Wagons
- 14.1: Bogie Rail and Swivel Bar Wagons ... 219
- 14.2: Glass and Well Wagons ... 221
- 14.3: Flat Wagons ... 223
- 14.4: Heavy Weight and Ingot Wagons ... 225
- 14.5: Gun Sets and Warflats ... 227

Chapter 15: Four- and Six-Wheeled Special Class Wagons
- 15.1: Glass Well Wagons ... 229
- 15.2: Locomotive and Boiler Wagons ... 231
- 15.3: Machinery and Agricultural Implement Wagons ... 233
- 15.4: Flat Wagons and Runners ... 237
- 15.5: Swivel Bar and Heavy Weight Wagons ... 239
- 15.6: Gunpowder Vans ... 241

Chapter 16: Goods and Mineral Brake Vans
- 16.1: Four-Wheeled Brake Vans and Wagons ... 243
- 16.2: Six-Wheeled Brake Vans ... 255

Chapter 17: Service Vehicles
- 17.1: Loco Coal and Ash ... 257
- 17.2: Ballast Wagons ... 265
- 17.3: Ballast Brakes ... 269
- 17.4: Gas Tanks ... 271
- 17.5: Tank Wagons ... 273
- 17.6: Breakdown Cranes and Associated Vehicles ... 275
- 17.7: Engineer's Department Vehicles ... 281

Appendices
- I: Types of Wagon and Numbers in Service ... 285
- II: St. Rollox Wagon and Service Vehicle Orders ... 287
- III: St. Rollox Non-Passenger Coaching Stock Orders ... 297
- IV: Known Orders Placed with Contractors ... 299
- V: St. Rollox and Contractors' Wagon and NPCS Drawings ... 305
- VI: Photographs in the 1900 Register of Wagon Plant ... 313
- VII: Information for the Modeller ... 315

Index ... 319

Published by LIGHTMOOR PRESS in conjunction with the CALEDONIAN RAILWAY ASSOCIATION
© Mike Williams, Lightmoor Press and the Caledonian Railway Association 2013
Designed by Nigel Nicholson. Cover design by Neil Parkhouse

British Library Cataloguing-in-Publication Data. A catalogue record for this book is available from the British Library
ISBN 9781 899889 74 7
All rights reserved. No part of this publication may be reproduced, stored in a retrieval system or transmitted in any form or by any means, electronic, mechanical, photocopying, recording or otherwise, without the written permission of the publisher

LIGHTMOOR PRESS
Unit 144B, Lydney Trading Estate, Harbour Road, Lydney, Gloucestershire GL15 5EJ
www.lightmoor.co.uk
Lightmoor Press is an imprint of Black Dwarf Lightmoor Publications Ltd.
Printed by Berforts Information Press, Eynsham, Oxford

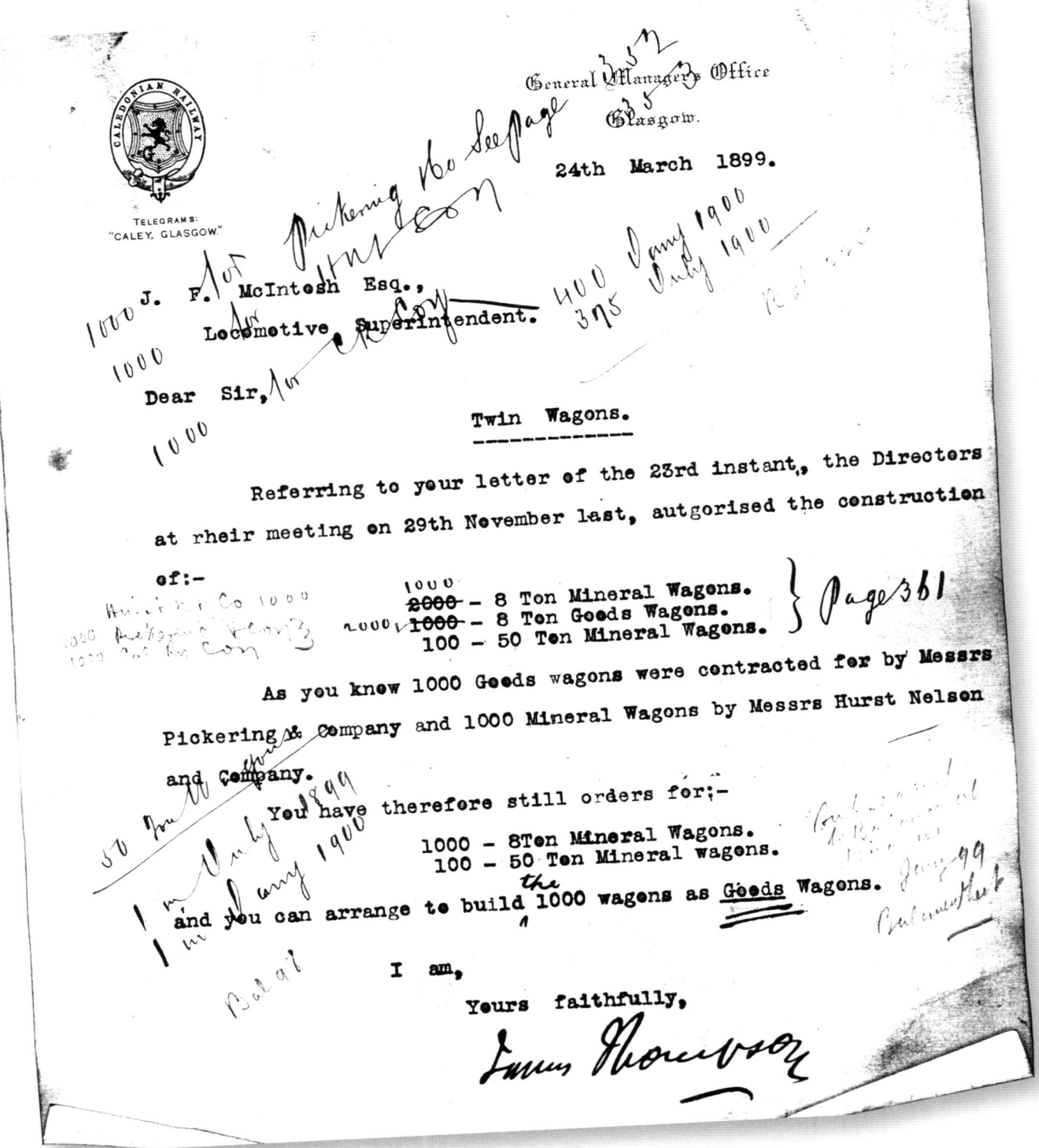

Plate 1.1
An example of the memos collected in the wagon renewal programme volumes. It is of particular interest because the original decision to build 100 50-ton ore wagons has been amended in the bottom left corner to one each in the periods ending July 1899 and January 1900. In the event only one 50-ton wagon was built and the other wagon appeared as the prototype Diagram 51 16-tonner. The 1,000 goods wagons outstanding were built to Diagram 24, order G176.

Chapter 1
Introduction and Sources of Information

1.1: Introduction

This book attempts to make sense of a complicated subject which has never before been studied in depth. It is part of a growing canon of work commissioned by the Caledonian Railway Association (CRA), which is registered in Scotland as an educational charity.

The book's primary aim is to record the scale and diversity of the wagon fleet owned by Scotland's major railway. As such, the author hopes that it will interest students of railway history in general and wagons in particular, as well as those whose interest is the Caledonian. Its second aim is to help modellers to make authentic replicas of Caledonian Railway (CR) goods and non-passenger coaching stock and to run them in typical formations.

Statements of fact are based on documentary evidence. Not unexpectedly for a railway that was born over 160 years ago and was merged into the LM&SR nearly ninety years from the time of writing, full documentation does not exist. To present as complete a picture as possible therefore requires reasonable supposition. Where deductions and interpretations are made, they are identified as such, and supporting reasons are given.

Structure of the Book

Chapter 1 deals with the sources of information which provided material for the book. It has three purposes. First, it serves as a bibliography. Second, it gives the reader an insight into the rich material that is available concerning a railway that ceased to exist three generations ago. Last, it may encourage students of rolling stock to delve still further and add to the information presented in this book.

The next chapter sets the scene. It deals with the commercial and industrial development of the area served by the Caledonian and its impact on the number and types of wagons in service. It also discusses some of the developments in railway infrastructure that were necessary to cope with the huge increase in traffic. It then describes the technical development of the CR wagon fleet, beginning with a brief historical overview.

The following two chapters deal with livery. Chapter 3 discusses the painting, lettering and numbering of goods stock. Non-Passenger Coaching Stock (NPCS) is dealt with similarly in Chapter 4. These chapters develop in more detail the overview set out in the chapter in *Caledonian Railway Livery*.[1]

From Chapter 5 onwards, the different types and designs of Caledonian wagons are discussed in detail. The chapters follow a common format. The development of each type of wagon is described in chronological order, with, where possible, the number of wagons built and when.

The basic division in the narrative is between wagons designed before and after 1882. Most, but not all, of the post-1882 wagon types were recorded in official wagon diagram books. The pre-diagram book wagons are described first. The description takes the form of a potted history of wagon development, cross-referenced to works drawings. Many of these early drawings have not survived; those that have are given their archive references in Appendix V for ease of further study.

Footnotes

Each sub-section concludes with a paragraph of references to source material. Primary sources, that is, original documents, have been used wherever possible. Secondary sources are clearly identified as such, and their use is justified in each case.

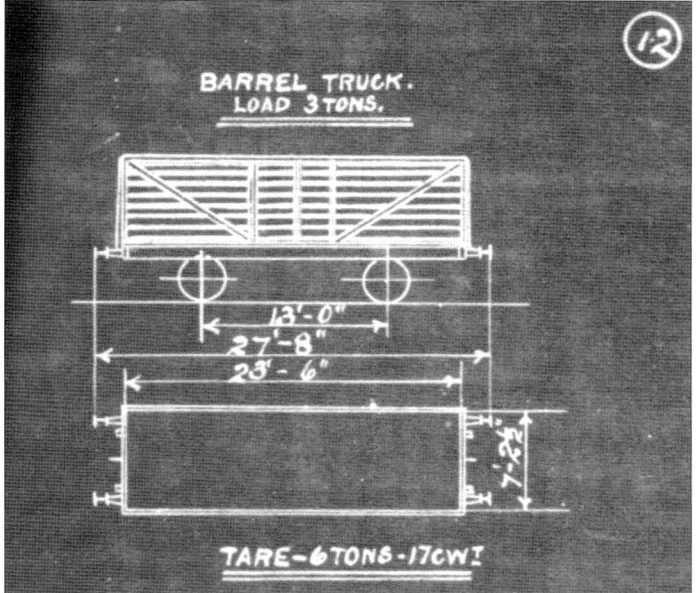

Above: Plate 1.2
These plates are reproduced from the small CR wagon diagram book. This sketch of the first type of empty barrel truck appears on page 12. This is a good quality drawing to a fairly large size.

Below: Plate 1.3
This is a poorer quality page showing a much larger wagon, which results in a smaller, harder to read, drawing. The St. Rollox order number G141 has been appended.

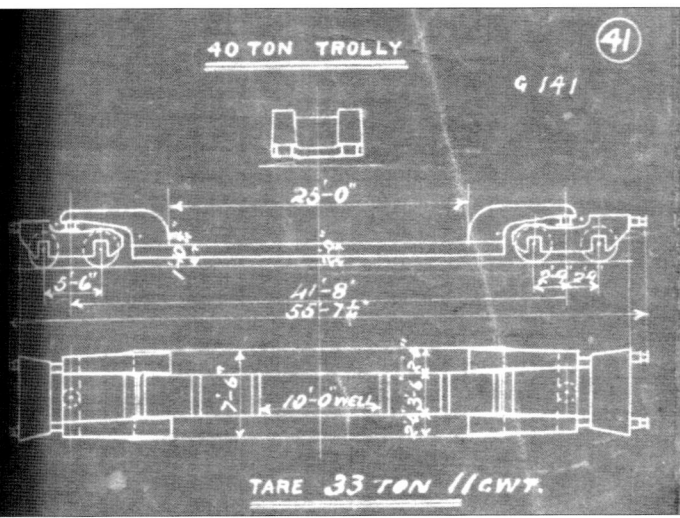

Photographs and Drawings

An attempt has been made to provide a photograph of every type of wagon described in the text. This has not proved possible, but over 90 per cent of the subjects are covered. Some of the photographs will be familiar to enthusiasts of the Caley, but every effort has been made to show pictures that have not been widely published. There are even some photographs of wagon types which cannot be related to what is known to have been built. Some photographs of complete goods trains and goods traffic infrastructure have also been included.

A selection of drawings issued by St. Rollox works and contractors will be found throughout the book. Some have been selected to compensate for the lack of a photograph of a particular wagon type. Others have been chosen because they record significant developments in the wagon fleet.

Most of the drawings were made at 1½ inches to the foot, so there is inevitably some loss of detail when they have been reduced to fit the page. As will be seen, some drawings are also in poor condition, which has further affected the quality of reproduction. They are nevertheless valuable source material which has not previously been published.

Appendices

Seven appendices contain a summary of information useful to the wagon researcher and modeller. Appendix I gives details of the wagons in service in 1874 as reported by two independent valuers, and the changes in the fleet's composition between 1907 and 1910. This supplements the information in Chapter 2. Appendices II and III deal with wagon and non-passenger coaching stock orders built by the Caledonian at St. Rollox works. Appendix IV records known wagon and NPCS orders built by outside contractors.

Appendix V lists the surviving St. Rollox and contractors' drawings, and their archive reference numbers. Appendix VI lists the wagon photographs collected in 1900 for the *Register of Wagon Plant*. It cross-references the photographs to diagram book numbers, and lists the plate number for those illustrated in this book. Finally, Appendix VII contains the list of wagon drawings for the modeller, and some specially commissioned drawings of characteristic Caley wagon details.

Acknowledgements

Books of this nature cannot be written without material help and perhaps more importantly encouragement, constructive criticism and counsel.

Archive staff at the following locations have kindly given access over a number of years to material, before, indeed, I knew that I was writing the book:

- National Records of Scotland, formerly National Archives of Scotland
- National Railway Museum
- Birmingham City Archives
- The Historical Model Railway Society

Two archives deserve special thanks. The Glasgow University Business Archive holds the Caledonian Railway Association Archive, as well as the order books and despatch records of R Y Pickering. At the time of writing, The Ballast Trust was working on the CRA's drawing collection and was also cataloguing a large number of St. Rollox drawings from the National Records of Scotland archive which had not been accessible in the past.

The freedom to browse in both these archives has led to many insights, especially about early wagon development, and saved a great deal of time. Thanks in particular to Andrew Swan, who made his catalogue entries of wagons available. This proved a valuable cross-reference source, and has cast new light on the development of the standard mineral and goods van designs of the early twentieth century.

Members of the Caledonian Railway Association have contributed generously from their collections of photographs, drawings and information. My thanks go especially to Angus McIntosh, who has produced a series of drawings based on often very poor quality originals that describe technical developments in CR wagon design, and record detail information which should be useful to the modeller. Ronnie Cockburn deserves a special mention for his work in collating CR wagon numbers and for compiling the transcription of the *Coaching and Non-Passenger Coaching Stock Register*. The wagon number list is being updated and should soon be available from the CRA website

Two other CRA members deserve special thanks. In late 2005, Tony Brenchley, a long time modelling colleague, published a proposal in *The True Line* for a series of guides for enthusiasts who wished to make authentic models of Caledonian Railway subjects. I volunteered to write the wagon book, and Tony provided me with a draft that he had started.

Some interest was shown in Tony's proposal, but little tangible was forthcoming. In 2009 the CRA committee decided to do something positive about *Modelling the Caley*, which had become the series title. The concept was for a series of part works, each about thirty pages long. At the 2009 AGM Jim Summers and I volunteered to start things off with signalling and wagons respectively. We both found quite quickly that the material available justified bigger publications than envisaged.

When, part-way through 2010, the wagon material had swollen to about fifty pages of text, some advice was needed – enter Jim MacIntosh. After talking with him, it was agreed that I should use what I had written as the basis for a history of CR wagons. Jim had written of the need for such a book in *Caledonian Railway Livery*.[1] Non-passenger coaching stock would be covered, as these vehicles were included in the wagon diagram book.

Without Jim's generous help and encouragement, I would still be writing this book in 2013. He has given me free access to material from his own researches which would have taken an inordinate amount of time (and expense) to extract from the original archive sources. He has made many helpful suggestions along the way, and read the draft manuscript – some parts more than once.

Finally, thanks to the CRA's publisher, Neil Parkhouse of Black Dwarf Lightmoor. He agreed, along with Jim, that the material should not be stinted in any way and that the illustrations and drawings should be commensurate with that aim. He and his team take all the credit for amalgamating the raw text and the collection of pictures and captions into the volume you are now reading.

Errors and Omissions

However hard one tries, there will be errors and misinterpretations when dealing with the wealth of material and the complex history of 80 years of wagon development. These are all my own work! There are several places in the text which leave loose ends. No doubt too, there is still information that has not yet come to light. Anyone with additional material or factual evidence that will add to the story of CR wagons is encouraged to get in touch via the Caledonian Railway Association. Significant information will be made available through the website.

References

1. By Jim MacIntosh, published in 2008 by Lightmoor Press in conjunction with the Caledonian Railway Association

1.2: Sources of Information – The Caledonian Railway

This section sets out the sources of information from the Caledonian Railway used in compiling the book. It is not a complete list of the surviving information, which can be accessed from the National Records of Scotland website. Some items can be also be consulted in the Caledonian Railway Association Archive.

Board and Committee Minutes

The full set of *Minutes of Meetings of Directors and Committees* starting in 1844 and continuing to 1923 is in the National Records of Scotland archive.[1] The volumes include decisions concerning the Locomotive & Stores and Traffic committees which dealt with rolling stock, either as renewals (paid for out of revenue) or capital expenditure. A similar set of officers' minutes is not known to have survived. Many of the decisions taken about modifications to wagons would have been taken at this level. Some of the loose ends left in this book, where there is no minuted record, would no doubt be tied up if the volumes ever became accessible.

The amount and detail of information in the existing minutes is uneven. In the early years reports on new rolling stock requirements are recorded as *'read and approved.'* Details are sketchy, and refer mainly to tenders let to outside contractors. From about 1890 onwards, the minutes are detailed enough to relate to specific orders for rolling stock, built either by St. Rollox or contractors. The half year ending 31st January 1893 was the first time that proposed rolling stock renewals were set out in detailed form. The situation becomes less clear again from 1918 to the Grouping, where totals of stock, but not the types, are mentioned.

There was a delay between authorisation and construction. In the early years of Drummond's tenure, the six-monthly programme was agreed immediately before the start of the period. By 1895, the go-ahead was given earlier, typically two months in advance. By 1900, the decision was taken earlier still. For instance, the programme for the half year which began on 1st August was agreed on 23rd March 1901. This typical timetable continued up to the end of the Caledonian's existence.

In Appendices II-IV, which record St. Rollox and contractors' orders, the authorisation date is given where known. The date that an order of wagons was actually put into service could be anything between nine and fifteen months later.

Plant built to the capital account was added to the balance sheet on the final day of the accounting period, which further extended the elapsed time from authorisation.

The minutes also record events such as the sale of old wagons and the fitting of dual brakes and steam heat pipes to non-passenger coaching stock. All these are grist to the mill of the rolling stock historian.

Indices to each volume show entries by subject matter. Even then, copying the relevant information would be a formidable task, but it has already been done. Jim MacIntosh extracted the relevant information some years ago, *'to develop a comprehensive record of the Goods and Mineral Wagons built by the Company over the period 1845 to 1923.'* The extracts can be downloaded from the Caledonian Railway Association Archive catalogue.[2]

The Wagon Renewal Programme

From 1903, the Caledonian embarked on a wagon renewal programme and a record was kept of the orders authorised by the Traffic Committee. Most of the wagons were charged to the revenue account, with a small minority regarded as capital expenditure. Committee meetings were held every six months and authorised renewals for the following half year. The Committee decisions were communicated to operating staff by memo, usually the day after the meeting. An example is shown in Plate 1.1.

These memos were collated into two volumes. The first volume runs to 1918.[3] The three half years ending January 1911, December 1914 and January 1918 are missing. The wagons authorised for 1911 and 1914 are however detailed in the board and committee minutes. It is possible that no wagons were authorised in 1918, which would account for the omission.

The second volume[4] continues to the Grouping. The information in this volume is complicated by alternative scenarios which were presented, dependent on government approval towards the end of, and after, the First World War, when all railways were under national control. These difficulties are discussed in Chapter 2.2.

References to these volumes have not been made in the text where they duplicate those made in company minutes. They have only been used if they add to or amplify facts in the main minutes.

Rolling Stock Returns and Censuses

Information about rolling stock changes was provided at six-monthly intervals for the shareholders of the Caledonian. Copies are held at the National Records of Scotland and the National Archive at Kew.[5]

The wagon and non-passenger coaching stock part of the returns records gives the following typical information. The example is for the half year ending July 1873. The wagon types varied according to what was added or withdrawn in any period.

Wagon Type	Worn Out	Replaced	Added
Ordinary	234	109	
Covered Vans	12	3	
Cattle	22	14	
Sheep	7		
Brake Vans	3	6	
Swivel	3	4	49
Mineral	106	106	1915
Ballast	6	1	
Horse Box	1		
Carriage Truck	2		

Statistics from these returns have been used to estimate the number of wagons built, particularly in the early days, when minute entries are scanty. The returns have also been used where possible to verify whether wagons were built to the capital or revenue accounts.

Another set of returns used the same shareholders' information to give the number of wagons in stock for the years 1868 to 1910 and, in more detail, the types of wagons in use in each July over the four years 1907 to 1910. The information formed part of *Miscellaneous Statements re Traders' and Other Wagons 1909-1910*.[6] The statements were produced as submissions to the Railway & Canal Commission Hearings of 1910, which was set to arbitrate on a dispute over demurrage between the Scottish railway companies and coal masters. The details in these returns are part of Chapter 2 and Appendix I. The *Miscellaneous Statements* book also contains information on the number of private traders' wagons running on the Caledonian system from 1867 to 1910.

Wagon Diagram Books

Various diagram books of CR wagons have survived. Every surviving copy (large and small) is different and the only printed date (1898) is on one copy of the large diagram book of carriages, vans and trucks. The date has been scored out as this particular copy of the book has clearly been updated.

The small CR book records the designs of wagon and non-passenger coaching stock built from just after the beginning of Drummond's tenure as Locomotive Superintendent in 1882 through to the end of the McIntosh period in 1914.

The book was not started in 1882, although the Board apparently requested that Drummond should set up the book. It was compiled later, with diagram numbers broadly, but not always, assigned in order of construction. One of several examples of diagrams assigned out of sequence is the medium and short horse boxes to Diagrams 8 and 9 respectively, which were actually built in the reverse order.

The special wagons numbered 1 and 2 pre-dated the Drummond era. Although built in the 1870s, they were assigned to pages 33 and 34 in the diagram book. Page numbers 35 and 36 were not assigned to wagons. They showed the maximum dimensions of CR rolling stock, and the dimensions of the authorised loading gauge. Oddly, the end dimensions of the various covered carriage and scenery trucks were set out on page 27 of the companion carriage diagram book. Reprints of both books are available for sale from the Caledonian Railway Association

Page 36 may have marked the end of the first part of the book, which would include all the wagons designed during Drummond's term of office.

The wagon designs then follow more or less in date order, with one major anachronism: the spindle buffer mineral wagon design was first authorised in December 1893.[7] It should have been allocated Diagram 38, but instead followed the Diagram 45 brake vans, which were authorised in December 1897.

Some copies of the book stop at 1914 with page 117, but others have additions from the Pickersgill era. An LM&SR version continues to Diagram 126, which was assigned to the bogie bolster wagons loaned to the Caledonian by the War Department in 1921.

The purpose of the book was to provide operating staff with information about dimensions, tare weight and capacity of the various wagons types on the system. Wagons were allocated diagram numbers which refer to the pages in the diagram book. In some cases order numbers are appended.

A diagram number could apply to one or more designs of vehicle of a similar type. As an example, the first six-wheeled brake vans were built with planks flush with the body framing. Later they were built with heavy outside framing, but the diagram number did not change because the dimensions remained the same. The same applied to the Diagram 67 10-ton covered goods vans.

The descriptions of wagons from Chapter 5 onwards use the sketches from the small diagram book as headings. The book was designed to fit into the pocket – the flat part of the page was landscape format, about 3½ inches by 2¾ inches. The pages were blueprints on quite thick paper, giving a white on blue image. The surviving examples have all received considerable use. For this reason, the original sketches when scanned vary greatly in quality. They have been redrawn for clarity and consistency in a style that reflects the original, with the tare weight and title removed. Sample pages from an original book are shown in Plates 1.2 and 1.3 on page 7.

St. Rollox Goods Order Numbers

Order numbers referred to particular batches of wagons within a diagram number that were built at St. Rollox. Contractor-built vehicles were not given an order number unless the contractor took over construction of an order that was authorised for building by St. Rollox. The order number system was begun by Drummond shortly after his arrival in 1882.

Two series of numbers usually applied to wagon stock. The G series was the most common. For example, forty Diagram 63 goods brake vans were built to order G210. The H series was the norm for coaching and non-passenger coaching stock. These are described in the next section.

Finally, some travelling gas tanks and other service vehicles were built to M series orders, as were the open brake wagons. Twelve tank wagons at least were built to a C series order, according to an annotation on the drawing.[8] Only fragments of the C and M series are known, from references on drawings.

A list of the goods order numbers forms Appendix II. The original list was compiled by Duncan Burton and Charles Underhill. The present author has cross-referenced the order numbers to diagram book numbers and has supplemented the information with the dates when the orders were authorised, where known, from the company minutes.

Coaching Stock Order Numbers

The full series of H numbers has survived in a coaching and non-passenger coaching stock register. The sole surviving copy is in the CRA Archive. Written up after the First World War and maintained until BR days, it therefore does not contain information about stock scrapped before the First World War. Earlier versions are not known to have survived. A typed version with added information is available as a reprint from the Caledonian Railway Association; this is a transcript by CRA member Ronnie Cockburn.[9]

The use of H order numbers started in 1885. Some goods stock built with running gear to passenger stock standards appears in this register. For instance, fish vans were goods Diagram 71, but built to order H210. Some wagons that were not built to NPCS standards received an H number because they were built on redundant coach underframes. The list of wagons built to H orders, cross referenced to diagram numbers, forms Appendix III.

The St. Rollox Drawings Registers

Six registers containing lists of drawings of rolling stock, machinery and other items survive in the NRS archive. Entries usually show the date of the drawing, the job number, the drawer number (its location in the drawing office filing system), a brief description and the name of the draughtsman. The description sometimes includes an order number. The drawer number appears on each drawing in the stencilled form of an extended letter D with a number written inside it.

The scope of the registers is shown in the table below. Register 5 is a rewrite of register 1 and part of 2. In register 1, the early drawings are the product of the Greenock works, which were leased by the CR. Drawings 399-420 contain many references to the fitting out of St. Rollox shed and works, where construction was concentrated after 1856. In register 6, the last drawing number in the Caledonian's existence was 22253. Although we know how many drawings were produced and brief details of the subjects, the final number of

CHAPTER 1.2: SOURCES OF INFORMATION – THE CALEDONIAN RAILWAY

surviving drawings is still to be determined. A sample page from register 4 forms Plate 1.4.

	DATES COVERED	JOB NUMBERS
Register 1[10]	pre-1850-1883	1-3508
Register 2[11]	1883-1892	3510-7134
Register 3[12]	1892-1899	7135-9622
Register 4[13]	1892-1907	9623-14327
Register 5[14]	pre-1850-1878	1-5621
Register 6[15]	1907-1938	14328-27288

SURVIVING ST. ROLLOX DRAWINGS

Surviving St. Rollox drawings are located in three archives. The National Railway Museum (NRM) has microfiche copies of all the railway drawings which were catalogued by the BR/Oxford Publishing Co. Joint Venture Group in the 1970s. These drawings were originally stored at Clapham museum and transferred to York when the National Railway Museum was opened. The original drawings are now lodged in Edinburgh, following a decision to store all Scottish material in the National Archive of Scotland (NAS).

The NAS has recently been renamed the National Records of Scotland (NRS). Its archive lists the original drawings in the Register House Plan (RHP) series. Requests for viewing are made to the Historical Search Room at General Register House in Edinburgh. Access is normally given to digital images of plans in the Search Room, rather than to the original plans. Where a plan has not been digitally imaged, the aim is to make an image available in the Historical Search Room within ten working days of the request being accepted.

The third repository of a limited, but growing, number of plans is the Caledonian Railway Association Archive. The wagon and NPCS drawings currently available are listed in the archive catalogue under the reference CRA6/1/2/1.

In the chapters on wagon types, St. Rollox drawing numbers are quoted. Appendix V cross-references the St. Rollox numbers to the Edinburgh and York archive collections as RHP and NRM respectively. At the time this book went to press, some NRS drawings were with The Ballast Trust for conservation and cataloguing. They had not yet been allocated RHP numbers, and are described in this book as 'not yet catalogued.' When numbers are allocated the list will be made available on the CRA website.

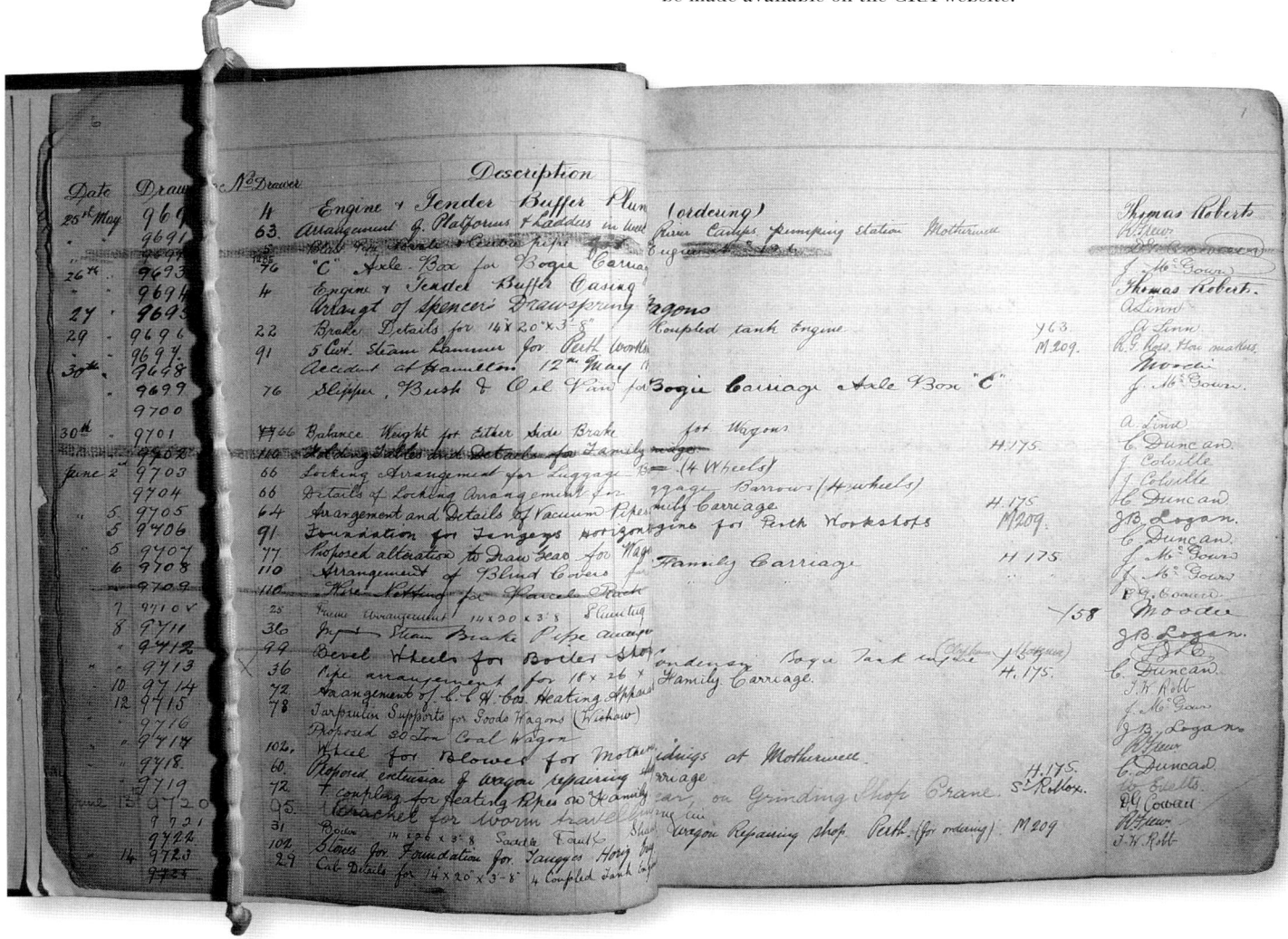

Plate 1.4
A sample spread of drawing register 4 showing entries between 25th May and 14th June 1899, some of which have order numbers assigned to them. Drawing 9716 is the first intimation that the Caledonian contemplated the construction of 30-ton bogie coal wagons. The entries crossed out in crayon were destroyed on 17th July 1939 in a fire at Derby Works, where the drawings were stored. The entry for drawing 9712 is annotated 'Clapham Museum'. These drawings formed the basis of the collection which went first to the National Railway Museum and then to Edinburgh.

Graeme Miller

Miller started work with the Caledonian as a premium apprentice in 1911, and was appointed as a draughtsman in 1916. After war service he was re-engaged in 1919.[16] He was instrumental in preserving, and perhaps contributing to, a technical history of CR wagons and carriages that is now in the National Railway Museum.[17] The history was compiled shortly after the Grouping and relates to rolling stock from 1872 onwards. It consists of dimensions and technical details for each type of wagon. A companion document for coaching stock was prepared at the same time. Neither document covers non-passenger coaching stock.

Official Photographs

Unlike the L&NWR, which seemed to have a photographer on hand to record every new type of wagon and carriage emerging from Earlestown and Wolverton, the Caledonian's official photographs are not a comprehensive record of the fleet.

An album of fifty-five photographs of CR wagons was assembled for the General Manager in 1900, entitled *Register of Wagon Plant with Photographs*.[18] The photographs sometimes depict a non-standard vehicle, or a type that had been superseded. For example, the cattle wagon is a pre-diagram book design and two more modern types had been produced by 1900. The register also gives numbers in service of the types of wagon photographed. Many of the photographs have found their way into the Historical Model Railway Society's collection. The list of photographs in the album, cross-referenced to diagram numbers where applicable, forms Appendix VI.

The National Railway Museum's collection of about 600 negatives from St. Rollox includes all types of rolling stock, plus scenes of interest on the railway, the Forth & Clyde canal, Grangemouth docks and the Clyde steamers. For Caledonian Railway researchers, West Coast Joint Stock vehicles are included in the L&NWR collection. Photographs of CR wagons built by contractors are described in Chapter 1.3.

Working Timetables and Appendices

Mineral and general working timetables give a picture of the volume of traffic, how it was organised and the way it flowed around the system.[19] The mineral timetables also list the names of traders who owned wagons working on the Caledonian and where they were based, and the owners of tank wagons.

Working timetable appendices provide information about goods train working practices. They list the running numbers of goods wagons fitted with continuous brakes. The numbers and dimensions of carriage and scenery trucks are set out, as are those for the special class wagons. The following years were consulted: April 1890, May 1891, November 1892, January 1894 and 1895, May 1896 and 1902, October 1906 and May 1915. These appendices are all held at NRS.[20] *The 1915 Appendix* is also in the CRA Archive,[21] and a reprint can be purchased.

Carriage Working and Marshalling Instructions

These documents provide some information about the regular working patterns of non-passenger coaching stock such as milk vans. Some give details about carriage gassing points and the allocation of the travelling gas tanks. A selection of these documents is in the CRA Archive, section reference CRA3/3/2.

Number Taker's Books

A book that records the numbers, ownership, loads, originating points and destinations of wagons passing Callander & Oban Junction is in the NRS archive.[22] This has provided sample numbers of certain types of wagon, as well as information on traffic flows and the composition of goods trains on the line in August/September 1920.

References
1. NRS BR/CAL/1/7 – 82
2. CRA Archive ref: 2/3/1/9 & 10
3. NRS BR/CAL/5/4
4. NRS/BR/CAL/5/5
5. NRS GD344/11/1, TNA: PRO RAIL 1110/48 and /49 respectively
6. NRS BR/CAL/4/134
7. NRS BR/CAL/1/36 entry 1509
8. St. Rollox drawing 6823, RHP 67547
9. CRA Archive refs: 3/4/1/14 (original), 1/6/40 (reprint)
10. NRS BR/CAL/5/113
11. NRS BR/CAL/5/114
12. NRS BR/CAL/5/115
13. NRS BR/CAL/5/116
14. NRS BR/CAL/5/117
15. NRS BR/CAL/5/56
16. Information taken from the *List of Special Apprentices*, NRS BR/CAL/15/13
17. NRM ref: C&W/CR/1 (C&W 109)
18. NRS BR/CAL/5/23
19. CRA Archive section 3/1/5 has four mineral timetables
20. In a series between NRS BR/TT/S/54/17 (1890) and /51 (1915)
21. CRA Archive ref: 3/1/4/2
22. NRS BR/CAL/5/60

Top Left: Plate 1.5
The Hurst Nelson builder's plate attached to a Diagram 14 swivel wagon built in 1896.

Bottom Left: Plate 1.6
This is the Leeds Forge patent plate, attached to the bogie of a 30-ton coal wagon built in 1903. Both bogies carried a plate, as well as the wagon underframe.

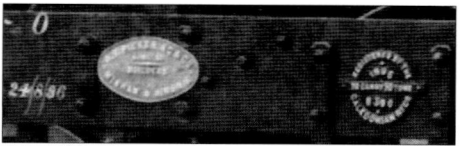

Top Right: Plate 1.7
An early R Y Pickering builder's plate, attached to an Oakbank Oil Co. tank wagon with an 1886 paint date. Also visible is the Caledonian Railway registration plate, which was attached to all private traders' wagons approved to run on the Caledonian system.

Bottom Right: Plate 1.8
The later version of the Pickering builder's plate, dating from 1899. It was attached to a coal wagon built for the private trader Malcolm MacCallum of Taynuilt.

1.3: Sources of Information – Outside Contractors

Up to the arrival of Dugald Drummond, the Caley relied heavily on contractors because the works at St. Rollox lacked sufficient capacity to build enough rolling stock to cope with the demands of rapidly expanding traffic. The problem was particularly acute in the 1870s and early '80s. This deficiency is discussed in Chapter 2.3.

After Drummond expanded and reorganised the company's works, most wagons were built in-house. This remained the case until the late 1890s, when old wagons had to be replaced in quantity and contractors provided the necessary extra capacity. Work continued to be let to contractors up to the Grouping, driven in part by the demands of the First World War. A list of orders for wagons and NPCS built by contractors forms Appendix IV. Orders from 1882 are cross-referenced to diagram book numbers, where known.

This section describes the surviving information from eight contractors who provided wagons and non-passenger coaching stock for the Caledonian, and who have left significant archive material.

Hurst Nelson

Hurst Nelson established a wagon and carriage works at Motherwell in 1880. The company first secured a contract with the Caledonian in 1895 for 800 wagons of four different types.[1] Hurst Nelson went on to build about 3,500 wagons and some carriages for the CR up to the Grouping. Plate 1.5 shows the builder's plate affixed to rolling stock.

The firm took publicity photographs of their output. The complete collection is held at the Motherwell Heritage Centre. Copies of the photographs also form part of the collections of the Historical Model Railway Society (HMRS) and the Caledonian Railway Association.[2]

Leeds Forge Co. Ltd

The Leeds Forge Co. Ltd was formed in 1873 to take over the existing business of toolmakers carried on by Messrs Samson and William Fox, and to erect works for the manufacture of iron and steel. The manufacture of rolling stock of patented pressed steel construction was commenced in 1887. This new technology was used extensively by the Caledonian.

Leeds Forge took an active part in the design, development and construction of all-steel carriage underframes. They specialised in the manufacture of pressed steel carriage and wagon bogies and underframes. The firm produced heavy and lightweight standard bogies for Caledonian carriage stock. Their wagons were of distinctive design with low tare weights compared with those built on conventional underframes.

The first Leeds Forge wagons for the Caledonian were the thirty experimental 30-ton bogie coal wagons of 1901. Most of their subsequent contracts were for bogie wagons. Leeds Forge also produced many of the pressed steel underframes for four-wheeled wagons, the bodies of which were built at St. Rollox or by other contractors.

The Leeds works closed after amalgamation with Metropolitan Cammell in 1923 and the business was transferred to Saltley. Drawings of carriages, wagons, pressed steel underframes and bogies for the CR are in the Metropolitan Cammell collection.

Metropolitan Cammell

The Metropolitan Railway Carriage and Wagon Company Ltd came into existence in 1862. It grew out of the firm of Joseph Wright who founded a carriage and wagon works in Saltley, Birmingham, in 1845. In 1902 the Metropolitan Amalgamated Railway Carriage & Wagon Company Ltd was formed to take over the business of the Metropolitan Company and to amalgamate with the following rolling stock companies:

– The Ashbury Railway Carriage & Iron Co. Ltd (founded as a public company in 1862)
– Brown & Marshall's Co. Ltd (1853)
– The Lancaster Railway Carriage & Wagon Co. Ltd (1863)
– The Oldbury Railway Carriage & Wagon Co. Ltd (1859)

These companies were major suppliers of wagons and NPCS to the Caledonian up to 1882. Various drawings of wagons and carriages built for the Caledonian have survived. They form part of the Metropolitan Cammell collection in the Birmingham City Archive.[3] Some of the drawings are also in the CRA Archive.[4]

R Y Pickering

In 1864, John Pickering, who originated from Yorkshire, chose Wishaw as the site for his wagon works. His son, Robert Young Pickering took over the business in 1878. Activities at that date included wagon repair and hire but, increasingly, Pickering became involved in the building of new wagons.

Pickering was encouraged to go for rapid expansion by Dugald Drummond. Drummond secured his own nominee, a Mr Robb, as Works Manager – but in 1891, by which time Drummond had left the Caledonian, the directors became dissatisfied by the low profits he was securing, in spite of his technical innovations, and he was replaced. The relationship with Drummond did not benefit Pickering financially – the Caledonian placed no orders with outside contractors between 1883 and 1895.

Pickering first secured a contract to build wagons for the CR in 1868, but, despite the relationship with Drummond, was not a major supplier of wagons until the renewal programme of the early 1900s. A number of carriage orders were also secured in the twentieth century. Pickering affixed two styles of builder's plate to wagons. They are shown in Plates 1.7 and 1.8.

The Glasgow University Business Archive holds the original enquiry books from 1896 and order books from 1888, plus wagon dispatch records. In many cases, the running numbers of the wagons are given. There is also some information about painting and lettering. An example is shown in Plate 1.9 overleaf. A few Pickering drawings are in the HMRS and CRA collections.

References
1. NRS BR/CAL/1/38 entry 1357
2. CRA Archive ref: 7/1/2
3. Birmingham City Archive ref: MS99
4. CRA Archive ref: 6/12/1
5. The generic reference for the Pickering collection is UGD12/

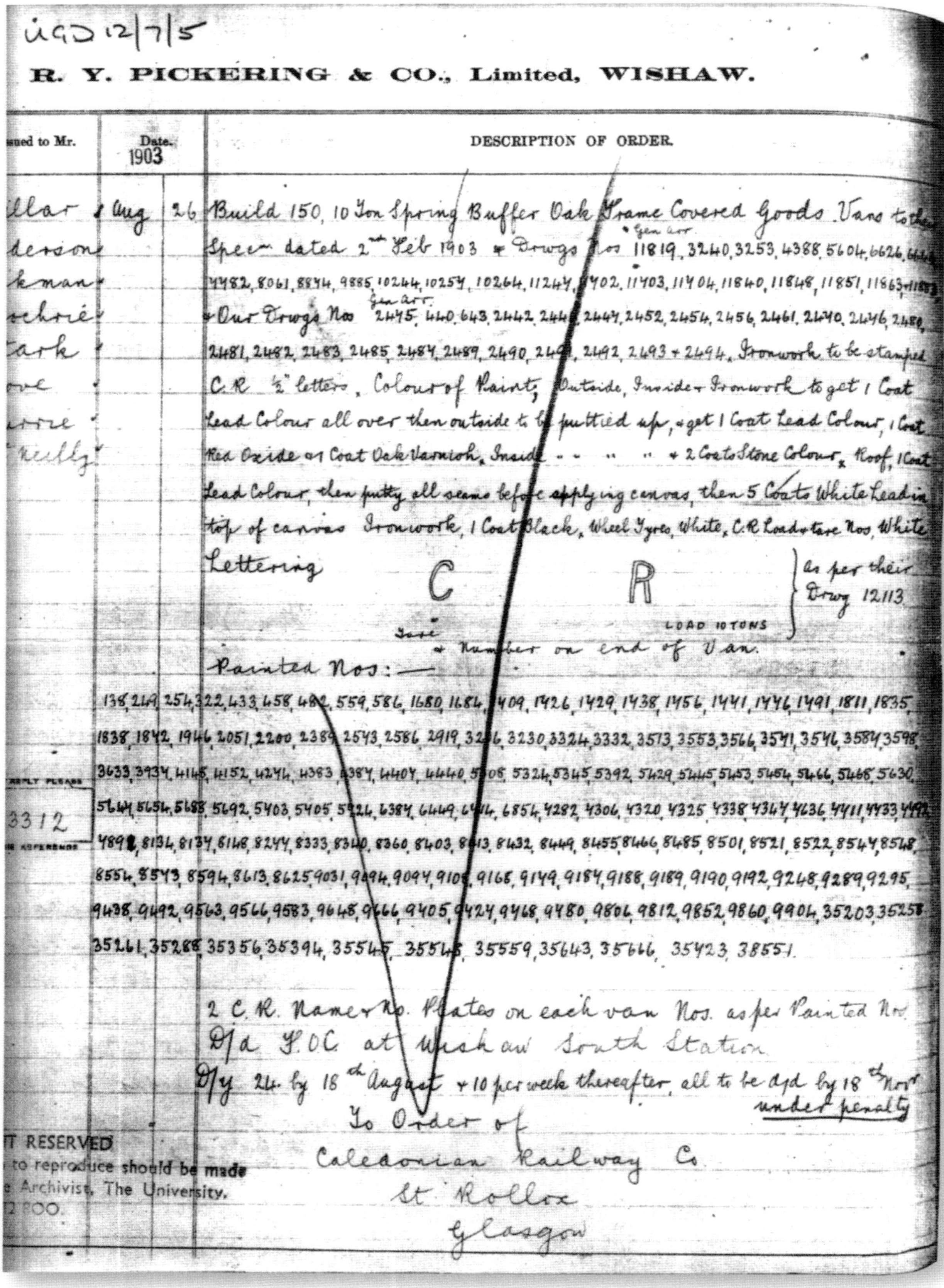
ÜGD 12/7/5

R. Y. PICKERING & CO., Limited, WISHAW.

...ssued to Mr.	Date. 1903		DESCRIPTION OF ORDER.
...llar / ...derson / ...kman / ...chré / ...ark / ...ove / ...rree / ...Reilly	Aug	26	Build 150, 10 Ton Spring Buffer Oak Frame Covered Goods Vans to their Specⁿ dated 2ⁿᵈ Feb 1903 & Drwgs Nos (Gen arr) 11819, 3240, 3253, 4388, 5604, 6626, ... 4482, 8061, 8874, 9885, 10244, 10257, 10264, 11247, 11402, 11403, 11404, 11840, 11848, 11851, 11863 & ... & Our Drwgs Nos (Gen arr) 2475, 440, 643, 2442, 244..., 2447, 2452, 2454, 2456, 2461, 2470, 2476, 2480, 2481, 2482, 2483, 2485, 2487, 2489, 2490, 24..., 2492, 2493 & 2494. Ironwork to be stamped C.R ½" letters. Colour of Paint; Outside, Inside & Ironwork to get 1 Coat Lead Colour all over then outside to be puttied up, & get 1 Coat Lead Colour, 1 Coat Red Oxide or Coat Oak Varnish. Inside " " " " & 2 Coats Stone Colour. Roof 1 Coat Lead Colour, then putty all seams before applying canvas, then 5 Coats White Lead in top of canvas. Ironwork, 1 Coat Black. Wheel Tyres, White. C.R Load & tare Nos, White Lettering

C R } As per their Drwg 12113

LOAD 10 TONS

tare & Number on end of Van.

Painted Nos:—

138, 249, 254, 322, 433, 458, 48..., 559, 586, 1680, 1684, 1409, 1426, 1429, 1438, 1456, 1441, 1476, 1491, 1811, 1835, 1838, 1842, 1946, 2051, 2200, 238..., 2543, 2586, 2919, 32..., 3230, 3324, 3332, 3513, 3553, 3566, 3571, 3576, 3587, 3598, 3633, 3934, 4145, 4152, 4274, 4383, ...387, 4407, 4440, 5...08, 5324, 5345, 5392, 5429, 5445, 5453, 5454, 5466, 5468, 5630, 5644, 5656, 5688, 5692, 5403, 5405, 5...24, 6387, 6449, 6...4, 6854, 4282, 4306, 4320, 4325, 4338, 4347, 4636, 4411, 4433, 449..., 489..., 8134, 8137, 8148, 8244, 8333, 83...0, 8360, 8403, 8...13, 8432, 8449, 8455, 8466, 8485, 8501, 8521, 8522, 8547, 8548, 8554, 8573, 8594, 8613, 8625, 9031, 9...4, 9097, 910..., 9168, 9179, 9184, 9188, 9189, 9190, 9192, 9248, 9289, 9295, 9438, 9492, 9563, 9566, 9583, 9648, 9666, 9405, 9424, 9468, 9480, 9806, 9812, 9852, 9860, 9904, 35203, 3525..., 35261, 35288, 35356, 35394, 3554..., 3554..., 35559, 35643, 35666, 35423, 38551.

2 C.R. Name & No. Plates on each van Nos. as per Painted Nos.

D/d F.O.C at Wishaw South Station

D/y 24 by 18ᵗʰ August & 10 per week thereafter, all to be d/d by 18ᵗʰ Novr under penalty

To Order of
Caledonian Railway Co
St Rollox
Glasgow

...PLY PLEASE ...3312 ...E REFERENCE

...T RESERVED ... to reproduce should be made ... Archivist, The University, ...2 8QQ.

Plate 1.9
One of the most detailed Pickering order book entries for a Caledonian Railway wagon contract – the first Diagram 67 covered goods vans. It includes the painting specification discussed in Chapter 3, and a list of the numbers to be applied to these wagons. Number 35394 was later erroneously re-issued in 1906 to a Pickering-built mineral wagon. Meticulous modellers should note the requirement to stamp all iron work with company initials ½ inch high. The lettering layout sketch refers to St. Rollox drawing 12113, which is reproduced in Chapter 3.

1.4: Sources of Information – The Technical and Enthusiast's Press

One of the Caledonian Railway Association's projects is to create a definitive list of published material about the company and to make it available to the researcher. The current catalogue is contained under the archive reference CRA9/2: Historical Publications Extracts. This section is confined to sources which have contributed material to this book.

References in the Contemporary Press

Developments on the Caledonian, in common with all other railway companies, were of great interest to railway professionals and enthusiasts alike. *The Railway Engineer* published drawings of the high capacity bogie coal and hopper wagons, plus the two versions of the McIntosh patent either side wagon brake. It also published an article on the issues concerning high capacity wagons. This has been used in the discussion of mineral wagon developments in the early twentieth century in Chapter 5.

Railway Gazette articles on freight distribution and CR marshalling yards have been used in Chapter 2. The *Locomotive Magazine* described goods and non-passenger coaching stock liveries in 1897. It also recorded the liveries of the 30-ton bogie coal wagons and the Diagram 63 brake vans in 1903 and 1920 respectively. Chapters 3 and 4 use this information.

The Railway Magazine published a special issue to celebrate the Diamond Jubilee of the Caledonian in 1907. This included an article by McIntosh on the evolution of rolling stock and provided material for Chapter 2. Four years later, there was an article on the development of the Scottish coal field which also provided information for this chapter. An illustrated article from 1903 on moving large castings by rail was used to amplify the development of special class wagons in Chapter 2. Another 1903 article on the new Railway Clearing House regulations for private traders' wagons informed Chapter 7.

Economic History

The material for Chapter 2.1 on the industrial and commercial developments affecting CR operations comes from three books. All were written by academics using primary sources, and are fully referenced.

The Industrial Revolution in Scotland[1] describes developments in two phases. The first, between 1780 and 1830, deals with the pre-eminence of the cotton industry. In the second phase from 1830 to 1880, cotton was ousted first by iron and coal, and later by shipbuilding, engineering and steel.

The Rise and Fall of Scottish Industry[2] overlaps the previous book to a certain extent, but provides added information on the links between shipbuilding and the development of the steel industry. It also explains how the abundance of raw materials allowed industrialists to remain wedded to outdated processes and to ignore advances in technology which would have improved productivity. It covers the period between 1707 and 1939.

The Origins of the Scottish Railway System 1722-1844[3] shows how the pioneering railways on the west coast of Scotland were intimately connected with the exploitation of coal and iron deposits. It also provides information on the amount of traffic carried by these lines.

The Enthusiast's Press

The Caledonian has been no better or worse served by the enthusiast's press than any other railway, but not much reference has been made to the wagon fleet. The Stephenson Locomotive Society published a book celebrating the centenary of the CR's formation, but confined its description of rolling stock to three pages. The photographic album *Caledonian Cavalcade* contained a few photographs of wagons and non-passenger coaching stock. Many had been published elsewhere.

An article in *the Journal of the Historical Model Railway Society* provided information on goods traffic which was used in Chapter 2. Another HMRS publication, *Oil on the Rails*, provided background material for the section on travelling gas tanks in Chapter 17.

The Caledonian Railway Association and its predecessor the Caledonian Railway Consortium of Modellers have helped to address the deficiency. Articles on wagons and goods traffic have been published in the CRA journal *The True Line*. These are acknowledged in the reference sections. *Caledonian Railway Livery* contains a chapter on wagons and non-passenger coaching stock. This material has been used throughout the book, but particularly as the basis for Chapters 3 and 4. *The Caledonian Railway in LMS Days* provided useful information about goods traffic and the wagon fleet after the Grouping.

The Caledonian and the L&NWR ran non-passenger coaching stock under the West Coast Joint Sock agreement. These vehicles are included in Chapter 10. Information has been taken from *West Coast Joint Stock*, published by the Historical Model Railway Society. Details of L&NWR and WCJS livery practice have been provided by *LNWR Liveries* and *An Illustrated History of LNWR Coaches*. This has been used in Chapter 4.

Modellers' Drawings

Coverage in model railway magazines has been patchy. The most reliable and prolific source of drawings was Kenneth Werrett, a member of the Historical Model Railway Society. Many of his drawings were originally to a large scale and were fully dimensioned. They were based on personal observation and measurements immediately after the First World War. A few were much less detailed and omitted information of the bolt heads which attached ironwork to the body. Most of his drawing appeared in *The Model Railway News*, with a few in *Railway Modeller*.

The other major source in quantity, but not in quality, was Sir Eric Hutchison. Born in 1892, he too was an eye witness of the railways in pre-Grouping days, and an early member of the HMRS. First published in *The Model Railway News*, his drawings later appeared in *Railway Modeller*.

He was a keen railway modeller, and therein lies a problem. His drawings almost invariably omitted underframe, buffer and brake detail. His rationale was that, as prototypically correct components were not available, there was no point in drawing them, because modellers would have to 'make do.' This could perhaps be forgiven if the information accompanying the drawings was trustworthy. In many cases it is not. Sample running numbers are often wrong, as is the number of wagons constructed. In some cases, the drawings are dimensionally incorrect.

Drawings by T. W. Bourne of a variety of Caledonian Railway and West Coast Joint Stock non-passenger coaching stock were published in *Model Railways* during the 1980s. Most have found their way into *Historic Carriage Drawings – NPCS*, published by the Pendragon Press. They are generally accurate, and are valuable because early vehicles built by Joseph Wright and the Metropolitan Carriage & Wagon Co. are included.

The Caledonian Railway Association Archive has CR wagon and non-passenger coaching stock drawings drawn by members. They carry only a few basic measurements, such as the wheelbase. The drawings which are available for purchase are listed in Appendix VII.

Finally, North British Railway drawings in *NBR Wagons, Some Design Aspects* have been consulted, because some of Drummond's design practices were carried over when he left the NBR and joined the Caledonian.

REFERENCES
1. By Dr David Hamilton, originally published in 1932. New impression published in 1966 by Frank Cass & Co. Ltd
2. By R. H. Campbell, Professor of Economic History at the University of Stirling, published in 1980 by John Donald Publishers Ltd
3. By C. J. A. Robertson, Lecturer in Economic and Social History, University of St. Andrews, published in 1983 by John Donald Publishers Ltd

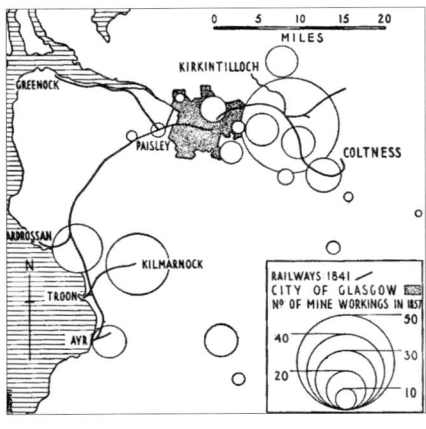

ABOVE: Figure 2.1
Map showing the early railways and the growing coal extraction industry in the west of Scotland.

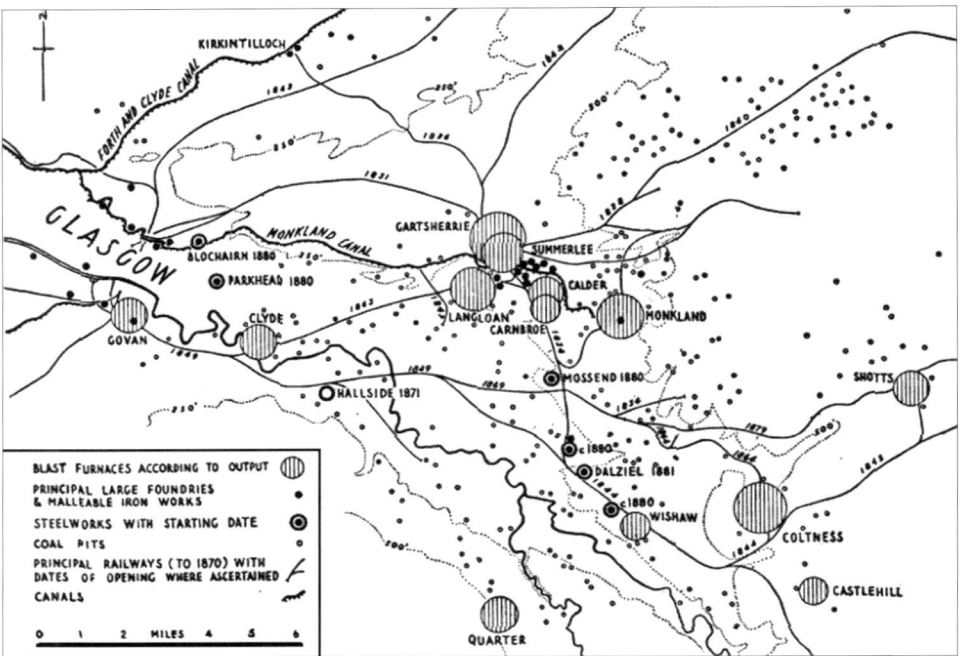

RIGHT: Figure 2.2
Map showing the extent of the iron industry with associated coal mines in the Clyde Valley, as it was in the early 1880s. The first steelworks had just been built.

ABOVE: : Plate 2.1
This typical colliery scene, taken at Bannockburn, near Stirling, is full of loaded CR 'bogies'. The pit belonged to the Alloa Coal Company. The photograph comes from the SCRAN archive, reference 014-925-R.

RIGHT: Plate 2.2
A scene at Coltness iron works with an assortment of 6- and 7-ton 'bogies.' Most of the wagons carry the early small lettering. In the foreground are two Diagram 13 rail wagons. This is another SCRAN picture, reference 581-500-R. A scene illustrating the loading of pig iron into wagons is shown in Chapter 6, Plate 6.10.

Chapter 2
The Growth and Development of the Wagon Fleet
2.1: Commercial Influences and Infrastructure

Sir James Thompson, the Caledonian Railway's General Manager, summed up the commercial and industrial forces which had driven the development of the company from the outset when he spoke on the occasion of its Diamond Jubilee in 1907.

'All over the country, we have been forced – but I must say willingly forced (although it sounds contradictory) – by the indomitable energy of the people of Scotland into making new and branch lines. The development of the Lanarkshire mineral fields has occupied a deal of our attention, the steel industry in Lanarkshire, the casting trade in Stirlingshire, and the suburban expansion in Glasgow, Edinburgh, Dundee and other towns have all claimed our attention and made inroads on our capital, but it goes without saying that Glasgow and the Valley of the Clyde have made the greatest and most deserved demands on our energy.'[1]

The first part of this chapter gives an overview of the sources of the Caledonian's traffic and its freight traffic infrastructure. It then relates traffic growth to the development of the wagon fleet. The development had two components. The first was an ever growing number of general purpose mineral and goods wagons. This fleet carried most raw materials and manufactured goods. The other component was an increasing diversity of specialist wagon types. Most of these wagons were used in the iron, steel, shipbuilding and general engineering industries.

It also examines the wagon depreciation policy, which was established on a less advantageous basis than the rest of the CR rolling stock. Insufficient funding meant that the wagon replacement programme, which was launched in the early 1900s, could not be implemented as quickly as the company wished. In 1911 the Caledonian Board finally addressed the problem, but its medium-term solution was not fully implemented, because of the outbreak of the First World War. Its ability to replace worn-out wagons was hamstrung during and immediately after the war, when all British railway operations were controlled by government through the Railway Executive Committee.

Scotland's Population Growth

In 1851, the population of Scotland stood at approximately 2,900,000. Over the next fifty years it grew to nearly 4½million. Much of this expansion was connected to industry, with a large influx of Irish immigrants forming the labour force. New housing in the industrialised area stimulated traffic in building materials, resulting in the construction by the CR of approximately 300 stone wagons. Many of these carried red sandstone from quarries around Dumfries. The wagons are discussed in Chapter 8.4. Traffic in foodstuffs and general household items also increased dramatically. As a result, the Caledonian built perishable goods vans and trucks.

Coal

The three industries of coal, iron and steel were inextricably linked, with coal and iron as the earlier components. They were well established before the arrival of the railways, and indeed were the stimuli for early railway construction in the west of Scotland. The modern steel industry started in Scotland in the late 1870s.

Up to the end of the eighteenth century, coal mining in Scotland was concentrated in Fife and Ayrshire, because high transport costs dictated that mining should be carried out near to the coast for export or around Glasgow close to its market. The coalfield around Coatbridge and Airdrie was not exploited at this stage.

Major expansion took place from 1790, when the Monkland Canal was opened. It linked collieries with Port Dundas on the north side of Glasgow, where it joined the Forth & Clyde Canal. One result was the opening of a large number of mines in the Coatbridge district during the first decade of the nineteenth century to meet the growing demands of the iron industry and domestic consumption. The intimate connection between the early railways and coal extraction is shown in Figure 2.1.

When the railway system was fully established, the output from Scottish coal mines was enormous. Tom Moffat, writing in *The Railway Magazine*[2] summarised the output from the various coalfields. The Caledonian had a major commercial interest in the Lanarkshire and Stirlingshire fields. The annual tonnages, shown in the following table, explain the preponderance of mineral wagons in Caledonian Railway stock and the number of private traders' wagons registered to run on the system.

	1886	1896	1911
Lanarkshire	11,414,904	15,805,301	17,504,906
Stirlingshire	1,134,294	1,980,139	3,112,939

The Lanarkshire field had by far the greatest output in the country, consistently accounting for about 55 per cent of the total tonnage. It had been worked at full capacity for a number of years, and in 1911 was starting to decline as seams became exhausted. Moffat saw the Fife and Lothians fields as the future of Scottish coal supply. He was *'happy to report'* that estimates showed that the part of the Fife field that did not lie under the Firth of Forth would supply the current level output for over 300 years!

In 1913 the Caledonian handled over 13 million tons of coal, coke or dross from collieries attached to the system, according to an article in *The Railway Gazette*, published in 1922.[3]

Iron

The iron industry got properly under way in Scotland with the foundation of the Carron Iron Company in 1759. Later in the century, Watt's development of the steam engine allowed the industry to be independent of water power. Furnaces could now be sited close to the raw materials.

In the late eighteenth century, Henry Cort invented the puddling process and the grooved roller, enabling iron to be shaped while hot into a variety of sections. This reinvigorated the wrought iron trade, which had been in the doldrums compared with the casting business.

Originally, iron ore was imported from England, until, in the early 1800s, David Mushet demonstrated the value of blackband ironstone, which lay in a deposit under a coal seam in the parish of Old Monkland. This local supply significantly reduced the costs connected with transporting raw material.

RIGHT: Plate 2.3
This picture is scanned from a *Railway Magazine* article on transporting castings by rail. The special train is leaving Stevenston station and consists of two of the five Diagram 43 30-ton bogie heavy weight wagons. The brake van has a brake stanchion on the verandah making it a Diagram 45 van. The similar Diagram 5 vans had one centrally located stanchion. HMS *Roxburgh* was a Devonshire Class cruiser, built by the London & Glasgow shipbuilding company in Govan. It was laid down in June 1902 and launched in January 1904.

BELOW: Plate 2.4
Another type of special load for the shipbuilding industry – the propeller shaft for HMS *Black Prince*. It is being transported from Beardmore's forge at Parkhead on two Diagram 43 heavy weight wagons, separated by a Diagram 14 swivel wagon with its bolster removed. It would have been sent to General Terminus, for onward transportation by sea. HMS *Black Prince* was laid down at the Thames Ironworks yard in February 1903 and was launched in March 1906. It sank with all hands at the battle of Jutland in 1916. The Diagram 43 wagons saw active service as well as part of the armoured trains, built to protect the east coast of Britain in the early days of the First World War.

The next stimulus in the growth of the Scottish industry was Neilson's discovery and patenting of the hot blast process in 1828. This, coupled with ironmaster William Dixon's use of coal rather than coke, tripled productivity and reduced costs by saving the amount of fuel consumed in the furnace. Scottish iron was, for a time, cheaper to produce than that in England and Wales.

As a direct result of these two inventions and the accompanying price advantage, many new furnaces were brought into production. By 1840 there were thirty furnaces in the parish of Old Monkland, producing on average 90 tons of iron per week.

The industry's growth was the stimulus for railway construction and, once lines were opened, further expansion was possible. The first lines on the west of Scotland supplemented the Monkland canal by penetrating further into the coalfield. Within a few years, the area around Coatbridge and Motherwell was dotted with ironworks, using the local coal and iron deposits delivered by the railway. Similar growth took place in Ayrshire. A map showing the extent of the iron and coal workings in the Clyde valley in about 1880 forms Figure 2.2.

The boom in the iron industry led to increased demand for coal and coincided with the rise of the railways. To a large extent each depended on the other. Indeed, the railways in the UK and overseas were major customers for wrought and malleable iron to build plant and equipment.

Production of pig iron peaked at 1,206,000 tons in 1870. It then fell to around half that figure, but rose again in the mid 1890s to over 1 million tons. This level of output was maintained until the First World War. The Caledonian carried pig iron from an early date. It is not possible to say how many wagons were used for this traffic up to 1890, as pig iron is not identified separately in the rolling stock returns. Orders show that the second peak in production stimulated the Caley to build over 1,500 wagons designed to carry pig iron between 1890 and 1912.

The malleable iron industry was superseded by steel, but pig iron was still required for castings and for the steel industry. The use of local iron ore declined as deposits became exhausted and its chemical content was unsuitable for the steel used in the shipbuilding industry.

The Lanarkshire blackband deposit was more or less exhausted by 1899, although 844,000 tons of ore were raised in Fife, Midlothian and Ayrshire. The industry resumed its dependence on imports from England and abroad. At the turn of the century over 1,400,000 tons of ore was imported.

SHIPBUILDING

The development of shipbuilding directly influenced the growth of the Scottish steel industry. During the time of the railways, three major developments influenced the composition of the wagon fleet. Steam power for ships became commonplace and the use of a propeller rather than paddles grew after SS *Great Britain* successfully crossed the Atlantic in 1845. This created a demand for marine engines, castings and components.

The second development was the use of iron rather than wood for ship's hulls. Clydeside was ideally placed to become the premier shipbuilding centre in the United Kingdom because of its proximity to the iron industry.

The third and last development was the substitution of steel for iron. Steel had greater strength and elasticity than iron and was easier to shape. Steel ships came to the fore from the late 1870s, following the pioneering work of Denny the shipbuilder. In 1879, one tenth of the tonnage of ships launched on Clydeside was made of steel, chiefly from the Denny yard. Ten years later, 97 per cent of the

2.1: COMMERCIAL INFLUENCES AND INFRASTRUCTURE

tonnage launched was steel. The invention of the triple expansion marine engine in 1882 was another major stimulus.

The shipbuilding industry required large quantities of platework and castings for such items as hull stems. It also required forged parts such as propeller shafts, as well as complete marine engines. This led the Caledonian to build a fleet of special wagons. Production started in earnest in 1890, although there were two wagons dating from the 1870s.

According to an article in *The Railway Magazine*,[1] the Caledonian handled weekly consignments of castings whose dimensions exceeded the loading gauge – for which reason they were conveyed on Sundays. The loads were transported from the Ayrshire Foundry at Stevenston, or the Newton works of the Steel Company of Scotland, to General Terminus on the south bank of the Clyde – see Plate 2.3 opposite. The wagons are discussed in Chapters 13 and 14.

STEEL AND GENERAL ENGINEERING

The steel industry in Scotland was driven by the demands from shipbuilding at a time when the malleable iron manufacturers were looking to diversify. Puddling and rolling were both labour intensive processes and rising labour costs were reducing competitiveness and profits.

At first the Bessemer process was tried, using the residue from the manufacture of sulphuric acid – one of the promoters of the Steel Company of Scotland was Charles Tennant who owned St. Rollox chemical works. The experiment was unsuccessful, and the local phosphoric iron ore was not suitable for steel making.

One of the earliest products made by the Steel Company was rails for the home and export markets. This led the Caledonian to build a fleet of six-wheeled wagons to transport the finished goods. These wagons are discussed in Chapter 8.1

The Steel Company diversified into shipbuilding materials. This dictated the use of acid steel produced by the Siemens-Martin open hearth process, rather than the Bessemer converter, because Lloyds banned the use of Bessemer steel in shipbuilding. Acid steel required the importation of iron ore from north-west England, Spain and, increasingly, from Sweden after 1900.

Steel eclipsed wrought and malleable iron, which changed the product from the iron works. This coincided with the exhaustion of Scotland's iron ore deposits, leaving the new industry dependent on imports. The ore was transported in ordinary mineral wagons. An attempt to develop a high capacity bogie wagon for this purpose did not progress beyond the prototype stage. The ore wagons are discussed in Chapter 5.

General engineering works turned out a wide variety of items. Worthy of note, because they stimulated developments in the Caledonian's wagon fleet, were locomotive builders, steel tubes and the manufacturers of structural steel for bridges, such as W. D. Arrol & Co. To serve the first, the CR built locomotive and boiler wagons. These, and other wagons built to carry various types of machinery, are covered in Chapter 15.

Tubes were probably carried in rail wagons at first, but later specialised wagons were built. This development was at the insistence of the managing director of Stewarts & Lloyds, the major tube manufacturer in the UK. The tubes were used as water mains to cater for the expansion of Glasgow. These wagons are described in Chapter 8.1.

Structural steel traffic was handled by a large fleet of swivel wagons, which were used in various combinations dependant on the size of the load. In 1885 there were about 750 of these wagons. After twenty years had elapsed, there were over 2,000 in service. The various designs are discussed in Chapter 8.2. An example of these wagons with a load is shown in Plate 2.5.

IMPORT AND EXPORT TRAFFIC

Coal for export was called 'shipment coal'. This was big business for coalmasters and the railways alike. According to Moffat, one quarter of the combined coalfield output was exported, amounting to over 10 million tons in 1911. This was an increase of 130 per cent over the shipments of only ten years earlier. The trade was mainly with the Baltic and Mediterranean ports. The major customers were Germany, Denmark, Sweden, Italy, France and Russia. There was also a significant west coast trade to Ireland, which left from the docks on the Clyde, Ardrossan and Stranraer.

The hoists and tipping arrangements for loading coal into ships' holds could only accept wagons of modest proportions. The dock concerns did not anticipate the railway companies' drive to maximise the load carrying capacity of mineral wagons which started at the end of the nineteenth century. Chapter 5.4 discusses the influence of loading and unloading infrastructure on CR mineral wagon design.

Aside from iron ore, wood was the major import into all the ports on the eastern seaboard of Scotland. When the enlarged Grangemouth dock was opened in 1882, it boasted 25 acres of timber storage ponds. The main exporters were the Baltic states. Timber

Plate 2.5
This is another type of load from a steelworks. Made by Alex Mather's Orwell works in Edinburgh, they are girders for the Murrayfield bridge in Edinburgh.

might arrive as whole trunks (round timber), as cut boards, or items such as pit props or railway sleepers. Round timber was transported by combinations of swivel wagons, while pit props and sleepers were conveyed in open goods wagons. The Caledonian built one lot of specialised wagons to carry 24-foot timbers, but no information about these wagons, apart from a sketch showing their basic construction, has survived. Timber-carrying wagons are discussed in Chapter 8.

Grangemouth docks and the associated Fouldubs marshalling yard handled heavy import/export traffic to and from continental Europe. The layout of the dock complex is shown in Figure 2.3. Plate 2.6 shows the arrangement for loading shipping coal. Plate 2.7 is a view of part of the dock complex and Plate 2.8 gives an impression of the extent of Fouldubs marshalling yard.

Delays in loading and unloading wagons caused congestion in marshalling yards and created considerable tension in the relationship between the Caledonian and private traders. The average mineral haul from pit to destination was 15 miles, and it was estimated that it took seven days for leaving its pit for a wagon to return.[5]

The CR and the traders were obliged to put more and more mineral wagons into service to compensate for the time that wagons were loaded but not moving. Railway companies tried to seek compensation for this inefficiency by charging traders for excessive delays. This resulted in the demurrage dispute of 1910, which is discussed in Chapter 7.

LIVESTOCK AND PERISHABLE GOODS

As soon as the railways developed beyond short lines dedicated to the carriage of minerals, they began to replace droving as a means of moving cattle and sheep to market. Once the Highlands were penetrated by rail, the change was complete. Buyers now travelled north by train to deal with graziers on their home ground, purchased animals in prime condition and sent them south by rail. The traffic was seasonal and heavy. This accounts for the large fleet of wagons which railway companies constructed to deal with livestock. This traffic and the wagons concerned are discussed in more detail in Chapter 11.

The same network of railways enabled fresh fish to be sent to markets in the south. The Caledonian built a fleet of wagons and vans to coaching stock standards for traffic within Scotland. With its west coast partner the L&NWR it used jointly-owned stock to transport fish to the major cities of England, which ran at express passenger train speed and was given priority in line occupation. Similar arrangements were made for meat traffic, which travelled by express goods train. Game, of course, provided seasonal traffic from August onwards each year.

Scotland's growing population increased the demand for milk and other foodstuffs. Much of the milk for Clydeside came onto the Caledonian system at Lockerbie from the dairy herds of Dumfries and Galloway. This required a small fleet of milk vans, which were attached to passenger trains. There was a return traffic in empty milk churns.

There was a significant seasonal traffic in fruit, which was divided into two types. Unlike some railways, the Caledonian did not build special vans for the purpose. Table fruit was transported in luggage vans by passenger train. Information about modifications to these vans is in Chapter 10.2. Fruit for jam making and confectionery was packed in barrels and transported in open goods wagons.

TOURISM AND THE CARRIAGE TRADE

Queen Victoria made the Highlands fashionable, ably abetted by Sir Walter Scott. The Caledonian built coaching stock to cater for the demand, plus a fleet of horse boxes to passenger stock standards which was well over 100 strong. It also built a number of open and covered carriage trucks to similar standards.

Some of the covered carriage trucks were dedicated to coachbuilders who, as the twentieth century progressed, moved into motor car body manufacture. Owners of early motor cars continued to use carriage trucks because their new steeds were not entirely reliable. There were two motor car factories on the system – Argyll Motors on the banks of the Clyde and Arrol Johnson near Dumfries. The horse boxes are discussed in Chapter 11 and the carriage trucks in Chapter 12.

At the opposite end of the market from the exclusive carriage trade, the start of the twentieth century saw the rise of electrified tramways operated by municipal transport undertakings. The traffic was sufficiently large for the Caledonian to build a fleet of six very long, but lightweight well wagons to carry tramcars from Glasgow manufacturers, as illustrated in Plate 2.9. The details are in Chapter 13.4.

RAILWAYS ON THE BANKS OF THE CLYDE

An album in the Caledonian Railway Association Archive[6] vividly illustrates Thompson's remarks about the enterprise of Glasgow and the Clyde Valley. Two lines were involved. The Lanarkshire & Dumbartonshire Railway was authorised in 1891 and was fully open in 1896. Its purpose was to exploit the traffic originating from the north bank of the Clyde, as the much earlier Glasgow, Paisley & Greenock line and its branches did on the south bank.

The album lists the engineering, shipbuilding and related works in the Clyde District to which the CR carried traffic. It consists of five maps showing private siding connections and a list of firms by location. This also includes the type of business and the method of invoicing full wagon loads and consignments weighing less than one ton. The list runs to fourteen pages, plus a page for traffic shipped overseas from Glasgow.

Two of the maps are included here. Figure 2.4/2.5 shows the lines west of Glasgow as far as Clydebank on the north side and Renfrew on the south, the centre of Glasgow and the lines east as far as Coltness. The sixth and last page of the Glasgow business list is also included – see Plate 2.10

GOODS AND MARSHALLING YARDS

The volume of traffic handled by the Caledonian dictated an extensive infrastructure. According to the previously quoted article in the 1922 *Railway Gazette*, the railway was divided into seventeen rolling stock districts. The bases for each region were:

1. Carlisle
2. Carstairs
3. Ross
4. Hamilton
5. Motherwell
6. Mossend
7. Polmadie
8. Ardrossan
9. Greenock
10. St. Rollox
11. Scotstoun
12. Edinburgh
13. Grangemouth
14. Stirling
15. Perth North
16. Perth South
17. Forfar

Marshalling yards acted as distribution and collection points for traffic within a district. An article in a Historical Model Railway Society series on goods and mineral traffic by Martin Waters[7] listed the major goods and marshalling yards on the Caledonian. They were described as follows, starting from the north of the system:

Aberdeen	*Guild Street* – general merchandise, warehouse, fish
	Clayhills – exchange with GNSR and NBR
	Craiginches – marshalling
Dundee	*West* – marshalling and general merchandise
	Buckingham Junction – exchange with NBR

Plate 2.6
Shipment of coal at Grangemouth was handled by the Gridiron yard. Shipment coal was loaded by tipping using coal hoists such as the one shown here. The dimensions of colliery loading sites and these hoists acted as a constraint to Caledonian mineral wagon development. Image SRX439C, courtesy of National Railway Museum / SSPL.

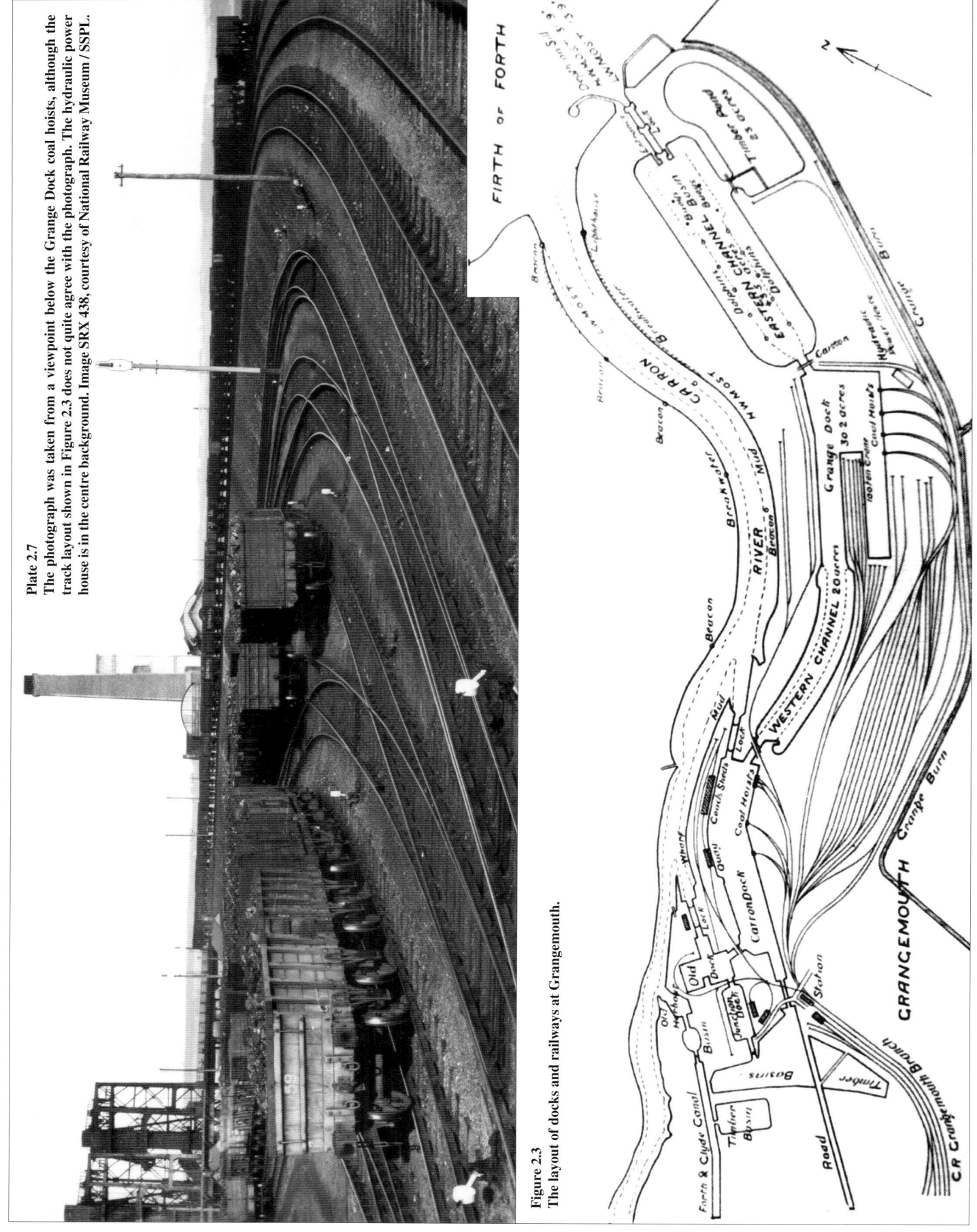

Plate 2.7
The photograph was taken from a viewpoint below the Grange Dock coal hoists, although the track layout shown in Figure 2.3 does not quite agree with the photograph. The hydraulic power house is in the centre background. Image SRX 438, courtesy of National Railway Museum/SSPL.

Figure 2.3
The layout of docks and railways at Grangemouth.

2.1: COMMERCIAL INFLUENCES AND INFRASTRUCTURE

Plate 2.8
Fouldubs yard was the marshalling point for Grangemouth's general goods and timber traffic. The timber was kept in a large holding pond at the Firth of Forth end of the docks – see Figure 2.3. Most of the stock that can be identified is North British or private trader, but there are some CR Diagram 22 solid buffer mineral wagons on the right with a CR 8-ton open goods beyond, and what looks like a newly-painted Diagram 3 goods van with a white roof further over again. The other covered goods vans with it are probably CR pre-diagram book 6-tonners, with roof doors. Looking to the left of the picture, the loading of pit props in low sided wagons was unusual; they were normally stacked vertically in mineral wagons. Image SRX 376, courtesy of National Railway Museum / SSPL.

Plate 2.9
Tram cars for Dundee. This picture shows 'Jumbo' 739 attached to the entire fleet of six Diagram 53 12-ton trolly wagons, which were built in 1902. The Dundee tramway system was electrified between 1899 and 1902. The tramcars ran on the Constitution Road route. They were probably made by Dick, Kerr at the Britannia Works in Kilmarnock.

Perth	*South and North Yards* – marshalling and general merchandise; exchange with NBR and HR	Greenock	Docks and shipyard sidings, local traffic
Stirling	Callander and Oban traffic, local sorting	Glasgow	*Buchanan Street* – yard and warehouse for Anglo-Scottish traffic
Grangemouth	*Gridiron Sidings* – shipment coal		*Robroyston* – marshalling
	Fouldubs Yard – marshalling and general merchandise, also extensive timber sidings		*General Terminus* – shipment coal
			Rothesay Docks – shipment coal

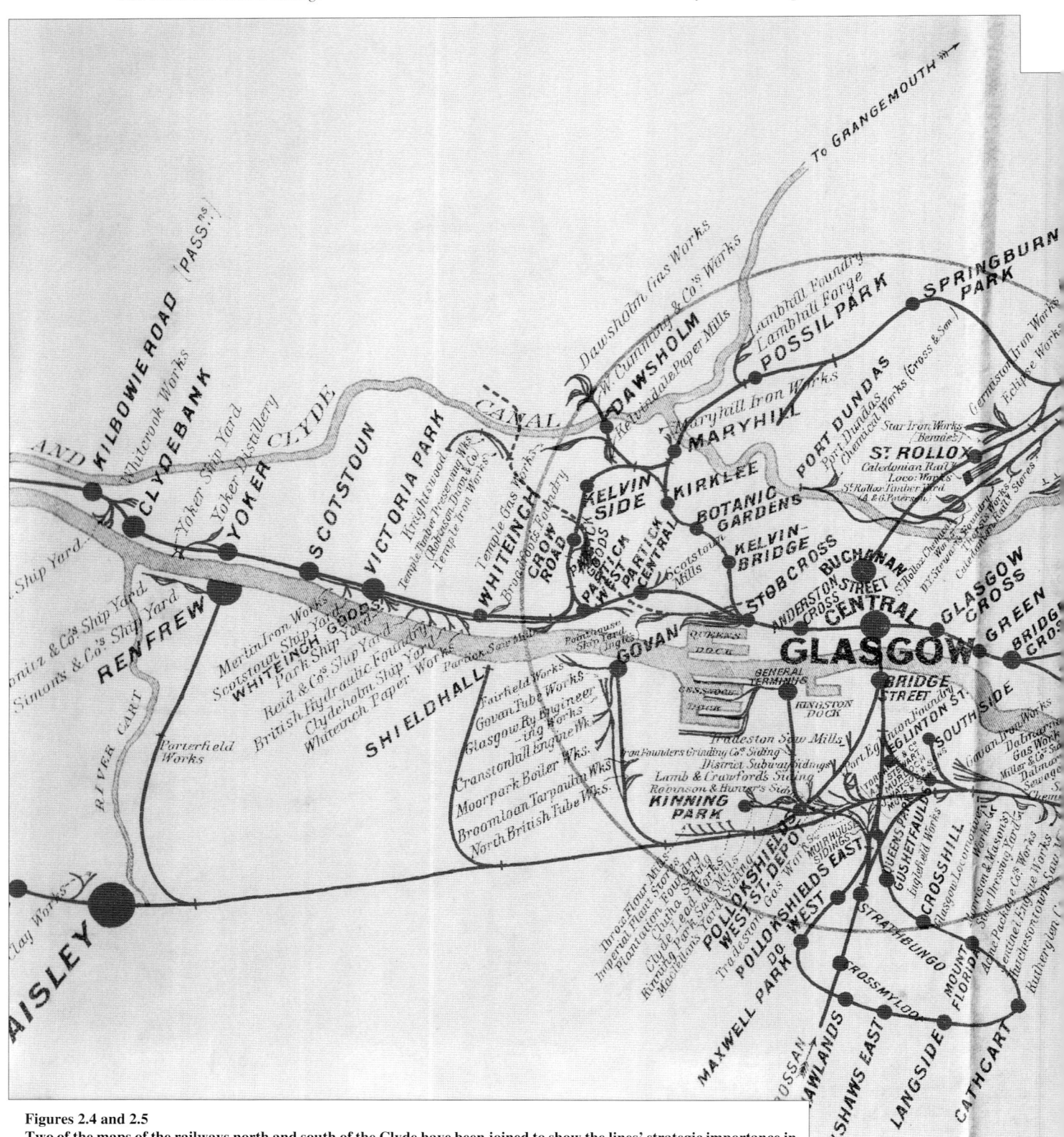

Figures 2.4 and 2.5
Two of the maps of the railways north and south of the Clyde have been joined to show the lines' strategic importance in serving the thriving industries in and around Glasgow. The sheer number of private sidings is impressive.

Hamilton	*Polmadie, London Road, St. Rollox (Sighthill)* – general
	Craighead and Ross Yards – coal traffic
Motherwell	*Lanarkshire New Yard* – steel works traffic
	Numerous works and colliery sidings
Mossend	Colliery and steel works traffic, general marshalling
Whifflet	Exchange with NBR
Edinburgh	*Lothian Road* – goods and warehouse
	Morrison Street – coal and marshalling
	Gorgie – livestock, general and Anglo-Scottish traffic
	Leith and Granton – extensive dock sidings
	Haymarket West Junction – exchange with NBR
Carstairs	general marshalling
Carlisle	*Viaduct Yard* – Anglo-Scottish traffic

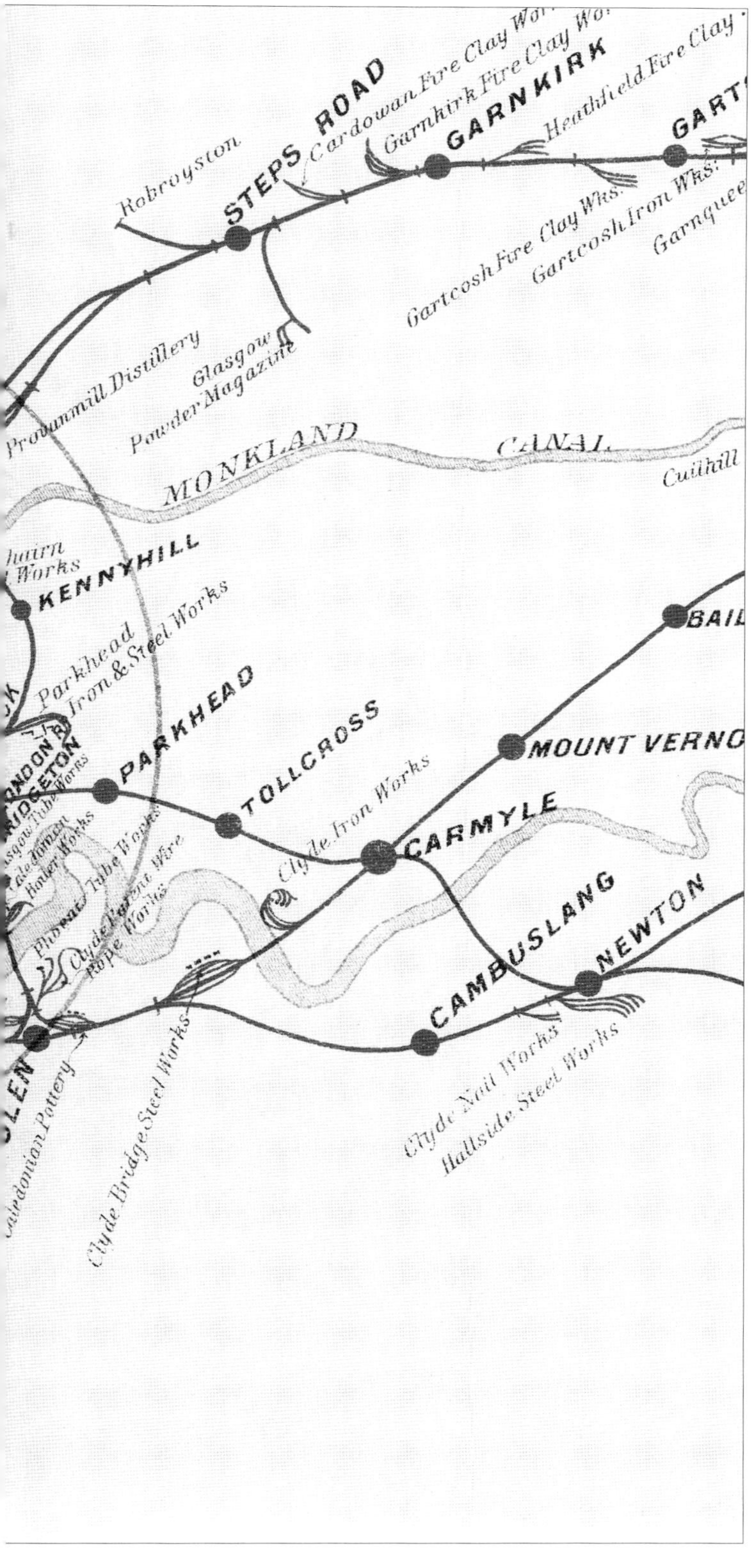

Charles Underhill submitted another article to *The True Line* from *The Railway Gazette* of November 1922 which detailed the workings of the five major marshalling yards around Glasgow.[8] Their locations are shown in Figure 2.7 (p. 30). The article stated that nearly three-quarters of the 100,000 wagons handled by the Caley every week went through these yards, although the figures tabulated below which are taken from the article only add up to two-thirds of the total. The yards' capacities and weekly throughputs are shown in the following table.

YARD	STANDAGE	THROUGHPUT
Mossend	2,000 wagons	20,000 wagons
Polmadie	2,300 wagons	17,000 wagons
Ross	1,400 wagons	10,000 wagons
Strathaven Junc.	2,200 wagons	10,000 wagons
Robroyston	1,100 wagons	10,000 wagons

A further yard for southbound traffic was built at Law Junction during the First World War, which probably accounted for the missing 8 per cent of wagons. The layout of the Craighead & Strathaven yard is shown in Figure 2.6. These combined yards handled traffic from the mines around Hamilton, Burnbank and Blantyre, plus Quarter and the Cadzow Branch.

Coupled with the number of trains contained in the Mineral Timetable of 1904[9] (available for sale from the CRA) there is a vivid picture of the sheer scale of mineral traffic, and the need for a large number of wagons to handle it. For example, Polmadie's daily mineral roster in 1904 involved over seventy engines, working eight-hour shifts.

TONNAGE CARRIED BY THE CALEDONIAN

According to the CR's deposition in the demurrage dispute of 1910,[10] the tonnage of minerals carried in 1909 was 19,356,568, increasing to over 20 million in the year ending 31st January 1910. In that year over 18 million wagons were dealt with. The 1909 tonnage was almost exactly double that carried in 1879. Goods traffic exhibited the same pattern. The 1909 tonnage was 4,725,505, compared with 2,424,307 in 1879.

REFERENCES
1. Published in *The Railway Magazine* special issue
2. 'Development of the Scottish Coalfield', in *The Railway Magazine*, August 1911, pp. 139-41
3. 'Freight Rolling Stock Distribution on the Caledonian Railway', reproduced in *The True Line*, issue 73, pp. 8-13
4. April 1903 issue, pp. 281-86
5. Quoted in the deposition to the demurrage dispute hearing, CRA Archive ref: 2/2/2/18, p. 157
6. CRA Archive ref: 3/7/2/34
7. *HMRS Journal*, Volume 9, pp. 14-20
8. 'Some Caledonian Railway Marshalling Yards', reproduced in *The True Line*, issue 72, pp. 22-26
9. CRA Archive ref: 3/1/5/2
10. In CRA Archive ref: 2/2/2/18

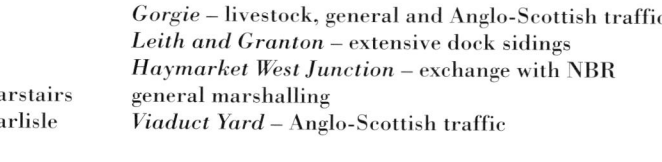

GLASGOW—Continued.

Route—"Via Carlisle & Caledonian Railway."

NAME OF FIRM.	DESIGNATION.	Traffic under One Ton and conveyed at Carted Rates.	Full Loads and Station to Station Traffic.
Rennie, Dugald, & Co.,	Camlachie Steel Works,	Buchanan Street,	Bridgeton.
Richmond, David,	City Tube Works,	do.	South Side.
*Risk, Moses, & Sons, Limited,	Provanmill Distillery,	do.	Buchanan St. (for Provanmill Distillery Siding).
*Robinson & Hunter,	Tar Distillers, &c.,	do.	South Side.
Rowan, D., & Son,	Engineers and Boilermakers,	do.	Stobcross.
Scotch and Irish Oxygen Co.,	Rosehall Works,	Buchanan Street,	South Side.
Scott, J. & J. G., Limited,	Crown Colour Works,	do.	Buchanan Street.
Scottish Oil and Chemical Co.,	White Lead, Paint, and Oil Manufacturers,	do.	Port-Dundas.
Shearer, John, & Son,	Kingston Dock Ship Repairing Works,	do.	General Terminus.
Do.	Kelvinhaugh Shipyard,	do.	Stobcross.
Smith, G. B., & Co.	Craighall Iron Works,	do.	Port-Dundas.
Smith, Hugh, & Co.,	Possil Engine Works,	do.	do.
Smith Brothers & Co.,	Engineers,	do.	Kinning Park.
Smith & M'Lean, Limited,	Clyde Galvanising Works,	do.	General Terminus.
Smith & Rodger,	Greenhead Paint and Varnish Works.	do.	Buchanan Street.
Springfield Steel Co.,	Steel and Ironfounders,	do.	London Road.
*Steel Co. of Scotland, Limited,	Blochairn Iron and Steel Works,	do.	Buchanan Street (for Blochairn Siding).
Sterne, L., & Co., Limited,	Crown Iron Works,	do.	Buchanan Street.
Steven, A. & P.,	Provanside Engine Works,	do.	do.
Steven & Struthers,	Brassfounders,	do.	Stobcross.
Stevens & Sons,	Railway Signal Manufacturers,	do.	Buchanan Street.
Stevenson, S., & Co.,	Polmadie Saw Mills,	do.	South Side.
Stewart, A. & C.,	Port-Eglinton Brass Foundry,	do.	do.
Stewart, J. & A.,	Kelvinhaugh Saw Mills,	do.	Stobcross.
Stewart, D., & Co., Limited,	London Road Iron Works,	do.	Bridgeton.
*Stewart, D. Y., & Co.,	Ironfounders and Engineers,	do.	Buchanan St. (for St. Rollox, West).
Stirrat, D., & Son,	Carriage Builders, &c.,	do.	Buchanan Street.
Stirrat, R., & Co.,	do.	do.	do.
Storer, James, & Co.,	Oil, Paint, & Varnish Manufacturers,	do.	Bridgeton.
Storrar Brothers,	Oil and Grease Manufacturers,	do.	Buchanan Street
Strathclyde Paint Co.,	Paint Manufacturers,	do.	Kinning Park.
Sutherland & Abercrombie,	Park Soap Works,	do.	do.
*Tennant, Charles, & Co., St. Rollox,	Chemical Works,	Buchanan Street,	Buchanan St. (for St. Rollox, West).
*Tharsis Sulphur & Copper Co., Ld.,	Copper Manufacturers,	do.	Buchanan St. (for St. Rollox, West).
Thomson, William, & Co.,	Engineers,	do.	Kinning Park.
*Torrance, J. Watt, & Co.,	Saw Millers,	do.	South Side.
Tradeston Tube Co.,	Tube Manufacturers,	do.	Kinning Park.
*United Alkali Co., Limited,	St. Rollox Chemical Works,	Buchanan Street,	Buchanan St. (for St. Rollox, West).
Ure, Allan & Co.,	Springbank Iron Works,	do.	Buchanan Street.
Ure, William,	Crownpoint Foundry,	do.	Bridgeton.
Walker, Henderson & Co.,	Engineers and Boilermakers,	Buchanan Street.	Buchanan Street.
Wallace, H., & Co.,	Lancefield Boiler Works,	do.	Stobcross.
Wallace & Connell,	Engineers, &c.,	do.	Buchanan Street.
Wallace, J., & Co.,	Agricultural Implement Makers,	do.	do.
Watson, Gow & Co.,	Etna Iron Works,	do.	South Side.
Watson, Laidlaw & Co.,	Brassfounders,	do.	Kinning Park.
*White, J. & J.,	Shawfield Chemical Works,	South Side (for Shawfield Chemical Works),	South Side (for Shawfield Chemical Works).
*White, J., & Co.,	Ibrox Flour Mills,	Kinning Park,	Kinning Park.
Willford & Co.,	Railway Spring Makers,	Kennyhill,	Kennyhill.
Wilson, William, & Co.	Lilybank Boiler Works,	Buchanan Street,	South Side.
Young & Co.,	Brassfounders,	Buchanan Street,	South Side.

* These Firms have direct Siding connection with Caledonian Railway.

Plate 2.10
This is the last of the 14-page list of companies on Clydeside which were served by the Caledonian and gives some idea of the diversity of industry on Clydeside. It includes the Steel Company of Scotland's Blochairn works. This was established in the 1850s to manufacture malleable iron. It was converted into one of the first Scottish steelworks in 1880. Further down the list is Charles Tennant & Co. The St. Rollox works was at one time the largest chemical company in the world. Tennants also controlled the United Alkali Company.

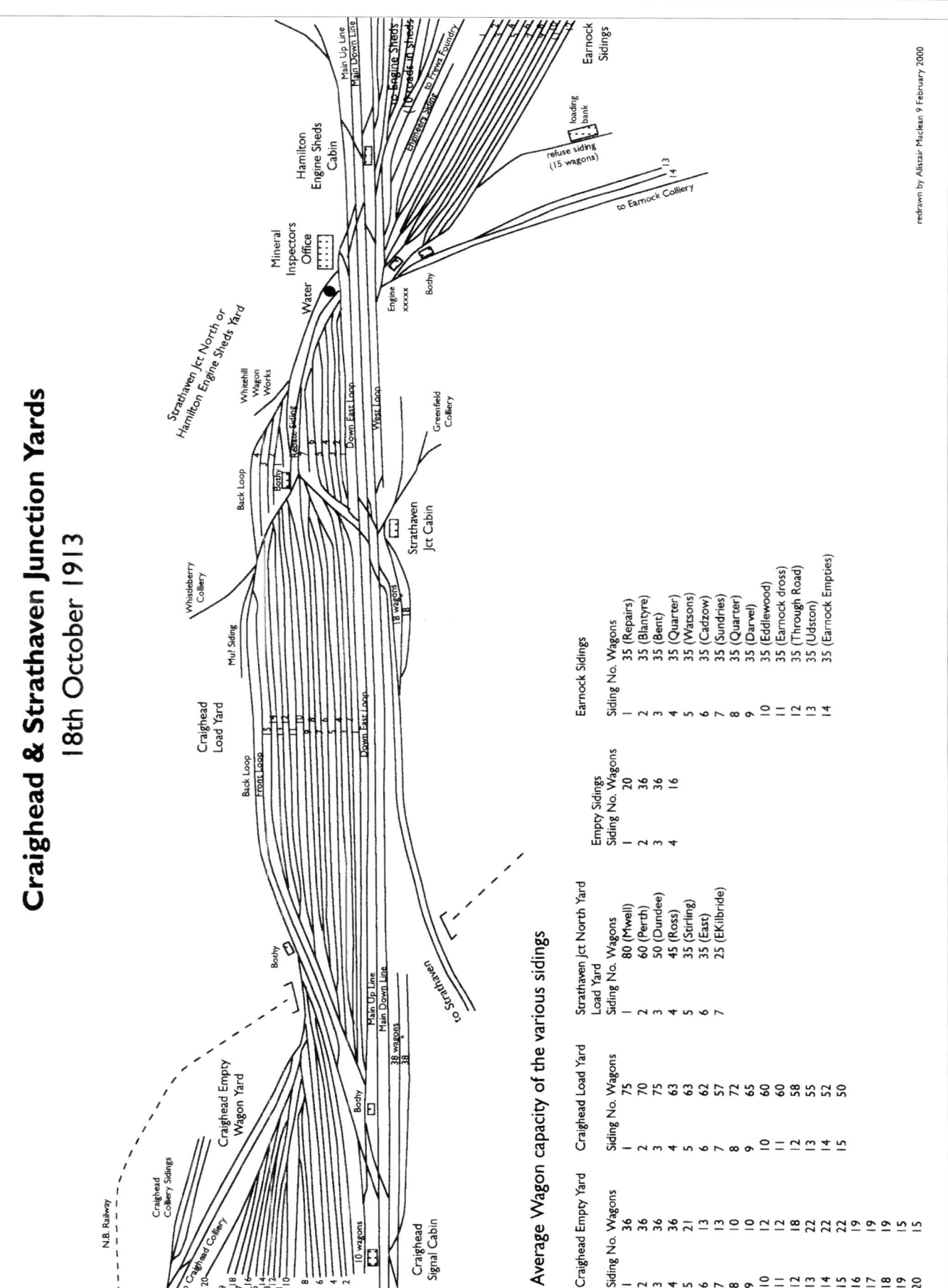

Figure 2.6 The layout of the Craighead and Strathaven marshalling yard in 1913.

Plate 2.11

One of a number of official pictures taken of Buchanan Street goods depot, image SRX 378, courtesy of National Railway Museum / SSPL. In 1903, the traffic record shows that Buchanan Street received 278,442 tons of goods, and despatched 345,974 tons. This did not all go through the depot; as Plate 2.10 shows, Buchanan Street was the invoicing point for most of the Glasgow Section goods traffic on the Lanarkshire & Dumbartonshire railway, as well as dealing with Anglo-Scottish traffic. Another picture shows a sign stating it was open from 6.00am to 5.40pm Monday to Friday, and until 3.30pm on Saturday.

In the right foreground is an empty barrel truck. The number 3074 is on the fourth plank from the top. The reinforcing rods between the doors and the standard wagon buffer identify it as one of the twenty-three Diagram 74 trucks built between 1903 and 1910. Another loaded barrel truck is in the left background, behind the Diagram 54 bogie wagon, which is in the daily service between Buchanan Street and 'Aberdeen, Dundee, Motherwell, Stirling, &c' mentioned in Chapter 9. The barrel truck is loaded to the full extent of the sides, which suggests that it is also a 6-ton capacity truck to Diagram 74. The other wagons are all Diagram 15 or 24 open goods, except for a Diagram 22 mineral wagon which is being emptied or loaded with straw.

The four wheeled road vehicles in the immediate foreground and over to the right are 'delivery lorries.' Although it cannot be discerned on the photograph, the words CALEDONIAN RAILWAY were probably written on the side rail in black. The overall livery was red. Immediately behind the lorry to the left is a wagon for carrying timber or pipes; these vehicles had an adjustable wheelbase to suit the load.

2.2: Types of Wagon and Numbers in Service

As we have seen in part 1 of this chapter, the Caledonian was ideally placed to meet the demands of the growing industrialisation of western Scotland. As soon as it opened for business, more industry was attracted to the area and more traffic was there to be exploited.

The result was a continual expansion in wagon numbers. For instance, in 1863 and again in 1865, the Board was asked to authorise the purchase of 1,000 wagons, charged to the capital account.[1] Five years later, 400 extra mineral wagons were requested to cope with the traffic arising from new pits on the Benhar branch.[2]

In 1871, loco coal wagons were routinely appropriated for revenue traffic.[3] This led to a decision to not only build wagons exclusively for loco coal, but to seek the urgent delivery of 3,000 new mineral wagons.[4] Still the situation was not resolved; in 1876 the General Manager reported details of a meeting with coalmasters concerning the scarcity of locomotives and wagons.[5] A further complaint was made in 1880.[6] More requests for stock were made in 1877 (for *'a few thousand wagons'*)[7] and 1881.[8]

Wagons Absorbed in 1866 and 1867

In 1865 the Caledonian amalgamated with the Scottish Central Railway. The Scottish North Eastern Railway followed suit a year later. Both contributed rolling stock to the Caledonian, which was recorded one year later in the traffic returns. A breakdown of wagons and NPCS is shown in the table below left. Neither railway contributed any mineral wagons, despite the fact that the Scottish Central served the Stirlingshire coalfield.

Trends 1870-1905

Half-yearly reports to shareholders give the stock of wagons over the period 1868-1910. The returns were tabulated as part of a series of statements to the Board of Trade about the CR rolling stock.[9] The results, shown at five-yearly intervals, are set out in the table below.

The figures show bursts of expansion interspersed by periods of consolidation. Between 1870 and 1875, the wagon fleet doubled, while the number of mineral wagons more than trebled. This was in response to the difficulties described earlier. The 1880s were relatively stable, followed by another large increase in stock during the 1890s, driven by a 35 per cent increase in mineral wagons.

The major changes between 1900 and 1905 were the increase in open and covered goods wagons, and swivel wagons. The 1905 figures are not quite the maximum; in 1907 the fleet peaked at 67,531 wagons, after which it steadily declined as high capacity mineral wagons replaced the old 8-ton wagons at the rate of two for one.

Details of the Wagon Stock in 1874

In 1874 the CR commissioned two independent experts to conduct an inventory and valuation of all its rolling stock.[10] Wagons were divided into more categories than appeared in the six-monthly returns, giving a partial picture of the growth in specialist traffic.

Open goods wagons were almost equally divided between solid and sprung buffer designs. Most were 6-ton (2,990) and 8-ton (4,003) capacity. The experts noted that, in 1870, 12,000 traders' wagons had been acquired by the company. The reports to shareholders recorded a transfer of 6,772 wagons to the CR stock in the period ending July 1872. The previous period is annotated *'plant taken over from traders is not included.'*

The Caledonian's attempts to eradicate private traders' wagons from the system by buying up the traders' stock are discussed further in Chapter 7.1.

Type	SCR	SNER	Total
Ordinary (i.e. goods wagons)	1,502	919	2,421
Covered Van	104	107	211
Cattle	126	65	191
Brake	32	13	45
Swivel	158	30	188
Ballast		24	24
10-ton (presumably goods)	262	18	280
Horse Box	21	7	28
Carriage Truck	15	3	18
Luggage Van	31	17	48
Fish and Milk Truck	5		5
Crane Wagon		1	1
Vitriol		4	4

	1870	1875	1880	1885	1890	1895	1900	1905
Open Goods Wagons	6,302	7,992	8,349	8,776	9,913	10,414	13,813	16,634
Covered Goods Wagons	868	1,051	1,224	1,290	1,315	1,369	1,459	1,928
Cattle & Sheep Trucks	648	837	836	875	875	875	875	990
Brake Vans	223	302	371	371	406	432	523	534
Swivel Wagons	539	750	745	753	1,053	1,053	1,853	2,152
Bar Iron/Round Timber		279						
Mineral Wagons	6,428	20,771	29,290	31,645	31,645	39,118	42,951	42,885
Gunpowder Vans	2	2	2	2	5	11	11	35
Tank Wagons	1	2	2	2	2	5	11	22
Ballast Wagons	104	244	248	254	254	254	254	349
Total	15,115	32,230	41,067	43,968	45,468	53,471	61,750	65,529

Twelve special class wagons were recorded of varying capacities, including one 30-ton trolley. Two furniture van wagons were also mentioned. There were 375 stone wagons, fifty beer wagons and eighty wagons that could carry either coke or sheep.

In the same census, the inventory of carriage stock identified 224 non-passenger coaching stock vehicles. They were all four-wheeled vehicles, except for one six-wheeled stores van. The 'Stranraer and Portpatrick' contributed a further nine – all four-wheeled. The total goods stock was therefore just under 33,800. The full details of the census are shown in Appendix I.

The Wagon Fleet in 1900

The next detailed snapshot of wagons in service is provided by the *Register of Wagon Plant with Photographs*, which dates from 1900.[11] The full list, cross-referenced to diagram numbers where applicable, forms Appendix VI. The stated total wagon stock of something over 69,000 considerably exceeded the rolling stock return of 1900, which was 61,750. In the shareholder's return, non-passenger coaching stock was omitted, as were special class and loco coal wagons, which accounts for the discrepancy.

The *1900 Register* shows for the first time the extent and variety of the special wagon fleet, which was expanded to serve the developing steel and engineering industries in the last decade of the nineteenth century. It highlights the importance of rail, swivel and twin wagons (about 600, 2,100 and 950 wagons respectively). Non-passenger coaching stock was also shown. Nearly 1,500 loco coal wagons were in service.

The 1902 Wagon Census

In April 1902, the Traffic Committee authorised a census of goods and mineral wagons.[12] Unfortunately, no details seem to have survived of its findings.

Details of the Wagon Fleet and Changes 1907-1910

As part of its submission to the Railway and Canal Commission in 1910, the Caledonian produced a statistical analysis of the complete wagon fleet, excluding non-passenger coaching stock.[13] Meat and refrigerator vans were included because they were numbered in the goods wagon series.

It gives by far the most detailed insight into the specialist wagons, and shows the impact of the increase in carrying capacity of the new standard mineral wagons that were built from 1903 onwards. It also coincides with the period when the wagon fleet was at its largest. The details are in Appendix I.

In 1907, the mineral wagon stock had decreased by over a quarter from the 1900 statement. The 'bogies' taken out of traffic were replaced by the 14, 16 and 30-ton wagons built in the first decade of the twentieth century.

The same effect occurred in loco coal traffic; the arrival of 300

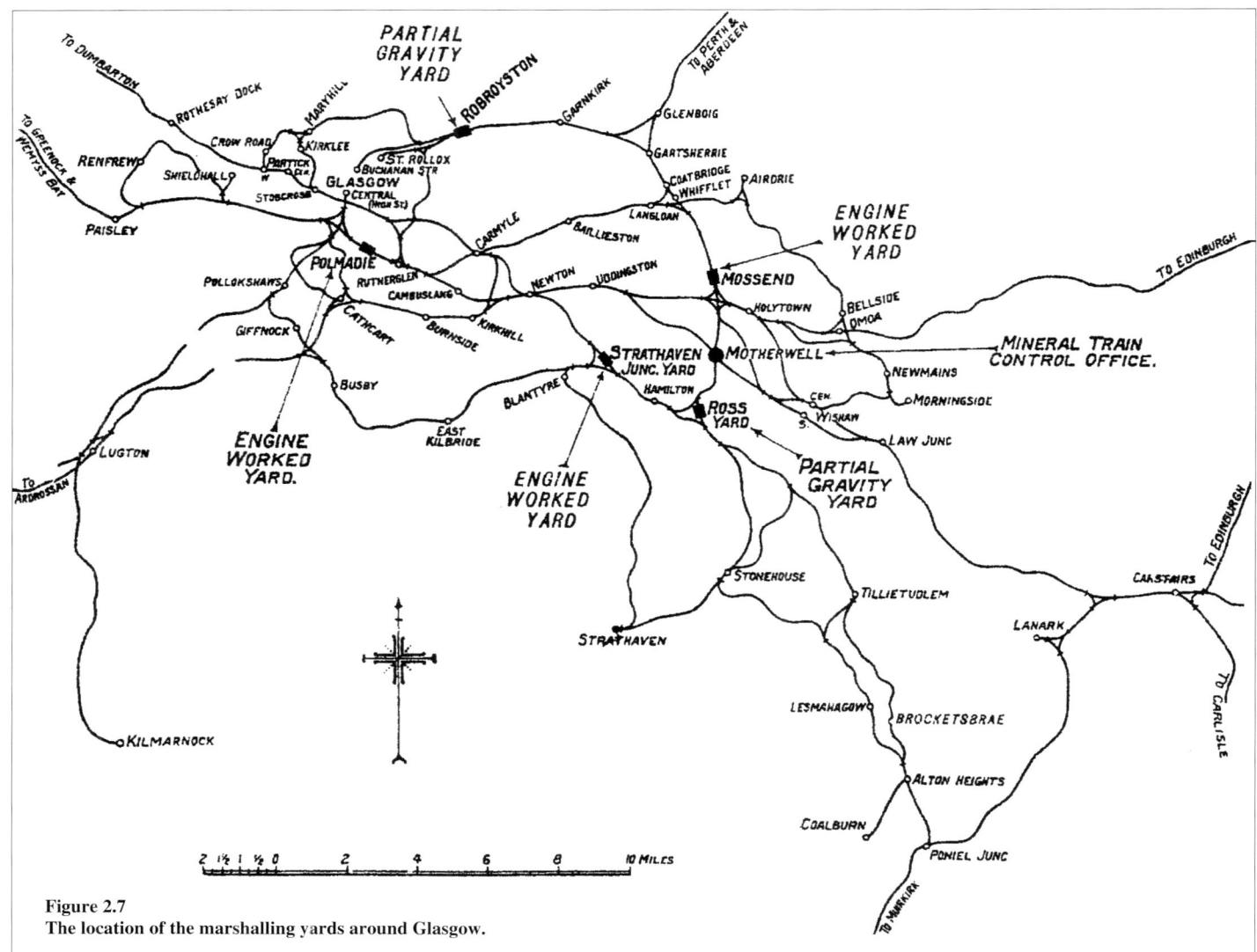

Figure 2.7
The location of the marshalling yards around Glasgow.

bogie wagons reduced the number of 10-ton wagons by nearly 500. There was some confusion between the return and reality as far as the other seventy 30-ton wagons were concerned. In the return they were classed as coal wagons; in fact they were used for a variety of traffic, as described in Chapter 5. The 50-ton iron ore prototype was included in the special class as a goods wagon.

Only 200 of the new 10-ton covered vans were in service, leaving the covered wagon fleet almost entirely in the hands of 6-ton vans. The number of rail wagons had increased by 50 per cent, with over 900 now in service. Swivel wagon numbers remained constant, but 133 30-ton bogie wagons had been introduced. There were approximately 400 more pig iron wagons than in 1900, with just under 800 14 or 15-ton wagons out of a total of approximately 1,800.

Not much changed between 1907 and 1910. There were 150 fewer open goods wagons of 8-tons capacity in 1910. The 6/7-ton 'bogies' further reduced by 7,500, halving the number on the books. This was partially counterbalanced by 1,300 more 16-ton Diagram 59 wagons. There were fewer 6 and 8-ton pig iron wagons, but they were not replaced by higher capacity wagons.

Wagon Depreciation Policy

As rolling stock, especially wagons, was replaced and upgraded from an early date, it is appropriate to describe how the work was financed and accounted for. The Caledonian did not write down the value of their wagons over forty years, as they did with locomotives and coaching stock. Instead, £32,000 per annum was set aside as a replacement fund.

This became a serious problem in 1904, when the company embarked on the wagon replacement programme. The number of replacements authorised in each half year suggests constraint. After the initial order of Diagram 67 covered vans built by Pickering on the capital account in 1903, only twelve more were authorised in the years up to 1910. Diagram 59 mineral wagons were built in batches of 208, 86 and 181, suggesting that the Traffic Committee was authorising what it could afford out of the £16,000 half-yearly budget.[14]

In 1911, the Directors decided to tackle the anomaly once and for all:

'The matter of the renewal of the Company's rolling stock has been repeatedly considered by the Chairman and Directors.'[15]

They reported that the stock of 46,470 wagons (the 6 and 7-ton 'bogies' were excluded from the count) was valued at £3,648,698. The £32,000 set aside was therefore significantly less than 1% of the capital value. At 2½% (i.e. on the basis of a forty-year accountancy life), the annual amount to be set aside would have been £91,217. The Board resolved gradually to increase the amount to be set aside, so that by 1917 it would be the necessary 2½%. The target was not reached, because during the First World War the government froze the sum for replacements at 1¾%, which was the 1913 figure.[16]

The situation did not improve immediately as a result of the Board decision. Part of the replacement programme for the period ending 31st December 1912 was postponed into the next half year.[17] As a result, ninety-one assorted wagons which had been authorised for July 1913 were not built.

In 1915 the limited wagon replacement budget was further eroded. The Board resolved:

'the amount of provision in respect of wagon renewals shall be reduced for 4 years from 1 January 1915, by a sum equal to the amount to be spent in extraordinary repairs of rebuffering and repairing the 10,000 Solid Buffer Wagons.'[18]

The decision, coupled with the government restriction, caused increasing problems with company accounts as the war progressed. Proposals about the wagon replacement programme in 1916 and 1917 were remitted for further consideration.[19]

In 1917 the Board resolved to rescind the 1915 decision,

'having regard to the difficulties which have arisen in connection with the accounts in respect of Rolling Stock Renewals ... to charge any wagons converted in 1917 direct against revenue.'[20]

The renewal programme for the half year ending 31st December 1917 was resubmitted and approved without the proposed expenditure on 800 conversions from solid to sprung buffers.[21]

At this point the Caledonian decided to take issue with government policy. The wagon replacement programme was only conditionally approved by the Traffic Committee. It included 380 mineral wagons, but renewal was only to be authorised,

'on condition that Company's claim to have renewal of wagons on 2½% basis is admitted by Government. Failing this the number will be reduced to 210. This number 210 can be authorised only if this Company's claim to have conversion of dead buffer wagons specially treated is admitted by the Government, failing this the number will be reduced to 60. This number of 60 16-ton wagons can be ordered at present, the rest being delayed pending settlement of the questions involved.'[22]

While it is not possible to be absolutely certain, the St. Rollox record for order G397 suggests that the government allowed the solid buffer conversion claim, but rejected the allowance of 2½%.

The Finance Committee seems to have finally resolved the wagon conversion problem in 1918, when it issued a statement about the inventory of rolling stock on the capital account.[23] It approved the proposal that:

'the Cost of Rebuffering wagons shall not enter into the renewal programme, and the Capital Valuation of rebuffered wagons shall be the original book value plus betterment reduced to 1913 basis. Inventory Valuations to be the original book value plus Total Cost of alterations.'

From 1918 it becomes difficult to reconcile the minuted decisions about wagon building with the order details at St. Rollox and outside builders. According to the late George Robin, in his article *The Rolling Stock Crisis of 1919*,[24] a backlog of replacements had built up from 1917, amounting to 1,610 wagons in total. The detailed list comprised:

1,165	16-ton mineral wagons
221	10-ton goods wagons
100	20-ton steel carrying wagons
60	10-ton goods vans
60	20-ton brake vans
2	20-ton implement wagons
1	each 20-ton and 40-ton trollies

The original proposal was to divide the work between St. Rollox and outside contractors in a ratio of approximately 1:2. In addition, the General Manager recommended construction of a further 1,207 wagons, comprising 1,000 16-ton minerals, 37 35-ton gondola wagons and 170 20-ton rail wagons.

Beginning with the half year ending December 1918 and continuing until the period ending December 1921, all proposals for wagon replacements were presented as Plan A or Plan B.[25] Plan A, the preferred option, took account of the backlog in the replacement programme. Plan B depended on the government's approval of expenditure equivalent to 2½% of the capital cost on the inventory.

The alternative proposals to the end of 1919, which would have almost exactly cleared the backlog of 1,610 renewals over three accountancy periods, were:

Half Year to	Plan A	Plan B
31st December 1918	512 wagons	391 wagons
30th June 1919	543 wagons	373 wagons
31st December 1919	551 wagons	381 wagons

It is clear that, if the government did allow 2½% to be used for the calculation in December 1918, the concession did not establish a precedent. A sub-committee was convened in June 1919 to consider the situation, along with a similar recommendation to overtake the backlog in construction of coaching stock.[26] It met on 7th July.

One recorded result was that five lots of wagons (a total of 456 vehicles) that had been allocated order numbers ready for construction by St. Rollox were cancelled.[27] The fifty 20-ton rail wagons to St. Rollox order G410 had been authorised as part of Plan B for the half year ending 31st December 1918, but had not been built by the time that the sub-committee met. The other orders, G417-G420, amounted to 406 wagons, which exceeded the Plan B figure for the half year ending 31st December 1919.

The Board approved the sub-committee's recommendation that 730 wagons be built. The major part of the programme was let to contractors. Pickering built 500 16-ton mineral wagons to card order 36083. Clayton & Shuttleworth built thirty six-wheeled goods brake vans.

At St. Rollox, the cancelled order number G417 was used to build sixty-six mineral wagons which were not among the 730 wagons authorised – they must have been accounted for in the next period. Orders G418 and G419 were re-authorised to a total of seventy-five wagons. It has proved impossible to trace the remaining fifty-nine wagons in the original list.

The practice of presenting alternative plans continued, as shown in the following table. In each case Plan B was approved, but always subject to Government agreement that a 2½% allowance could be applied:

Half Year To	Plan A	Plan B
30th June 1920	527 wagons	320 wagons
31st December 1920	549 wagons	364 wagons
30th June 1921	533 wagons	368 wagons
31st December 1921	576 wagons	413 wagons

The December 1921 proposal was delayed *'until further instruction is given.'*[28] These wagons do not seem to have been built. When Government control of the railways ceased in 1921 the Board felt free to implement the original 2½% calculation for rolling stock replacements, but not for wagons. A minute in May 1922 recorded the Board's agreement,

'to continue charge at 2½% on Rolling Stock Inventory Values to include £20,000 p.a. replacement of old wagons.'

This allowance was of course much less than the £32,000 p.a. which had originally been allowed before the Board resolved to address the accounting anomaly in 1911. The inflation which began during and after the First World War further eroded its purchasing power. For instance, the cost of a Class '498' 0-6-0 tank doubled between 1915 and 1918.[29] The CR established a new valuation of £3,855,464 for the wagon fleet in 1915, but only increased it by £34,000 in 1918.[30] Despite these constraints, 455 wagons were authorised in April 1922 for the half year ending 30th June 1922.[31]

The Situation Immediately Prior to Grouping

By 1922, the size and composition of the wagon stock had changed again. An article in *The Railway Gazette* in 1922[32] gave the total number of wagons as 54,458. This did not include non-passenger coaching stock. While direct comparisons for all the types of wagon are not possible, the number of the following increased: covered goods 2,710 (over one third more than 1910), cattle trucks 1,475 (over 40 per cent increase), brake vans 647 (plus 10 per cent).

Mineral wagon numbers had decreased by about 2,000 or 7 per cent (presumably the 6/7-ton wagons that were not yet stored in 1910). The total included 255 hopper wagons. Swivel wagons had decreased by about 600 (one quarter of the 1910 total). The number of traders' wagons working on the system had fallen to 22,000; the traders' load-carrying capacity did not decrease as larger wagons replaced those built in the 1880s and 1890s.

When the Caledonian finally became part of the London Midland & Scottish Railway on 30th June 1923, it handed over 51,356 wagons, plus 1,778 service vehicles. Less than 5 per cent of the total stock was under 8 tons capacity, and most of these were covered goods vans.[33]

References
1. NRS BR/CAL/1/13 entry 480,
   NRS BR/CAL/1/14 entry 580
2. NRS BR/CAL/1/18 entry 305
3. NRS BR/CAL/1/19 entry 1286
4. NRS BR/CAL/1/19 entry 1729
5. NRS BR/CAL/1/22 entry 1730
6. NRS BR/CAL/1/26 entry 306
7. NRS BR/CAL/1/13 entry 1235. The Board authorised 1,000 wagons in response to this expansive request
8. NRS BR/CAL/1/26 entry 349
9. Held in the national archives at Edinburgh and Kew – NRS GD344/11/1 and TNA: PRO RAIL 1110/48 and /49 respectively
10. NRS BR/CAL/5/15
11. NRS BR/CAL/5/23
12. NRS BR/CAL/1/46 entry 79
13. In NRS BR/CAL/4/134
14. Information about renewals in the twentieth century is summarised in NRS BR/CAL/5/11
15. NRS BR/CAL/1/60 entry 1105
16. Quoted in 'The Rolling Stock Crisis of 1919', in the *Caledonian Journal Number 3*, pp. 22-24. The author, the late George Robin, did not include references, but he was clearly using primary sources
17. NRS BR/CAL/1/62 entry 631
18. NRS BR/CAL/1/66 entry 723
19. NRS BR/CAL/1/68 entry 98,
    NRS BR/CAL/1/69 entry 605
20. NRS BR/CAL/1/69 entry 619
21. NRS BR/CAL/1/69 entry 696
22. NRS BR/CAL/1/69 entry 799
23. NRS BR/CAL/1/71 entry 97
24. *Caledonian Railway Journal Number 3*, p. 23
25. NRS BR/CAL/1/71 entry 229,
    NRS BR/CAL/1/71 no entry number,
    NRS BR/CAL/1/72 entry 906,
    NRS BR/CAL/1/74 entry 23,
    NRS BR/CAL/1/75 entry 566,
    NRS BR/CAL/1/76 entry 442,
    NRS BR/CAL/1/77 entry 2070
26. NRS BR/CAL/1/73 entry 110
27. NRS BR/CAL/1/73 entry 374
28. NRS BR/CAL/1/77 entry 2070
29. Quoted in *Forty Years of Caledonian Locomotives*, p. 175
30. NRS/BR/CAL/4/6, *Statement of capital expenditure as at 31st December 1915*. This was periodically updated and used to negotiate the compensation to shareholders when the CR was absorbed into the LM&SR
31. NRS BR/CAL/1/79/259
32. 'Freight Rolling Stock Distribution on the Caledonian Railway', reproduced in *The True Line*, issue 73, pp. 8-13
33. Figures from the Directors' report of 31st December 1922, quoted in *The Caledonian in LMS Days*, p. 67

2.3: Technical Development – Historical Overview

So far, this chapter has discussed the commercial factors which influenced the development of the Caledonian wagon fleet. These led to increasing numbers of wagons and to greater specialisation as wagons were built to suit particular traffic needs. We have also seen that financial constraints within the company compounded by the demands of the First World War slowed the modernisation programme that was started early in the twentieth century.

The following sections deal with developments in the design and construction of wagons. There were two main drivers for change. The first was the constant search for improvements in operational efficiency. One aspect of this was the growing need for effective management of the company as it became established in the second half of the nineteenth century. The need to improve cost-effectiveness became more pressing towards the end of the nineteenth century, when operating costs rose, in part owing to the greater influence of organised labour and a general reduction in working hours. This stimulated various technical innovations.

The second driving force came from regulatory bodies. They were concerned with establishing standards of technical design, and the need to improve safety for passengers and railway staff. For instance, effective continuous brakes were needed to cope with the greater speed of passenger trains and to prevent the recurrence of serious accidents caused by brake failures. This obviously affected non-passenger coaching stock. Also, towards the end of the nineteenth century, in the interest of railway staff safety, it was not enough for ordinary wagons to have a brake that could only be operated from one side.

We begin with a brief overview of how CR wagon design evolved and continue with a discussion of the main technical developments as applied to the wagon fleet. This deals in turn with running gear, brakes, buffers and drawgear.

The Early Days

As far as wagons were concerned, during the first thirty-five years of its existence, the Caledonian Railway was running to stand still, and did not really control its own destiny. Despite the fact that the Caledonian opened for business with *'substantial vehicles carrying from 4½ to 5-tons of loose coal'*[1] the first mineral wagons were found to be inadequate soon after they entered service. Steps were taken to replace them with wagons of double the capacity.[2] In two years between July 1856 and July 1858, 1,442 wagons were declared to be 'worn out' and their carrying capacity was replaced by 675 new stock. The scrapped wagons represented 36 per cent of the mineral fleet.

As we have seen earlier in this chapter, minutes also frequently record that expanding traffic demands caused the company to lack sufficient rolling stock. There was another side to this problem. For most of their wagon construction during this period, the Caledonian had to rely on outside contractors. The works at St. Rollox lacked the capacity and/or the organisation to keep up with demand. The necessary tendering process took time, and most wagons seem to have been contractor, rather than company, designs. Late delivery was often a problem; it was particularly acute in 1874, when minutes refer to arrears from several contractors.

The first of two turning points in the history of the Caledonian wagon fleet took place in 1882, when Dugald Drummond was appointed as Locomotive Superintendent. By this time the rolling stock situation was not good. Under George Brittain development of all types of rolling stock had stagnated, the adoption of continuous brakes for passenger stock had barely started, and he became increasingly unwell, as had Benjamin Conner before him.

The wagon building capacity at St. Rollox works was totally inadequate, at a time when the number of wagons in stock was increasing dramatically. Between 1860 and 1869, 8,230 wagons had been built, of which 1,528 (under 19 per cent) came from contractors. In the decade 1870-79, contractors built over 80 per cent of the wagons authorised by the Board – the returns show that 26,400 wagons were built, of which contractors are known to have accounted for 22,004.

Repair capacity was also a problem. On 30th January 1875 the Traffic Committee reported that the number of wagons waiting repair had increased to 1,788 from 715 on 12th December.[3] In 1877, St. Rollox again could not keep up with repairs and contractors took up the shortfall.[4] Something similar happened in 1880 when over one quarter of the horse boxes were reported to be awaiting repair.[5]

The Drummond Revolution

Dugald Drummond was headhunted from the North British Railway with the promise of a salary nearly two and a half times greater than that of the current incumbent, George Brittain.[6] Brittain resigned five months after Drummond's arrival in July 1882.[7]

By the end of 1882, Drummond had convinced the Board to invest £60,000 on the modernisation and extension of St. Rollox works[8] and had been authorised to spend £30,000 over a three-year period to clear the backlog in fitting existing passenger stock with the Westinghouse brake.[9]

The last orders to contractors for wagons were authorised in July 1883.[10] There is no record of further outside tenders until 1895. During these twelve years the Caledonian met its own needs, constructing over 26,000 wagons. Gas lighting was fitted to carriages during the first few years of Drummond's tenure. Dual brakes were fitted to non-passenger coaching stock, starting in 1887.[11]

Drummond also made a huge impact on wagon design. The mineral 'bogies' and other designs with outside axle guards and wooden brake blocks were replaced by the mineral wagons, cattle trucks, open goods wagons and vans with up-to-date suspension and improved brakes that would last well into the twentieth century. He resigned in 1890.

Modernisation at the Turn of the Nineteenth Century

After the brief tenure of Hugh Smellie, John Lambie continued the construction of Drummond-designed goods stock. The major development in his time was the adoption of spindle (that is, sprung) buffers for mineral wagons.[12] This signalled the end of solid buffer wagon construction. Unfortunately in 1895, he, like Smellie, died suddenly in office. John McIntosh succeeded Lambie, and remained in post until 1914. During his command, the second turning point in Caledonian wagon design history took place.

In 1899 the search began for a mineral wagon design to carry the greatest paying load while minimising dead weight. This eventually resulted in the 30-ton bogie coal wagons and the new four-wheeled standard mineral wagon to Diagram 59. Both had steel underframes, effecting a reduction in dead weight. The weight reduction was especially marked when Leeds Forge patent pressed steel underframes were used, rather than conventional steel channel. Experiments with wagon brakes that could be applied from either side also started in 1899. From 1903, all wagons were built with either side brakes.

Steel underframes became the norm for mineral and open goods wagons. The wagon replacement programme was launched in 1903, with the two new designs of Diagram 59 mineral wagon and Diagram 67 van as the backbone, along with modernised designs of open goods and pig iron wagons. The only Drummond design to be built in the renewal programme was the Diagram 10 cattle wagon. It too was fitted with modern brakes. All these designs were built up to the end of the Caledonian Railway's existence.

The rebuilding of 6,000 solid buffered mineral wagons to Diagram 22 was set in motion. The brake van fleet was also modernised with the construction of four- and six-wheeled designs to Diagrams 62 and 63. The latter had much greater braking capacity than previous brake vans. New designs of non-passenger coaching stock and perishable goods vehicles appeared. The special wagon fleet was extended and diversified.

While St. Rollox was not able to supply all the company's rolling stock needs, McIntosh could look back in 1907 and say that, since he took office in 1895, the works had built 33,098 wagons, as well as 549 locomotives and 1,208 carriages.[13]

REFERENCES

1. Quoted from 'The Evolution of the Rolling Stock', written by John McIntosh for the Caledonian Railway Diamond Jubilee edition of *The Railway Magazine* in 1907
2. Taken from rolling stock returns in six-monthly reports to shareholders, held at Edinburgh and Kew, NRS GD/344/11/1 and TNA: PRO RAIL 1110/48 respectively
3. NRS BR/CAL/1/22 entry 435
4. NRS BR/CAL/1/23 entry 951
5. NRS BR/CAL/1/25 entry 1144
6. NRS BR/CAL/1/22 entry 1991 gives Brittain's starting salary as £700 p.a. Drummond was appointed at £1,700, according to NRS BR/CAL/1/27 entry 858. His salary was increased by £400 with effect from August 1888 (NRS BR/CAL/1/32 entry 973). Smellie was appointed his successor in 1890 at a salary of £1,500 (NRS BR/CAL/1/33 entry 1442)
7. NRS BR/CAL/1/27 entries 1465 and 889 respectively
8. NRS BR/CAL/1/27 entries 1302 and 1334
9. NRS BR/CAL/1/27 entry 1441
10. NRS BR/CAL/1/27 entries 577 and 578
11. NRS BR/CAL/5/11 entry 35. Drummond added a note 'The best stock only to be fitted.'
12. NRS BR/CAL/5/11 entry 117
13. Quoted in the *Railway Magazine* CR Jubilee edition

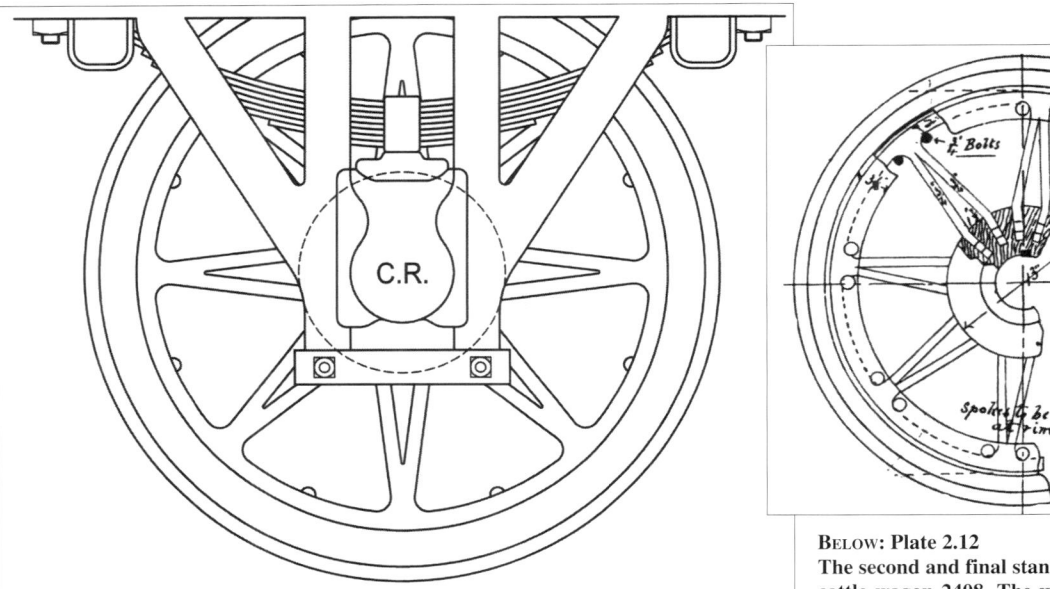

FAR LEFT: Figure 2.8
The first type of wagon wheel had a cast set of spokes, riveted to the wheel tyre. This is taken from St. Rollox drawing 1540, shown in full as Figure 5.1. The enlargement was redrawn by Angus McIntosh.

LEFT: Figure 2.9
A section through the second type of wagon wheel, showing the welded and bolted joints between the wrought iron spokes and the tyre. This is taken from Figure 5.2, which shows St. Rollox drawing 2558.

BELOW: Plate 2.12
The second and final standard types of wagon wheel, under large cattle wagon 2408. The welded type with reinforcing bolts is on the left, the later type is on the right. The complete wagon is shown in Plate 11.3.

2.4: Running Gear

Wheels

The first Caledonian wagons had cast iron wheels. In September 1856, the company decided to replace them gradually with wheels made of malleable iron, which were better able to withstand shocks and vibration in traffic.[1] In January 1861 the CR General Manager wanted to give notice that private traders should make a similar change, but the Board considered it to be premature.[2] Presumably by this time all the company's wagon wheels had been replaced.

The standard wagon wheel from very early days was 3 feet 2 inches diameter with eight open spokes. The first type had a cast centre, which was riveted to the tyre – see Figure 2.8. This type of wheel was eventually outlawed in the Railway Clearing House wagon specification of 1887.

The next variation had welded joints between the wrought iron spokes and tyre – see Figure 2.9. Each joint was reinforced by two bolts. The final type, which Drummond may have introduced, had the tyre pressed on. The second and the final types are shown under one wagon in Plate 2.12. A 2 feet 9 inches diameter version of the later wheel was used on the bogie coal wagons and many of the bogie wagons in the special wagon fleet. Some brake vans were fitted with 3-foot 9-inch disc wheels – see Chapter 16 for details.

At first, a 3-foot 6-inch open spoke wheel was used for goods vehicles rated for passenger traffic. This was superseded in modern (post 1900) construction by the Mansell coach wheel, also 3 feet 6 inches in diameter. Some late-constructed vehicles were fitted with 3-foot 9-inch disc wheels. Examples of all these wheels can be found in photographs in Chapter 12.

Suspension

The early mineral wagons had short springs, only 3 feet 1 inch long between attachment points. This type is shown in Figure 2.10. Some mineral and loco coal wagons in 1872 and 1873 were probably built with *'the patent cushioned bearing spring.'* This device had an action like a self-contained spring buffer and dispensed with spring hangers. It appears on St. Rollox drawings 1251 (Figure 17.1, p. 258) and 1540 (Figure 5.1, p. 82). The latter drawing shows the patented device on one axle and a conventional spring on the other, so it looks as if the experiment was short lived. The mineral wagon suspension was also used on timber and ballast wagons of the period. Plate 2.13 shows a typical arrangement. Other axle guard shapes are shown in Appendix 7.

Early goods wagons had longer springs, with the axle guard inside the solebars – see Figure 9.1 (p. 142). The 6-ton covered goods vans also had the longer springs, but the axle guards were outside the solebars, as shown in Plate 9.15 (p. 154). Some wagons, such as the 1876 design of cattle wagon, had wagon springs suspended from swing links. See Figure 11.2 (p. 186).

The standard wagon spring introduced by Drummond and used for most goods and mineral stock, was 3 feet 4 inches between attachment points and had eleven leaves. It is shown in Figure 2.11. From the Drummond era onwards, axle guards were bolted to the inside face of the solebars.

Early non-passenger coaching stock and wagons built on redundant coach underframes had axle guards bolted to the face of the solebar and long springs, attached to their pivot points with swing links – see Plate 2.14. A later form of suspension is shown in Figure 2.12.

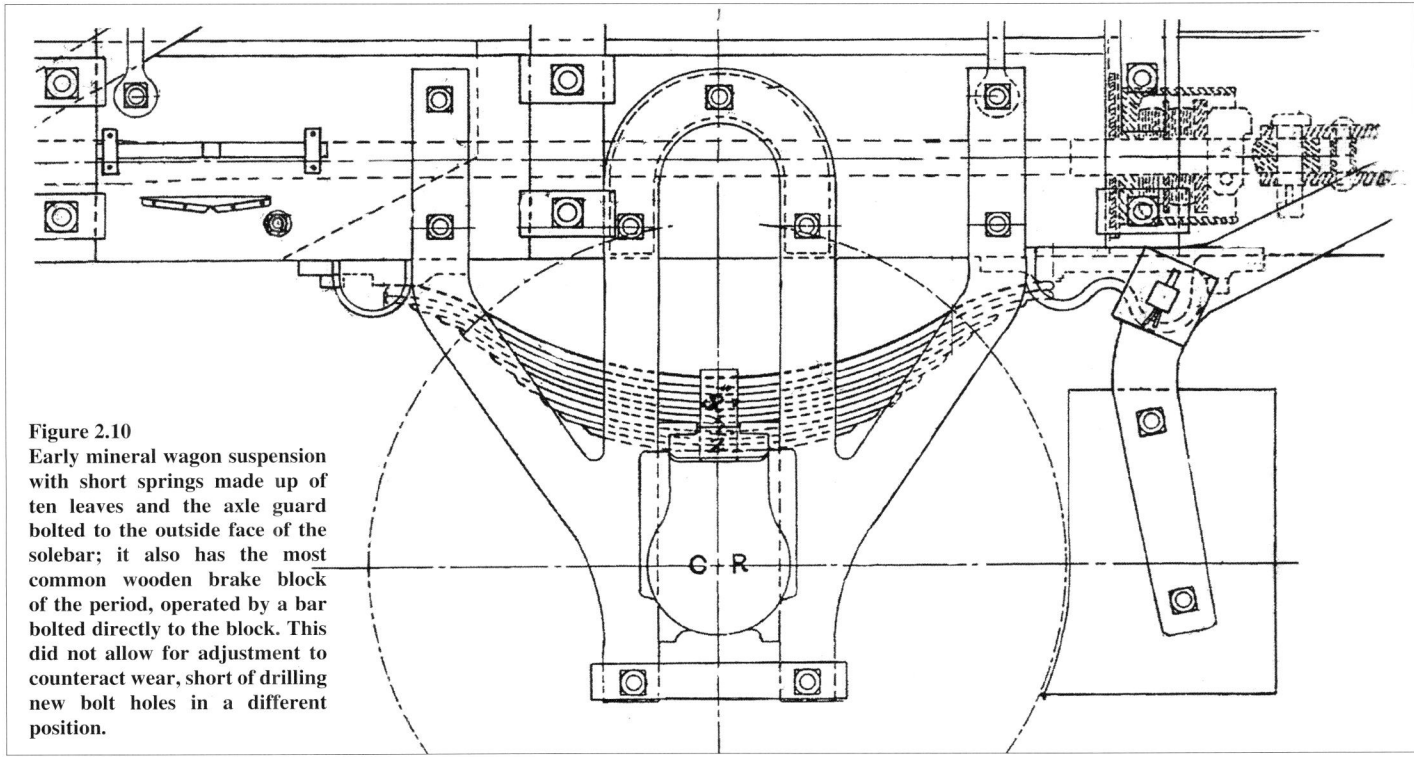

Figure 2.10
Early mineral wagon suspension with short springs made up of ten leaves and the axle guard bolted to the outside face of the solebar; it also has the most common wooden brake block of the period, operated by a bar bolted directly to the block. This did not allow for adjustment to counteract wear, short of drilling new bolt holes in a different position.

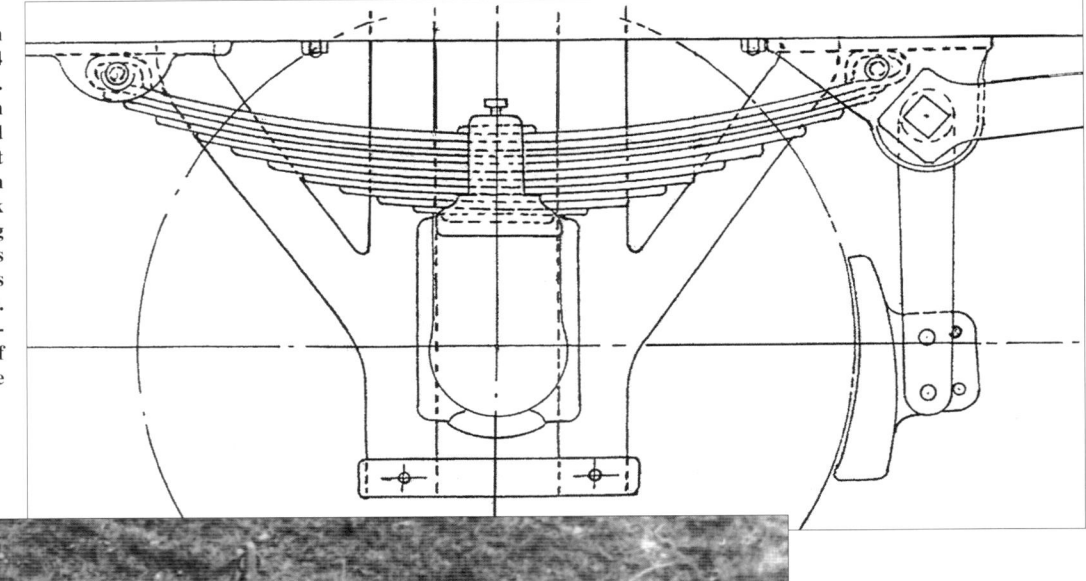

RIGHT: Figure 2.11
The standard Drummond wagon spring with eleven leaves, 3 feet 4 inches between suspension points. The drawing also shows the iron brake block which Drummond introduced. The lever pivot is cast integrally with the spring suspension point. When new, the brake block was 3 inches at the bottom, tapering to 1 inch at the top. The hanger was 18½ inches long. The block was adjustable to accommodate wear. The brake lever boss was lozenge-shaped and twice the thickness of the lever itself. It was attached to the shaft by a prominent square bolt.

LEFT: Plate 2.13
This photograph shows the most common type of early axle guard with both outside legs vertical, bolted to the outside of the solebar. Swivel wagon 36036 was built on a mineral wagon-type underframe, evidenced by the short springs.

RIGHT: Figure 2.12
This shows the modern style of NPCS suspension, as fitted to open and covered carriage trucks.

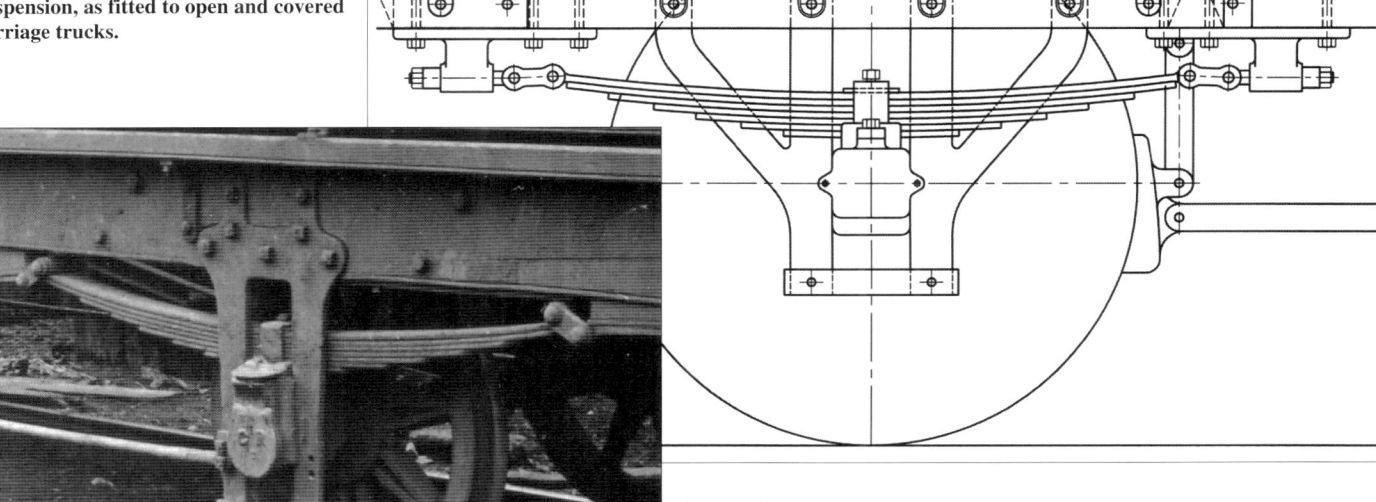

LEFT: Plate 2.14
Old-style carriage and NPCS suspension. Many fish trucks and the first design of empty barrel truck were built on redundant carriage underframes like this. Figure 2.12 (above) shows the modern version of NPCS suspension.

2.4: RUNNING GEAR

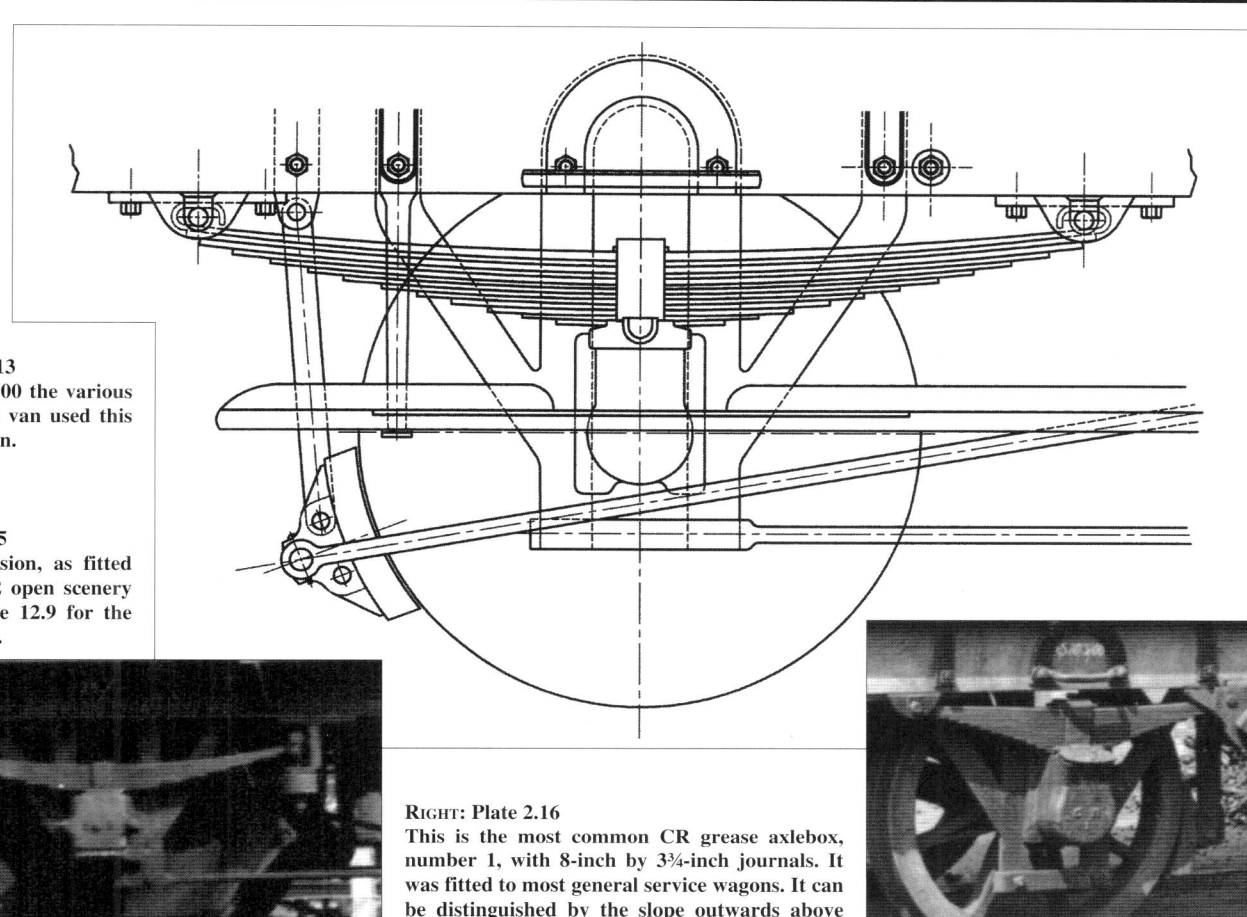

RIGHT: Figure 2.13
From 1883 to 1900 the various designs of brake van used this type of suspension.

BELOW: Plate 2.15
J-hanger suspension, as fitted to a Diagram 92 open scenery truck – see Plate 12.9 for the complete picture.

RIGHT: Plate 2.16
This is the most common CR grease axlebox, number 1, with 8-inch by 3¾-inch journals. It was fitted to most general service wagons. It can be distinguished by the slope outwards above the round bottom which received the axle. This increased its capacity for lubricant.

Other vehicles had springs attached to J-hangers – for instance, the standard six-wheeled underframe used for non-passenger coaching stock had 4-foot 6-inch five-leaf springs, as in Plate 2.15. The brake vans built after 1900 also used this system, but with eight leaves. Prior to 1900 the brake vans had the suspension design shown in Figure 2.13.

AXLEBOXES

Most CR wagons had grease axleboxes. The company initials were cast into the face and most boxes also bore a number. The usual number was 1, which identified an axlebox with 8-inch by 3¾-inch journals. The larger dimension showed the length of axle supported in the axlebox. The smaller dimension was the axle diameter. This size was sufficient for most wagons from the start of the Drummond era – see Plate 2.16. It was specified by the Railway Clearing House for 10-ton capacity wagons.[3] Wagons carrying heavier loads were fitted with 9-inch by 4-inch journals, as in Plate 2.17.

Grease lubricated axles had a high rolling resistance, and required frequent stops for examination to avoid overheating. The Caledonian followed the North Eastern Railway in exploring the benefits of an anti-friction device. An official photograph records this as fitted to Diagram 59 mineral wagon 12696. Unfortunately, the paint date is indistinct.

Plate 2.18 shows the device. It consisted of two large diameter rollers resting on the ends of each axle. The roller pivots revolved at one fifth of the axle speed. The rollers ran on a gudgeon pin, on which bore a brass-lined steel cap which was separately lubricated to reduce static friction. The device was fitted from December 1902 to over 6,000 NER wagons, but it was progressively removed from 1910 onwards.[4] The added weight of the device seems to have negated any benefits to running.

There is no record of this development in CR company minutes, or of how many wagons were modified. There is no drawing in the St. Rollox registers. Its main application on the NER was to high capacity (20 tons plus) wagons, so it may have not been widely adopted by the CR, which did not own any four-wheeled mineral wagons of over 16 tons capacity.

From the early 1900s oil axleboxes were fitted to many new wagons and older wagons that were up-rated to carry heavier loads. Plate 2.19 shows an Iracier patent box and Plate 2.20 shows the more common standard oil box. By this time the journals were 9 inches by 4½ inches, following the Clearing House specification of 1903 for 12-ton wagons.

The CR fitted the Iracier style of axlebox to wagons, NPCS and carriage bogies from 1912 to 1913. On four- and six-wheeled wagons they were associated with steel underframes. The springs were 3 feet 2 inches long. The North British and Highland railways also used them for a period. The Caley fitted them to about 400 wagons, NPCS and carriages. They were removed in 1920, to be replaced by conventional oil axleboxes.[5]

REFERENCES
1. NRS BR/CAL/1/11 entry 216
2. NRS BR/CAL/1/12 entry 1342
3. Quoted in 'The New Regulations for Private Owners' Wagons', by an anonymous private owner, in *The Railway Magazine*, October 1903 issue
4. Information is taken from *North Eastern Record Volume 2*, p. 110
5. NRS BR/CAL/1/75 entry 528

ABOVE LEFT: Plate 2.17
The 9-inch by 4-inch axlebox was fitted to wagons designed to carry a heavier than normal load. It is distinguishable by the prominent ridge across the face of the casting.

ABOVE CENTRE: Plate 2.18
The antifriction device, mounted on 16-ton mineral wagon 12696. One of the device's drawbacks was the increase in weight, but the painted tare weight does not reflect this.

ABOVE RIGHT: Plate 2.19
An Iracier patent oil axlebox, under a Diagram 110 pig iron wagon built in 1912.

RIGHT: Plate 2.20
This is a CR 9-inch by 4½-inch oil box fitted to a Diagram 59 16-ton mineral wagon built in 1922. This was the largest oil box fitted to general service wagons. Diagram 87 goods wagons, which only loaded to 10 tons, were fitted with 9-inch by 4-inch axleboxes.

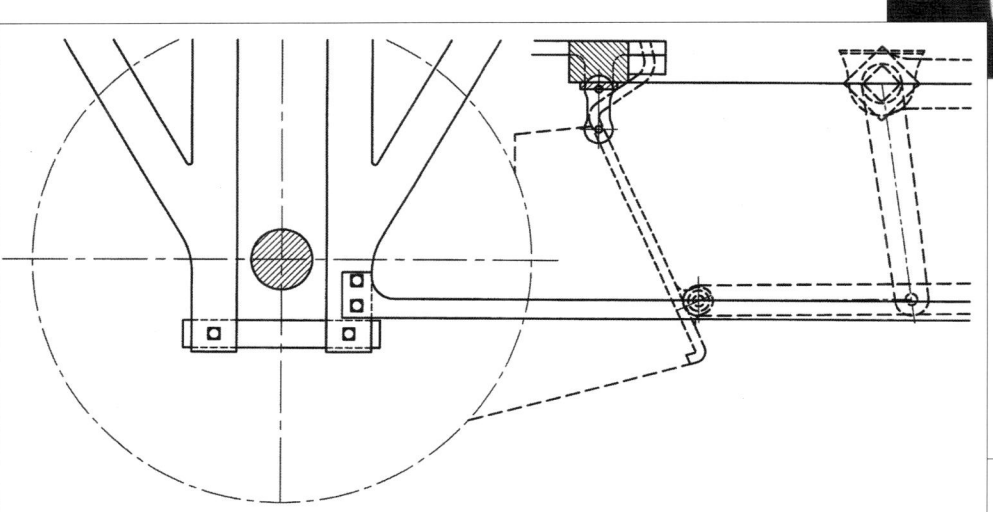

LEFT: Figure 2.14
This shows the push-rod operated version of the wooden brake block. The holes in the push-rod allowed adjustment for wear on the brake block.

BELOW: Figure 2.15
The first version of the McIntosh patent brake, which was introduced in 1899. The long handle was loose on the V-hanger pivot. The brakes were applied by the short handle with the perforated end, to which the long lever was pinned. The perforations were used to take up wear in the brake blocks.

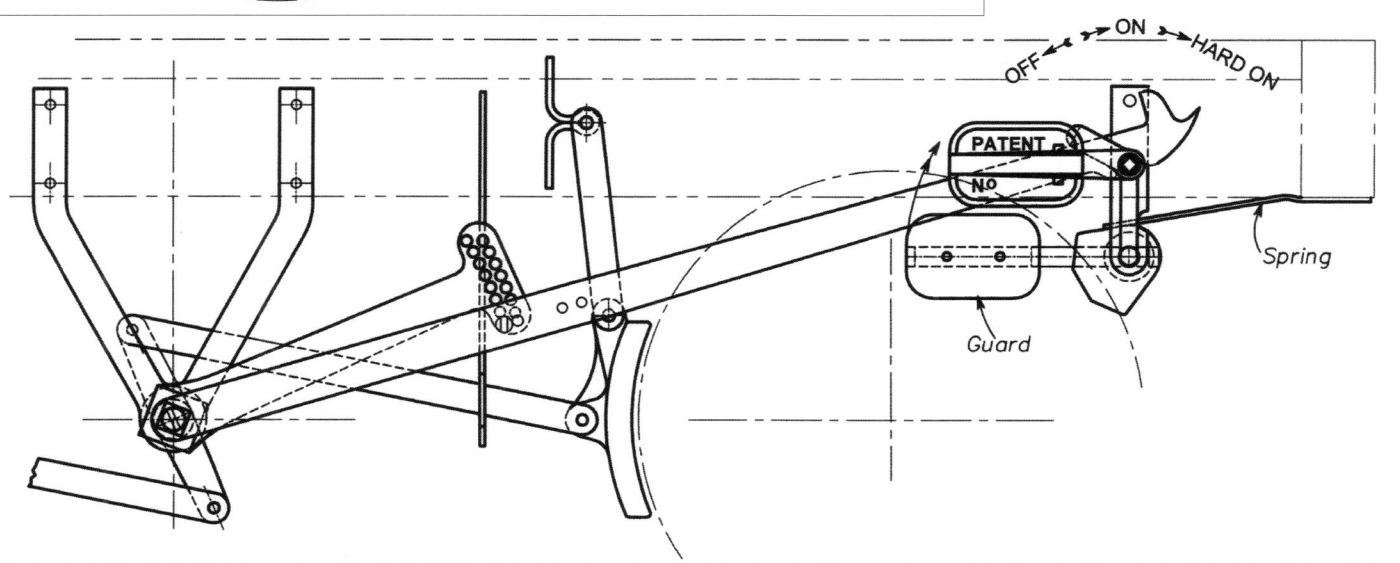

2.5: Brakes

Early Brakes

The first brake was a wooden block applied to the left-hand wheel on one side of the wagon. The actuating lever was bolted to the face of the block. It is shown in Figure 2.10 and Plate 2.13. Mineral wagons with an end door had the brake block at that end of the wagon. This rule also applied to the iron brake block that succeeded it.

In a more sophisticated, but less commonly used version, the wooden block was screwed to a strip of metal, and actuated by a push-rod. This increased the leverage that could be applied. The push-rod also had holes to take up wear on the block. This version was fitted to pre-diagram book cattle wagons, the early iron gunpowder vans and fish and game trucks manufactured by the Metropolitan Carriage & Wagon Works. Figure 2.14 depicts the arrangement, based on St. Rollox cattle wagon drawing number 2035. It is illustrated in Plates 9.15 and 15.16 (pp. 154 and 240 respectively)

The Drummond Iron Brake

The next development, instituted by Drummond, used an iron block working on one wheel. The brake lever pivot casting formed part of the wagon spring retainer. This was the most common brake on wagons constructed from the mid-1880s. It is shown in Figure 2.11. It was used until the end of the nineteenth century, when it was superseded, first by the McIntosh patent brake and eventually by the Morton brake, applied to two wheels on one side of the wagon.

The Patent Either Side Brake

From the late 1890s the Board of Trade put pressure on all railways to improve wagon brake gear. A specification for private trader's wagons was issued in 1899.[1] This required each wagon to have a double brake with brake blocks of cast iron, and the lever guard with a pin and chain or rack to hold the brake down.

Secondly, the Board of Trade issued an order for railways to adopt brake gear that could be applied from either side of the wagon. This was to reduce the large number of accidents in goods yards when shunters had to cross the rails to apply brakes which could only be actuated from one side.

Various attempts were made to meet these requirements. In 1899 the Caledonian adopted a brake patented by McIntosh. It was a modification of the Morton double brake which could be applied from either side of the wagon. The main feature of the brake, quoting from the patent document, was

'... an attachment whereby the lever may be actuated to apply or release the brakes from either side of the wagon and be held in either of these positions without the aid of pins, wedges or other means usually employed.'[2]

The brake had three positions – off, on and hard on. 'Off' needs no explanation. 'On' partially applied the brake to help control trains when running down a steep incline. Goods trains were required to stop before descending in order to 'pin down the brakes.' 'Hard on' immobilised the wagon.

Photographs show the brake on open goods and mineral wagons, plus a cattle wagon and the special wagons to Diagram 58. Drawings specify it for the last order of Diagram 3 covered vans and the Diagram 49 heavy weight wagons. A general arrangement drawing of the brake and a full set of dimensioned components appeared in *The Railway Engineer*,[3] from which Figure 2.15 is derived. In some cases a cast hanger was used to suspend the operating mechanism. This is shown in Plate 2.21.

It is reasonable to suppose that the brake was fitted to wagons constructed from 1899 to 1903, when the wagon replacement programme started. The brake was not adopted for the new standard mineral wagons and goods vans to Diagrams 59 and 67. From 1903, photographs show newly-built wagons fitted with the Morton double brake to one side only.

The arrangement was also used to apply the hand brake to continuous braked vehicles. The last instance of this application seems to have been the six-wheeled horse boxes built in 1907/8.

McIntosh developed a modification to the patent brake in 1900, which was accepted in 1901.[4] It was applied progressively by a sprung tooth which engaged in a series of notches. The means of actuating the brake was also modified:

'we may employ a short actuating arm or lever keyed to the transverse shaft, the motion given to which lever may be transmitted to the brake lever through the medium of a short link pivoted at one end to any convenient point upon the operating lever and at the other end to two toggle links secured to the side of the wagon and the brake lever respectively, so that motion in one direction distends the toggle links and in the other collapses them.'

Diagram 24 wagon 9818 and Darngavil private trader 688 built by Pickering[5] were photographed with this modification. The CR wagon was part of an order for 300 replacement wagons, authorised in 1899.[6] *The Railway Engineer*[7] carried a drawing, which is redrawn as Figure 2.16 and shown under 9818 in Plate 2.22. At the same time,[8] St. Rollox built 1,000 more Diagram 24 wagons, fitted with the Morton double brake on one side only, which is the first authenticated example of this type of brake gear on the Caledonian.

It is difficult to see what advantage either brake offered over the much less complex brake lever guide with a series of holes and a pin operating the Morton style brake which first appeared in the 1890s. This actually offered more gradations of leverage than the patent

Plate 2.21
This shows the first patent brake, in this case with a cast V-hanger. Note how the long lever is pinned to the shorter operating lever. The other style of V-hanger is shown in Figure 2.15 opposite.

brake. In particular, the number of pivot points on the modified version of the patent brake would have been very vulnerable to wear and consequent loss of motion.

In 1906, the Board of Trade set up a committee to consider the question of either side brakes. In 1907 it ruled that none of the either side brakes submitted for scrutiny were satisfactory. The McIntosh brake had not been submitted. All the brakes were banned. The Great Western Railway, who had submitted the Dean-Churchward brake, appealed against the ruling.

Despite the Board of Trade ruling, and the availability of the approved Morton either side brake, the Caledonian persisted with experiments, based on the original patent. One variation is shown in Plate 2.23. There does not appear to be a mechanism to link the brake to the other side of the wagon. There is no evidence that this modification was implemented on any scale.

As a footnote to this episode in CR wagon development, many readers will know that McIntosh influenced locomotive design in Belgium to the extent that more McIntosh-style locomotives ran on the continent than in Scotland. The relationship started with the Traffic Committee's approval in February 1898 for McIntosh to supervise in person the construction in Glasgow of five locomotives based on the Dunalastair II design.[9] Belgium also seems to have adopted the patent brake. St. Rollox drawing, 9966, dated 17th November 1899, which has not survived, is described as *'either side wagon brake for Belgian State Railways.'*

Modern Wagon Brakes

In 1911, the Board of Trade published the Prevention of Accidents Rule, which settled the brake question once and for all. This stated that:

– Brake levers were to be on each side, of like pattern and placed so that each was to the right of a man facing the wagon. The brake had to be capable of application from either side.
– Levers were to be fitted so that sufficient power could be conveniently applied with one hand. Two brake shoes were required, one on each axle.

The rules were to be immediately applied to new wagon construction, but railways owning more than 20,000 wagons, such as the Caledonian, were allowed twenty year's grace to put their house in order. Effectively, that meant that the problem would disappear as wagons wore out and were scrapped. The Dean-Churchward brake was exempted from the ban following a successful appeal by the GWR.

As previously mentioned, the Caledonian had fitted the Morton double brake arrangement on one side of the wagon only to an order of 1,000 Diagram 24 wagons in 1898/99, while experimenting with the patent brake. To comply with the 1911 ruling it adopted the development of the Morton brake which could be so applied. The patent brake was also eventually replaced by the simpler arrangement.

Continuous Brakes on NPCS

After a long delay, caused at least in part by the poor health of successive Locomotive Superintendents, the Caledonian adopted the Westinghouse system for the continuous brake in late 1880.[10] This decision affected goods stock and non-passenger coaching stock (NPCS) that often ran in passenger trains.

Two options were possible for goods stock and NPCS. A complete set of Westinghouse apparatus could be fitted, or a through pipe to give continuity between the locomotive and the carriages if the wagon was marshalled at the head of the train.

The 'piped only' option was implemented in May 1882, when the Traffic Committee reported that just under half the carriage stock had been fitted with the brake,[11] and approved a proposal *'to put in pipe connectors on Horse Boxes, Carriage Trucks and Fish & Game Trucks.'* A minute recorded a decision to fit five *'additional'* covered carriage trucks and twenty fish vans with vacuum pipes *'as well as the Westinghouse brake'*[12] in 1885. Stock built post 1900 to full NPCS standards was usually fitted with the full braking system.

Dual Brakes

Vacuum brake fittings were necessary for through traffic to England, primarily via the L&NWR. This company adopted the automatic vacuum brake in 1888 after a long dalliance with the Clark patent chain-operated continuous brake. Following a serious accident at Lockerbie in 1883 the Caledonian insisted that all West Coast Joint Stock vehicles should be fitted with the Westinghouse brake. The L&NWR adopted the simple vacuum brake, which in its turn was proved inadequate in an accident caused by a runaway train at Carlisle in December 1886.[13]

The Caledonian reacted to the L&NWR's decision to adopt the automatic vacuum brake by authorising dual brakes to be fitted to ten horse boxes, thirty-seven carriage trucks, twelve milk trucks, seventy-five fish trucks and the sole corpse box.[14] Against the horse box entry, Drummond wrote *'only the best stock to be fitted.'*

Steam Heating Pipes

Although not strictly a braking matter, steam heating is mentioned here because the pipes were part and parcel of the arrangements necessary for NPCS to run in passenger trains, when coupled in their usual position immediately behind the engine. Pipes were fitted to twenty horse boxes, ten covered carriage trucks and forty fish vans in 1901.[15] From then on pipes were routinely fitted to stock that was designed to run in passenger trains.

Stock built before that date was gradually fitted with the pipes. In 1904, six open carriage trucks were fitted *'for the conveyance of motor omnibuses by passenger trains.'*[16] In 1914 a further ten open carriage trucks were fitted.[17] Finally, 123 vehicles were fitted with steam heating pipes in 1920.[18] This was connected with a programme to provide over 600 existing carriages with steam heat over a three-year period from 1919. The full list consisted of:

'61 Horse Boxes, 19 6-wheel Fish Vans, 11 4-wheel Fish Vans, 7 4-wheel Covered Carriage Trucks, 5 4-wheel Open Caravan Trucks, 2 6-wheel Open Trucks, 2 4-wheel Open Trucks, 16 Gas Tanks.'

References
1. Quoted in *The Railway Magazine*, October 1903, p. 326
2. Patent 23849, applied for in November 1898, accepted 31st May 1899
3. *The Railway Engineer*, October 1900 edition, p. 294
4. Patent 4019, applied for in March 1900, accepted 16th February 1901
5. Pickering card order 4412, for 50 10-ton wagons numbered 639-688, is dated 10th August 1900
6. NRS BR/CAL/1/42 entry 1033
7. April 1901 edition, p. 108
8. NRS BR/CAL/5/11 entry 361
9. Minute quoted in *The Caledonian Dunalastairs*, pp. 50-51
10. NRS BR/CAL/1/26 entry 130
11. NRS BR/CAL/1/27 entry 816
12. NRS BR/CAL/5/11 entry 25
13. Both accidents and their causes are described in *West Coast Joint Stock*, pp. 286-87
14. NRS BR/CAL/5/12 entry 23
15. NRS BR/CAL/5/11 entry 35
16. NRS BR/CAL/1/50 entry 302
17. NRS BR/CAL/1/66 entry 156
18. NRS BR/CAL/1/74 entry 317

2.6: Buffers and Drawgear

Unsprung Buffers

Early wagons were fitted with solid, that is, unsprung or 'dumb', buffers. They were formed as extensions to the solebars with thickening pieces of a similar width on the inside to produce a rectangular pad 1 foot high and 9 inches wide. The assembly was bolted together and bound with metal strapping. The construction is shown in Figure 2.17.

In 1889 the Railway Clearing House recommended that all wagons should be built with sprung buffers, with a view to eliminating solid buffers by 1910. Builders and operators of private traders' wagons opposed the recommendation, and the deadline for abolition was postponed until 1915.

The Scottish railway companies were given extra time to comply but wagons with solid buffers were banned from travelling into England. The *1915 Working Timetable Appendix* also records that the wagons were banned from the steeply graded portion of the Callander & Oban line, west of Balquhidder, and banned altogether from running in mixed trains on the line.[1]

Early Sprung Buffers

The Caledonian continued to build solid buffer mineral and ballast wagons until well into the 1890s. Goods and livestock vehicles, however, were fitted with sprung buffers from an early date. Two types of sprung buffer were fitted to pre-Drummond wagons and vans and their application continued into the Drummond era.

The first type to be considered was a self-contained buffer, seen in Figure 2.18 and Plate 2.24. The buffer stock was unusually short. It was bolted to a wood pad, which in turn was bolted to the headstock.

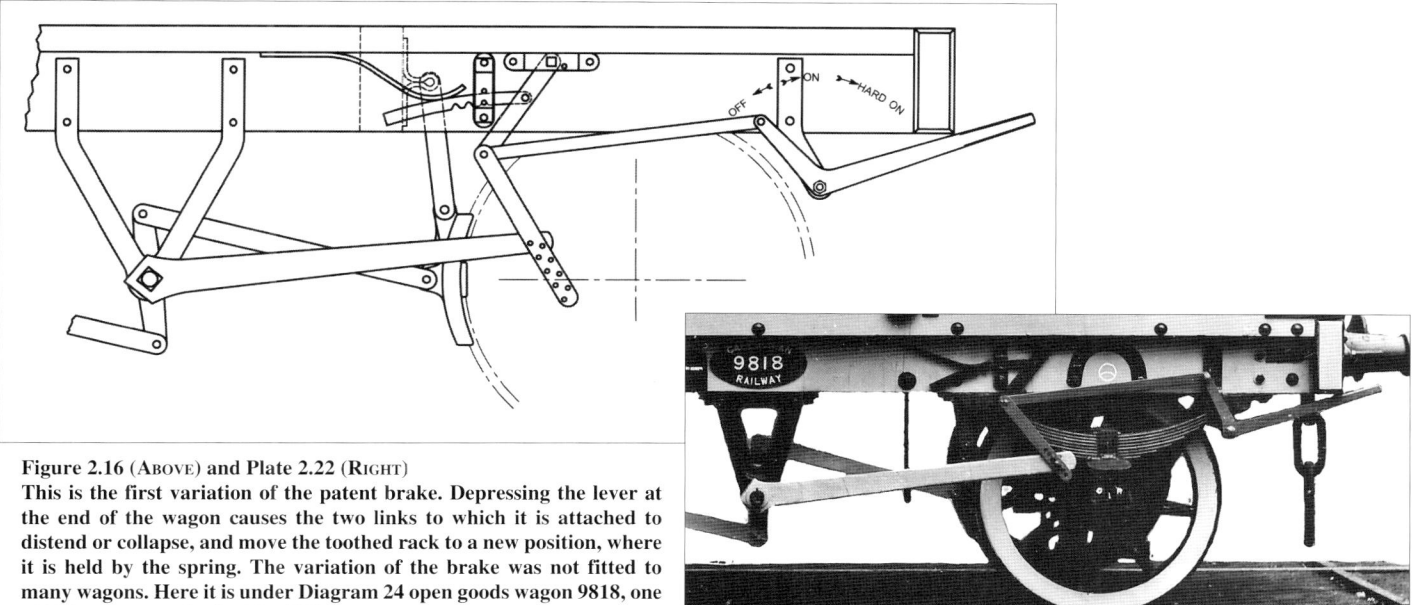

Figure 2.16 (Above) and Plate 2.22 (Right)
This is the first variation of the patent brake. Depressing the lever at the end of the wagon causes the two links to which it is attached to distend or collapse, and move the toothed rack to a new position, where it is held by the spring. The variation of the brake was not fitted to many wagons. Here it is under Diagram 24 open goods wagon 9818, one of 300 wagons authorised in 1899.

Below: **Plate 2.23**
A different version of the patent brake variation, photographed a short time after 12th September 1907, according to the paint date on the solebar. 70433 was a Diagram 24 wagon, built by Pickering in 1900 with the first type of McIntosh patent brake. It was one of the 1,000 wagons that were to be painted steel grey. Various toothed rack mechanisms were drawn in the patent documents, but not this one.

The buffer spindle was thicker (probably 6 inches diameter) than a normal wagon buffer. Some, as in the photograph and drawing, were made with a step cast in the top.

The second type, which was used at the same time as the four-bolt version, and probably superseded it, had an elaborate ribbed casting and a three-bolt attachment to the headstock. It is shown in Figure 2.19 and Plate 2.25. Like all wagon buffers except those fitted to bogie wagons, the buffer head was 1 foot in diameter.

The Drummond Standard Wagon Buffer

The buffer introduced by Drummond as standard also had a three-bolt fixing, with a strengthening rib on the outside. It is shown in Figure 2.20 and Plate 2.26. A variation of the buffer was applied to vehicles with drop ends that were not fitted with continuous brakes, such as rail and twin wagons. A step was cast on the top. It is shown in Plate 2.27.

Self-Contained Buffers

In 1903, a few solid-buffered mineral wagons to Diagram 22 were upgraded by fitting self-contained buffers on new headstocks. This buffer is shown in Figure 2.21 and Plate 2.28. In 1905 conversion began in earnest. The programme to modify all these wagons was given added momentum in 1914, as a result of the deadline imposed by the Railway Clearing House. The conversion of these wagons is discussed further in Chapter 5.5. The buffer was also fitted to Diagram 37 twin wagons.

A heavy duty self-contained version of the standard Drummond three-bolt buffer was fitted to a variety of wagons, including the Diagram 14 swivel wagons, Diagrams 62 and 63 brake vans and Diagram 110 pig iron wagons. The buffer head had thicker spindles than standard – see Figure 2.22 and Plate 2.29.

Buffers for Wagons with Steel Underframes

The early lots of Diagram 59 mineral wagons were fitted with the Drummond standard buffer – see Plates 5.19 and 5.20 (pp. 102

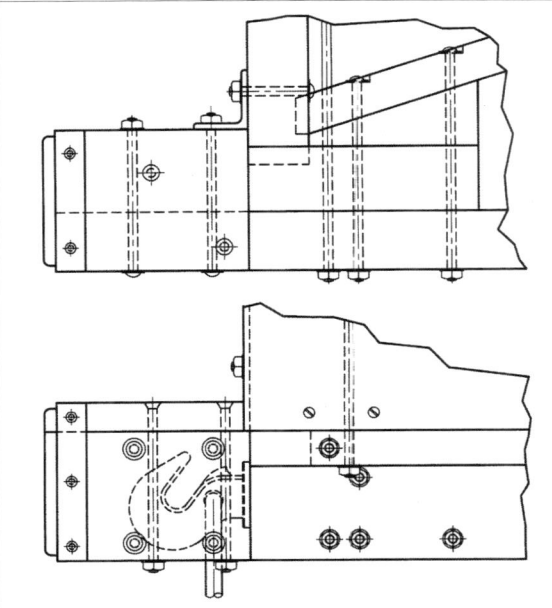

Above: Figure 2.17
Early wagons were fitted with buffers that were extensions of the solebar. The top plan view shows that the width of the buffer face was increased by bolting an extra piece of wood inside the solebar extension. It was further strengthened by an angle bolted to the headstock. The lower side view shows that an extra piece of wood was bolted to the top. The ensemble was bound together at the end by a hooped metal strip.

Figure 2.18 (Right) and Plate 2.24 (Far Right)
The first type of self-contained sprung buffer was attached to the headstock by four bolts. It had a short buffer casing, so it was always packed out from the solebar. Sometimes the packing was square; sometimes it was shaped to match the buffer base. The drawing shows a cast step on the top, the photograph shows the buffer without the step.

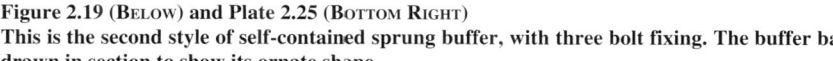

Figure 2.19 (Below) and Plate 2.25 (Bottom Right)
This is the second style of self-contained sprung buffer, with three bolt fixing. The buffer base is drawn in section to show its ornate shape.

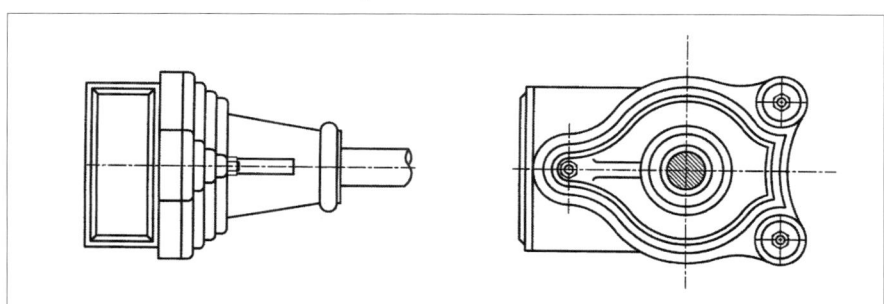

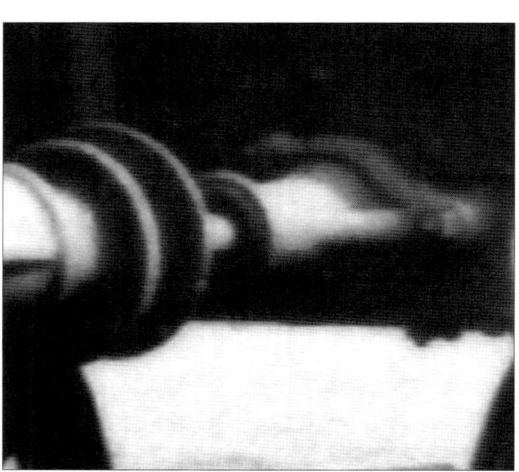

2.6: BUFFERS AND DRAWGEAR

and 104). Subsequently, a new style of buffer was fitted to wagons with steel underframes. Its slightly tapering body had two small reinforcing ribs. Two bolts each side attached it to the headstock. Plate 2.30 and Figure 2.23 show the buffer.

Finally, the 30-ton bogie minerals and most of the bogie special class wagons had a non-standard buffer with an 18-inch head. Examples are shown in Chapters 5 and 13. The Diagram 43 30-ton heavy weight wagons were fitted with what seems to be the standard Drummond locomotive buffer.

NPCS Buffers

Two different types of carriage buffer were fitted to non-passenger coaching stock, but were not universally applied. The first type pre-dated the Drummond era, and was inherited by vehicles that were built on redundant carriage underframes. It is shown in Plate 2.31. This type of buffer was also fitted to the first design of all-metal gunpowder van – see Plate 15.16 (p. 240).

The second type was the standard buffer used for coaching stock from the Drummond period onwards. A version with a step welded to the top was fitted to open carriage trucks built on new underframes and covered carriage trucks with end doors – see Figure 2.24 and Plate 2.32. The buffer face projected 1 foot 10 inches from the headstock, giving an overall length 3 feet 8 inches greater than the length over body. The increase in overall length with wagon buffers was 3 feet 4 inches, so vehicles fitted with carriage buffers can be readily identified from the dimensions in the diagram book.

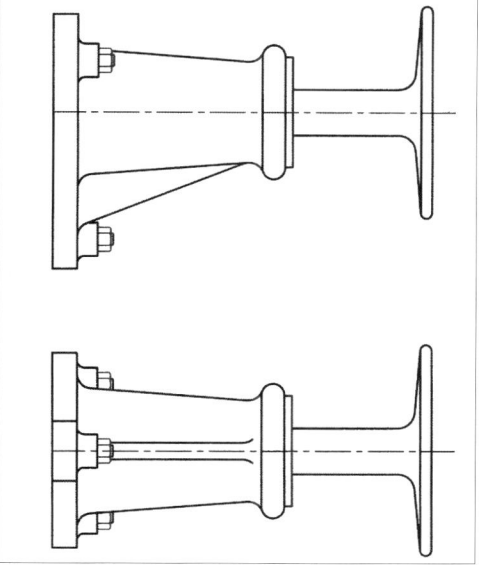

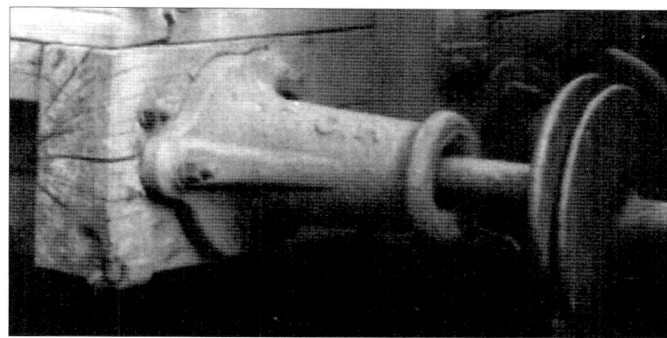

Figure 2.20 (ABOVE) and Plate 2.26 (ABOVE RIGHT)
The previous sprung buffers were superseded by the Drummond standard buffer shown here. This also had a three bolt attachment. In the plan view (top drawing) the reinforcing flange is to the outside of the wagon. The photograph shows that the company initials were cast into the buffer base.

RIGHT: Plate 2.27
The Drummond standard buffer with a step welded to the top was used for wagons with drop ends.

Plate 2.28 (BELOW) and Figure 2.21 (BELOW RIGHT)
The self-contained buffer as fitted to the Diagram 22 solid buffer mineral wagons when they were rebuilt during the twentieth-century wagon replacement programme. In this photograph of a twin wagon, the cast company initials appear twice for good measure.

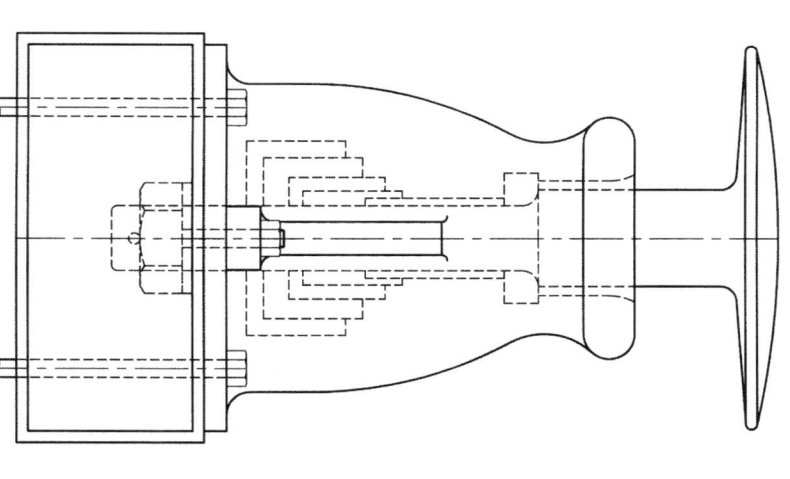

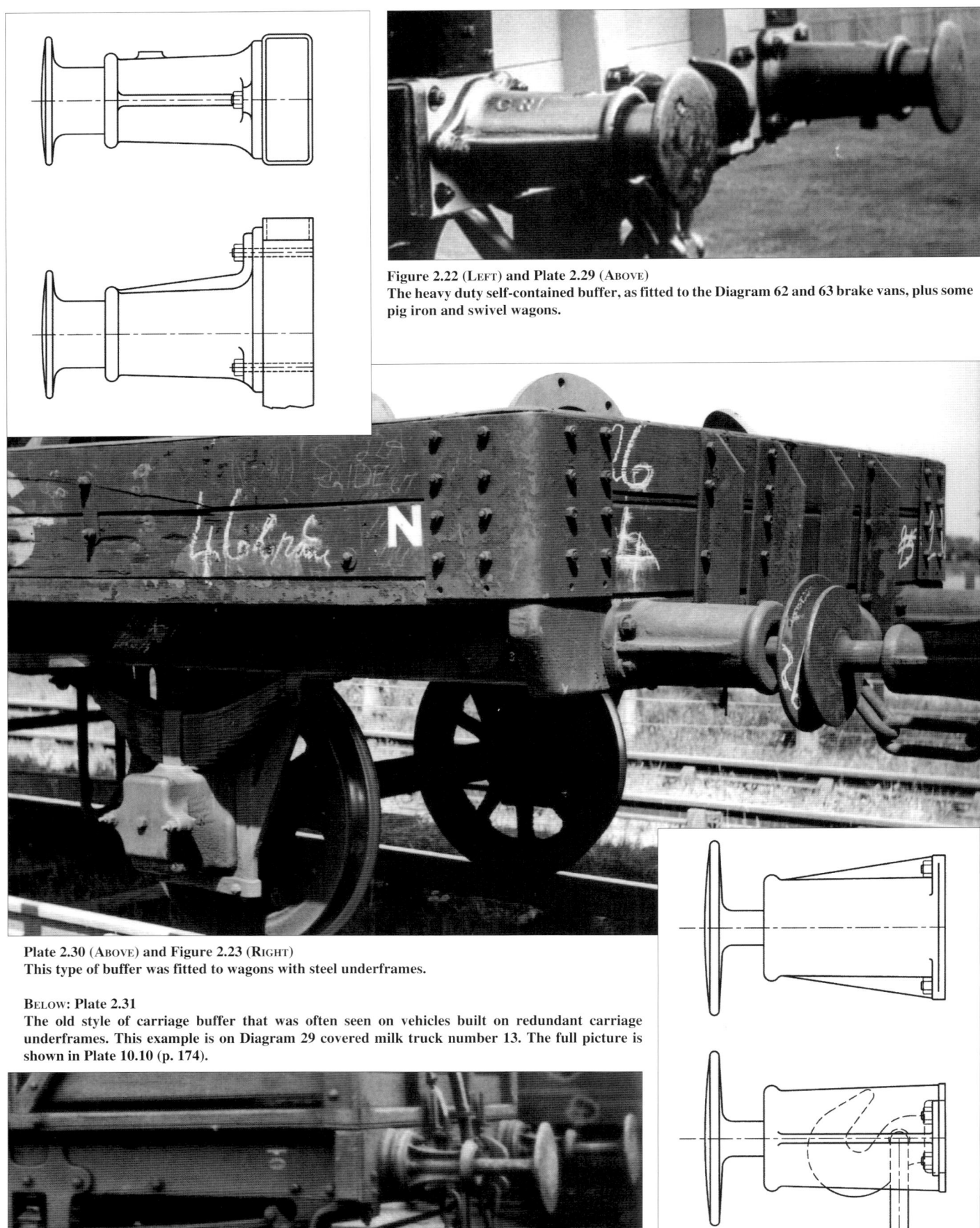

Figure 2.22 (Left) and **Plate 2.29** (Above)
The heavy duty self-contained buffer, as fitted to the Diagram 62 and 63 brake vans, plus some pig iron and swivel wagons.

Plate 2.30 (Above) and **Figure 2.23** (Right)
This type of buffer was fitted to wagons with steel underframes.

BELOW: **Plate 2.31**
The old style of carriage buffer that was often seen on vehicles built on redundant carriage underframes. This example is on Diagram 29 covered milk truck number 13. The full picture is shown in Plate 10.10 (p. 174).

2.6: BUFFERS AND DRAWGEAR

Plate 2.32 (Above) and **Figure 2.24** (Right)
The standard coach buffer was fitted with a step when the ends of carriage trucks folded down. This provided a firm platform for end loading.

Bottom Right: **Figure 2.25**
This shows the shackle coupling that was fitted to early wagons. It is redrawn from an early mineral wagon general arrangement.

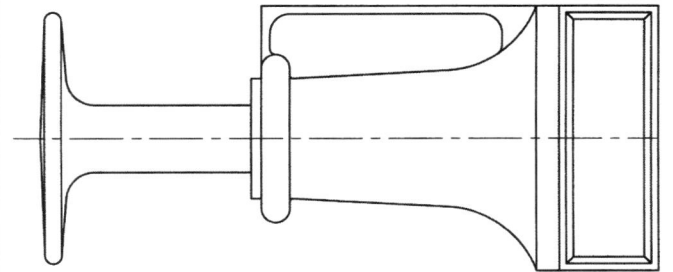

Drawgear

The early wagon coupling consisted of a hook and shackle arrangement, plus safety chains. It is shown in Figure 2.25. It was used until 1873 when the Traffic Committee gave authority

'to abolish the chain and hook coupling and to proceed at once to substitute for it the hooked bar and long linked couplings, but without withdrawing the wagons from traffic for this sole purpose.'[2]

Some solid buffered wagons retained a 6-inch middle link, which reduced the overall length of the coupling to 2 feet 6 inches. A Diagram 21 loco coal wagon was photographed for the *1900 Register* and is depicted in Plate 5.5 (p. 88).

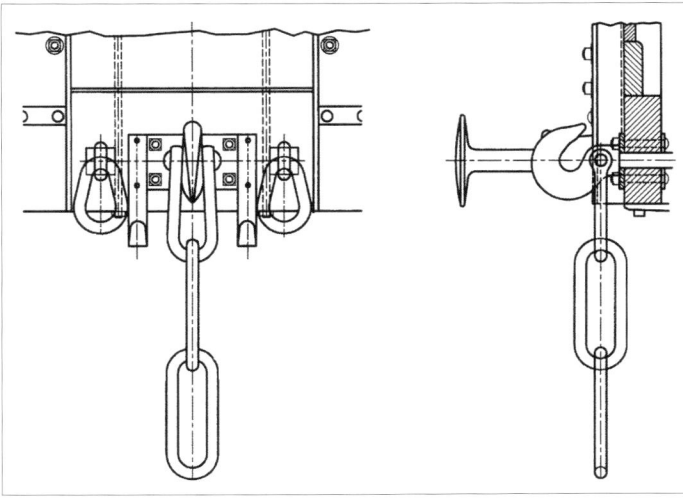

References
1. *1915 Working Timetable Appendix*, p. 82
2. NRS BR/CAL/1/20 entry 1302

ABOVE: Plate 3.1
Black buffers are clearly visible on this Diagram 14 swivel wagon in a Hurst Nelson publicity photograph. Everything, including the bolt heads on the solebar, has been given special treatment.

RIGHT: Plate 3.2
This St. Rollox publicity photograph of a Diagram 46 mineral wagon also shows special treatment for every detail, including black buffers. Other aspects of note are the tare numerals centred under the C, which is 12 inches high. The load information has been displaced to the left by the writing indicating the three positions of the McIntosh patent brake. The 2¾ inches high load and tare characters are condensed.

BELOW: Plate 3.3
One of a number of publicity photographs of Diagram 24 goods wagon 9818, fitted with the improved McIntosh patent brake.

Chapter 3
Wagon Livery and Numbering

3.1: Livery

First of all, an apology to readers who already have a copy of *Caledonian Railway Livery*. The Caledonian Railway Association decided that this book should stand alone, and that the material in Chapter 6 of the previous publication should be used as a starting point for this chapter. Inevitably, some of the illustrations will be familiar.

As the author said in the introduction to 'the livery book,' Chapter 6 was intended to be a broad brush commentary on the subject of carriage and wagon livery as an addition to what was essentially a publication about locomotives. While some of the material in *Caledonian Railway Livery* has been re-used in this chapter, it has also been amplified with new material, and in some cases reinterpreted.

This chapter deals with goods and special class wagons. Non-Passenger Coaching Stock (NPCS), which was also touched on in Chapter 6 of *Caledonian Railway Livery*, is covered in Chapter 4 of this volume.

Contemporary Historical References

No official minute or reference exists concerning the painting of wagons until 1899. The first authoritative reference to wagon livery is in an 1897 issue of the *Locomotive Magazine*:

> 'The goods wagons are a brick red, with white letters, black ironwork and white tyres ... Goods brakes are a similar colour with vermilion ends.'

In default of evidence to the contrary we can only assume that this colour scheme was adopted at the inception of the railway. Although the quotation mentions wagons, we must also assume that it applied to covered vans as well, plus the few special class wagons then in existence.

The black ironwork reference needs clarification. It obviously referred to ironwork on the inside and outside of wooden bodied wagons, the capping strip along the top of open wagons, and the running gear below the solebar. It could also be construed that metal buffer casings were black. This was certainly the case for grey-painted North British wagons. Examples of NBR practice can be found in *Wagons on the LNER No. 1 – North British*, published by the Irwell Press.

Five photographs of newly-built Caledonian wagons support this theory. The first two are Hurst Nelson publicity photographs. One depicts the last of 100 Diagram 14 swivel timber wagons, completed in 1896 – see Plate 3.1. The other is the last of fifty Diagram 13 rail wagons built at the same time. This is shown in Plate 8.3 (p. 127). The wagons are in 'photographic grey' livery with details and the company initials picked out in black. In both cases the buffers are obviously black.

The next example is a Pickering publicity photograph of a Diagram 24 open goods wagon, part of a contract for which was completed in 1900. It is shown in Plate 9.7 (p. 147).

The other two photographs depict St. Rollox-built wagons. The first is Diagram 46 8-ton mineral wagon number 63872, which was part of an order for 291 wagons completed in 1900. The second is Diagram 24 open goods wagon 9818, also built in 1900 (Plates 3.2 and 3.3). In these photographs of wagons in traffic livery, the tone of the buffer casings is darker than the body paint and matches adjacent black ironwork.

The author suggests that the Hurst Nelson photographs do not represent the wagons as they appeared in service. These wagons were two of the first four contracts awarded simultaneously to Hurst Nelson by the Caledonian and were obviously treated as something special. The same treatment was used on the official photograph of Hurst Nelson's share of the Diagram 54 bogie coal wagon contract – see Plate 5.12 (p. 97) and a Diagram 59 mineral wagon (Plate 3.5).

The photographs of the 6-ton covered vans built by Hurst Nelson at the same time appear in traffic livery. They do not show a tonal variation between the body and the buffers. These vans had very little visible ironwork to highlight. See Plate 9.20 (p. 157).

Similarly, the Pickering photograph is a representative of a very large contract, which was also given a non-standard paint specification, and was fitted with the McIntosh patent brake. This wagon order is discussed in the sub-section on official painting specifications below.

The St. Rollox wagon examples were probably also specially selected for the photographer because they showed the two variations of the McIntosh brake. At least five photographs were taken of wagon 9818, from different angles. The patent brake was first fitted to these wagons and the order for Diagram 24 wagons built by Pickering. Both the St. Rollox wagons are fresh out of the works.

All the other pictures of CR wagons suggest that the buffers were painted the same colour as the wagon body. This includes mineral wagon 63951 from the same lot as 63872, which was photographed for the *1900 Register*. The stains on the axleboxes and a layer of light dirt clearly show a wagon in traffic. The buffers are the same tone as the body and the ironwork is considerably darker – see Plate 3.4.

Wagons with steel underframes invite similar alternative interpretations. However, the painting specification for the Diagram 59 mineral wagon contract that was sent to Pickering specifically states that the underframe was to be painted red oxide. Photographs of these wagons show no variation between the tone of the buffers and the underframes. See Plate 3.5 and the photographs in Chapter 5. The paint specification is discussed in detail in the next sub-section.

Taking the evidence as a whole, the author concludes that the buffers of goods wagons were normally painted red oxide and that the few exceptions were examples of special treatment for wagons that were in some way out of the ordinary.

Wagon tyres were indeed white as stated in the *Locomotive Magazine*. This practice can be seen in many photographs of newly built and repainted wagons, but the paint quickly became obscured by dirt, as evidenced by photographs of wagons in traffic.

Official Painting Specifications

Three entries in the Pickering order book contain the only extant wagon painting instructions from the Caledonian. The earliest departs from common practice. The Pickering contract mentioned above[1] for 1,000 goods wagons fitted with the McIntosh patent brake was ordered to be painted '*steel grey*'. The publicity photograph shows a wagon with paint significantly lighter than the black ironwork, but it is impossible to determine whether the colour was indeed grey. The wagon and the paint specification are shown in *Caledonian Railway Livery* on pp. 291 and 292 respectively.

Plate 3.4
This in-service photograph of a Diagram 46 mineral from the same order as that in Plate 3.2 shows a similar pattern of lettering, but the buffers are the same colour as the wagon body.

There is no record of such a change to the specification in company minutes. Earlier Pickering card orders for Diagram 22 mineral wagons[2] do not specify a livery. The first states *'letter, colour and samples as sent.'* The other two refer back to the first. There is no reason not to accept the steel grey specification as a record of what actually happened, especially as this is not among Pickering's repertoire of colours applied to wagons. The livery may have been applied to highlight the patent brake which was introduced that year. It is of course quite possible that when the wagons were due for a repaint, they took the red oxide livery.

The other two specifications from 1903, one for covered goods vans to Diagram 67 and one for mineral wagons to Diagram 59, put us on more familiar ground.[3] The instructions seem to have been part of a wish on the Caledonian's part to codify painting and lettering practise around the introduction of the new standard wagons in the early years of the twentieth century.

The specification for the mineral wagons reads as follows

'body outside 1 coat lead colour, 2 coats red oxide with varnish added for the last coat. Inside one coat of lead colour. Underframe 3 coats red oxide with varnish added for the last coat. Wheels and ironwork one coat lamp black, with a little japan added. Wheel tyres and number plate letters white.'

The same wording appears on Pickering card order 19105 of April 1911. The pig iron wagons built in 1912 to card order 21679 and the twin wagons to order 22691 were identically painted, save for an extra coat of lead colour to the exterior.

The covered van specification was essentially the same with slight differences and some additions

'outside, inside and ironwork to get 1 coat of lead colour all over and then puttied up, the outside to get 1 coat lead colour, 1 coat red oxide and 1 coat oak varnish. Inside to get two coats of stone colour. The roof five coats of white lead on top of the canvas. Iron work 1 coat of black.'

A Note on Red Oxide

Ferric oxide, one of the oxides of iron, is a common, naturally-occurring mineral. It is often called haematite, after the Greek word for blood. Rust is another form of the same oxide. Red oxide pigment was originally made by grinding the ore and allowing it to dry naturally. The colours obtained varied on a spectrum from yellow (various shades of ochre) through red oxide to deepening shades of brown (raw sienna, umber and Vandyke brown). The colour obtained is governed by trace elements present in the ore.

Its use declined around the start of the twentieth century, when it was found that some grades of the paint promoted corrosion rather than inhibited it.[4]

Synthetic red iron oxide pigments were first made in a laboratory setting in the eighteenth century by heating copperas or ferrous sulphate, the pigments obtained varying from light red to dark purple. The colour depended on the degree of heat applied. This explains references in Pickering orders for private traders' wagons to brown and red oxide.

The synthetic pigment was consistent in colour and cheap to produce, because the raw material could be obtained as a by-product from industrial processes, such as sulphuric acid production (the ferrous compound) and galvanising (the copperas starting point). Exposure to the elements tended to turn red oxide to a pinker shade.

There is no good match among the British Standards Institution colours in BS 2660, or in its replacement, BS 381C. The best matches to the author's eyes are RAL International colours in the range RAL 2010 (most intense, therefore newly painted), to RAL 2003 (weathered to a lighter shade).[5]

Wagons of All-Metal Construction

The Diagram 54 bogie coal wagons were, according to a contemporary report, *'painted dark red, the lettering being very prominent, being in white block.'*[6] Publicity photographs, except that commissioned by Hurst Nelson, suggest that the wagons were painted all-over red, with black running gear. The Hurst Nelson wagon (Plate 5.12, p. 97) is in photographic grey with the ironwork around the doors and the body reinforcing angles in a darker colour, presumably intended to signify black.

Photographs of the bogie coal wagons in traffic support the

one-colour body assertion, but the mention of dark red remains a mystery. A specification for painting these wagons has not survived. If painting had followed the requirements for the metal part of the Diagram 59 wagons, the application of varnish may have made the overall colour scheme look darker. Plates 5.11-5.14 (pp. 96, 97 and 99) show the differences between the Hurst Nelson publicity photograph and the wagons in traffic.

The Diagram 66 hopper wagons also appear in photographs to have been painted all over red – see Plate 6.7 (p. 112). By analogy, the Diagram 121 hopper wagons would also carry this livery, but there is no photographic evidence of them in Caledonian days. The various wagons of metal construction in the special series also seem to have received the all-over livery. Examples can be seen in Chapters 13 and 14.

Open Goods Wagon Interiors

We have seen that the 1903 specification required that the Pickering order for Diagram 59 mineral wagons should receive one coat of lead colour inside. The rare examples of pictures showing the interiors of goods wagons suggest that the normal practice might be to leave the wood unpainted, and for the ironwork to be painted black – see Plates 8.2, 8.4 and 9.2 (pp. 124, 127 and 144). Such was common practice on other railways, for instance the Midland.

Gunpowder Vans

There is no record of a special livery for gunpowder vans, as was the case on some railways, including the Caley's partner the L&NWR. The two early iron gunpowder vans and the Diagram 78 vans built in 1922 look in photographs to have been painted all-over red oxide. The wooden bodied vans to Diagram 4 seem to have been painted like the Diagram 3 vans from which they were developed. Examples of all these vans are in Chapter 15.

Wagons with Continuous Brakes or Through Pipes

Some general goods wagons were fitted with, or were piped for, continuous brakes, but were not built to full non-passenger coaching stock standards. The vehicles concerned were 10-ton covered vans to Diagram 67 and 10-ton open goods wagons to Diagram 87.

In date order, forty Diagram 67 vans were fitted with oil axleboxes and dual brakes in 1911 as part of St. Rollox order G307. Thirty were built in 1912 to order G325 and another forty in 1914 to order G360. Forty Diagram 87 wagons were up-graded in 1914, and a further forty-five to Diagram 67 in 1915/16. Finally the 300 Diagram 67 vans built to carry explosives in 1917 were fitted with continuous brakes. These orders are discussed in more detail in Chapter 9.

While it is not possible to be absolutely certain, these wagons were probably painted in goods, rather than non-passenger coaching stock, livery. This assertion is based on photographs of two Diagram 67 vans built to carry explosives, which almost certainly have white lettering – one example is shown in Plate 9.22 (p. 161); the other is in *Caledonian Railway Livery*, p. 273. In support of the theory, similar wagons on the North British and L&NWR remained in ordinary goods colours.

The other goods wagons fitted with continuous brakes were the thirty-one Diagram 54 bogie wagons modified for goods traffic, and the four Diagram 91 road vans for the Callander & Oban line. The only clear picture of a Diagram 54 wagon in goods traffic is of a very traffic-worn example. The Diagram 91 vans were only photographed at the head of a train, and it is impossible to determine livery details from pictures taken at an oblique angle. It is reasonable, but it cannot be definitely proved, to suggest that they were also painted red oxide.

Meat Vans

St. Rollox drawing 2533 was issued in 1879. It depicted the lettering for dead meat vans. This probably related to an order for forty dead meat vans from Oldbury, Ashbury and Brown & Marshall.[7] The drawing has not survived. The vans in Plate 9.19 (p. 157) may carry this lettering.

The Diagrams 1 and 2 and the modified Diagram 3 vans were not built to full NPCS standards, in that they retained wagon buffers, brake gear and suspension. They were, however, fitted with screw couplings and safety chains. These features, with the addition of a through brake pipe, allowed them to travel in passenger trains. In these respects they were similar in construction to West Coast Joint Stock and L&NWR meat vans. They were all numbered in the general goods wagon series.

All the photographs of these vans show them in traffic-stained condition, but the livery treatment of dead meat vans adapted from ordinary vans in the West Coast Joint Stock suggests that the Caledonian vans received standard goods livery and lettering

Plate 3.5
Another Hurst Nelson publicity photograph showing a steel underframe Diagram 59 mineral wagon. The underframe and the buffers are the same colour as the body, in conformity with the 1903 painting specification.

Brake Vans

The sides, solebars and ironwork of brake vans were painted in the same way as ordinary wagon stock according to the *Locomotive Magazine*. The ends were painted vermilion in the same style as the brake ends of passenger stock – some sources mention '*regal red*.'[8] Presumably the colour was the same as that applied to locomotive and tender buffer beams and the ends of passenger brake vans.

It has been suggested,[9] based on the personal recollection of CR goods guards, that this practice was discontinued in the years prior to the Grouping. To counter this suggestion, the enlargement (Plate 3.6) of the photograph of the Diagram 104 combination goods and brake van probably taken in 1923 strongly suggests a vermilion brake end. The headstock looks to be the same colour. The description in *The Locomotive Magazine* of the Diagram 63 brake vans built in 1920 also mentions vermilion ends.[10]

According to *The Locomotive Magazine* article, the inside of brake vans was stone colour, with dark stone seats and lockers. The ceiling was light blue. This may well have recorded standard practice, as the interior of the Diagram 67 goods vans was specified as stone colour.

Ballast Brakes

Following the publication of a drawing in the *Model Railway News*,[11] there was some speculation in the letters pages about the livery of these vans.[12] The starting point for the debate was that contemporary published information made no mention of livery and that there was no discernible difference in colour between the sides and ends of the vans. This led the first correspondent to conclude that the likeliest colour was black, and that the livery also applied to the ballast hoppers. The suggestion was based on the assumption that the livery was not likely to have been the same as for ordinary goods stock. The second writer, while not disagreeing, reiterated the description of the ordinary brake vans published in *The Locomotive Magazine*.

In the three-quarter view in *The Railway Engineer*, the colour of sides and ends does indeed appear the same. Both this picture and the side view of the brake van show a glossy finish to the paintwork. This may suggest that the vans were painted all-over red oxide, with a coating of oak varnish, as in the contemporary order for Diagram 67 covered vans built by Pickering.

On balance, the suggestion of black livery does not really add up. All brake vans were classed as service vehicles anyway, and the ballast brakes were not numbered in a special series. Likewise, the ballast hoppers were numbered as ordinary goods wagons. The standard livery would not warrant a remark, whereas a different colour, such as black, would. It is reasonable to conclude, therefore, that the brake vans and hoppers were painted in standard goods livery. It does seem, however, that the ends of ballast brakes may not have been painted vermilion.

References
1. Pickering card order 3352
2. Orders 1687, 1702 and 1730 of 1895/96
3. Pickering card orders 6673 and 6708 respectively
4. Noted in the *Mechanical Engineer's Pocket Book* (1899) and *Transactions of the Institute of Civil Engineers* (1907)
5. http://www.icomsps.co.uk/colour_chart.htm
6. In *The Locomotive Magazine*, 14th July 1903
7. NRS BR/CAL/1/24 entry 1616
8. John Boyle, in livery notes on CRA modeller's drawings
9. Letter in *Model Railway News*, January 1963
10. *The Locomotive Magazine*, 14th August 1920
11. Drawing in November 1962 issue, pp. 426-27
12. Letters in January 1963 and March 1963

ABOVE: Plate 3.6
This enlargement of the only known photograph of a Diagram 104 combination goods and brake van suggests that the brake end and the headstock were painted vermilion. It is possible, however, that the variation in tone is the effect of strong sunlight. The photograph can be dated to after 1922, because the locomotive is a Class '191' 4-6-0, delivered to the Caledonian at the end of that year.

RIGHT: Plate 3.7
This is part of one of the publicity photographs of the Diagram 65 ballast brake with spreading plough. The end and side seem to be the same colour. The number is sited above the verandah; on other brake vans it was below. The tare weight has been chalked on the end for the benefit of the painter.

3.2: Letter and Number Styles

An indication of company ownership must have been applied to wagons from the start of the Caledonian's existence. The company was in contact at Carlisle with the London & North Western Railway from 1847, and wagons were travelling into England from then on. For instance, a minute in January 1848 recorded the need to make arrangements for cattle wagons travelling into England from Dumfries.[1] It would be necessary to identify company ownership to ensure that wagons were easily identified for return.

Some companies used symbols to show ownership of its wagon stock. The North British had a quatrefoil mark as well as letters. The L&NWR used two diamond shaped marks and no letters until the first decade of the twentieth century.[2] There is no photographic or written record to suggest that the Caledonian used a symbol rather than company initials. It is reasonable to assume that the CR used letters from the outset.

It is only possible to discuss the general principles and development of lettering in this chapter. Throughout the book, the captions to pictures point out lettering details and variations.

Script Numerals and Letters

While there are numerous pictures of early wagons, nearly all have been repainted and re-lettered, some of them probably more than once. Four photographs show goods stock with script style numbers. These are shown in Plates 3.8-3.11. In one case, the company initials are also visible, and in script.

It has been suggested that this was the original lettering style.[3] A persuasive analogy can be drawn with the script lettering and numbers usually, but not exclusively, applied to engines up to the beginning of the Drummond era.[4] The letters and number styles are similar, except for the fancifully shaped figure 7 applied to two of the wagons. Following the analogy to its conclusion, Drummond replaced the script style with the block lettering and numbering style on locomotives and wagons alike.

There is also supporting evidence for this theory from the Caledonian's west coast partner, the London & North Western Railway. Locomotives originally carried painted numbers, then engraved plates. In both cases a script style was used, which was very

Plates 3.8-3.10
These are examples of script writing on wagons. Plate 3.8 (Above) is the only one to show company initials as well as numbers. Plate 3.9 (Left) is an example applied to a pre-diagram book 6-ton goods van, fitted with the three-bolt self-contained buffer. The relief effect suggests that shading may have been applied to the numerals. Plate 3.10 (Lower Left) shows a more ornate version of numbering on a CR mineral 'bogie' – compare the figure 7s in this and the previous picture. The florid style of numbering also appears on mineral wagons belonging to private trader Robert Addie & Sons, which figure in the background to special class wagon 54 in the *1900 Register* – see Plate 15.13 (p. 240).

Right: Plate 3.11
This shows the script number on the end of a cattle wagon design that was built from 1876. Unfortunately, the lettering on the side of the wagon is obscured. In the original photograph, which is shown in Plate 11.4, *Cardean* is in the foreground, fitted with a superheater. This dates the photograph to after 1911.

similar to the CR wagon examples. A similar style was applied to NPCS in the early years, according to *LNWR Liveries*.[5] Ordinary L&NWR goods wagons were lettered in block style, but it should be remembered that lettering came late to the North Western. Diamond marks were exclusively used as the company identifier up to 1908.

The photograph of mineral wagon 30460 (Plate 3.8) shows the company initials and number in script style. *Caledonian Railway Livery*[6] entertained the possibility that the wagon was Scottish North Eastern Railway in origin. This is incorrect. The return for January 1867, which details all the rolling stock absorbed from the SNER, shows that no mineral wagons were included.

The wagon is rated at 7 tons and has CR cast on the axleboxes. The diagonal body bracing identifies it as a wagon built from 1878 to St. Rollox drawing 2558 – see Figure 5.2 (p. 84). The company initials and number look freshly painted compared with the other writing on the wagon. This suggests that the style was either common practice at the time or a recent innovation.

The next two photographs do not offer much clarification about common practice. Only the end of the van 37170 in Plate 3.9 is visible, so we do not know the size and style of the company initials. It was a standard pre-diagram book 6-ton van, built in large numbers in the 1870s and early '80s. The highest known number for one of

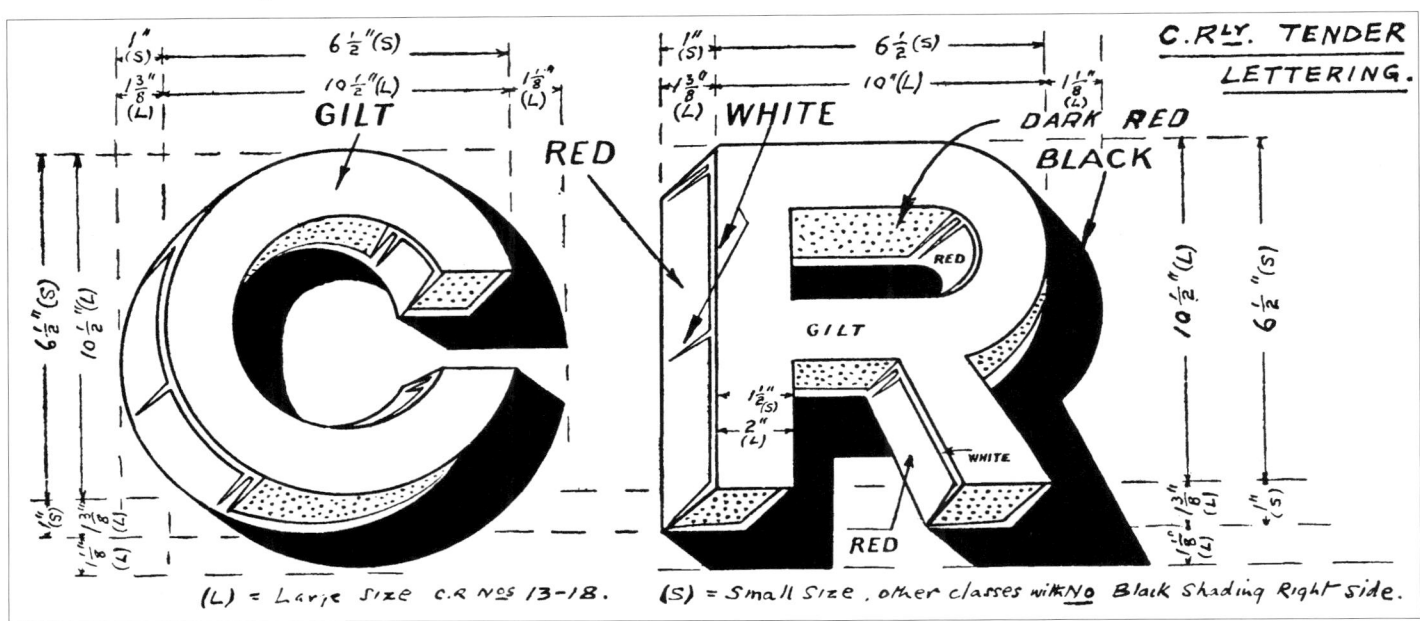

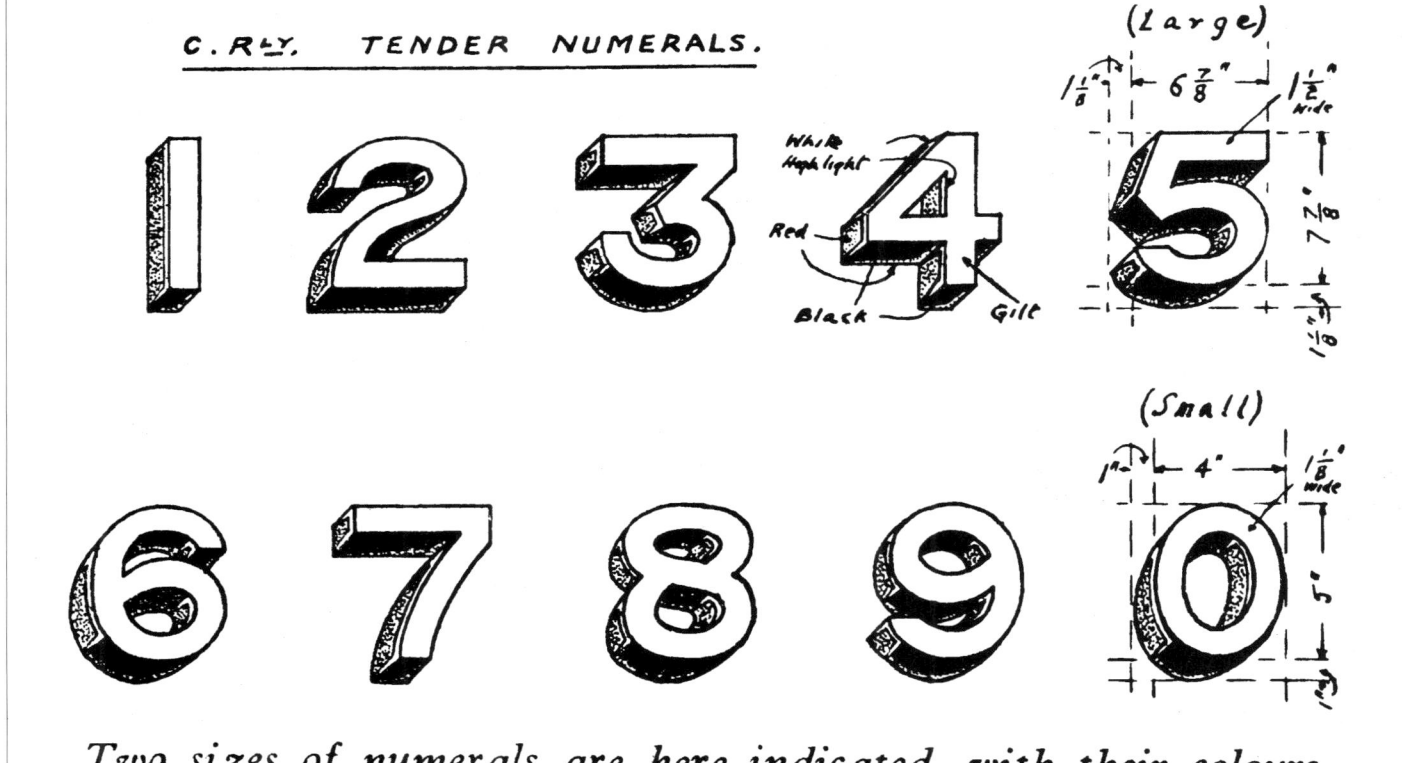

Figures 3.1 (Above) and 3.2 (Below)
A B MacLeod's drawings of letters and numerals as applied to locomotives, which first appeared in *The Model Railway News*.

these vans is 37250, which was built after Drummond took office, and has the first style of block lettering – see Plate 9.17 (p. 154). A photograph of van number 37155,[7] which must have been built at more or less the same time as 37170, also shows block lettering.

A similar story applies to mineral wagon 47418 in Plate 3.10. Again, only the number is visible. A photograph at Ardrossan harbour (see Plate 5.4, p. 87) shows a rake of new-looking mineral wagons with the first style of block lettering. It is highly unlikely that three newly repainted wagons would appear coupled together. The wagon nearest the camera is 46296, which must have been built earlier than 47418.

The cattle wagon in Plate 3.11 is more difficult to interpret. The design was current from 1876 until it was replaced by Drummond's Diagram 10 wagon in 1883. Other photographs (Plates 11.2 and 11.3, pp. 183 and 185) of pre-Drummond cattle wagons show them with obviously repainted block lettering and numerals. There is nothing to suggest, either that this wagon was an aberration, or that it represented current practice.

Was script the original style or a short-lived variation? The wagons were all built around the same time, but the evidence of only four photographs is inconclusive. Script style numbers are more difficult to read than block, and would have seriously inconvenienced number takers in marshalling yards. It is easy to understand why it would be phased out, but hard to believe that it would replace a more legible style.

One thing is certain; block lettering on goods stock was the norm from the start of the Drummond period until the Grouping, and wagons with script writing should have been block lettered when they were repainted.

How the script number on van 37170 survived until 1900, when it appeared in the background of photograph number 30 in *The Register of Wagon Plant*, is a mystery. The cattle wagon example is even more remarkable, as it was in the background of a photograph of *Cardean* after it had been fitted with a superheater in 1911.

Locomotive, Coach and Wagon Lettering Compared

The first printed record of any Caledonian letter and number style was published in 1944 by A B MacLeod in *The Model Railway News*. Macleod was a senior railway manager who was a highly respected commentator on Scottish railways. He wrote a history of the Caledonian Railway locomotives designed by McIntosh. The Historical Model Railway Society used *The Model Railway News* article as the foundation for its *Livery Register No. 1, Caledonian Locomotives*, published in 1965.

Caledonian Railway Livery used MacLeod's drawings to establish that the coach lettering and numbers applied when the two-colour livery was reintroduced were the same style as that used on locomotives and tenders.[8] The shapes of the characters were identical, but the shading and shadow effects differed. MacLeod's drawings are reproduced here as Figures 3.1 and 3.2.

Enlargements of the initials on locomotives and tenders were examined in *Caledonian Railway Livery*.[9] The letter C varied between a true circle and an oval.[10] In the latter case, the letter was narrower than it was high. The author did not suggest that either style was the official version.

Re-examination of these enlargements shows that only six (Plates 15, 17, 22, 28, 29 and 31) of the nineteen examples were condensed. This suggests that the true circle as drawn by MacLeod was the approved style, and supports the suggestion that the condensed letter style was caused by human variation.

The author of *Caledonian Railway Livery* did not investigate a possible connection between the locomotive and carriage styles and wagon letters and numbers. Wagon letters were first applied to the solebars. Judging by the space available on a 12-inch solebar overlapped at the top by the curb rail which retained the floor boards, the height was the same as the smaller size of tender lettering without shading, that is, 6½ inches. The numerous photographs suggest that the letter C was truly circular.

Removing the shadows and shading from MacLeod's drawings or the colour re-creations in *Caledonian Railway Livery*[11] leaves block letters and numbers identical to the small lettering first applied to wagons. The present author concludes that the original letter and numbering style on wagons was linked to that on locomotives and carriage stock.

Drawings Specifying Lettering and Numbering Styles

There are no early drawings of ordinary rolling stock letters and numbers in the St. Rollox registers. Official drawings of 12-inch, 15-inch and 18-inch letters were issued to contractors. Examples of the three sizes have survived.

The 12-inch lettering drawing 18740 was issued to Pickering in 1916 for a contract to build Diagram 87 open goods wagons.[12] This is shown as Figure 3.3. Only the vertical measurement of the company initials is specified, but the horizontal dimension is identical. The lettering therefore shows a truly circular C.

The 15-inch letters were the subject of drawing 16708, issued to Hurst Nelson for the construction of 20-ton Diagram 108 rail wagons in 1912.[13] The letters are in the condensed style.

Two St. Rollox drawings setting out the measurements of the condensed 18-inch lettering style for the mineral wagon and covered goods van accompanied the painting specifications issued to Pickering in 1903.[14] These drawings are Figures 3.4-3.7.

The weight of letters (i.e., the stroke thickness) varied with their height. The C and the upright of the R were always the same. The cut out forming the C was the same width as the stroke. If letters were condensed, the loop of the R was ½ inch lighter than the upright. The tail of the R tapered from bottom to top. The table shows the sizes, most of which are scaled from drawings.

Height	C/R Upright	C Cut Out	R Loop
6½in	1½in	1½in	1½in
9in	2in	2in	2in
12in	3in	3in	3in
15in	3½in	3½in	3in
18in	4in	4in	3½in

Finally, a 1912 drawing[15] specified the lettering for an order of Diagram 109 twin wagons. It showed very lightweight company initials 12 inches high and a C with a serif at the top – see Figure 3.8 (p. 58). Photographs, including Plate 8.16 (p. 140), show that 12-inch block lettering of normal weight was applied.

Evidence from Photographs

Official drawings record intention; what happens in practice is often different. When the *Register of Wagon Plant* was produced in 1900, the standard letter height was 12 inches and 15-inch letters were beginning to appear. The photographs in the album provide an opportunity to ascertain what was happening at a fixed point in time. To make doubly certain, the letter R was also checked. If the C is part of a true circle, lines drawn touching the extremities of the R will enclose a square.

Only broadside, or very nearly so, photographs were selected. The sample was supplemented by other views, often seen in the background of photographs. In all, fifty-two examples were examined. The table on page 55 summarises the results. 'T' indicates a C which is a true circle and an R that occupies a square; 'C' indicates condensed letters. Examples of all the sizes and styles are shown in Plates 3.12-3.20.

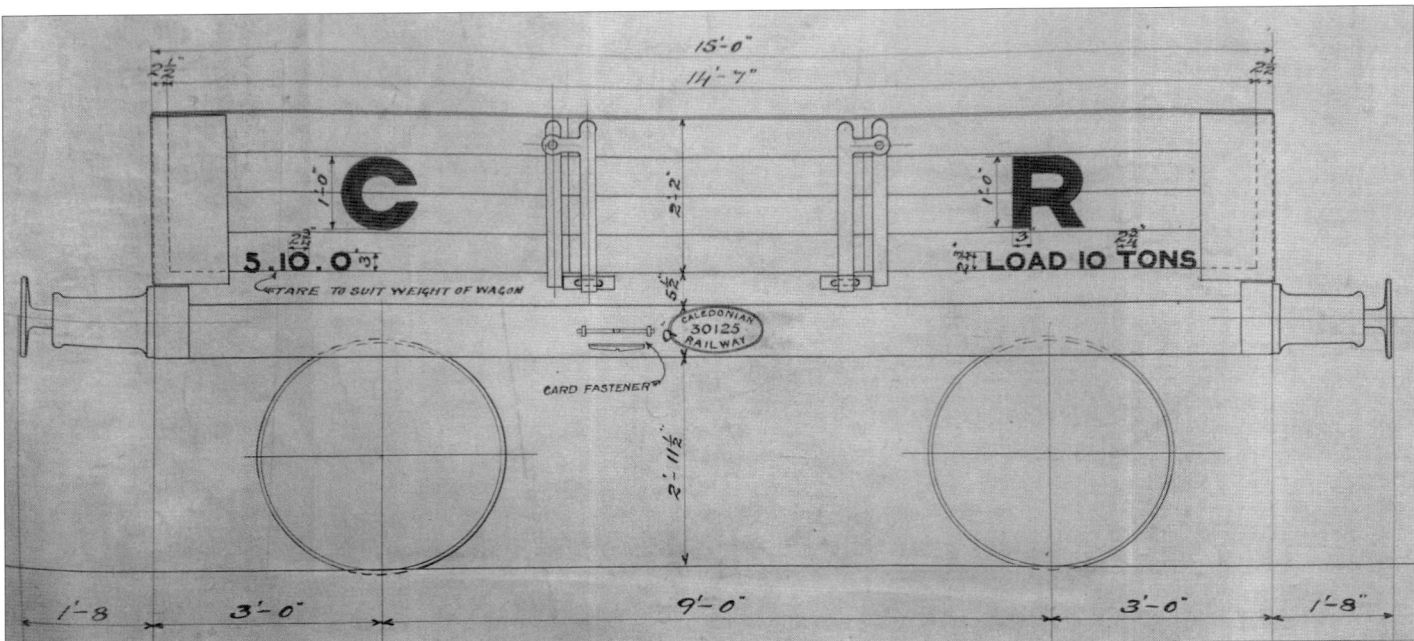

ABOVE: Figure 3.3
St. Rollox drawing 18740 was issued to R Y Pickering in 1916 for a Diagram 87 open goods wagon contract, which St. Rollox intended to build to order G.383. It shows 12-inch lettering and a truly circular C. The load characters are 2¾ inches square, as in the 1903 specifications – see Figures 3.4-3.7. The tare characters are 3 inches high, rather than the specified 2¾ inches. Why a mineral wagon series number appears on the cast plate is a mystery.

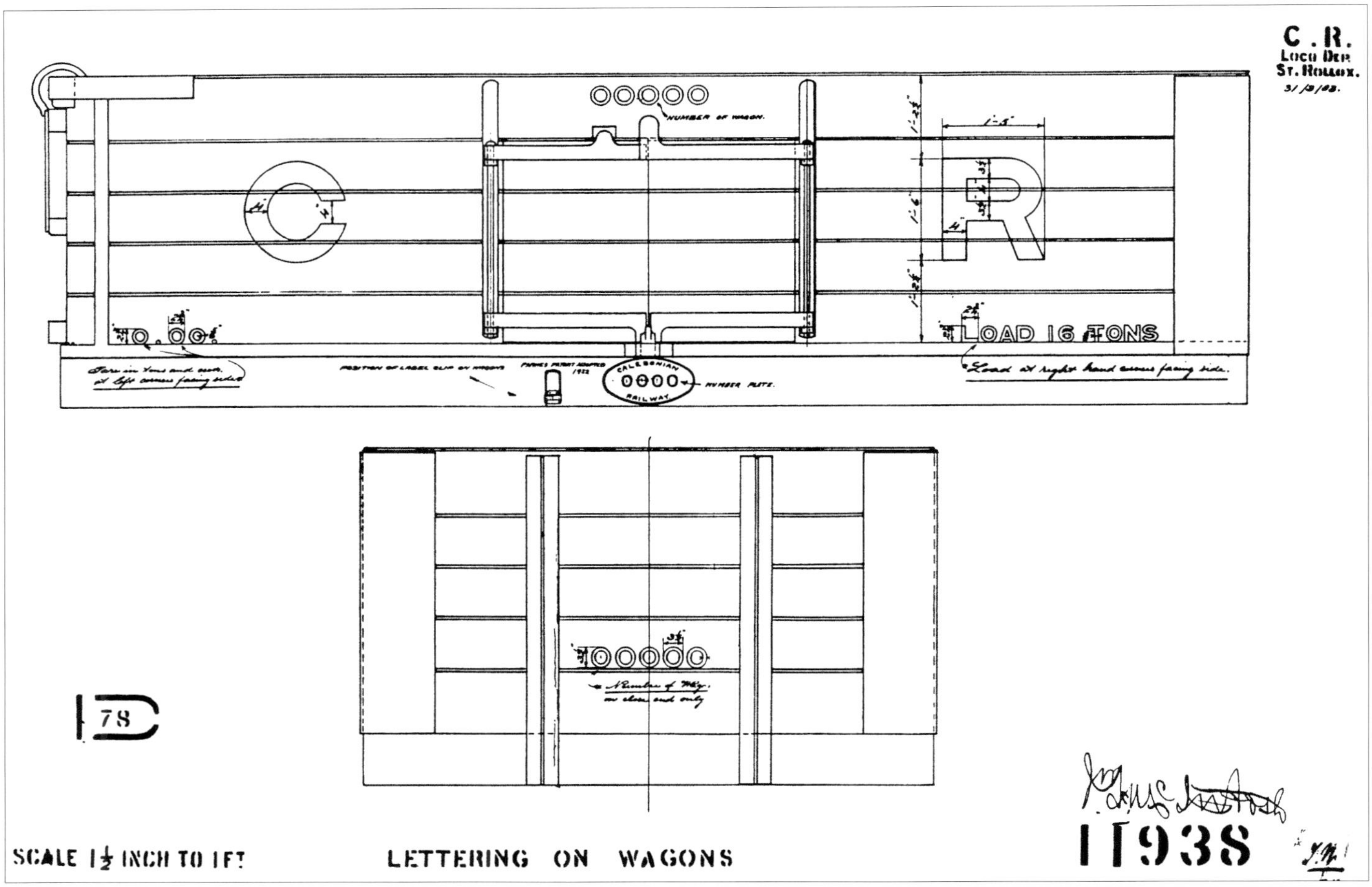

Figures 3.4-3.7
Figures 3.4 (ABOVE) and 3.5 (FACING PAGE TOP) show the lettering specifications for the new designs of mineral wagon and covered van issued to Pickering. The St. Rollox numbers are 11938 and 12113 respectively. Figures 3.6 (FACING PAGE, BOTTOM LEFT) and 3.7 (FACING PAGE, BOTTOM RIGHT) are enlargements showing that the company initials were condensed – i.e., taller than wide.

3.2: LETTER AND NUMBER STYLES

Size	9 Inches		12 Inches		15 Inches	
Shape	T	C	T	C	T	C
1900	3	1	10	12	0	3
Other	2	0	10	8	0	3
Total	5	1	20	20	0	6

Among the photographs are two instances of wagons with 12-inch letters painted in 1906 (the ballast hopper in Plate 17.11, p. 266), and a Diagram 110 pig iron wagon, photographed when newly built in 1913 – see Plate 6.14 (p. 116). The fact that these wagons were painted with circular letter Cs after the establishment of the condensed 15-inch letter style tends to confirm that this was the approved style of 12-inch lettering.

The Evolution of Letter Size and Shape

Based solely on the drawings of the condensed 18-inch letters, the author of *Caledonian Railway Livery* suggested that previous writers had been mistaken when they said that the letter C was part of a true circle.[16] Analysis of all the available drawings and photographic evidence shows that previous writers were not entirely mistaken. On the evidence of the drawings and a sample of photographs which is tiny in comparison with the number of wagons in the fleet, the size and shape of company initials seems to have evolved as follows.

The letters and numbers painted on the solebars of early wagons were 6½ inches high. When they migrated from the solebar to the wagon body, the height was usually 9 inches. In many cases these

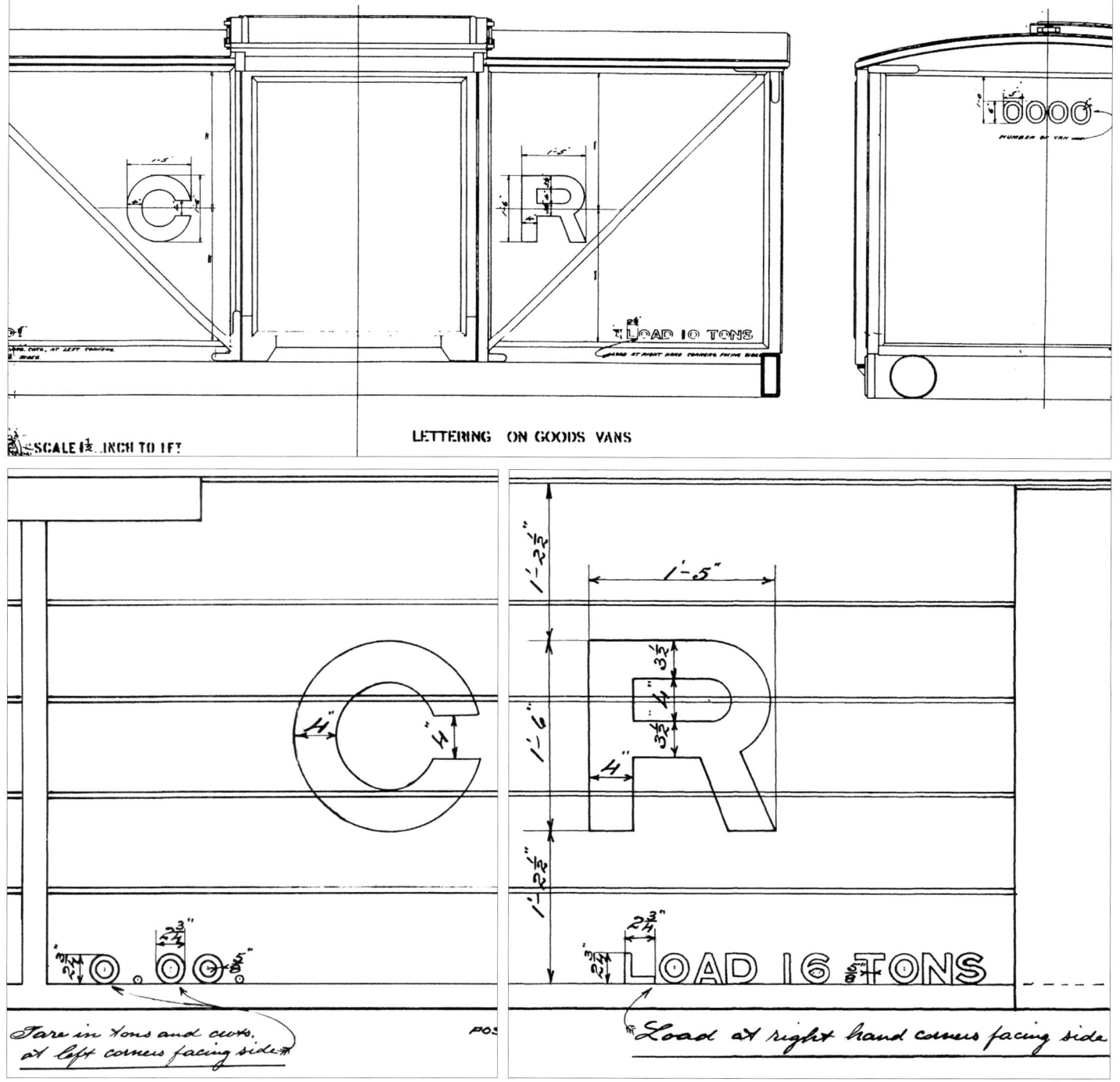

Plate 3.12
A truly circular 9-inch C on pre-diagram book swivel wagon 36036.

Plate 3.13
The only condensed version of 9-inch lettering identified for certain – on pre-diagram book rail wagon 37413. Wagons 36036 and 37413 were freshly lettered and photographed for the *1900 Register*.

Plate 3.14
Diagram 46 mineral wagon number 63951.

Plate 3.15
One of a pair of twin wagons to Diagram 47.

Plate 3.16
Diagram 46 mineral wagon, number 59078. The wagons illustrated in Plates 3.14-3.16 are all 12-inch letters with the C describing a true circle.

Plate 3.17
This is an example of 12-inch condensed letters on a Diagram 24 open wagon, photographed in 1907.

3.2: LETTER AND NUMBER STYLES

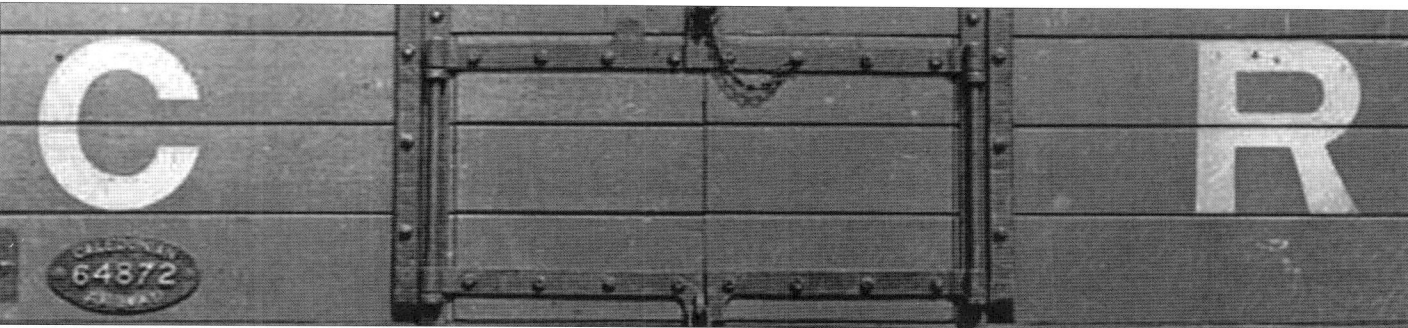

Plate 3.18
An example of the 15-inch condensed style, on the prototype Diagram 51 ore wagon 64872.

Plates 3.19
Another example of the 15-inch condensed style, on Diagram 52 14-ton mineral wagon 13036.

Plate 3.20
Finally, we return to a truly circular 12-inch letter C, on Diagram 86 ballast wagon number 35272, built in 1906.

LEFT: Plate 3.21
The first 9-inch lettering style, as applied to a 'bogie' with centre doors. The company initials are separated by a dot.

BELOW: Plate 3.22
This fuzzy enlargement shows the arrangement for an offset door wagon.

letters were replaced by larger lettering when rolling stock was repainted. The 6½-inch and 9-inch letter Cs were circular.

The circular C was the official 12-inch letter style, but what actually appeared on wagons depended on individual letterers' interpretation of the 'right shape'. It was just as likely to be condensed as circular.

The 15-inch letters, as seen around the turn of the twentieth century on the Diagrams 50 and 51 iron ore wagons and a Diagram 52 mineral, established the condensed style as standard for letters over 12 inches high. This was perpetuated and codified when the 18-inch letter became the preferred size from 1903 onwards, unless lack of space precluded its use.

The bogie coal and hopper coke wagons used 30-inch letters – see Plates 5.14 and 6.7 (pp. 99 and 112). A drawing was not issued, even though this was a completely new letter and most of the wagons were built by contractors. Scaling from the photographs suggests that a hypothetical 24 inches high condensed style letter was used, with the height increased to 30 inches by the addition of a 6-inch straight section in the middle of the C. The cut-out section of the C only increased from 4 inches to 8 inches rather than 10 inches, giving it a more closed appearance than the smaller letters.

Tare Weight and Load Lettering

Block letters and numbers was used for the tare weight and the permitted load. Photographs suggest that the style was used from at least the start of the Drummond period. The 1903 drawings required these letters and numbers to be 2¾ inches high and the same width. This, of course, created a circular zero. The same size was specified on the Diagram 109 twin wagons built by Pickering in 1912. The Diagram 87 open goods wagons built by Pickering in 1916 had the load characters at 2¾ inches high, but the tare characters were 3 inches high and 2¾ inches wide.[17]

References

1. NRS BR/CAL/1/8 no entry number
2. *LNWR Liveries*, p. 129
3. *Caledonian Railway Livery*, p. 267
4. See examples in *Caledonian Railway Livery*, Chapter 5
5. *LNWR Liveries*, Plate 109
6. *Caledonian Railway Livery*, p. 272, caption to Plate 14
7. *Caledonian Railway Livery*, p. 274, Plate 17
8. *Caledonian Railway Livery*, pp. 16, 18
9. *Caledonian Railway Livery*, pp. 77-79
10. *Caledonian Railway Livery*, p. 71
11. *Caledonian Railway Livery*, p. 16
12. Not yet catalogued, Pickering card order 30872
13. RHP 69651
14. St. Rollox 11938 and 12113 respectively
15. St. Rollox 16710, not yet catalogued
16. *Caledonian Railway Livery*, p. 265, caption to Plate 2
17. St. Rollox 16710, Pickering card order 22691

Left and Below: Figure 3.8
Drawing 16710 is dated 25th December 1912, according to the St. Rollox register. It was issued to show the lettering on the new Diagram 109 twin wagons, but in fact standard 12-inch letters were used, rather than this light, serif, style. The publicity photographs of these wagons (for example Plate 8.16, p. 140) were all taken at an angle, so it is not possible to be certain about the shape of the letters.

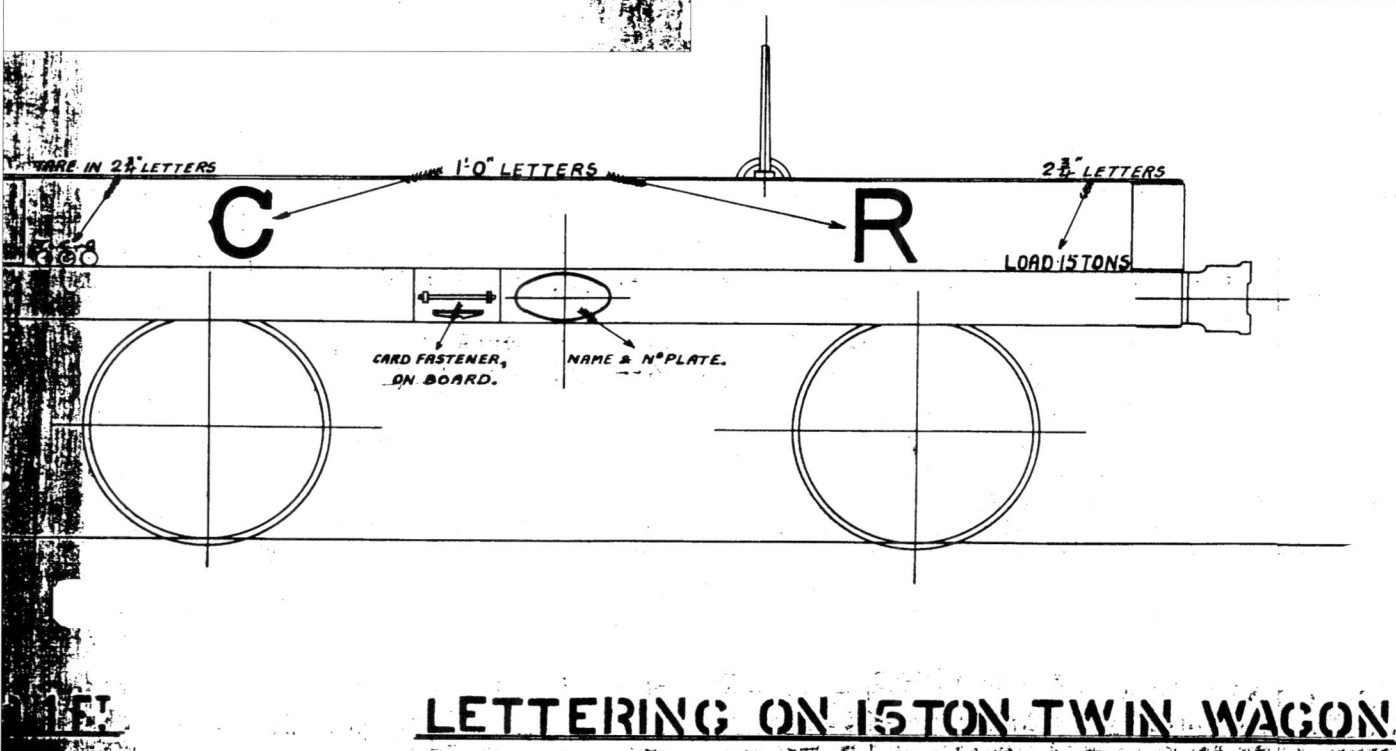

3.3: Location of Letters and Painted Numbers

Small Company Initials on Early Wagons and Vans

The heavy outside framing on the early mineral wagons dictated the location of the company initials and numerals, as did the side doors, if any. Plates 3.21-3.23 show the various dispositions. Whatever the option adopted, the letters were originally 9 inches high. If the company initials were not separated by framing, they were separated by a dot. The letters were located on the horizontal centre line of the wagon body.

The wagon number was located to the right, and aligned with the bottom, of the company initials. The numerals could be 4 inches or 6½ inches high. The load details were similarly located on the left. The 4 inches high writing was on two lines to fit the narrow space between the frame members.

The style also applied to covered vans, but the numerals and company initials were both 6½ inches high, as in Plate 3.24. The load information was located at the bottom of the wagon body towards the right-hand end. At some point that cannot be determined, 12-inch

ABOVE: Plate 3.23
When a wagon had no doors, it was possible to move the load information to a more usual position.

BELOW: Plate 3.24
The early style and size of lettering and numerals applied to a 6-ton van.

ABOVE: Plate 3.25
This enlargement from a picture of a freight train crossing the Tay Bridge at Perth shows an open wagon with a four digit number, possibly 1333, so it must be a goods wagon. This is the only evidence for this lettering position, apart from the loco coal wagons.

BELOW: Plate 3.26
This depicts a pre-diagram book open goods wagon with the second, later, style of lettering. The company initials (including a truly circular C) are 12 inches high. The numbers on the solebar are 6½ inches high. The condensed load lettering has been moved to the centre because it would have been to close to the bottom of the R.

company initials were applied, and the wagon number was moved to the centre of the solebar. Plates 3.25 and 3.26 give examples of this style. An example of a covered van with this lettering style is shown in Plate 9.17 (p. 154). It may have been an interim arrangement at the start of the Drummond period.

SMALL COMPANY INITIALS ON OTHER WAGONS

On the evidence of one photograph (see Plate 3.25) and many examples on loco coal wagons, the company initials on early open wagons were written in 6½-inch characters to the left of centre of the wagon solebar, with the number alongside. The letters were separated by a square dot. The area described by the letters and numbers was arranged symmetrically about the wagon centre line. Later, the company initials were applied to the body of the wagon, with the number remaining at the centre of the solebar – see Plate 3.26.

LARGE COMPANY INITIALS LOCATED ON THE WAGON BODY

The layout of larger company initials on the body side coupled with a cast number plate was a Drummond initiative. The standard locations from 1903 formed part of the drawings issued to Pickering. The specification seems to have codified practice dating from Drummond's accession. The basic rule was that the letters should be set around the horizontal centre line of the space that they occupied.

The space did not include the curb rail of the mineral wagon. The letters were centred vertically in the space left by the body ironwork. In the case of mineral wagons to Diagrams 21, 22 and 46, the corner plate at the fixed end occupied more space than the ironwork at the end with the door. The letters' spacing from the vertical centre line of

Plate 3.27
This enlargement of the lettering on a Diagram 22 mineral wagon shows that the letter R was symmetrically placed in the space between the side door ironwork and the corner plate. The distance from the side door to the centre line of the letter dictated the positioning of the letter C. As a result, the C is not centred in the horizontal space available.

CHAPTER 3.3: LOCATION OF LETTERS AND PAINTED NUMBERS

the wagon was dictated by the position of the right-hand letter – see Plate 3.27.

The horizontal centre line rule applied to vans, except gunpowder vans. The space to be occupied was inside the half round beading which covered the joints between the body planking and the body framework. The letters could not be positioned on the vertical centre line of the space, because ironwork ran diagonally across it. This displaced the letters towards the centre door, as seen in Plate 3.28.

WAGONS WITHOUT COMPANY INITIALS

A small number of special class wagons did not carry company initials at all, leaving the number plate as the only means of identifying ownership. The wagons fell into two categories. The pre-diagram book runner wagons and the heavy weight wagons to Diagram 49 had no space available for the initials. The Diagram 113 ingot wagon side members were crowded with rivets and shackles, occupying the available space. The three Diagram 56 trollies built in 1902 and the two Diagram 94 boiler wagons did have space available, but for some unknown reason, the letters were not applied.

The lack of easy identification was not really a problem, as the traffic for these wagons was short haul around Glasgow and the wagons would not have left the Caley system. The return depot served to identify company ownership if necessary.

WAGONS LETTERED FOR SPECIFIC SECTIONS OF THE SYSTEM

The number range from 50000 included newly built CR loco coal and mineral wagons, to Diagrams 21 and 22, some of which were designated and lettered for the Hamilton (1,851 wagons), Lesmahagow (2,250) and Law (126) sections. This practice did not start with these wagons. There is photographic evidence (see Plates 3.29 and 3.29a) of early wagons lettered 'LAW'. In this case the letters were applied to the centre of the wagon body, in one case on the side door. The

ABOVE: Plate 3.28
Pickering built Diagram 67 van of the 1903 contract, lettered on the side exactly to the specification in Figure 3.4, although there is no sign of a number on the end. The ironwork running diagonally across the body displaces the letters from centre of the body element.

LEFT: Plates 3.29 and 3.29a
These two enlargements are from the background to the photograph of the Oakbank Oil Co. tank in Plate 7.8. It shows two early wagons lettered for the Law Section. The tare weight numbers are in script style. The photograph dates from 1896, according to the paint date on the tank wagon's underframe.

ABOVE: Plate 3.30
The Diagram 22 wagon in the foreground is lettered for the R&C SECTION. It is flanked by two 7-ton 'bogies' with offset doors. All the wagons in the picture have 12-inch company initials. In each of the two rows of wagons behind is another Diagram 22 lettered for the Lesmahagow Section. The coal loads extend above the sides of the wagons. Filling the cubic capacity of wagon body never exceeded the design load.

LEFT: Plate 3.31
When a wagon was lettered for a particular section of the system, the space available for the company initials was reduced. The company initials were centred in the available space, and therefore dropped half a plank width.

letters were in the standard block style. A later wagon, built in 1896 and lettered for the Hamilton Section is shown in Plate 5.6 (p. 88).

In 1895, mineral wagons were also branded for the Carfin & Cleland Section. Diagram 46 wagons, which had been introduced a year previously, were originally earmarked for this section. Some must have been lettered for the service, because a minute records a letter in October 1895 to McIntosh which confirmed verbal instructions *'to cease painting the new spindle buffered wagons and instead to set aside our older type of solid buffered wagons for the Carfin and Cleland Section.'*[1] This explains the continued construction of Diagram 22 wagons by Hurst Nelson and Pickering in 1895 and 1896.

There is one photograph (Plate 3.30) of a Diagram 22 wagon at Netherton lime works, lettered R & C SECTION. This presumably stood for Rutherglen and Coatbridge, but there is no official reference to an order for wagons to be so lettered.

When section lettering was applied to the top plank, the rule that company initials should be placed in the centre of the space available still held good. As the top plank was now occupied, the initials were displaced downwards by half a plank's width – Plate 3.31 shows this.

The practice of lettering mineral wagons for specific sections of the system was officially discontinued by the Traffic Committee in 1908.[2]

On the limited evidence of one photograph (the left-hand wagon in Plate 17.20, p. 278), the lettering was crudely painted over.

Part of an order for Diagram 3 vans built in 1896 by Hurst Nelson was lettered for the newly opened Lanarkshire & Dumbartonshire Section. The spelling of the county with an 'n' which is customary to our eyes was only adopted in 1913. The company initials were moved to the left-hand side and separated by a dot in order to accommodate the location lettering, which was written on two lines on the right-hand side in 4-inch letters. Plate 9.20 (p. 157) illustrates this lettering.

Early in the twentieth century, superannuated 'bogies' were marked with a white cross in a circle about 12 inches in diameter for certain types of traffic on restricted parts of the system. The details of the traffic are in Chapter 5.5 and a wagon features in the background of Plate 6.7 (p. 112). The practice continued at least until 1915, as the information was included in the *Working Timetable Appendix* of that year.

LETTERING ON WAGONS FOR SPECIFIC TYPES OF TRAFFIC

Coke wagons modified from Diagram 46 minerals were lettered FOR COKE TRAFFIC along the bottom extension plank, using

6-inch letters. Each word was centred in the space between the uprights supporting the spars. Plate 6.5 (p. 110) illustrates one such wagon. Presumably, this style also applied to modified Diagram 22 wagons, although there is no photographic evidence.

The lettering on modified Diagram 21 loco coal wagons was different. The words COKE TRAFFIC ONLY were written on the left-hand top plank, using 4-inch lettering. A location WHEN EMPTY filled a similar space on the right-hand side. Unfortunately the location is indecipherable in the only picture of these wagons where lettering is visible. The photograph and the history behind the modification can be found in Chapter 6.

The 40-ton hopper wagons had COKE WAGON written high up in the centre of the body side, using 6-inch letters. This prevented the application of extra numbers on the side of the wagon. It is not known if the numbers were repeated on the ends. A photograph is in Chapter 6.

On the evidence of one photograph (Plate 6.3, p. 106) four-wheeled hopper wagons were specifically identified in 6-inch letters across the top plank of the body.

Pig iron wagons had the two words written in 4 inches high condensed letters, applied on the centre line of the body. The words were usually on the single body plank, but could be on the curb rail. This lettering was the subject of a drawing in 1916 – see Figure 3.9.[3] Photographs show that the lettering was current before 1900. A wagon so lettered for the *1900 Register* is in Plate 6.10 (p. 114), and there is an earlier example in Plate 6.9 (p. 113). The 4-inch condensed letters were also used for the Diagram 25 lime wagons. There is a picture of this wagon in Chapter 9.

The Diagram 50 bogie iron ore wagon and the prototype of Diagram 51 were lettered 50 TON and 16 TON IRON ORE WAGON respectively. The 6-inch letters were centred on the top plank of the wagon. There are pictures of both wagons in Chapter 5. Photographic evidence shows that the lettering was not applied to the other Diagram 51 wagons.

Loco Coal Wagons

Lettering of loco coal wagons followed two styles. A drawing of 1876[4] has letters, number and designation roughly sketched in pencil. The company initials and number were on the solebar in the usual position for the time, with LOCO COAL ONLY in 6½-inch letters on the wagon body. The side door separated the first two words, creating an asymmetrical effect. This seems to have been the first style of lettering and is shown in Plate 3.32. The words LESMAHAGOW SECTION often appeared on the top plank.

Wagons built later had the company initials in 12-inch letters separated by a dot on the left-hand end of the body, with LOCO on the right – see Plate 3.33. This layout also applied to Diagram 21 mineral wagons in loco coal service – see Plate 5.5 (p. 88). The earlier wagons would have been lettered to the new style when they were repainted.

The extra lettering applied to the 30-ton bogie mineral wagons carrying loco coal was centrally located on the body panels on either side of the centre door. The letters scale at 10 inches high. Part of the lettering can be seen in Plate 5.14 (p. 99).

Above: Figure 3.9
This is taken from St. Rollox drawing 18741, which codified earlier practice. Note that the letters were condensed, and the two centre points for striking the arcs of the G and the O.

Left: Plate 3.32
This shows the first style of lettering for loco coal wagons, but is not entirely typical – the LESMAHAGOW SECTION wording was usually on the top plank. Above the word LOCO there is also ghost writing: CARSTAIRS is written in the same size block lettering. It may be that the wagon was attached originally to Carstairs locomotive depot, but was reassigned to Lesmahagow traffic. This would explain the very cramped new lettering, which almost obscures the right-hand tare numeral.

Brake Van Lettering

Company initials on brake vans were located by reference to the space created by the open verandahs, thus placing them higher than on vans in ordinary traffic. The letters were 12 inches high. If no outside framing or lookout intervened, the letters were separated by a dot as usual. Two examples are shown in Plates 3.34 and 3.35. Others are shown in Chapter 16.

The standard practice for wagons was followed as far as painted numbers were concerned. If a footboard support was attached on the centre line of the solebar, the number was painted on the bottom plank of the body.

When cast number plates were introduced they were most often fitted on the right of the centre of the solebar with the tare weight an equal distance away from the centre line to the left.

Brake vans were allocated to specific locations, in letters about 3 inches high. The information was located on the centre line of the body if possible, but outside framing or handrails prevented this in some designs. Some, but not all, vans also carried the name of the brakesman at the bottom of the body, in the centre. Examples are shown in Chapter 16.

Gunpowder Van Lettering

The company initials on the first two iron gunpowder vans and their Diagram 4 successors was conventional, but placed higher up the van body compared with their general revenue counterparts. In the case of the iron vans a safety notice was applied to the bottom of the door. This displaced the special purpose lettering to slightly above the horizontal centre line of the side.

On the Diagram 4 vans the special purpose lettering was applied on the two planks above the door handle ironwork. The GUNPOWDER VAN lettering used the same height of lettering as the company initials, but lighter and condensed, and with a rather peculiar letter G. An example is shown in Plate 3.36.

The only photograph of a Diagram 78 van shows very lightweight lettering, but the same block style. The positions of the company initials and the special purpose lettering were reversed from the previous gunpowder van layout. Photographs of the two types of metal gunpowder vans can be found in Chapter 15, p. 240.

Additional Painted Numbers

In conjunction with the cast number plates, wagon numbers were usually, but not always, repeated on the ends. This practice was extant in 1882, according to *LNWR Liveries*,[5] which quotes a minute of August in that year requiring the number of L&NWR wagons to be painted on the ends *'in the same manner as on the Caledonian Railway.'*

The specified position for open wagons in the 1903 drawing was centred on the second plank from the floor. Presumably this was to avoid their being obscured by a tarpaulin. Each digit filled a space 3½ inches square. This was repeated on Pickering card order 22691 for the Diagram 109 twin wagons built in 1913. On mineral wagons numbers were applied to the fixed end only.

Some, but not all, Diagram 59 mineral wagons had additional numbers on the centre of the body above the side door. The St. Rollox drawing specified 3½-inch numerals for both sides and ends, but this is directly contradicted by a Pickering card order[6] which specified 3½-inch numbers on the end and 5½-inch on each side, as in Plate 3.5. The larger size seems to have been commonly adopted.

The Diagram 54 bogie coal wagons had the number repeated in the larger size over the centre door. The number was usually, but not

Above Left: Plate 3.33
These are examples of the second style of loco coal lettering at Perth. The left-hand wagon carries the Lesmahagow Section lettering in the normal place across the top plank. Also of interest is the number on the cattle wagon end, painted in the space described by the arc of the roof, and the ballast wagon in the foreground, which is lettered for Laurencekirk.

Plates 3.34 (Top Right) and 3.35 (Right)
These enlargements show the position of the 12-inch company initials in relation to the opening in the sides which formed the verandah. The Diagram 5 van in Plate 3.35 also shows the location of the home depot, in this case Polmadie.

CHAPTER 3.3: LOCATION OF LETTERS AND PAINTED NUMBERS

always, repeated on the ends of these wagons in the same size. The Diagram 66 bogie hopper wagons were lettered COKE WAGON on the top centre of the body side, preventing the addition of a painted number. There is no photograph of the ends of these wagons.

On the Diagram 67 vans, the specification required the bottom of the numbers to be located 1 foot down from the top of the area on the end that was enclosed by the half frame beading. The numbers were to be 5 inches high and 6 inches wide. In practice the numbers were often located in the centre of the arc described by the roof. The Diagram 67 vans built to carry explosives in 1917 carried duplicate numbers on the second plank from the bottom of the sliding doors – see Plate 3.37.

The duplicate number on brake vans could be placed just under the roof or immediately under the verandah opening. See, for example, Plates 16.2 (under the roof arc) and 16.11 (below the verandah opening) (pp. 245 and 255 respectively).

ADDITIONAL NUMBERS ON CATTLE WAGONS

The wagon number was repeated on each body side, centred on the top plank of the body above the letter R, as in Plate 3.38. The size of numeral was the specified as 3½ inches. This may have been a late development which paralleled a similar addition on the London & North Western Railway. *LNWR Liveries*,[7] quoting an unattributed primary source, mentions that in 1896 the inspector of Irish cattle traffic:

'drew attention to the difficulties in ascertaining the numbers

ABOVE: Plate 3.36
Lettering style and location on Diagram 4 gunpowder van number 18. The special purpose lettering is the same height as the company initials, but lighter and condensed to fit the available space.

RIGHT: Plate 3.37
An enlargement from Plate 9.23, showing the extra numbers painted on the doors of Diagram 67 vans that were built to carry explosives.

FAR RIGHT: Plate 3.38
An additional number was painted on cattle wagons in 3½-inch numerals. This may have been a relatively late development, but it was certainly extant by the time of the *1900 Register*. This picture is an enlargement from the background of a photograph, which dates from 1913, of 4-2-2 123 and inspection saloon number 1. The cattle wagon is the standard Drummond design to Diagram 10, which was still being built in 1914.

of cattle trucks owing to the numbers being on the ends of the vehicles only, and that it was ordered that as cattle wagons entered the works for repair their numbers should be painted on the sides also.'

At first sight, this is a curious statement, as L&NWR wagons carried cast number plates on the solebar, as did the Caledonian. It was probably necessary because the cast number plate was obscured by the cattle dock when loading. The plates were also often covered by spillage from the lime wash used to clean and disinfect the interiors.

The book goes on to state that the number was painted in 3½-inch characters over the right-hand diamond, in other words in the same position as adopted by the Caledonian. The practice was said to be discontinued during the First World War.

OTHER WAGON MARKINGS

A puzzling feature found on many, but not all, wagons was a sign consisting of a circle about 2 inches diameter with a curved line dividing it. It was stencilled in white paint on metal wagons (Plate 3.39). In the case of wooden wagons, it was only sometimes picked out in white, and was usually incised or branded (Plate 3.40). It was therefore obscured by the body paint. It always appeared at the right-hand end. On wooden wagons it sometimes appeared on the body curb rail, but its more usual position was in the semicircle described by the crown plate on the solebar.

The first appearance to which a date can be attached is on the mineral wagons built by Hurst Nelson in 1897 that were originally destined for Dunn Brothers (Plate 5.7, p. 88). Many of the wagons photographed for the *1900 Register* carried it. The last date on photographic evidence is 1906, when it appeared on the hopper ballast wagons (Plate 17.11, p. 266).

The North Eastern Railway used a very similar symbol, described as '*circle and bar*', which identified mineral wagons that were fitted with a special arrangement to allow them to be hauled up steep inclines by cable. It was prominently displayed towards the top right of the wagon body. [8]

So far, the symbol's significance on the Caledonian is unclear. It was applied to a wide range of wagon types from old mineral 'bogies' to special class wagons, with grease and oil lubrication alike. It does not seem to have had an operational purpose, as it was not easily seen, especially on wood underframe wagons. It may possibly have been a census or stock-taking mark, but it does not appear on every wagon. Its appearance on contractor and St. Rollox built wagons precludes it being a company or wagon builder's identification mark.

REFERENCES
1. NRS BR/CAL/5/11 entry 242
2. NRS BR/CAL/1/56 entry 1217
3. St. Rollox 18741, not yet catalogued
4. St. Rollox 2044, not yet catalogued
5. *LNWR Liveries*, p. 135
6. Card order 10164 for 300 steel underframe mineral wagons, dated 25th May 1906
7. *LNWR Liveries*, p. 136
8. Described in *North Eastern Record Volume 2*, p. 111

Plates 3.39 (ABOVE LEFT) and 3.40 (ABOVE CENTRE)
The significance of this mark has not yet been explained. It is shown on a Diagram 66 hopper wagon and one of the two 15-ton special class machinery wagons.

Plates 3.41 (LEFT) and 3.42 (ABOVE RIGHT)
These are submitted as a record of the last wagon in original Caledonian Railway livery, unless someone knows otherwise. As you can see from George Stilley's note, he saw this van body in 1959. It was a Diagram 67 van built before 1912 when heavy outside framing was adopted, making its state of preservation even more remarkable. On a final note, measurement of the company initials does indeed suggest that Stilley was right and that he had found an exception to the condensed 18-inch letter rule – the C is truly circular!

3.4: Cast Number and Builder's Plates

Shortly after Drummond took up office in 1882, the painted number was superseded for new construction by an oval cast plate, bearing the words CALEDONIAN RAILWAY in two arcs above and below the wagon number in the centre. Wagons with painted numbers retained the style until withdrawal. There are numerous photographs in the *1900 Register* depicting early wagons in this state, some of them newly painted for the occasion.

The oval of the wagon plates was flatter than those fitted to locomotives. Although the latter progressively increased in size, the ratio of height to width remained almost identical at between 0.62:1 and 0.64:1. The wagon plates' ratio was constant at 0.51:1. Wagon plates had to accommodate five digit numbers, which no doubt dictated the extra width. The Drummond locomotive number plate is shown in Plate 3.43, with a wagon plate in 3.44 for comparison.

There were two types of plate. Their dimensions were identical. The block style numerals used for painted wagon numbers were used for both types of plate. The background was painted black with the raised elements picked out in white.

The plates were individually cast. The consistency of spacing of the letters that make up the words suggests that they were on two blocks of metal that were used repeatedly. The numbers were added individually in the centre of the mould. These factors led to variations, the most frequent being misalignment of the numbers. Plate 3.45 shows a particularly poor example.

The First Style of Cast Number Plate

Drummond introduced the first type of plate, although painted numbers were still applied to wagons and vans built in 1882/83, as he was beginning to stamp his mark on all aspects of Caledonian design. Some pre-Drummond era wagons received cast plates after rebuilding. This plate did not have a raised rim. It was still in use when Diagram 46 wagon 63951, built in 1899/1900, was photographed for the *1900 Register*.

One of these plates is in Kidderminster Railway Museum, carrying the number 37255. It is illustrated in Plate 3.44. The caption in *Caledonian Railway Livery* said that the type of wagon to which it was attached was not recorded. It was certainly a goods wagon, built before the 100 Diagram 13 rail wagons of order G9, whose numbers started at 37336. Thirty dead meat vans were authorised to the capital account a month before the rail wagons, so they presumably occupied numbers 37306-37335. Previous to that was order G5 for 100 swivel wagons. These appeared in the July 1885 returns as additions, so would have been numbered to the capital account in a block from 37206-37305, which included the

Plate 3.43 (Top Left) and 3.44 (Left)
The lower plate is the first style of cast number plate introduced shortly after Drummond took office, with the contemporary locomotive number plate for comparison. The cast number plate of wagon 37255 probably dates from 1885.

Above: **Plate 3.45**
An example of very poorly aligned numbers on the first version of the cast number plate. This was on a Diagram 3 6-ton covered van. The full picture is Plate 10.8.

Plates 3.46 (ABOVE) and 3.46a (BELOW)
These show the two different styles of lettering used on the first version of the cast number plate. The early style, on the plate for 37255 is above; the later style, on 70517, is below. The later plate was originally attached to one of the 1,000 Diagram 24 open goods wagons, built by St. Rollox in 1899/1900 to order G176.

Kidderminster plate. Plate 8.10 (p. 135) shows two of this type of wagon, which originated in late 1882.

Unlike the letters used on the contemporary locomotive number plates, the company name on this first plate originally used slightly more extended block lettering, as in the case of number plate 37255. Later, a condensed form of block lettering was adopted, which was the same as that on the locomotive number plate. The two styles are compared in Plates 3.46 and 3.46a.

THE SECOND STYLE OF CAST NUMBER PLATE

The second version, which had a raised rim, used the condensed style of letters first seen on Drummond locomotive number plates and perpetuated by McIntosh on his garter style locomotive plate. It is shown in Plate 3.47.

Its first authenticated appearance was on the Diagram 52 mineral wagons to St. Rollox order G186, which was authorised in March 1901 but it may have been fitted to order G180, authorised in the previous August. St. Rollox drawing 11247 of 30th January 1902,[1] therefore, codified existing practice. It seems to have been part of a package associated with the new standard wagons. The drawing is shown in Figure 3.10 (opposite).

For no obvious reason, the two Diagram 89 trolley wagons numbered 217 and 218 were fitted with rectangular plates with raised rims – see Plate 3.48. The lettering and number styles were the same as on the standard plate. Plate 13.9 (p. 216) shows one of the wagons.

LOCATION OF CAST PLATES

From the outset, the cast plates were normally bolted on the centre line of the solebar – see Plates 3.2 and 3.3, for example. This practice was codified by the 1903 mineral wagon drawing. If an underframe component prevented the normal position, the plate was offset, usually to the right, as in Plate 3.28. For the same reason, the number plate was fitted to the body planking on rail and swivel wagons that were fitted with stanchions – see, for example, Plate 8.3 (p. 127).

The second version of the plate could not be fitted in the narrow channel solebars of the production batch of Diagram 51 ore wagons, so it was attached to the wagon body. The drawing shows a ⅜-inch radius to the back to allow it to fit snugly into the wider channel solebars which were introduced on the Diagram 59 mineral wagons.

BUILDER AND CAPACITY PLATES ON BOGIE WAGONS

Starting with the order for the Diagram 53 trollies in 1900, St. Rollox applied cast builder and/or load plates to some, but not all, steel underframe bogie wagons. The plates had raised lettering and a border, anticipating the second style of wagon number plate by two years. Where a load was indicated on a plate it was not painted on the wagon. The list of wagons on which plates have positively been identified is:

DIAG.	TYPE OF PLATE
53	Load 12 tons, the rest indecipherable
54	Caledonian Railway, builder and year
56	2 plates: Load 20 tons distributed and builder plate
66	Caledonian Railway, builder and year
89	Load 30 tons, builder and year
94	Load 40 tons, builder
112	Load 35 tons, builder and year
113	Load 35 tons, builder and year

A drawing was issued by St. Rollox in 1902,[2] which is shown as Figure 3.11. An example of a typical builder's plate is shown in Plate 3.49. A different style of plate was fitted to the Diagram 54 bogie coal wagons and the Diagram 66 40-ton hoppers. This is shown in Plate 3.50.

REFERENCES
1. RHP 69655
2. St. Rollox 11467, not yet catalogued.

LEFT: Plate 3.47
McIntosh introduced the modified version of the cast plate with a raised rim. This example is carried by a Diagram 87 10-ton open goods wagon. The snug fit in the channel solebar, thanks to the radius on the back of the plate, is evident. The St. Rollox drawing is shown in Figure 3.10.
CENTRE: Plate 3.48
One of the rectangular number plates used only on the Diagram 89 trolly wagons, built in 1908.
RIGHT: Plate 3.49
A builder's plate attached to Diagram 89 trolly number 217, one of the two wagons with a rectangular number plate. Plate 13.9 shows the complete wagon.

3.5: Allocation of Numbers

Ordinary Service Wagons

In October 1910, a rolling stock return[1] described the wagon numbering sequence set out in the table below. Photographs of early goods and mineral wagons strongly suggest that the numbering scheme was long established, and extended as the wagon fleet increased.

Goods	Mineral
1-10000	10001-35070
35071-35083	35084
35085-35090	35091
35092, 35094-45000	45001-65172
	66219-66530
69451 upwards	

The return stated that wagon 35093 had been broken up. 65173-66218 and 66531-69450 were said to be unallocated and were treated as blanks. In fact, the numbers from 66001-30 and 66031-66100 had been allocated in the early 1900s to batches of Diagram 54 mineral wagons from the Leeds Forge Company and St.Rollox respectively.

This was not an error that had been rectified by 1910; wagons with original numbers in these ranges were recorded in an LM&SR document of 1931.[2]

In effect, the mineral wagon series was closed at 65172, because the block 66219–66530 was allocated to 30-ton bogie coal wagons and 40-ton hoppers. The 8,000 stored 'bogies' that were mostly numbered in the first mineral wagon block would provide more than enough spare numbers for their Diagram 59 replacements, which were built in considerable numbers until 1922. The increased capacity of the new mineral wagons meant that, as well as replacing an old wagon and taking its number, another wagon's number was released as a spare.

A full list of numbers correlated to types of wagon has not survived, but over 20,000 have been identified from photographs and sub-contractors' orders. The list will be made available on the CRA website. Sample numbers of wagons, where known, are included in the descriptions of the various types of wagon as an aid to modellers.

Allocation of Numbers Within the Series

Wagons built to the capital account were numbered consecutively within the goods and mineral series. A wagon built as a replacement took the number of a wagon that was written off,

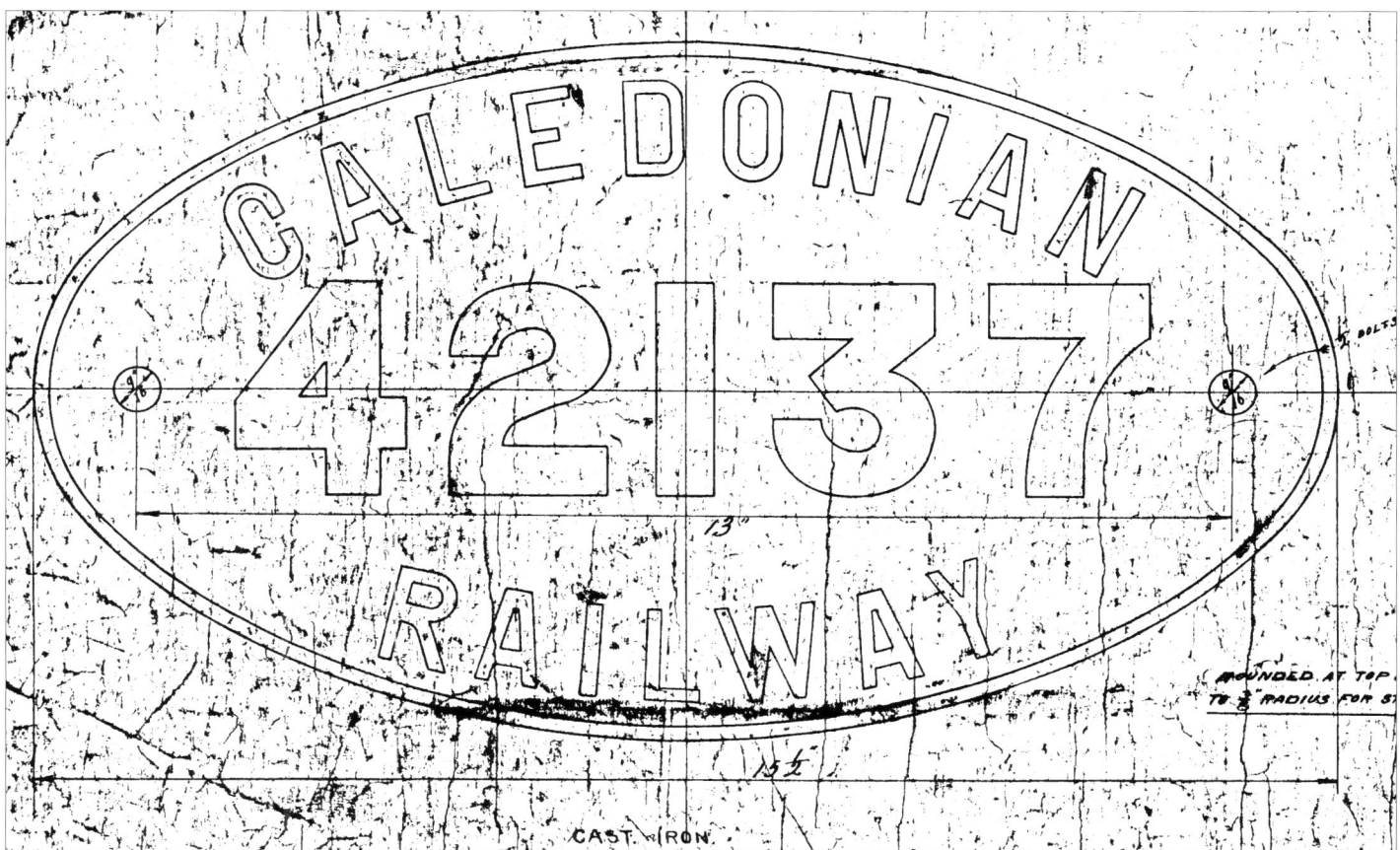

Figure 3.10
The St. Rollox drawing 11247 for the cast plate illustrated in Plate 3.47.

RIGHT: Plate 3.50
This is an example of the railway builder and year of build plate attached to a Diagram 54 mineral wagon.

BELOW: Figure 3.11
The St. Rollox drawing for the builder's plate, dated August 1902.

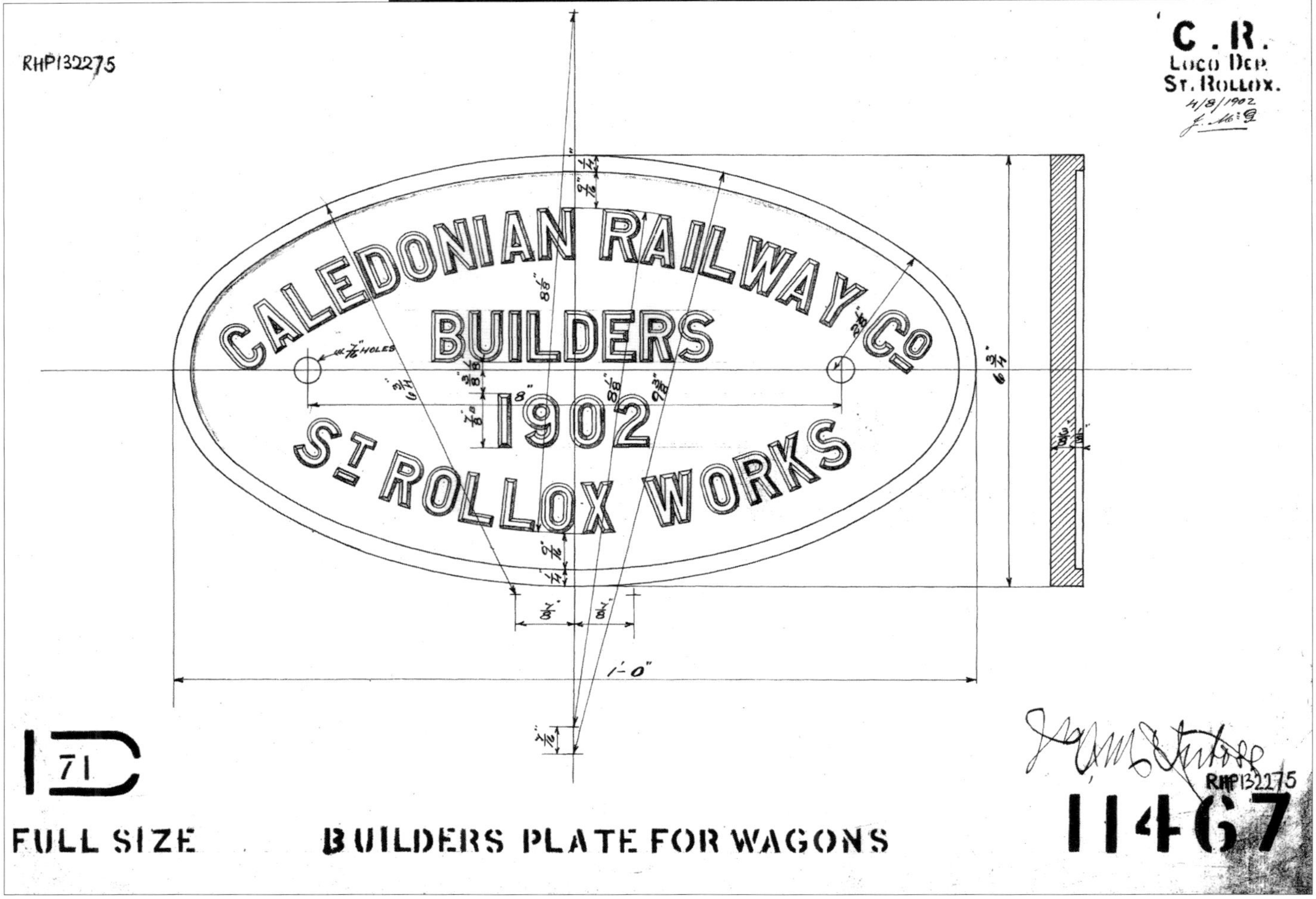

creating a random element in what was originally a sequential numbering system. The original wagon may have been the same type as its replacement, but that was not necessarily the case. The practice was exemplified in 1897, when 400 wagons were purchased from Hurst Nelson. McIntosh described the numbers to be allocated as *'Capital Nos. 100 high; Revenue 300 mixed.'*[3]

The replacement and upgrading of wagons started very early in the Caledonian's history, and continued into the twentieth century. If the numbering system above was established from the outset, early numbers must have been used at least twice, culminating in the allocation in 1916 of numbers such as 10096 to Diagram 59 wagons lettered for loco coal.[4]

By the time Drummond took office, mineral wagon numbers had gone beyond 50XXX in the second major block outlined on the previous page. One of the last 'bogies,' number 50677, was photographed for the *1900 Register*. Goods wagons too were into the second block of numbers, as shown in photographs that included pre-diagram book 6-ton van number 37250 – see Plate 9.17 (p. 154). By the start of the twentieth century mineral wagon numbers had reached 639XX and goods wagons 712XX, on the evidence of publicity photographs and contract details.[5]

The highest mineral wagon number apart from the bogie coal wagons and the solitary 50-ton iron ore wagon was 65172, the last of an order of 1,000 Diagram 52 mineral wagons, built to the capital account in 1902/3.

The highest goods wagon number known for certain is 74072. The type of wagon cannot be identified, but it was an open wagon, recorded delivering a Pickering-built brake van at Stobcross Quay in

3.5: ALLOCATION OF NUMBERS

1921; the brake van was destined for the Bengal to Nagpur Railway. The highest number identified in a photograph is 74015, which was a Diagram 124 rail wagon, built in 1919.

It is possible that the number series extended further. In 1922, the Caledonian purchased from the government 300 vans for carrying explosives. Two hundred were charged to the capital account. If standard practice was followed, numbers would have been allocated above the highest existing goods vehicle number. What little is known about these wagons is set out in Chapter 9.2, at the end of the description of the Diagram 67 vans.

There are two cases of apparent illogicality (at least to the author, if not to the Caledonian) in the number allocation. Stone wagons as photographed for the *1900 Register* were allocated goods numbers when the mineral series might have been expected. Pig iron undergoes a more complicated refining process than that of blasting from rock and was actually traded as a commodity. The wagons, were, however, numbered as minerals.

The only known instance of a deliberate 'breach of the rules' is the 50-ton ore wagon 72000, which received a special number in the goods series, significantly beyond the highest number that had been allocated at the time of its construction in 1899. It may have been intended as the start of a new number series for the 100 wagons that were originally authorised. The anomaly was corrected when it appeared as a special goods wagon in the 1910 breakdown of Caledonian goods stock.

Three lots of mineral wagons authorised as renewals were allocated high numbers, which would imply that they were in fact charged to the capital account. The wagons were to orders G178 (the prototype Diagram 51 four-wheeled ore wagon), G179 (291 Diagram 46 mineral wagons) and G180 (the production lot of 201 Diagram 51 wagons). There is no obvious explanation for this apparent anomaly. The rolling stock returns show that equal numbers of wagons were withdrawn and built as replacements, so vacant low numbers were available.

There was one recorded case of unintentional misallocation of numbers. In Pickering card order 10164 for 300 Diagram 59 mineral wagons, the dispatch record for 15th August 1906 gives the following numbers: 35015, 35049, 35069, 35094, 35159, 35245, 35321, 35344 and 35394. All but the first three are in the goods series. To compound the error, the number 35394 had already been appropriately allocated to a Diagram 67 goods van built by Pickering as part of card order 6673 in 1903 – see Plate 1.9 (p. 14).

The mineral wagons were treated as replacements, so the numbers used by Pickering would have been allocated by the Caledonian accounts department. Presumably numbers from the correct series were allocated and the wagons were repainted and fitted with new cast plates to correct the error.

SPECIAL CLASS WAGONS

A separate number series existed for trolley, well, machinery and heavy weight wagons, plus furniture van wagons. This probably originated in 1868, when *'boiler wagon, trolly number 1'* entered service, followed by trolly number 2 in 1876 and machinery wagon number 3 in 1883. These wagons and their origins are discussed in more detail in Chapters 13 and 15. The *1890 Working Timetable Appendix* listed the three wagons at the start of the special series, followed by twenty other special purpose wagons numbered as goods wagons. The first rail wagons were also included, numbered in the goods wagons series, but not the ten locomotive wagons.

Plate 3.51
Here is a Caledonian Railway wagon in LM&SR livery carrying original and LM&SR numbers, with the two sets of company initials also visible. It is a Diagram 59 mineral wagon with oak underframe, built as part of Pickering card order 36083, delivered to the CR in the week of 26th June 1920.

By 1894, the flat, machinery and furniture van wagons had been renumbered into the special series, followed by eight gunpowder vans. In the *1895 Working Timetable Appendix* the number of special wagons had risen to fifty and the gunpowder vans had been allocated a separate number series starting from 1.

The fleet of special wagons continued to increase, until by the *1915 Working Timetable Appendix* the series ran from 1 to 363. The gunpowder van series had extended to 35. Later the special list reached 380 with a Diagram 96 trolley built in 1918.

The large fleet of six-wheeled rail wagons was included from the outset in the special wagon list, but they were never renumbered into the special series, retaining their original numbers in the goods wagon block.

Brake Vans

Brake vans were classed as service vehicles and had a number series of their own. A complete record of the numbers has not survived. The stock of vans reached its peak in 1908 with 596 vehicles. The highest known number is 671, recorded by an eyewitness. This was a Diagram 63 brake van allocated to Hamilton. A photograph of Diagram 63 van number 600 is of an inside framed van. It must have been one of the twenty built on the capital account in 1907, because later vans had heavy outside framing.

As before, replacements took the number of a withdrawn van. For instance, an eyewitness reported that Diagram 62 brake van number 105 was allocated to St. Rollox.

Service Vehicles

As well as goods brake vans, this category included tank wagons, ballast and loco coal wagons, according to the return of 1910. All these wagons were regarded as general service vehicles for numbering purposes. Tank and ballast wagons were included in the goods wagon number series, and loco coal wagons were treated as minerals. Ballast brakes took numbers in the ordinary brake van series.

Wagons in Departmental Use

This group included wagons used in loco depots and works for ash disposal and moving materials. They were wagons that had been taken out of revenue service when they were replaced by more modern vehicles. Most of these wagons seem not to have been numbered, but several wagons appear in photographs at Perth with locally issued numbers. It is not known whether this practice was unique to this depot.

Engineer's department vans and wagons did not exhibit a consistent pattern. Old mineral wagons used in ballast trains retained their original mineral wagon numbers, even after repainting to show their new, restricted use. Some runner wagons attached to breakdown cranes took the number of the crane; others had no number. The converted mineral wagons used as tenders for small tank engines were sometimes numbered and sometimes not. In one case, the wagon took the number of the locomotive to which it was attached.

Wagon Renumbering After the Grouping

According to George Dow, the LM&SR allocated CR wagons numbers between 300001 and 352999, including the special wagons.[6] There are no pictures of CR wagons in LM&SR livery that contradict this assertion.

Comparing the CR numbers with the range allocated by the LM&SR shows that wagons with CR numbers below 52999 had 300000 added, and those from 53000 upwards were renumbered into the gaps created by the wagons scrapped in the replacement programme. This implies that no numbers were duplicated when adding 300000 to wagons in the ordinary service, special class and gunpowder van series. It seems likely that the gunpowder vans were renumbered into the general goods wagon series.

As a result of the renumbering policy, surviving goods vehicles had 300000 added to their original numbers, apart from those in the block from 69451 onwards, which started with wagons built in 1899.

Mineral wagons from 53000 upwards were renumbered. This included a large quantity of the modified solid buffer minerals to Diagram 22, all the Diagram 46 minerals, about half the Diagram 52 wagons which had been built to the capital account and the Diagram 51 ore wagons. All the Diagram 59 wagons built under the renewal programme had been allocated numbers originally carried by old wagons, so they were already numbered below 52999.

The only documented new numbers were those allocated at random to the surviving 30-ton bogie mineral and 40-ton hopper wagons. The numbers were recorded in an LM&SR diagram dating from 1931.[7]

Brake vans were renumbered at the end of the wagon series by adding 353000 to their CR numbers. This avoided duplication with the special class wagons, which also had three-digit numbers. A photograph of a Diagram 62 brake van in LM&SR livery can be found in Chapter 16.

References
1. In BR/CAL/4/134
2. *LMS Diagrams of Bogies used for Heavy Weight and Mineral Wagons*, CRA Archive ref: 3/4/1/24
3. NRS BR/CAL/5/11, entry 290
4. Pickering dispatch records for card order 29760
5. 63951 was photographed for the *1900 Register*. 71283 was the last of 1,000 Diagram 24 wagons to Pickering card order 3352, which was begun in August 1899
6. *HMRS Journal*, Volume 6, p. 48
7. *LMS Diagrams of Bogies used for Heavy Weight and Mineral Wagons*, also published in *The True Line*, issue 73, pp. 27-29

Plate 3.52
As an introduction to the chapter on Non-Passenger Coaching Stock livery, here is *Dunalastair I* 4-4-0 number 729, heading an Up train south of Stirling. Behind the engine is a Diagram 84 refrigerator van for meat, followed by three Diagram 39 vans, all in plain brown livery. The Diagram 39 vans are part of the group numbered in the carriage, fish and milk van series, because they have louvred sides. Possible numbers are between 145 and 148, which were designated as meat vans. Why the front van is running with open doors is a mystery. Details of the vans can be found on pages 168 and 175.

Chapter 4
Non-Passenger Coaching Stock Livery and Numbering
4.1: The NPCS Livery

The wagons and vans discussed in this chapter were built with braking systems, running and drawgear which allowed them to be marshalled in passenger trains, as well as in block trains running at passenger train speed, such as fish trains. They were also marshalled behind the locomotive in Class A express goods trains. The vehicles fell into four categories of traffic, shown in the following table. Goods vans and wagons to Diagrams 67 and 87 that were fitted with continuous brakes have been discussed in section 3.2.

Type	Diagram Numbers
Livestock	8, 9, 40, 70, 73
Meat	84, 90, 102
Fish, fruit and milk	15, 29, 30, 39, 55, 71, 72, 76, 116
Carriage and scenery	11, 11A, 44, 68, 69, 83, 88, 101

There were also pre- or non-diagram book vehicles in each category. Some of these vehicles, dating back to the 1870s, were still in traffic at the Grouping. The types are dealt with in the order above, after a general discussion on liveries.

Early Livery

Non-passenger coaching stock (NPCS) made its appearance almost from the start of Caledonian Railway operations. Thirty horse boxes and the same number of carriage trucks were ordered during 1846.[1] Three of the horse boxes and a luggage van were involved in the accident to the Scottish mail train at Rockcliffe in 1849, while travelling at the rear of the train.[2]

There is no information about the livery of these early vehicles, but they may have been painted lake or 'dull brown' like the third class carriages mentioned in *Caledonian Railway Livery*.[3] In 1873, the decision was taken to 'Paint the Carriages a uniform colour';[4] this was presumably some shade of brown, which may also have been used for NPCS, but there is no firm evidence. It is only from the Drummond era, i.e. after 1882, that we are on more certain ground.

The Standard NPCS Livery

As with ordinary goods wagons, the key contemporary reference to Caledonian Railway practice is the 1897 article in the *Locomotive Magazine*, which stated:

'Horse boxes are a similar colour to the older carriages, but have plain yellow lines only, whilst passenger fish trucks have no lining, and plain yellow letters.'

The fish trucks referred to fell into three categories. In date order, pre-diagram book open and covered trucks were designated for fish, milk and game traffic. Secondly, there were at least thirty open trucks built on old carriage underframes between 1887 and 1891. This was the type photographed in the *1900 Register*, and reproduced as Plate 10.17 (p. 180). Last, there were Diagram 15 open goods wagons, upgraded to carry fish by passenger trains in the 1890s, amounting to 159 in the *1900 Register*. All these wagons are discussed in detail in Chapter 10.

Although not specifically mentioned, it is reasonable to assume that the livery also applied to the covered carriage trucks of Diagrams 11 and 11A, which had panelled bodies and were built to NPCS standards.

By 1897 white had been re-introduced for the upper panels of coaches superseding the '*older carriages*' livery referred to by the *Locomotive Magazine*. The exact date of this development is uncertain, but the practice was extant in 1892, when it was mentioned in an internal memo from James Thompson to John Lambie.[5]

Its re-introduction may have been motivated by the introduction of bogie carriages in 1887. Minutes in June and July 1888 refer to stores contracts for colours,[6] and there is specific reference to 'marine white'. Tenders were obtained from two suppliers and samples were submitted to analysis. The contracts were finally agreed in July 1889.[7]

The older carriage livery was described in the same article as '*a dark purple lake, with yellow striping, having a fine vermilion edge.*' The 'striping' obviously referred to the lining. The livery described is that carried by the tri-composite carriage built by the Midland Carriage Company in 1882, which is shown in *Caledonian Railway Livery*.[8]

Caledonian Railway Livery discussed in detail the nature of the purple brown colour and the confusion caused by the various names that have been applied to it.[9] The salient points can be summarised as follows. There were two components to the colour after the undercoat had been applied – the base coat and the top coat. This was followed by three coats of varnish, which had a yellow tint.

The base colour was brown, which railway companies created by mixing a red pigment with black. A coat of 'lake' was applied over this. Lake pigments were all in the red colour range. They were semi-transparent, allowing the base coat to contribute to the final colour. The result after varnishing was described by David Jenkinson in *British Railway Carriages of the 20th Century* as a slightly lighter version of the shade used by the L&NWR.

Caledonian Railway Livery did not define the lake colour beyond stating that all 'lakes' were in the red colour range. In fact, the Caledonian used crimson lake as a top coat. In 1889 the Loco & Stores Committee

'*submitted correspondence with Mr Drummond in reference to the supply of Crimson Lake required for painting carriages. Mr.Lorimer to arrange with Mr Drummond.*'[10]

The suggested British Standard 2660 shade is 3-039 '*which may lack a reddish tint*' and '*probably somewhere between*' 8017 chocolate and 8016 mahogany brown in the RAL International series.[11] The British Standard colour quoted was defined by BR Scottish Region in 1957 as part of a project to record the liveries of the five Scottish pre-Grouping railways.

Conclusions about Lining

On the cumulative evidence of photographs of the various types of Caledonian NPCS, it seems reasonable to state that all NPCS with panels received lining. The '*fine vermilion edge*' was probably present, but does not show up in photographs. Open stock and vans of boarded construction were unlined. Horse boxes which had a mixture of boarded and panelled sections were only lined on the panelled elements.

A Later Livery

When the Stephenson Locomotive Society (SLS) published its book to celebrate the Caledonian Railway centenary in 1947, a chapter on *'Locomotives and Rolling Stock Colours'* was included.[12] The whole subject was covered in fewer than three octavo pages, so the material was extremely simplified. For instance, only the second type of cast wagon number plate was mentioned, and no reference was made to painted numbers.

That said, every effort seems to have been made to ensure the accuracy of what *was* written. The livery of non-passenger coaching stock was described in the passenger stock section as purple brown, echoing the *Locomotive Magazine* statement, but, as part of the goods stock entry, refrigerator vans, fish vans and trucks were recorded as

'painted brown (not purple-brown, but more of a chocolate shade) with white roofs, black ironwork and running gear, and were lettered in medium chrome yellow unshaded letters.'

This does not contradict the statement in the *Locomotive Magazine*. All the vehicles cited by the SLS were built after the 1897 article. It refers to a different livery, which may have been introduced in line with a change in L&NWR practice. According to *LNWR Liveries*, writing about NPCS in the nineteenth century,

'it is believed that carriage trucks (whether open or covered) and horseboxes were painted in carriage lake, but after 1900 they were painted in a colour known as "quick brown". This colour was made from a mixture of Indian red and black (possibly with the addition of a quantity of burnt turkey umber) and was probably the same as was used for undercoating on the passenger vehicles. At a distance, this dark chocolate colour was barely distinguishable from the lake of the carriages, but at a closer range it was less lustrous and transparent. The colour was in fact a dark purple brown which was intended as a close approximation of the expensive lake.'[13]

The livery for L&NWR fruit, milk and fish vans was changed at the same time as the carriage trucks. Those that were

'constructed similarly to passenger vehicles were painted in the passenger style, but thereafter [i.e. post-1900] they were all-brown, with yellow lining.'

Livery Descriptions in the Carriage Register

The pages of the register had a column headed *'Colour Painted'*. Against each item of rolling stock in the luggage and brake van numbering series, an initial W or B was entered. These letters stood for White and Brown. The former referred to the white upper panels on coaches and vans, associated with dark purple lake lower panels. Brown was the NPCS purple brown livery. The horse box, and carriage, fish and milk truck numbering series did not record livery details. The gas tanks were described as *'purple lake'* or *'brown'*, referring to the carriage stock and NPCS liveries respectively. The numbers of the gas tanks in each livery are shown in tabular form in Chapter 17.4.

Conclusions about Liveries

From the 1880s until 1897 when the article in the *Locomotive Magazine* was published, there was only one livery for Caledonian NPCS – purple brown, either lined or unlined, depending on whether the vehicle was panelled or of boarded construction. At some time later, perhaps from 1900, another, chocolate brown, livery was introduced for vehicles of boarded construction that were not built to the full NPCS specification. Panelled stock continued in lined purple brown livery, unlike the adoption of 'quick brown' by the L&NWR. The choice of livery dictated the style of lettering, as will be discussed in Chapter 4.3.

Although it is not mentioned anywhere, photographs of newly painted vehicles show that they were varnished – see for instance Plate 12.5 (p. 205) for a panelled, purple brown covered carriage truck, and 10.5 (p. 170) for a chocolate brown painted refrigerator van.

There is no official definition of the chocolate brown colour. Hutchison variously describes it as *'coach brown'* and *'chocolate brown'*.[14] It may have followed the same development as the L&NWR livery, that is, a similar but cheaper version of the coaching stock livery. The formulation for the L&NWR version was given in *LNWR Liveries*. The pigments in 'body brown' were drop black and Indian red, in the proportions of 20:19.[15] The paint was applied over a lead undercoat. For passenger stock, a top coat of carmine lake was then applied, followed by carmine lake-tinted varnish. These coats were omitted for NPCS.

Ironwork and Underframes

The *Locomotive Magazine* article did not mention the colour of NPCS underframes or ironwork. In the section on passenger stock livery in the SLS book, it was stated that *'the entire underframe, bogies, footboards and buffer bodies were black.'* Duncan Burton confirmed that carriage underframes were black in his article on 45-foot non-corridor coaches published in *Model Railways*.[16] It is reasonable to assume that NPCS in lined passenger livery were treated similarly.

The SLS chapter gave black ironwork for NPCS and the brown painted vans and trucks. This was reiterated in the notes accompanying Hutchison's drawings. The non-panelled stock would probably have followed ordinary goods stock practice for painting ironwork, with underframes and buffers the same colour as the body.

Van Roofs

In all cases, van roofs were painted white, according to the *Locomotive Magazine*. Ventilators, where fitted, were also white – see the newly painted Diagram 2 meat van in Plate 10.9 (p. 173). If the 1903 Diagram 67 van painting specification quoted in Chapter 3 represented established CR practice, roofs received five coats of white lead over a canvas covering. The white lead quickly oxidised to grey.

Plate 4.1
An enlargement from a photograph of a Diagram 73 six-wheeled horse box, showing lining on the panels of the groom's compartment. The company initials and number are shaded carriage characters.

LOUVRES AND VENTILATORS

Louvres consisting of angled slats of wood were applied to openings in the bodies of some vans as a ventilation aid. They were fitted as shown in the table below. The livestock and meat vans were not panelled; the vans for the remaining two types of traffic were panelled.

TYPE	DIAGRAM NUMBERS
Livestock	8, 9, 40, 70, 73
Meat	90 and pre-diagram book vans
Fish, fruit and milk	30, 39, 71
Carriage and scenery	11A, 68, 83

Photographs of vans without panels (Plates 10.7, 11.6 and 11.9) suggest that the louvres were painted in the body colour. The louvres fitted to the livestock compartments of the Diagram 8 and 73 horse boxes obeyed this rule; the part of the body in which they were located was not panelled – see Plates 11.6 and 11.9 (pp. 190 and 198 respectively).

When louvres were fitted to panelled vans, painted either in purple brown or full passenger livery, photographs show that they were light coloured – see Plates 4.4 and 4.5 (p. 77). The colour has been described as 'varnished pine'[17] or 'painted yellow',[18] which come to much the same thing.

The carriage type ventilators fitted above the doors of horse box passenger compartments seem from photographs to have been painted body colour, and not lined as in coaching stock, as in Plates 11.10 and 11.13 (pp. 195 and 198).

NPCS INTERIORS

On the limited evidence of two photographs in the *1900 Register*, the interior of fish and milk trucks and open carriage trucks was painted body colour. This may have been a special treatment for official photographs which appeared in the *1900 Register*. The trucks are shown in Plates 10.17 and 12.2 (pp. 180 and 200).

It is likely that the Diagram 55 fish trucks and the Diagram 15 adaptations for fish traffic had unpainted interiors, in common with other open goods wagons. Interior ironwork would have been black according to specification.

Insulated vans lined with zinc (Diagrams 72, 76, 102 and 116) were presumably unpainted. The colour of wooden van interiors is not known for certain. It may well have been the same as ordinary goods vans, which were given two coats of 'stone colour' according to the 1903 Pickering card order 6673 for the first Diagram 67 covered vans.

LIVESTOCK VEHICLES

Vehicles carrying horses and valuable cattle were built to full NPCS standards and ran regularly in passenger trains, or in block trains with other NPCS. Their details are discussed in Chapter 11. The horse boxes, mentioned explicitly in the *Locomotive Magazine* article, were painted purple brown. Photographs show that the panelled elements of the Diagrams 8 and 73 bodies were lined – see Plate 4.1 (opposite).

The Diagram 9 horse boxes and the two types of cattle van to Diagrams 40 and 70 had no panelling. Very few photographs exist of these vehicles – none at all in the case of Diagram 70, and the Diagram 40 van is in filthy condition – see Plate 11.6 (p. 190). The cleanest example is the pair of Diagram 9 horse boxes shown in Plate 11.9 (p. 193). These horse boxes and the pre-diagram book horse box just behind them are not lined. On this limited evidence, it is suggested that the Diagram 40 and 70 vehicles were painted chocolate brown. The Diagram 9 horse boxes would have been originally purple brown and the survivors may have been repainted chocolate brown after 1900.

MEAT VANS

The livery of Diagrams 1 and 2 meat vans has been discussed in Chapter 3. The small number of vans to Diagrams 84, 90 and 102 were all fitted with dual system continuous brakes and screw couplings, and had large diameter axle box journals, which were oil lubricated. Wheels 3 feet 9 inches diameter also matched coaching stock standards. These vans, none of which had panels, were painted chocolate brown with plain chrome yellow letters; Plate 4.2, which shows a close up of lettering on a Diagram 84 refrigerator van, is an example.

Hutchison (who was one of the contributors to the SLS book, and may well have provided information for the livery section) put forward an alternative livery when he drew the body of a Diagram 84 refrigerator van in the March 1957 *Railway Modeller*. His accompanying notes stated that they were painted '*body and underframe rather dark grey; all ironwork black; writing primrose yellow.*' He added that the vans were varnished.

The credibility of these observations is seriously undermined because Hutchison drew attention to a CR trumpet ventilator that

Plate 4.2
Another enlargement, this time showing the livery and lettering details of a Diagram 84 refrigerator van. The company initials are 12 inches high and the small lettering is 3½ inches.

the vans did not carry, stated that there were thirty vans, not ten, and gave them a block of numbers in the mineral wagon series.

It is just possible that he confused them with West Coast Joint Stock refrigerator vans, which were probably painted dark grey, but with no markings, according to Casserley and Millard, who made their observation on limited photographic evidence.[19]

Fish, Fruit and Milk

Nine diagrams made up the fish, fruit and milk carrying vehicles, plus a number of other vehicles, either pre-diagram book or constructed outside the diagram book system, that survived into the twentieth century. They are all described in Chapter 10.2, pp. 173 and 180.

Most of the vehicles were vans, with the exception of the numerous fish trucks to Diagrams 15 and 55 and most of the non-diagram vehicles. All the vans were built to full NPCS standards. The non-diagram book vehicles were also to these standards, as they were constructed on redundant carriage underframes.

Dealing first with the vans, the diagrams can be further divided into those with panelled or boarded bodies. The panelled vans were Diagrams 30, 39 and 71. Vans of either slatted or boarded construction comprised Diagrams 29, 72, 76 and 116.

Some Diagram 30 and 39 vans were painted in full passenger livery; and are dealt with separately in section 4.2. None of the photographs of these vans that were painted all-over purple brown is helpful in determining whether they were lined, or what style of lettering was applied. Lining would, however, be expected.

The only photograph of a Diagram 71 fish van (Plate 10.16, p. 179) is in bright sunlight, again preventing any conclusion about lining or lettering. The commentary to Hutchison's drawing[20] said that yellow lining was present, as would be expected.

As to the vans of boarded construction, a photograph of a Diagram 29 milk van was recorded for the *1900 Register* – see Plate 10.10 (p. 174). This shows a van in plain colours with no lining and plain block letters. The fish vans to Diagrams 72, 76 and 116 seem to have escaped the photographer. All these vans would have been painted chocolate brown.

The modified Diagram 15 open fish trucks were photographed on at least three occasions. Examples are shown in Plates 10.16 and 10.18 (pp. 179 and 180). As expected, the trucks are in all-over chocolate brown livery. There is no reason to think that the Diagram 55 trucks were treated otherwise.

Carriage and Scenery Trucks

As with the previous category, this was a mixture of open trucks and covered vans, which were also confusingly called trucks. Among the covered trucks, Diagram 101 was the only design of boarded construction. The rest, comprising Diagrams 11, 11A, 68, 83 and 88, were panelled.

Good quality photographs exist of all these vehicles, except for Diagram 11, the first body style of Diagram 11A and Diagram 88. They can all be found in Chapter 12. The panelled trucks are in lined purple brown, and the boarded truck numbered in the NPCS series is in all-over chocolate brown. An enlargement of a Diagram 11 van is shown in Plate 4.3.

The two Diagram 88 covered scenery trucks do not appear in photographs. There are two livery possibilities. The equivalent L&NWR vehicles to D.442 were painted in full passenger livery.[21] They were dual fitted and built at around the same time as the Caledonian vehicles. It is tempting to think that the CR and L&NWR practices for these vehicles were the same. The alternative possibility is that they were painted in all-over purple brown with yellow lining like the six-wheeled Diagram 83 covered carriage trucks, with which they shared body construction details.

The Diagram 101 truck (Plate 12.7, p. 206) numbered in the goods series poses a problem. The vehicle is very traffic stained, and the lettering could be either yellow, indicating brown livery, or grubby white to go with red oxide paintwork.

For the open trucks we have to rely on a photograph of pre-diagram book truck number 1618, which was freshly painted when photographed for the *1900 Register*. Plate 12.2 (p. 200) shows it in all over unlined brown. This may have been the original purple brown, or it may have been one of the first manifestations of the new chocolate brown livery.

The trucks to Diagrams 69 and 92 were only photographed in LM&SR livery and those to Diagram 44 seem to have escaped attention altogether. It is reasonable to assume that they received the chocolate brown livery. Hutchison drew a Diagram 92 truck, which appeared twice in the model press, described both times as a carriage truck.[22] One set of notes describes the livery as '*chocolate brown*', the other as '*coach brown*'.

References
1. NRS BR/CAL/1/7 p. 359, NRS BR/CAL/1/7 p. 360
2. Article in *The True Line*, issue 72 and letter in issue 73.
3. *Caledonian Railway Livery*, p. 243
4. NRS BR/CAL/1/20 entry 1782
5. NRS BR/CAL/5/11 page 110, quoted in *Caledonian Railway Livery*, p. 246
6. NRS BR/CAL/1/32 entries 449 and 513
7. NRS BR/CAL/1/33 entry 264
8. *Caledonian Railway Livery*, p. 244, Plate 4
9. *Caledonian Railway Livery*, p. 246 'Brown Pigments'
10. NRS BR/CAL/1/33 entry 1235
11. *Caledonian Railway Livery*, pp. 247, 294
12. *Caledonian Railway Centenary 1847–1947*, pp. 56-58
13. *LNWR Liveries*, pp. 105-6
14. *The Model Railway News*, July 1945, p. 131 and *Railway Modeller*, November 1959, p. 248
15. *LNWR Liveries*, p. 125
16. *Model Railways*, May 1975, pp. 246-7
17. Hutchison, *Railway Modeller*, April 1956, p. 86
18. *Caledonian Railway Livery*, caption to Plate 44, p. 263
19. *West Coast Joint Stock*, p. 273
20. *Railway Modeller*, April 1956, p. 86
21. Photograph in *An Illustrated History of LNWR Coaches*, p. 163
22. *The Model Railway News*, July 1945, p. 131 and *Railway Modeller*, November 1959, p. 248

Plate 4.3
This time, an enlargement of a Diagram 11A covered carriage truck, which shows yellow lining to the panels, light painted (or varnished) louvres, and shaded carriage style numerals.

4.2: NPCS in Passenger Livery

A small number of vans are known to have been painted in full passenger livery, with white upper panels, lining and shaded lettering. The *Locomotive Magazine* article recorded the livery as follows:

'the lower portion the same colour as the above [i.e. the dark purple lake of the older coaches], and the upper panels white, with lines in yellow and fine white edge; in each case the lettering is in gold, shaded with red and black, and the coat of arms is put on the lower panels.'

The coat of arms was not carried on NPCS, on the limited photographic evidence available to us. Although not mentioned in the above quotation, the ends were also purple lake. There was no lining on the ends.

The underframe and running gear was black, according to the SLS book and Duncan Burton's notes in the May 1975 edition of *Model Railways*, previously quoted in Chapter 4.1.

The details of the livery are discussed in *Caledonian Railway Livery*.[1] The British Standard Institute colour equivalents established by British Railways Scottish region were BS 3-039 (Sepia) for the lower panels and BS 9-093 (New Grey Mist) for the upper panels. According to *Caledonian Railway Livery*, the sepia shade may lack a slight red tint which would have been provided by the final 'lake' coat. The upper panel shade reflected the consensus that a small amount of blue pigment was added to the white to prevent the yellowing effect of the varnish coat. This was similar to L&NWR/WCJS practice, which added 2oz of ultramarine blue to 14lb of white lead, giving the proportion of 1 part blue to 112 of white.[2]

The Vans Involved

Those recorded as painted *'white'* in the *Carriage Register* were the seven Diagram 39 vans built in 1897 to order H150, numbered 197-203 in the luggage van series. As the carriage register was compiled after the First World War and updated until some way into the Grouping, we must assume that these vans carried this livery until the end of their lives in CR colours.

Caledonian Railway Livery[3] mentions a reference to the two linen vans numbered 214 and 234 which were used by the CR to transport laundry as painted white, but the *Carriage Register* records them as brown.

A photograph, reproduced as Plate 10.14 (p. 177), shows that another Diagram 39 van, number 81 in the carriage, fish and milk truck series, was painted with white panels. This van was built in 1898 to order H168. The *Carriage Register* section for this number series does not record livery details, so we cannot know if all ten vans to this order were painted with white upper panels.

Reasons for the Livery

One possible reason for using the full carriage livery starts from the reasonable assumption that the NPCS livery was always some shade of brown. The white panelled livery must then have been applied to certain vans for a special reason. It was not connected with the dedication of some vans to particular firms, as a number of these vans were recorded and/or photographed in brown livery as well as with white upper panels.

It may have been connected with the introduction of the

Plate 4.4
Painted (or varnished) louvres and lined panels on a Diagram 83 covered carriage truck.

Plate 4.5
The full passenger livery, applied to Diagram 39 van number 81. The complete picture is Plate 10.14 (p. 177).

Caledonian's prestige twelve-wheeled coaches, commonly known as *'Grampian Stock'*. These coaches were introduced from 1905 on the most important express trains. White panelled NPCS would have presented a uniform train. The serif lettering on the Lipton's van in Plate 4.9 (p. 81) would support this theory, as a similar style of lettering was used exclusively on the Grampian stock.[4] The 1913 train marshalling circular has a fish van marshalled in the 5.30pm service to Glasgow and Edinburgh, which was composed of Grampian coaches. This could explain the full carriage livery on Diagram 39 van number 81.

It is also possible that all panelled NPCS built from the early 1890s onwards were originally white, coinciding with the reintroduction of white upper panels on carriage stock. This would include the Diagram 30 vans built to orders H75, 123 and 128. In support of this theory, one of the H123 vans was photographed with white upper panels. For Diagram 39, it would comprise orders H135, 141, 146 and 168, plus order H150, which was numbered in the luggage van series and is recorded as white in the *Carriage Register*.

Diagram 39 vans figured frequently in photographs at the head of passenger trains, and they were without exception all-over purple brown. This would suggest that, if the theory is correct, all but order H150 were repainted. This would accord with L&NWR practice. The contemporary L&NWR D.108 fish vans received the full WCJS passenger livery when new, but were later repainted in the joint stock version of purple brown.[5] In this scenario, certain vans would have retained the white livery for marshalling with Grampian stock.

None of the foregoing is supported by records in minutes. It is based on circumstantial evidence only and offered as an interpretation of a puzzling aspect of Caledonian livery practice.

References
1. *Caledonian Railway Livery*, pp. 246-47
2. *LNWR Liveries*, p. 125
3. *Caledonian Railway Livery*, p. 261
4. *Caledonian Railway Livery*, pp. 252-54, gives details of the Grampian stock lettering style
5. *West Coast Joint Stock*, p. 277, shows the original livery

4.3: Lettering and Numerals

Style of Lettering and Numerals

On the evidence of photographs of the Diagrams 8 and 73 horse boxes and the Diagrams 11A and 83 covered carriage trucks, vans with coach type panelling and lining on the body had shaded writing for the company initials and number. The shaded lettering was applied despite the fact that the panel in which it was painted was purple brown, not white as in carriage stock (see Plates 4.1, 4.3 and 4.6).

As already mentioned in Chapter 3, carriage stock letters and numbers were in the same style as that used on locomotives and tenders (Figures 3.1 and 3.2). The *Locomotive Magazine* article described the letters as '*gold, shaded with red and black.*' The SLS book reiterated this statement. The overall height of the letters and numbers was 4 inches including the shading. When the company initials occupied an uninterrupted space they were separated by a square dot.

Open trucks and vans of boarded construction which were painted chocolate brown had plain yellow writing – see Plates 4.2 and 4.7 in this chapter, and Plates 10.10 and 12.2 (pp. 174 and 200 respectively). The colour of the letters was described as '*medium chrome yellow*' by the SLS.

The load and tare characters were white on open carriage truck 1618, newly painted for the *1900 Register*. They were yellow in the case of the Diagram 84 refrigerator vans – see Plate 10.5 (p. 170).

There are no photographs of gas tanks in CR livery, and information about their lettering has not survived. One would assume that plain block chrome yellow characters were used for the brown vehicles, and shaded lettering for those painted purple lake. Their base depot may have been painted as well. This was the case for the North British.[1]

Location of Shaded Lettering and Numerals

On panelled vehicles, company initials and numbers were located in the small waist panels on the body side. They were spaced symmetrically around the vertical centre of the vehicle. They were located on the sliding doors of the Diagram 39 vans – see Plate 10.14 (p. 177).

The running number was not repeated on the ends of lined out NPCS, but *was* repeated on wagons and vans. The exception to the rule seems to have been the covered carriage trucks with wagon numbering, where the join between the two end doors would have interfered with a number in the centre.

Location of Plain Lettering and Numerals

Early fish, milk and carriage trucks echoed the prevailing wagon custom of painting company initials and number on the solebar – see Plates 10.10, 10.17 and 12.2.

The size and shape of the company initials on vehicles built after 1883 followed contemporary wagon practice, with large letters on the body. Cast number plates were not applied to stock in the various NPCS number series, but both versions of plate were applied to goods stock built to NPCS standards.

The small letters on fish trucks as seen in Plate 4.7 were the same size as the load and tare characters, that is, $2\frac{3}{4}$ inches. The small lettering on refrigerator and fresh meat vans was slightly larger, scaling from the photographs in Plate 4.2 and 10.7 as $3\frac{1}{2}$ inches.

Special Lettering on Vans

Details are given in the *Carriage Register* of vans in Diagrams 11A, 30 and 39 that were allocated to specific types of traffic. There is evidence that two styles of lettering were applied to diagrams 30 and 39. There are no photographs of the Diagram 11A vans in dedicated traffic.

In the more common style, the company name and sometimes the type of traffic was written in serif letters. They were evenly spaced along the side of the van with no regard for raised panelling – see the Lipton's van in Plate 4.9 and the Mitchell's tobacco van in Plate 10.13 (p. 177). The Lipton's letters scale to about 1 foot 9 inches high and the Mitchell's letters to about 9 inches. A plain block style of the large lettering was used for the Waddell's sausage van in Plate 10.12. There are no photographic records of the other dedicated vans.

On the vans in full passenger livery, the letters show up as dark – perhaps they were the same purple brown as the panelling. It is not possible to tell whether shading was present. It would be reasonable to assume that the lettering on purple brown vans was the same colour as the company initials and numbers, that is, middle chrome yellow.

Other Markings

All non-passenger coaching stock and wagons fitted with continuous brakes had small block letters painted on the solebar to indicate the location of the release cords for the vacuum and Westinghouse brakes. Comparison with the chrome yellow lettering suggests that these letters were white. This mirrors L&NWR/West Coast Joint Stock practice.

References
1. *Wagons On the LNER Volume 1, North British*, p. 70

Facing Page Top: **Plate 4.6**
Shaded carriage style characters, applied to the drop door of a Diagram 9 horse box.

Facing Page Bottom: **Plate 4.7**
The more common layout of lettering applied to Diagram 15 and 55 open fish trucks. A variation is shown in Plate 10.18. The company initials are 12 inches high.

Plate 4.8
This atmospheric picture was taken at Aberdeen between 1913 and 1915, when the Joint station was being rebuilt. From the left, the NPCS consists of the following stock. Two purple brown painted Diagram 39 vans – the one with the open doors is lettered for Stephen Mitchell's Tobacco Traffic; there is a clearer view of this van in Plate 10.13. The Lipton's sausage traffic van is number 203, the only Diagram 39 Lipton's van painted in full passenger livery, according to the *Carriage Register*. To the far right are two West Coast Joint Stock Diagram 107 fish vans.

4.4: Allocation of Numbers

Early Non-Passenger Coaching Stock

Wagon running numbers were not recorded in the inventory of rolling stock conducted in 1874,[1] but they *were* given for non-passenger coaching stock. Horse box numbers ran from 1 to 100. The 'Stranraer and Portpatrick' railway contributed six horse boxes, which were allocated numbers 21-26. It is not known whether they were part of the 100 strong block.

The thirty-five carriage and sixty-two fish and game trucks were numbered in another series from 1 to 106. Three 'Stranraer and Portpatrick' carriage trucks were included in the list.

Twenty-three milk trucks were numbered randomly between 54 and 949 in yet another series. The stores and bullion vans were numbered 1 and 2, and 1-3 respectively.

Later in the Caledonian era, the different types of NPCS were numbered in four series, all starting at 1. They were recorded in the *Coaching and NPCS Register*.[2] These number series are discussed in the following paragraphs.

The Luggage and Brake Van Series

This series was mainly composed of passenger brake vans running on four, six or eight wheels. Some of, but not all, the Diagram 39 vans, which actually were mainly used for meat and fish traffic, were included. They were allocated three blocks of numbers – 197-203, 210-222 and 234-239. Confusingly, the Diagram 71 and 72 fish vans were also allocated numbers in this series, rather than taking fish, fruit and milk truck numbers. The fish vans were allocated a block of numbers from 248 to 269.

Horse Boxes

Horse boxes had their own series, which included the two types of special cattle box that were built to NPCS standards. Numbers eventually ran from 1 to 141 on the completion of the Diagram 73 construction. Another series starting at 1800 accommodated Diagram 9 horse boxes that were renumbered to make way for their Diagram 8 successors. This number series extended to 1856, and included some pre-diagram book vehicles.

Plate 4.9
This is a closer look at the Lipton's van. The letters are evenly spaced along the van and positioned with complete disregard for either doors or panels. The worst example is the letter P, which is partly on the sliding door and partly on the adjacent body. Three havock ventilators are positioned along the centre line of the roof.

Carriage, Fish and Milk Trucks

The most extensive number series was assigned to carriage, fish and milk trucks. This seems to have been established in mid-1891, because vehicles built earlier were assigned four-digit numbers upwards of 1500, whereas all those built after the second half of 1891 had numbers below 195. Order H51 spanned the changeover period. It comprised five fish trucks built in January 1891 with four-digit numbers and one built in July that was assigned number 123.

Full details are in the *Coaching and NPCS Register*. The list includes the Diagram 55 fish trucks built to H205 and numbered in the goods wagons series in a block from 7901 to 7940, but not the modified Diagram 15 trucks that were used for fish and milk traffic. The numbers of these trucks are listed in the *1915 Working Timetable Appendix*. The covered carriage trucks built to goods orders G324 and G346, numbered 73283-73291 and 73537-73542 were also included in the *Coaching and NPCS Register*.

Travelling Gas Tanks

Gas lighting was first put on trial on the CR in late 1882.[3] A separate number series from 1 to 27 was assigned to gas tanks. One tank had been on the system since 1883, but this may have been purely for internal use and did not receive a number. The series seems to have started in the early 1890s when construction of the travelling tanks began. The list is included in the *Coaching and NPCS Register*. It is discussed in more detail in Chapter 17.4.

NPCS Renumbering After the Grouping

The fish and meat vans numbered in the Caledonian luggage and brake van series and the stock in the carriage, fish and milk trucks series were renumbered by the LM&SR, seemingly at random, into a block of numbers between 6400 and 6705.

Numbers were allocated to the surviving Diagram 9 short horse boxes in a block from 6707 to 6822, following their original Caledonian numbers up to 100, with gaps where withdrawals had taken place. The gaps were filled with the survivors of the larger Diagram 8 vehicles. Diagram 9 boxes renumbered into the series starting at 1800 received LM&SR numbers between 6848 and 6877. The six NPCS specification cattle boxes, which also had CR numbers below 100, were included in this block of numbers.

The Diagram 73 horse boxes were renumbered in order in a block between 6823 and 6846. The surviving Diagram 9 boxes with Caledonian numbers in the 18XX series were allocated numbers in order between 6848 and 6877.

The seventeen travelling gas tanks, which had their own CR number series between 1 and 27, were allocated a block of numbers from 6901 to 6917, closing the gaps in the Caledonian sequence.

Full details of the LM&SR renumbering, and the second LM&SR renumbering where applicable, are included in the *Coaching and NPCS Register*.

References
1. NRS BR/CAL/5/15
2. CRA Archive ref: 3/4/1/14
3. NRS BR/CAL/1/27 entry 1076

LEFT: Plate 5.1
An early mineral wagon with side door offset to the opening end. The wheels have very light wrought iron spokes. The picture was published in McIntosh's article *The Evolution of the Rolling Stock* in the Caledonian Railway diamond jubilee issue of *The Railway Magazine* in 1907.

BELOW AND FACING PAGE: Figure 5.1
The next three figures depict the evolution of the 7-ton coal 'bogies'. St. Rollox drawing 1540 dates from 1873. It shows a wagon with offset doors and a patent spring device on the left-hand bearing. This seems to work on the same principle as a self-contained buffer.

Chapter 5
General Mineral Wagons

5.1: Introduction

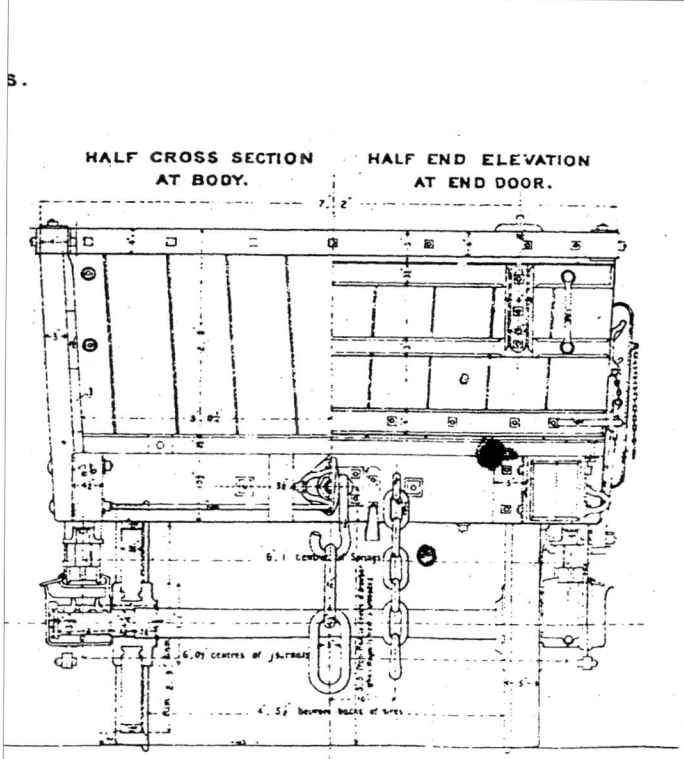

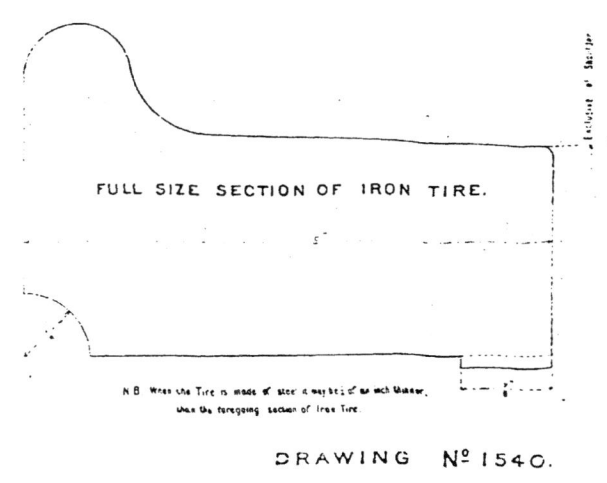

The Importance of Mineral Traffic

As discussed in Chapter 2, the prime purpose of the Caledonian's constituents was the carriage of minerals, and for the rest of its existence it was first and foremost a mineral carrier. In 1910, the railway carried approximately 23 million tons of minerals and 5 million tons of goods.

The sheer volume of mineral traffic is striking. An article in *The True Line*[1] mentions that, at the end of the nineteenth century, there were about 250 pits in Lanarkshire alone, with an output of 17 million tons of coal per annum, of which the Caledonian carried 12 million tons. Ross yard, one of several receiving output from the coalfield, handled 2,000 wagons per day and was open round the clock.

The mineral traffic on the Caledonian was virtually a railway within a railway. It had its own timetable and pay rates for operating staff. It had a dedicated traffic control centre at Motherwell. At any given time most Caledonian locomotives were hauling or sorting mineral wagons

The following tables show the number of wagons scrapped, replaced and added to the fleet. The numbers are aggregated from the six-monthly wagon returns that formed part of the reports to shareholders.[2] The relative importance of mineral traffic compared with all other traffic is plain to see.

In the first table almost twice as many mineral wagons were built as the rest of the wagon types combined. In the second table only 50 per cent more mineral than other wagons were built, but from 1903 the capacity of the new wagons was far greater than those that they replaced. From 1913 to the Grouping, just under 3,000 more 16-ton mineral wagons were built.

1858-1895	Replaced	Added	Total
Mineral	39,372 (56%)	39,080 (80%)	78,452 (66%)
Other	31,025 (44%)	9,819 (20%)	40,844 (34%)
Total	70,397	48,899	119,296

1895-1912	Replaced	Added	Total
Mineral	17,733 (53%)	10,209 (76%)	27,942 (60%)
Other	15,907 (47%)	3,268 (24%)	19,175 (40%)
Total	33,640	13,477	47,137

Wagon Descriptions and Capacities

By 1900, the early mineral wagons were called 'bogies'. This seems to have been a generic term, like 'pug' for any small or not so small tank engine. An addition of Collins Concise Dictionary defines 'bogie' as *'a small railway truck of short wheelbase, used for conveying coal, ore etc. (19th century).'* As the century progressed, the pre-diagram book loco coal wagons were also given the same name in company minutes.

The official descriptions of the various wagons in the mineral wagon fleet are confusing. Some were called coal wagons, others mineral, and yet others iron ore, but wagons were loaded indiscriminately. The capacity descriptions in the diagram book and on the sides of wagons confuse the issue further. Iron ore is much denser than coal (about 30 cubic feet per ton, compared to 42 cubic feet).

The table on the right applies this information to the cubic capacities of the different types of CR wagons. It shows that the design load was always slightly more than the cubic capacity of the wagon. It also shows that the load as written on mineral wagons was the iron ore weight, except for Diagrams 22, 46 and 54.

Some commentators have drawn unfair conclusions about the merits of the bogie coal wagons and the Board's decision to authorise their construction because they have used the four-wheeled wagon iron ore load as a comparator, rather than the coal capacity.

	CAPACITY (CU FT)	IRON ORE (TONS)	COAL (TONS)
Earliest mineral	130	4½	3¼
Renewal	180	6	4½
Later 'bogie'	200	6¾	5
Diagram 22	288	9½	7
Diagram 46	312	10½	7¾
Diagram 51	465	15½	11½
Diagram 52	415	14	10
Diagram 54	1190	40	28½
Diagram 59	480	16	12

References
1. 'The Caley's Bread and Butter', by Fred Landery, in *The True Line*, issue 56, pp. 7-10
2. NRS GD344/11/1, TNA: PRO RAIL 1110/48 and /49

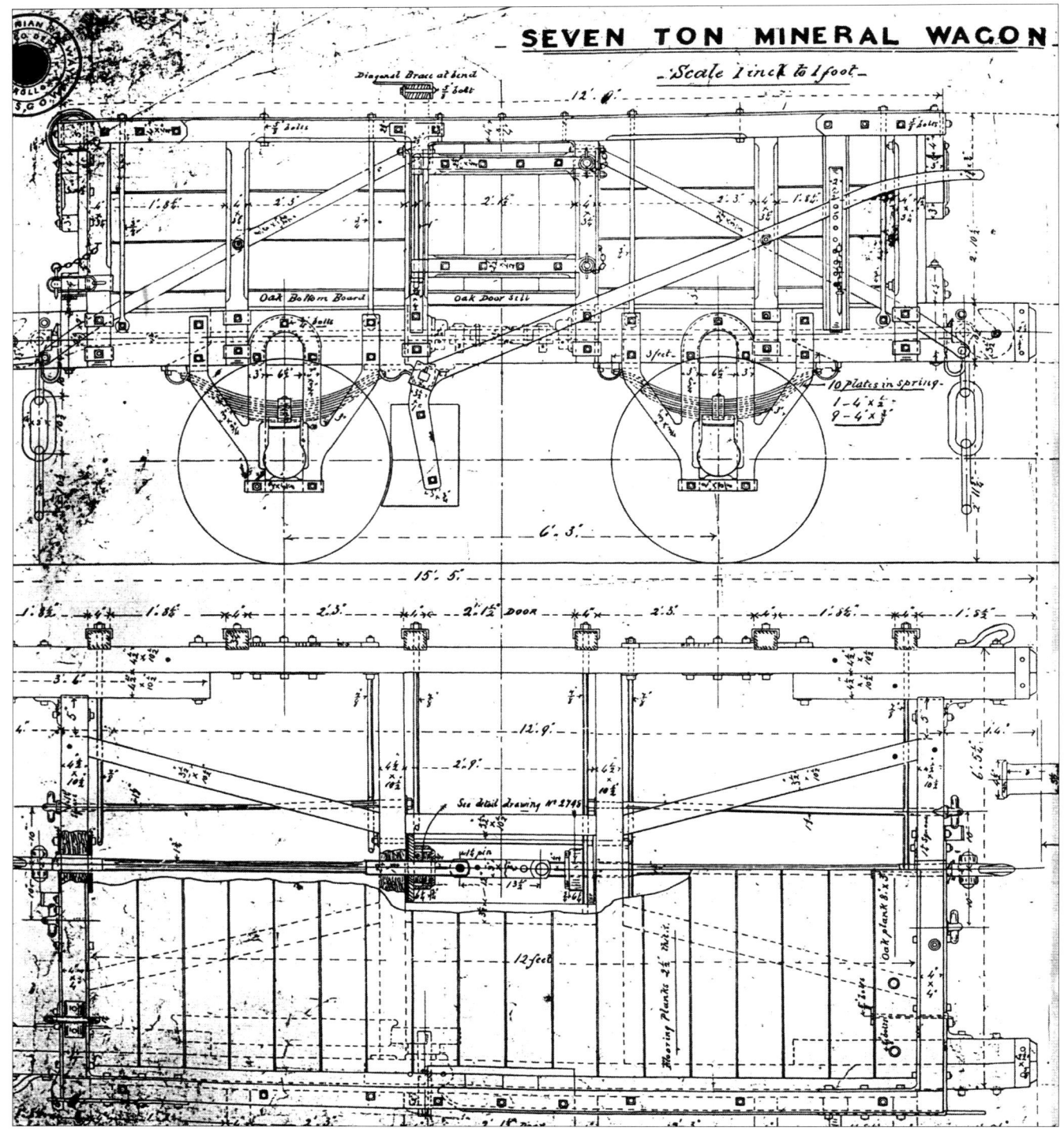

5.2: The Early 'Bogies'

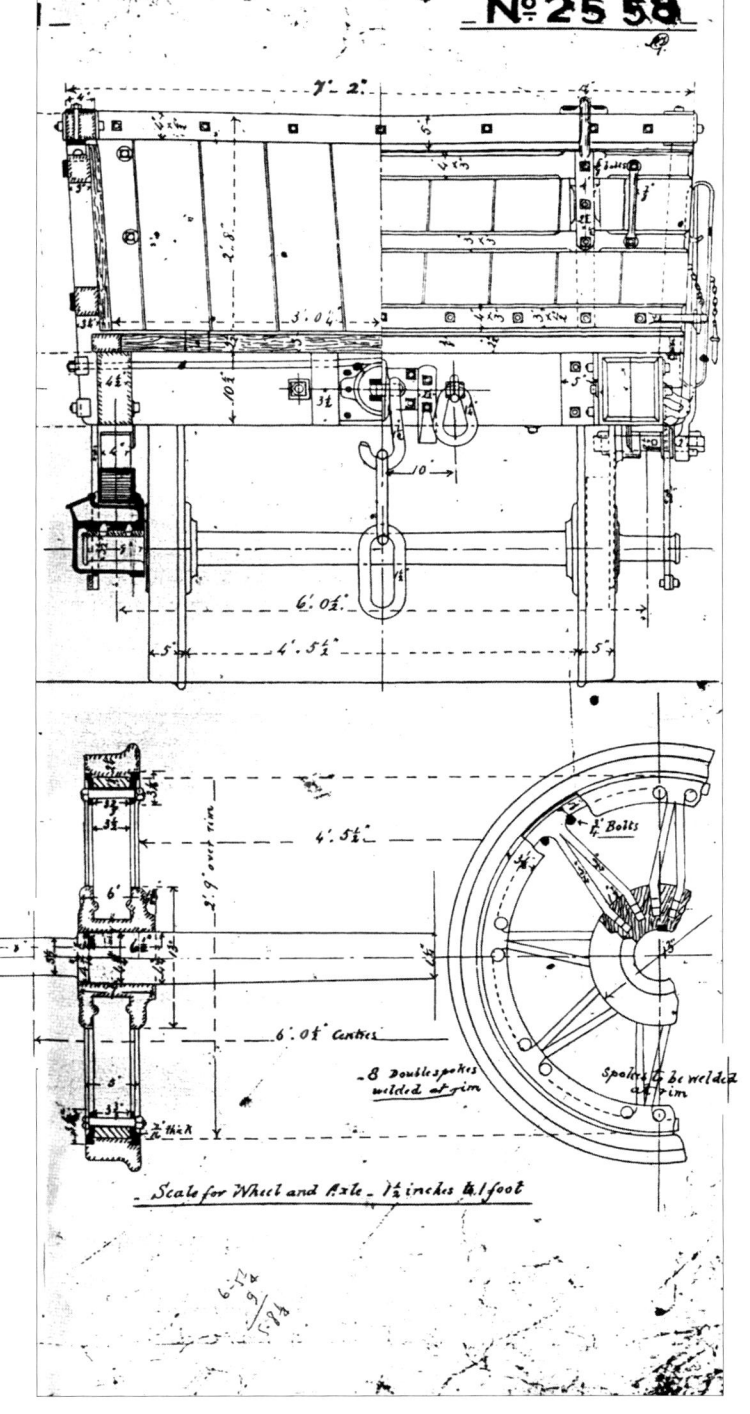

FACING PAGE AND BELOW: Figure 5.2
The wagon in drawing 2558 is to the same dimensions as the drawing 1540 design, but with centre doors and diagonal bracing to the body sides. The drawing dates from 1878.

The first mention of wagons appears in a minute of 14th July 1846 when it was reported that none had been ordered. The situation was remedied by ordering 600 from contractors, which must have included coal wagons, '*All @ £72 each and the whole to be delivered on the line on 1st May 1847.*'[1]

In November a further 400 were to be ordered. The type of wagon was not specified. The first reference to coal wagons was on 20th November 1846, when a minute instructed that '*200 coal wagons for the Garnkirk Railway be contracted for.*'[2]

The Caledonian quickly recognised the importance of relatively high capacity wagons. The rolling stock returns of 1857 and 1858 refer to mineral wagons that were worn out and their renewals as being 6 tons capacity. The 1858 wagons were said to be averaging 3¼ tons. This must have been the designated load as the 252 wagons deducted from stock were replaced by 137 new 6-ton wagons. In fact, the coal carrying capacity of these wagons was only 4½ tons, as evidenced by the cubic capacity and by John McIntosh's article in the *1907 Railway Magazine* celebrating the company's diamond jubilee.

Further withdrawals of the old wagons took place up to the half year ending July 1863, by which time 2,153 wagons had been written off. The half year figures of wagons in service, taken from the reports to shareholders, show the progression to higher capacity wagons between 1857 and 1863.

1853	1855	1857	1859	1861	1863
3,450	4,000	4,000	3,423	3,223	4,007

By 1867, the Directors of the Company were satisfied that the capacity of plant was now sufficient. In November a minute,[3]

'*Resolved that in future renewals the following principle be adopted viz.: to replace vehicle for vehicle of at least equal carrying capacity.*'

Records of the dimensions and constructional details of the early contractor-built wagons have not survived, although they must have had a capacity of about 130 cubic feet for the coal load to be 3¼ tons. Similarly, the cubic capacity of their nominally 6-ton renewals must have been around 180 cubic feet, giving a coal load of 4½ tons. Prices of the wagons varied quite widely. In 1857, Ashbury charged £50 each for an order for 250 wagons and £57 10s for an order of 137 later the same year.[4] The price was £52 in 1858 and only £39 in 1859.[5]

DESIGN DEVELOPMENTS

Benjamin Connor was asked to take estimates for mineral wagons of '*not less than 8 tons each*' in 1870.[6] Despite this directive, the Caledonian persevered with smaller capacity wagons. The first drawing for a 6-ton wagon dates from 1871 (St. Rollox 1104).[7] The wagons were 11 feet long by 7 feet wide with sides 2 feet 6 inches deep. The sides sloped outwards towards the top and were supported by heavy wooden frames outside the planking, braced with iron rods. Wagons had side doors in central or offset positions. An end door was provided for unloading by tipping. The door's heavy framing and its pivot using two hooped hinges was a design feature of Caledonian wagons up to and including the first pattern of Diagram 59 wagons in 1903. Solid buffers were fitted and the single wooden brake shoe was operated by a long lever with the brake lever guard attached to the wagon body.

The design was slightly enlarged, although the load remained at 6 tons, with St. Rollox drawing 1293 of 1872.[8] The inside length was 12 feet, and the body was 2 feet 8 inches deep. The width was 6 feet 1 inch at floor level, tapering to 6 feet 6 inches at the top.

The first 7-ton wagon drawing also appeared late in 1872 (St. Rollox 1424).[9] This was followed in 1873 by drawing 1540.[10] The capacity had increased by 1 ton, but the wagons were still to the same dimensions as drawing 1293. This particular drawing showed an offset door version. Drawing 2558 showed a centre door version to the same dimensions with diagonal iron bracing to the body sides.[11]

The final development in 1882 was a '*new 7 ton wagon*' to St. Rollox drawing 3141.[12] This was significantly larger at 12 feet 9 inches long on a 6-foot 3-inch wheelbase, with an external width of 7 feet 2 inches at the top of the body. The sides were now 3 feet deep. The increased depth was achieved by widening the bottom board.

Like their predecessors, the bottom board on the sides, the door sill and the two floor boards adjacent to the headstocks were made of oak. One of the copies of drawing 3141 has the hand-written note '*build quantity 250.*' The rolling stock returns do not record any new wagons in 1882 or 1883, so these must have been part of the 2,000 plus wagons that were replaced in these two years.

Well over 20,000 of these early wagons were built. Their very robust construction meant that there were still more than 10,000 on the books in 1910, although 8,000 were stored out of service, occupying over 20 miles of siding space. Their eventual fate is discussed in Chapter 5.5.

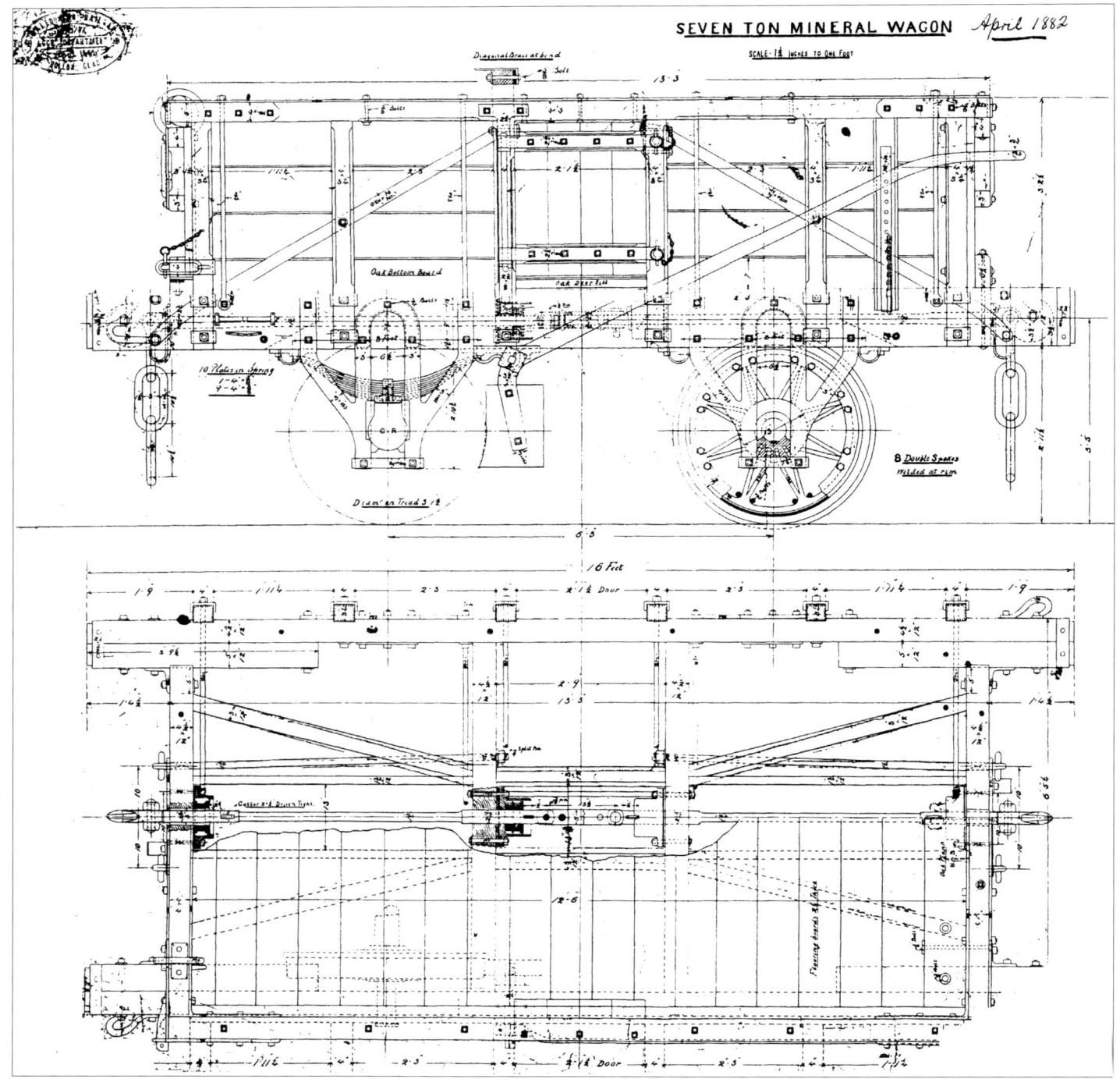

References

1. NRS BR/CAL/1/7 p. 360
2. NRS BR/CAL/1/7 p. 490
3. NRS BR/CAL/1/16 entry 241
4. NRS BR/CAL1/11 entry 551,
   NRS BR/CAL1/11 entry 1048
5. NRS BR/CAL1/11 entry 1851,
   NRS BR/CAL/1/12 entry 218
6. NRS BR/CAL/1/18 entry 1514
7. Not yet catalogued
8. Not yet catalogued
9. Not yet catalogued
10. NRM 13747/W
11. NRM 8059/W, RHP 69151
12. NRM 8050/W, RHP 69139

Plate 5.2
An offset door example with a heavy version of the old type of wheel. The door was offset towards the fast end of the wagon.

Plate 5.3
A late built example of the first type of mineral wagon (the poorly aligned painted number is over 50000) with centre doors. Despite the fact that this type of wagon had been outdated by two successive designs by the beginning of the twentieth century, they still formed a significant part of the mineral wagon fleet. For this reason, number 50677, which did not have diagonal iron bracing, was photographed for the *1900 Register of Wagon Plant*.

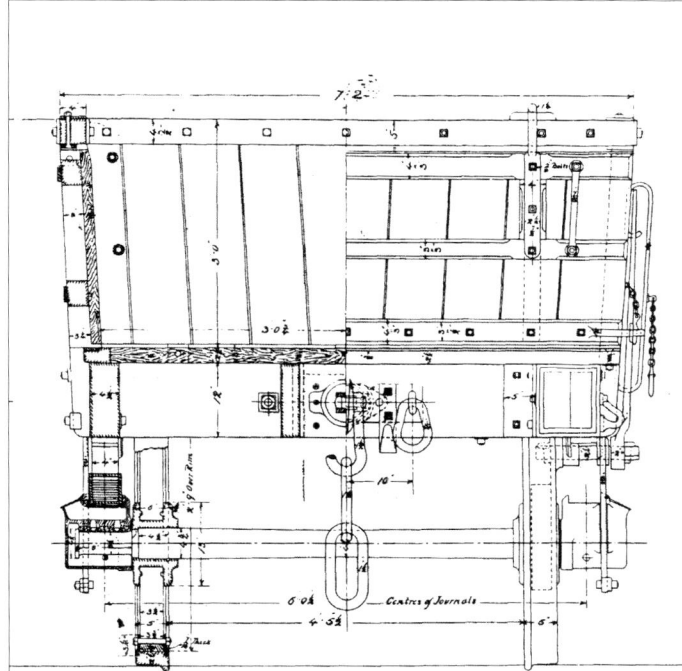

ABOVE AND FACING PAGE: **Figure 5.3**
This is the final version of the 'bogie', drawing 3141 dated 1882. Although the dimensions and therefore cubic capacity are increased, the designated load remained the same as the earlier designs.

RIGHT: **Plate 5.4**
On the quayside at Ardrossan, with three new-looking centre door 7-ton wagons in the foreground. The high running numbers suggest that they were built around 1880. The furthest of the three has diagonal bracing matching St. Rollox drawings 2558 and 3141, which has displaced the company initials and number. Two earlier and smaller 7-ton wagons are visible in the rear. The massive construction of the wagon body framing is very obvious and the hooped end door hinge arrangement, which was used on all mineral wagon construction into the twentieth century, can be seen. The wagon in the immediate foreground has the more widely-spread end door hinge, which was ultimately adopted for most private traders' wagons

ABOVE: Plate 5.5
A Diagram 21 wagon in loco coal service, photographed for the *1900 Register of Wagon Plant*. The early lettering for wagons in this traffic was LOCO COAL ONLY, with the company initials on the solebar. Photographs of this style are in Chapter 17. The low number, 21519, means that it replaced an earlier wagon – by the time this wagon was built, mineral wagon were numbered beyond 50000. It has the old style of coupling with short centre link used with solid buffer wagons. The heavy duty springs are almost straight.

Plate 5.6
61693 was part of an order of 1,000 Diagram 22 wagons numbered 61171-62170, built by Pickering between November 1895 and May 1896. The Pickering builder's plate has not yet been fitted. The initial letters of HAMILTON SECTION are slightly larger than the rest. The company initials are centred in the space left below the section lettering and therefore half a plank lower than normal. The brake lever guard on the Diagram 22 and 46 wagons was secured to the curb rail rather than the solebar.

Plate 5.7
In 1897 the Caledonian took over 400 wagons that had been built by Hurst Nelson for Dunn Brothers. The Hurst Nelson drawing, number 2801, is in the NRM archive, reference 11922/W. This photograph depicts one of the 300 that were treated as replacements. Although built to Diagram 22 dimensions, there were the following variations from the norm: spindle buffers similar to the NBR pattern were fitted; there were five body planks, not four; the doors were vertically planked, not horizontal; the brake lever guard is attached to the solebar; the running gear had CR 33 axleboxes and eight-leaf springs whilst Diagram 22 had CR 1 axleboxes and twelve-leaf springs. Finally, there was a problem about the buffers – the CR casting was 13 inches long, whereas the Railway Clearing House specification was 10 inches. Hurst Nelson was given the option of reducing the headstock thickness or to revert to dead buffers.

5.3: Four-Wheeled Wagon Development 1883-1899

The early mineral wagons had a poor payload to tare weight ratio, caused by their very robust wooden framed body construction. A wagon carrying 5 tons of coal weighed a total of nearly 10 tons. A larger wagon to cope with increased traffic demands was required that had a lighter but sufficiently robust body. Loco coal wagons with flat sides attached to the underframe by wrought iron knees and ironwork bolted to the planking had been built from the early 1870s. This type of construction was adopted for general mineral traffic.

These wagons introduced a design feature which characterised Caledonian mineral wagons almost to the end of its existence. The central planks of the cupboard doors had no visible means of support. In fact the doors were in two parts. The outer planks, made of pine, were 2 inches thick. Inside, the door was lined with 1-inch thick planks of oak running vertically, which were screwed to the outer planks.

Mineral Wagon Load 10 Tons – Diagram 21

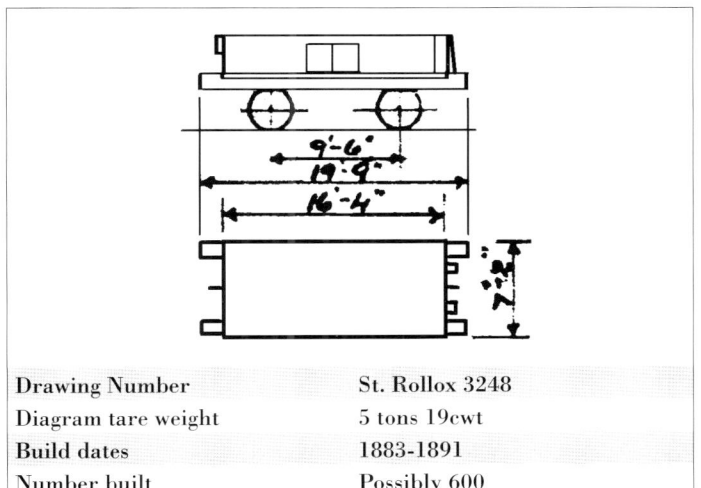

Drawing Number	St. Rollox 3248
Diagram tare weight	5 tons 19cwt
Build dates	1883-1891
Number built	Possibly 600

Two types of mineral wagon appeared in 1883, shortly after Drummond's installation as Superintendent. The Diagram 21 design was a development of the 10-ton loco coal wagon of 1874, slightly enlarged in length and height (5 inches and 2 inches respectively). It had an end door as well as side doors. The axle guards were fitted inside the solebars, and the iron brake, applied to one wheel. The loco coal wagon drawing (St. Rollox 1690) is shown in Chapter 17.

Craven Brothers' offer of 400 wagons '£63 at Carlisle' was accepted by the Locomotive & Stores Committee on 3rd July 1883.[1] For clarification, the cost was £63 each! Others may have been built at St. Rollox, for example to orders G3 and 17, but the descriptions do not mention the wagon capacity. Order G92 in 1891 for 200 wagons was lettered for the Lesmahagow Section.[2]

One copy of the diagram book says that they were later fitted with self-contained buffers, making the overall length 20 feet 3 inches. St. Rollox drawing 12980 of 1905 depicts this modification.[3] They may have been part of the solid-buffered wagon rebuilding programme, but there is no photograph of a wagon with this modification.

Mineral Wagon Load 8 Tons – Diagram 22

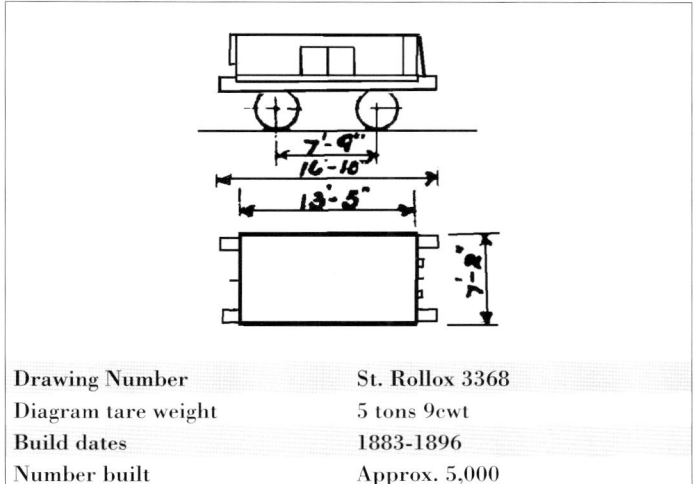

Drawing Number	St. Rollox 3368
Diagram tare weight	5 tons 9cwt
Build dates	1883-1896
Number built	Approx. 5,000

The second type of wagon was to Diagram 22. The body construction and design set the pattern for future Caledonian four-wheeled mineral wagons up to the introduction of the steel underframe designs in the early 1900s. They were similar to Diagram 21, but were 14 feet 0 inches long by 7 feet 8 inches wide externally and 3 feet deep. The small radius curves of colliery lines dictated the 7-foot 9-inch wheelbase. They had solid buffers and the now standard single lever iron brake block was fitted. The axle guards were inside the solebars, rather than outside as in the pre-diagram book 'bogies'. The 8-ton wagon became the preferred standard, particularly for 'land sale' or retail trade traffic, because the wagons could be unloaded quickly by hand, avoiding demurrage charges.

The Locomotive & Stores Committee accepted offers from contractors for 600 wagons on the same date as the Diagram 21 offer. The combined total of 1,000 Diagram 21 and 22 wagons is substantiated as capital expenditure by the rolling stock return for the twelve month period ending July 1884, which records the addition of 1,011 mineral wagons.

Production of the Diagram 22 wagons from St. Rollox ceased in 1894, when the first Diagram 46 sprung buffer minerals were constructed, but they were still being built by Hurst Nelson and Pickering in 1895/96.[4] This was because dedicated wagons were required for the Carfin & Cleland Section. The original intention was to use Diagram 46 wagons, but the decision was countermanded late in 1895, when a minute recorded the decision *'to cease painting the new spindle buffered wagons and instead to set aside our older type of solid buffered wagons for the Carfin and Cleland Section.'*[5]

The Diagram 22 wagons were reconstructed with sprung buffers in the twentieth century to conform to the Railway Clearing House edict that solid buffered wagons should be abolished. This modification is discussed in section 5.5.

LEFT: **Plate 5.8**
A Diagram 46 wagon built in 1900, according to the paint date. It was one of the last of these wagons, built at St. Rollox to order G179. It is fitted with the McIntosh patent brake, but is otherwise typical of this design. The brake lever is in the 'hard on' position, with the lever pointing slightly below horizontal. The wagon springs have only eight leaves, twelve were more usual. The tare weight is in three figures. It and the load lettering are centred under the C and R. The letters are 12 inches high, not 15 inches as suggested in *Caledonian Railway Livery*. These wagons were recorded as renewals in the minutes, despite the high numbers which suggest that they were treated as capital expenditure.

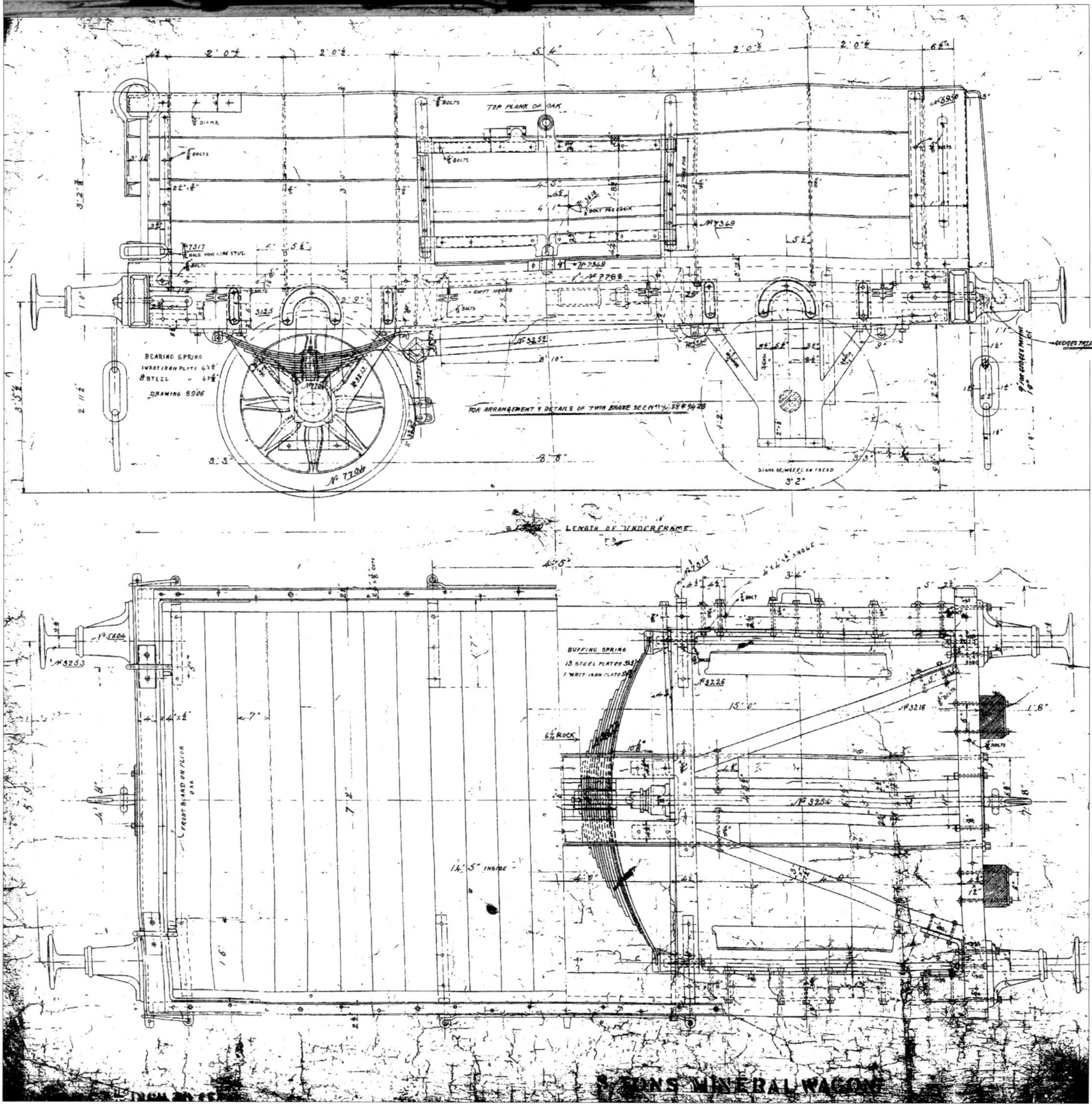

8 Tons Mineral Wagon – Diagram 46

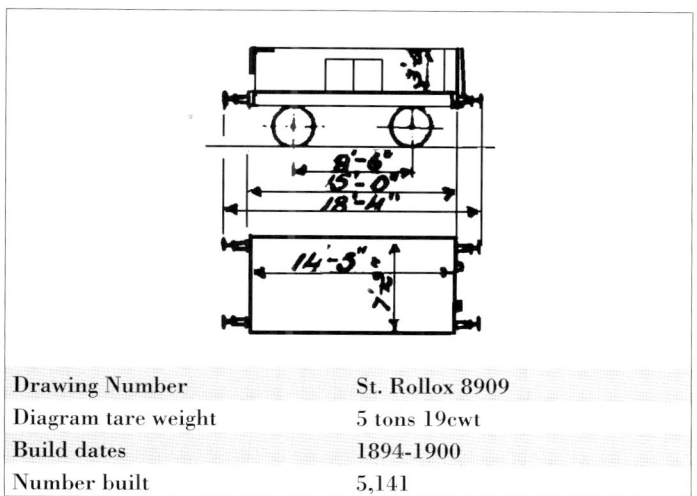

Drawing Number	St. Rollox 8909
Diagram tare weight	5 tons 19cwt
Build dates	1894-1900
Number built	5,141

In May 1893 the Traffic Committee tabled a proposal to construct all new mineral wagons with spring buffers, *'the same as the Goods Plant.'*[6] The additional cost was £4 per wagon, when a typical wagon was reported to cost £55.

The proposal was obviously accepted, because the Diagram 22 design was upgraded to include sprung buffers, or *'spindle buffers'*, as the diagram book and St. Rollox order records describe them. The spindles referred to extensions to the buffer rams that bore on two sets of leaf springs fitted near to the centre line of the wagon. The original St. Rollox drawing was number 7312, which has not survived. The later drawing quoted above only differed in the type of cotter pin securing the door.

In December 1893, 250 wagons were authorised as renewals,[7] with a further 1,950 (1,500 to the capital account) in 1895.[8] Over 5,000 were built, all at St. Rollox except for 1,000 built by Hurst Nelson in 1899-1900.

They were slightly longer (15 feet on an 8-foot 6-inch wheelbase), but otherwise identical to the Diagram 22 wagons. Although they supplanted the Diagram 22 design, the number series of the two types overlapped because contractors continued to fulfil orders for the earlier type of wagon after St. Rollox went over to building the Diagram 46 design.

The sprung buffer design was also tested out as a new standard type of wagon for private traders. In December 1894, Pickering built a sample wagon for Thomas Muir, Son & Patton of Dundee.[9] This was followed by nine more in June 1895.[10]

In their original state with the single iron brake the only improvement over the Diagram 22 wagons was the provision of sprung buffers, in accordance with Board of Trade requirements, which required the elimination of solid buffers. Overall they were marginally less effective that the Diagram 22 wagons, as they were heavier for the same capacity and the sprung buffers were more liable to breakage.

The last production batch of 291 wagons from St. Rollox was fitted with the McIntosh patent brake, which acted on two wheels and could be operated from either side of the wagon. This went part way to meeting Board of Trade requirements, but at the cost of a further increase in weight and complication. Production ceased in 1900, when the Diagram 52 wagons were introduced. These and subsequent four-wheeled designs are discussed in Chapter 5.5.

References
1. NRS BR/CAL/1/28 entries 577 and 57
2. NRS BR/CAL/5/11 entry 87
3. Not yet catalogued
4. Hurst Nelson photograph, HMRS collection ref:ABP103 and Pickering card orders 1687, 1702 and 1730
5. NRS BR/CAL/5/11 entry 242
6. NRS BR/CAL/5/11 entry 117
7. NRS BR/CAL/1/36 entry 1509
8. NRS BR/CAL/1/37 entry 444
9. Pickering card order 1476
10. Card order 1590

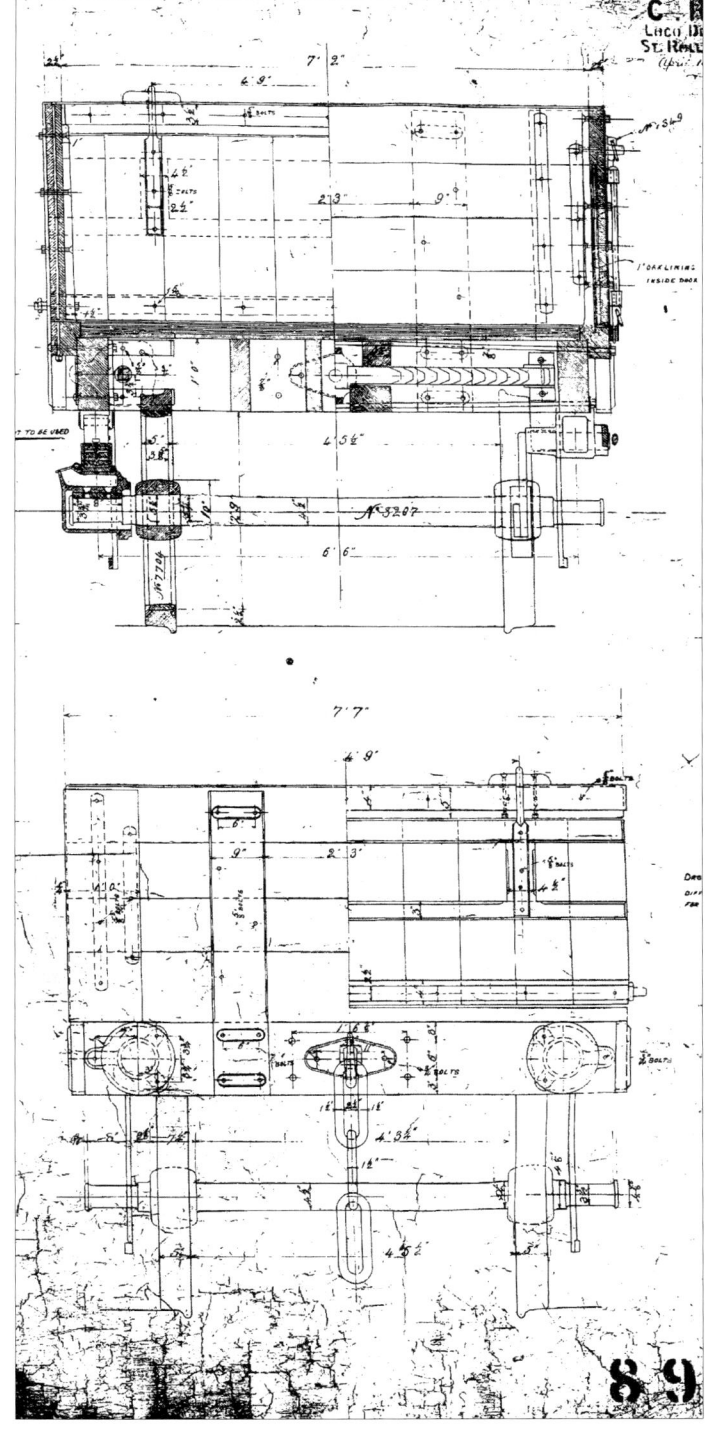

FACING PAGE AND RIGHT: **Figure 5.4**
St. Rollox drawing 8909 for the Diagram 46 mineral wagon. This dates from 1898, but only differs in minor detail from the original drawing of 1893, number 7312, which has not survived.

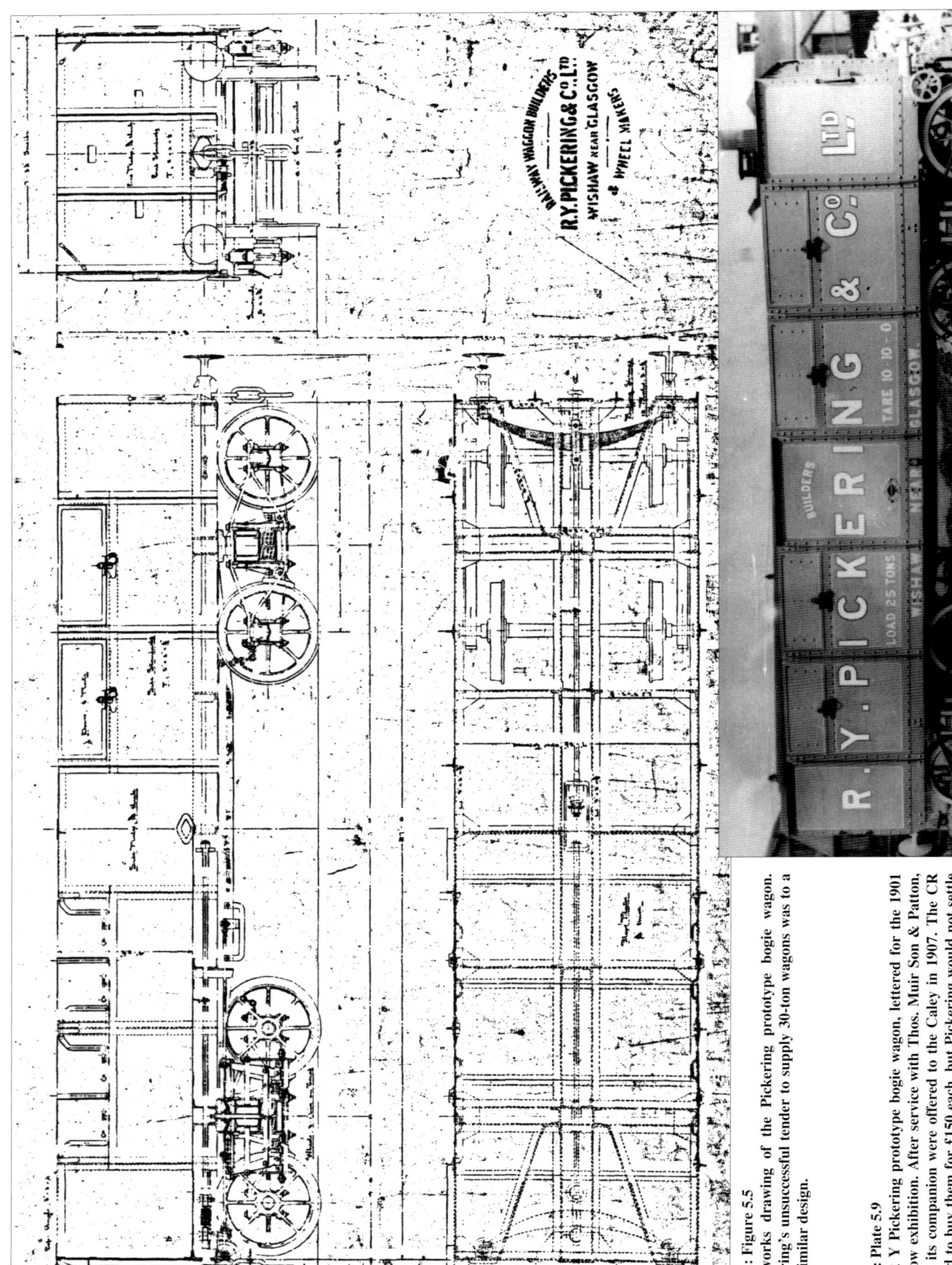

ABOVE: Figure 5.5
The works drawing of the Pickering prototype bogie wagon. Pickering's unsuccessful tender to supply 30-ton wagons was to a very similar design.

RIGHT: Plate 5.9
The R Y Pickering prototype bogie wagon, lettered for the 1901 Glasgow exhibition. After service with Thos. Muir Son & Patton, it and its companion were offered to the Caley in 1907. The CR offered to buy them for £150 each, but Pickering would not settle for less than £175. This offer was declined by the Traffic Committee.

5.4: Bogie Mineral Wagons

At the turn of the century the railway companies were under pressure. An article in *The Railway Engineer* summarised the action required, having stated that between 1889 and 1899 average working expenses had grown from 52.3 per cent to 59.6 per cent of gross receipts,

'First: That there is a pressing need for retrenchment in dealing with the conveyance of goods traffic … and in particular with the mineral traffic
Second: That such retrenchment can only be effected to any considerable extent by increasing the paying loads of mineral trains thus diminishing the number of miles run by such trains
Third: That in order to augment the paying load of mineral trains it is necessary to increase the carrying capacity of individual mineral wagons.'[1]

As well as these commercial pressures, the Caledonian urgently needed to replace its ageing mineral wagon fleet, most of which were still 'bogies' whose payload was not much greater than their tare weight. The most modern wagons to Diagrams 22 and 46 loaded to eight tons, with a tare weight approaching six tons. There were two choices – evolution or revolution. The Caledonian went down both routes, but tried revolution first.

50 Ton Ore Wagon – Diagram 50

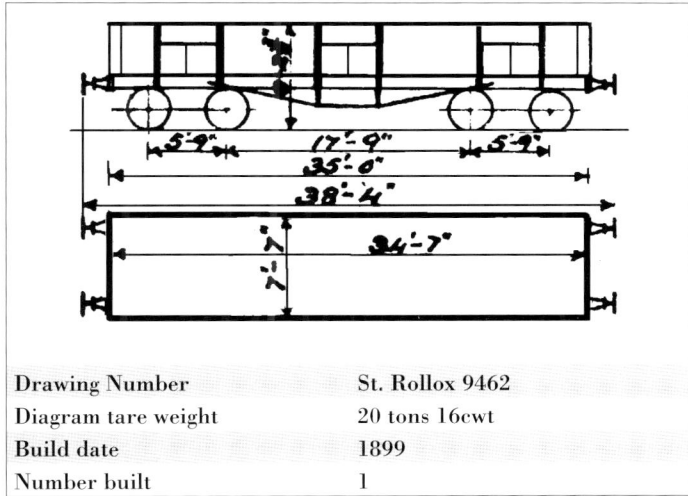

Drawing Number	St. Rollox 9462
Diagram tare weight	20 tons 16cwt
Build date	1899
Number built	1

In March 1899 the Board authorised the construction of 100 50-ton wagons, amended to a single wagon in the half year ending July 1899 and another in the period ending January 1900[2] – see Plate 1.1 (p. 6). In the event, only one was built, numbered 72000. This number was not in the mineral wagon series and was beyond the range applied to goods wagons. This had reached 71283, the last in a block of numbers allocated to 900 wagons built by Pickering to card order 3352, starting 12th August 1899.

The second wagon probably appeared as the prototype Diagram 51 wagon, number 64872, which was built for comparative purposes. This statement is supported by the fact that the bodies of both types were of similar construction, and the official photographs were taken in the same location. The wooden floor of the bogie wagon was plated over. It was fitted with oil axleboxes and the Westinghouse brake. The wheels were 3 feet 2 inches diameter.

The table below compares the 50-ton wagon with three Diagram 51 wagons coupled together. It is clear that the 50-ton wagon's advantage lay in a reduction in train length (or more load in the same train length) and lower rolling resistance per ton payload, attributable to the reduced number of axles. The tare weight, and thus the overall weight of a loaded train, was only slightly reduced, because conventional wooden construction was adopted for the bogie wagon.

	Tare	Length	Axles
Diagram 50	20 tons 16 cwt	38ft 4ins	4
Diagram 51	21 tons 6 cwt	58ft 0ins	6

The company seems to have accepted that the idea was ahead of its time. McIntosh said as much in his review of the rolling stock for the Caledonian Railway Jubilee.

'Eight years ago the CR put a 50 ton wagon in traffic: but, although found to be very useful, it so far remains the sole representative of its race. Most probably it is a case of taking time by the forelock.'[3]

It did not appear as a mineral wagon in the 1907-1910 stock statements, where it was described as *'open goods special class.'*[4] This incidentally corrected the anomaly of a mineral wagon with a number in the goods wagon series. It was still available for traffic in 1915, as the Appendix to the working timetable for that year notes that it *'must not be propelled round sharp curves.'*[5] Here it was described as an ore wagon, suggesting that its use in goods traffic had ceased. It did not survive to be renumbered with the other bogie wagons by the LM&SR in 1931.

Wagons Made of Steel

The need to increase payload and reduce tare weight was leading to experiments with high capacity wagons made entirely of steel. In Scotland, R Y Pickering exhibited a 25-ton bogie wagon at the Glasgow Exhibition in 1901.[6] It and another of the same type were registered with the CR (registration numbers 13751 and 13806). They were handed over to the Scottish Wagon Company and then hired out to Thos. Muir Son & Patton, the Dundee coal merchants. Also in 1901, the Darlington Wagon Co. built 30-ton side door coal wagons and 32-ton hopper discharge wagons for the North Eastern Railway.[7]

30 Ton Bogie Coal Wagons – The First Experiment

At the same time as the 50-ton wagon was authorised, a wagon to carry 30 tons of coal was actively considered. St. Rollox drawing 9716 for a *'proposed 30 ton coal wagon'* appeared in June 1899. The drawing has not survived.

On the Caledonian, the Locomotive and Stores Committee in October 1900,

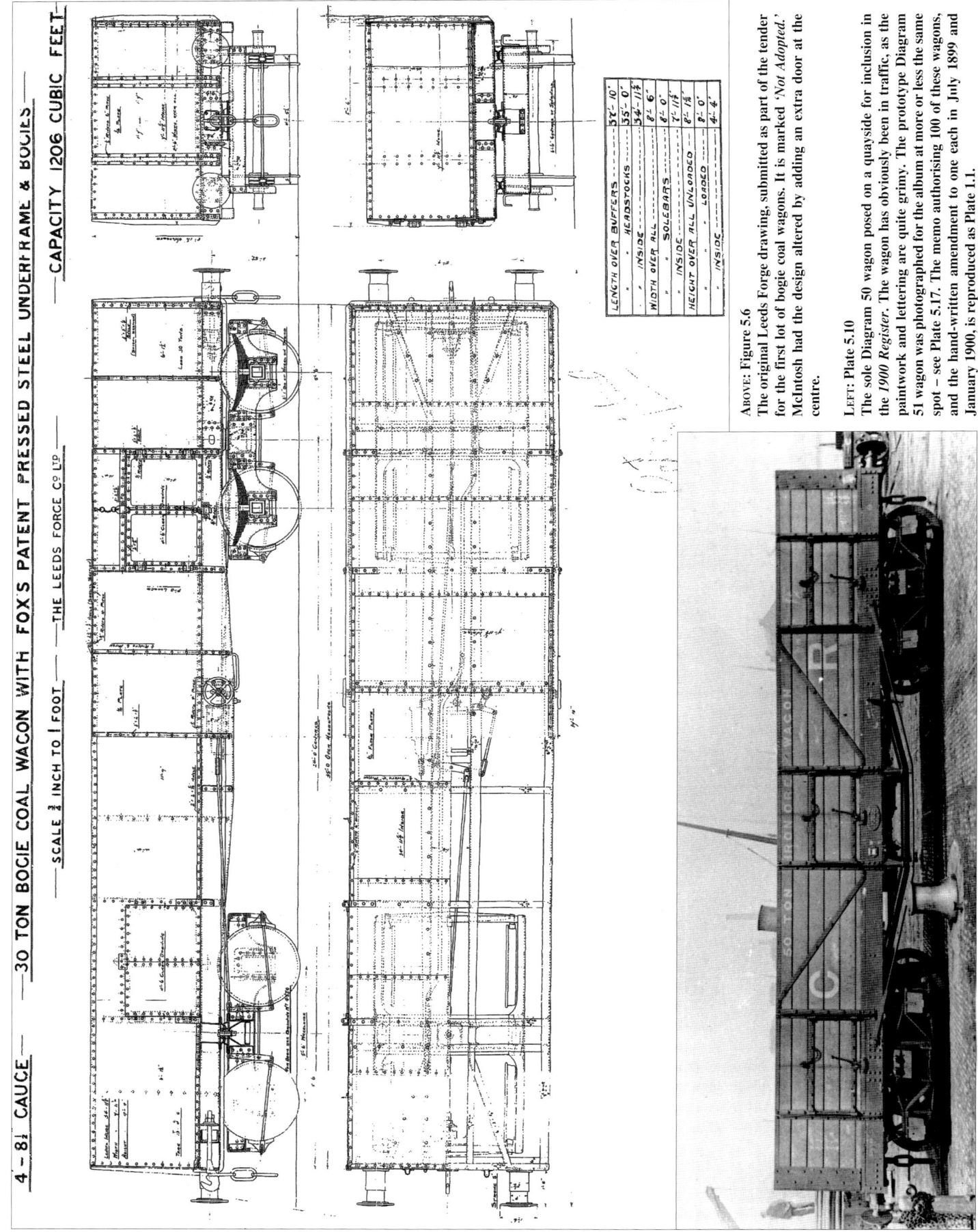

ABOVE: Figure 5.6
The original Leeds Forge drawing, submitted as part of the tender for the first lot of bogie coal wagons. It is marked *'Not Adopted.'* McIntosh had the design altered by adding an extra door at the centre.

LEFT: Plate 5.10
The sole Diagram 50 wagon posed on a quayside for inclusion in the *1900 Register*. The wagon has obviously been in traffic, as the paintwork and lettering are quite grimy. The prototype Diagram 51 wagon was photographed for the album at more or less the same spot – see Plate 5.17. The memo authorising 100 of these wagons, and the hand-written amendment to one each in July 1899 and January 1900, is reproduced as Plate 1.1.

'agreed to approve of the principle of the Company obtaining wagons with a much larger capacity for the conveyance of loco coal and other suitable traffics, and recommend in the first instance fifty wagons with a carrying capacity of thirty tons of coal be obtained for experimental purposes, and that offers be taken from makers in this country and the United States.

Also that notice be given to the coalmasters and the owners of the docks connected with the line of the intention of the Company to introduce a larger class of wagon and requesting their co-operation ... The new wagons to be charged to revenue.'[8]

In January 1901 offers were considered for '50 ton [changed in pencil to 30 ton] Wagons, 20 from American Car and Foundry Coy @ £235; 30 from Leeds Forge @ £360.' The alteration suggests that this might have been part of the order for ore wagons, with 72000 regarded as the prototype. McIntosh was instructed 'to arrange details to his satisfaction with builders and secure any possible reduction in price.'[9] Leeds Forge drawing 4761 dated 4th January 1901 no doubt formed part of the tender documentation.[10]

Pickering also tendered unsuccessfully for this contract in a document dated November 1900, according to their register of enquiries.[11] The drawing associated with the tender shows a wagon that was very similar to the 25-ton wagons which were built at the same time.[12]

On the 5th February the minutes recorded 'Thirty ton Wagons Ordered:- 20, American Car and Foundry @ £250; 30, Leeds Forge @ £355, as per designs arranged with the builders by McIntosh.'[12] The Leeds Forge drawing mentioned above has two doors per side and is marked 'not adopted'. The wagons as built had three doors, no doubt a modification required by McIntosh. A drawing in The Engineer[13] shows the design with three doors and specified 2 feet 9 inches diameter wheels.

Leeds Forge delivered its order of thirty wagons promptly and they were allocated numbers 66001-66030. These were blank numbers in the CR numbering scheme, which perhaps reflects the experimental nature of the order. The wagons had Fox patent pressed steel solebars and bogies. They were fitted with oil axleboxes and the Westinghouse brake. Photographs show that they had 3 feet diameter wheels when delivered. They later ran on 2-foot 9-inch wheels.

The wagons were originally all metal, but a planked white pine floor was fitted soon after they entered traffic, according to a minute of April 1902.[14] The steel plate work of the body and original floor was three-sixteenths of an inch thick.

The American part of the order was a disaster. According to The Railway News, writing after the event in August 1903, the wagons

'arrived in sections, being put together on the dock rails in Glasgow. After being put together, however, the wagons had to be cut to pieces and practically rebuilt, ... as the workmanship was found to be so defective.'

The CR Board had decided in July 1902 to 'decline to take the wagons under any circumstances.'[15] In 1903 an MP interceded with the Caledonian's General Manager on behalf of The American Steel Trust asking that 'the Company should enter into negotiations with a view to taking over the twenty large capacity wagons which were recently rejected.' The Loco & Stores Committee declined.[16]

The Leeds Forge wagons obviously proved satisfactory because the Board decided to go ahead with more bogie wagons. The dimensions had not yet been decided. Drawing 11082, dated 24th October 1901, is described in the register as 'proposed 30 ton coal wagons (1) 35ft x 8ft x 4ft 4in (2) 28ft 4in x 8ft x 5ft 4in.' A further 1901 drawing (11161) was of 'diagrams of large capacity wagons (proposed).' Neither of these drawings has survived.

In December 1901 the Traffic Committee[17] reported that the General Manager had submitted a draft letter to the Coal Masters intimating the introduction of 'Large Capacity Mineral Wagons.' Two weeks later, the Board authorised the construction of 500 wagons to the capital account 'to be built own workshop.'[18] By this time, the Traffic Committee had authorised the installation of an 80 tons capacity weighing machine at Mossend to accommodate the new wagons. This was originally destined for Polmadie.[19]

30 Ton Bogie Coal Wagon – Diagram 54

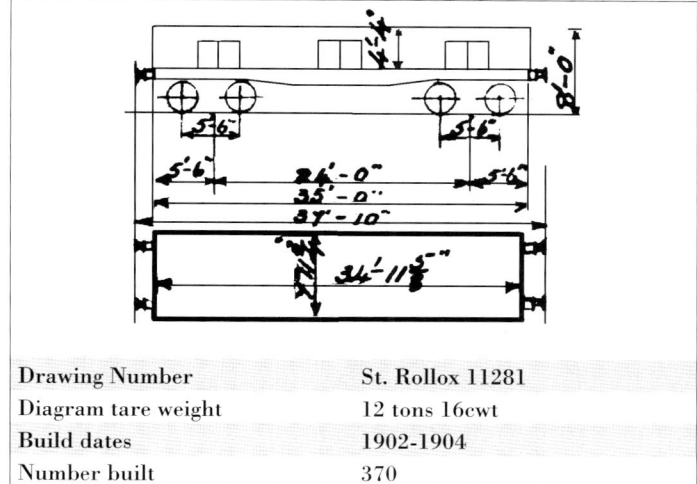

Drawing Number	St. Rollox 11281
Diagram tare weight	12 tons 16cwt
Build dates	1902-1904
Number built	370

Fifty wagons were built between July 1902 and April 1903.[20] The number series tabled below suggests that this was the major part of St. Rollox order G195. When construction got properly under way in 1903, most of the wagons were built by outside contractors because St. Rollox had devoted most of its capacity to building 1,000 Diagram 59 mineral wagons against order G207.

In January 1903 the Loco & Stores Committee minutes recorded the order of '100, 30 ton Wagons from Leeds Forge at £270 and tare not exceeding 13 ton, delivery within 5 months. Mr McIntosh to make further enquiries at other makers and submit report.'[21] On 17th February offers for a further 200 wagons were agreed.[22]

Two types of wagon were produced. Those from Leeds Forge were identical to the 1901 order. The company had supplied the Midland Railway with wagons to the same design in 1902. The more common design to drawing 11281 from St. Rollox and contractors had a truss-rod underframe and diamond frame bogies. Oil axleboxes were fitted, giving a further reduction in rolling resistance compared with Diagram 46 wagons. Wheels were 2 feet 9 inches in diameter. Non-standard buffers were fitted with 18 inches diameter heads. The St. Rollox drawing specified a steel floor, but the increased tare weight of the wagons in service suggests that they too were fitted with wooden floors

Only 370 wagons were actually built, with a further twelve of the authorised 500 appearing from St. Rollox as Diagram 66 hopper wagons. Blocks of numbers were allocated as follows:

	QTY OF WAGONS	NUMBER RANGE
St. Rollox	70	66031-66100
Leeds Forge	100	66231-66330
Metropolitan	100	66331-66430
R Y Pickering	30	66431-66460
J Renshaw	10	66461-66470
Birmingham R C & W	30	66471-66500
Hurst Nelson	30	66501-66530

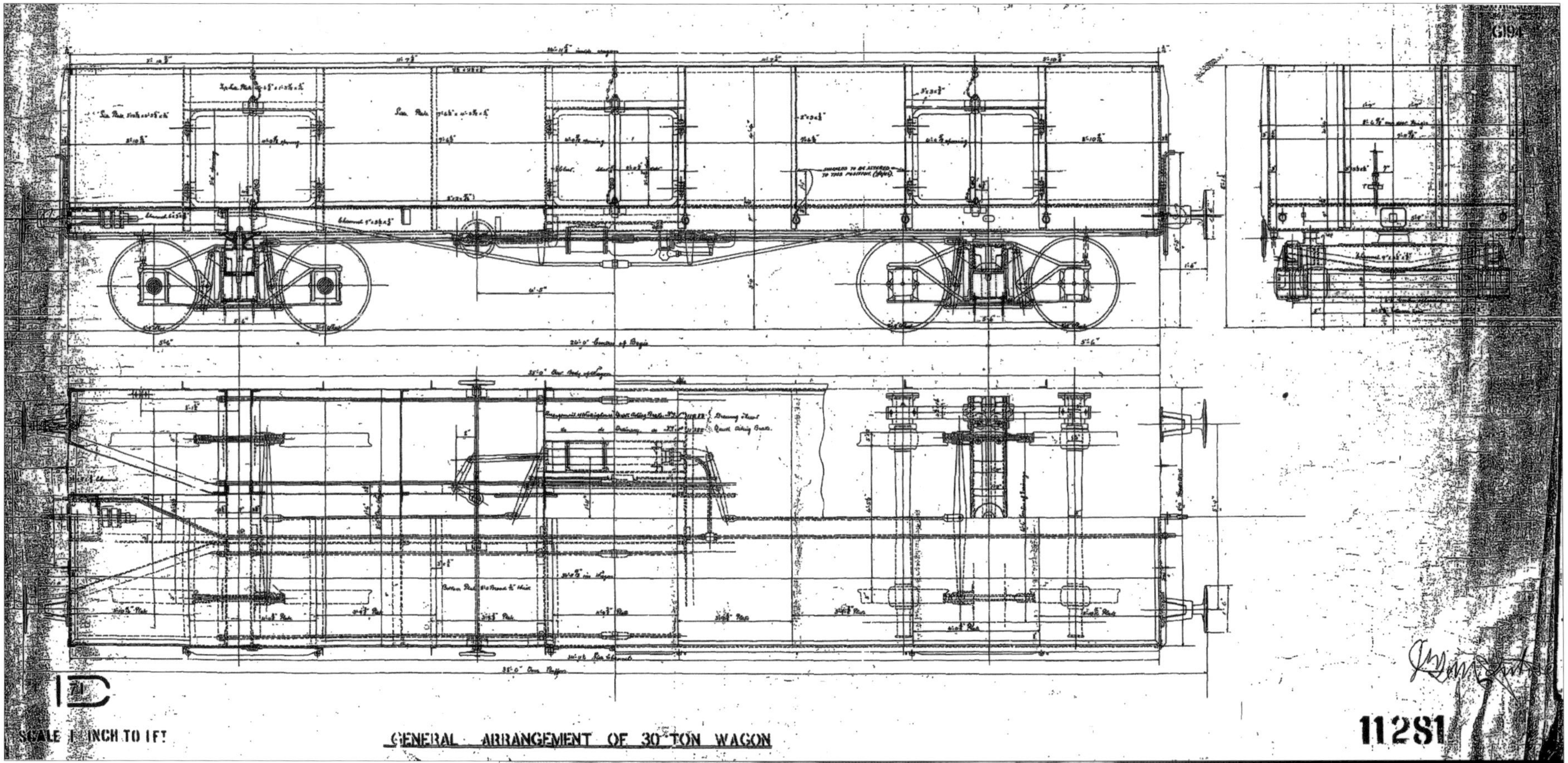

ABOVE: Figure 5.7
The St. Rollox drawing for Diagram 54. This was the design used for the majority of the wagons, even though the design was heavier than the pressed steel construction used by Leeds Forge.

RIGHT: Plate 5.11
This picture of a wagon from the first batch of bogie coal wagons built by Leeds Forge shows the original 3 feet diameter open spoke wheels, as specified in Leeds Forge drawing 4761. Later, 2-foot 9-inch wheels were substituted. The depth of the pressed steel underframe allowed the number plate to be fitted on the centre line of the wagon. This was not possible with the other, more common, design of bogie wagon.

5.4: BOGIE MINERAL WAGONS

Plate 5.12
A typical St. Rollox pattern wagon, in this case built by Hurst Nelson. The photographic grey livery suggests that the iron work reinforcing the body was black. Photographs of the wagons in service and the Pickering building specification show that they were painted all-over red oxide.

Plate 5.13
A representative of the R Y Pickering order for thirty wagons, card order 6638, despatched to the Caledonian in 1905. The ripples in the plating bear witness to the thinness of the metal. The large lettering is set on the horizontal centre line of the plate; the lettering on the Hurst Nelson wagon in the previous plate is above it.

On the same date as the Leeds Forge wagons were authorised, the first 20-ton six-wheeled goods brake vans were given the go-ahead, again to the capital account.[23] The Caley originally envisaged block trains of 30-ton wagons with Westinghouse-fitted brake vans, hauled by the Class '600' 0-8-0 locomotives that were built at the same time. In support of this assertion, an article in *The Locomotive Magazine* for 4th July 1903 describes

> '*a trial trip with 30 of (the wagons) and drawn by 602, one of Mr. McIntosh's eight-coupled goods engines, ... recently run to Perth from Motherwell.*'

However, only one continuous braked van was built in 1903, with the rest of the order of forty vans postponed until 1907. The twenty vans that were finally authorised appeared without the continuous brake.[24]

In December 1901 the original intention was that the 30-ton Mineral Traffic Wagons

> '*will be chiefly employed for conveyance of Locomotive Coal and that 1,500, 10 ton wagons ... be transferred to stock of ordinary minerals.*'[25]

In fact, 300 exchanged roles with part of an order of 1,000 16-ton wagons that had been intended to carry loco coal. A further twenty-three were used to carry railway sleepers, and forty-six were designated for coal traffic to blast furnaces.

Some but not all of the wagons were designed to carry general merchandise from the outset, evidenced by the rings for securing tarpaulin ropes which were fitted to the T-angles reinforcing the body. The remaining thirty-one wagons were routinely used for this traffic from 1903.[26] The alterations to the wagons for goods traffic are discussed and illustrated in Chapter 9.

A wagon from the original Leeds Forge batch, number 66022, had its body removed, possibly as a result of accident damage, and became a flat wagon. It was assigned to Diagram 77. There is no record of this alteration in company minutes, but the diagram number suggests that it took place in 1905. The wagon is described in Chapter 14.3

In 1916 a further twenty-five were authorised. These may have been replacements for wagons which were sent overseas. James McEwan mentions that bogie coal wagons and six-wheeled brake vans to Diagram 63 were sent to France, although the source of his information was not recorded. The order was amended in favour of sixty 16-ton wagons, '*due to difficulties of getting timeous deliveries of steel.*'[27]

CONCLUSIONS

The Diagram 54 design concept was more radical than the Diagram 50 design and had greater potential for success. The tare weight was considerably reduced by using all-metal construction, although, according to photographs, the St. Rollox-style wagon exceeded the diagram weight by about half a ton. Indeed, a photograph of Leeds Forge wagon 66297 from the production lot shows a tare weight of 14 tons 1cwt, presumably after the wooden floor had been fitted.

The 30-ton wagons were clearly fit for purpose. If twenty-five wagons were sent overseas, they and the rebuilt 66022 reduced the fleet to 344. If this was the case, over three quarters (266 of the 344) survived to be recorded by the LM&SR in 1931.[28] They continued to carry loco coal in LM&SR colours and, like Caley locomotives, were seen on the former Highland Railway system.

In its booklet on the Caledonian Railway centenary in 1947, the Stephenson Locomotive Society reported that while the wagons were no longer in normal service,

> '*some are still used by the Permanent Way Department as sleeper wagons, and some have been acquired by the Carrongrove Paper Co. for transporting esparto grass from the ports to their mills.*'

One of the conversions to sleeper traffic (LM&SR 321305, original CR number 66305) was photographed in 1954 at Workington, although it was condemned at the time.[29]

The benefits of the wagons could not be realised in mineral revenue service because the infrastructure was geared to the design and dimensions of 8-ton wagons. In the June 1901 shareholders report, James Thompson the General Manager set out the problems in introducing the high capacity wagons that would produce operating efficiencies. He pointed out that in America the infrastructure had grown up side by side with railway developments, whereas in the UK the railways had to conform with the restrictions of old infrastructure. He stated,[30]

'The difficulty which British railways have now to contend with was not simply to reform their own methods, but to wait for the alterations and improvements of the established conditions of the country. There is not, at the present time, a single shipping port, iron or steel works, or gas works, or any works in Scotland, capable of dealing with a wagon carrying 30 or even 20 ton of coal, and there are not half-a-dozen collieries capable ... of admitting a wagon of the height of a 30 ton wagon. In spite of these drawbacks ... [the Caledonian] ordered 50 wagons capable of carrying 30 ton of coal or 50 ton of iron ore, which they will meantime use for certain classes of traffics, in the hope that ... [users] will see it to be their interest to gradually adapt their appliances to the new plant.'

The colliery owners did not adapt. In 1910 there were only 450 private trader's wagons over 12 tons capacity – less than 1½ per cent of the total number registered to run on the Caledonian.[31] The bogie wagons in loco coal traffic made savings in line occupancy and coal consumption because the locomotive hauling the train did not work so hard. It did not improve the revenue earning equation, because loco coal traffic was an operating cost.

The ultimately effective compromise for revenue earning traffic was to improve the load carrying capacity of conventional wagon designs within the constraints imposed by mine owners and end users, first with the Diagram 52 design, then with Diagram 59.

This brings us back to the *Railway Engineer* article cited earlier, which summed up the writer's preferred solution to the problem as follows:

'the ideal wagon for mineral traffic is one that will secure the largest proportion of paying load to total weight, whilst necessitating the smallest alteration of, or additions to, the accommodation and appliances of colliery proprietors and railway companies. As compared with a wagon of the bogie type, a 4-wheel 20-ton coal wagon possesses advantages ... whilst being free from certain disadvantages which must always accompany the use of long bogie wagons upon the railways of this country.'

The paper advantages of the bogie coal wagon design over the Diagram 46 wagon are summarised in the table below, assuming, for ease of calculation, a 600-ton load. Dimensions to calculate the cubic capacity are taken from the diagram book. The coal load is the rated capacity of the wagon. The train weight is the tare plus the coal load, multiplied by the number of wagons. The tare weight is that shown in the diagram book, and was greater in practice for the Diagram 54 wagons, thus reducing the theoretical advantage. The train of high capacity wagons is 17.5 per cent lighter, very much shorter, and the rolling resistance attributable to the axleboxes is almost halved.

The reduced length of the train made up of bogie wagons contradicts one of the alleged failings of the design – that the trains of these wagons were too long to be accommodated in refuge sidings. On the contrary, the trial run of thirty bogie coal wagons mentioned previously would have needed 112 Diagram 46 wagons, forming a train over 2,000 feet long. The rolling resistance of such a train fitted with grease axleboxes does not bear thinking about.

The advantages of the four-wheeled wagons to Diagrams 52 and 59 compared with a train of Diagram 46 stock are also shown in the table. A load of 600 tons in Diagram 59 wagons afforded an 11½ per cent improvement in train weight, a 33 per cent reduction in the number of wagons and therefore rolling resistance, and approximately 27½ per cent less train length. There is a marked increase in operational efficiency between Diagrams 52 and 59. Two tons of extra payload was carried at the cost of 5cwt extra tare. In this case, the extra weight of the enlarged wagon body was partially offset by the change from a wood to a lighter steel underframe.

THE HIGH CAPACITY WAGON ON OTHER RAILWAYS

The high capacity concept was not widely adopted in the UK in the early 1900s. The Caledonian was not only the early adopter, but the greatest user. Leeds Forge built thirty wagons for the Midland Railway in 1902. Hurst Nelson built vacuum braked wagons for the Great Northern in 1903. The Great Western built twenty-seven 40-ton wagons between 1904 and 1910.[32] Most of these wagons seem to have been in loco coal traffic.

In Scotland, the Scottish Cooperative Society took delivery in 1905 of 30-ton hopper discharge wagons from Leeds Forge to carry coal from the Hamilton district.[33] The other major coal carrier in Scotland, the North British, did not go down the high capacity route.

REFERENCES
1. February 1902 issue
2. NRS BR/CAL/5/11 entry 361
3. Quoted in *The Railway Magazine*, September 1907
4. NRS BR/CAL/4/134 p. 6
5. *1915 Working Timetable Appendix*, p. 75
6. Pickering card order 5158, March/April 1901
7. Described in *Locomotive Magazine*, Vol. VI, p. 210
8. NRS BR/CAL/5/11 p. 437
9. NRS BR/CAL/1/44 entry 558
10. NRM 11907/W
11. Pickering Enquiry Book UGD12/6/2, ref: G2094, Glasgow University Business Archive
12. Pickering drawing 1693, dated 7th January 1901, HMRS collection ref: 8
13. Issue dated 4th October 1901
14. NRS BR/CAL/1/44 entry 847
15. NRS BR/CAL/1/46 entry 77
16. NRS BR/CAL/1/46 entry 580
17. NRS BR/CAL/1/47 entry 326
18. NRS BR/CAL/1/45 entry 668
19. NRS BR/CAL/1/45 entry 3
20. The statement giving delivery dates of the wagons to Diagrams 54, 66 and 81is in BR/CAL/4/134
21. NRS BR/CAL/1/47 entry 441
22. NRS BR/CAL/1/47 entry 566
23. NRS BR/CAL/1/47 entry 464
24. NRS BR/CAL/1/54 entry 209
25. NRS BR/CAL/5/12 pp. 48-49
26. NRS BR/CAL/4/134 p. 33
27. NRS BR/CAL/1/67 entries 1221 and 1268
28. Information contained in *LMS Diagrams of Bogies used for Heavy Weight and Mineral Wagons*, CRA Archive ref: 3/4/1/24
29. Reproduced in *The True Line*, issue 69, p. 35
30. Reported in *The Railway Engineer*, February 1902
31. In the returns contained in BR/CAL/4/134
32. Information in *History of Great Western Wagons*
33. Scottish Coop wagon quoted in Pickering's Estimate Cost Books, UGD12/3/7 p. 251, Glasgow University Business Archive

DIAGRAM	TARE	CAPACITY	COAL LOAD	TRAIN WEIGHT	WAGONS	AXLES	LENGTH
54	13 tons 3cwt	1,190cu ft	30 tons	863 tons	20	80	757ft
46	5 tons 19cwt	312cu ft	8 tons	1,046 tons	75	150	1,373ft
52	6 tons 5cwt	386cu ft	10 tons	975 tons	60	120	1,098ft
59	6 tons 10cwt	485cu ft	12 tons	925 tons	50	100	992ft

5.5: Four-Wheeled Wagon Development Post 1900

The Fate of the Early 'Bogies'

Early in the new century, the Caley began to make inroads into the old mineral wagon stock. A Loco & Stores Committee minute in July 1901 recorded the following recommendation:

'Old 6 & 7 ton Wagons – for the next 6 months, to break up old wagons on which the cost of repair would exceed £10 and replace by larger wagons of equivalent tonnage.'[1]

A special committee of Caledonian Railway directors was set up to oversee the process. The rolling stock return for the period ending January 1902 records 1,258 wagons as worn out, replaced by 815 new wagons. The renewals would have been Diagram 52 wagons. The capacity of the new wagons more than accounted for the loss attributable to the scrapped wagons. A company minute in April 1906 stated, this time citing the Diagram 59 wagons as renewals,

'In view of the general working of mineral traffic, that the 4,884, 6 ton wagons be taken at once out of stock and the value be placed to a suspense a/c and that they be replaced with wagons of larger capacity say 16 ton, of equal value.'[2]

On 5th March 1907 it was recommended and agreed that the *'7 ton Mineral Wagons [be] included with the 6 ton wagons in the Special Committee's brief.'*[3]

Disposal of wagons started in 1908 and continued until 1912. By then, approximately 13,000 had been sold, mostly in lots of four figures. During the same period, over 6,000 Diagram 59 wagons had been built by St. Rollox and outside contractors, easily maintaining the carrying capacity of the mineral fleet.

Many went to P & W McLellan Ltd for scrap. Those that were acquired by coal and iron masters were banned from running on the Caledonian system, and were restricted to internal use. According to the *1915 Working Timetable Appendix*[4] these wagons were painted dark green, with either the firm's initials or the name of the works, lettered in bold on the side.

Above: Plate 5.14
The two types of Diagram 54 wagon coupled together. The Leeds Forge design on the right now has 2 feet 9 inches diameter wheels and the wagon rides lower than the other wagon as a result. The Leeds Forge wagon has much larger buffer heads. The St. Rollox-built wagon on the left is not fitted with tarpaulin rings. In the background the right-hand wagon is to Diagram 21. It has been re-lettered for loco coal use and the company initials from when it was in general mineral service are still visible.

Left: Plate 5.15
From right to left, Diagrams 46, 54, 50 another Diagram 46 and some old 'bogies' provide a potted history of Caledonian Railway mineral wagon development at Netherton lime works. The difference in size between the Diagrams 54 and 46 wagons vividly illustrates the advantage that existed on paper in favour of the bogie wagon. The end of the Diagram 54 wagon does not carry a number. Facing the photographer in the right background is a Diagram 21 wagon, adapted to carry coke, identifiable by the four raves. Only three were fitted to the deeper bodied Diagram 46 adaptations.

Some of the old wagons remained in service with the Caledonian. In May 1910 it was resolved, in response to a request made the previous November, that

'1,000 6 & 7 ton old wagons to be stored and repaired and put into traffic if the necessity should arise.'[5]

The *'necessity'* was for internal use around locomotive depots and in the various engineering sections of the line. These wagons are discussed in greater detail in Chapter 17.

Some wagons were marked with a white cross to show that they were reserved for certain areas on specific traffic. This practice seems to have been adopted early in the twentieth century, judging from the official photograph of a Diagram 66 hopper wagon which appears as Plate 6.7 in the next chapter. Quoting again from the *1915 Appendix*[6] the wagons were:

'For mineral traffic on the section between Ardrossan and Lugton Junction;
For slag from Chapelhall and Kilgarth to places on Western Section;
For mineral traffic on the section between Kirtlebridge and Brayton; and
For manure traffic on the section between Dundee and stations between Perth and Forfar.'

The continued use of these wagons on this traffic was confirmed by the Board of Directors in November 1915.[7] There is no record of its cessation.

UPGRADE OF DIAGRAM 22 WAGONS

Diagram 22 wagons were converted by fitting new headstocks and self-contained sprung buffers in order to conform to Railway Clearing House regulations. The St. Rollox drawing number was 12972,[8] issued in March 1905, although rebuilding may have started in a small way during the half year ending July 1903.[9]

In 1912/13 over 3,000 of these wagons had been liberated into general traffic by the expiry of the various thirling arrangements agreed in the 1890s. John Watson purchased his 1,000 thirled wagons for private use after threatening to take legal action to possess them.[10] In October 1914 a minute authorised a major reconstruction programme, which was stimulated by the impending Railway Clearing House deadline for the abolition of solid buffered wagons. The details are in Chapter 2.6

'1250, Solid Buffer Wagons to be converted by rebuilding into 10 ton Goods & Mineral Wagons, being part of the whole stock of 10,000 Solid Buffer Wagons to be dealt with in 4 years from January 1st 1915.'[11]

The 10,000 was the combined total of the wagons in CR traffic and the thirled wagons. By 1917 just over 6,000 had been rebuilt. In May 1918, the remaining 3,800 wagons were authorised for conversion by the Board of Directors.[12]

In 1919 some wagons were modified by the addition of a bottom door. This was the subject of drawing 20062.[13] A double door covered an aperture 4 feet by 2 feet 3 inches between the cross members of the underframe. There is no record in the minutes of the number of

RIGHT: Plate 5.16
58660 was one of 200 Diagram 22 wagons numbered 58471-58670 that were originally 'thirled' in the service of the Clyde Coal Company. This photograph was taken just after the Grouping. The wagon has been rebuilt with sprung self-contained buffers. The rebuilding specification was for 'a double brake put on opposite side to existing brake', but in this case a single brake block has been added. The brake on the near side is the original, as the convention was for the brake ratchet to be at the fixed end of the wagon. The designated load is now 10 tons, the capacity when loaded with iron ore.

LEFT: Plate 5.17
64872 was the prototype Diagram 51 wagon, built by St. Rollox in the first half of 1900. A further 201 were authorised in August the same year. These wagons are easily identified by the narrow channel solebars, compared with Diagram 59. They could not accommodate the standard cast number plate, hence its displacement to the body. The buffer beams are made of the same channel as the solebars. Another distinguishing feature is that the top two planks are continuous, rather than the top plank only of the Diagram 59 wagons. The McIntosh brake with cast hanger is fitted. The axleboxes are number 12 type, with 9-inch by 4½-inch journals. The grab handle on the fixed end is an unusual feature for the Caledonian, although it was not uncommon on private traders' wagons.

5.5: FOUR-WHEELED WAGON DEVELOPMENT POST 1900

wagons that were modified and no order number in the St. Rollox list.

16 Tons Iron Ore Wagon – Diagram 51

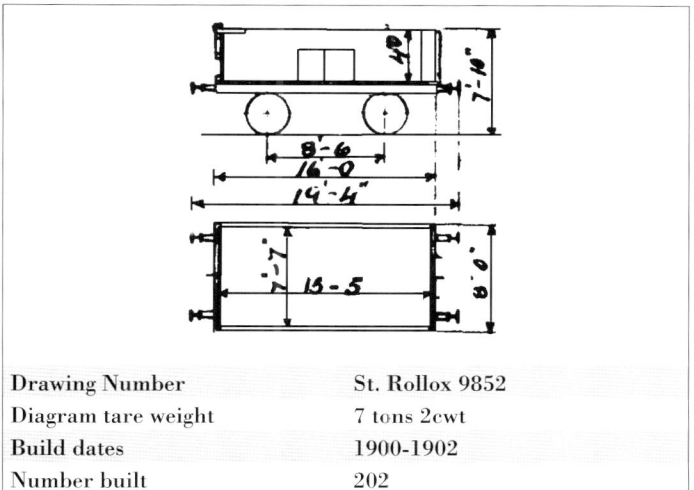

Drawing Number	St. Rollox 9852
Diagram tare weight	7 tons 2cwt
Build dates	1900-1902
Number built	202

At the same time as the Diagram 50 wagon was built, McIntosh designed a four-wheeled ore wagon. The prototype Diagram 51 wagon was authorised late in 1899 and built at St. Rollox as part of an order for 300 mineral wagons to G178.[14] The order was described as a rolling stock renewal for the half year ending July 1900 in the minutes.

It was a significant advance over the Diagram 46 wagon, with almost 50 per cent greater cubic capacity. This was achieved by raising the sides by 1 foot and increasing the length and width by 1 foot and 5 inches respectively. The axlebox journals were enlarged from 8 inches by 3¾ inches to 9 inches by 4½ inches to cope with the extra load.

The prototype was the first mineral wagon to be built with a metal underframe. The narrow metal channel solebars and buffer beams accounted for the slightly lower overall height compared with the Diagram 59 wagons that superseded them. The production order numbers continued from 64872, so all these wagons were treated as capital expenditure.

The Search for an Optimum Capacity Wagon

The stated goal was a four-wheeled wagon that would carry 50 per cent more coal than a Diagram 46 wagon, within the constraints of existing infrastructure. The October 1900 minute authorising the experimental 30-ton bogie wagons stated:

> 'with regard to the wagons used for shipment coal, the Locomotive Superintendent submitted particulars of a wagon capable of carrying twelve tons of coal and sixteen tons of iron ore [the Diagram 51 design], and he is instructed to look further into the matter and report, with a view to reducing the tare and increasing the load, keeping in view the existing conditions at ports and collieries.'[15]

Evidently, Diagram 51 was not regarded as the solution, probably because the tare weight was excessive.

14 Ton Mineral Wagon – Diagram 52

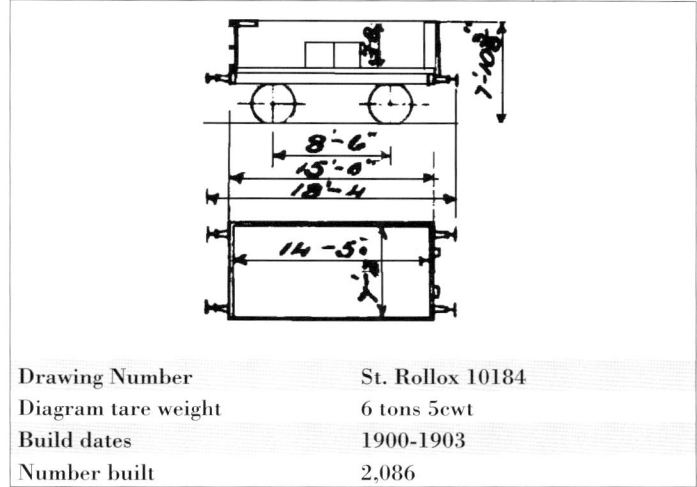

Drawing Number	St. Rollox 10184
Diagram tare weight	6 tons 5cwt
Build dates	1900-1903
Number built	2,086

The Diagram 52 design was first authorised in August 1900.[16] The original intention was to build 300 wagons to Diagram 46.[17] It was a development of the Diagram 46 design with the height of the body increased by one plank to 3 feet 8 inches. The side door opening remained three planks high. The axle box journals were heavier at 9 inches by 4 inches compared with 8 inches by 3¾ inches. These changes allowed 10 tons of coal, or 14 tons of ore, to be carried. Some, and maybe all, the wagons were fitted with the McIntosh patent brake.

All were built at St. Rollox. About half were treated as replacements. Although the wagons were built in quantity over a relatively short period, the design was only an interim step in improving the carrying

Plate 5.18
Diagram 52 wagon 17303 was fitted with the McIntosh patent brake. Coupled with the low running number, this suggests it was from the first replacement order to G186, authorised in March 1901. The V-hanger is the cast version, and the brake push rods are of unequal length. These wagons may have been the first to carry the second version of the cast number plate. The LOAD 14 TONS lettering is smaller than that of the tare weight, and is centred in the space between the door and the end ironwork. The load lettering is more widely spaced than usual.

Plate 5.19
An example of the first 1,000 wagons built by contractors in 1903 to drawing 11950 – in this case by Hurst Nelson. It is fitted with CR 12 grease axleboxes with 9-inch by 4½-inch journals. It has the traditional heavy framed two-hinge end door and horizontally planked side doors. The double brake on one side only was new to Caledonian mineral wagons, although the McIntosh brake was still being fitted to NPCS after this date.

BELOW AND FACING PAGE: Figure 5.8
St. Rollox drawing 12014 shows the heavy framed end door which was used on the Diagram 59 wagons from 1903 to 1905.

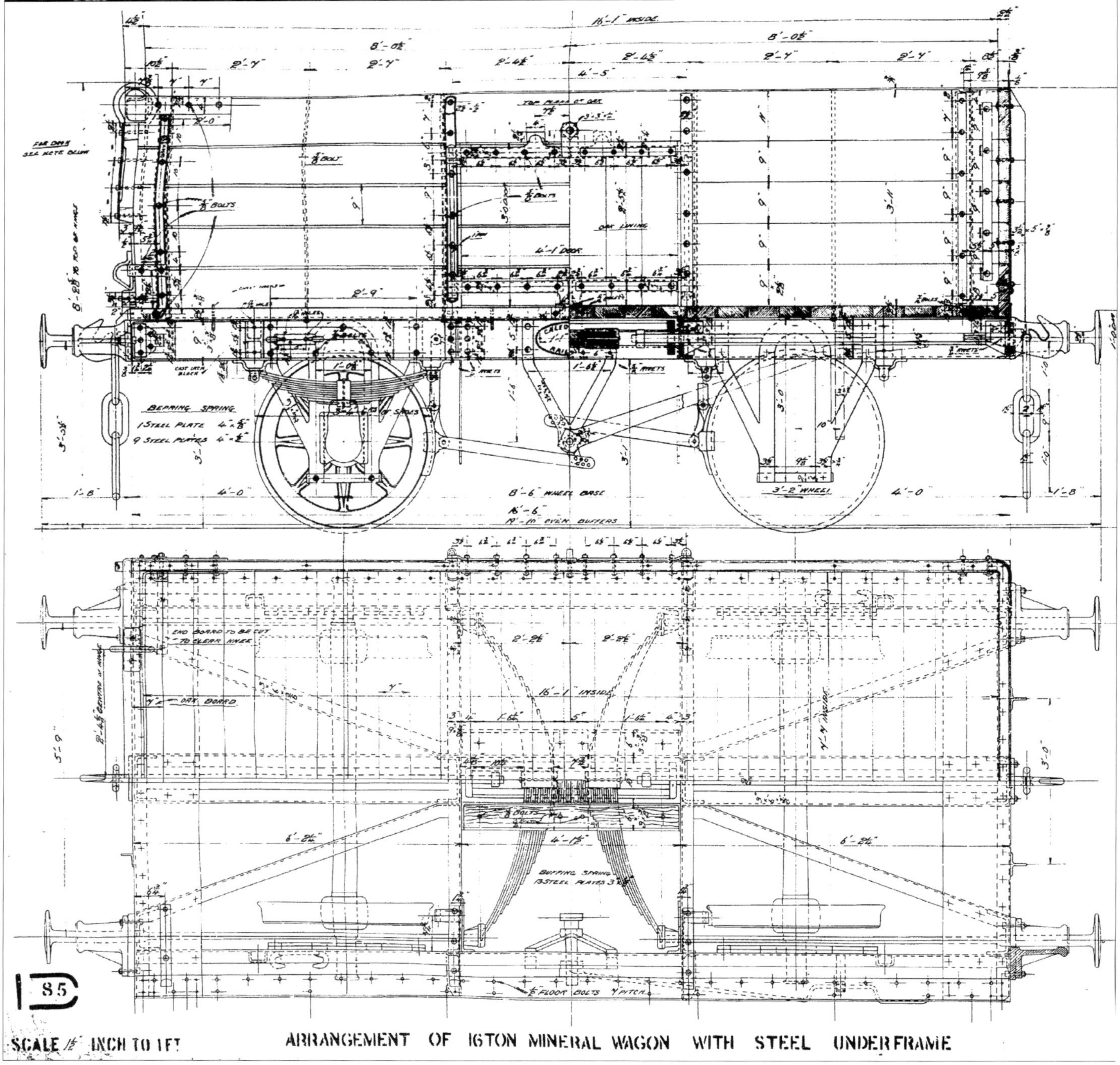

5.5: FOUR-WHEELED WAGON DEVELOPMENT POST 1900

capacity of four-wheeled wagons. Other designs were considered, but the solution which made the most of carrying capacity in the prevailing conditions was the Diagram 59 wagon.

UNIMPLEMENTED DESIGN PROPOSALS

In 1903, while the Diagram 52 wagons were still under construction, and the first drawing for the Diagram 59 wagons had been prepared, two proposals for increased capacity wagons emanated from the drawing office. Drawing 11815 was for a 12-ton mineral wagon with doors at both ends. This was a common design on the Glasgow & South Western Railway and 12-ton examples were running on its system in 1899.[18]

Harking back to the ideal wagon in the *Railway Engineer* article, drawing 12005 was for a 20-ton coal wagon. If this design had been built to RCH guidelines, the minimum wheelbase would have been 10 feet. Internal dimensions would have been 21 feet by 7 feet 6 inches, with 5 feet high sides, giving an overall height of over 9 feet. In fact, when the Lancashire & Yorkshire Railway designed a 20-ton steel underframe shipping coal wagon, its external dimensions were 21 feet 6 inches long by 8 feet wide, and the overall height was 10 feet 1 inch. The wheelbase was 12 feet.[19]

Neither of the CR designs was approved. The restrictions imposed by infrastructure which prevented the 30-ton wagons' use in revenue service would probably have applied to the 20-ton wagon design. The drawings have not survived.

16 TON IRON ORE WAGON – DIAGRAM 59

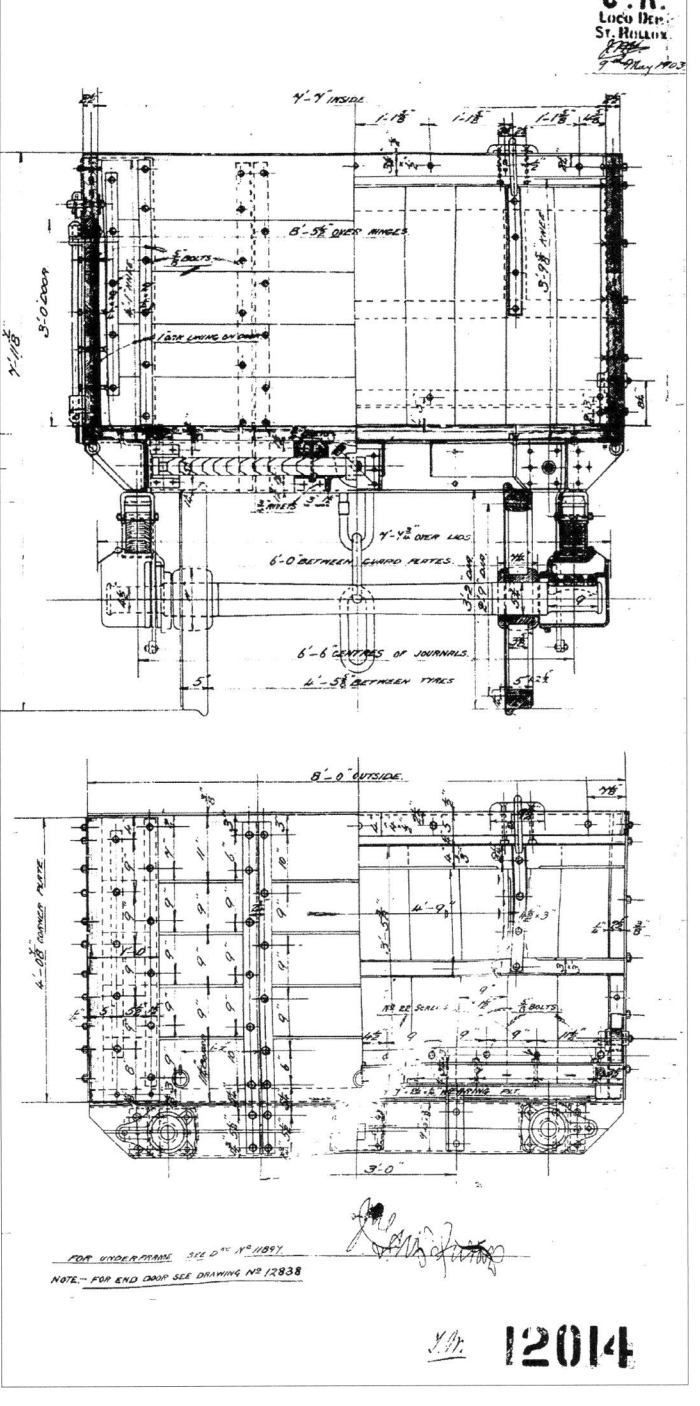

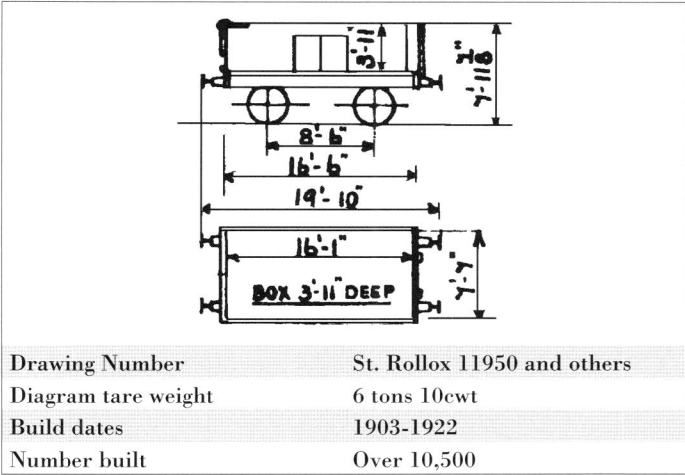

Drawing Number	St. Rollox 11950 and others
Diagram tare weight	6 tons 10cwt
Build dates	1903-1922
Number built	Over 10,500

This was the final mineral wagon development, which achieved the aim of the original instruction to McIntosh. The following table shows how the Caledonian worked around the restrictions imposed by colliery and docks infrastructure. The comparison is with the recommended dimensions for a 12-ton coal/16-ton ore wagon that were issued by the Railway Clearing House.

	RCH 12-Ton	CR Diagram 59
External length	15ft 0in	16ft 6in
External width	7ft 11in	8ft 0in
Overall height	8ft 8in	8ft 0in
Depth of box	4ft 7in	3ft 11in
Wheelbase	9ft 0in	8ft 6in
Cubic capacity	500 cu ft	485 cu ft

The first order was authorised in the renewal programme for the first half of 1903[20] and construction continued until 1922. The twenty-nine wagons to order G428 were the last Caledonian wagons to be built at St. Rollox. The Caledonian built about 6,000 wagons, and outside contractors a further 4,500.

The original intention was to use wood underframes. Drawing 11664,[21] dated 23rd February 1903, showed a wood underframe wagon and was annotated for order G204. On 3rd April, drawing 11950 was issued, also annotated for G204, with a pressed steel underframe.

Most of the wagons were built with steel underframes, which were frequently supplied by contractors to St. Rollox to fulfil their orders. Wood was substituted for steel between 1916 and 1918, when steel became difficult to obtain or dearer than wood.[22] Contractors built wood underframe wagons up to 1922.[23]

St. Rollox drawings document differences in end door hinges and

Plate 5.20
21402 exhibits the simplified end door with three hoop hinges that became the standard. It was one of 100 built by Hurst Nelson in 1906 as part of an order of 1,000 placed with various contractors. The St. Rollox drawing number was 13082.

BELOW AND FACING PAGE: **Figure 5.9**
This is the St. Rollox drawing for the modified end door arrangement used on Diagram 59 wagons after 1905.

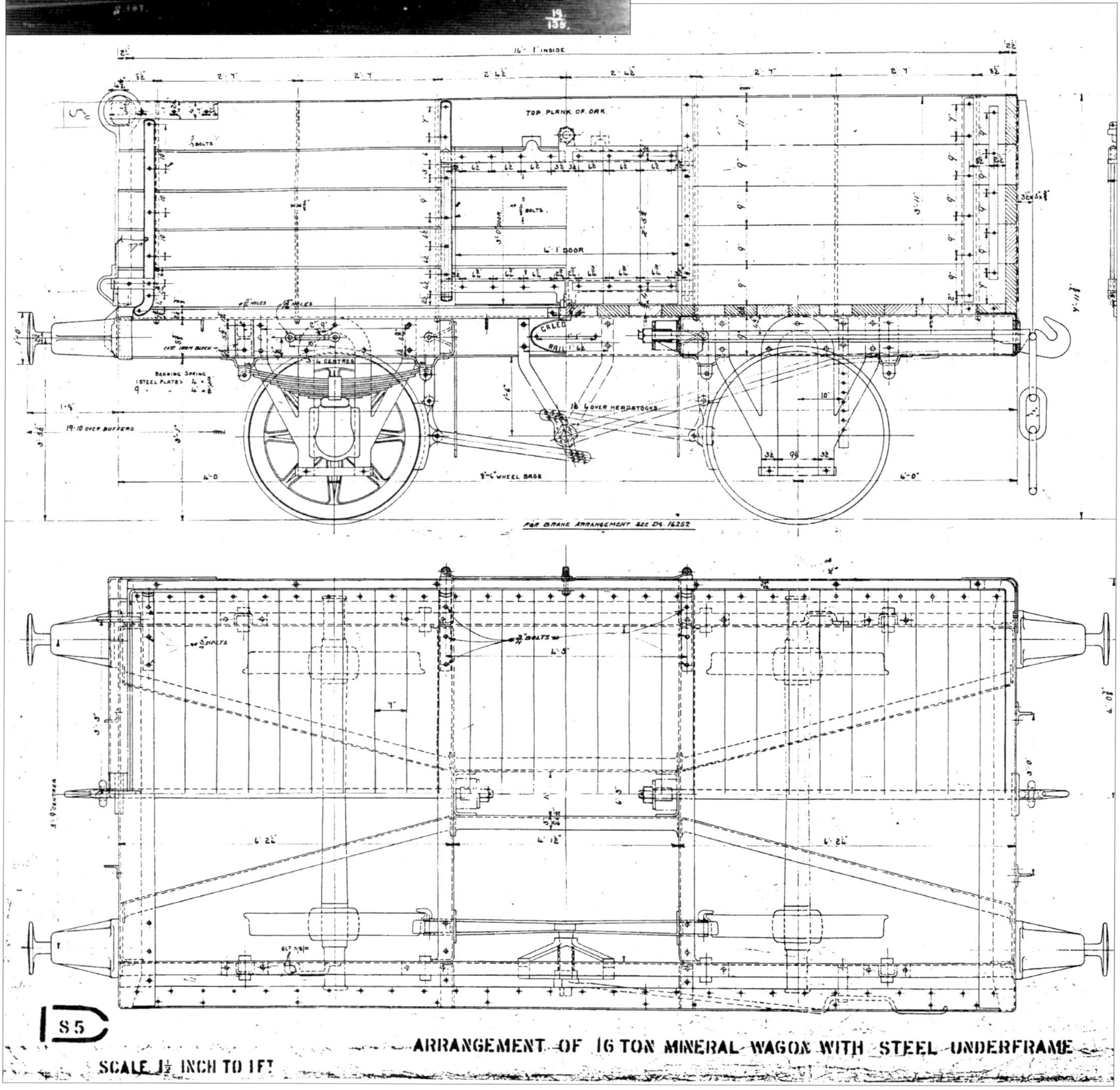

5.5: FOUR-WHEELED WAGON DEVELOPMENT POST 1900

Plate 5.21
The paint date on the wooden solebar is 14/11/22. This wagon was built by the Hamilton Wagon Co. as part of an order of 400 to drawing 18698. It has vertically planked side doors and the end door has additional L-iron reinforcement, although T-section was specified in the drawing. Heavy duty buffers, the Morton design of either side brake and 9-inch by 4½-inch oil axleboxes are fitted. The clutch arrangement that reverses the motion of the transverse brake rod is very clear. The weight is now nearly half a ton greater than in 1903. The execution of the letter C leaves something to be desired!

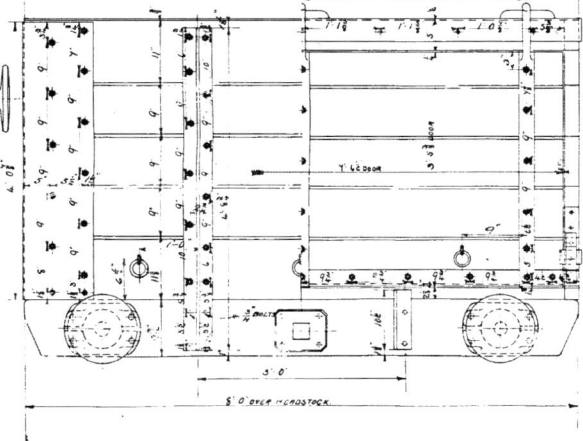

framing, side door planking, axleboxes, brake gear and underframes. The first type of wagon was built from 1903 to 1905 to drawing 11950. It had the heavy framed end door with two hoop hinges, similar to the Diagram 46 wagons. St. Rollox built 1,070 of these wagons to orders G204 and G207. Six contractors shared an order for a further 1,000. Order G204 used Leeds Forge pressed steel underframes.[24] Steel channel underframes were used for the remainder.

In 1905 the end door was simplified. The heavy wooden bracing was replaced with conventional ironwork, and three hoop hinges were used. Wagons with this door arrangement and side doors with horizontal planking were built up to 1915. The St. Rollox drawing was 13082.[25] St. Rollox built most of the wagons to this design – 3,839 in all to twenty-two order numbers. Order G330 for 250 wagons was built with Iracier axleboxes. Contractors built a further 1,250. The drawing specified the steel underframe buffer.

As previously mentioned, oak underframes were substituted for metal in 1916. The drawing for these wagons was St. Rollox 18698.[26] The first St. Rollox order for 100 wagons to G384 was actually built by the Clayton Wagon Works. St. Rollox is known to have built at least another 555 wood underframe wagons, and it may have been 705 if St. Rollox order G397 is correct as recorded. In the renewal programme for the period ending December 1917, 380 wagons were authorised, subject to Government rulings on two counts. The Traffic Committee noted, authorising sixty wagons pending the decision:

> *'As to wagons the renewal of 380, 16 ton Mineral Wagons is authorised only on condition that Company's claim to have renewal of wagons on 2½% basis is admitted by Government. Failing this the number will be reduced to 210.'*[27]

Contractors built a further 960 wagons with wood underframes up to 1922, including the sixty built by Pickering in 1916 as substitutes for the 30-ton bogie wagons for loco coal.[28] The decision was made partly because steel was not readily available, but also on price. The 30-ton wagons would have cost £11,000 and the four-wheeled wagons cost £10,620.[29] These wagons were actually built to the original drawing 11664, but with the later three hoop door. They are discussed further in Chapter 17.

Self-contained buffers were fitted to the wood underframe wagons. Wagons built to drawing 18698 also had side doors with vertical, rather than horizontal, planking. The end doors were reinforced with two vertical pieces of angle iron. Oil axleboxes were fitted and the Morton either side brake became the standard. Up to 1916, the double brake operated from one side only was fitted.

Finally, between 1918 and 1922 St. Rollox built 405 wagons, the underframes of which were not specified in the order book. Given that contractors continued to build wooden underframe wagons until 1922, it is probable that St. Rollox did the same.

References

1. NRS BR/CAL/1/44 entry 1571
2. NRS BR/CAL/1/52 entry 1102
3. NRS BR/CAL/1/54 entry 767
4. *1915 Working Timetable Appendix*, p. 70
5. NRS BR/CAL/1/59 entry 141
6. *1915 Working Timetable Appendix*, p. 70
7. NRS BR/CAL./1/67 entry 729
8. NRM 11923/W
9. NRS BR/CAL/1/46 entry 1363
10. NRS BR/CAL/1/60 entry 1106
11. NRS BR/CAL/1/65 entry 1041
12. NRS BR/CAL/1/71 entry 515
13. NRM 11919/W
14. NRS BR/CAL/1/43 entry 449
15. NRS BR/CAL/5/11 entry 437
16. NRS BR/CAL/1/43 entry 2075
17. NRS BR/CAL/1/43 entry 1689
18. Photograph and narrative in *HMRS Journal*, Vol. 16, No. 1, pp. 3-4
19. A drawing of this design appeared in *Model Railway News*, March 1964, p. 257
20. NRS BR/CAL/1/46 entry 1363
21. NRM 11898/W
22. NRS BR/CAL/1/67 entry 1268 records the cancellation of the last order of 30-ton wagons because of difficulties in steel supplies. NRS BR/CAL/1/69 entry 605 specifies wood underframes for the substitute 16-ton wagons.
23. For example, Pickering card order 36083 of 1919
24. NRS BR/CAL/1/47 entry 121
25. NRM 11914/W
26. NRM 11913/W
27. NRS BR/CAL/1/69 entry 799
28. Pickering card order 29760
29. NRS BR/CAL/1/67 entry 1268

LEFT: **Plate 6.1**
Hopper ancient. The iron brake block and cast number plate suggest that 23473 may be one of those altered according to the 1885 drawing, at the same time losing its original wooden brake block and painted number. However, the weight is 7 tons rather than the 5 tons stated on the drawing description. Standard Drummond mineral wagon springs with an integrally-cast brake pivot have replaced the original suspension. This may well explain the increase in capacity and the addition of the cast number plate. The modifications amounted to a rebuild.

RIGHT: **Plate 6.2**
Hopper modern. A Diagram 121 hopper in LM&SR service. Apart from the open spoke wheels, it looks a very modern design. It has oil axleboxes and the standard steel underframe buffer. The brake lever is cranked to clear the hopper operating mechanism. As these wagons were built as renewals, it would probably have been numbered 27189 in CR days.

Chapter 6
Specialised Mineral Wagons
6.1: Hopper Wagons

In the very early days of the Caledonian, hopper wagons were not required, because the company did not have the infrastructure to deal with them. A minute of May 1849 declining to purchase 200 iron bodied coal wagons offered by the L&NWR stated that the wagons

'are intended to discharge from the bottom, whereas the CR do not ship and have no drops at their sidings.'[1]

Nearly forty years later, the mineral 'bogie' design included a hopper version (St. Rollox drawing 4484 of 1st July 1885).[2] The drawing register described it as *'alteration of 7 ton mineral wagon to 5 ton hopper wag[on].'* According to the *1900 Register* there were twenty of these wagons. This included six that were recommended in a Traffic Committee minute of 3rd November 1891 for coal traffic to the Central Hotel in Glasgow.[3]

These wagons remained in service until 1911, when they were replaced by adapted Diagram 59 16-ton mineral wagons. St. Rollox drawing 15710, which has not survived, is recorded in the drawing register as a *'16 ton wagon underframe with centre bottom door for Central Station.'*

An unknown number of Diagram 22 mineral wagons were also fitted with two bottom doors, operated by catches at the side of the wagon, to drawing 5721 of 1888.[4] The door openings were 4 feet long by 2 feet wide.

Order G179 included eight hopper wagons as part of an authorisation for 300 mineral wagons in the renewal programme for the period ending 31st July 1900.[5] There is no record of a drawing for such wagons, although drawing 10385, dated 1st August 1900 refers to a *'guard for mineral wagon with hopper bottom.'* This would suggest a modification to a standard mineral wagon design. This drawing has not survived. It is possible that the order was actually fulfilled by the purchase of *'eight tipping wagons for the Muirkirk section'* authorised in May 1900.[6] There is no mention of the builder of these wagons.

The first reference in company minutes to hopper wagons in more modern times was in 1901, when the hopper bottom ballast wagons were introduced.[7] These are discussed in the chapter on service vehicles. In 1902 a number of drawings for hopper coal wagons were made. St. Rollox numbers 11292 and 11395 were for a 30-ton wagon. Drawing 11396 was for a wagon of 10 tons capacity. None of these designs were adopted and the drawings have not survived.

Eventually both wooden and metal bodied hopper wagons were produced for revenue service. The different designs and the small numbers built suggest that they were probably used for traffic to particular locations. The 40-ton bogie hoppers are dealt with in the section on coke traffic later in the chapter.

FACING PAGE, BOTTOM: Plate 6.3
The two wagons to the foreground are probably built to drawing 12668, which has not survived. They do, however, match Graeme Miller's description. The 8 tons load is much more realistic than the 16 tons ascribed to order G233. Note that the side doors are only three planks high, like the Diagram 51 and 52 mineral wagons. Behind the wagons is a Diagram 45 brake van, distinguishable by the brake wheel in the verandah area. The similar Diagram 5 vans had one brake wheel inside the body of the van.

10 Ton Hopper Wagon – Diagram 75

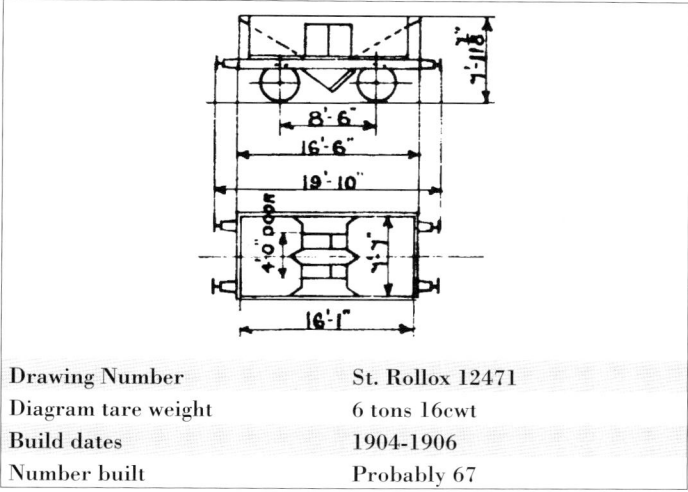

Drawing Number	St. Rollox 12471
Diagram tare weight	6 tons 16cwt
Build dates	1904-1906
Number built	Probably 67

Diagram 75 wagons were a modification of the Diagram 59 mineral wagons, with both ends fixed. They retained the side cupboard doors. The hopper arrangement reduced the cubic capacity to 10 tons of coal.

In January 1904 the Traffic Committee tabled a proposal *'to construct 12 Standard 12 ton Coal Wagons with Hopper Bottoms for the United Turkey Red Company.'*[8] The Diagram 59 coal load was 12 tons, so this may be the first reference to the Diagram 75 design, although the hopper bottom would have reduced the payload considerably. The only record of an order for twelve such wagons is part of G180, which was actually authorised as 400 mineral wagons in 1900.[9] One can only assume that the hopper wagon part of the order was not built until three and a half years later.

Twenty hopper bottom wagons were authorised in the renewals programme for the half year ending January 1906.[10] In the St. Rollox order book G239 refers to 14 ton (the iron ore load capacity) hopper wagons.

The last order for these wagons was G245, authorised according to the renewals memos, but not mentioned in the minutes. This order was for forty wagons in the renewals memo, but the St. Rollox order list states that thirty-five were built. The drawing for these wagons, St. Rollox 13359,[11] was dated 29th November 1905. The capacity was stated as 12 tons. There is no photograph of a Diagram 75 wagon; numbers are not known.

In July 1904 drawing 12668[12] for a 12-ton capacity wagon was issued, which seems to have been a variation of Diagram 75. The dimensions are identical apart from the wheelbase, which was 10 feet. Miller stated that they were *'the same design of chute and door as the former [i.e., to drawing 12471] wagon, wood underframe, self contained buffers.'*

As part of the renewal programme for the first half of 1905, forty *'hopper bottom coke wagons'* were authorised.[13] The wagons were built to order G233 and were described as 16-ton coke wagons. The low density of coke makes the stated capacity impossible within the loading gauge for a wagon of the length of Diagram 75.

20 Ton Hopper Wagon – Diagram 97

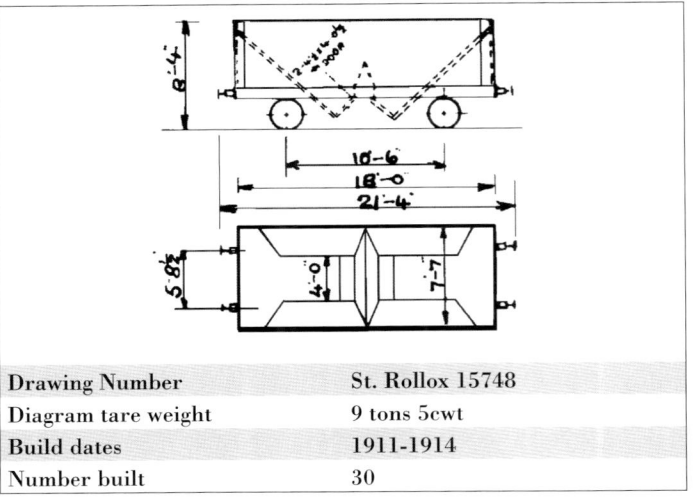

Drawing Number	St. Rollox 15748
Diagram tare weight	9 tons 5cwt
Build dates	1911-1914
Number built	30

The Diagram 97 and 98 wagons were similar to each other, in that Diagram 98 (order G311) was a shortened version of 97 (G300), with only one set of discharge hoppers rather than two. Both types had wooden bodies. Ends were fixed and there were no side doors.

St. Rollox issued drawing 14049 for a 20-ton hopper ore wagon in 1907. This was probably only a proposed design, as there is no mention of such a wagon in the minutes, and no build order from St. Rollox or contractors. The drawing has not survived.

A Traffic Committee minute in January 1911 recorded the decision that *'35 of the 110, 16 ton Mineral Wagons authorised 15 Nov 1910 should be replaced by 20, 25 ton Hopper wagons.'* They were to be used on Glengarnock Iron and Steel Works ore traffic from Ardrossan.[14] The capacity according to the drawing was 499 cubic feet. This only equates to 17 tons of ore or about 12 tons of coal.

Miller records that they had 10-inch by 5-inch oil lubricated journals. They were built on pressed steel underframes from Leeds Forge, according to a further Traffic Committee minute of 24th January 1911.[15] The buffers were set half an inch closer than normal. The Diagram 98 dimension was the standard 5 feet 9 inches.

The later lot of ten wagons to order G345 was authorised for the period ending June 1914.[16] An annotation to the original drawing says that they were to be fitted with iron hopper doors and that the either side brake was to be used. Numbers are unknown; the wagons were allocated random numbers as renewals, and no photograph exists.

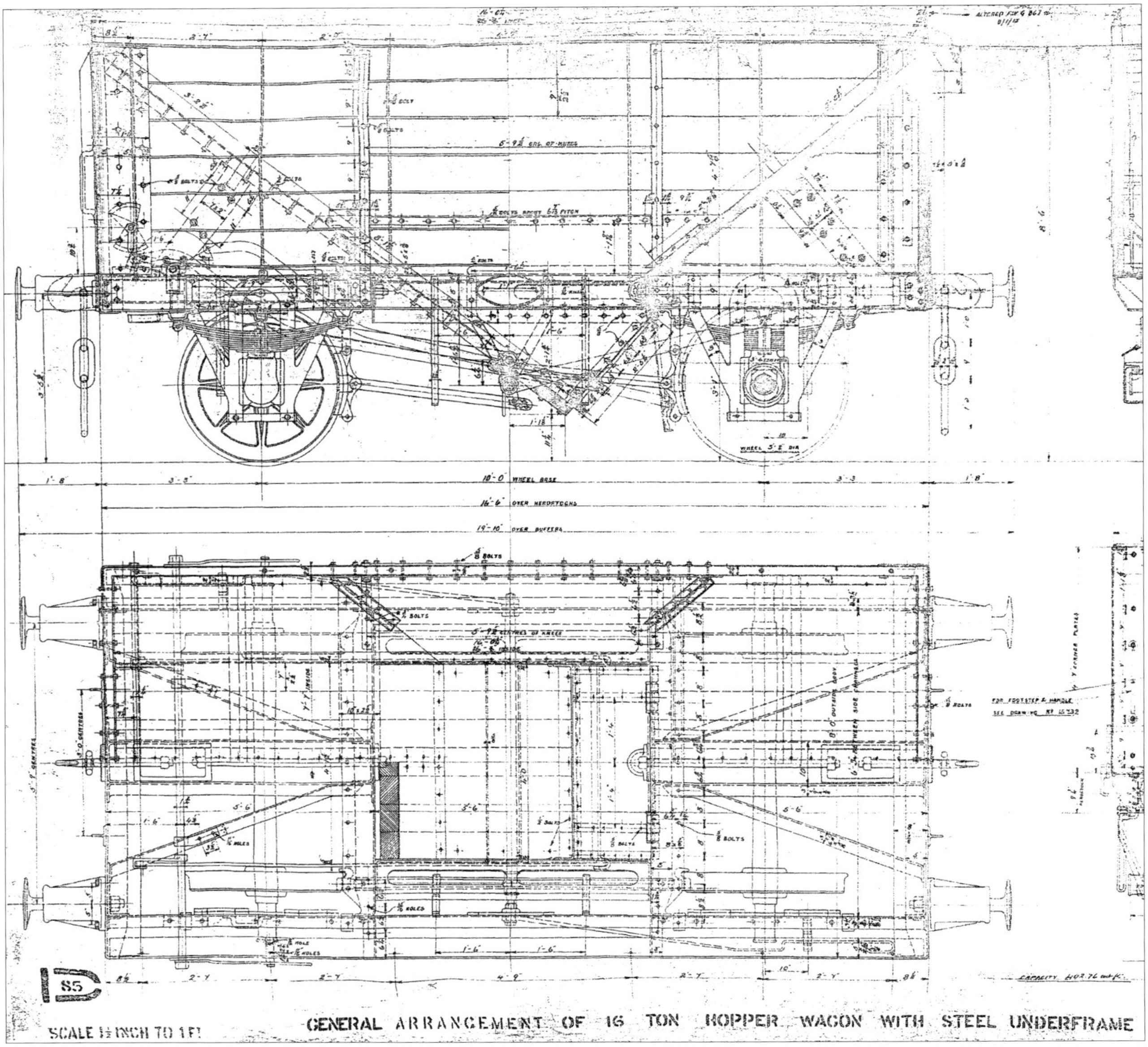

16 Ton Hopper Wagon – Diagram 98

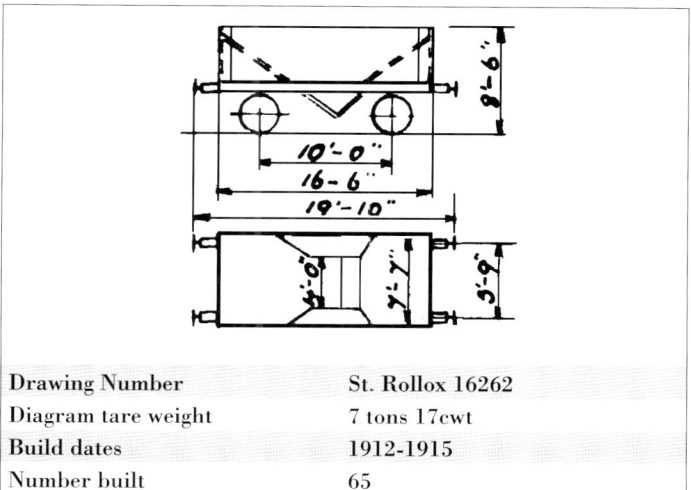

Drawing Number	St. Rollox 16262
Diagram tare weight	7 tons 17cwt
Build dates	1912-1915
Number built	65

The wagon renewal programme for the period ending July 1912 authorised St. Rollox to build this shortened version of Diagram 97.[17] The diagram load designation was for coal traffic, as their capacity of 402 cubic feet does not equate to 16 tons of iron ore. Like the Diagram 97 wagons, pressed steel underframes were used, this time with 9-inch by 4½-inch journals and grease lubrication. The Morton either side brake was fitted. The hopper slopes were asymmetrical and the discharge door was offset to avoid fouling the transverse brake shaft.

The first lot of 25 was built in 1912 to order G311. A further forty were built to order G367 in the renewal programme for the period ending 30th June 1915.[18] The minute and the St. Rollox order list both describe the wagons as 10 tons capacity, which was their iron ore loading. This suggests that the wagons were used for carrying both types of mineral. The numbering of these wagons is not known.

10 Ton Hopper Wagon – Diagram 121

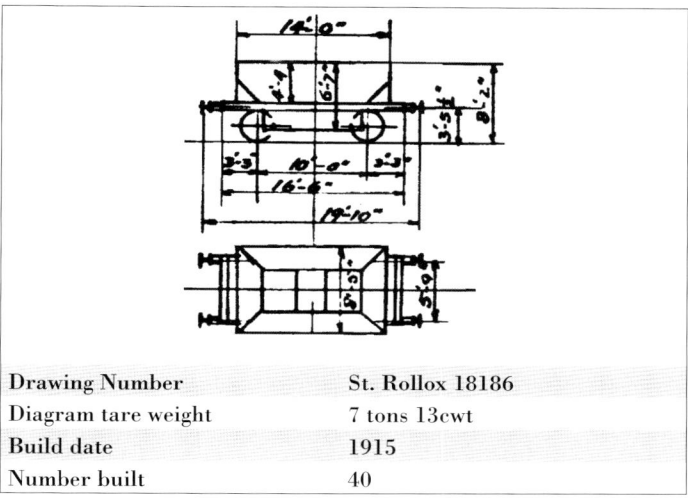

Drawing Number	St. Rollox 18186
Diagram tare weight	7 tons 13cwt
Build date	1915
Number built	40

The renewal programme for the period ending 31st December 1915[19] included authorisation for twenty 16-ton hopper bottom wagons, presumably of this type, but St. Rollox order G372 was for the same number of 10-ton hopper wagons to Diagram 121. This is confirmed by the drawings register book, where General Arrangement 18186 and detail drawings 18159, 18168 and 18177 all refer to a 10-ton steel hopper wagon to order G372.

This was the only small all metal hopper design. The discharge mechanism consisted of *'two longitudinal folding doors on bottom'*, according to Miller. The oil lubricated journals were 9 inches by 4½ inches. The design was first built at St. Rollox in 1916. A Locomotive & Stores Committee minute of 19th October 1915 accepted Hurst Nelson's offer of a further twenty wagons.[20] Presumably these were also treated as renewals. The only known number is 27189.

References
1. NRS BR/CAL/1/8 no entry number
2. RHP 68457
3. NRS BR/CAL/5/11 entry 91
4. NRM 11981/W RHP 70038
5. NRS BR/CAL/1/43 entry 449
6. NRS BR/CAL/1/43 entry 1707
7. NRS BR/CAL/1/45 entry 453
8. NRS BR/CAL/1/48 entry 1099
9. NRS BR/CAL/1/43 entry 1737
10. NRS BR/CAL/1/51 entry 102
11. NRM 11214/W
12. Not yet catalogued
13. NRS BR/CAL/1/56 entry 217
14. NRS BR/CAL/1/59 entry 1252
15. NRS BR/CAL/1/59 entry 1318
16. NRS BR/CAL/1/63 entry 1383
17. NRS BR/CAL/1/61 entry 66
18. NRS BR/CAL/1/65 entry 1041
19. NRS BR/CAL/1/66 entry 568
20. NRS BR/CAL/1/67 entry 396

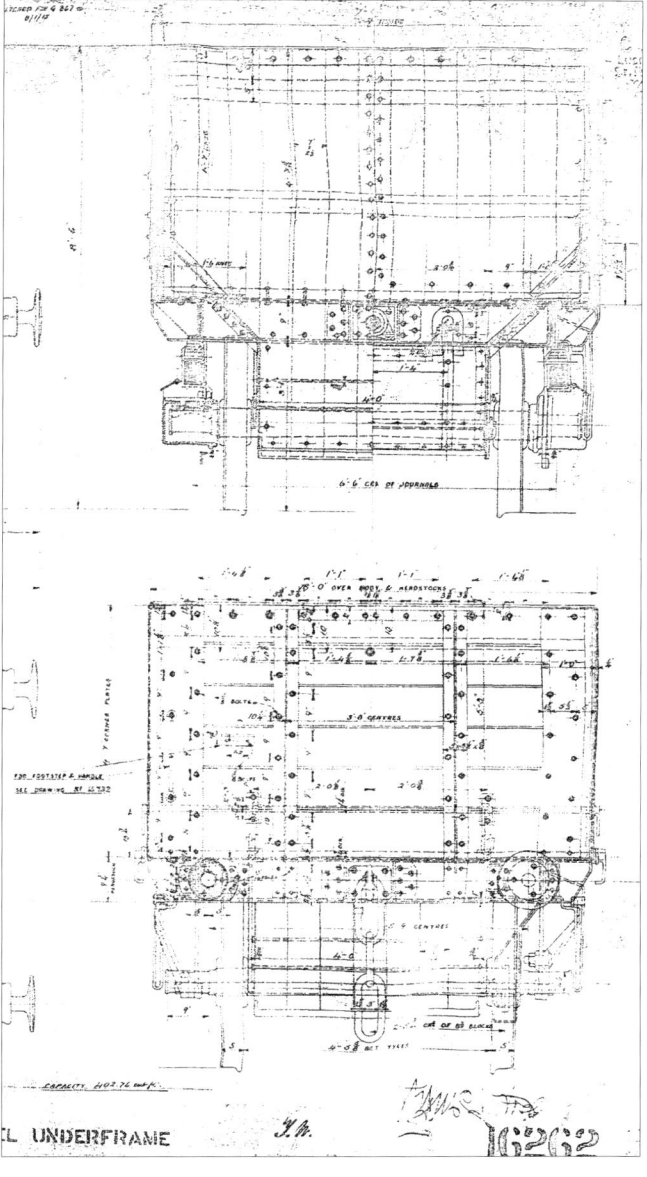

Left and Facing Page: Figure 6.1
The St. Rollox drawing of the Diagram 98 hopper wagon. The Diagram 97 wagons were similar in construction.

ABOVE: Plate 6.4
This early picture at the cattle dock in the Caledonian goods yard at Peebles probably shows a dual purpose sheep or coke wagon on the right. Judging by the medium cattle wagon alongside, it is not long enough to be one of the coke wagons that were converted from large cattle wagons.

BELOW: Figure 6.3
The 1911 St. Rollox drawing 15685 showing the modifications to be made to a Diagram 21 wagon to fit for coke traffic, but only showing the addition of three spars, giving an 8-ton, rather than a 10-ton, capacity. These were the wagons requested by the Alloa Coal Co.

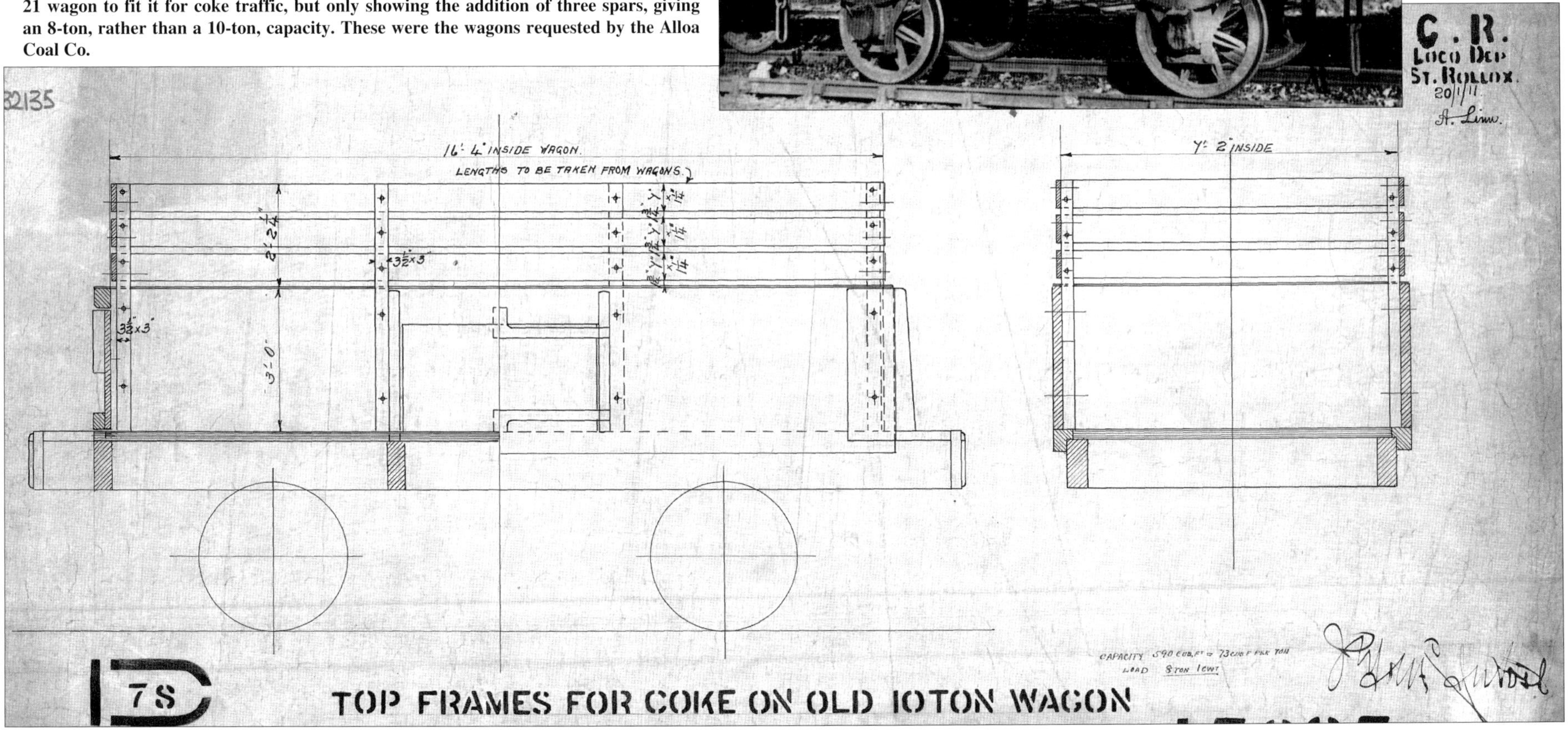

BELOW: Plate 6.5
This photograph shows a Diagram 46 wagon modified to carry coke. The extra bolts to secure the uprights are visible at either side of the doors on the top and bottom planks. It is just possible to see that the bottom end spar had cut-outs to clear the end door pivot hinges, thus allowing continued use of the door. The FOR COKE TRAFFIC lettering is centred in the spaces between the bolts that attach the bottom spar, except for the word TRAFFIC, which is displaced to the left. Converted wagon 58903 was also recorded for posterity.

6.2: Coke

The Pre-Diagram Book Period

Specialised coke wagons were used from the start of the Caledonian's existence. The original fuel for locomotives was coke and in one sense these wagons were the forerunners of the loco coal wagons discussed in Chapter 17. As early as 1848 a minute

'Resolved that the attention of the Goods Manager. be drawn to the propriety of taking steps for immediately cultivating Coke Traffic.'[1]

The early returns show the following significant changes in the stock of coke wagons. In the intervening years the stock remained more or less constant.

Year	1853	1854	1856	1862	1865
Number	52	110	161	144	108

Early St. Rollox drawings for coke wagons were a dual purpose coke and cattle wagon (drawings 193/4), 220, 221 and 339, which was for a wagon with a circular end. All these drawings were pre-1860 but none survive. There were 107 coke wagons in July 1867, but the inventory of November that year records none. They must have been subsumed into the mineral wagon numbers and subsequent returns no longer recorded them as a separate category. It seems that they were replaced as they wore out by non-specialised wagons. A Loco & Stores Committee minute in 1873 stated:

'Wagons to replace Coke Wagons worn out. Replace by Wagons of similar value, Mineral or others.'[2]

One year later a new design for carrying coke also had a dual purpose. St. Rollox drawing 1588[3] of 1874 is for a *'Sheep or coke wagon, spindle buffers, 4ft deep, 16ft inside.'*

The next development in the 1880s was St. Rollox order G23, for 65 medium cattle wagons and (G24) the same number of coke wagons *'to be converted from large cattle wagons.'*

Adaptations to Coal Wagons

Diagram 46 wagons, and the earlier Diagram 22, were adapted to carry coke by fitting 'raves' above the sides to accommodate the load, which occupied a greater volume than the same weight in coal. The raves were three 7-inches wide planks, attached by vertical spars to the inside iron work of the wagon. There is no record of a St. Rollox drawing for the modification.

Numbers recorded in the 1920 traffic book on the Callander & Oban[4] were 11872, 46425, 46479, 58839, 61443, 62204, 63253 and 64356. The second and third numbers suggest that they were Diagram 22 wagons. Number 61443 definitely was to Diagram 22, built by R Y Pickering in 1896.[5]

There were 150 coke wagons in service in 1900, according to the *Register of Wagon Plant*. More were required later. In 1904 a Board minute authorised the alteration of *'100 closed end old loco coal wagons for coke traffic.'*[6] These were no doubt Diagram 21 wagons which had become surplus following the introduction of the bogie coal wagons. This type of wagon had been modified before, because one appears in the background of a photograph in the *1900 Register* – see Plate 6.6 below.

In 1911, a further *'100 10 ton bogie wagons to be fitted with capes for coke traffic'*, following an application from the Alloa Coal Company for additional wagons.[7] As a reminder, 'bogie' was Caledonian terminology for any old solid buffer mineral wagon. They loaded from Bannockburn, where the Alloa Coal Co. was based. The station there had a coke ovens siding.[8]

This modification did merit a drawing – St. Rollox number 15685,[9] dated 21st January 1911. The wagon body and underframe is only sketched, but it shows a Diagram 21 10-ton loco coal wagon. Only three raves are drawn, and a hand-written note gives the capacity as 8 tons, using a density for coke of 73 cubic feet per ton. Photographic

Plate 6.6
This picture shows a Diagram 21 wagon modified for coke traffic. The lower sides compared with those of Diagram 46 required four spars to render the wagon capable of carrying a 10-ton load. It is lettered COKE TRAFFIC ONLY on the left and an indistinguishable destination WHEN EMPTY on the right. It is tempting to interpret the letters as BANNOCKBURN, given that the wagon to the left is from the Alloa Coal Company, and that extra coke wagons of this type were requested for their traffic in 1911 – this picture is an enlargement from the *1900 Register of Wagon Plant*.

evidence shows that four raves were fitted, which allowed the full 10-ton load to be carried.

Possible numbers for the modified wagons were 15650, 23189, 27054 and 35828. They were all recorded in a number taker's book[10] at Panmure in 1911, delivering coke from Bannockburn to Taymouth.

40 Ton Hopper Wagon – Diagram 66

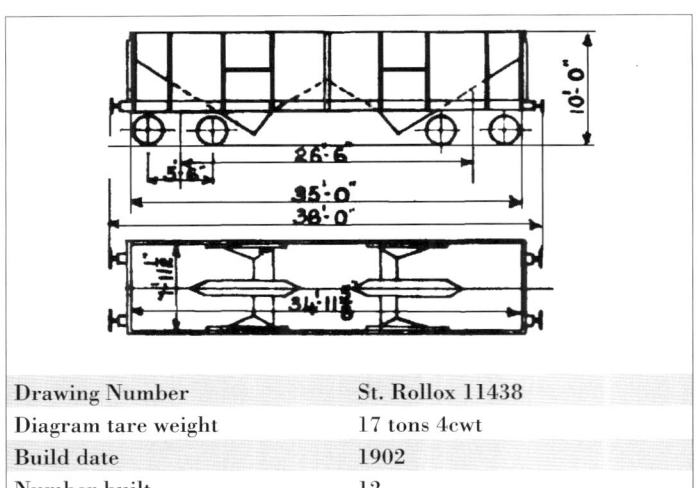

Drawing Number	St. Rollox 11438
Diagram tare weight	17 tons 4cwt
Build date	1902
Number built	12

The original order for Diagram 54 wagons to be built at St. Rollox was for 100, but only seventy were built. Another twelve emerged in 1903 as 40-ton hopper wagons to Diagram 66.[11] The CR numbers were 66219-66230, immediately preceding the block of numbers allocated to the 300 Diagram 54 wagons that were built by contractors.

The underframe was the same as the Diagram 54 wagons, but without the truss rods. The sides were 2 feet higher than the Diagram 54s and there were only two doors on each side. A short ladder was welded to the underframe and body at the left-hand end of each side. The Westinghouse brake was fitted.

Their original purpose was to carry coke from Plean colliery in Stirlingshire to the iron and steel industry in West Cumberland. This was an attempt to break into a new source of traffic according to *The Colliery Guardian*, which stated in 1903 that:

> 'the iron and steel furnaces in Furness and West Cumberland area have previously relied on the South Durham Collieries, whose coal and coke is conveyed, for the most part, in private wagons of the colliery proprietors ... the smaller 10 ton type.'

It looks as if the attempt to cultivate this traffic failed. In 1914 a Traffic Committee minute recorded that the Chief Goods Manager

> 'recommended that the 12 wagons built in 1903 should be reduced in height from 10ft to 8ft 4in, to be suitable for conveyance of fuel from Messrs Wilson & Clyde Coal Coy's Law Collieries to Dalzell Steel Works.'[12]

The modification, which would lower the height to the level of the top of the side doors, reduce the capacity to 30 tons and effectively turn the wagons into hopper versions of Diagram 54, was approved as a revenue expense. The St. Rollox drawing is annotated '*the height has been reduced by 1ft 8¾in*', but only 66223 was recorded as modified among the ten surviving wagons that were renumbered by the LM&SR in 1931.[13]

References

1. NRS BR/CAL/1/8 no entry number
2. NRS BR/CAL/1/21 entry 494
3. Not yet catalogued
4. NRS BR/CAL/5/60
5. R Y Pickering card order 1702
6. NRS BR/CAL/1/50 entry 124
7. NRS BR/CAL/1/59 entry 1254
8. *1915 List of Goods Stations* CRA Archive ref: 3/7/2/9
9. Not yet catalogued
10. The book is privately owned
11. NRS BR/CAL/1/46 entry 1223
12. NRS BR/CAL/1/65 entry 440
13. Information contained in *LMS Diagrams of Bogies used for Heavy Weight and Mineral Wagons*, CRA Archive ref: 3/4/1/24

Above: Plate 6.7
An official photograph of Diagram 66 hopper 66226. The tare weight for once is less than that set out in the diagram book. The load as a percentage of the total wagon weight was the same as that of Diagram 54. A section of angle iron has caused the word WAGON to be written asymmetrically on the side. There is no room for an additional number to be written on the side. It is not known if the number was repeated on the ends, as was the case with the Diagram 54 bogie coal wagons. Behind it is one of the superannuated 7-ton 'bogies' marked with a cross in a circle for traffic on designated sections of the system. This is discussed in Chapter 5.5. The symbol has been painted over the R.

Right: Plates 6.8a and 6.8b
Enlargements of Plate 6.7 to show the hopper operating instructions and perfectly aligned characters on the cast number plate. The paint date is 10/7/03.

6.3: Pig Iron Wagons

Pre-Diagram Book Designs

The carriage of pig iron began very early in the company's existence. A minute in May 1848 records that the price of transporting pig iron from Glasgow to Carlisle had been fixed at 1s 2d (6p) per ton.[1]

Pig iron wagons were not separately identified in the wagon returns; the only firm information consists of a few entries in the minutes. In 1857, 100 wagons were ordered from Ashbury[2] and a further eighty-eight in 1866.[3] Seventeen wagons required renewal in 1869-70,[4] and 250 were required in 1871, again supplied by Ashbury.[5]

Early drawings in the register were probably 222 ('*a truck for iron*'), 470 and 614. All these were prior to 1868. These drawings have not survived, nor has 937, dating from 1870. Drawing number 1396 dates from 1872. According to Miller, it was for a dead buffer 10-ton wagon, 12 feet 6 inches by 6 feet 8½ inches over ends and sides and 1 foot 2 inches deep inside. Sides and ends were fixed. The permitted load was said to be 10 tons, but photographic evidence contradicts that.

Pig Iron Wagon (8 and 14 Tons) – Diagram 16

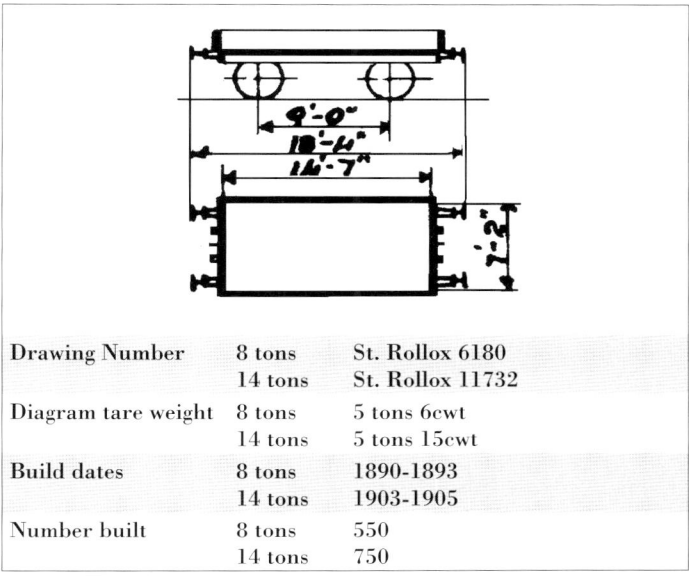

Drawing Number	8 tons	St. Rollox 6180
	14 tons	St. Rollox 11732
Diagram tare weight	8 tons	5 tons 6cwt
	14 tons	5 tons 15cwt
Build dates	8 tons	1890-1893
	14 tons	1903-1905
Number built	8 tons	550
	14 tons	750

Built to Diagram 16, the pig iron wagons used the same underframe as Diagrams 15 and 24 open goods wagons. An earlier drawing which has not survived (6148 of July 1889) specifically stated that

Plate 6.9
Loading pig iron. Pig iron's density was 450lbs per cubic foot, so a great deal of physical effort was involved. The new-looking wagons are more examples of the 1872 design. There is a good view of the solid buffer style of horse hook attached to the nearer wagon. This type of wagon would have been replaced in the twentieth century by wagons to Diagrams 16 or 110.

Plate 6.10
Six-ton pig iron wagon 12853 with piles of locomotive tyres in the background, built to drawing 1396. The underframe was 'similar to swivel wagon'. The running gear is also similar to the contemporary mineral wagons, with 3-foot 2-inch springs.

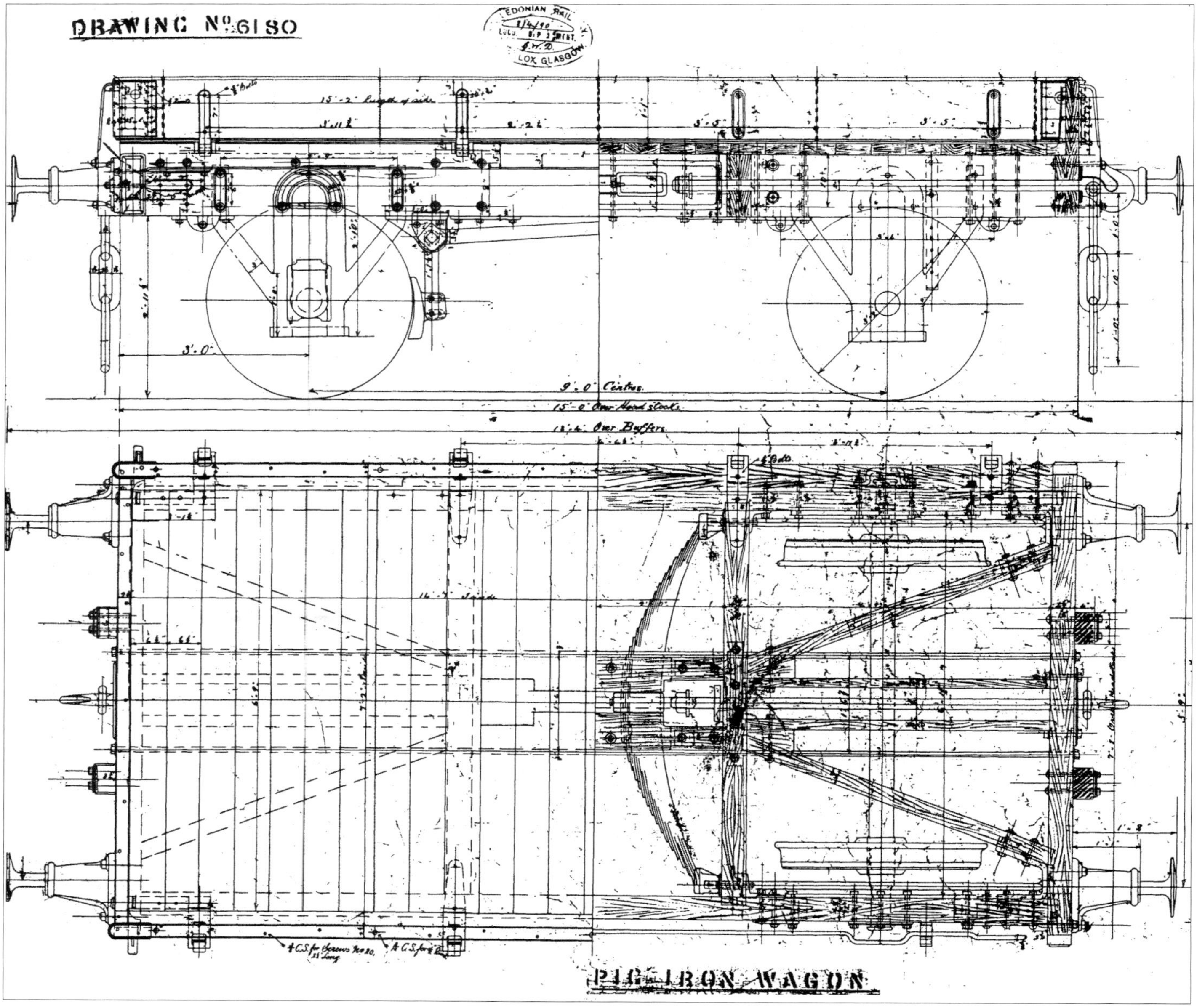

BELOW: **Figure 6.2**
St. Rollox drawing 6180 for the first sprung buffer pig iron wagon to Diagram 16.

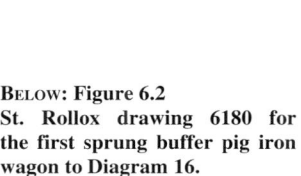

Plate 6.11
A Diagram 16 wagon rated at 8 tons. It has a single iron brake block and the standard Drummond wagon buffer. The lettering and load are positioned in the centre of the single-plank body.

Plate 6.12
This Diagram 16 example is rated at 12 tons. It has twelve leaf springs and larger axlebox journals than the 8-ton wagon in Plate 6.11. It has the Morton brake on one side only, and is fitted with self-contained buffers. The words PIG IRON and the load are written on the curb rail. The two-plank body construction is a variation from the norm.

the design was based on an altered goods wagon. The single plank falling side was 13 inches high. The ends were fixed.

The official capacity was 8 or 14 tons, suggesting that larger axlebox journals were fitted to the 14-ton version. Drawing 11732, dated 21st November 1902, gave the load as 10 tons.[6] The first order for the higher capacity wagon was G203 on the evidence of this drawing. Two further orders of 300 and 250 wagons were built at St. Rollox in 1903-1904.[7] The design was superseded by Diagram 85 in 1906.

In 1906 a drawing was issued detailing *'addition to the sides and ends of pig iron wagons.'*[8] Two 6½-inch planks doubled the body height, giving the cubic capacity of a standard open goods wagon. The planks were attached by 4-inch by 3-inch oak stanchions inside and out, which disabled the falling sides. The forty wagons replaced by Diagram 85 may have been modified. There is no record in the minutes, or a photograph.

15 Ton Pig Iron Wagon – Diagram 85

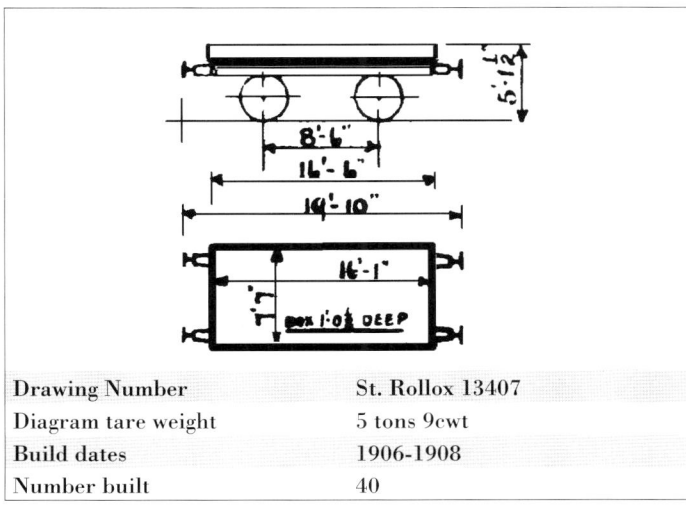

Drawing Number	St. Rollox 13407
Diagram tare weight	5 tons 9cwt
Build dates	1906-1908
Number built	40

The Diagram 85 wagons were the first steel underframe pig iron wagons. They used the same underframe as the Diagram 59 mineral wagons, which had been introduced two years earlier. They had falling sides and fixed ends, like all the modern pig iron wagons.

They were authorised in the rolling stock renewal programme for the half year ending 31st July 1906.[9] They were fitted with Leeds

Forge pressed steel underframes as shown in Plate 6.13. A Loco & Stores Committee authorised the purchase of forty frames at £18 10s each.[10] Wagon number 12910 was also photographed.

16 Ton Pig Iron Wagon – Diagram 110

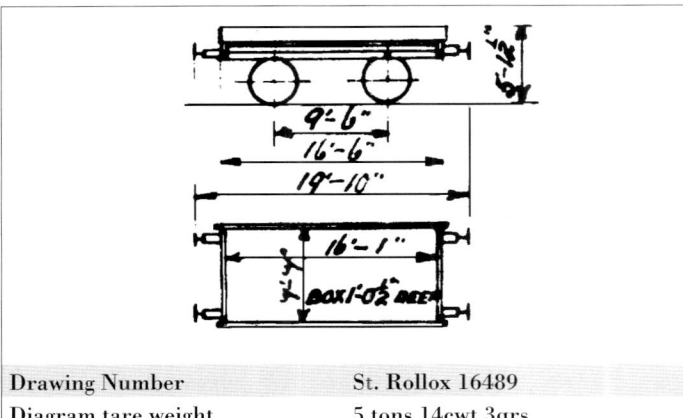

Drawing Number	St. Rollox 16489
Diagram tare weight	5 tons 14cwt 3qrs
Build date	1912
Number built	520

Diagram 110 wagons had similar bodies to Diagram 85, but a 1 foot longer wheelbase and bigger axle journals allowed a 1 ton greater load with less than 6cwt increase in tare weight. The drawing shows Iracier axleboxes. They were originally authorised as 15-ton wagons,[11] but, when tenders for 300 wagons were accepted from Pickering and Hurst Nelson, the stated capacity was 16 tons.[12]

Two months later, the order was increased by 100, equally shared between the contractors.[13] Numbers from the Pickering order were in the range from 27015-34649.

Like the Diagram 59 wagons, a wooden underframe version was built in 1916,[14] to drawing number 18733.[15] This order for 120 wagons was given St. Rollox order G385, but the wagons were actually built by Hurst Nelson. These wagons were fitted with heavy duty grease axleboxes.

At the same time as the wooden underframe wagons were built, Leeds Forge produced a version of their patent underframe for these wagons, which combined solebar and side rail in one pressed steel section.[16] The records do not show whether any wagons were built using these components.

References
1. NRS BR/CAL/1/8 no entry number
2. NRS BR/CAL/1/11 entry 1058
3. NRS BR/CAL/1/14 entry 1421
4. NRS BR/CAL/1/17 entry 1503, NRS BR/CAL/1/18 entry 562
5. NRS BR/CAL/1/19 entry 1314
6. NRM 11932/W
7. NRS BR/CAL/1/47 entry 464, NRS BR/CAL/1/47 entry 1127
8. St. Rollox 13972, NRM 11930/W
9. NRS BR/CAL/1/51 entry 1131
10. NRS BR/CAL/5/12 entry 190
11. NRS BR/CAL/1/62 entry 133
12. NRS BR/CAL/1/62 entries 148 and 225
13. NRS BR/CAL/1/62 entry 468
14. St. Rollox order G393
15. NRM 11915/W
16. Drawing dated 21/11/1916, in the HMRS collection, reference 12746

RIGHT: Plate 6.13
This photograph depicts a Diagram 85 wagon in LM&SR days. Note the angle brackets supporting the floor under the two inboard side hinges. Pig iron was an extremely heavy commodity which could easily distort or break a floor which significantly overhung the solebar. This feature was common to all modern pig iron designs.

LEFT: Plate 6.14
The last design of pig iron wagon, to Diagram 110. It was one of eight despatched by Pickering on 20th February 1913 to complete an order of 200. The cost was £99 17s 6d each. The wagon is fitted with the Morton brake and Iracier axleboxes. The weight of the strokes on the R of the 12-inch company initials is much lighter than the C, which is a true circle. The tare, which is in three figures, and the load lettering are on the body, rather than the curb rail as in the example in Plate 6.15.

RIGHT: Plate 6.15
A wooden frame Diagram 110 wagon, built by Hurst Nelson. It has been suggested that this order originated in 1912, but it seems more plausible to date it to 1916, when order G385, originally intended to be built in-house, was sub-contracted to Hurst Nelson. This was the year that construction of wood underframe Diagram 59 wagons also began because of steel shortages.

Chapter 7
Private Traders' Wagons

7.1: Wagons Owned by Private Traders

Private traders' wagons played a vital part in transporting the mineral traffic carried by the Caledonian Railway. The associated loading and unloading infrastructure influenced the dimensions, design and size of the company's own wagon fleet, as was discussed in Chapter 5. The first two sections of this chapter deal with the Caley's relationship with private traders and their wagon stock. The final section deals with the construction and hire of tank wagon underframes for use by private traders.

Like most railway companies, the Caledonian had an uneasy relationship with the private traders who ran their wagons over the system. The one advantage – that the traders invested their money in part of the wagon fleet rather than the railway company – was outweighed by a number of disadvantages. The first concerned maintenance.

Enforcing Maintenance and Construction Standards

Inadequate maintenance was a serious problem until enforced by regulation. At Penistone in 1885 the axle of a private trader wagon fractured. The subsequent derailment wrecked several coaches of an excursion train that was passing in the other direction. There was one fatality and numerous injuries.[1] The accident led the Railway Clearing House to draw up detailed technical standards for all aspects of wagon construction. The standards came into force in 1887.

Despite the improved mechanical specification, the failure rate of private traders' wagons was still higher than those owned by the railway companies. These incidents caused, at the very least, considerable disruption to traffic. The 1902 *Railway Engineer* article on high capacity wagons, quoted in Chapter 5, pointed out a disproportionately high rate of wagon tyre failure attributable to private owners' wagons, even after the issue of a more stringent specification in 1899.

The 1899 specification had tried to address the maintenance problem by introducing an inspection system for traders' wagons. The wagon design had to be accepted by the railway company over which the wagon was to run. A cast registration plate was fitted to the wagon's solebars. Regular maintenance and a general overhaul every seven years were conditions of registration.

Maintenance and repairs were usually the responsibility of the wagon builder. The Caledonian regularly issued lists of traders who had permission to run wagons over the system, and who should be informed if repairs were needed.[2]

The Clearing House specifications encouraged very robust construction, leading to a high tare weight compared to wagon capacity. It was not unusual for a trader's 8-ton capacity wagon to have a tare weight which approached 6 tons. An equivalent CR Diagram 22 wagon's tare weight was as low as 5 tons 6cwt. This problem was addressed in a further Railway Clearing House specification in 1903.[3] The tare weight of 10-ton wagons was not to exceed 6 tons 2cwt, and that of 12-ton wagons should not exceed 6 tons 12cwt. This was a timely intervention; there are photographs dating from the early 1900s of Pickering-built 10-ton wagons weighing over 6½ tons and some 12-ton wagons weighing over 7 tons. The mechanical specifications of wagons, such as the strength of headstocks and drawgear, were also upgraded at the same time.

Inefficient Working and Congestion

Private traders' wagons were only used for their owners' traffic. This guaranteed 50 per cent empty working and the time-consuming necessity to split and re-marshal trains of wagons for return to their point of origin. A side effect of excess shunting was the increase of wear to wagons. The shocks of shunting were much more injurious than ordinary running. These problems, and the difficulties described below, were a major bone of contention in the demurrage dispute of 1910. By this time, the number of traders' wagons running on the CR was equal to the number of company wagons – see later in this section. Some of the dispute proceedings are in the Caledonian Railway Association Archive.[4]

At the dispute hearing, the L&NWR representative gave evidence that all railway companies tried to return 'foreign' (other company) wagons loaded to the parent system. The L&NWR currently returned about one third of wagons with a load. Exhaustive calculations were put forward by various railway companies to show the excess hours of shunting caused by splitting trains composed wholly or partly of traders' wagons.

Secondly, in the view of the railway officials at the hearing, coalmasters used wagons as mobile stores. Wagons were filled with

---

ABOVE: Plates 7.1-7.3
Three examples of private traders' wagon registration plates, courtesy of Michael Dunn. They show three different ways of identifying the registering railway company. The 40-ton example may have been attached to a bogie tank wagon. According to a return in 1909, there were nine 40-ton wagons registered on the CR.

coal, but were not immediately dispatched to their destination. Guy Calthrop, the CR representative at the hearing, stated that circulars had been issued periodically since 1868 about *'the undue retention of company wagons by traders.'* He went on to say that in 1908 7,500 wagons were standing under load for longer than three days. After issuing a further circular, this had reduced to between 1,500 and 2,000 wagons. There had been 500-600 wagons standing under load for between twenty-one and sixty-five days. After the circular was issued, this reduced to fifty. The inference was that the traders were to blame.

A variation of the use of wagons as mobile stores concerned the practice of 'staging forward'. This relieved congestion at pits, but only moved the loaded wagon part way to its final destination. Calthrop gave as an example the traffic from James Dunlop & Co.'s Carmyle pit to Queen's Dock on the north bank of the Clyde. Wagons were used as stores for up to three months until the coal was sold. This caused congestion in marshalling yards to the detriment of all traffic.

Calthrop stated that the Caledonian had tried to address this problem in 1880. A circular was issued stating that company wagons must not be used for storage. The traders must provide their own wagons for the purpose, but they could not be kept in CR sidings. The coalmasters had counterclaimed for failure on the company's part to provide sufficient wagons.

The Caledonian now wished to charge the equivalent of siding rent for the use of wagons as mobile storage, at the rate of 1s 6d per day for a company wagon and 6d per day for a trader's wagon. The charge would come into effect after the wagon had been loaded for two days. This had already been put into practice, but Calthrop admitted that *'we have not recovered from a single trader one of these charges as yet.'*

All these complaints were, of course, contested by the traders. They said that there was no room to accommodate storage for coal other than in wagons. Double handling would break coal up, and open air storage would cause it to deteriorate.

The problem of delays in unloading shipment and bunker coal was usually not of the traders' making. The railway companies were informed that a ship was 'open for loading' in advance of its actual arrival. Arrangements were then made to transport the coal so that it could be loaded with the least delay. In fact, ships were often delayed through weather and mechanical mishaps. The practice at the quayside was to load the first ship that arrived, even though it had in effect 'jumped the queue'.

The Coltness Iron Co., a major customer of the Caledonian, turned one of the company's complaints against itself. The Coltness representative stated that the CR regularly sent loaded wagons before the contents were actually required, creating the very operational inefficiency that it complained of.

The last development that impacted on operational efficiency from the railway companies' point of view was the new practice of sorting coal into different types according to size. Loads were originally of two types – 'coal' and 'dross'. Since about 1900 washing and separating plants had been installed at pits. Loads were now divided into coal and nuts, which were further subdivided into trebles, doubles, singles, etc. The railway companies said that this was a source of delay. Each type required its own wagon and could not be mixed.

The traders did not reply to this complaint. From the writer's perspective, the railway companies' objection seems unfounded. The customer had developed a new way of working, and the railway company as a common carrier would have to adapt to its customers' needs. If that involved a change in operational practice, so be it.

Attempts to Eliminate Traders' Wagons

The Caledonian was not unusual in having a large number of private traders' wagons registered to run on its system. Given the rapid expansion in traffic when new collieries were opened in the 1860s and '70s, the company would have risked over-capitalisation if it had built all the wagons itself.

Of the problems outlined above, the major difficulty identified by the company was re-marshalling. In the half-yearly report to shareholders for the period ending January 1871, the Directors reported on steps that had been taken during the previous year to take control of all the wagons running on the system:

'The [use of traders wagons] worked tolerably well so long as the trade was in the hands of a comparatively small number of iron and coal masters, each of whose traffic was sufficient for full train loads; but, as the traders increased and with them the number of wagons, the sidings and depots became so overcrowded with wagons requiring continual shunting and marshalling – those of each individual owner, however few, having to be separated from the others, and forwarded, loaded or unloaded, from and to the different pits – that it was only with difficulty the traffic could be kept moving. If all were under the control of the Company, to be used according to the exigencies of the service, a larger traffic, conducted much more easily and economically than hitherto, would be developed and accommodated, to the mutual advantage of the Company and of the Traders.'

In early 1870 the Caledonian Board had received a letter *'urging that the Company should themselves own all the wagons on their line.'*[5] In May there were complaints about lack of mineral wagons. Five hundred were recommended for purchase immediately and *'an arrangement be made if possible for the purchase of all the wagons belonging to the Traders on the line.'*[6]

In October the Board sanctioned a Committee on Traders' Wagons *'to consider and report on a suggestion that the wagons be bought up by a Joint Stock Company in order to their being employed on the Caledonian.'*[7]

Within two days the Committee reported back[8] with a list of the rate abatements traders received for carrying goods in their own wagons and a list of traders owning wagons. In some cases the Caledonian was under an obligation to use its own wagon stock. The Committee were

'in favour of some arrangement being made for the Company obtaining, if not at once the property, at least the possession and control of the wagons and their ultimate absolute property.'

One complication was that some traders did not technically own their wagons. The Committee reported on an interview with a director of the Scottish Wagon Company which provided wagons under 'purchase lease' (hire purchase) arrangements. The Wagon Company *'might be able to advance the [Caledonian] the necessary amount to take up the wagons from the traders.'* The Committee was instructed to see if they could get a better deal elsewhere.[9]

On 1st November the Board of Directors authorised the Committee

'to endeavour to arrange for the purchase of the wagons, the property of the Traders, and to transact for the necessary money accommodation – also to arrange for the acquisition of the wagons on the line leased by Traders from Wagon Companies and the Manager was instructed as far as possible to prevent additional Traders Wagons being put on the line.'[10]

A meeting was held the next day with traders who were willing to negotiate the sale of their wagons. After a further meeting in the following week, the Committee (now renamed the Wagon Purchase Committee) was given the remit to purchase as many wagons as it could.[11]

At that point there were over 17,000 traders' wagons running exclusively on the Caledonian or on the CR and North British.[12] This prompted the resolution that the company should go to Parliament to raise the money to buy wagons 'say £600,000 in stocks and shares, £200,000 by borrowing.'[13]

Some traders were willing to sell their stock immediately. A Mr Simpson offered 300 wagons at £40 each. At the same time, Hamilton and McCulloch offered their fleet of about 700 wagons, without naming a price. It was agreed that the wagons should be inspected and bought

'if the price is considered fair. If considered too high have the price of the wagons settled by reference.'[14]

In early December a circular was sent to all traders outlining the Caledonian Board's intentions to purchase their wagons, coupled with a request that no additional traders' wagons should be placed on the line.[15] A copy of the letter is shown in Plate 7.4.

The offer was partially successful; the 1874 wagon census reported that 12,000 wagons had been taken over, which would have left 7,700 still in private hands. However, the rolling stock return for January 1872 does not record a transfer of wagons, stating *'plant taken over from traders is not included.'* The July 1872 return states that 6,772 traders' wagons were transferred. This tallies with the reduction in traders wagons between 1870 and 1875 in the table at the foot of the page.

The Caledonian tried to maintain the momentum of sales. In March 1873 the Traffic Committee asked the Board to consider:[16]

'1st whether the present allowance to Traders for providing wagons shall continue, or be reduced say to an 1/8th of a penny per ton mile.
2nd whether the Traders who have not sold their wagons to the Company shall be bound to accept this allowance or sell their wagons at a price to be mutually agreed upon, or, failing agreement to be settled by arbitration.'

The decision was postponed, but the next month it was agreed to adopt the English Companies' rate of ⅛th of a penny.[17] Then the wagon purchase policy was compromised. Instructions were sought in September 1873 about the continued supply of mineral wagons to traders. The Board replied that traders could continue to supply their own wagons at the reduced allowance.[18]

To compensate for the ban on further traders' wagons on the system, the Caledonian had stated in the December 1870 letter that *'an ample supply of new Plant is being provided by the Company.'* The company was as good as its word. The returns between 1871 and 1874 show that 6,838 new mineral wagons were added to the Caledonian fleet.

These efforts were not enough. Wagons continued to be in short supply. Only ninety-eight wagons were added in 1875. Traders convened a meeting about the problem in December 1875,[19] and further complaints were made in November 1877. This complaint prompted the Glasgow Committee to seek estimates for 2,000 additional mineral wagons.[20]

Earlier in the year, Merry & Cunningham had threatened to withdraw 750 wagons from service and the Glasgow Committee laid contingency plans to purchase 1,000 wagons.[21] Merry & Cunningham's wagons were eventually sold to the Caledonian at £37

10s each.[22] The rolling stock returns show that over 8,600 mineral wagons were added to stock in between 1876 and 1878. Two thousand wagons were also replaced during this period.

INFRASTRUCTURE IMPLICATIONS

In early 1872, the company formally identified the need to build new workshops to repair the increased stock of wagons. The Caley had found itself short of repair capacity in 1870, when the lack of serviceable wagons had forced an approach to the L&NWR for 200

Caledonian Railway Company.

SECRETARY'S OFFICE,
Glasgow, 10th Dec., 1870.

DEAR SIR,

The Directors being satisfied that the working of the Railway would be facilitated, and the Traders be benefited, if all the Wagons employed in the conduct of the Mineral Traffic were the property of the Company, I am instructed to inform you that they are prepared to treat with you, if you are so disposed, for the purchase of the Wagons owned by you, at a valuation to be mutually agreed on; or, if you prefer it, at a price to be fixed by arbitration, the Wagons being valued as the stock of a going concern.

The Directors are also prepared to acquire Wagons which may be on the Line under purchase leases, provided the terms are not too onerous.

In order to the attainment of the object in view with as little delay as possible, I am directed to request that no additional "Traders' Wagons" may be placed on the Line; but, that the Trade may not suffer inconvenience by this condition, an ample supply of new Plant is being provided by the Company.

Until a sufficient number of "Traders' Wagons" shall have been acquired to admit of their use for the Traffic generally, without detriment to the interests of the Traders from whom they have been purchased, the Directors will secure to the Traders individually a supply equivalent to the number each may have made over to the Company.

I am,
Yours faithfully,
ARCH. GIBSON,
Secretary.

Plate 7.4
The letter sent by the CR to coalmasters in December 1870, also courtesy of Michael Dunn. The company only partially achieved its aim of eliminating traders' wagons from the system.

	1867	1870	1875	1880	1885	1890	1895	1900	1905	1910
Caledonian Mineral Stock	6,673	7,160	21,068	22,866	25,515	27,253	32,273	35,929	38,361	31,088
Traders CR Only					9,330	13,115	15,349	18,266	23,588	24,839
Traders CR and Other Lines					3,266	5,773	4,493	5,480	4,935	6,514
Traders Total	9,571	17,127	10,460	12,576	12,596	18,888	17,948	23,746	28,523	31,353

wagons on loan. The Glasgow Directors instructed Benjamin Conner to:

> 'report without delay on the number of the Company's wagons waiting repair distinguishing as far as he can those wanting heavy repair from those wanting slight repair.'

It was also to be suggested to Mr Conner that *'if he cannot at once overtake the repairs, some of the Plant wanting repairs might be sent to Mr Pickering.'*[23]

Conner contracted the repairs to Pickering and Faulds. The Permanent Way & Traffic Committee noted this and recommended:

> 'that additional accommodation be got without delay so as to allow more repairing to be done by the Company.'[24]

In June 1871 John Watson offered to sell his wagon repair workshops at Motherwell. The asking price was far higher than the valuation. It was agreed to negotiate, providing a satisfactory agreement could be reached on the purchase of his wagon fleet.[25] Watson accepted a conditional offer for the works and to *'give his 700 wagons at £31,171 10s, the Company's valuation being £773 1s below the price put on them by him.'*[26]

It took until the end of August 1872 to finalise the deal with Watson.[27] In the meantime, the Traffic Committee accepted tenders for wagon repair workshops at Lesmahagow Junction[28] and Perth[29] at a cost of £2,158 and £1,095 respectively.

A further difficulty at this time was the lack of skilled labour. In April 1872, the Traffic Committee received a report that *'these men cannot be got and that the English companies are in the same position.'*[30]

Number of Traders' Wagons on the Caledonian

The drive to eliminate traders' wagons from the system was only partly successful, and only for a short period of time. Even after the purchases, which were recorded in the half year ending July 1872, there were half as many traders' wagons as Caledonian minerals. The number of traders' wagons began to increase steadily again from 1885 to 1890.

Following a reduction in numbers when the Caley made further purchases, the increase in traders wagons resumed until, by 1910, the number of traders' and Caledonian's wagons was almost exactly equal. The CR mineral stock decreased sharply between 1905 and 1910, as a result of the withdrawal of the old 'bogie' wagons.

The table on the previous page shows the number of private trader wagons compared with the number of Caledonian Railway mineral wagons. Up to 1885, traders registered solely by the Caledonian were not identified separately. The Caledonian figures for 1872 and 1890 include wagons acquired from traders (6,772 in 1872 and 1,313 in 1890). The purchases are reflected in the reduction in the traders' totals for those years.

Caledonian Wagon Designs Used by Traders

As previously mentioned, the design of wagon used by traders had to be approved before registration for traffic. Anticipating the Railway Clearing House specification in 1887, in the January St. Rollox produced drawings covering the general arrangement of an acceptable wagon (number 5491) and the recommended designs for ironwork and brake gear (5492-95). The drawings were based on the then standard Diagram 22 solid buffered mineral wagon. McCorquodale & Co. published them commercially for traders and outside wagon builders.

The design was adopted as the standard by a number of colliery owners, including those who owned the old wagons which became part of the thirling arrangements discussed in the next section.

In 1889 the Railway Clearing House recommended that the construction of solid buffered wagons should be discontinued, but allowed railway companies and traders to carry on with their construction after protests. The Caledonian ceased to build solid buffered mineral wagons in the mid 1890s. In 1900 St. Rollox issued drawing 10284 for private traders for the alteration of this type of wagon from solid to sprung buffers. The drawing has not survived.

References

1. http://www.railwaysarchive.co.uk/eventsummary.php?eventID=5306
2. For example, *Caledonian Railway Mineral Timetable 1904*, pp. 47-49, CRA Archive ref: 3/1/5/2
3. Quoted in 'The New Regulations for Private Owners' Wagons', by an anonymous private owner, in *The Railway Magazine*, October 1903 issue
4. CRA Archive refs: 2/2/2/17-20
5. NRS BR/CAL/1/18 entry 496
6. NRS BR/CAL/1/18 entry 678
7. NRS BR/CAL/1/18 entry 1333
8. NRS BR/CAL/1/18 entry 1339
9. NRS BR/CAL/1/18 entry 1340
10. NRS BR/CAL/1/18 entry 1401
11. NRS BR/CAL/1/18 entry 1451
12. In NRS BR/CAL/4/134
13. NRS BR/CAL/1/18 entry 1451
14. NRS BR/CAL/1/18 entry 1466
15. NRS BR/CAL/1/18 entry 1539
16. NRS BR/CAL/1/20 entry 1207
17. NRS BR/CAL/1/20 entry 1437
18. NRS BR/CAL/1/20 entry 1857
19. NRS BR/CAL/1/22 entry 1653
20. NRS BR/CAL/1/23 entry 642
21. NRS BR/CAL/1/23 entry 957
22. NRS BR/CAL/1/23 entry 1087
23. NRS BR/CAL/1/18 entry 203
24. NRS BR/CAL/1/18 entry 461
25. NRS BR/CAL/1/19 entry 594
26. NRS BR/CAL/1/19 entry 717
27. NRS BR/CAL/1/20 entry 377
28. NRS BR/CAL/1/20 entry 123
29. NRS BR/CAL/1/20 entry 348
30. NRS BR/CAL/1/19 entry 1751

Facing Page: Plate 7.5
A wagon to the Diagram 22 design as built for a private trader, with vertically-planked doors and simplified end door framing. This example was built by R Y Pickering for Archibald Russell Ltd. The paint date on the solebar reads 18/5/99. The livery was described in the card order as *'brown oxide, white letters shaded black. Top plank vermilion.'* Close examination reveals that the top plank was not completely vermilion, only the part covered by lettering.

Left: Plate 7.6
An enlargement of the Archibald Russell wagon in Plate 7.5, which shows the plate recording registration with the Caledonian. This version has the company name in full. The registration date is 1899 and the registration number is 10995. Also visible is the brake pivot plate that the Caley recommended for contractor-built wagons.

7.2: Thirled Wagons

According to an article in *Railway Archive*[1] which was based on primary sources, the practice of thirling originated on the North British Railway in 1887. The NBR purchased nearly 6,000 wagons from traders, and then assigned them exclusively to the trader's traffic.

The thirling agreement's main purpose was to prevent the threat of competition for traffic by the Caledonian around New Monkland. As the reader will remember from Chapter 2, this area was rich in coal and blackband iron ore deposits. Thirling ensured that, where more than one railway company might carry a load, the wagons were exclusively to be moved by the railway company signing the agreement. A by-product of the agreement was that it ensured that the wagons were maintained to railway company standards.

The Caledonian retaliated by entering thirling agreements with some coalmasters in the Lanarkshire coalfield. The arrangements were made in the early 1890s and were to last for twenty-one years.[2] This was the last development in thirling; the general managers of the North British and Caledonian agreed not to enter any more arrangements with effect from March 1892. Presumably the agreement with the Clyde Coal Company which is shown in the table on the next page was already under negotiation.

Details of the Thirling Agreement

The following extract from the agreement with John Watson covers the salient points of the relationship. The first party was the Caledonian Railway; the second party was Watson. The CR General Manager reported in July 1890 that the agreement had been signed.[3]

'The first party shall, with all reasonable despatch, provide and thereafter maintain and renew at their own expense not less than 750 eight-ton coal wagons, that is to say, 500 during this season, or by 31st December, 1890, and the remaining 250 in the following spring, or by 31st March, 1891, which wagons shall, during the subsistence of this Agreement, be appropriated to and used or employed by the parties hereto exclusively for the traffic of the second party's collieries at Eddlewood, aforesaid, and at Earnock on the first party's Railway, consigned by the second party on and by the first party's Railways, and shall not be used or employed for any other traffic than that of the second party on or via the first party's Railways.

The said wagons shall be the exclusive and absolute property of the first party, and shall at all times be maintained and renewed by them, and shall bear their ordinary nameplate, and shall also be marked as follows, vizt., John Watson's Eddlewood and Earnock Collieries.'

The Wagons Involved

Eight coal companies entered thirling arrangements with the Caledonian. The CR numbers of 4,371 wagons and their dedicated users are shown in the table overleaf. The numbers allocated to these wagons occupied two large blocks from 51725-54124 and 57200-58670, plus 56500-56999. These numbers indicate that they were charged to the capital account.

The 900 old wagons in the table overleaf were taken over by the Caledonian from the coal companies. The new wagons were all built by the Caley except for one batch of 200 from Pickering. The CR numbers were 52825-53024, originally Cadzow Coal numbers 500-699, but probably taken over by the CR as soon as they were built.

Owner	Built		Numbers
Bent Colliery Co.	5/91-6/92	New	53525-53824
		Old	53825-54124
		New	58371-58470
Cadzow Coal Co.	4/91-5/93	Old	53225-53524
		New	52725-53224
Clyde Coal Co.	3/92-9/92	New	58471-58670
		New	56500-56999
James Dunlop & Co.	12/91-6/94	New	57400-57899
Flemington Coal Co.	11/91-3/92	New	57900-57999
		Old	57200-57399
Kerr & Mitchell	4/91-4/93	Old	58175-58270
		New	58271-58370
John Watson Ltd	9/90-12/91	New	51725-52724
Wishaw Coal Co.	12/91-1/92	New	58000-58174

Solid buffered wagons to Diagram 22 predominated, with the exception of the 800 wagons numbered 57400-57999, 58271-58370 and 58371-58470, all of which were built to Diagram 46, the sprung buffered development of Diagram 22. Random numbers, mostly in the 50XXX series, were allocated to a further 749 wagons, making 5,120 wagons in total.

When the thirling arrangements reached their expiry date, John Watson Ltd threatened legal action over a claim to purchase the 1,000 thirled wagons from the Caledonian. The Board of Directors wrote to Watson, stating their willingness to facilitate settlement.[4] The remaining parties to the thirling agreements seem to have handed the rights to their wagons back to the Caledonian.

References
1. 'Scottish Traders' Wagons', by Ed McKenna, in *Railway Archive*, issue 34
2. Documentation on the Caledonian's involvement with thirling, including copies of contracts, is included in the 1910 *Miscellaneous Statements*. NRS BR/CAL/4/134
3. NRS BR/CAL/1/33 entry 1741
4. NRS BR/CAL/1/60 entry 1106

ABOVE: Plate 7.7
This photograph, part of a picture taken at Perth mineral depot, shows one of the 1,000 Diagram 22 design wagons thirled to John Watson Ltd. Comparison with the Diagram 22 mineral in Caledonian livery to its left shows that the CR lettering remained in its usual position. JOHN WATSON LTD was added to the top and EARNOCK lettering to the bottom planks.

Plate 7.8
No photographs of a private trader's tank mounted on a CR underframe have come to light, but this is a typical example of a wood underframe tank wagon, built by Pickering in 1896 and registered with the Caledonian. The wheels have discs over the front of the spokes to prevent shunters from immobilising the wagon by 'spragging', that is, jamming the spokes with a piece of wood.

7.3: Tank Wagons

Chemical manufacturers and oil refiners normally bought tank wagons from established wagon builders. For instance, the Oakbank Oil Co. and Youngs Oil Co. had fleets of wagons of varying capacities, built by Pickering over a number of years. Hurst Nelson also built a considerable number of tanks.

A variation of this approach was for the private trader to commission a tank from a wagon builder and mount it on an underframe provided by a railway company. The Caledonian offered this facility, as did the Glasgow & South Western. Registration with the railway company was necessary, as with all private traders' wagons.

Between 1862 and 1867 the Caledonian owned four and then eight vitriol tanks, according to the rolling stock returns. It is possible that these wagons were sold to Charles Tennant & Co., whose chemical works was at St. Rollox.

Caledonian Construction of Tank Frames

The first mentions of this arrangement are late in 1896 and early 1897 when the St. Rollox order register records underframes built for the United Alkali Co., Charles Tennant, Robinson & Hunter and Alex Cross & Sons. Details of all the orders are included in Appendix II.

The underframes remained the property of the Caledonian and were hired out to the user on an annual rental. In 1896 the charge per annum was £2 10s.[1] The charge was the same in 1900.[2] By 1914 it had risen to £3 10s for a wood underframe and £4 10s for steel.[3]

In June 1902, 28 tank wagons belonging to James Ross & Co. were taken over by the Caley.[4] They are not recorded as additions in the rolling stock returns. Six numbers of James Ross tanks are known from the *1907 Working Timetable*: 449, 1696, 3943, 7287, 8534 and 71689.[5] The Callander & Oban traffic records of 1920 mention seven tar tanks: 61, 112, 462 and 720 from Grangemouth, 34 and 146 from Camelon and 142 from Falkirk.[6] Presumably these too were part of the James Ross fleet. It is not clear whether the numbers refer to the frames or to the tanks.

The rolling stock returns of 1907-10 recorded 140 *'frames carrying tanks.'*[9] This figure may or may not include the ex-James Ross vehicles.

In 1917 the company decided to get out of the business of hiring underframes. The General Manager recommended an annual charge of £14 for wood underframe tanks and £16 for steel.[8] The steep increase from the 1914 rate was presumably intended as a lever in the *'endeavour to sell the underframes to the tanks' owners.'*

Later the same year the board approved the recommendation that the company should discontinue building underframes to let out on hire.[9] In 1918, a memo referring to the 1917 decisions concerning the sale of underframes and the increased hire charges was approved.[10]

Tank Underframe Users

The *1904 Mineral Time Table* listed the private traders who had tanks running on the Caledonian system.[11] James Ross & Co. figured in the list, suggesting that the tanks taken over by the Caledonian two years previously remained in Ross traffic.

St. Rollox building records show that underframes were constructed for traders as set out in the next table. Not all were allocated G order numbers. Some of the frames contributing to the total were only mentioned in company minutes. Where the location column is blank, the company was not recorded in the mineral timetable, but did appear in company minutes. Two of the companies did not use wagon underframes built at St. Rollox. The Oakbank Oil Company purchased complete tank wagons, mainly from R Y Pickering. There are no photographs of Cox Brothers tank wagons in the HMRS collection, but an open wagon is photographed in the Hurst Nelson collection.

It is worth mentioning that Charles Tennant of Tennant & Co., whose St. Rollox chemical works was at one time the largest in the world, was one of the prime movers in the development of early railways around Glasgow. He was one of the founders of the Steel Company of Scotland and president of The United Alkali Company. This eventually became a consortium of forty-five chemicals businesses, which included the original St. Rollox works.

Company	Location	Built
Wm Briggs	Arbroath	2
Cox Brothers	Lochee	
A Cross & Son	Port Dundas	12
Oakbank Oil Company	Midcalder	
Robinson & Hunter	West Street	2
James Ross & Co.	Falkirk	7
Richard Smith	West Street	2
Tennant & Co.	St. Rollox & Panmure	6
United Alkali		19
Maxwell		1
Coltness Iron Co.		4
Alex Hope Jnr & Co.		27
E B Robinson & Co.		2
Glengarnock Chemical Co.		1
D M McQueen		1
Scottish Oil Fuel Co.		3
George Miller & Co.		2
John Miller, Aberdeen		2

Drawings

The table overleaf lists the surviving drawings from St. Rollox concerning private trader tank wagons. Where the drawings can be tied to an order number this is included. Details of the tanks are taken from company minutes.

References
1. NRS BR/CAL/1/40 entry 293
2. NRS BR/CAL/5/11 entry 415
3. NRS BR/CAL/1/65 entry 342
4. NRS BR/CAL/1/46 entry 389
5. CRA Archive ref: 3/1/2/9, Northern Section, p. 77
6. NRS BR/CAL/5/60
7. NRS BR/CAL/1/71 entry 698
8. NRS BR/CAL/1/70 entry 124
9. NRS BR/CAL/1/70 entry 417
10. CRA Archive ref: 3/1/5/2, p. 49
11. In BR/CAL/4/134

Order	Date	Detail	SRX
G146	1896	Underframe for Vitriol tank. C. Tennant & Co.	8121
G192	1901	10-ton sulphuric acid tank wagon for United Alkali Co.	10648
	1904	Underframe for 10-ton tanks	12611
G227	1904	Tank only Alexander Hope, Provanmill. Underfame is drawing 12638	12649
G229	1904	Proposed 10-ton sulphuric acid tank wagon for United Alkali Co.	12725
G235	1904	Underframe for tank for Wm Briggs & Sons, Arbroath	12789
G255	1906	Underframe for tank for David M'Queen. Drawings 13888/9 are for the tank	13887
G262	1907	Arrangement of tank wagon. Alex Cross & Sons	14119
	1910	Underframe for cylindrical tank	15643
G301	1911	Tank for Scottish Oil and Fuel Co.	15697
G369	1914	Acid tank for Richard Smith's executors	17724
G375	1915	10-ton tank wagon. United Alkali Co. Ltd	17899
	1915	Tank for J Ross & Co.	17925
	1916	Arrangement of tank wagon for Messrs Richard Smith's executors	18547

Plate 8.1
This is an example of the first type of rail wagon, to drawing 2209. It had 12-inch falling sides and fixed ends. Although the drawing specifies brakes *'on one centre and one end wheel'*, the wagon has one wooden brake block operated by a push rod. If the number had been painted in the centre of the wagon, it would have been partially obscured by the brake lever, so it has been displaced to the right. The tare weight is on the body plank, but the smaller load lettering is on the curb rail. The springs for the centre wheels only are suspended from J-hangers. The left and centre wheels are of the old type, with a more modern set on the right. Enough is visible of the buffers to indicate that they are the pre-Drummond three-bolt variety. There is a broken cast plate to the right of the brake lever. The lettering is indecipherable, but it may be a Cravens Ltd plate. Cravens successfully tendered for 100 of these wagons in 1881. In support of this theory, the brake gear and long lever are very similar to that on a contemporary Cravens covered van mentioned in Chapter 9.

Plate 8.2
This is one of the rail wagons built to drawing 2209A and up-rated to 25 tons capacity. It has three-bolt self-contained spring buffers and a wood brake block operated by a pushrod on one wheel only. It is lettered ST ROLLOX WHEN EMPTY, although the Working Timetable Appendices state that they were allocated to Bridgeton station. This photograph was taken for the *1900 Register*. By 1902 the sides had been removed, according to the Working Timetable Appendix of that year. Another wagon of the same type is directly behind it, which shows the position of the company initials. In the background are three types of Caledonian 6-ton covered vans, a Diagram 6 brake van and a cattle wagon of the 1876 design to drawing 2035.

Chapter 8
Steel, Timber and Stone Wagons

8.1: Four- and Six-Wheeled Rail and Tube Wagons

Pre-Diagram Book Designs

Rail wagons with six wheels first appeared in 1877, to St. Rollox drawing 2209.[1] A copy of this drawing (2209A) has a pencil note *'altered to 9in by 5in journals and heavier springs for Special Wagon.'* This annotation probably dates from between 1896 and the *1900 Register of Wagon Plant*, when six of the wagons were recorded separately. The underframe of both types of wagon was strengthened by transverse truss rods on the centre line and just inboard of the outer spring attachments.

The sides folded down, but the ends were fixed. The wheelbase was 18 feet. The drawing shows wood brake blocks applied to the centre and one end wheel, with the pushrods operated through a bell crank. The first three-bolt sprung buffer was fitted. A later drawing, number 2220, has not survived.

Rail wagons were not separately identified in the rolling stock returns. There were only two references in the pre-1882 minutes. In October 1878 six rail wagons were part of a proposed renewal programme for the half year ending in January 1879.[2] The decision to go ahead was postponed until the next meeting. In December authority to proceed was requested.[3] The Locomotive & Stores Committee decided to delay taking tenders. No further reference is made to this proposal. The rolling stock returns for 1879 do not correlate with the wagons contained in the proposed programme. In January 1881, Cravens Ltd successfully tendered for 100 15-ton rail wagons at £100 each.[4]

They were designed to carry 24-foot lengths of rail, but were not capable of carrying the longer sections which had been authorised by the Board of Directors in 1885, when they resolved

'... to adopt the 90lb rail for the districts where the Traffic is heavy and to adopt the proposal to increase the length of each rail to 32 feet, also to adopt the proposal to use steel bolts and fish plates.'[5]

Despite this partial exclusion from the traffic for which they were nominally intended, wagons to similar dimensions were built until the end of the Caledonian's existence. It begs the question as to how the longer rail sections were transported before the introduction of the bogie rail wagons in 1912.

There were two alternatives. Provided that rail wagons with folding ends were used, a flat wagon could take up the overhang. Company instructions provided for this.[6]

'Bars ... rails ... etc., projecting beyond the ends of wagons must in all cases be securely bound and must be protected by guard wagons (runners) where necessary, projecting ends being towards the rear of the train.'

The longer rails could also be carried on a pair of swivel wagons. In Plate 8.6 two pre-diagram book swivel wagons are loaded with 32-foot rail sections.

Information on the numbering and dimensions of these and subsequent rail wagons is contained in the appendices to various working timetables. Although they were considered to be special class wagons, they were all numbered in the ordinary revenue service goods wagon series. The number series of the pre-diagram book wagons ran from 37336 to 37455 – 120 wagons in all. In the appendices between 1890 and 1896, the inside dimensions of 37336 were 26 feet 5¼ inches by 7 feet, with 9-inch deep sides. The rest were 25 feet 1 inch by 6 feet 6 inches with 6½-inch sides.

By 1902 all the wagons had been brought into line with 37336, at 26 feet 5¼ inches by 7 feet. Now, 37336-37355 had 9-inch sides. The rest had 1 foot high sides, except for 37356, 37358, 37378, 37397, 37400 and 37409, which had no sides at all. The dimensions were the same in the *1915 Appendix*.

The wagons without sides were up-rated to 25 tons capacity, presumably thanks to the increased bearing size and stronger springs mentioned on drawing 2209A, and lettered BRIDGETON STATION WHEN EMPTY. When one of these wagons was photographed for the *1900 Register*, it had sides and was lettered for St. Rollox – see Plate 8.2.

Bullhead rail is 6 inches high and 3 inches wide in round figures, so even at 80lbs per yard, about fifty 24-foot rails was the load limit. It would take nine wagons to carry the rails for one mile of track. When carrying rails, therefore, the load was contained within the wagon sides. Continued construction despite their partial exclusion from rail carrying traffic, coupled with inclusion in the general goods numbering series are evidence that these wagons were not confined to this traffic. Any light steel sections which fell under the generic term 'rail' could be loaded, limited only by the length of the wagon.

It also follows that wagons that were fitted with stanchions must have been dual purpose vehicles. There is photographic evidence that they carried timber – see Plate 8.4. In this guise they were the natural successors to the pre-diagram book round timber and bar iron wagons discussed in the next section.

Rail Wagon Load 15 Tons – Diagram 13

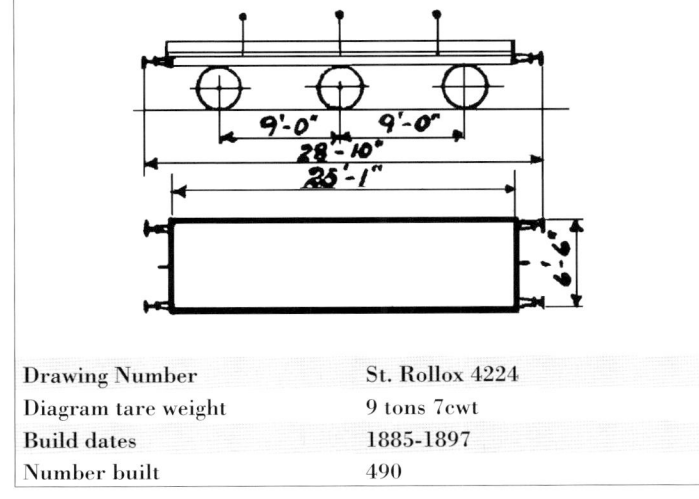

Drawing Number	St. Rollox 4224
Diagram tare weight	9 tons 7cwt
Build dates	1885-1897
Number built	490

St. Rollox drawing 4224 dates from 1884. In April the following year the Traffic Committee considered the addition of 100 rail wagons.[7] This was not the first order for these wagons in the records. St. Rollox order G4 was for 150 flexible six-wheeled wagons, but there is no record of these wagons in the special class number series. Order G9 was the execution of the April 1885 minute.

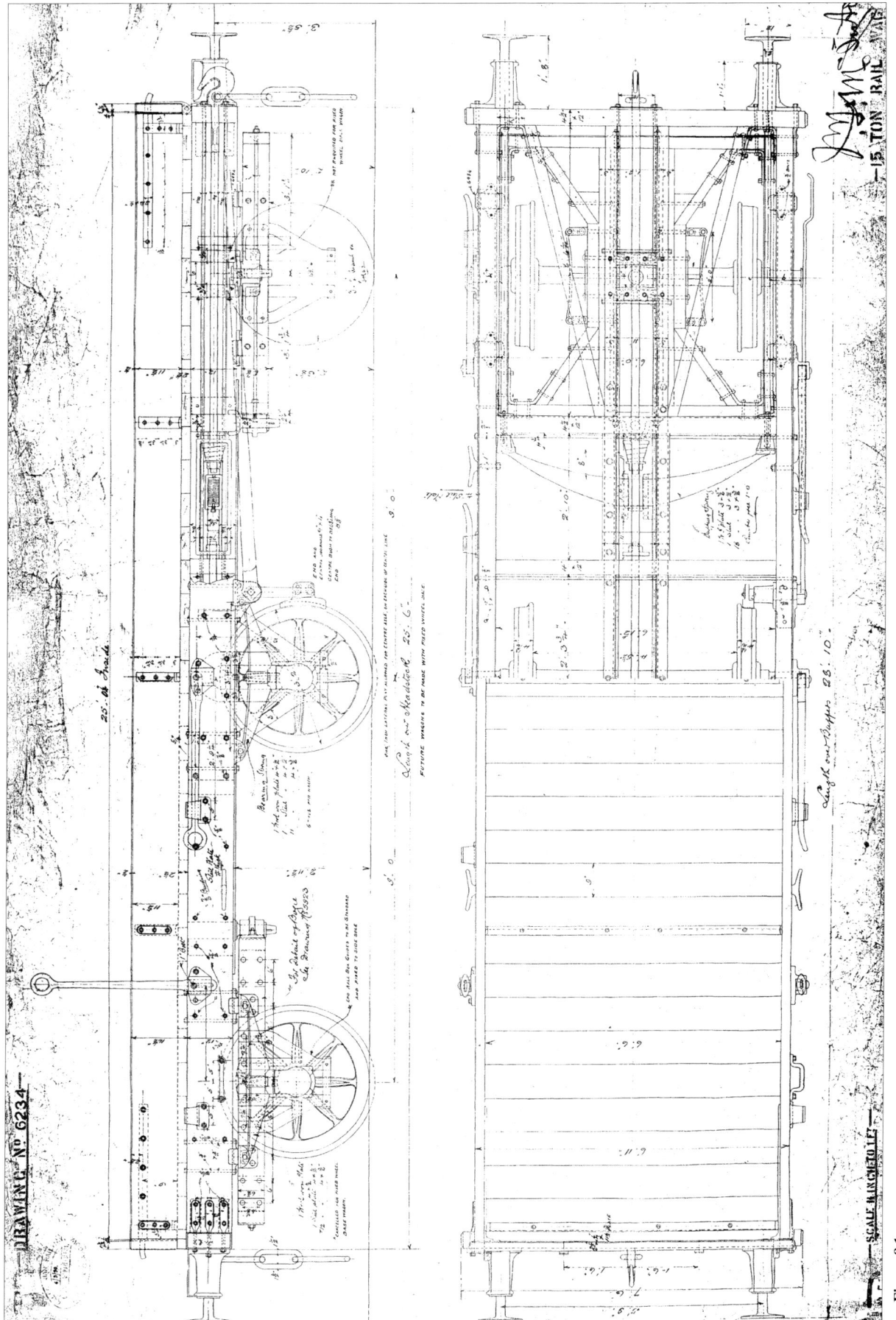

Figure 8.1
St. Rollox drawing 6234, showing the original flexible wheelbase design for Diagram 13. The left-hand stanchion is shown in the raised position, and the centre one folded. The annotation changing future production to a rigid wheelbase is just below the length over headstock measurement.

8.1: FOUR- AND SIX-WHEELED RAIL AND TUBE WAGONS

Plate 8.3
This was the last in the lot of fifty Diagram 13 rigid wheelbase wagons built by Hurst Nelson in 1896-98. Notice the step welded to the top of the standard wagon buffer casting to accommodate the end when it was dropped. The brake is now a single cast iron block. Despite the rigid wheelbase, only one wheel is braked. The first type of cast number plate is fixed to the body side to avoid the centre stanchion.

The wagons were 25 feet 1 inch long by 6 feet 6 inch externally (i.e., the same width as the outer dimension of the solebars), with a one-plank side 6½ inches high. The wooden solebars were faced with a ¼-inch iron plate. Three stanchions each side enabled them to carry bulkier, but lighter, loads such as timber. These were folded down when not in use. The floor was made of 9-inch planks. Like the Diagram 14 swivel wagons and the Diagram 37 twin wagons, the headstocks were wider than the body. The hand brake operated on the centre wheel on each side, because the outer axles were mounted on pony trucks.

The numbers of the first order were 37705-37804. Wagons 37795-37798 had fixed sides and ends. The remaining six had folding ends; stepped buffers would have been fitted to these wagons, as shown in Plate 8.3. At some point between 1902 and 1915, 37752 was broken up.

A further order of forty flexible wheelbase wagons was built to G58 in 1888/89. There is no record of a minute authorising these wagons, which were allocated numbers 38092-38131. Length and width were the same as their predecessors, but the fixed sides and folding ends were 12 inches high. Order G64 for 300 wagons followed

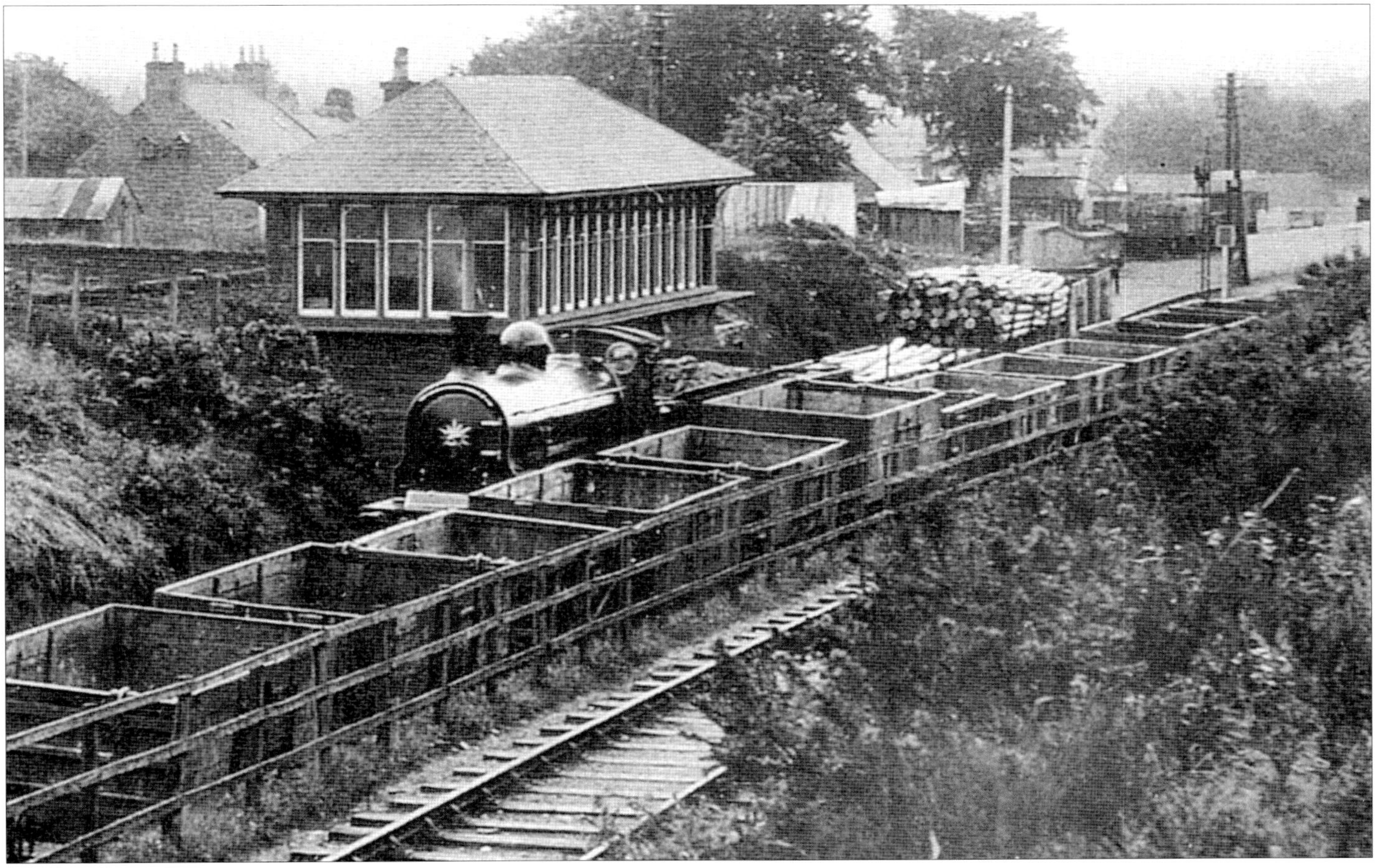

Plate 8.4
This is Locharbriggs station, said to be in 1910. An immaculate class 812 0-6-0 with elaborate smokebox decoration draws out from the yard, hauling two Diagram 13 wagons carrying felled timber and two empty mineral wagons. At the front of the train are four Diagram 22 wagons sandwiching a 7-ton 'bogie'. The nearest wagon to the camera has been rebuilt with self-contained buffers. A Diagram 59 wagon is followed by another 'bogie' and more Diagram 22s. There is no visible lettering on any of the wagons, and all seem to have unpainted interiors. The use of the 'bogies' in revenue traffic suggest that the date may be rather earlier than 1910.

shortly afterwards. They were authorised in a minute of January 1889.[8] Numbers were 38880-39179. Between 1906 and 1915, wagons 39146 and 39158 acquired 15-inch sides.

In 1895 the design was modified. Drawing 6234[9] of 1890 for a flexible wheelbase wagon was annotated *'future wagons to be built with fixed wheelbase.'* The modification was applied to an order for fifty wagons authorised to the capital account in September 1895.[10] They were built by Hurst Nelson, twenty-five each in the periods ending July 1896 and January 1898. Dimensions were the same as previously. Numbers were 41866-41915.

15 Ton Rail Wagon – Diagram 60

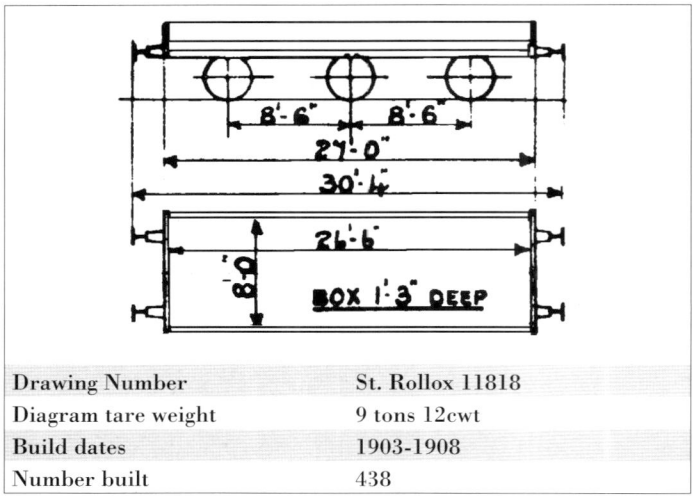

Drawing Number	St. Rollox 11818
Diagram tare weight	9 tons 12cwt
Build dates	1903-1908
Number built	438

In January 1903 tenders were sought for 300 *'15 ton steel carrying rail wagons.'*[11] The contract was initially to be divided between Pickering, Hurst Nelson and the Motherwell Wagon & Rolling Stock Co. at £95 each.[12] In the event, Motherwell and Pickering declined to supply and the entire contract was awarded to Hurst Nelson *'for delivery by end September under penalty of 5s per wagon per week.'*[13] The wagons had 15-inch sides, folding ends and no stanchions. Four shackles were added in 1912, according to an annotation on the drawing. They were authorised as capital expenditure and numbered 72683-72982.

A further 138 were authorised as renewals for the half year ending January 1905.[14] Presumably they were intended to replace the wagons built in 1881, but there is no record of their being built at St. Rollox or by contractors.

Two wagons were built as renewals to order G271 in the half year ending July 1908.[15] They replaced Diagram 13 wagons which had been appropriated for use as runner wagons for the new Cravens-built 20-ton steam breakdown cranes. As they took existing numbers, the records do not show which wagons were replaced. Plate 17.20 (p. 278) shows that one at least of the wagons taken out of revenue service had a flexible wheelbase. They may have been built to Diagram 13 as a like for like replacement, or to the newer Diagram 60. The replacement wagons have not been included in the numbers built for either design.

20 Ton Rail Wagon – Diagram 108

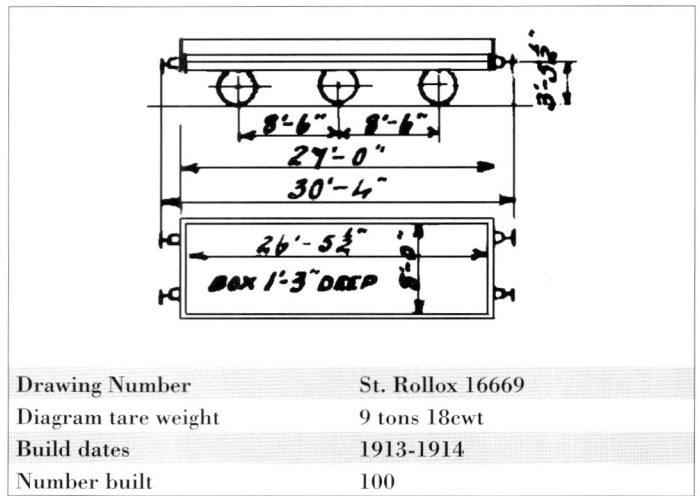

Drawing Number	St. Rollox 16669
Diagram tare weight	9 tons 18cwt
Build dates	1913-1914
Number built	100

Wagons to Diagram 108 were ½ inch shorter than Diagram 60, but were otherwise dimensionally identical with fixed sides and folding ends. They were authorised as capital expenditure in December 1912 for the Clydebridge Steelworks traffic, along with 100 Diagram 109 swivel wagons.[16] The order was split equally between Cravens and the Motherwell Wagon & Rolling Stock Co. Delivery was at the rate of ten per week from 1st April 1913 at £182 each. They had a double brake on each side. The tare weight was not given in the diagram book. The weight shown is taken from the *1915 Working Timetable Appendix*. Numbers were 73183-73282.

Plate 8.5
The next development in rail wagon design to Diagram 60, again built by Hurst Nelson. This time the first wagon in the contract of 300 was photographed. Stanchions were not fitted, so the number plate could return to the solebar. It could not be fitted centrally, however, as one of five iron angles supporting the floor was in the way. A double brake is fitted on one side of the wagon only. The company ownership letters are 15 inches high. The numbers on the end are larger than the 6 inches specified in drawing 12113.

20 Ton Rail Wagon – Diagram 124

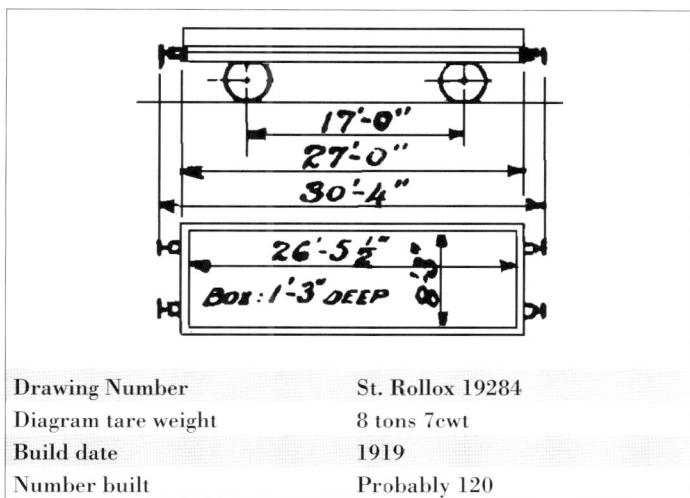

Drawing Number	St. Rollox 19284
Diagram tare weight	8 tons 7cwt
Build date	1919
Number built	Probably 120

The final development in rail wagons increased the width of the Diagram 108 body by 3 inches and mounted it on the same design of four-wheeled steel underframe as the Diagram 114 tube wagons, with 10-inch by 5-inch, rather than 9-inch by 4½-inch, journals. The new underframe effected a 1½ ton saving in tare weight. Oil lubrication replaced grease. The Morton brake was fitted to one pair of wheels. Shackles for securing chains were fitted inside the wagon on the side planking over the axle centre lines.

The wagons were authorised as part of the renewal programme for the half year ending 31st December 1918. One hundred wagons were authorised, restricted to an initial fifty,

'*pending settlement of claims (1) to have renewals based on 2½% and (2) conversion of Dumb Buffers to be treated as Special Repairs.*'[17]

The St. Rollox order G410 for fifty wagons, which had still not been built in July 1919, was cancelled and reappeared as G419. A further seventy wagons described as '*20-ton iron and steel carrying wagons*' were probably built to this diagram by Cravens. This order was authorised in April 1920.[18] Known numbers are 6316, 9001, 9003, 37631, 40972. A further three numbers, 74013–74015, suggest that part of one of the orders was charged to the capital account.

16 Ton Tube Wagon – Diagram 114

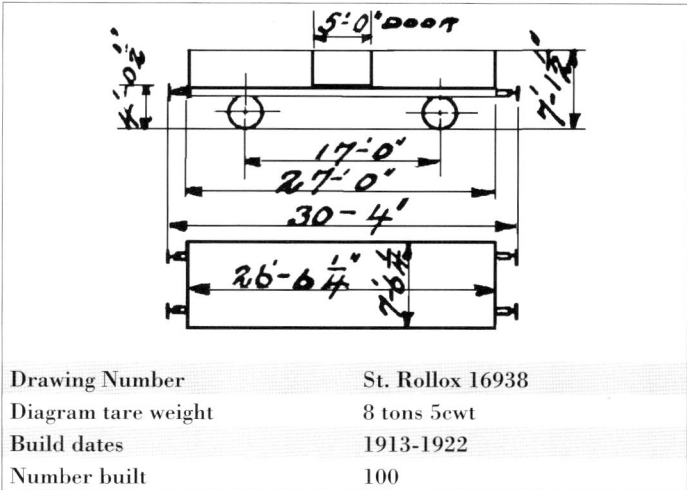

Drawing Number	St. Rollox 16938
Diagram tare weight	8 tons 5cwt
Build dates	1913-1922
Number built	100

These wagons looked like enlarged versions of the Diagram 24 open goods wagon. The four-plank body was 3 feet 1 inch high. The bodies were built on a steel underframe reinforced with short truss rods. The drawing shows that the first lot was built with Iracier axleboxes and heavy duty springs. The rest had 10-inch by 5-inch oil axleboxes. The Morton double brake was applied to two wheels on one side.

Twenty-five were authorised to the capital account in 1913, order G340. They were built in response to a complaint by Mr Barman, the Managing Director of Stewarts & Lloyds, about the failure to supply suitable wagons for his traffic, which was the carriage of pipes for the replacement of Glasgow's water supply system.[19] Twenty-five were ordered for period ending 31st December 1914, to order G355.[20] Twenty more were authorised in 1916 and built to G379.[21] A further

LEFT: Plate 8.7
This is the final design of rail wagon to Diagram 124, in use as a boiler wagon. The underframe is the same design as the Diagram 114 tube wagon, with channel underframes reinforced with short truss rods. Heavy duty springs, oil axleboxes and solid spoke wheels are fitted. The number is not repeated on the ends of the wagon because the reinforcing angles do not allow enough space.

RIGHT: Plate 8.6
One of the ways that 32 feet long rails were carried before the advent of the bogie rail wagons in 1912.

thirty were built to order G423 almost at the end of the Caledonian's existence, authorised for the half year ending 31st December 1922.[22] These three lots were part of the renewals programme.

The only known number from the capital expenditure lot is 73348. Presumably this was part of a block allocation. Other numbers are 3182, 3347, 3592, 3655, 35950 and 40798.

References
1. This drawing and 2209a are not yet catalogued
2. NRS BR/CAL/1/24 entry 1318
3. NRS BR/CAL/1/24 entry 1383
4. NRS BR/CAL/1/26 entry 392
5. NRS BR/CAL/1/30 entry 336
6. quoted from the CRA reprint of the *General Directions ..with Regard to the Conveyance of Merchandise Traffic* paragraph 138. Archive ref: 3/3/1/11
7. NRS BR/CAL/1/29 entry 1207
8. NRS BR/CAL/1/32 entry 1178
9. NRM 11894/W RHP 70052
10. NRS BR/CAL/1/38 entry 1357
11. NRS BR/CAL/1/47 entry 464
12. NRS BR/CAL/1/47 entry 567
13. NRS BR/CAL/1/47 entry 693
14. NRS BR/CAL/1/49 entry 769
15. NRS BR/CAL/1/45 entry 1143
16. NRS BR/CAL/1/62 entries 1004 and 1025
17. NRS BR/CAL/1/70 entry 335
18. NRS BR/CAL/1/74 entry 876
19. NRS BR/CAL/1/63 entry 508
20. NRS BR/CAL/1/64 entry 1149
21. NRS BR/CAL/1/67 entry 1010
22. NRS BR/CAL/1/80 entry 869. Part of an authorisation for 461 replacement wagons

Left: Plate 8.8
A Diagram 114 tube wagon with a four-figure number, which indicates that it was not one of the first twenty-five built to the capital account in 1913. The company initials are 18 inches high, and the TUBE WAGON letters are 6 inches. The number plate is just visible, displaced to the right to avoid the door spring. Disc wheels are fitted.

Below and Facing Page: Figure 8.2
This drawing dates from 1916, and shows a modification to drawing 1359. The modification had already been made in 1900, as wagon 5483 appeared in the background of a photograph in the *1900 Register*; this photograph is reproduced in Chapter 14 as Plate 14.6.

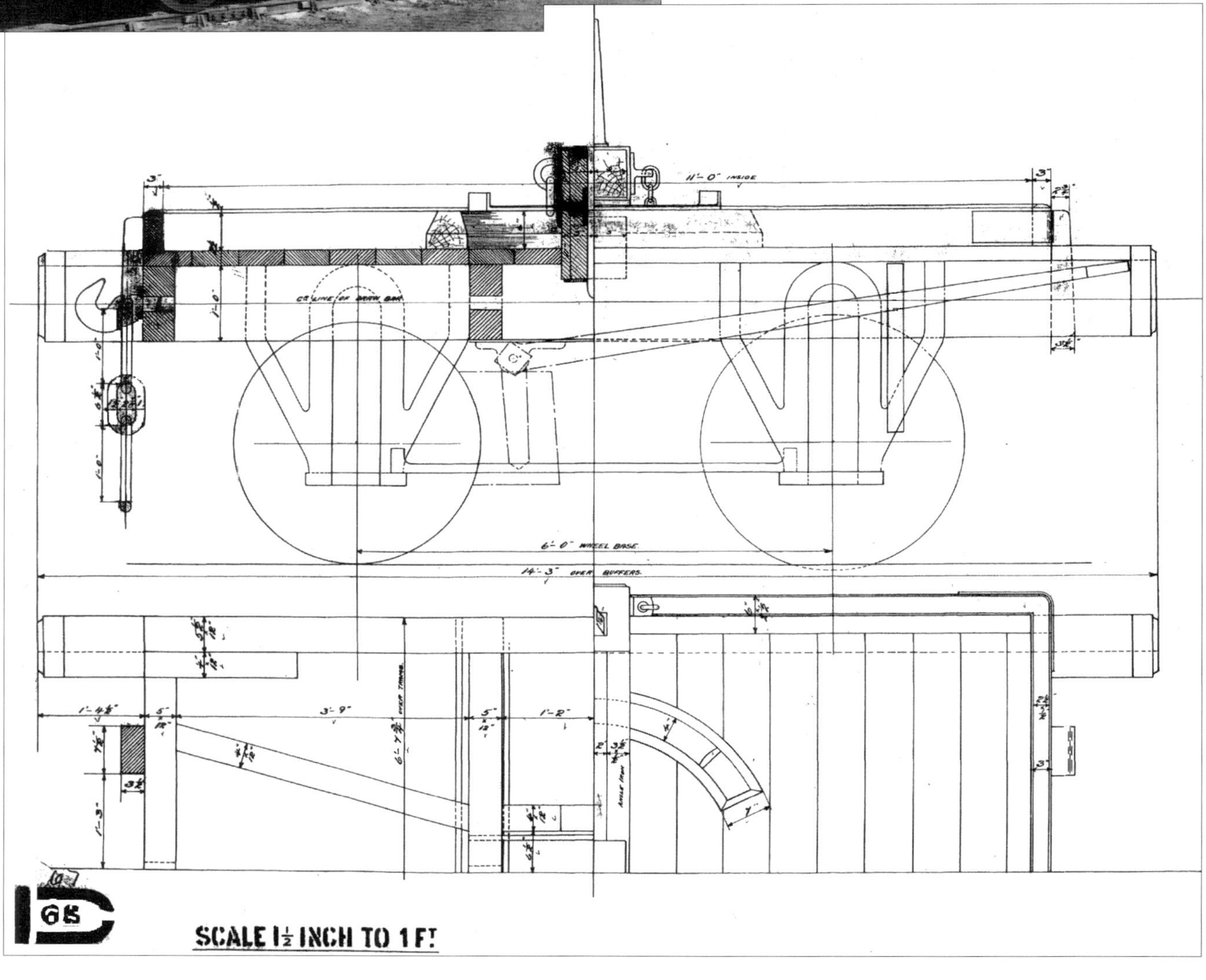

8.2: Timber and Swivel Wagons

Pre-Diagram Book Designs

Early drawings of timber wagons (St. Rollox numbers 180, 208, 334 and 337) have not survived. One of these drawings was used in 1857 to build a prototype wagon for a contract for nineteen pairs of wagons.[1] Ashbury was awarded the contract at a price of £116 per pair.[2] The prototype was recorded in the January 1857 rolling stock return as a swivel wagon '*under construction.*' The Ashbury wagons cannot be identified in the subsequent return.

The first wagons in the rolling stock returns that are specifically for timber date from 1866, when wagons originally built from 1854 to carry bar iron were redesignated as round timber/bar iron wagons. These wagons were built by contractors to their own design, as there are no St. Rollox drawing register entries for bar iron wagons. At the time of the change of use, there were ninety-nine such wagons. The stock rose to 127 in 1868. The last mention of these wagons in the rolling stock returns was in July 1876.

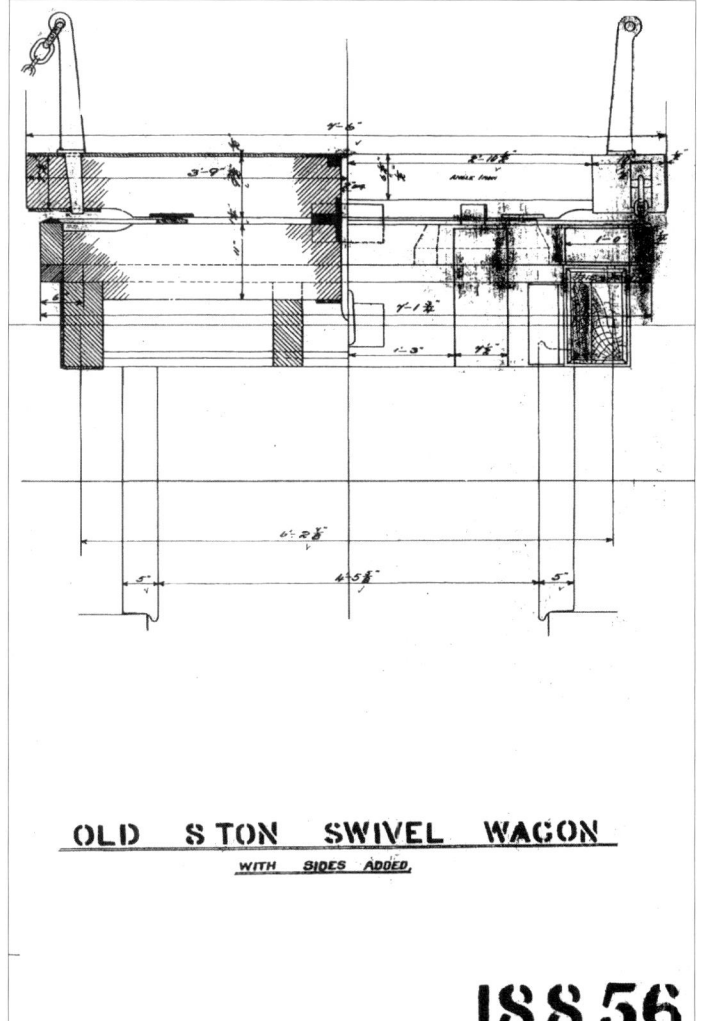

The wagons had fixed sides of two planks and, scaling off the photograph of 3386 in the *1900 Register of Wagon Plant*, were 1 foot 3 inches or 1 foot 4 inches high. The ends folded down. Two stanchions were fitted to extend the load-carrying height. These could be folded down onto cradles. The wheelbase was 9 feet 6 inches.

Swivel wagons were first mentioned in a minute of 1861 when Ashbury supplied forty at £64 10s each.[3] By 1865, when they supplied a further fifty, the price had fallen to £59 10s.[4] In total, contractors supplied 495 wagons up to 1872, when a St. Rollox designed wagon appeared. The Caledonian also inherited 158 swivel wagons from the Scottish Central and thirty from the Scottish North Eastern.

The precursor of the Diagram 14 swivel timber wagon appeared in 1872 to drawing 1359. The wheelbase was 6 feet and the springs were only 2 feet 11 inches long. The external dimensions of the body were 11 feet 5½ inches by 7 feet and 14 feet 3 inches long over the solid buffers. They had a single swivelling bolster with two stanchions. In the ten years from 1873 to the arrival of Drummond, 345 wagons were replaced with this design, and 200 additional wagons built. Originally these wagons had no sides. At some time before 1900, sides 6 inches high were added – see Plate 14.6 (p. 224), which shows wagon 5483 in the background, and Plate 8.9 in this chapter. The modification was recorded in 1916 by St. Rollox drawing 18856, reproduced here as Figure 8.2. A further alternative number is 5503.

Drummond Era Wagons not in the Diagram Book

The first timber wagon of the Drummond period was not recorded in the diagram book. Drummond signed St. Rollox drawing 3242, which is dated 20th September 1882.[5] It depicts a wagon with 6-foot wheelbase and the single cast iron brake. The buffers, however, are the pre-diagram book self-contained sprung variety. The external dimensions were 13 feet 10 inches by 6 feet 11½ inches. There was a centrally mounted swivelling bolster and two folding stanchions on each side. The sides were 9½ inches high.

Company minutes do not record authorisation to build wagons to this design, but in the period January 1883-1890, each six-monthly return showed renewals to a total of 217 wagons. In addition, 100 were built to capital in the period ending July 1885, 150 in the period ending January 1889 and a further fifty in the next six months.

The numbers in the returns may include wagons built to drawings 3609-11 for a '*Dundee timber wagon.*' The drawings date from 1883 and have not survived. There is no order number for these Dundee wagons, or reference to them in minutes.

The next design of timber wagon also missed inclusion in the diagram book. A minute in April 1885[6] authorised 100 '*round timber and bar iron*' wagons to be built to the capital account. Drawing 4410 of May 1885 was for a solid buffer round timber wagon.[7] It was essentially a modernised version of the pre-diagram book design with axle guards inside the solebars and the standard iron brake. It was a two-plank wagon with sides 1 foot 4 inches deep. The sides were fixed and the ends folded down. Two folding stanchions were fitted on either side, centred above the axles. External dimensions were 17 feet 4 inches long by 7 feet 7 inches wide. The wheelbase was 9 feet 6 inches. The St. Rollox order was G12.

The final wagon missing from the diagram book was designed for the Montrose timber traffic. Drawing 5581 is dated 21st December 1888. It is annotated as being '*for 24ft boards.*' This was the standard

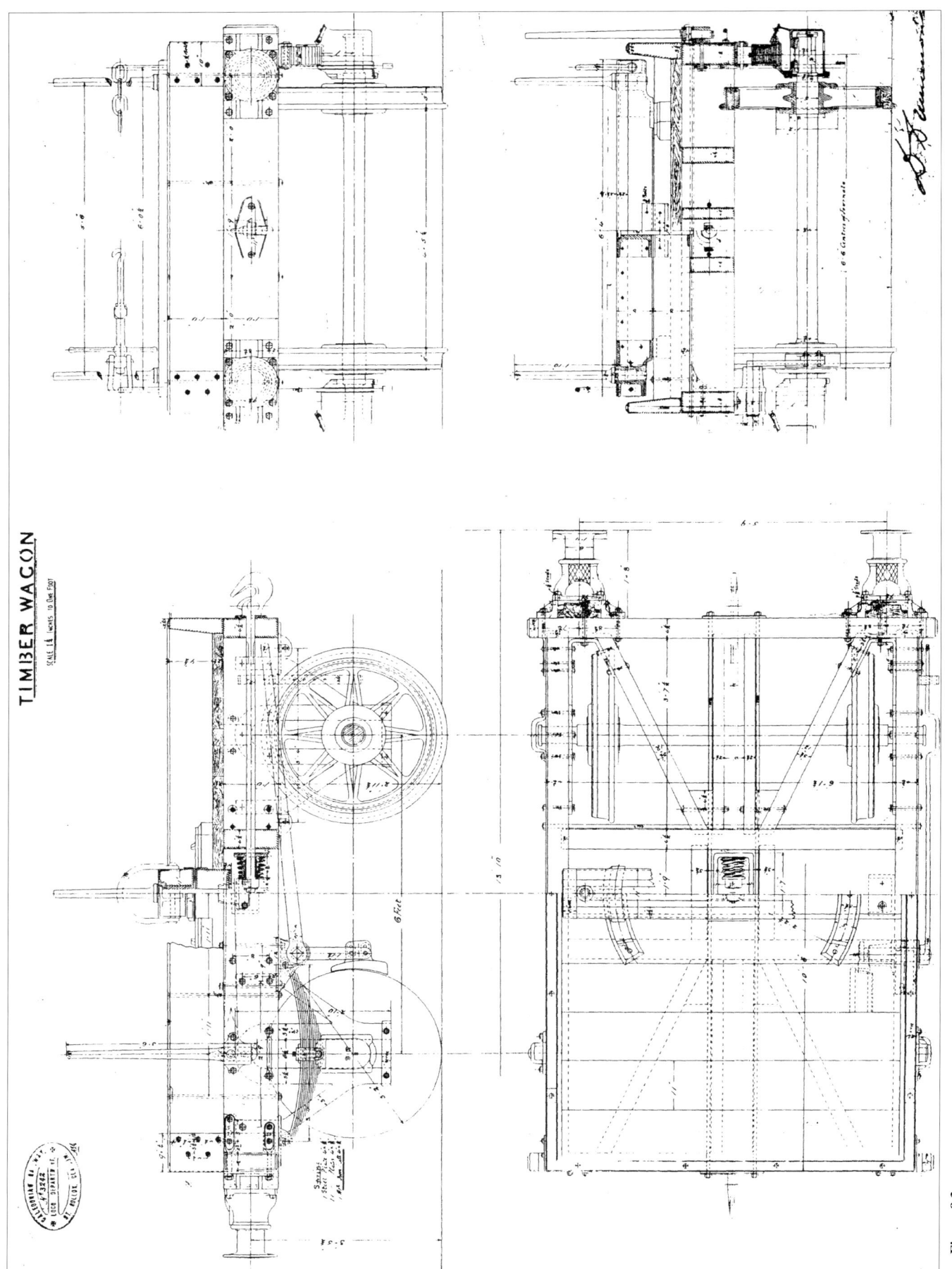

Figure 8.3
St. Rollox drawing 3242 was for a timber wagon that, although signed off by Drummond, was not included in the diagram book. Note that the sides and ends were thicker at the bottom than the top. It also shows the early four bolt self-contained buffer with a step cast in the top, and the packing piece between it and the headstock.

8.2: TIMBER AND SWIVEL WAGONS

Plate 8.9
The fixed sides and ends of this wagon built to drawing 1359 were only 6 inches high, which meant that the 9-inch letters covered the edge of the curb rail that retained the floor, as well as filling the side. Centring the letters over the axles does not allow enough room for the tare weight or the load in their normal positions. Note the very short springs. Number 36036 was one of the 200 wagons built as additions to the fleet. Other photographs show numbers 5483 and 5503 which were replacements.

length for sawn wood, which might be 11 inches wide ('deals'), or 'battens' which were 7 inches wide. Both widths were 2½ or 3 inches thick. Incidentally, pine sawn to the batten size was used for wagon floors. The wood, from Norway and the Baltic States, came through all the east coast ports.

The design was of open boarded construction, similar to the empty barrel trucks. The sides were 3 feet high. The ends were peaked, rising to 4 feet 1 inch at the apex. A wooden rail connected the two peaks, presumably acting as a tarpaulin support. The internal body dimensions were 24 feet 3 inches by 7 feet 5 inches. The drawing does not show underframe detail, apart from the wheelbase (13 feet) and the length over headstocks (24 feet). The body, therefore, overhung the headstocks. Parts of the drawing are reproduced overleaf.

St. Rollox order G49 was for seventy-six wagons. They were probably authorised in October 1887 or July 1888. Details were not given of the rolling stock to be constructed in either case.

Swivel Timber Wagon Load 8 Tons – Diagram 14

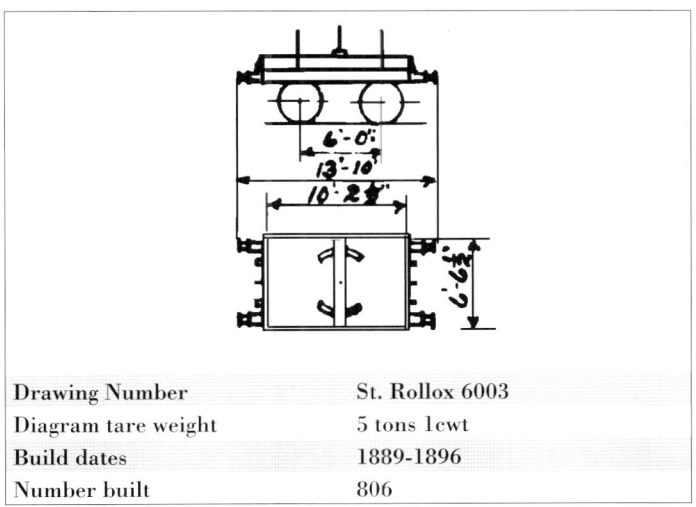

Drawing Number	St. Rollox 6003
Diagram tare weight	5 tons 1cwt
Build dates	1889-1896
Number built	806

The first Drummond timber wagon design to figure in the diagram book was allocated Diagram 14. It was a swivel timber wagon 10 feet 2½ inches long by 6 feet 6½ inches wide externally, i.e., to the outside dimension of the solebars. The sides were one plank (9½ inches) high. The headstocks were wider than the ends, although the diagram book suggests that this was not the case. They were fitted with one swivelling bolster, heavy self-contained buffers and screw couplings. The drawing and diagram book show a pair of folding stanchions fitted to the sides, but these do not appear on wagons in photographs.

The first order was for 200 wagons to St. Rollox G69. These were charged to the capital account.[8] A further 306 were built as renewals to orders G79, 97 and 150. These orders were authorised in 1890, 1892 and 1896 respectively.[9] Finally, 300 were authorised in 1895/96 to the capital account, 200 built at St. Rollox to order G153 and 100 by Hurst Nelson.[10] The Hurst Nelson block of numbers may have run on from their order for Diagram 13 rail wagons, in which case the series ran from 41916 to 42015.

Sixteen wagons of similar design were built with larger journals and stronger springs. They were allocated numbers in the special wagon series, where they were described as swivel bar wagons. Four appeared in the special wagons list in 1895 and in the 1902 list the remainder were recorded. These wagons are discussed in Chapter 15, section 5.

8 Ton Timber & Ore Wagon – Diagram 48

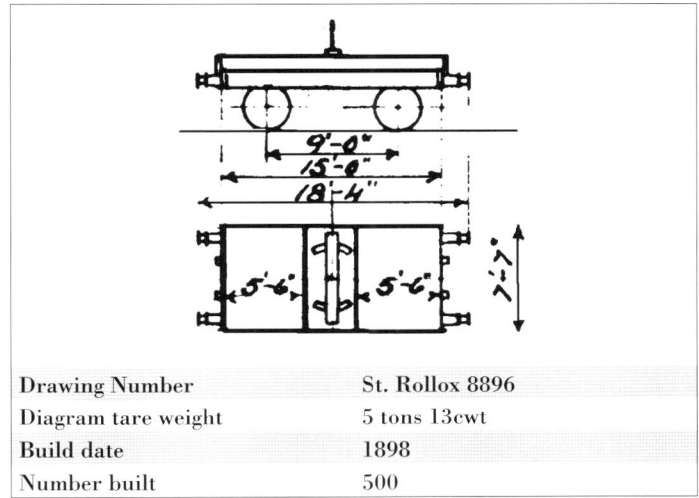

Drawing Number	St. Rollox 8896
Diagram tare weight	5 tons 13cwt
Build date	1898
Number built	500

The wagons to Diagram 48 were confusingly described as for 'timber and ore' in the diagram book. They were built in one lot to order G167 in 1898 and charged to the capital account.[11] The underframe and bodies were the same as the Diagram 47 twin

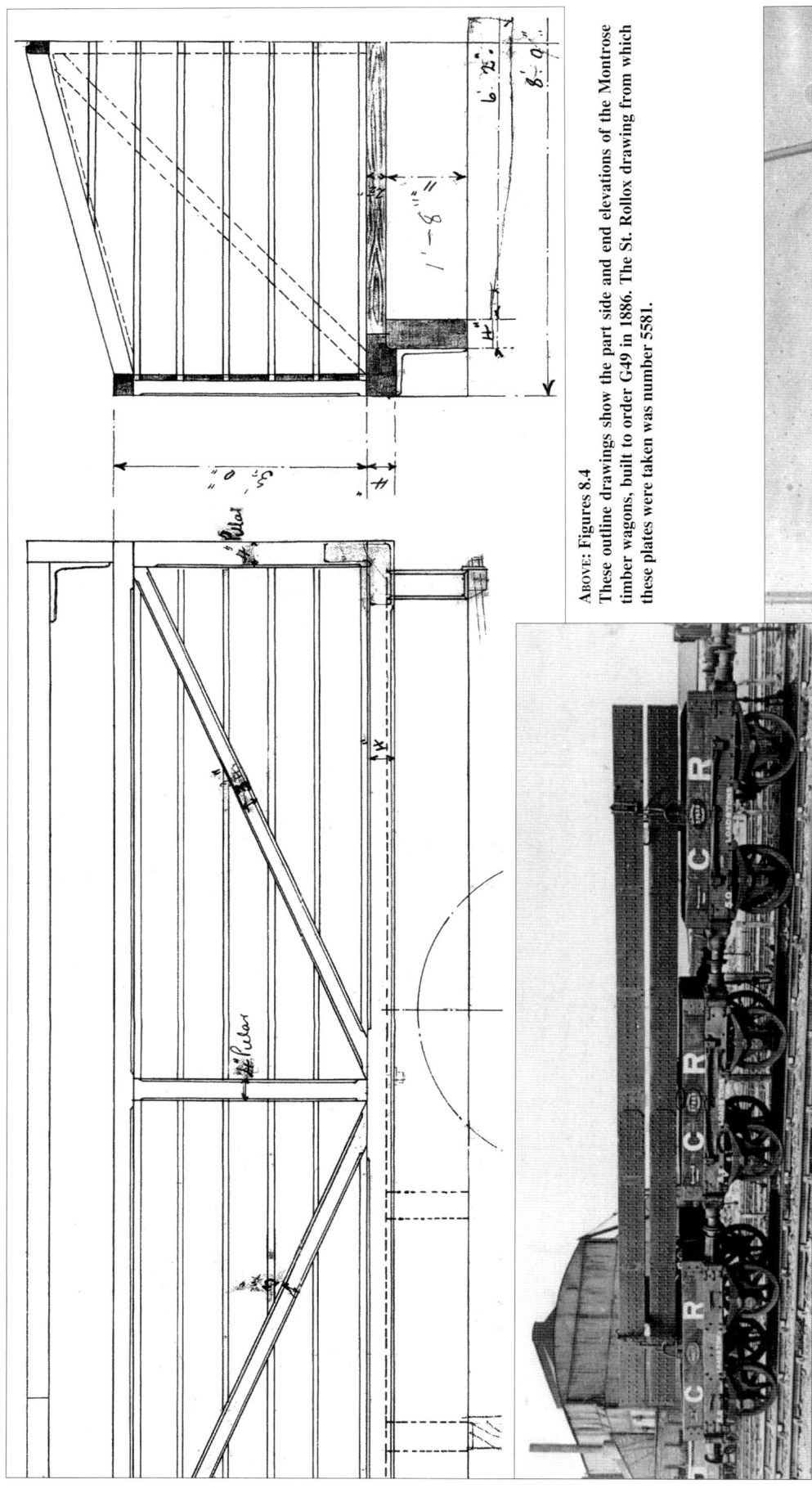

ABOVE: Figures 8.4
These outline drawings show the part side and end elevations of the Montrose timber wagons, built to order G-49 in 1886. The St. Rollox drawing from which these plates were taken was number 5581.

ABOVE: Plate 8.10
The two wagons to the right are built to drawing 3242. The numbers suggest that they were charged to the capital account. They are coupled to a Diagram 14 wagon, which was their modern successor. The middle wagon has the early four-bolt heavy duty self-contained buffer without step. The right-hand wagon has the version with the step cast in. The wood packing pieces follow the shape of the buffer bases. The lettering and numbering arrangements are the same for all three wagons.

RIGHT: Plate 8.11
One of 100 round timber and bar iron wagons, built to drawing 4410 in 1885. The order was charged to the capital account, but the number implies a replacement wagon. One axle guard has a curved bridle, the other is straight. The position of the right-hand stanchion has displaced the load lettering onto two lines.

wagons, but both ends were fixed and the one-plank 13-inch sides folded down. They had screw couplings and the heavy self-contained buffer. The journals were 8 inches by 3¾ inches. The swivelling bolsters were centrally mounted.

REFERENCES
1. NRS BR/CAL/1/11 entry 1146
2. NRS BR/CAL/1/11 entry 1166
3. NRS BR/CAL/1/12 entry 1388
4. NRS BR/CAL/1/14 entry 1421
5. NRM 8048/W RHP 69163
6. NRS BR/CAL/1/29 entry 1207
7. NRM 8057/W RHP 69180
8. NRS BR/CAL/1/32 entry 1178
9. NRS BR/CAL/1/33 entry 1038, NRS BR/CAL/1/35 entry 263, NRS BR/CAL/1/40 entry 15
10. NRS BR/CAL/1/38 entry 1357
11. NRS BR/CAL/5/11 entry 321

ABOVE: Plate 8.12
Another Hurst Nelson publicity photograph, this time for one of 100 Diagram 14 timber wagons built in 1895/96. It was the last wagon built, if the numbers continued from the contract for Diagram 13 rail wagons and ran from 41916 to 42015. The heavy duty buffers, coupled with the short wheelbase, give a massive appearance. The company initials are 9 inches high. Bolt heads on the flitched solebar have displaced the first style of number plate to the body plank. The body is of insufficient length to accommodate the load lettering, which has been moved to the centre of the solebar.

Plate 8.13
The 500 Diagram 48 wagons were built in 1898. The 12-inch company initials are centred in the spaces left by the side hinges, with the load lettering on the centre line of the wagon.

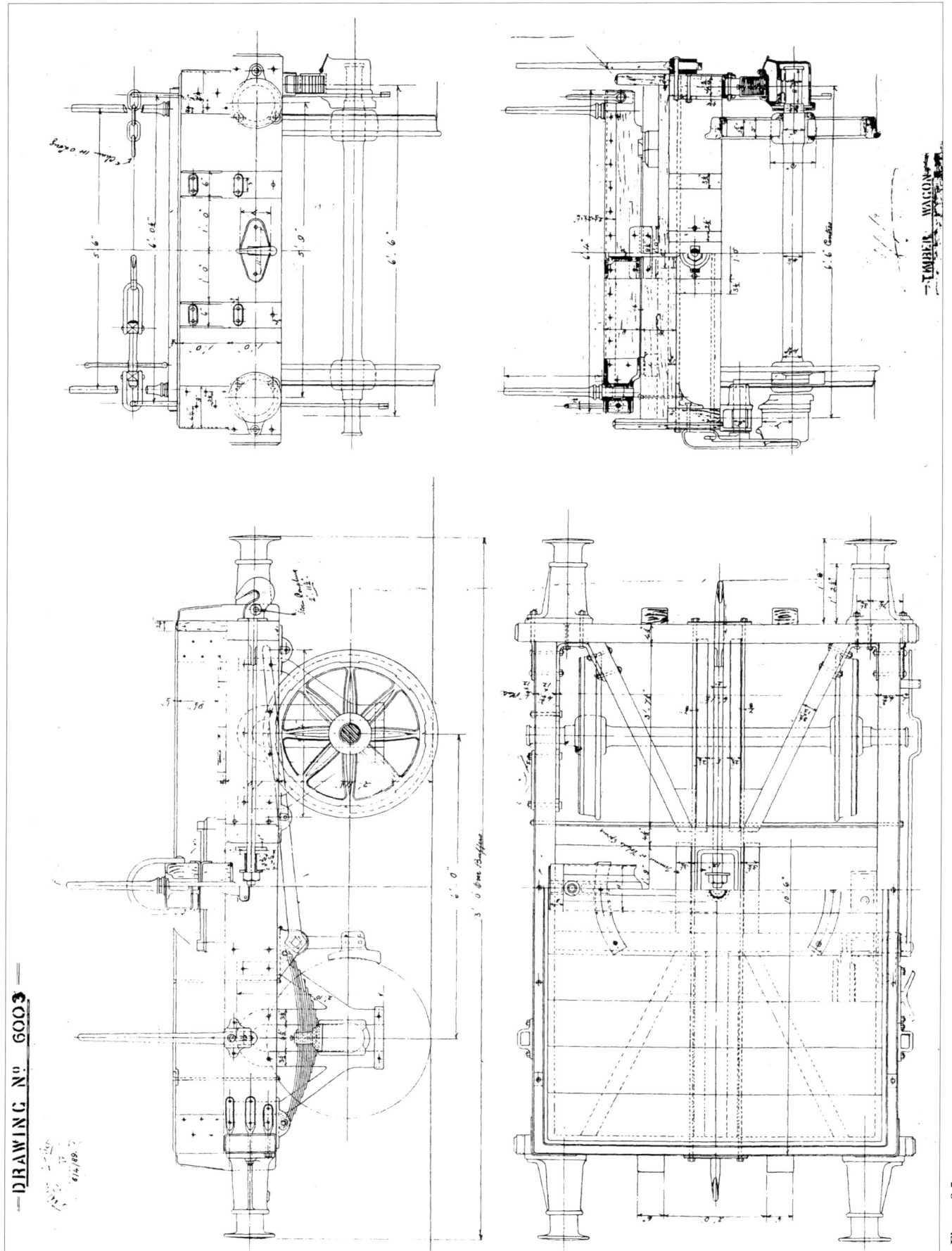

Figure 8.5
This is the drawing for the Diagram 14 swivel timber wagon, St. Rollox number 6003. It was the modernised version of the wagons built to drawing 3242, shown in Plate 8.10. The folding stanchions on the sides echo the earlier design, but photographic evidence suggests that they were not fitted.

8.3: Twin Wagons

20 Ton Twin Wagon – Diagram 37

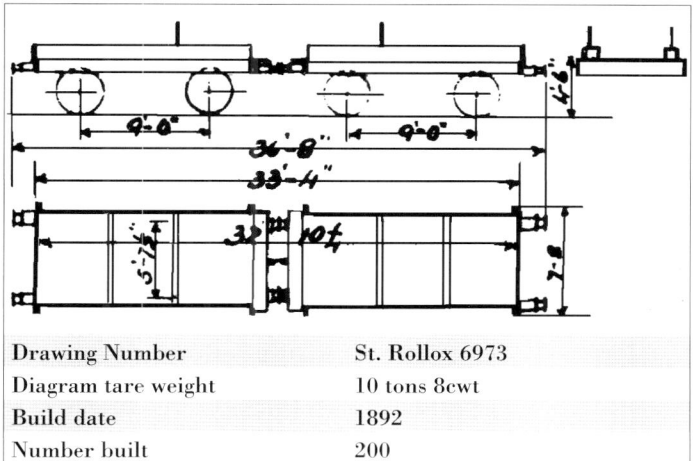

Drawing Number	St. Rollox 6973
Diagram tare weight	10 tons 8cwt
Build date	1892
Number built	200

The St. Rollox drawing describes these wagons as '*Single bolster timber wagon fold down ends between twins.*' They were built within six months to order G98, authorised in January 1892.[1] It had previously been minuted that swivel and twin wagons with spindle buffers were urgently required.[2] They were authorised as renewals, and are recorded as such in the rolling stock return, but the number on a wagon in a photograph suggests that they were built to the capital account.

Like the Diagram 14 swivel wagons, they were shortened versions of the Diagram 13 rail wagons. The individual bodies were 15 feet long by 6 feet 6 inches wide. The single plank body was 13 inches high. The outer ends of the set were fixed and the inner ends folded down. The bolster did not swivel.

The axlebox journals were heavier duty than usual at 9 inches by 4 inches. Rather than the spindle buffers mentioned in the minutes, the buffers were the heavy duty self-contained type; despite the fact that the inner ends folded down the inner pair was not the stepped variety. The wagons were semi-permanently coupled in pairs with a special shackle coupling that compressed the buffers to form a semi-rigid unit – see Figure 8.7.

The diagram book sketch does not show folding stanchions fitted to the solebar, but the St. Rollox drawing and photographic evidence shows that they were so fitted. The wagons were numbered in a block; photographic evidence shows this included 43219 and 43245.

Plate 8.14
One half of a pair of Diagram 37 wagons. One hundred pairs were built during 1892. The combination of fixed bolster and folding stanchions is unique among Caledonian wagons. This wagon has the self-contained buffer that was used to convert the Diagram 22 mineral wagons, rather than the heavy duty version shown on the drawing. The company initials are centred in the space left by the ironwork on the body. Lack of space has caused the load lettering to be written on two lines. Both these and the Diagram 47 wagons were rated at 20 tons in the diagram book, but show individual capacities of 8 tons each.

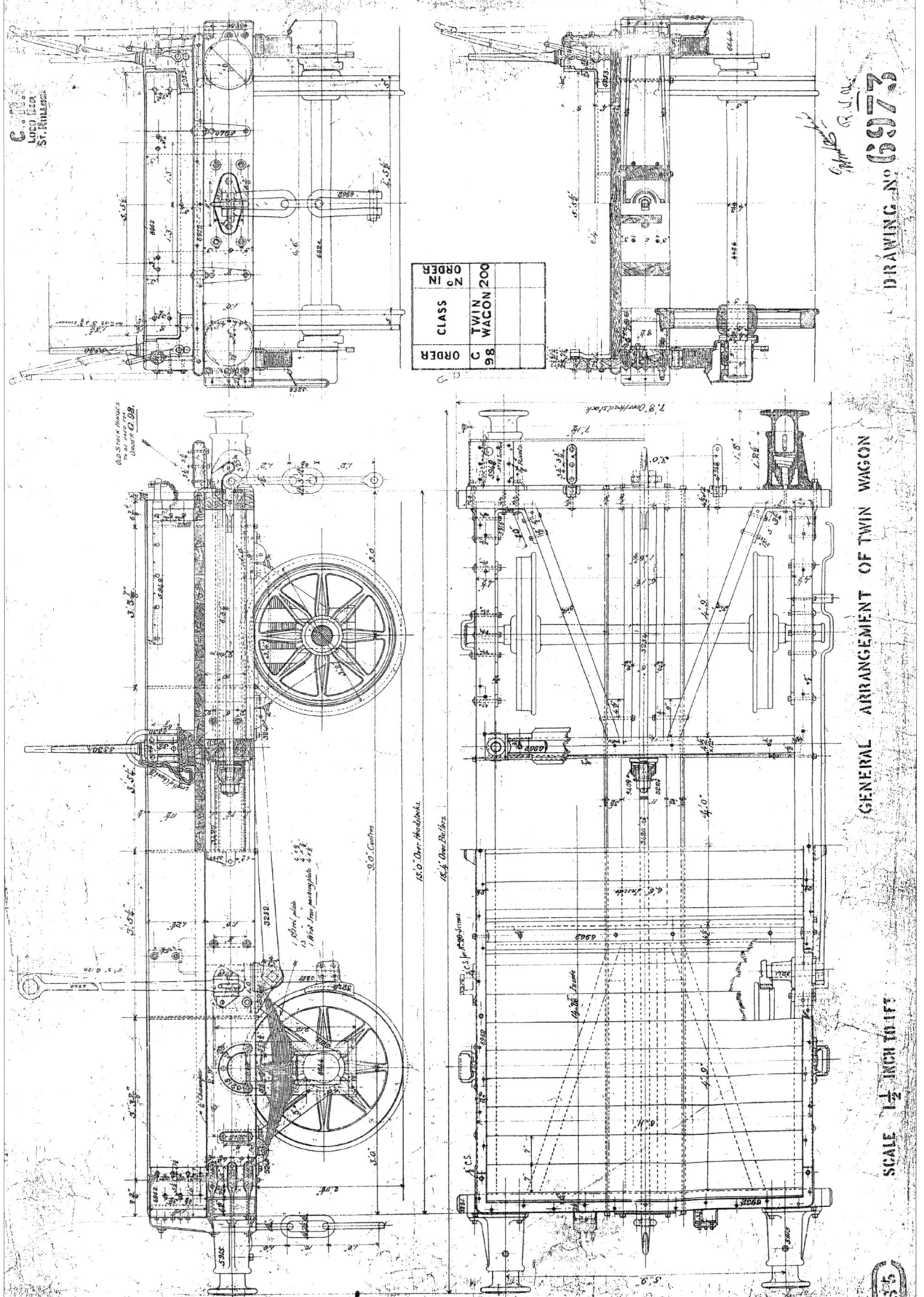

Figure 8.6
St. Rollox drawing 6973 for the Diagram 37 twin wagons. Although the underframe and body construction strongly resembled the Diagram 13 rail wagons, the presence of crown plates and other iron work shows that the solebar was not flitched. Note the semi-permanent shackle coupling between the pairs of wagons.

20 Ton Twin Wagon – Diagram 47

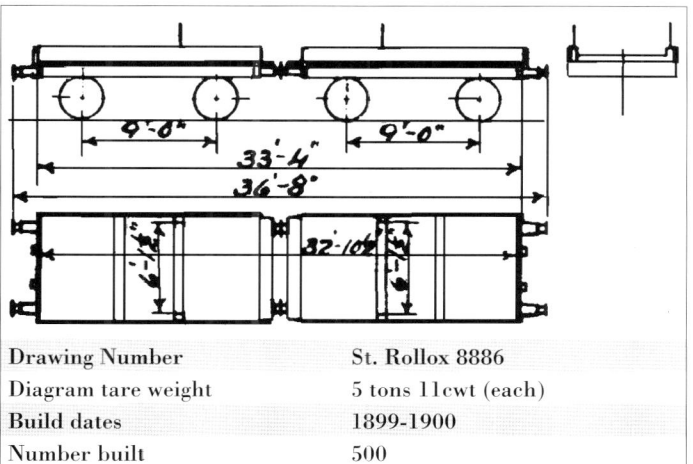

Drawing Number	St. Rollox 8886
Diagram tare weight	5 tons 11cwt (each)
Build dates	1899–1900
Number built	500

The individual wagons of Diagram 47 shared a common underframe with the Diagram 48 timber and ore wagons, except that the axlebox journals were heavier at 9 inches by 4 inches, rather than 8 inches by 3¾ inches. The bolsters were offset towards the centre of the pair of wagons and did not swivel. The inner ends folded down.

A single capital expenditure order (St. Rollox G166) was authorised at the same time as the Diagram 48 wagons.[3] In the period ending July 1899, 452 were built. The balance was completed by the end of January 1900. They were fitted with the McIntosh brake with the cast V-hanger. Heavy duty self-contained buffers were fitted. The wagons were semi-permanently coupled, as Diagram 37, and consecutive numbers with the lower number an even number. Like the Diagram 37 wagons, they would have been allocated a block of numbers, including 43640/41 on photographic evidence.

15 Ton Twin Wagon – Diagram 109

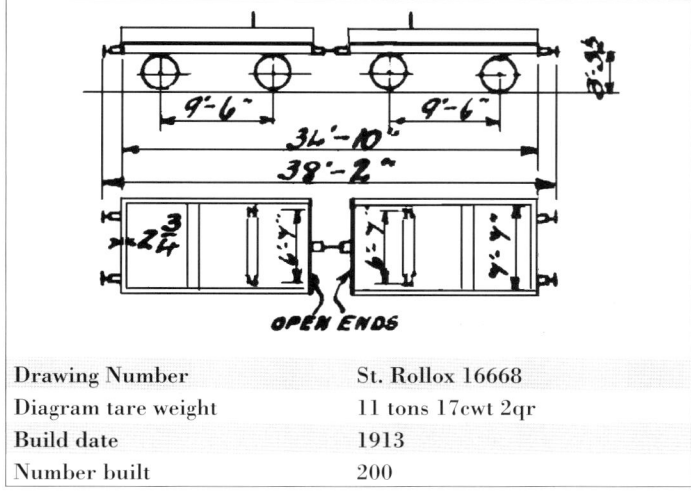

Drawing Number	St. Rollox 16668
Diagram tare weight	11 tons 17cwt 2qr
Build date	1913
Number built	200

These wagons were enlarged and modernised versions of Diagram 48. The capacity in the diagram book refers to each wagon, so the load was actually 30 tons. The wheelbase was 6 inches longer and the

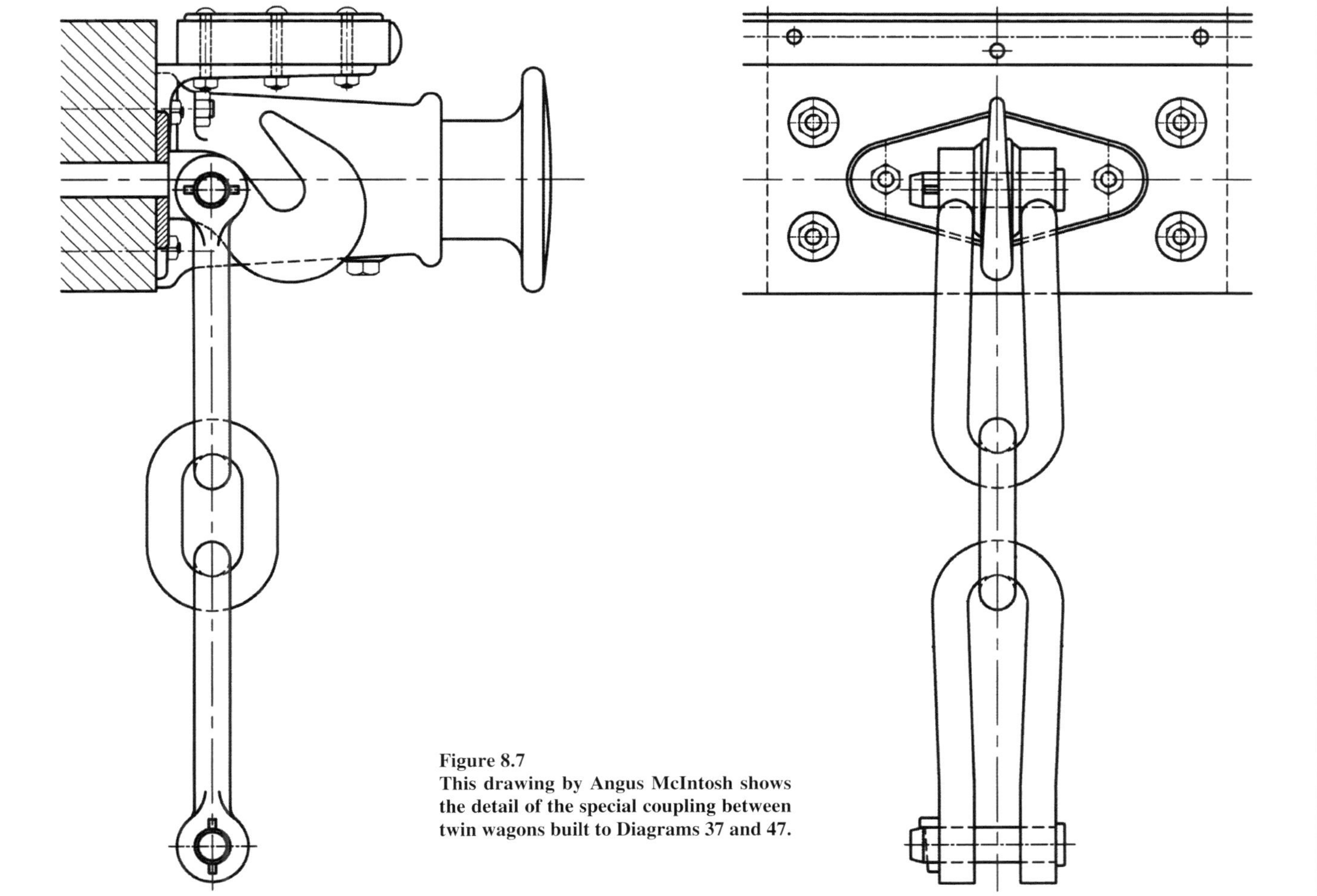

Figure 8.7
This drawing by Angus McIntosh shows the detail of the special coupling between twin wagons built to Diagrams 37 and 47.

overall width was 8 feet 0½ inch. There were no ends between the two wagons. The sides, outer ends and stanchions were fixed. The body was made of American red pine, with a white pine floor, according to the card order.

They were carried on steel underframes. The journal size was 9 inches by 4½ inches. They were built with Iracier axle boxes, but these were later removed. Each wagon had double brakes on both sides which could be operated from either side of the wagon. They were semi-permanently coupled in pairs by a pin and central buffing plate arrangement. They had the larger self-contained buffer at the outer ends.

The Board authorised 100 pairs of Diagram 109 twin wagons in November 1912, along with the 100 15-ton rail wagons for the Clydebridge Steelworks traffic.[4]

A subsequent minute[5] states that offers were accepted from Pickering and Hurst Nelson for fifty pairs each, with delivery starting in March 1913. The Pickering dispatch book records that their delivery started on 22nd March and the order for fifty pairs was completed on 17th April.[6]

A slightly later card order[7] shows that Pickering completed the remainder of the contract as well. Batches of wagon frames were received from Leeds Forge and the running gear and bodies were built at Wishaw. This order ran on from the end of the previous order and was completed on 10th May.

REFERENCES
1. NRS BR/CAL/1/35 entry 263
2. NRS BR/CAL/5/11 entry 68
3. NRS BR/CAL/5/11 entry 321
4. NRS BR/CAL/1/62 entry 1004
5. NRS BR/CAL/1/62 entry 1026
6. Pickering card order 22691
7. Pickering card order 22699

ABOVE: Plate 8.15
This pair of wagons, numbers 43640/41, to Diagram 47 was built in 1899/1900. The McIntosh patent brake is fitted, but the arrangements differ. The left-hand wagon has a cast hanger and equal length push rods. The right-hand wagon has an ordinary V-hanger but offset, giving unequal length push rods. This variation was also seen on a Diagram 52 wagon, which was built at roughly the same time. In both cases the brake actuating levers are in odd positions, suggesting that brake block wear has not been taken up.

BELOW: Plate 8.16
This photograph shows the final development of twin wagon to Diagram 109, with a steel underframe and Iracier axle boxes. These examples should have been built by Hurst Nelson, but were actually built by Pickering, using Leeds Forge underframe parts. Fifty pairs numbered 73083/4-73181/2 were ordered for the Clydebridge Steelworks traffic in 1913 at a cost of £242 per pair. Braking follows the twin wagon convention of sets of brakes on alternate sides of the pair of wagons. Pickering built another order of fifty pairs on their own account, using Leeds Forge underframes, numbered 72983/4-73081/2.

8.4: Stone Wagons

Pre-Diagram Book Era Wagons

Wagons to carry stone were first constructed in 1869. The rolling stock return for the period ending July 1869 records the addition of 101 wagons, annotated *'one (pattern) built at Coy works at expense of Revenue.'* In the next period a further forty-nine were built to the capital account.

The only reference to these wagons in company minutes was in December 1870, when Ashbury was authorised to build 200 as part of a tender for a number of different types of wagon.[1]

St. Rollox drawing 1082 dates from 1871.[2] The drawing register described it as a 10-ton wagon with 14-foot sides The rolling stock returns for the periods ending July 1871 and January 1872 record the addition of 225 wagons, suggesting that the balance of twenty-five were built at St. Rollox. No further wagons were built.

These wagons were long lived. One was photographed for the *1900 Register of Wagon Plant* where it was stated that 171 were in service. It shows a wagon of typical construction for the period, with folding centre doors and fixed ends. The sides were of two narrow planks, total height about 12 inches. The wagons are not identified in the 1907-10 statements.

Later Period Wagons

Two other drawings which have not survived (St. Rollox 8502 and 9212) are for road metal wagons. The first, which dates from 1897, was a 10-ton wagon specifically for Lanarkshire Council. The second, drawn a year later, was described as a road metal wagon. These wagons were built by Pickering.[3] They were originally unpainted, according to the card order; instead, the bodies received one coat of gold size and two of coach varnish. Ironwork was black, as was the lettering.

The wagons were sold to the Scottish Wagon Co. and subsequently hired to the council. In April 1899, Pickering assumed ownership of the wagons:

'We are to take over from and fulfil the Lanarkshire County Council's obligations to the Scottish Wagon Company in respect of 25 wagons (10 ton spring buffer for Road Metal with folding sides) 26/58150–50/58174 built by us in 1897 until 75 new wagons are delivered to them.'[4]

The wagons were lettered for Dunduff quarry and were then painted slate colour *'same as Hurst Nelson Co's Dunduff Quarry.'*

References
1. NRS BR/CAL/1/17 entry 1570
2. Not yet catalogued
3. Pickering card order 2186
4. Pickering card order 3586

Plate 8.17
A pre-diagram book stone wagon built to drawing 1082 and photographed for the *1900 Register*. According to the rolling stock returns, 225 were built in 1871/2 and 171 were still in stock in 1900. The painted number is 35399. The load is written on the curb rail to avoid the company initial, but there is room on the body for the tare weight. The old-style shackle coupling with small centre link is still in use. This is another example (see also Plate 8.11) of curved and straight axle guard bridles on the same wagon.

ABOVE: Plate 9.1
This picture of a train crossing the Tay at Perth shows some of the early short-wheelbase goods wagons, unfortunately covered by tarpaulins. The running number of the third wagon back has four digits, indicating a wagon in the goods number series.

BELOW AND FACING PAGE: Figure 9.1
St. Rollox drawing 1659 dates from 1874. The underframe is modern-looking compared with contemporary mineral wagons, with axle guards inside the solebars, spindle-sprung buffers and laminated sprung drawgear.

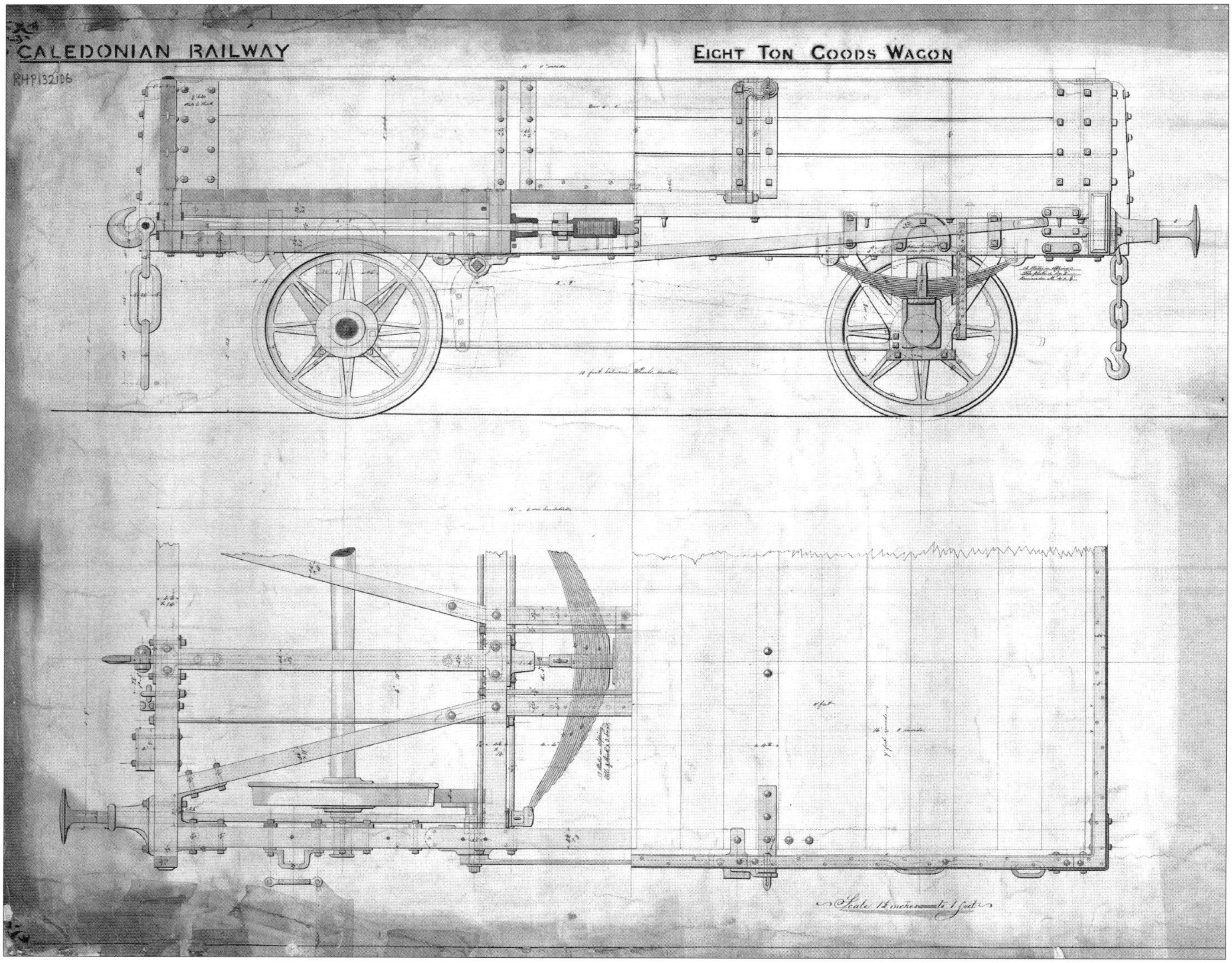

Chapter 9
Ordinary Goods Wagons and Vans

9.1: Open Goods

This chapter deals with wagons that carried general merchandise. Specialist vehicles for perishable goods and livestock are discussed in Chapters 10 and 11. The rolling stock returns described open goods wagons as *'ordinary'*. Covered goods vans were separately identified.

Eight hundred wagons were ordered from contractors in the summer of 1846, but they were probably a combination of coal and goods types.[1] When the rolling stock returns began in 1853 there were 900 ordinary goods wagons, compared with about 3,500 mineral wagons.

By 1857 the goods wagon stock had increased to over 1,350. The mineral stock had only increased by 500 wagons over the same period. As was explained in Chapter 5, higher capacity mineral wagons were built as renewals, reducing numbers while maintaining capacity. Many of the orders in the late 1850s were for specialised wagons, such as timber and bar iron carriers. A typical order for ordinary wagons of the period was from Faulds of Glasgow, who tendered for eighty-four goods wagons at £29 15s, less 5%.[2]

In 1861, Ashbury supplied 100 deep sided goods wagons, 100 deep sided with round ends, and twenty of 10 tons capacity. The prices were £73 10s, £74 10s and £66 respectively. At the same time, Faulds supplied 100 ordinary wagons at £63 each.[3] According to the returns, most of these replaced worn out wagons.

The next major addition to the goods wagon fleet was in 1865, when 240 wagons were added to stock. These were probably built by the CR, as there is no record of a tendering process. The stock stood at 1,692 in July 1865. Amalgamation with the Scottish Central Railway added 1,500 more, with a contribution of over 900 from the Scottish North Eastern in 1867. The fleet was also increased by a large order from Ashbury, which included 125 ordinary wagons at a price of £61 each and sixty-two with round ends for £69 10s.[4]

Three hundred wagons were added in the period ending July 1869. They had been ordered from Ashbury. The cost was £54 each. Part of the payment was made in 5% company stock.[5] The additional wagons were in response to complaints by the Coltness Iron Co. and the Haywood Gas Coal Co. that mineral wagons meant for their traffic had been diverted to carry general goods.[6]

In the period ending January 1871, 420 ordinary wagons were added to the fleet. Again, most were supplied by Ashbury in the form of 350 *'deep sided wagons'* at £63 each.[7] In the same period Ashbury supplied wagons as renewals, at £67 each for 300 round ended wagons and 150 ordinary wagons at £54 each.[8]

The years 1874, 1877 and 1881 saw further additions of 351 wagons, 197 and 205 respectively. As well as the additions, 4,984 wagons were replaced between 1869 and 1882. Nearly two-thirds of the total was built in the five calendar years set out in the following table:

1874	1877	1880	1881	1882
581	482	643	941	479

The capacity of these wagons is not always specified, but the earlier designs were probably 6 tons, based on one mention in a tender accepted in 1869. Seven and 8-ton wagons were first mentioned in tenders starting from 1870.

Wagons, of course, were also constantly replaced. The table below shows the returns, aggregated over five-year periods from 1865, plus the years 1880-82, when Drummond was appointed. Contractors did not build all these wagons. Apart from 1877, successful tenders account for about one third of the additional wagons.

1865-69	1870-74	1875-79	1880-82
155	1,476	1,450	2,063

Pre-Diagram Book Designs

References to drawings of ordinary goods wagons abound from the earliest times, although they have not survived. Some were for low sided wagons, some mentioned falling sides. Around 1870, 6 tons capacity was mentioned for three drawings and 10 tons in another. Two drawings were for round end wagons with laminated

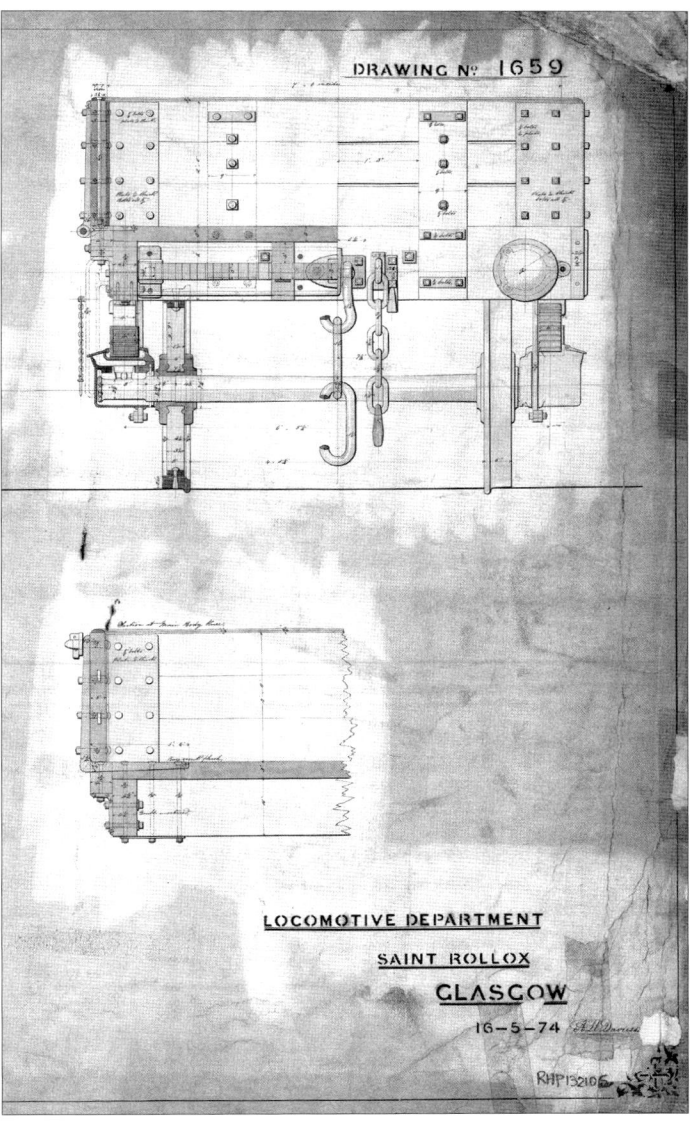

LEFT: **Plate 9.2**
This picture, taken at Muchalls station goods yard, shows an early design of open goods wagon to drawing 1522. Note the tiebar between the axle guards, a common design feature on goods and loco coal wagons of the 1870s and early '80s. The load writing on the left-hand side is in italic script and there does not seem to be any indication of the tare weight. Also of great interest is the open goods wagon next to it. It is a Port Patrick Railway wagon, one of 39 *'ordinary 6-ton wagons with buffers'* absorbed into Caledonian stock, according to the rolling stock inventory of 1874. Was the trefoil the PPR's illiterate mark?

BELOW AND FACING PAGE: **Figure 9.2**
The St. Rollox drawing number 3504 of the Diagram 24 wagon, dated 3rd April 1883 in the drawings register. The Diagram 15 wagons were identical in dimensions. Like all goods wagons, the bolt heads were on the outside to avoid damage to loads.

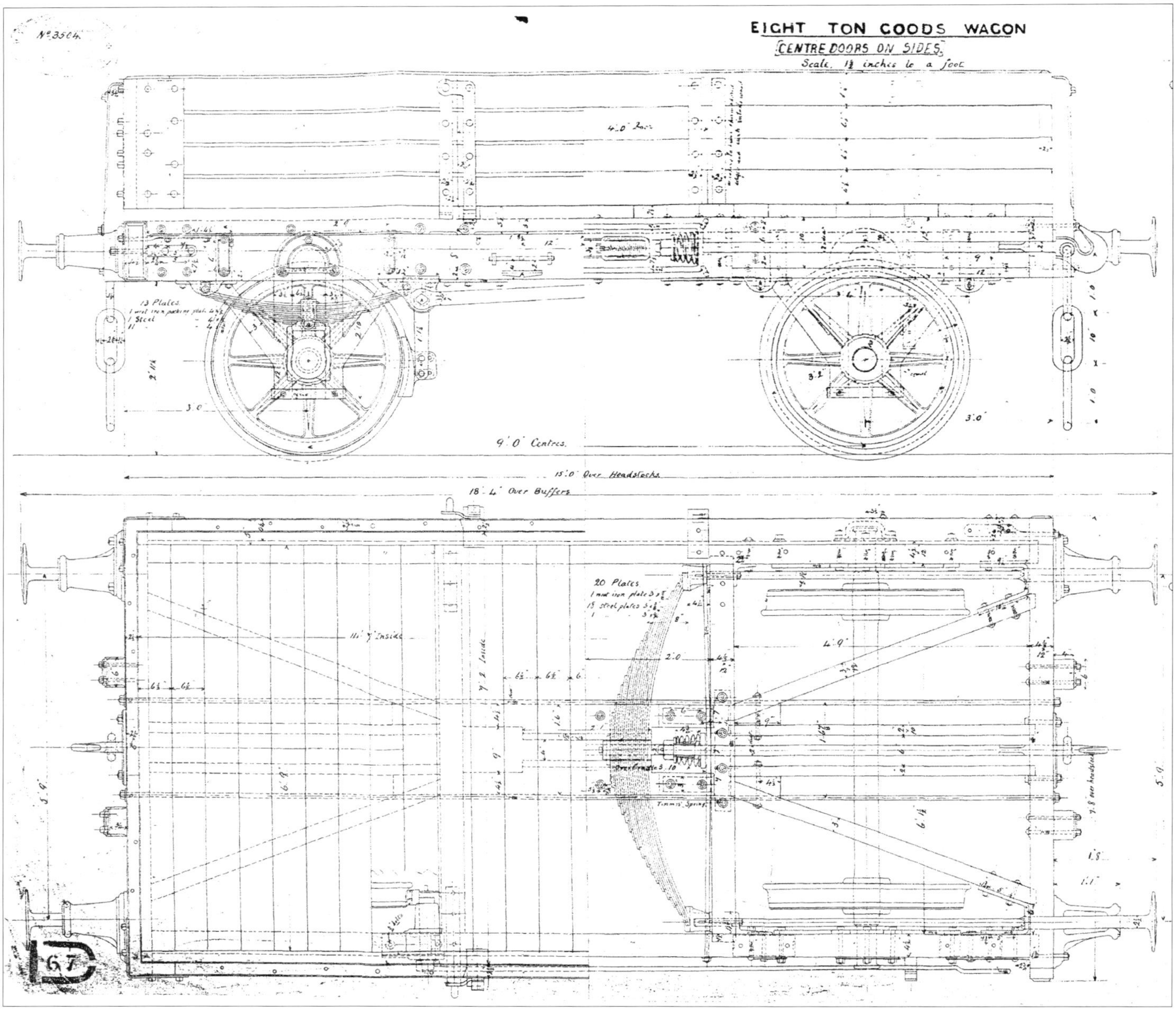

Plate 9.3
The later style of pre-diagram book goods wagon with self-contained three-bolt sprung buffers. The 12-inch letters are condensed. The lack of tie bar between the axle guards and the Drummond pattern cast iron brake block suggest that it may well be one of the *'reconstructed'* wagons of 1906. These wagons were originally built to drawing 1659. The ironwork looks heavier than that used on Diagram 24 wagons, which also supports the reconstruction theory.

spring buffers. Another dating from 1871 was for a 10-ton wagon with 2-foot sides.

The first surviving drawing (number 984) dates from 1870 on the evidence of a note requiring the solebars to be ¼ inch thicker for a contract in November of that year.[9] It is for an 8-ton wagon with solid buffers, with 1 foot 6 inches deep sides, measuring 15 feet over body. This drawing was probably used for the Ashbury contract for 350 wagons, which was agreed in December 1870.

A drawing (St. Rollox 994) for a very similar wagon was produced at the same time for carrying beer.[10] It had 1-foot 9-inch single-plank sides, with a 4-foot 6-inch drop door. Four-bolt spindle buffers were fitted. The rolling stock returns record that fifty of these wagons were put into traffic in 1871

This was followed in 1872 by a sprung buffer version to drawing 1397. The dimensions are given by Miller as 14 feet 6 inches by 7 feet 6 inches, and 1 foot 6 inches deep – but these were the internal dimensions. The wheelbase was 8 feet 6 inches.

In 1873 the St. Rollox register records two designs. Drawing 1502 depicted an 8-ton wagon. Internal dimensions were 16 feet 6 inches by 7 feet 6 inches. The sides were 1 foot 6 inches deep. Side doors were fitted. The wheelbase was 10 feet. Drawing 1659, issued in 1874,[11] was for a similar wagon with sides 2 feet high. It had the three-bolt self-contained buffer. Safety chains were fitted and there was a tie bar between the axle guards.

Also in 1873, a slightly shorter wagon without doors was the subject of drawing 1522. It was 15 feet 4 inches by 7 feet 6 inches, with 1 foot 9 inches deep sides. The wheelbase was 9 feet. One of these wagons is shown in Plate 9.2. Subsequent drawings that have not survived were 2131 and 3202.

The Drummond and McIntosh eras saw the mass scrapping of old wagons. From Drummond's arrival up to 1899, nearly 9,000 goods wagons were replaced and over 2,000 added to the stock.

	1883-84	1885-89	1890-94	1894-99
Renewed	1,393	2,305	1,855	3,369
Added	0	469	501	1,283

The figures included every type of general goods wagon except the swivel wagons, but St. Rollox and contractor orders show that about 9,000 of the general goods type were built. The designs for these new wagons were to Diagrams 15 and 24. One or the other may have the distinction of being the first recorded order built by St. Rollox under the G system, as order G0 was for six goods wagons, type unspecified. The first certain order was for 400 wagons to order G10, authorised in April 1885.

Plate 9.4
This photograph shows a Diagram 15 wagon loaded with coal in LM&SR days. It still has the original single lever brake gear, although by the time of the photograph there was probably a set of double brakes on the other side. The view clearly shows how the strapping folded back round the inside of the body at the ends, and the simple hinge arrangement. The sides were secured by a pin on a chain. The knob lower down on the ironwork contacted the end of the headstock to prevent damage to the brake gear when the sides were dropped. The effect of age on the headstock, solebar and top plank is noteworthy.

Plate 9.5
This is the only known photograph of a wagon in CR livery with a tarpaulin bar. The 6-inch letters also depart from the standard practice of the time. The number, unfortunately, is not visible. Another Diagram 15 wagon with a tarpaulin bar was photographed as a tool wagon in LM&SR bauxite carrying the number 338203, but the bar was fixed in the upright position and may have been a post-Grouping modification. A 1912 drawing (St. Rollox 16591) was entitled *'sheet support for 8-ton mineral wagon'* but has not survived.

Plate 9.6
St. Rollox built 2,900 Diagram 15 and 24 wagons in 1898/99. Judging by the number, which is repeated on the body rather than on the end, this was one of the 1,000 built to G176 and charged to the capital account. It has a double brake on one side only. The door spring was attached off-centre to accommodate the number plate in its usual position on the centre line of the wagon between the V-hanger legs. The company initials are poorly shaped.

9.1: OPEN GOODS

Goods Wagon Load 8 Tons – Diagram 15

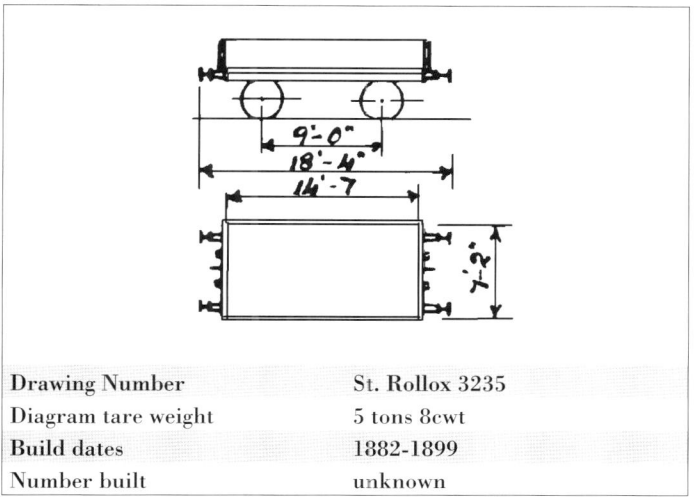

Drawing Number	St. Rollox 3235
Diagram tare weight	5 tons 8cwt
Build dates	1882-1899
Number built	unknown

The Diagram 15 and 24 wagons were identical, except that Diagram 15 had falling sides and Diagram 24 had 4 feet wide doors in the centre of the side, hinged at the bottom. The sides and ends were 2½ inches thick, giving external dimensions of 15 feet by 8 feet. The 2 feet 2 inches high body had four equal planks.

Nearly 200 Diagram 15 wagons were fitted with oil axleboxes and continuous brakes to carry fish and milk by passenger train. These are described and illustrated in Chapter 10.

It is not possible to be sure of the numbers that were built of each type, because most orders and minutes do not specify the type of wagon. The number of Diagram 24 wagons shown in the next table is based on specific references in minutes.

Plate 9.7
The next photograph shows one of the order of 1,000 Diagram 24 wagons built by R Y Pickering in 1899/1900 fitted with the McIntosh patent brake. They were also charged to the capital account and the painting specification was 'steel grey'. This livery is discussed in Chapter 4.

Goods Wagon with Side Doors Load 8 & 10 Tons – Diagram 24

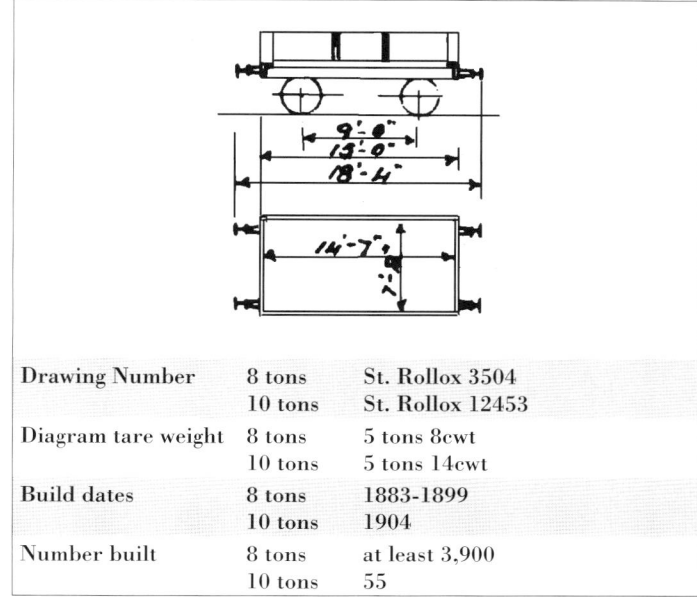

Drawing Number	8 tons	St. Rollox 3504
	10 tons	St. Rollox 12453
Diagram tare weight	8 tons	5 tons 8cwt
	10 tons	5 tons 14cwt
Build dates	8 tons	1883-1899
	10 tons	1904
Number built	8 tons	at least 3,900
	10 tons	55

Originally these wagons, like Diagram 15, were fitted with 8-inch by 3¾-inch journals and the standard single iron brake block. The capacity was 8 tons. Drawing 7059[12] was issued in 1892 for the construction of 500 renewal wagons to St. Rollox order G101. It was also used for an order of 1,000 wagons built by Pickering in 1899/1900, but this contract specified the McIntosh patent brake.[13] The brake increased the tare weight to 5 tons 15cwt. This order was built to the capital account and allocated numbers 44834-44933 and 70384-71982.

In 1904 the design was upgraded. The register entry for the original St. Rollox drawings of 1882 is annotated

'stronger underframe, steel or wood, stronger bearing springs and self-contained buffers and either side brake, journals 9in x 4in and capacity 10 tons, increase of width 5in.'

Self-contained buffers and either side brakes were fitted. Fifty were built to St. Rollox order G219. The order was part of the half-yearly renewal programme authorised in November 1903.[14] The last five wagons were authorised in October 1904.[15] Both diagrams were then superseded by Diagram 87, which was, in effect, the steel underframe version of the upgraded design.

About 300 Diagram 24 wagons were adapted to carry sheep by extending their sides with spars, rather like mineral wagons adapted to carry coke. Presumably the modification was reversible as the carriage of sheep was seasonal traffic. This modification is discussed in Chapter 11.

Reconstruction of Old Wagons

At the same time as the Diagram 87 wagons were introduced, some, perhaps all, surviving pre-diagram book wagons were '*reconstructed*.' Drawing 13938[16] of November 1906 depicts a wagon with the same dimensions as that to drawing 1659, with the exception of the wheelbase, which is the peculiar measurement of 9 feet 10 inches rather than 10 feet. The 1906 drawing shows the Drummond single iron brake and standard three-bolt buffer. There is no tie bar between the axle guards. The location of bolt holes on the body planking was dictated by the original wagon ironwork, which was '*to be reused if in good condition.*'

There is no mention of these wagons in the minutes, and the word '*reconstruction*' suggests that this was a way of building what were in effect new wagons without an impact on the balance sheet. The wagon returns for the periods ending July 1907 and January 1908 record the replacement of 260 wagons. Only forty of these were to Diagram 87 order G250, authorised on 24th April 1906. It is reasonable to assume that the remainder were the reconstructed wagons. It is also possible that the reconstruction programme continued throughout the next two half-year periods. One hundred Diagram 87 wagons were authorised, but 394 open goods wagons were replaced. Plate 9.3 is a possible example.

Plate 9.8
This typical steel underframe Diagram 87 wagon with falling sides was part of a batch of twenty-five built by St. Rollox and charged to the capital account. The paint date is 3/7/22. The steel underframe is the pressed steel version with the curb rail included. Under magnification, the small oval plate to the right of the number plate reads '*Leeds Forge*' (probably) across the top and '*Motherwell*' (certainly) underneath. If correct, Leeds Forge must have licensed production of their patent underframe to a manufacturer more convenient for delivery to St. Rollox than the factory in Leeds.

10 Ton Goods Wagon (with Steel Underframe) – Diagram 87

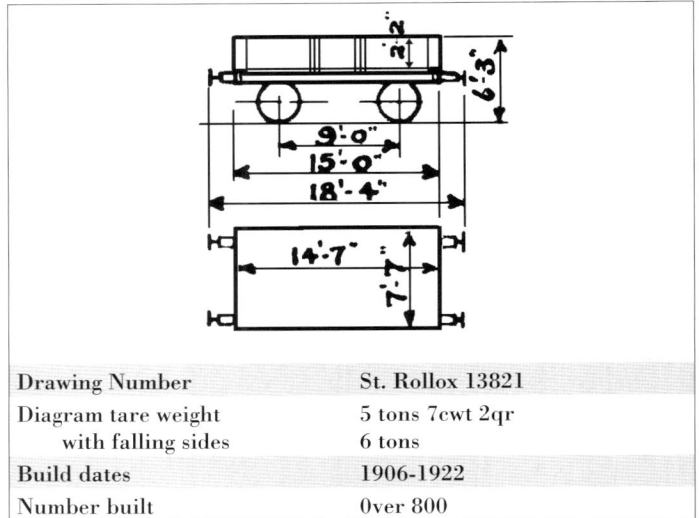

Drawing Number	St. Rollox 13821
Diagram tare weight	5 tons 7cwt 2qr
with falling sides	6 tons
Build dates	1906-1922
Number built	Over 800

These wagons were 5 inches wider than the original version of Diagram 24, fitted with steel underframes and pressed steel headstocks. The self-contained steel underframe buffer was fitted. Most had oil axleboxes, although two orders which included 72013 and 73302 were fitted for grease lubrication.

Steel underframes had been adopted as standard from the early 1900s, but war-time restrictions in supply caused both these and the 16-ton mineral wagons to revert to wood construction for a short time. St. Rollox drawings 18851[17] (centre door) and 18882[18] (drop side version) depict the modification. Both date from November 1916.

Order G383 for 100 renewal wagons with side doors was originally to have been built by St. Rollox, but was actually built by Pickering in 1916/17 on oak underframes.[19] Sample numbers from this order include 1508, 1986, 2046, 4234 and 8895. Although not specified as such, order G392 for eighty wagons with falling sides was also probably built on wood underframes, because a subsequent order for 16-ton mineral wagons (G394) had them specified.

Known orders for wagons with falling sides were G268, 338 and 392, amounting to 315 wagons. Most were authorised under the renewal programme. Orders with centre doors included G250 and G383, totalling 140 wagons. A total of 261 wagons were not specified. There was at least one further order for this type. A Hurst Nelson photograph, taken in 1919, shows a wagon with falling sides. It would

have been built in the renewals programme for one of the two halves of that year, when the minutes did not show the details of the wagons to be built.

Order G368, authorised in 1914[20] and built in 1915, was fitted with dual brakes and steam heat pipes. The St. Rollox drawing number is 17741.[21] These forty wagons, which also had falling sides, were allocated random numbers between 1186 and 3271. The full set of numbers is on page 119 of the *1915 Working Timetable Appendix*.

12 Ton Goods Wagon – Diagram 79

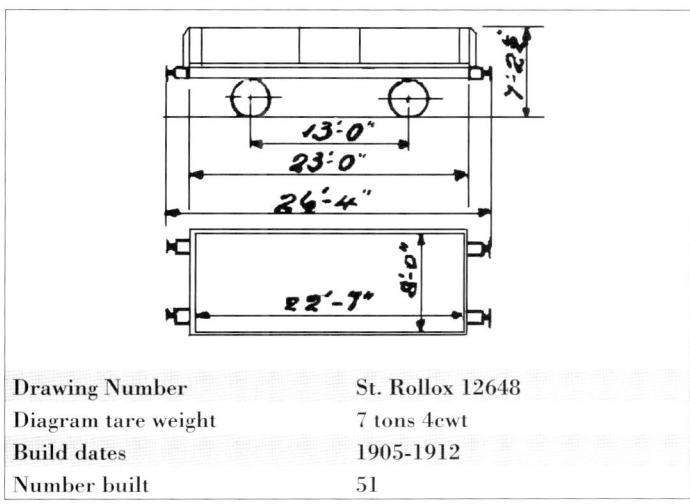

Drawing Number	St. Rollox 12648
Diagram tare weight	7 tons 4cwt
Build dates	1905-1912
Number built	51

The thirty-six Diagram 79 wagons authorised for construction in the half year ending January 1905[22] were enlarged versions of the Diagram 24 wagons, with a capacity of 12 tons. The sides were 3 feet deep, with a drop door opening of 5 feet. It was fitted with 9-inch by 4½-inch journals and self-contained buffers. A further fifteen were built in 1912. The Morton brake was fitted on one side only to this lot. The only known number is 8592. Other numbers were random as they were part of the wagon renewal programme.

12 Ton Goods Wagon – Diagram 120

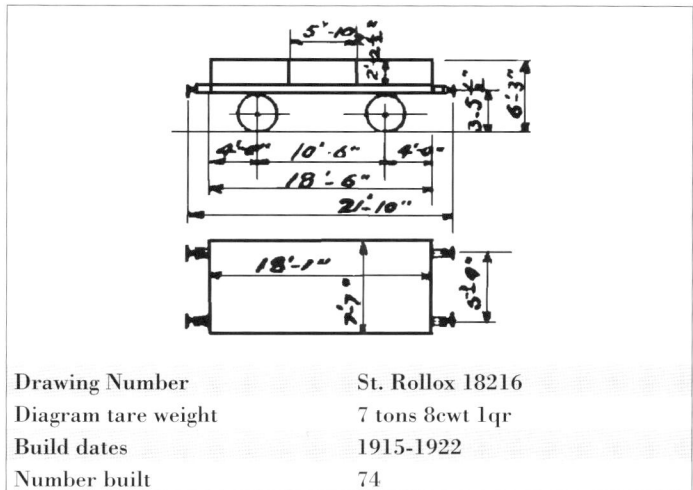

Drawing Number	St. Rollox 18216
Diagram tare weight	7 tons 8cwt 1qr
Build dates	1915-1922
Number built	74

The first twenty-four wagons to this design were built in 1915 to order G373. A further fifty were authorised in 1921.[23] The wagons retained the 2 feet 2 inches high sides of Diagrams 15 and 24, but were 18 feet 6 inches long externally and 8 feet wide. The

Plate 9.9
This is a Diagram 87 wagon built on a wood underframe in 1916. It can be distinguished from the Diagram 15 and 24 wagons by the wider headstocks, caused by the 5 inches increase in body width. The side away from the camera is dropped down. It is fitted with the Morton brake arrangement and oil axleboxes. The latter may have been an LM&SR addition. The CR number may have been 1588, as all the wooden underframe Diagram 87 wagons were replacements. The number does not appear in the despatch records of the wagons to order G383 that was built by Pickering in 1916, so it is probably one of eighty built by St. Rollox to order G392, authorised later the same year.

Plate 9.10
This Diagram 79 wagon was one of the first order of thirty-six built to G222, authorised in May 1904 with a double brake on one side only. The 1911 order to G312 had either side brakes. It has self-contained buffers and the less common horse hook, which were more usually seen on wagons with steel underframes. Twelve-leaf springs are fitted and 9-inch by 4½-inch journals. The door spring is mounted slightly off centre – see the position of the metal patch on the door. The tension of the chain securing the load has pulled the spring out of vertical. The number plate is displaced to the left of centre rather than the more usual right.

door opening was 5 feet 10 inches. They were fitted with pressed steel underframes, grease axleboxes with 9-inch by 4½-inch journals, heavy duty springs and self-contained buffers. The Morton brake acted on one side. The only known number is 38380 in Plate 2.11 (p. 28).

Proposed 12 Ton Open Wagons

In November 1918, sketches were made of ten different styles of 12-ton wagon, all with steel bodies.[24] Lengths varied from 17 feet to 20 feet, and the depth of the sides were 3 feet, 1 foot 9 inches and 9 inches. Nothing seems to have come of these radical proposals.

Diagram 54 Wagons in Goods Traffic

Thirty one of the bogie wagons were routinely used for general goods traffic from 1903.[25] As part of the rolling stock renewal programme for half year ending December 1914, an order for another six 30-ton bogie goods wagons was proposed.[26] The Traffic Committee decided to alter six of the existing loco coal wagons, rather than build new.[27] The alteration to these wagons consisted of making the plates above the side doors removable to allow staff to carry consignments into the wagons and welding a small lidded box for invoices to the body. Presumably, the modifications applied to all the wagons in general goods traffic.

An article in *The Railway Gazette* in 1922 mentions a daily service between Buchanan Street and *'Aberdeen, Dundee, Motherwell, Stirling, &c'*. The wagons carried *'returned empties'* back to Glasgow. Each wagon could carry a load equivalent to at least three Diagram 15 or 24 wagons. It is difficult to be more precise, as these and the smaller wagons were routinely loaded higher than their sides, with the load secured by tarpaulins.

There is no record of a drawing for the alterations, or a full set of numbers for the modified wagons, except for two photographs. Plate 2.11, a photograph of Buchanan Street goods station, shows 66413 in the background. This wagon was one of the 100 built by the Metropolitan Carriage & Wagon Co. Birmingham Railway Carriage & Wagon Co.'s 66498 shows the modifications for carrying goods in Plates 9.12-9.14.

References
1. NRS BR/CAL/1/7 p. 360
2. NRS BR/CAL/1/11 entry 551
3. NRS BR/CAL/1/12 entry 1388
4. NRS BR/CAL/1/14 entry 1421
5. NRS BR/CAL/1/17 entry 117
6. NRS BR/CAL/1/17 entry 28
7. NRS BR/CAL/1/18 entry 1570
8. NRS BR/CAL/1/18 entry 860
9. Not yet catalogued
10. Not yet catalogued
11. Not yet catalogued
12. NRM 8041/W, RHP 69143
13. NRS BR/CAL/5/11 entry 361, Pickering card order 3352
14. NRS BR/CAL/1/48 entry 691
15. NRS BR/CAL/1/50 entry 217
16. Not yet catalogued
17. NRM 12001/W
18. NRM 11999/W
19. Pickering card order 30872
20. NRS BR/CAL/1/65 entry 1041
21. NRM 11997/W
22. NRS BR/CAL/1/49 entry 769
23. NRS BR/CAL/1/80 entry 869
24. Not yet catalogued
25. NRS BR/CAL/4/134 page 33
26. NRS BR/CAL/1/64 entry 1149
27. NRS BR/CAL/1/80 entry 1335

Plate 9.11
This is a 10-ton goods wagon to Diagram 120. Twenty-four were authorised in 1915, and a further fifty in 1922. It is fitted with a Morton brake, acting on the two wheels on the far side of the wagon. Although the number is not clear, the photograph was annotated as 38380.

9.2: Covered Goods

Covered goods vans made an early appearance on the Caledonian. A minute in February 1851 stated that material was in hand to work up upwards of thirty covered wagons, and that the Traffic Committee had ordered ten for Glasgow–Manchester traffic.[1] The rolling stock return for July 1853 shows the total as twenty-two. Numbers did not increase significantly until 1858 when the total was forty-one. By 1862 it was just over 200. The Scottish Central contributed 104 and the Scottish North Eastern 101 at their respective amalgamations.

Over the twenty-five year period from 1857 to 1882, just over 1,100 vans were added to stock, while a further 400-plus were replaced. Faulds supplied 121 renewals at £99 10s each as part of a tender which was accepted in February 1861.[2] Analysis of the tenders over the period alongside the half-yearly shareholders' reports suggests that nearly all the remaining renewals were built by St. Rollox in small numbers during each six-month period, while contractors built the additions charged to capital expenditure. Ashbury and Oldbury were the major contractors, supplying 465 and 312 vans respectively. Drawings of these early contractor-built vans have not survived, but an advertisement with a picture of an Ashbury van built in 1863 looks very like the slightly later standard Caledonian design, apart from running gear and buffers. The picture is unfortunately unsuitable for reproduction in print, but can be viewed at http://www.metcam.co.uk.nstempintl.com/ashbfull.htm.

Pre-Diagram Book Designs

Early St. Rollox drawings of goods vans have not survived. Drawing 2090 of 1875 was redrawn in 1916 and numbered 19471.[3] This design was adopted as standard and built until the Diagram 3 vans were introduced. The bodies were almost identical to the contemporary L&NWR 6 and 7-ton designs.[4]

The drawing depicts a 6-ton van measuring 16 feet 9 inches by 7 feet 8 inches, on a 10-foot wheelbase. The axle guards were outside the solebars. Both types of early self-contained sprung buffer were fitted. Examples are: four-bolt buffer 4956, 4995, 5126; three-bolt buffer 1931, 37155, 37228, 37250.

The van had heavy outside framing not dissimilar to the Ashbury design of 1863. There was a door opening of 5 feet 10 inches on one side only, with a roof door above. The two side doors slid behind the body sides. Reinforcing rods were fitted between the top and bottom rails of the body, echoing the construction of the 7-ton mineral 'bogies'.

The last recorded order from contractors was authorised in July 1882, when S J Claye tendered for eighty vans as part of a larger contract.[5] In March 1883, St. Rollox designed a variation of the current design, with an iron body and Drummond details.[6] The body and floor was a self contained unit which sat on a conventional underframe. There is no certain photographic record of the iron

Plates 9.12, 13 and 14
One of the thirty wagons built by the Birmingham Railway & Carriage Works in merchandise service. The sections of plating over the doors are removable for ease of loading. Immediately below the 'C' is a small hinged box with 'INVOICES' cast into the lid. The load was protected by tarpaulins which were attached to rings part way up the T-angle bracing. The use of tarpaulins also allowed the load to extend above the height of the wagon body. There is no evidence of a wood floor, which would be visible through the open doors. Plate 9.13 (*left*) shows the alterations to the door and 9.14 (*right*) the invoice box in more detail.

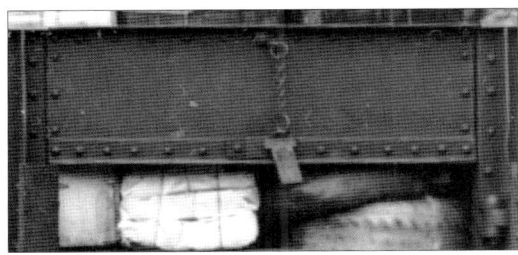

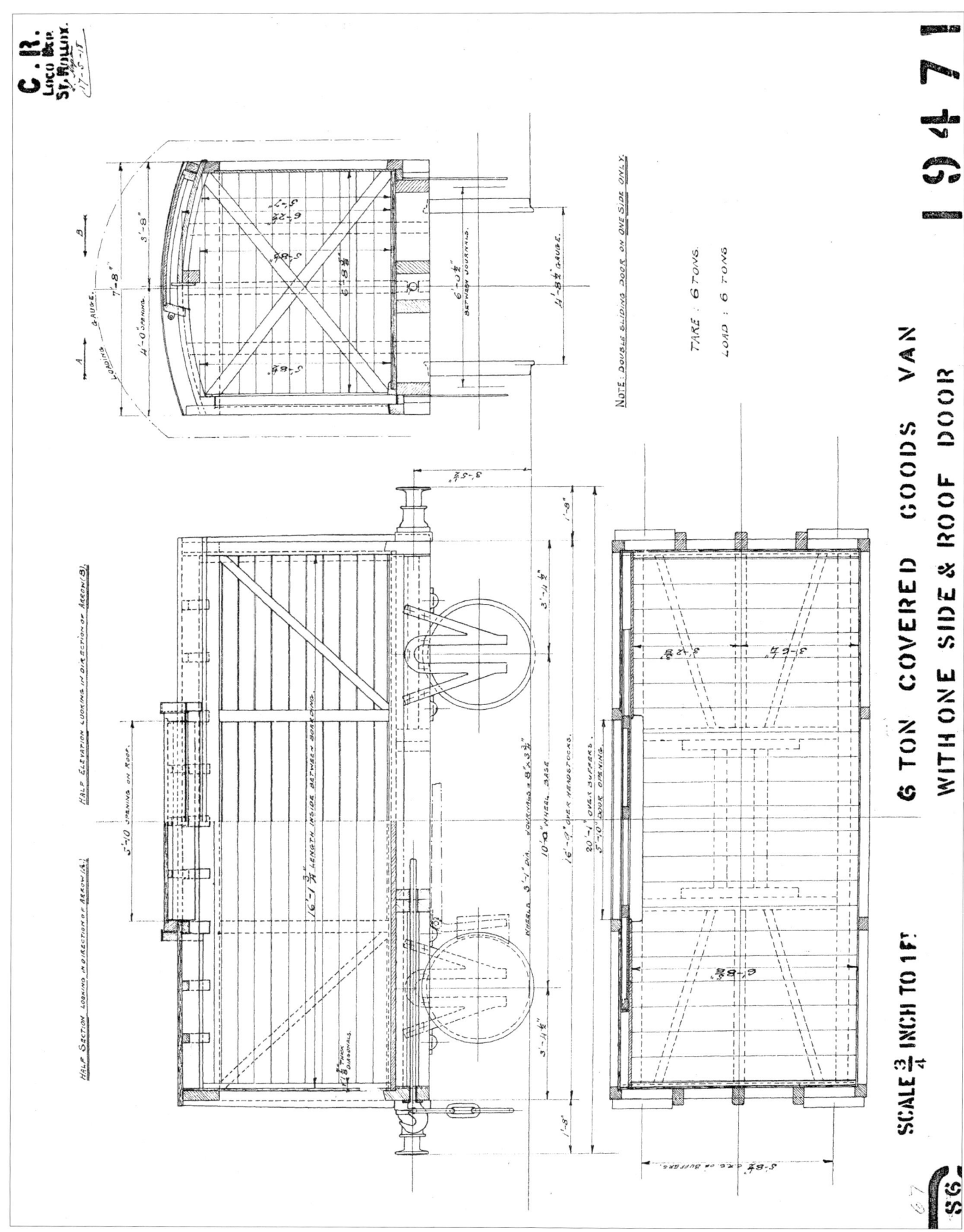

bodied design, although they may be the vans shown in Plate 9.19.

St. Rollox continued to build wooden bodied vans to the original design. The returns record just under 200 replacements up to the half year ending January 1885. Vans of this type built after Drummond's arrival had modern running gear with axle guards inside the solebars.

Covered Goods Van Load 6 Tons – Diagram 3

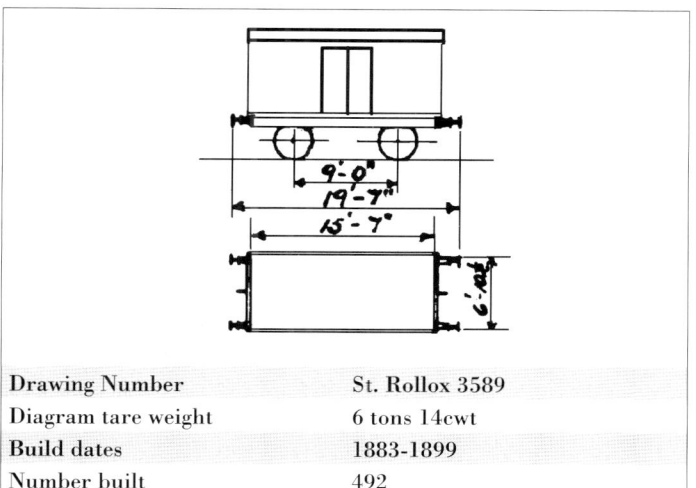

Drawing Number	St. Rollox 3589
Diagram tare weight	6 tons 14cwt
Build dates	1883-1899
Number built	492

This diagram was built to two different body styles. Both had double swing doors with an opening of 5 feet. They were 16 feet 2 inches over headstocks and the body was 7 feet 6 inches wide. The sides were 6 feet 4 inches high to the eaves. The first type was identical to an NBR design,[7] which Drummond originated in 1880 before his move to the Caledonian in 1882, but with CR buffers, running gear and iron brake. The sides were vertically boarded with mouldings covering the joints.

St. Rollox built 224 vans to this style.[8] Order G126 of 1895 included six vans *'with ventilator for yeast traffic.'* A drawing was not made of the modification. No other information is available about these vans. A further 150 were built to the capital account by Hurst Nelson. Some of the latter vans were lettered for the nominally independent Lanarkshire & Dumbartonshire Railway. Another photograph of a van in the same order was not lettered for a specific section of the system.[9]

Starting with order G159, authorised in September 1897, the vans were horizontally planked with flush boarding. The St. Rollox drawing for the first style carries a hand-written note detailing the alteration. The joints with the framing were covered with half-round beading. Order G159 was for thirty-eight vans, and a further eighty were built to G173 in 1899. The horizontally boarded style was continued in the first Diagram 67 design.

Six vans additional to the thirty-eight ordinary vans on order G159 were adapted to carry gunpowder. This modification is discussed in Chapter 15. The last St. Rollox order (G173) was fitted with the McIntosh patent brake. This variation was the subject of drawing 8703.[10] Some of these vans were modified for perishable goods traffic. These are discussed in Chapter 10.

Facing Page: Figure 9.3
St. Rollox number 19471 of 1918 was a redrawing of the original, number 1090, which dated from 1875. It shows a wagon with heavy self-contained buffers. Unfortunately it does not show the door side of the van. It is hard to imagine that any of these vans still survived in 1918, given the construction under the renewal programme of the Diagram 67 vans.

10 Ton Covered Goods Van with Sliding Doors – Diagram 67

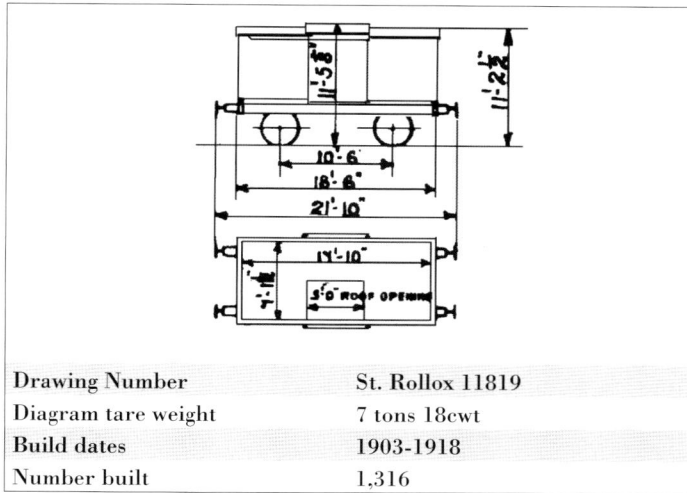

Drawing Number	St. Rollox 11819
Diagram tare weight	7 tons 18cwt
Build dates	1903-1918
Number built	1,316

These vans were originally plain boarded with 5-foot sliding doors on both sides and a single roof door. Half-round beading covered the joints between the boarding and the framework, like the later design of Diagram 3. They were originally fitted with a brake which acted on both wheels on one side only.

They first appeared in 1903, when a contract was split between R Y Pickering, who built 150, with the Motherwell Wagon & Rolling Stock Co. and Renshaw each contributing a further twenty-five.[11] The price was £93 10s each. Two publicity photographs of 254 and 3937 show that they were fitted with CR 14 grease axleboxes. The low random running numbers suggest that they replaced earlier vehicles.

In 1907, the Traffic Committee authorised the modification of three vans for Argyll Motor Company traffic by fitting *'a small aperture or slip door.'*[12] There is no record of a drawing for this intriguing modification, which presumably was applied to the end of the vans.

By the time order G290 was authorised in late 1907,[13] the roof door had been abandoned and end ventilators were fitted. These modifications are recorded on drawing number 14457.[14] In 1909, Morton brakes on both sides of the van were fitted for the first time;[15] this was order G280, to drawing 14789.[16] These were the first vans with wooden outside framing. They were fitted with a sliding flap on the left of each end, and a ventilator covered with a bonnet.

The twenty vans to order G290, authorised for the half year ending July 1910,[17] had 3-foot 9-inch wheels and tie rods between the axle guards. These vans were the subject of drawing 16215.[18] In 1912 the order for 100 vans to G307 was built with Iracier axleboxes.

There is a record of 107 dual brake fitted vans in the *1915 WTT Appendix*. They were first authorised in 1911, when forty of an order of 100 were modified.[19] These vans had oil axleboxes and screw couplings. Numbers in the Appendix include 1040, 4256, 5761, 7190, 8126, 8451, 9169, 9824 and 35693. The total does not exactly match the information on the St. Rollox orders. G307 (the original forty vans), G325 and G360 (thirty and forty vans respectively) were recorded as built with the dual brake. St. Rollox drawing number 17335 refers to order G360. It has not survived.

A further forty-five (orders G371 and 391) were built with dual brakes in late 1915/1916. Some of these vans were probably insulated to carry frozen meat at the request of the Ministry of Food. This development is discussed in Chapter 10.

In July 1915 the Traffic Committee[20] authorised the conversion of seventeen vans to carry cordite paste. This, the propellant for artillery shells, was made at the newly-opened factory at Gretna.

(Continued on page 160)

LEFT: Plate 9.15
This photograph of 5126 shows the construction of these wagons well, but is not entirely typical. The most common version has diagonal framing on the doors, as in the next photograph. The brake on this van is actuated by a pushrod, whereas the brake arm was normally attached direct to the brake block. The earliest type of four-bolt sprung buffer is fitted with a packing block behind it, and the first type of open spoke wheel. The lettering on this and the next two vans is the later style, which lasted until cast number plates were introduced. The number on the solebar is offset to the right probably because CR was originally painted left of centre.

BELOW: Plate 9.16
This photograph shows how the doors slid behind the body side on these early vans.

BELOW: Plate 9.17
The photograph of 37250 shows the non-door side of the wooden covered vans. This is one of the last orders for this type, built after Drummond took office and before he introduced the Diagram 3 design. 37250 has the early three-bolt self-contained sprung buffer and modern running gear with the springs outside the axle guards. The springs are very light, with few leaves. The ends of the headstocks are chamfered in a similar style to L&NWR wagons, but without the reason for it being done – the L&NWR had brake levers that projected beyond the headstocks. Other numbers were 37155 and 37229. 37170 was numbered in script style and is shown in Chapter 3.

9.2: COVERED GOODS

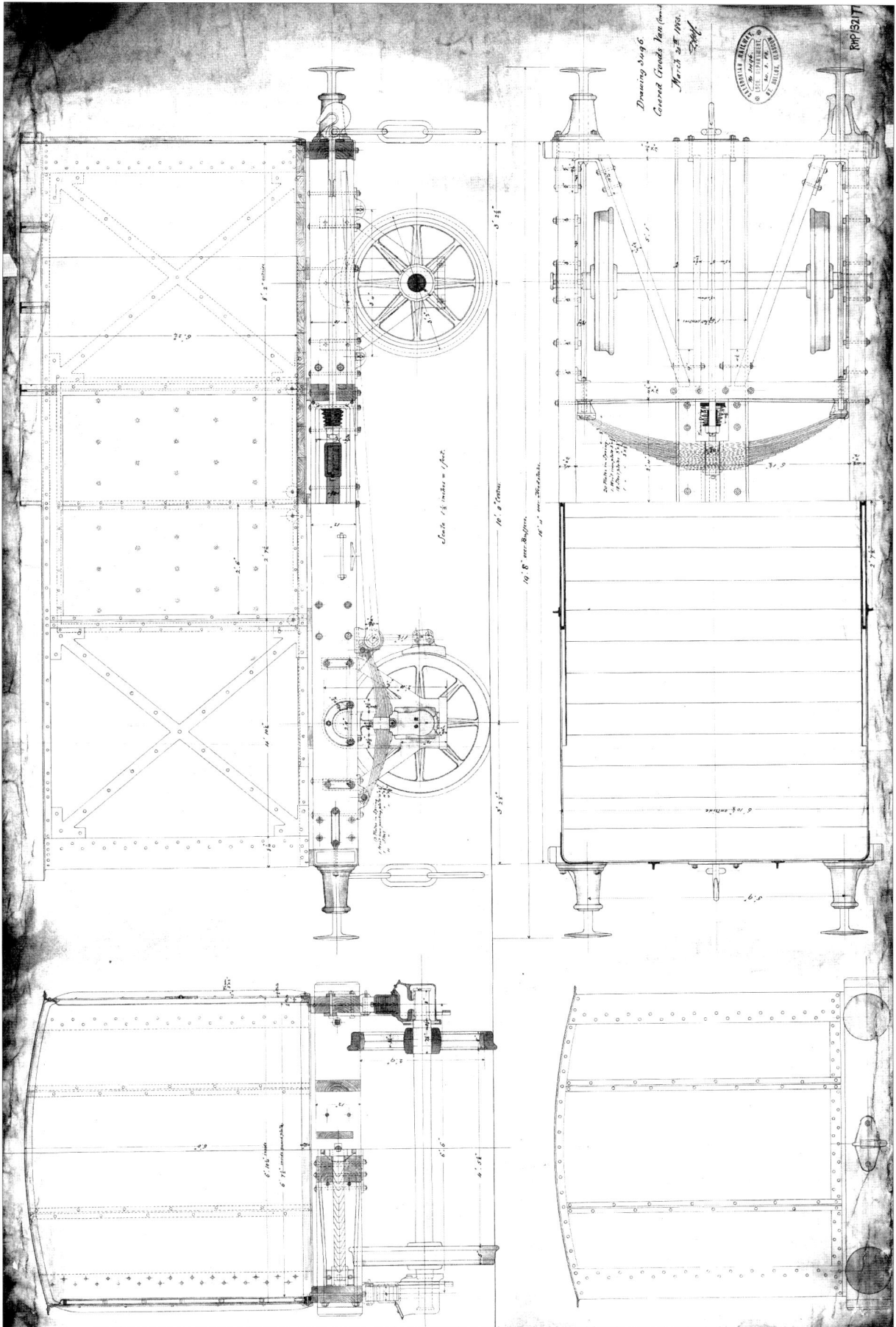

Figure 9.4
This drawing of an iron-bodied van on a wood underframe is a mystery, so far. It dates from shortly after Drummond's arrival at St. Rollox, at the time when the pre-diagram book 6-ton goods vans were still being built. Comparison with Figure 9.3 shows that the dimensions of the two vans were very similar, once allowance has been made for the different materials used. The main differences are this van's use of standard Drummond spindle buffers, running gear and the iron brake.

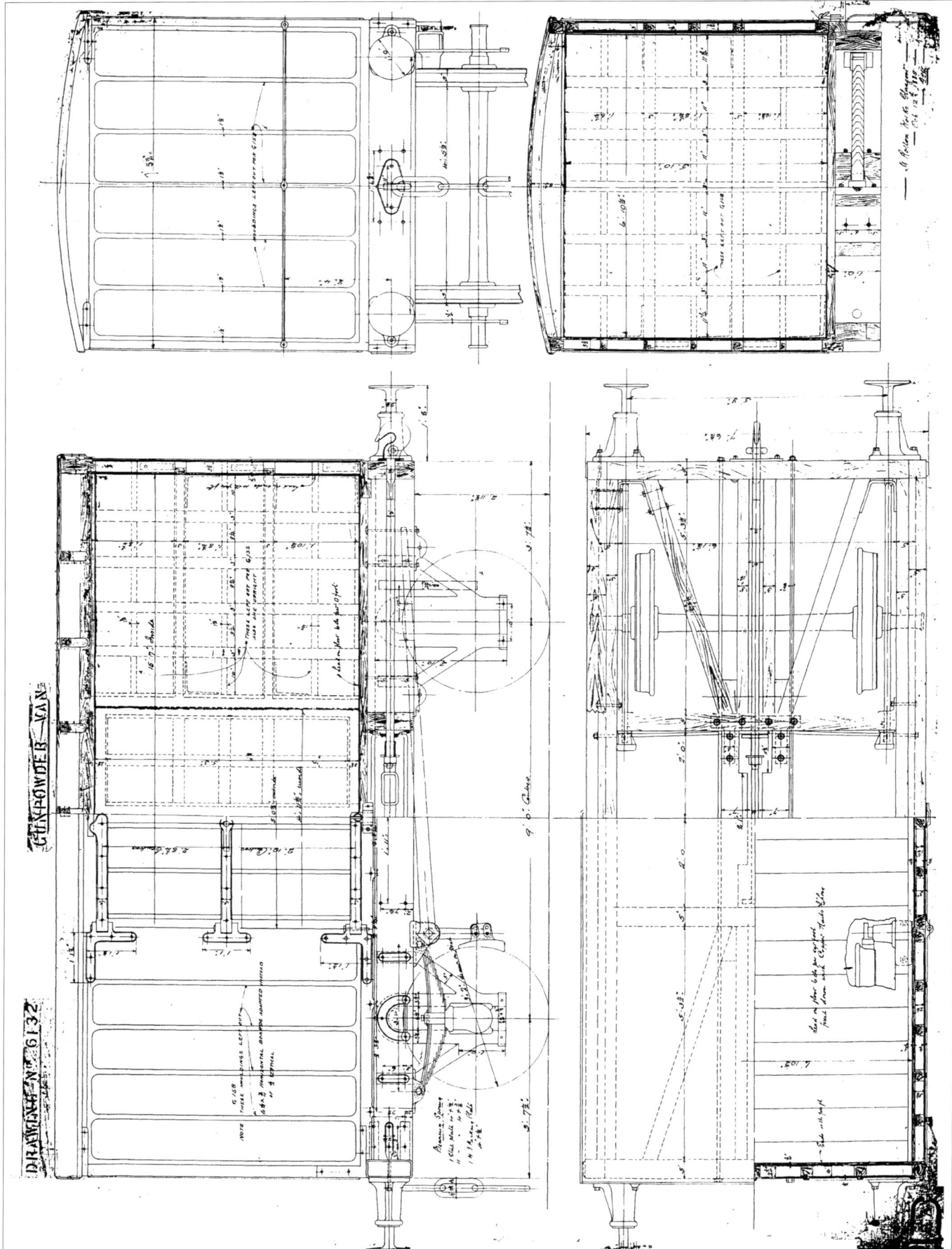

Figure 9.5
This is St. Rollox drawing 6132, which shows the first style of Diagram 3 goods van and the alterations required to make a Diagram 4 gunpowder van.

ABOVE AND RIGHT: Plates 9.18a and 9.18b
These two enlargements show the different styles of lower body ironwork dictated by the two styles of early sprung buffer.

BELOW: Plate 9.19
David Lochrie provided a photograph of the quayside at Oban, from which this enlargement has been made. It may show four of the covered vans made of iron to St. Rollox drawing 3496. The overall dimensions and wheelbase look correct, the roof looks thin, which suggests metal rather than boards, and there is no sliding door on the roof. The writing on the left-hand side of the body cannot be read, but it must describe some special purpose. It is also possible that they are dead meat vans. A drawing for special lettering of meat vans was issued by St. Rollox in 1879. Information about the drawing is in Chapter 3.

Plate 9.20
The first style of Diagram 3 van, built by Hurst Nelson in 1896, lettered for the newly opened Lanarkshire & Dumbartonshire section. Other vans in this contract were not lettered for a specific part of the system.

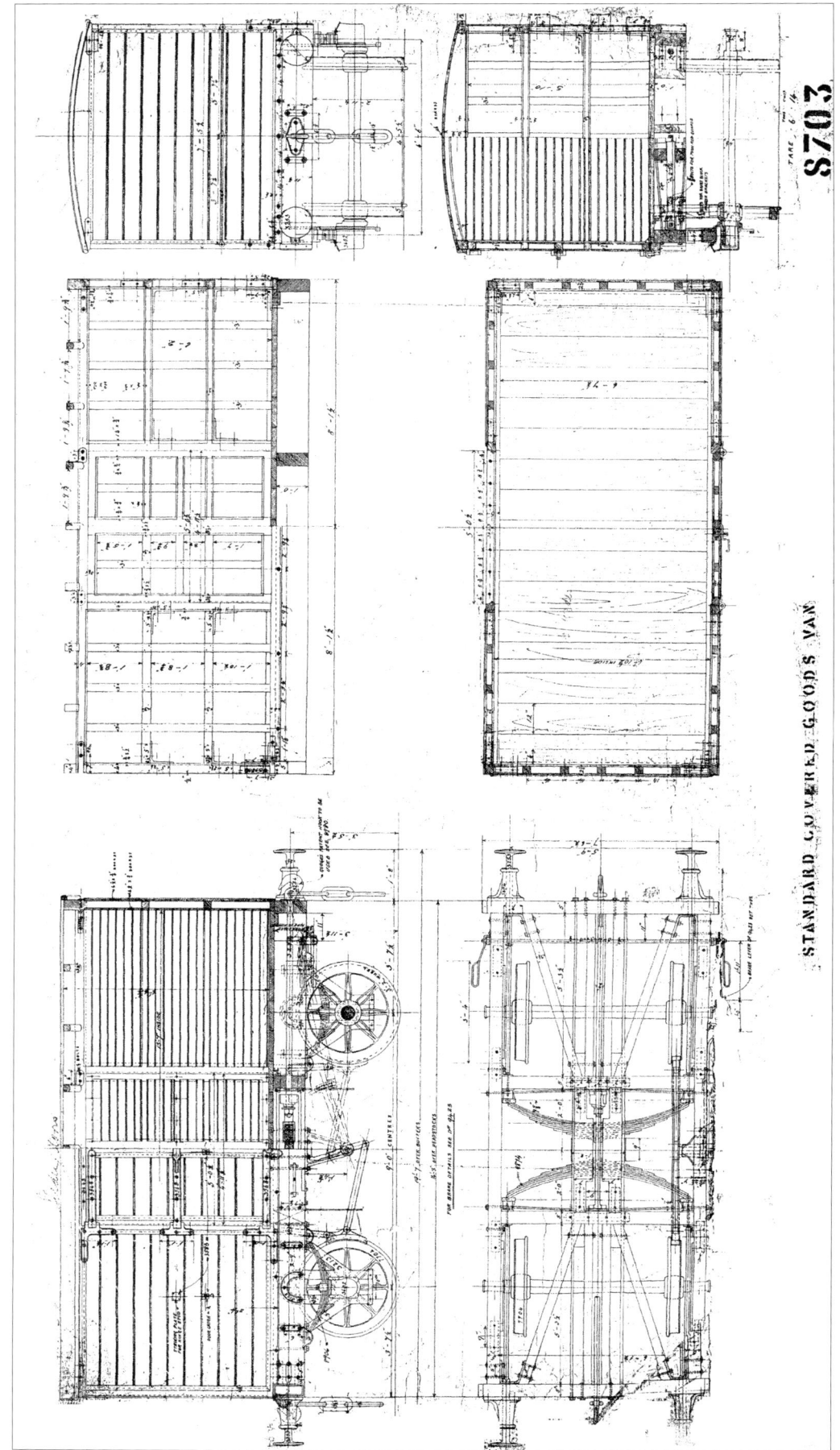

Figure 9.6
St. Rollox drawing 8703 shows the later style of horizontal planking applied to Diagram 3 vans, plus the McIntosh brake fitted to order G173. Plates 10.8 and 15.17 show examples of this type of van built to the horizontally boarded style.

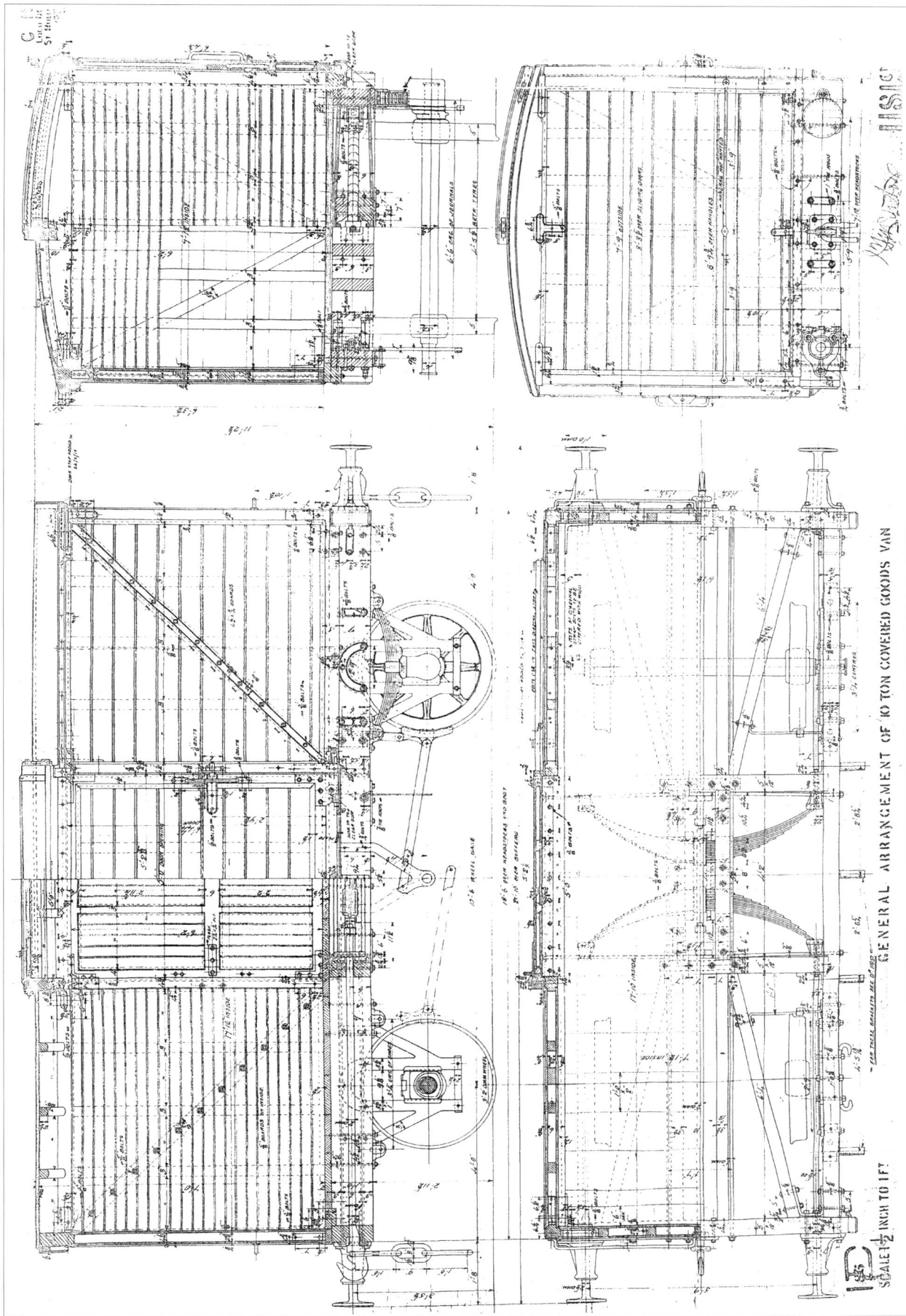

Figure 9.7
The St. Rollox drawing for the new standard 10-ton van to Diagram 67, built from 1903 onwards. This is the original version with roof door. Later versions had heavy outside framing and side doors only.

(Continued from page 153)

'Vans will be insulated, have oil axle boxes, screw couplings, the outside to be covered with fire resisting material and the sheeting inside to be secured with copper nails.'

Continuing the armaments theme, two orders for 150 vans were built to the capital account in 1917 to carry explosives.[21] They were fitted with dual brakes and oil axleboxes. Wheels were 3 feet 6 inches in diameter and the five-leaf springs were 4 feet between centres.

The original intention was to divide the order between five contractors, but the Loco & Stores Committee was not confident that the Motherwell Wagon Co. could fit the dual brake. It was suggested that their share of the contract might be divided equally between the other four tenderers.

Eventually the contract was shared equally between Pickering and Clayton & Shuttleworth.[22] The Pickering vans were numbered 73659-73808 inclusive.[23] Photographs of 73809 and 73814 suggest that the Clayton contract numbers followed immediately afterwards.

Three hundred more wagons for explosives traffic were purchased from the Disposal and Liquidation Committee in 1922.[24] Two hundred were charged to the capital account and 100 to revenue.[25] Nothing more is known about these wagons.

Proposed Bogie Van

Shortly after the introduction of the Diagram 67 van, a design for a 20-ton van mounted on bogies was considered. This was the subject of drawing number 12578, dated 27th April 1904. The design might have been a covered version of Diagram 54, if a comparable 30-ton iron van first built by the GWR in the same year is anything to go by.[26] There is no further mention of this design, and the drawing has not survived. Its application would have been limited to large consignments of parcels on express goods trains between cities, and the modified Diagram 54 wagons covered with a tarpaulin served the same purpose.

15 Ton Covered Goods Van with Sliding Doors – Diagram 80

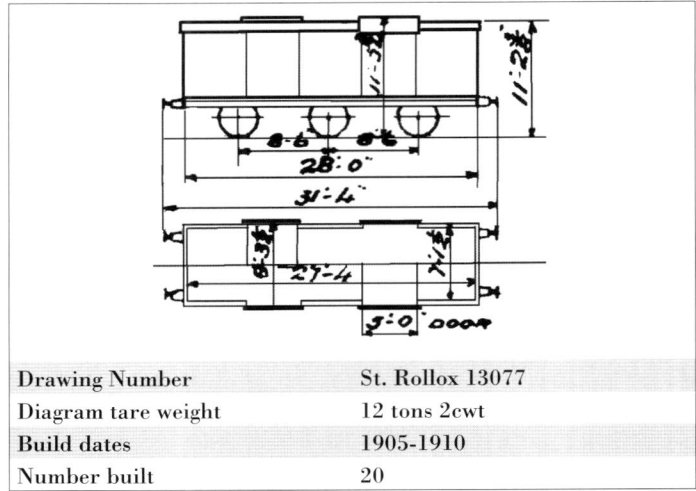

Drawing Number	St. Rollox 13077
Diagram tare weight	12 tons 2cwt
Build dates	1905-1910
Number built	20

Ten Diagram 80 vans were built to order number G237 in the half year ending January 1906.[27] Four more were authorised in 1908 to G274, and a final six in 1910 to order G291.[28] They were all classed as renewals. The underframe was steel and the 9-inch by 4-inch journals were oil lubricated. Ordinary wagon suspension was fitted. The wheels were 3 feet 9 inches in diameter. A double brake acted on the centre and right-hand wheel.

Essentially, the bodies were enlarged versions of Diagram 67. The body had outside framing. They were 28 feet long externally and when built had two sliding doors per side. The drawing is annotated *'originally with roof doors'* but the date of their removal is not recorded. The roof doors were located over the right-hand door in each case. Drop slides were fitted on the left of each end, again echoing Diagram 67. The G274 order was built to drawing 14653.[29] Ladders were fitted at the end of these vans. Running numbers are not known.

9.2: COVERED GOODS

Plate 9.22
The later style of Diagram 67 van, with outside framing to the body. This example was part of an order of 300 vans built in 1917 to carry explosives. One half of the order, including this van, was built by Clayton & Shuttleworth, the other half came from Pickering. They were fitted with dual brakes and oil axleboxes. This example has solid spoke wheels. The van's numbers were repeated on the sliding doors. At the right-hand end of the solebar is a Ministry of Munitions cast plate.

15 Ton Six Wheeled Goods Van with Sliding Doors – Diagram 115

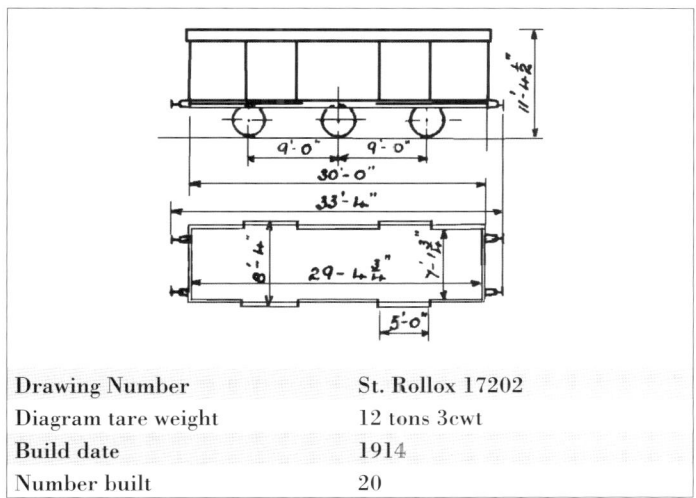

Drawing Number	St. Rollox 17202
Diagram tare weight	12 tons 3cwt
Build date	1914
Number built	20

The Diagram 115 vans continued the sliding door configuration of the Diagram 80 vehicles, but were built on the now-standard 30-foot six-wheeled underframe, and fitted with wagon buffers. The springs were suspended from J-hangers. Wheels were 3 feet 6 inches in diameter and the Morton either side brake acted on two pairs of wheels. They did not have roof doors. Twenty were built to order G344 as part of the renewal programme.[30] The only known number is 815, and probably 6198, on the evidence of a photograph in LM&SR livery.

Facing Page: Plate 9.21
The photograph shows a Renshaw-built example of Diagram 67, number 1630. It is fitted with Iracier axleboxes, which suggests that it was part of an order for 100 vans to G307, built in 1911. The number plate has been offset to avoid the metal bracket under the centre of the door. This feature was common to all these vans. The horse hook is not the usual Caledonian pattern, although it was common on the North British Railway. All the Diagram 67 vans seemed to have this feature.

Lime Wagon Load 8 Tons – Diagram 25

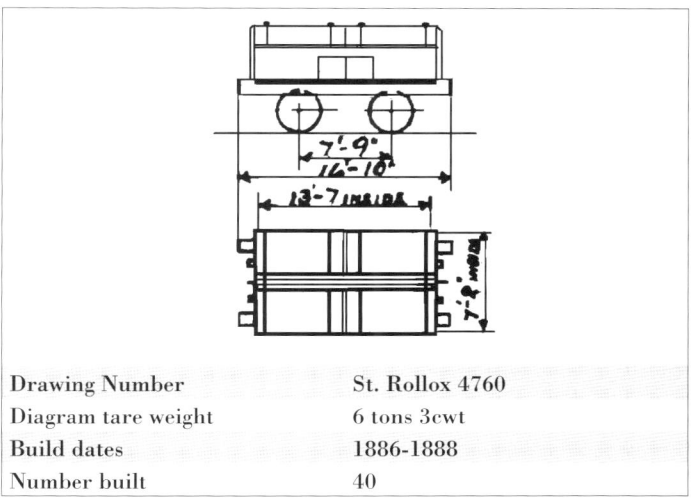

Drawing Number	St. Rollox 4760
Diagram tare weight	6 tons 3cwt
Build dates	1886-1888
Number built	40

These wagons carried sacks of quicklime, which reacts violently to moisture. A Pickering card order for lime wagons for the Owen Stone Company required the body *'to be perfectly watertight'* and each wagon was subject to inspection by the purchaser.[31] Quicklime was the basis of the disinfectant wash applied to cattle wagons. Limestone, from which it was made, was used as a flux in the iron and steel industry; this was carried in ordinary mineral wagons.

The CR design was a Diagram 22 mineral wagon with a peaked roof to protect the contents from the elements. The roof hinged on the longitudinal centre line of the wagon, and was split into two halves each side. The hinge line was protected by a canvas strip.

The minutes do not record authorisation of these wagons. They were built to three orders (ten of each to G25 and G40, plus twenty to G54). The 1900 and 1910 returns also record forty of these vehicles. The general arrangement drawing, St. Rollox 4760, detail drawing 4767 and detail drawing 6140 of July 1889 have not survived.

Known numbers are 38612-38621, suggesting that this was the block number series of one of the first two lots. The numbers imply that the wagons were built to the capital account. Wagon 38613 was photographed for the *1900 Register*.

Plate 9.23
This is probably a Diagram 80 van. The angle of intersection of the bracing suggests a shorter centre section than the Diagram 105 van 306198 in Plate 9.24. The springs are wagon springs rather than suspended on J-hangers. The wheels are a mixture of solid spoke and disc.

Plate 9.24
This Diagram 105 van was photographed in LM&SR livery. The body design is the same as the second style of Diagram 67 covered van. The LM&SR number suggests that the van was originally CR 6199.

Plate 9.25
One of the forty Diagram 25 lime wagons that were built at St. Rollox between 1885 and 1889. They were essentially Diagram 22 wagons with a peaked roof. Each side of the roof was in two sections, split on the centre line of the side doors. The hinge along the top of the roof was covered in canvas. The securing clips for the roof sections are very prominent. The GENERAL TERMINUS WHEN EMPTY lettering has displaced the tare weight to the solebar. The coupling is the old style with a short centre link.

References

1. NRS BR/CAL/1/9 entry 207
2. NRS BR/CAL/1/12 entry 1388
3. NRM 8053/W NRS RHP 69162
4. L&NWR Diagram 32
5. NRS BR/CAL/1/27, no entry number
6. Drawing 3496, RHP132177
7. Cowlairs drawing 44W, not assigned an NBR or L&NER diagram number
8. Order numbers between G1 and G129 – see Appendix II
9. HMRS collection ref ABP705
10. St. Rollox drawing 8703, NRM 8049/W, RHP 69177 shows the standard van with the patent brake. Another version of the drawing, NRM 11902/W, RHP 70109, shows the perishable goods modifications
11. NRS BR/CAL/1/47 entry 568
12. NRS BR/CAL/1/55 entry 129
13. NRS BR/CAL/1/55 entry 1143
14. NRM 11959/W
15. NRS BR/CAL/1/57, no entry number
16. NRM 11969/W
17. NRS BR/CAL/1/58 entry 731
18. NRM 11964/W
19. NRS BR/CAL/1/61 entry 65
20. NRS BR/CAL/1/66 entry 1362
21. NRS BR/CAL/1/68 entry 1416
22. NRS BR/CAL/1/69 entry 379
23. Pickering card order 31321
24. NRS BR/CAL/1/79 entry 274
25. NRS BR/CAL/1/79 entry 748
26. Details in *All About GWR Iron Minks*, pp. 47–48, published by the HMRS
27. NRS BR/CAL/1/51 entry 102
28. NRS BR/CAL/1/56 entry 425 and 1/59 entry 125
29. NRM 11970/W
30. NRS BR/CAL/1/63 entry 1383
31. Card order 2159

9.3: Empty Barrel Trucks

One major source of traffic for these wagons was through Edinburgh (Lothian Road) goods yard and Port Dundas in Glasgow. In Edinburgh, the Caledonian Distillery branch served Distillers Co. In Glasgow, Port Dundas grain distillery was the largest supplier of grain whisky for blending in Scotland.[1]

Empty barrels were also needed for preserved fish. For instance, there was regular traffic in cured herrings between Oban and Leith – 900 tons of fish was despatched in January and February 1911. Jam makers were another source for this traffic.

Barrel Truck Load 3 Tons – Diagram 12

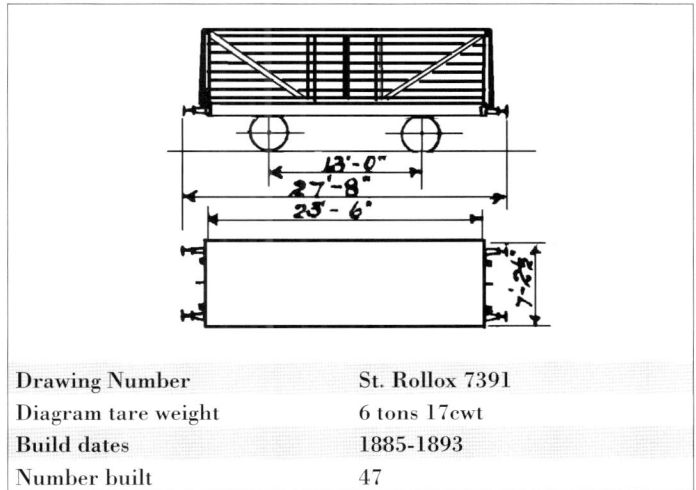

Drawing Number	St. Rollox 7391
Diagram tare weight	6 tons 17cwt
Build dates	1885-1893
Number built	47

These and the Diagram 74 trucks were similar in construction to cattle wagons and milk trucks. The Diagram 12 trucks were 24 feet long and 7 feet 8½ inches wide externally. The sides comprised seven 8-inch planks which were 3 inches thick, each separated by a 2-inch gap. The gap between the third and fourth planks from the top was filled in to accommodate the company initials.

Construction started in 1885 to St. Rollox drawing 4655. A further drawing (number 6200) was issued in 1890. These have not survived, but drawing 7391 from 1893 has. Some, if not all, of the trucks were built on redundant carriage underframes, including 1704, an early example with the number painted on the solebar, which appears in the *1900 Register of Wagon Plant*.

The wheelbase is given on the diagram as 13 feet, but varied depending on the coach underframe. The *1900 Register* gives the number in stock as fifty-five, rather than the forty-seven identified in the order numbers. By 1910, the rolling stock return records forty-six in stock.

These wagons could only carry empty barrels and were lettered to that effect. Even with empty barrels, the 3 tons capacity meant that the wagons could not be fully loaded. This led the Caledonian to build 6 tons capacity wagons of a similar size, which allowed them to carry a full load. These wagons formed Diagram 74.

Barrel Truck – Diagram 74

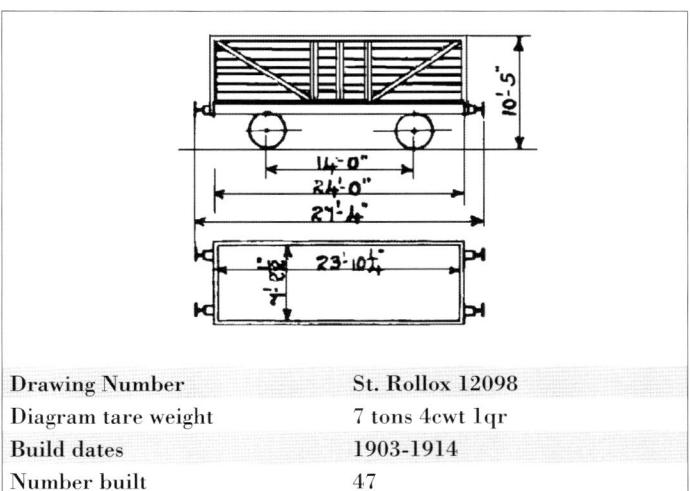

Drawing Number	St. Rollox 12098
Diagram tare weight	7 tons 4cwt 1qr
Build dates	1903-1914
Number built	47

According to the wagon renewal minutes, twenty six-wheeled empty cask wagons were authorised for the half year ending 31st January 1904.[2] The extra pair of wheels would have allowed the capacity of the Diagram 12 design to be increased to 6 tons. Six-wheeled underframes might have been available through the carriage renewal programme, but instead the wagons were built on new steel four-wheeled underframes with channel headstocks.

Construction of the four-wheeled wagons was the same as

Plate 9.26
Empty barrel truck number 8267 to Diagram 12 was built on an old carriage underframe. The wheelbase looks to be 14 feet 6 inches. It retains the original safety chains, screw couplings and coach buffers. The wheels, however, are 3 feet 2 inches diameter in place of the 3-foot 6-inch coach version that would have originally been fitted. It carries the first type of cast number plate, offset to clear a bracket supporting the floor at the centre of the door opening. A McIntosh patent brake lever operates a push rod brake block on the left-hand wheel only. As the brake was patented in November 1898, the wagon was probably one of fifteen built to order G177, authorised in May 1899. The additional lettering reads 'EMPTY CASKS ONLY.' on the left-hand side) and 'LEITH WHEN EMPTY.' on the right.

Diagram 12. The standard wagon buffer was fitted rather than the steel underframe version. They had oil axleboxes, screw couplings and the double Morton brake on one side only. The modern running gear doubled the permitted load compared with Diagram 12 trucks. Twenty-three were built to orders G203 (1903) and G287 (1910).[3]

Originally, a tube and bolt arrangement to prevent the sides from bowing out tied the body together across the top of the framework that formed the 5-foot door opening. Plate 2.11 (p. 28) shows an example, numbered 3074. The works drawing is annotated with changes starting with order G349, authorised in 1913. Angle iron tie bars in a shallow arc replaced the tube and bolt arrangement and an either side brake was fitted. A further twenty-four were built to the modified design to two orders of twelve each (G349 and G363).[4]

References
1. Information from the *1910 List of Sidings*
   An article in *Sou' West Journal* issue 43, pp. 11-18 also provided background information
2. NRS BR/CAL/5/4
3. NRS BR/CAL/1/47 entry 1127 and BR/CAL/1/58 entry 731 respectively
4. NRS BR/CAL/1/63 entry 1383 and BR/CAL/1/65 entry 1041 respectively

Plate 9.27
303300 was a Diagram 74 empty barrel truck photographed in LM&SR days, by which time the screw couplings had been replaced by three links. It was one of twenty-four wagons built to the modified design from 1913 onwards, with angle iron bracing in an arc between the sides. The original number was probably 3300, as the trucks were all built as replacements.

Plate 9.28
One of the four Diagram 91 road vans in its usual position just behind the engine on a Callander & Oban goods train in the LM&SR era. The 'Jumbo' has been fitted with a vacuum brake and lamp brackets on the buffer beam and smokebox. It does not yet have a front number plate. With age, the road van's body has developed a marked bow upwards towards the centre. This was a common feature of six-wheeled vehicles late in life.

9.4: Road Vans

Pre-Diagram Book Designs

Road vans carried general merchandise, such as parcels and packages, that did not constitute a full wagon load. Many companies built specialised vans for this traffic. In the Caledonian's rolling stock returns, four road vans were recorded in the period ending January 1859. These vans were converted from fish vans which had been built in 1853. The number of road vans rose to 23 by January 1864.

The first reference to this type of vehicle in the minutes was in 1879, when the Glasgow Committee accepted a tender from Brown & Marshall for ten Roadside Covered Goods Vans at £94 10s each.[1] In 1880 the Committee accepted a tender for a further twelve from Craven Bros at £86 each.[2] In 1882, ten *'Roadside Parcels Vans'* were ordered as replacement vehicles from S J Claye.[3] No further information exists about these vans.

10 Ton Goods Van (Callander & Oban) – Diagram 91

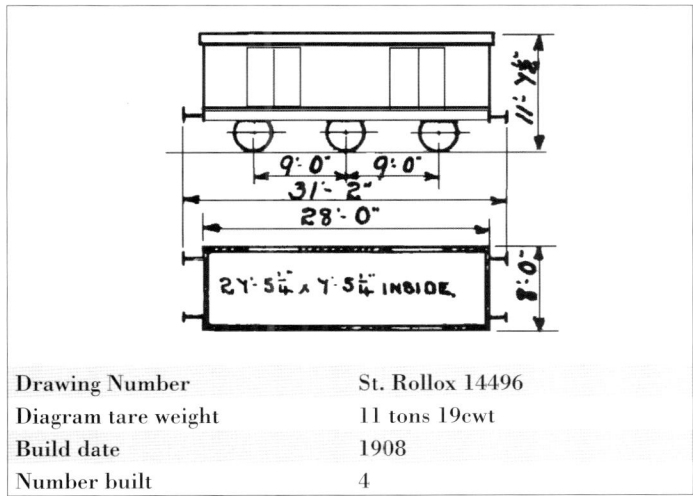

Drawing Number	St. Rollox 14496
Diagram tare weight	11 tons 19cwt
Build date	1908
Number built	4

The eight vans to Diagrams 91 and 104 were the only CR vehicles in modern times specially designed for that purpose. This contrasts with the North British Railway, which designed a broadly similar van to the Caledonian Diagram 91 design in 1904, eventually building 100.[4] Caledonian Railway working timetables show that road vans ran throughout the system, using ordinary goods vans. The Diagram 104 design served as a brake van as well as a road van and is discussed in Chapter 16.

Although they were described as goods vans in the diagram book, the Diagram 91 vans were known as road vans by the number takers who recorded their passing at Callander & Oban Junction in 1920.[5] The four vans were built to order G270.[6] They were horizontally planked and flush boarded, similar in style to the first version of the Diagram 67 goods van. Two sets of double hinged doors with window openings were fitted. The left-hand pair had vertical bars on the inside of the glass. The right-hand pair was boarded over.

They were carried on six 3-foot 6-inch disc wheels, which ran in oil boxes. The 4-foot springs were suspended on J-hangers. The Westinghouse brake was fitted, plus hand brakes on each side applied to the left-hand wheel. They had standard wagon buffers, screw couplings and safety chains. Steps and handrails at one end gave access to four oil lamps on the roof centre line.

As can be seen in Plates 9.28 and 9.29, the vans were marshalled at the front of goods trains, where the continuous brake supplemented the locomotive's braking power. The vans made one trip per day each way on north and southbound afternoon departures from Stirling and Oban. Numbers were recorded as 1233, 1280, 1483 and 1578 in the C&O traffic book in 1920.[7]

The vans lasted well into the Grouping era; a picture in *Steam in the Western Highlands* shows one at Luib in 1939. The oil lamps and steps had been removed by then. There is special lettering in the centre of the body, but it is indistinct. LM&SR numbers were presumably the above plus 300000.

References
1. NRS BR/CAL/1/25 entry 703
2. NRS BR/CAL/1/26 entry 44
3. NRS BR/CAL/1/27 entry 353
4. Cowlairs drawing 404W, NBR Diagram 48
5. NRS BR/CAL/5/60
6. NRS BR/CAL/1/55 entry 1143
7. NRS BR/CAL/5/60

Plate 9.29
Two goods trains ran between Stirling and Oban every day from Monday to Saturday. This is the afternoon train, which had a road van marshalled behind the locomotive. It is on the main line near Cornton level crossing between Stirling and Bridge of Alan. Behind the road van is either a Diagram 15 or 24 open goods wagon and three Diagram 46 minerals, followed by the second style of Diagram 67 van with outside framing. The train is an average length for the C&O; the maximum load was thirty wagons for a Class '55' 4-6-0.

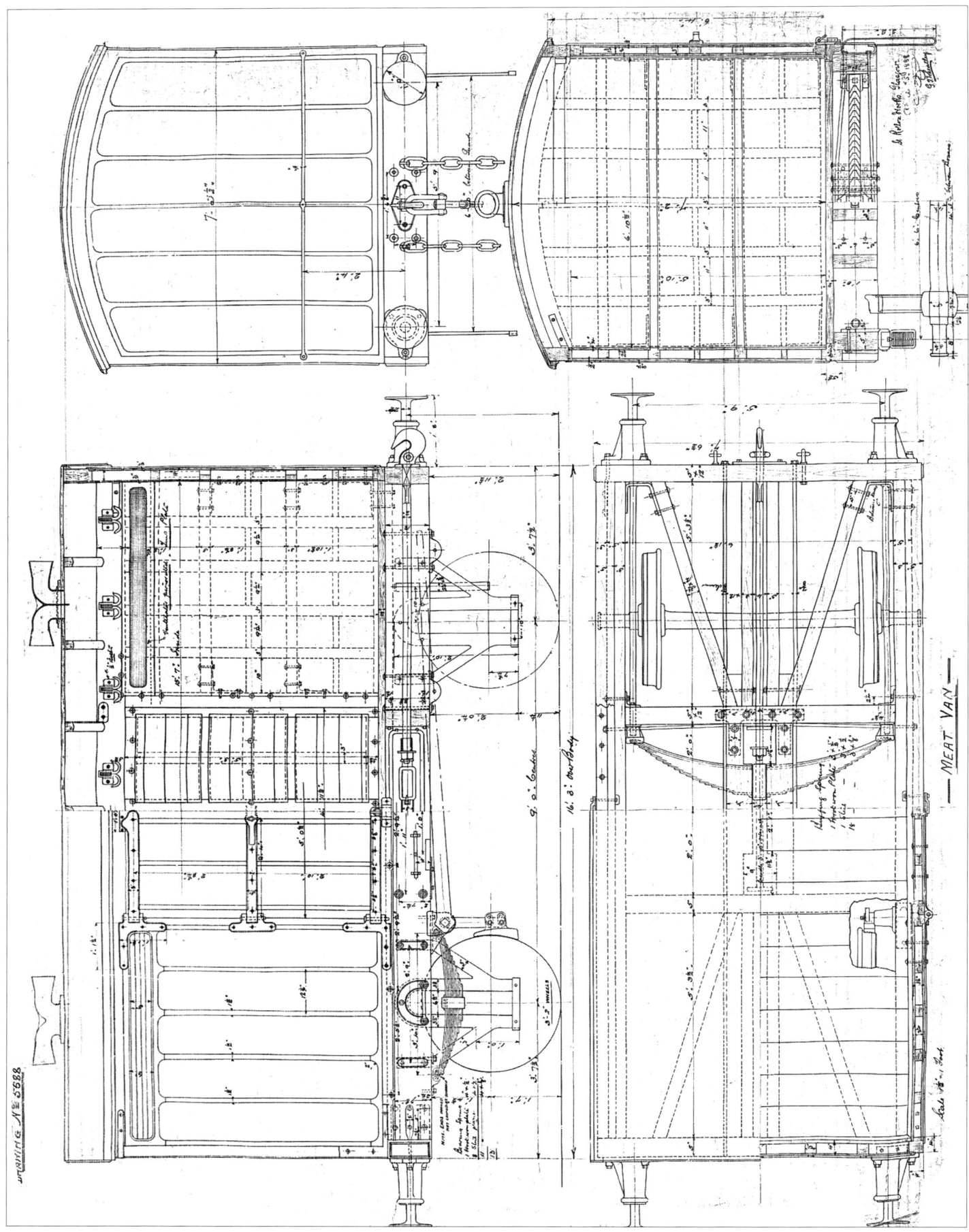

Chapter 10
Perishable Goods

10.1: Meat Vans

Pre-Diagram Book Designs

The Caledonian seems to have carried meat traffic from the opening of its main line from Glasgow to Carlisle in 1848. In a minute dated 26th May of that year

'Attention was called to the traffic in Dead Meat from Edinburgh to London twice weekly. Enquire if arrangements can be made for this traffic to be sent to the Newgate and Leadenhall Markets on Mondays & Fridays, to be combined with Salmon from the Tay on the opening of the line from Perth.'[1]

That said, there are no references to meat vans in the rolling stock returns, in early orders from contractors or in the St. Rollox drawing register. If they existed, which seems unlikely, they must have been subsumed into the covered van category.

The first specific reference in the minutes dates from February 1879, when a total of forty dead meat vans were ordered from Oldbury, Ashbury and Brown & Marshall.[2] In November the same year, a tender for eighteen four-wheeled and ten six-wheeled fresh meat vans was accepted from Brown & Marshall at £106 10s and £183 each respectively.[3]

The first St. Rollox drawing is 2347, dated 1878. It may have been used for the four-wheeled vans built by contractors. The dead meat vans had the same underframe as the ordinary open and covered goods vehicles described in Chapter 9. They were designed to run in passenger trains, being retro-fitted with through pipes, and with the springs suspended from swing links. The push rod version of the wooden brake block was fitted.

They strongly resembled the goods vans, but with slightly different framing, a small louvre ventilator in each end, and two trumpet ventilators on the roof centre line. They had the first type of three-bolt spring buffer. The *1900 Register* states that 121 dead meat vans were in service in 1900, but that must include the vans to Diagrams 1 and 2, leaving perhaps twenty-one of the older vans as survivors.

The contemporary fresh meat vans had no louvres or roof ventilation, and standard goods wagon running gear. They were, however, fitted with through pipes, indicating that they were eligible for passenger train traffic.

Dead Meat Van – Diagram 2

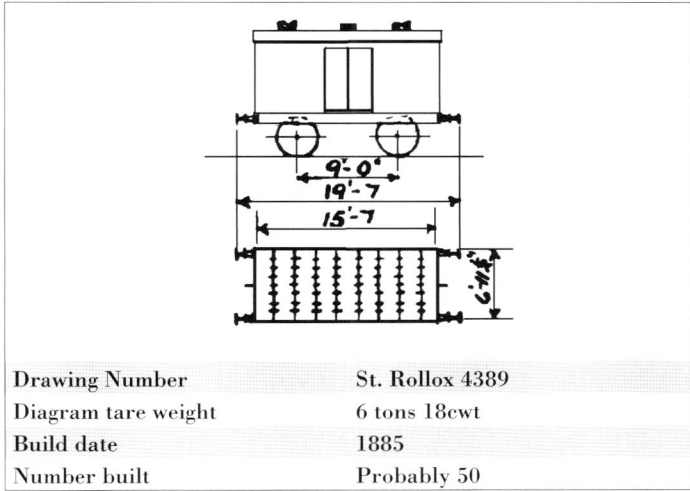

Drawing Number	St. Rollox 4389
Diagram tare weight	6 tons 18cwt
Build date	1885
Number built	Probably 50

Diagrams 1 and 2 are discussed in date order of construction, which was the reverse of their position in the diagram book. The drawing states that the vans were built on the same underframe as the Diagram 3 goods vans that first appeared two years earlier. The double door opening was 4 feet, compared with 5 feet 0½ inch for Diagram 3. The sides and ends were originally fully panelled, although photographs of these vans show them with horizontally planked sides. This may have been a similar style evolution to that of the Diagram 3 vans. Ventilation louvres were fitted in the panels under the eaves, another echo of carriage stock.

The drawing shows a single circular ventilator on the roof centre line, but the diagram book, drawn up long after the wagons were built, shows two trumpet ventilators as well. The van's capacity was 112 carcasses, hung on double hooks that were fixed to eight transverse bars fitted at eaves height.

The wheels were 3 feet 9 inches diameter, and ran in oil-lubricated axleboxes. Screw couplings and side chains were fitted, indicating their suitability for passenger trains. Standard wagon buffers were

RIGHT: Plate 10.1
This is a pre-diagram book dead meat van, fitted with louvres on the ends and trumpet ventilators. It was photographed for the *1900 Register*, where it was stated that 121 vans were in service. The design was based on the standard covered van of the period, without a sliding roof door, with the following modifications to suit it for passenger train traffic: through brake pipe, screw couplings and safety chains and short heavy duty wagon springs suspended on swing links. It is fitted with three-bolt self-contained buffers. The wood brake block is operated by a pushrod. The headstocks have chamfered ends in L&NWR style. The painted number, which may be 7984, has been displaced to the right by what looks like a cast plate. Lettering is either non-existent or completely obscured.

FACING PAGE: Figure 10.1
This is the St. Rollox drawing of the Diagram 1 design of dead meat van.

Plate 10.2
This van exhibits a different approach to roof ventilation from that in Plate 10.1, but the rest of the van is identical. A supplementary roof is fitted, spaced from the real roof by blocks. In motion, this would create a forced airflow which cooled the main roof and thus the interior. Again, there is no sign of lettering. The number on the end seems to be 8027.

fitted, and the single iron brake block was operated by a push rod.

Minutes in March and April 1885[4] authorised the construction of thirty and twenty dead meat vans, in both cases parts of orders for new (capital expenditure) plant. St. Rollox orders G7 and G13 correspond.

Meat Van – Diagram 1

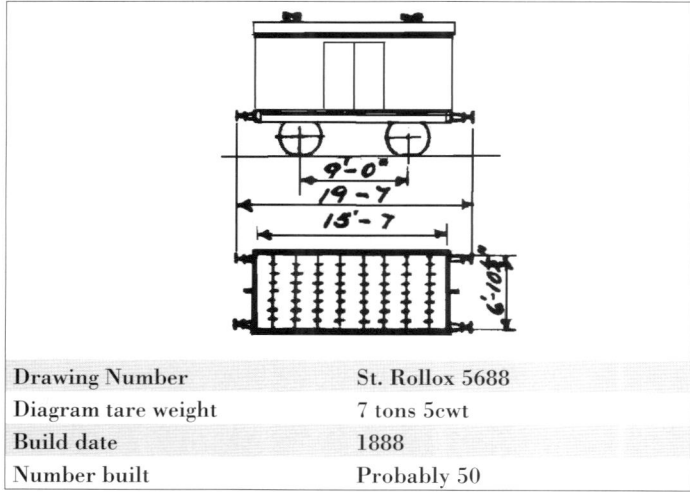

Drawing Number	St. Rollox 5688
Diagram tare weight	7 tons 5cwt
Build date	1888
Number built	Probably 50

The Diagram 1 meat vans were one inch wider than the Diagram 2 vans, but length and height were the same. The double doors reverted to the 5-foot 0½-inch opening of Diagram 3. They could also carry 112 carcasses on fifty-six double hooks. The general arrangement drawing shows that the bodies were vertically planked and covered with half-round beading at 12-inch centres, like the first variant of Diagram 3. Louvres were fitted at the top of each side. There were two trumpet-shaped ventilators on the longitudinal centre line. They had standard wagon running gear and the single iron brake, but were fitted with screw couplings and side chains, indicating that they were considered suitable for running in passenger trains.

Traffic Committee minutes in 1888/9 do not provide details of the wagons authorised, but St. Rollox orders G50 and G55 were for a total of fifty vans to carry fresh meat.

The *July–September 1907 Working Timetable* lists the numbers of fifty-one short wheelbase meat vans, plus the Diagram 84 vans discussed in the next paragraph. The numbers were 37331/2, 37805-37847 and 37849-37854. This suggests that the first two were from the Diagram 2 orders, with the remainder a fifty-strong block for the Diagram 1 vans.

Refrigerator Van - Diagram 84

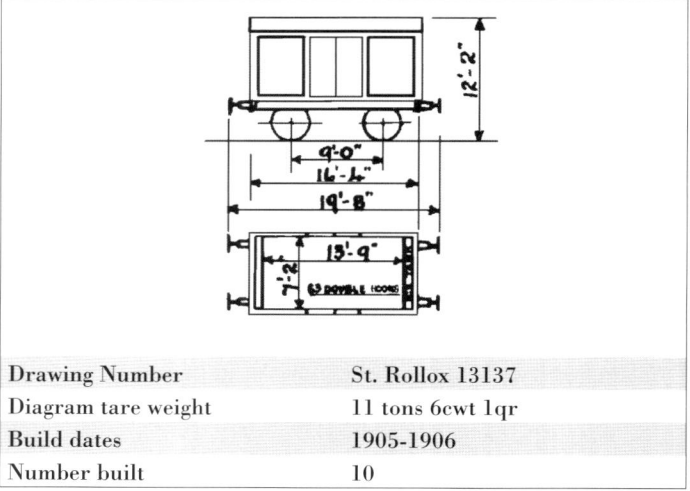

Drawing Number	St. Rollox 13137
Diagram tare weight	11 tons 6cwt 1qr
Build dates	1905-1906
Number built	10

The body construction of these vans was similar to the Diagram 67 covered vans, but with folding, rather than sliding, doors and no roof door. They could carry 126 carcasses on sixty-three double hooks. The ends were lined with ice tanks which were filled through hatches on the roof, accessed by ladders.

They had 3-foot 9-inch spoked wheels and 9-inch by 4½-inch oil axleboxes. The McIntosh patent hand brake was fitted, and dual system continuous brakes, supplemented by side chains. The only deviation from the full NPCS specification was the use of wagon buffers. The vans were built to order G238 as renewals.[5] The numbers are recorded in the *1907 Working Timetable* as 1844, 2181, 2530, 5593, 7179, 7594, 9493, 35754, 35814 and 37990.[6]

ABOVE: Plate 10.3
Contrasting with the two dead meat vans in the previous plates, this is a van with the same basic body design, lettered for fresh meat traffic. It does not have louvres or roof ventilation. Ordinary wagon springs are fitted, plus the Drummond cast iron brake, and a through pipe to run in continuous braked trains. The company lettering is in the usual position for covered vans. The painted number is unfortunately in shadow.

RIGHT: Plate 10.4
A pair of perishable goods vans at Biggar. The van in the rear is to Diagram 2, but with horizontally planked sides, rather than panelling. It is fitted with oil axleboxes. The nearer van is probably a pre-diagram book dead meat van like that in Plate 10.1, viewed from the other side. The bracing to the non-door side of the body differs from the standard pre-diagram book goods wagons shown in Chapter 9.

FACING PAGE: Plate 10.5
This is an often-seen photograph of one of the ten Diagram 84 refrigerator vans. The paint date is January 1906. The hatches to access the ice boxes are just visible on the roof. Points of interest are the scalloped ends to the headstocks, L&NWR style, the footboards, which were not fitted to any other meat van, and the pair of lamp brackets low down on the end. The letters are 18 inches high. The livery is almost certainly brown with chrome yellow lettering. The letters definitely differ in tone from the white letters on the solebar and the cast number plate. The additional number can just be detected under the roof arc. The writing indicating the three positions of the McIntosh patent brake is in a straight line rather than the usual curve. No doubt the body beading prevented the usual arrangement.

TOP RIGHT: Plate 10.6
This Diagram 90 refrigerator van built to order G273 carried number 1745 in Caledonian Railway days. The N letters indicate that it is not part of the common user arrangement.

MIDDLE RIGHT: Plate 10.7
Coincidentally, a picture of the same van in CR ownership also exists. This enlargement shows the CR lettering layout. The tare weight then was 10.13.2. The company initials have been displaced from their usual position by the 'FRESH MEAT TRAFFIC' lettering and are centred under the louvres.

BOTTOM RIGHT: Plate 10.8
Diagram 3 standard goods van number 3046 was part of order G173, built in 1891. All eighty vans were fitted with the McIntosh patent hand brake with cast hanger. This was one of the vans that were modified for perishable goods traffic. It has oil axleboxes and is piped for vacuum and Westinghouse brakes. Eyelets are fitted along the roof edge to accommodate the Harrison cord alarm system used by West Coast expresses. Its use on this van is odd, as the system was phased out from 1899, following condemnation by the Board of Trade a year earlier. The timber solebars and headstocks are 'flitched' – i.e. faced with a thin sheet of metal; this explains the lack of the usual ironwork and crown plates. There is no sign of a number on the end. The low running number shows that it was a replacement vehicle. The cast number plate bears a seriously misaligned row of numbers. The photograph was taken for the *Register of Wagon Plant*.

6 Ton Meat Van – Diagram 90

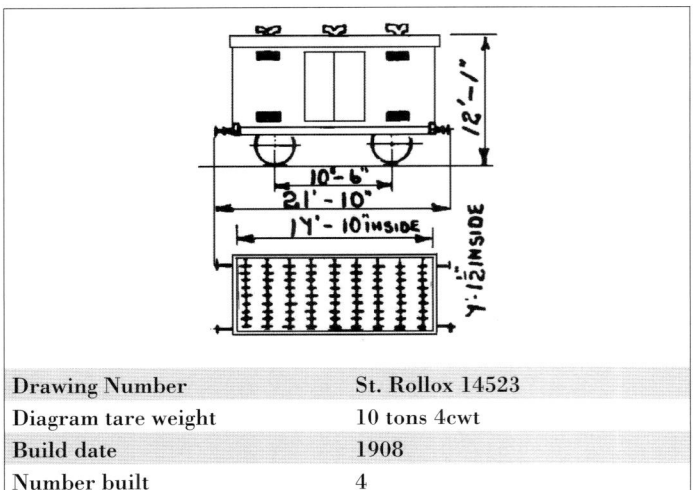

Drawing Number	St. Rollox 14523
Diagram tare weight	10 tons 4cwt
Build date	1908
Number built	4

Four Diagram 90 refrigerated meat vans were built as part of the renewal programme for the half year ending July 1908 to G273.[7] They were 18 feet 4 inches long externally by 7 feet 6½ inches wide. The capacity was 162 carcasses. They were fitted with louvres on the sides and ends and had three trumpet ventilators on the roof centre line. They had dual brakes, 9-inch by 4½-inch oil axleboxes and wagon buffers. Numbers were 1745, 1748, 1757 and 1777.[8]

10 Ton Meat Van – Diagram 102

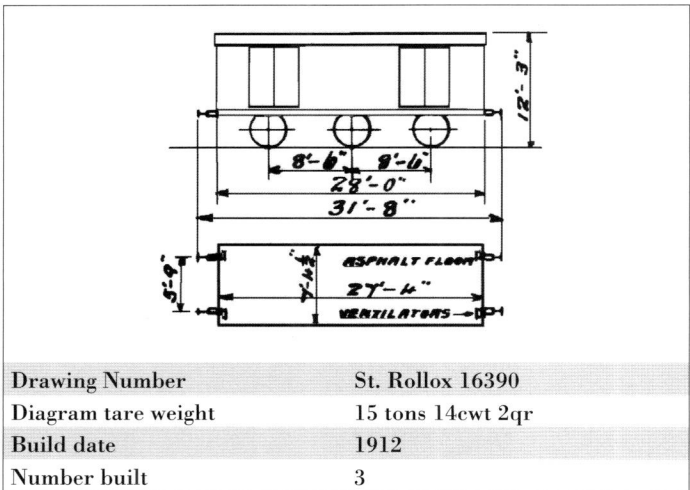

Drawing Number	St. Rollox 16390
Diagram tare weight	15 tons 14cwt 2qr
Build date	1912
Number built	3

Six-wheeled 28 feet long meat vans to Diagram 102 were built to order H301 as part of the renewal programme,[9] and numbered 188-190. They were the only meat vans to be fitted with carriage buffers, and thus to the full NPCS specification. This is probably why they were also the only meat vans to be built to an H order. They were vertically planked and had two sets of swing doors per side. The floors were covered with asphalt and the sides and ends were lined with zinc. Two louvre ventilators were fitted on each end. They survived until the end of the Grouping period.

Other Caledonian Meat and Refrigerator Vans

As mentioned in Chapter 9, some of the Diagram 3 goods vans built in 1899 were modified for perishable goods traffic. One of two versions of the drawing for order G173 shows '*insulating of ends and side doors for Vans for Meat Traffic, roof double skinned for Insulated Vans.*'[10]

The number of vans so modified is unknown. There is no mention of the modification in company minutes and the rolling stock return only records the order as '*covered wagons*'. One of the modified vans, numbered 3046, was photographed for the *1900 Register*.

In 1918 the Ministry of Food asked the Caledonian to insulate covered goods vans for the conveyance of frozen meat. The Traffic Committee approved the conversion of fifty-one vans at no cost to the company.[11] Presumably the vans selected were from the 100-plus dual brake fitted examples of Diagram 67.

West Coast Joint Stock

The Caledonian also had an interest in West Coast Joint Stock meat vans. The full, but not entirely accurate, story is told in Chapter 14 of Casserley and Millard's book *West Coast Joint Stock*. In summary, the Caledonian built fifty vans to the Joint Stock account in 1880, numbered 212-261. This order was discussed in a CR Traffic Committee minute in January of that year.[12] They were later fitted with through pipes. *West Coast Joint Stock* says that they were banned from express passenger trains by 1892, but the *July-September 1907 Working Timetable* lists them with the Diagram 1, 2 and 84 vans as suitable for passenger traffic.

The dimensions given in the text (16 feet long, 9-foot wheelbase) do not match the picture described as a CR dead meat van in *West Coast Joint Stock*.[13] This picture probably depicts a van to St. Rollox drawing 2347.

A further batch of vans, numbered 262-286, was added in 1886, and twenty-five more (387-402) two years later. These vans were dual braked. Casserley and Millard erroneously attribute the building of these vans to the Caledonian. In fact they were an L&NWR design; the drawing in the HMRS collection[14] is annotated 'Earlestown'.

The next addition was a batch of fifty refrigerator vans, built at Earlestown in 1893, numbered 287-336.[15] They were identical to L&NWR Diagram 46, but fitted with Mansell wheels and the Westinghouse, as well as vacuum, brake. Vans 308, 317 and 334 were destroyed in accidents in 1907. They were replaced by six-wheeled versions of the Diagram 46 vans, measuring 30 feet overall.

The final fifteen vans were built in 1913/14, numbered 337-351. They were identical to L&NWR Diagram 46A, but dual fitted. They were of similar construction to the previous vans, but were 2 feet longer.

The WCJS meat vans were painted dark grey, but do not seem to have been lettered.[16] The refrigerator vans were painted white with a grey curb rail. They did not carry any identification apart from the words 'Refrigerator Van' and an oval ownership plate on the solebar reading 'West Coast Joint Stock' above the number.[17]

References

1. NRS BR/CAL/1/8 no entry number
2. NRS BR/CAL/1/24 entry 1616
3. NRS BR/CAL/1/25 entry 703
4. NRS BR/CAL/1/24 entries 1117 and 1207
5. NRS BR/CAL/1/51 entry 102
6. CRA Archive ref: 3/1/2/9
7. NRS BR/CAL/1/55 entry 1143
8. CRA Archive ref: 3/1/2/17
9. NRS BR/CAL/1/61 entry 66
10. St. Rollox 8703, NRM 11902/W RHP 70109, shows the perishable goods modifications
11. NRS BR/CAL/1/71 entry 854
12. NRS BR/CAL/1/25 entry 992
13. *West Coast Joint Stock*, p. 271
14. HMRS ref: 1129
15. HMRS ref: 1169
16. *West Coast Joint Stock*, p. 273
17. Earlestown official photographs, reproduced in *LNWR Liveries*, p.131 (D.46) and p.133 (WCJS 6-wheeled replacements)

10.2: Fish, Fruit and Milk

Pre-Diagram Book Designs

Ten fish and game vans were recorded in the rolling stock return for 1853 as part of merchandise and minerals. In 1858 two were converted to cheese vans and four to road vans. The remaining four fish vans disappeared from the record in the July 1863 return.

Six fish and game trucks appeared in the coaching section of the return in 1865. Twelve were added in 1866, and a further five when the Scottish North Eastern Railway was absorbed in 1867. These latter trucks may have been scrapped immediately, as in the November 1867 census the number was back down to eighteen. Amazingly, one of the 1866 trucks survived until the end of the Caley's existence. The *Carriage Register* records it as having fixed sides and ends, 15 feet 5 inches long and 7 feet 2 inches wide on a 9-foot 6-inch wheelbase. Its final number was 1521.

Four milk trucks were added in the period ending July 1870. These were the product of Metropolitan Carriage & Wagon Co., at £75 10s each.[1] Two were for the Lesmahagow line and two for Strathaven traffic.[2] A drawing for these trucks is in the Birmingham City Archive.[3] This shows a vehicle with solid sides and ends, 16 feet long on an 8-foot wheelbase. Mansell wheels 3 feet 6 inches in diameter are fitted. They did not survive long enough to figure in the updating of the Carriage Register.

The first mention of fish and game traffic in the minutes is in November 1870,[4] when thirty-two additional trucks were applied for. Benjamin Connor was asked to report how many could be built in-house. The rolling stock return for the period ending July

Plate 10.9
Immediately behind 179 class 4-6-0 number 181 is one of the four Diagram 90 meat vans, built in 1908. The vans are distinguishable by the pairs of small louvres at the top and bottom of the side and the row of three trumpet ventilators. These are in a line along the centre of the roof, although the angle of the picture might suggest otherwise. A horizontally-planked Diagram 2 meat van follows. It is newly painted, and may have lettering along the centre of the side. The third vehicle is a Diagram 11A or 68 covered carriage truck, which suggests that this could be an empty stock train rather than one carrying perishable goods. Unfortunately we cannot see whether a green disc is visible on the other side of the cab. This would designate the train as Class A express goods. Positive identification of stock further back is not possible, although there is one open wagon, presumably either a fish truck or an ordinary wagon with continuous brakes. The cove roof profile of one van towards the end of the train suggests a Diagram 107 West Coast Joint Stock fish or meat van.

1871 confirms that twenty-six were built as additions to stock, with a further six in the next period. A Joseph Wright & Sons drawing depicts these trucks,[5] although there is no record of a tender from the contractor in the minutes. Perhaps the Wright drawing was used by St. Rollox for in-house construction.

Two of the trucks, renumbered 1541 and 1543, survived to be recorded in the Carriage Register as carriage trucks. Four others to the same design were converted to carriage trucks in 1881. These trucks are discussed further in Chapter 12.

In 1872 tenders were sought for twelve fish and game vans. The Metropolitan Carriage & Wagon Co. was successful.[6] The vans were built to drawing 2265 (Birmingham City Archive reference). They were 16 feet 6 inches long and 7 feet 6 inches wide on a 10-foot wheelbase. They had heavy vertical outside framing and planked sides. The single wooden brake block operated by push rod was standard for Metropolitan designs of the period.

One van, renumbered 1568, survived until 1924. Its dimensions are not recorded in the Carriage Register, where it is described as a '*game van – open*'. Its withdrawal date is not known. Two more, numbered 166 and 167 in the luggage and brake van series, survived into LM&SR ownership. Lacking brake pipes and steam pipes, they would not have run in express passenger trains in their later years, or have carried perishable goods. It is likely that they were used as covered goods vans. They were withdrawn in 1924 and 1925 respectively.

Ten milk trucks were added in the rolling stock return of July 1876. There is no surviving drawing, or any details of these trucks. Later additions and renewals were classified as fish/milk trucks.

25Ft Covered Milk Truck – Diagram 29

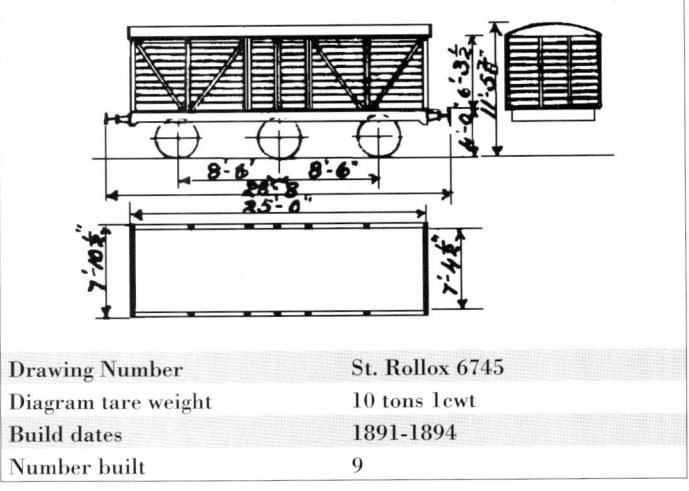

Drawing Number	St. Rollox 6745
Diagram tare weight	10 tons 1cwt
Build dates	1891-1894
Number built	9

Construction of this design started with two trucks to order H60. The slatted sides and ends were 3 inches thick. The numbers of these trucks have not been traced. Later in 1891 two more were built to order H69. Numbers 12, 13 and 15, built to order H95 in 1893, ran on old four-wheeled coach underframes, with outside axle guards on a 14-foot wheelbase, and retained the old type of carriage buffer.

The last order was H113. These trucks, numbered 3-5, 19, 20 and 127, were mounted on new underframes with six wheels. This

Left: Plate 10.10
One of the four Diagram 29 covered milk vans built on old carriage underframes to order H95 in 1893. The remaining seven trucks ran on six-wheeled underframes. Safety chains and old style carriage buffers are fitted – a survival from the underframe's days as a passenger carriage. The Westinghouse pipe has been pushed backwards, breaking the plank behind it. Lamp irons are fitted on the right-hand end post on each side. There seems to be a pair of brackets for a destination board on the top right-hand plank.

Below: Plate 10.11
A brown painted Diagram 30 van is immediately behind the engine of this north-bound train leaving Stirling.

10.2: FISH, FRUIT AND MILK

Plate 10.12
An enlargement of a scene at Glasgow Central, with a Diagram 30 van block lettered 'Waddell's Sausage Van'. The van is fitted with trumpet ventilators. The three Waddell's vans, numbered 46-48 in the carriage, fish and milk truck series, were not recorded as having ventilators in the *Carriage Register*.

increased the carrying capacity from three tons to six. They were fitted with carriage buffers. All the trucks were dual brake fitted and number 127 received a steam heat pipe at some point. The whole class was withdrawn shortly after the Grouping.

FISH, FRUIT AND MILK VAN - DIAGRAM 30

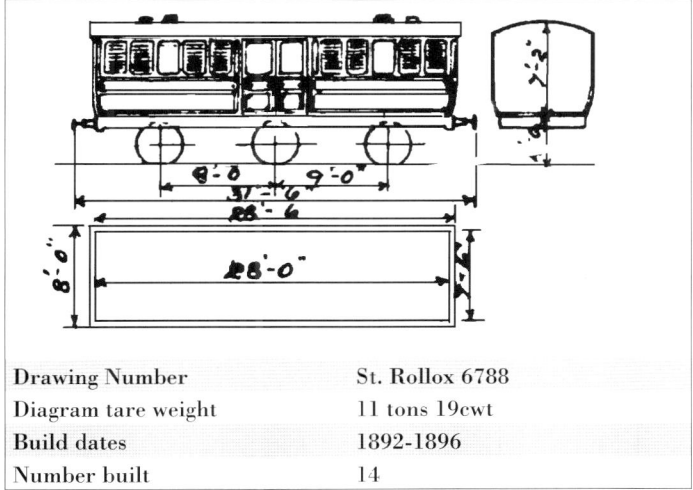

Drawing Number	St. Rollox 6788
Diagram tare weight	11 tons 19cwt
Build dates	1892-1896
Number built	14

The six-wheeled Diagram 30 vehicles were described as fish, fruit and milk vans. The external dimensions were 28 feet 6 inches long by 8 feet wide. They had carriage buffers and 3-foot 9-inch disc wheels were fitted. The sides were panelled with a pair of swing doors in the centre and had ventilation louvres.

Of the first order of four vans to H75, numbers 1 and 2 were for the use of Howietoun Fisheries, Stirling. These were the vans annotated *'built for carriage of live fish'* in the NPCS list. Portable tanks were carried, fitted to the floor and/or resting on shelves. Vans numbered 130/131 were reserved for Annacker's sausage traffic.

Of the second lot of five to order H123, two (49 and 50) were built with sliding shutters and glass in panels each side. These were designated fish, fruit and milk vans. The remaining three (46-48), designated fish vans, had wooden panels instead of glass. They were for Waddell's sausage traffic. At least one of these vans was painted with white upper panels – see Plate 10.12. The last order (H128), of general purpose fish vans, was numbered 51-55.

Ten of the fourteen vans received an LM&SR number. They were withdrawn in the mid to late 1920s.

LUGGAGE, FISH, FRUIT AND MILK VAN – DIAGRAM 39

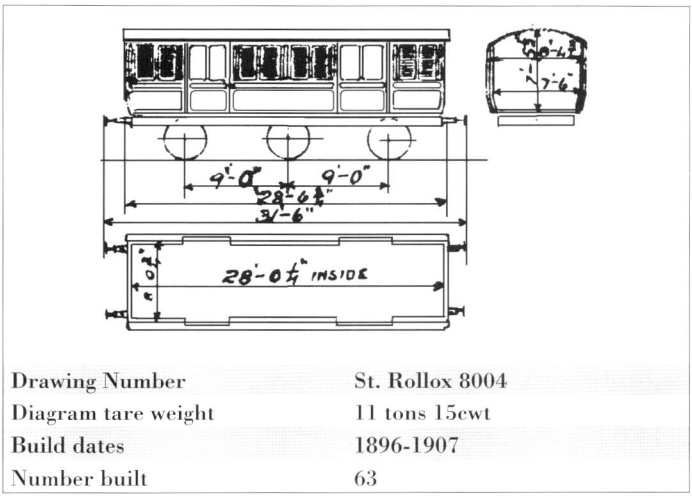

Drawing Number	St. Rollox 8004
Diagram tare weight	11 tons 15cwt
Build dates	1896-1907
Number built	63

Thirty-seven Diagram 39 vans were built in small batches and numbered between 56 and 151 in the carriage, fish and milk truck number series. They were similar to the Diagram 30 vans, apart from a 3½ inches higher roof, with two sliding doors per side, rather than a pair of swing doors in the centre. They were fitted with 3-foot 9-inch disc wheels and carriage buffers.

Numbers 145-148 were designated meat vans; the rest were for fish traffic. Although the last lot of three built to order H254 in 1907 were described as fish vans, they were fitted with plain floors for the Lockerbie milk traffic. Their numbers were 149-151. The tare weight of these vans was reduced by 6 cwt.

A further twenty-six were built in 1897 (order H150) and in 1900 to orders H181 and H191. They were numbered in the luggage and brake van series. This group was not fitted with louvres. The first seven (197-203) were painted in passenger livery with white upper panels and the remainder (210-222 and 234-239) were all-over purple brown. Number 201 was painted purple brown in 1902.

The vans in the luggage and brake van series were variously described as for fish, meat, tobacco or linen traffic. The latter (two vans numbered 214 and 234) plied between Slateford laundry and CR hotels in Glasgow and Edinburgh. The meat vans (203, 210-212, 236 and 237) were branded for Lipton's sausage traffic. One of these vans, painted with white upper panels, is shown in Plate 4.8 and the enlargement 4.9 (pp. 80, 81). Vans 200-202 were described as Stephen

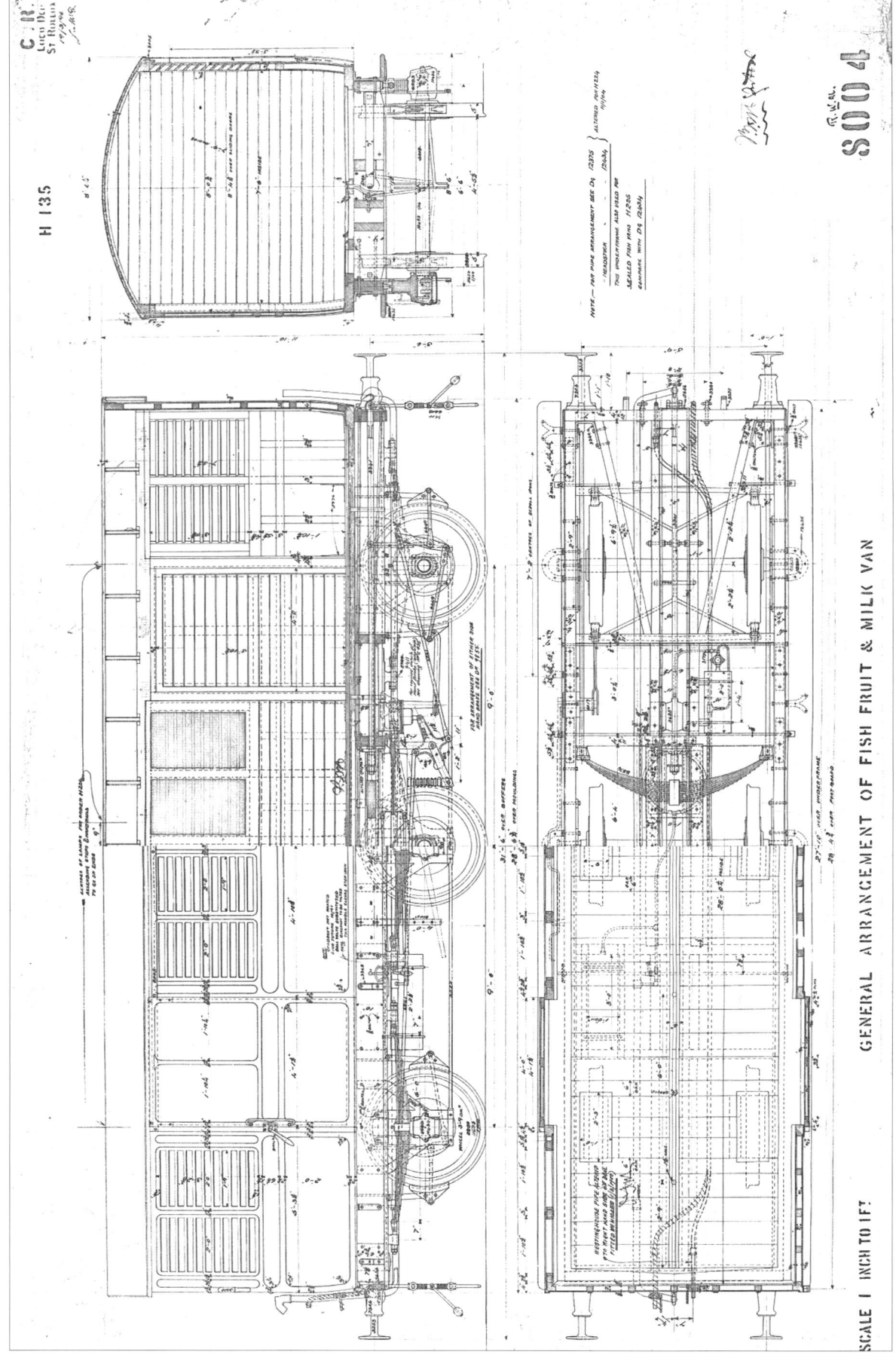

Figure 10.2
St. Rollox drawing 8004 depicts the sliding door Diagram 39 van with louvre ventilation. Some of the vans did not have this feature. An example in full passenger livery is shown in Plate 10.14. The drawing also states that the underframe was to be used for the four sealed fish vans to Diagram 76.

10.2: FISH, FRUIT AND MILK

Plate 10.13
Another enlargement, this time at Bridge Street, showing two Diagram 39 vans with dedicated traffic lettering. Both vans have four havock ventilators on the roof centre line. The brown van is lettered for Stephen Mitchell's tobacco traffic, probably making it 201 in the luggage and brake van number series. The *Carriage Register* noted that this van was painted brown in 1902, although it was later white. The white van behind is the other Mitchell van, therefore number 200. The brown van has letters with serifs, while the white van has block lettering.

Mitchell's, Mitchell's and F & J Smith's tobacco vans respectively. One of the Mitchell vans had white upper panels (number 200) and the other was originally brown, but painted with white panels later. A photograph of both these vans is reproduced as Plate 10.13. All lasted until the mid to late 1920s and were allocated LM&SR numbers.

MODIFICATIONS TO DIAGRAMS 30 AND 39

Although not mentioned in the minutes, some designated fish vans to Diagrams 30 and 39 were modified to St. Rollox drawing 13925 in 1906. This entailed the fitting of hooks and bars for meat traffic. This ante-dated a similar conversion of twenty-five West Coast Joint Stock fish vans to Diagram 107, which were converted in 1913. The numbers of the modified vans are not recorded in the *Carriage Register*.

In April 1907 the Traffic Committee authorised the fitting of twenty six-wheeled vans with shelves for table fruit traffic between Scotland and England.[7] Drawing number 14132 dated 1st May 1907 was an *'arrangement of shelves for carrying fruit in fish, fruit and milk vans (folding doors)'* and thus applied to Diagram 30. Drawing 14138 dated two days later was for *'fish, fruit and milk vans (sliding doors)'* and applied to Diagram 39. It is not known which vans were modified. Presumably the modifications were reversible, as fruit traffic was seasonal. None of the drawings mentioned in this section have survived.

FISH TRUCK WITH FALLING SIDES – DIAGRAM 55

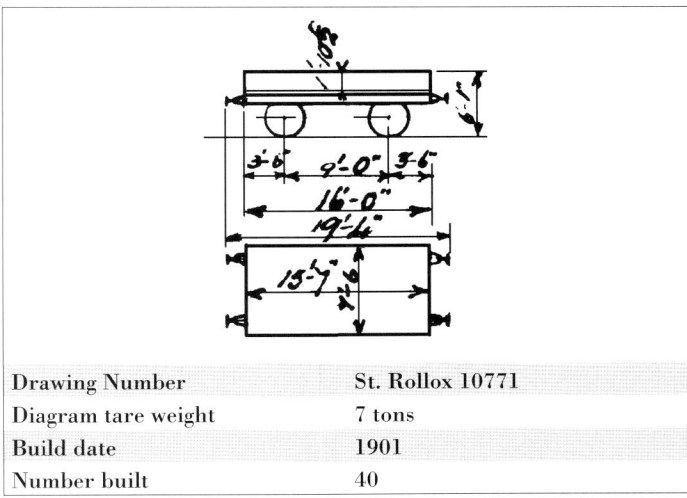

Drawing Number	St. Rollox 10771
Diagram tare weight	7 tons
Build date	1901
Number built	40

Open fish trucks to Diagram 55 were built to order H205. The sides had three planks, from top to bottom 6½ inches, 9 inches and 6 inches. Wheels were 3 feet 9 inches. The St. Rollox drawing does not specify the type, but they were probably spoked, as in the

Plate 10.14
Diagram 39 fish van number 81 was built to order H168 in 1898. The sliding doors opened towards the centre of the van. The van is painted in full passenger livery, which is rather travel stained. The ventilation louvres are either painted yellow or varnished pine.

Plate 10.15
A brown painted Diagram 39 van, propelled by a Carlisle station pilot de luxe. The background to the number plate of the shunter is vermilion, which dates the picture to before 1906, when the name *Cardean* was applied and the number plate's background was changed to blue to match the locomotive livery.

photographs of modified Diagram 15 trucks. They were dual fitted, piped for steam heat and had safety chains as well as screw couplings. The drawing shows the McIntosh patent hand brake.

They were allocated a block of numbers from 7901-7940. The LM&SR numbers are unknown, but Sir Eric Hutchison, writing in the January 1946 *Model Railway News*, stated that this type and the adapted Diagram 15 wagons could still occasionally be seen.

Fish Van with Sliding Doors – Diagram 71

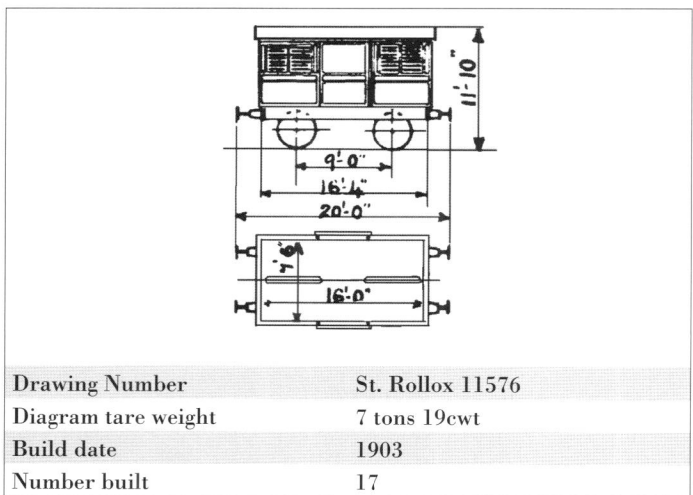

Drawing Number	St. Rollox 11576
Diagram tare weight	7 tons 19cwt
Build date	1903
Number built	17

The dimensions of the Diagram 71 and 72 fish vans were identical. Eight to Diagram 71, order H210, were numbered 248-255 in the luggage and brake van series. A further nine (260-266, 268 and 269) were built later the same year to order number H212. There is no record in the minutes of these or the Diagram 72 vehicles being authorised either as capital or in the renewal programme for the first half of 1903.

The vans had panelled sides, louvres and sliding doors. They were dual fitted and had steam heat pipes. The running gear was to passenger stock standards with 4-foot springs. The axle guards on each side of the van were tied together. The open spoked wheels were 3 feet 9 inches diameter.

Nine of the vans just survived into the LM&SR era. They were allocated, but did not receive, an LM&SR number. Another two ran with an LM&SR number, but were scrapped in 1925.

Four vans (CR 255, 263, 265 and 268) were probably the subject of a complete rebuild as the Caledonian's independent existence was drawing to a close. In September 1922 drawing 21861[8] described the construction of '*new fish bodies on old underframes.*' The underframes were dimensionally identical to the Diagram 71 vans. The new bodies were vertically planked with sliding doors to the same dimensions as those of Diagram 71. Two sets of louvres were fitted to each side. The vans cited actually carried LM&SR numbers according to the *Carriage Register*. Their withdrawal dates are not recorded, but they do not seem to have received numbers under the 1931 renumbering scheme.

Sealed Fish Van – Diagram 72

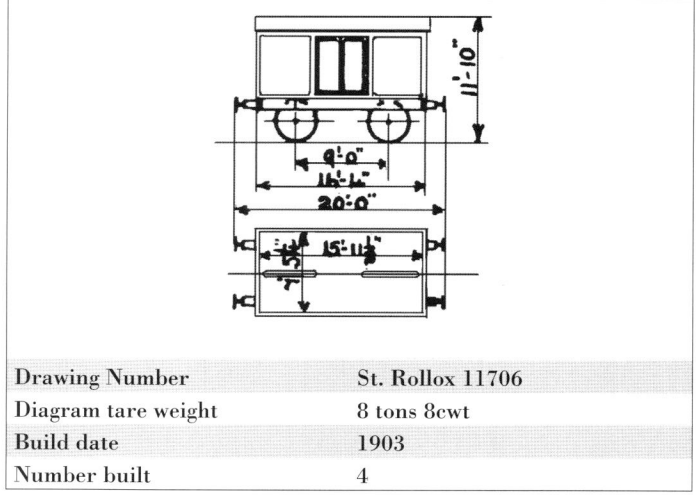

Drawing Number	St. Rollox 11706
Diagram tare weight	8 tons 8cwt
Build date	1903
Number built	4

These vans were built for frozen fish traffic to Southampton. This was a long established service; the agreement with the South Western Railway was drawn up in 1841.[9] They were part of order H210 and numbered 256-259. The drawing was for the body only, so one assumes that the underframe was the same as for Diagram 71.

They had horizontally boarded sides and ends with half round beading covering the joints between the planks and the body frame.

10.2: FISH, FRUIT AND MILK

Plate 10.16
In the daylight outside the goods shed stands a Diagram 71 fish van. Next to it inside the shed is a Diagram 15 wagon, modified for fish traffic. The lettering is in the standard layout and differs from the wagon shown in Plate 10.18. The load designation is in the centre of the wagon, rather than the right-hand side. This seems to have been the preferred location for these and the Diagram 55 trucks. Also worthy of note are the CR long case clock with access ladder for winding purposes and the notice over the door, encouraging staff to 'Keep Smiling' with three exclamation marks.

BELOW: **Figure 10.3**
Part of St. Rollox drawing 11706, which shows the sealing arrangement of the doors on vans to Diagrams 72 and 76.

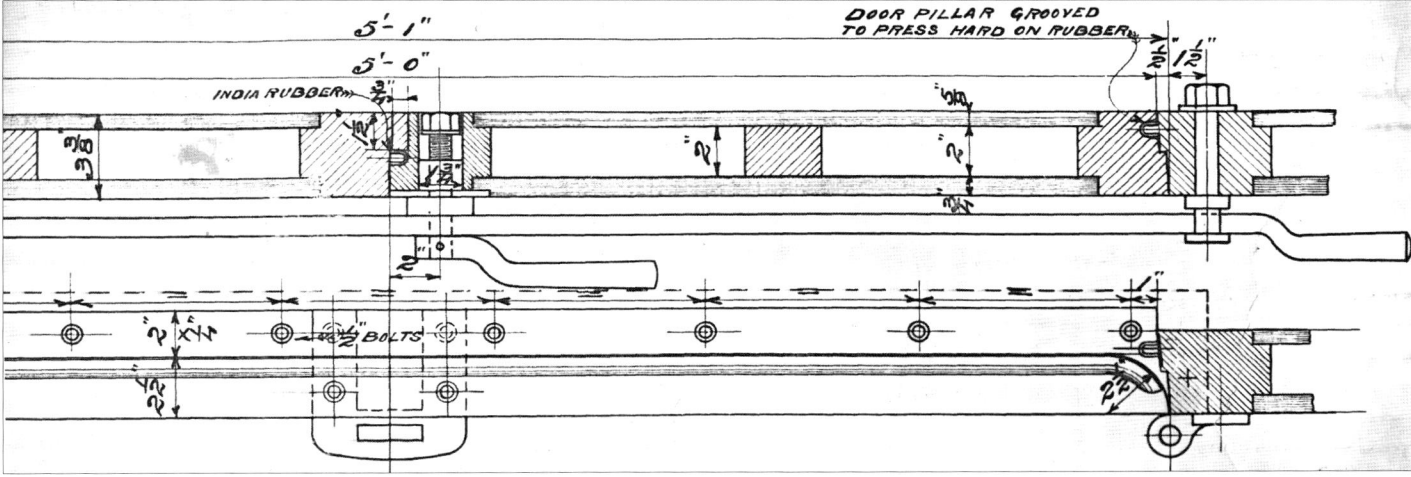

This was the same style as the later variation of the Diagram 3 goods vans. The seal was effected by India rubber sections which fitted into grooves around the doors. They were lined throughout, including the roof, with zinc. All received an LM&SR number. The last example was withdrawn in 1928.

SEALED FISH VAN – DIAGRAM 76

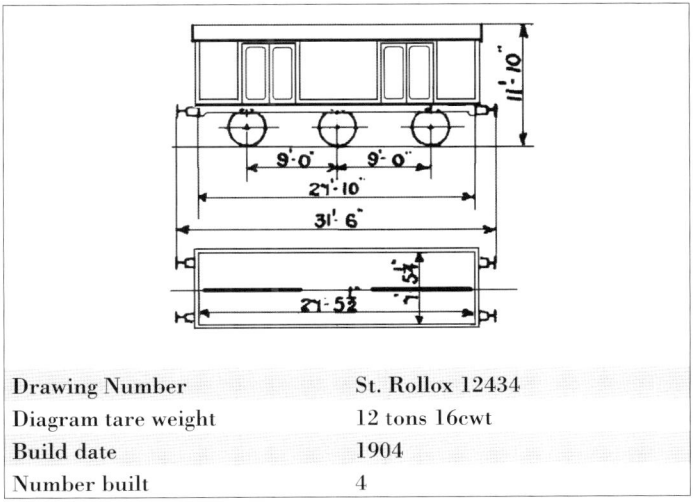

Drawing Number	St. Rollox 12434
Diagram tare weight	12 tons 16cwt
Build date	1904
Number built	4

The Diagram 76 vans built to order H225 were six-wheeled versions of Diagram 72, again for the Southampton traffic. They were built on the same underframe as the Diagram 39 vans. The body construction was similar to Diagram 72. CR numbers were 59, 113-115. All received an LM&SR number and three lasted into the 1930s.

FISH VAN – DIAGRAM 116

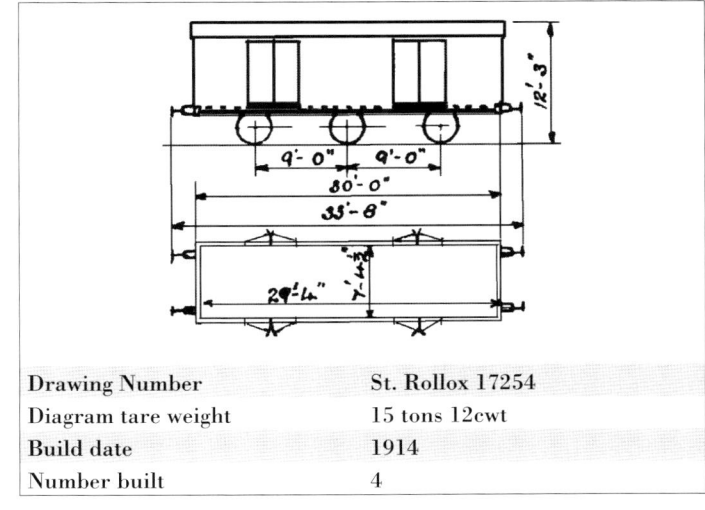

Drawing Number	St. Rollox 17254
Diagram tare weight	15 tons 12cwt
Build date	1914
Number built	4

The Traffic Committee minute authorising these vans as additions to the renewals for the half year ending 30th June 1914 described them as

Plate 10.17
Open fish or milk truck 1614 was built to order H45 in 1891 on a redundant coach underframe. It retains the original buffers, drawgear and suspension. It has been fitted with dual brakes for traffic south of the border. The small letters W and V indicate the position of the release cords for the two brakes. Although it has falling ends and a hinged vacuum pipe, it would not have been used as a carriage truck, because there is no means of securing such a load.

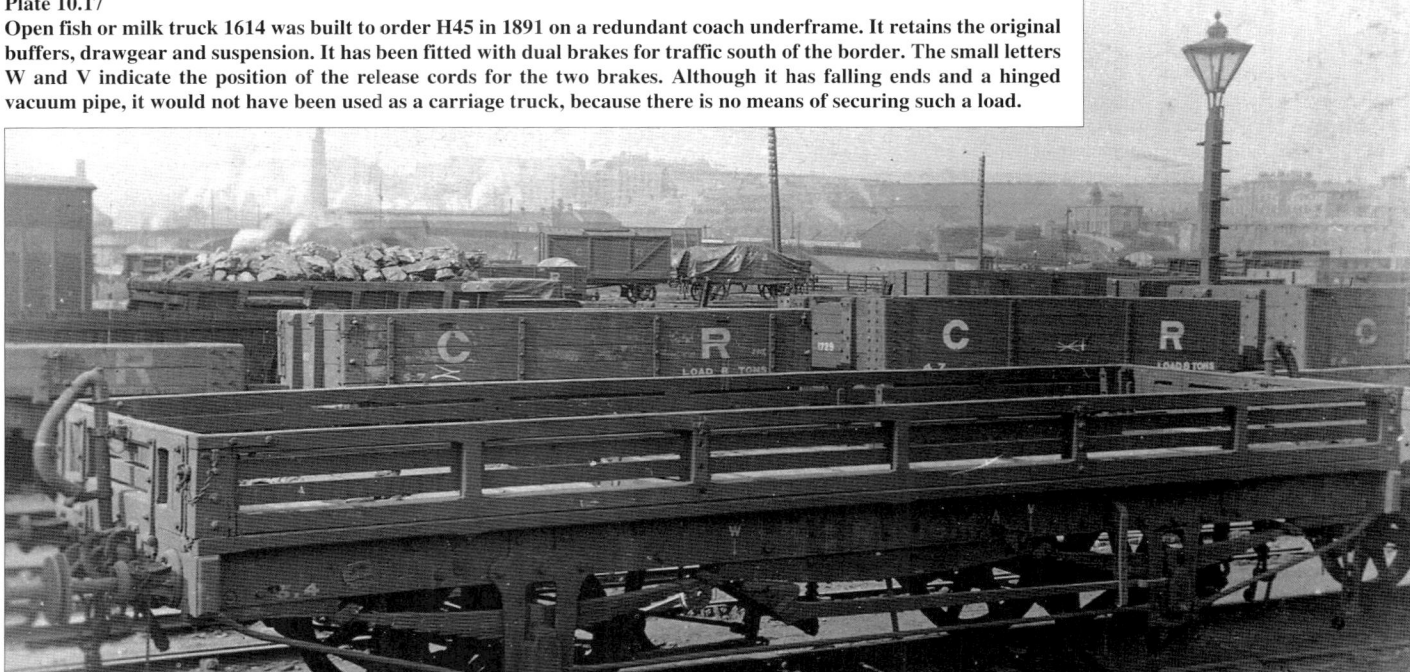

'*six wheel Vans fitted with ice tanks for Frozen Fish from Aberdeen to Southampton and Tilbury.*'[10]

The bodies were similar to the Diagram 102 meat vans, but 2 feet longer on a 1 foot longer wheelbase. The vans were built to NPCS standards using the same underframe as the Diagram 101 covered carriage trucks. Iracier axleboxes were originally fitted, but these were removed in 1920. The four-holed disc wheels were 3 feet 6 inches diameter.

Ice tanks were fitted in each corner and between the doors on both sides. Like the Diagram 102 meat vans the floor was covered with a layer of asphalt. The interior of the sides and ends was lined with zinc.

They were numbered 73585-73588 in the goods stock series, which suggests that they were in fact charged to the capital account. LM&SR numbers are unknown.

OTHER CALEDONIAN FISH, FRUIT AND MILK VEHICLES

In the late 1880s and early 1890s, open trucks were built on old carriage underframes. They were not referred to in company minutes. There is no record of drawings for them in the St. Rollox

Plate 10.18
One of the Diagram 15 goods wagons adapted for fish traffic by passenger train by fitting dual brakes, screw couplings and oil axleboxes. It is very traffic-worn and may have been taken out of service, judging by the white crosses indicating splits in the top plank and, more critically, in the solebar adjacent to the left spring bearing. The normal lettering 'FISH TRAFFIC BY PASSENGER TRAIN' is on the top two planks. The words 'FISH TRAFFIC' are repeated on the bottom plank. The chalked date 7/4/22 has been written over the tare weight numerals. Another modified wagon is shown in Plate 4.7 (p. 78).

register and they did not receive diagram numbers. Some, but not all, were recorded in the St. Rollox order book. The open fish trucks details are:

Date	Order	Known Numbers
1887/8		1509, 1648, 1655, 1661, 1663
1891	H51	(10 built) 124, 1513, 1524, 1528/9, 1548, 1551, 1575

The fish and milk trucks' details are:

Date	Order	Known Numbers
1889	H36	(8 built) 1505, 1507, 1516, 1623
1891	H45	(17 built) 116, 1578, 1579, 1583, 1614

Nearly 200 Diagram 15 open goods wagons were upgraded for working fish and milk traffic by passenger train. This was not a new idea. In 1880 four drawings (St. Rollox 2810-2813) were made for alterations to an early goods wagon design for the Montrose fish traffic. These drawings have not survived and the minutes do not mention the modifications required.

The Diagram 15 wagons were fitted with oil axleboxes and 3-foot 6-inch open spoke wheels. They had screw couplings and all but twenty were fitted with dual brakes, which suggests that they were employed in traffic on to the L&NWR system. The remainder had the Westinghouse brake only, or through pipes. The modification is not mentioned in company minutes, and no drawing was made.

There were 192 such trucks listed in the *1915 Working Timetable Appendix*. They all had three or four-digit numbers, suggesting that the trucks were part of an early renewal programme. They may have been adapted from the 330 goods wagons, type unspecified, authorised as renewals in 1890 to orders G77 and G86. The 1900 *Register of Wagon Plant* gives the total in service as 159. This leaves thirty-three trucks which must have been modified between 1900 and 1915.

In February 1921, eight four-wheeled meat vans were authorised for conversion to carry fish by fitting ice tanks. The Traffic Committee minute stated:

'In recent years traffic in preserved fish from Aberdeen for export to the Colonies has considerably increased. The fish is conveyed from Aberdeen to London, Southampton, etc. The Company have only 4 refrigerator vans and this number is insufficient. The Traders will supply the ice.'[11]

Presumably the four vans referred to were the Diagram 72 sealed fish vans, which were used for this traffic. The candidates for conversion must have come from Diagrams 1, 2, or 3, as all the other four wheel meat van designs already had ice refrigeration.

West Coast Joint Stock Fish Vans

Fish traffic was carried in company vehicles until the late 1870s. In November 1877, George Findlay, the L&NWR Goods Manager, wrote to Irving Kempt, the Caledonian Railway General Superintendent, about the need for specialised fish vans for the West Coast route. A tracing of a six-wheeled open vehicle was included. The Traffic Committee agreed to invite tenders for six trucks.[12] When built, these would become the first non-passenger vehicles in the West Coast Joint Stock.

Although the minute described them as trucks, the L&NWR built them as four-wheeled vans in 1878. They were 25 feet long. Numbers in the WCJS series were 167-172. They were on page 47 of the L&NWR diagram book. The Diagram 106 vans described below replaced them in 1898. Two were handed over to the Caley. They were recorded as additions in the January 1899 rolling stock return. They are not recorded in the *Coaching and NPCS Register*. CR numbers are not known.

In 1878, the Traffic Committee considered an application for a special fish train from Perth to the south.[13] The Committee delayed a decision, pending further information. In May 1879, the Committee agreed to run a special train as an experiment for that season only.[14] It is reasonable to assume that the WCJS vans were used on this train, supplemented by company vehicles as needed.

As with the meat vans, the full story of WCJS fish vans, numbering details and withdrawal dates are in Casserley and Millard's book.[15] Unlike the meat vans, all the fish vans were specially built for the joint traffic at Wolverton to L&NWR design principles.

Thirty-four vans to L&NWR Diagram 108 were built between 1891 and 1895. They were also 25 feet long on a 16-foot wheelbase six-wheeled underframe. They were fully panelled in L&NWR style, with arc roofs and louvred sides. They were fitted with torpedo ventilators. Numbers were 471-482 and 539-560. Two were destroyed in accidents before 1923, but the rest received the first LM&SR number. Four survived to be renumbered by the LM&SR, but were withdrawn by 1936. A block plan and photograph appear in *West Coast Joint Stock*.[16]

The renewals for the P47 vans were built to L&NWR Diagram 106. They were built on a 30-foot 1-inch underframe and ran on six wheels. They were identical to the four WCJS Diagram 103 parcels sorting vans, but without corridor connections. They took the numbers of the vans that they replaced. They all received the first LM&SR number. Two were renumbered in 1933 and were withdrawn in 1938 and 1944. There is a block plan in *West Coast Joint Stock*, and a photograph of the parcels van.[17]

The final type of van was the most numerous. One hundred were built to L&NWR Diagram 107 between 1908 and 1910. They were fully panelled with cove roofs and louvred sides. Numbers were 595-694. In 1913, twenty-five were altered to carry meat. Almost all received the second LM&SR number, and some survived beyond nationalisation. Drawings and photographs appear in *West Coast Joint Stock*.[18]

The first vans' livery is not known. The Diagram 106 renewals may have been in full passenger livery like the parcels vans, but no proof exists. The Diagram 108 vans were in full WCJS passenger livery when built, but were later (at the first repaint?) in the joint stock version of NPCS brown. The Diagram 107 vans were brown from the outset. Louvres were varnished pine (or yellow) in all cases. The only lettering was FISH VAN *London and Scotland* in two rows below the fleet number. This was centrally positioned below the waist for Diagram 108, and centred in the left-hand lower body panel for Diagram 107.[19]

References
1. NRS BR/CAL/1/17 entry 1005
2. NRS BR/CAL/1/17 entry 1064
3. Birmingham City Archive ref. 2260
4. NRS BR/CAL/1/18 entry 1517
5. Birmingham City Archive ref. 2281
6. NRS BR/CAL/1/19 entry 1562
7. NRS BR/CAL/1/54 entry 1070
8. Not yet catalogued
9. NRS BR/CAL/1/8 dated 23/2/1849, no entry number
10. NRS BR/CAL/1/63 entry 1448
11. NRS BR/CAL/1/16 entry 826
12. NRS BR/CAL/1/24 entry 9
13. NRS BR/CAL/1/24 entry 776
14. NRS BR/CAL/1/24 entry 1836
15. *West Coast Joint Stock*, Chapter 14
16. *West Coast Joint Stock*, pp. 276/77
17. *West Coast Joint Stock*, pp. 249 and 276
18. *West Coast Joint Stock*, pp. 279 and 280
19. *West Coast Joint Stock*, p. 49

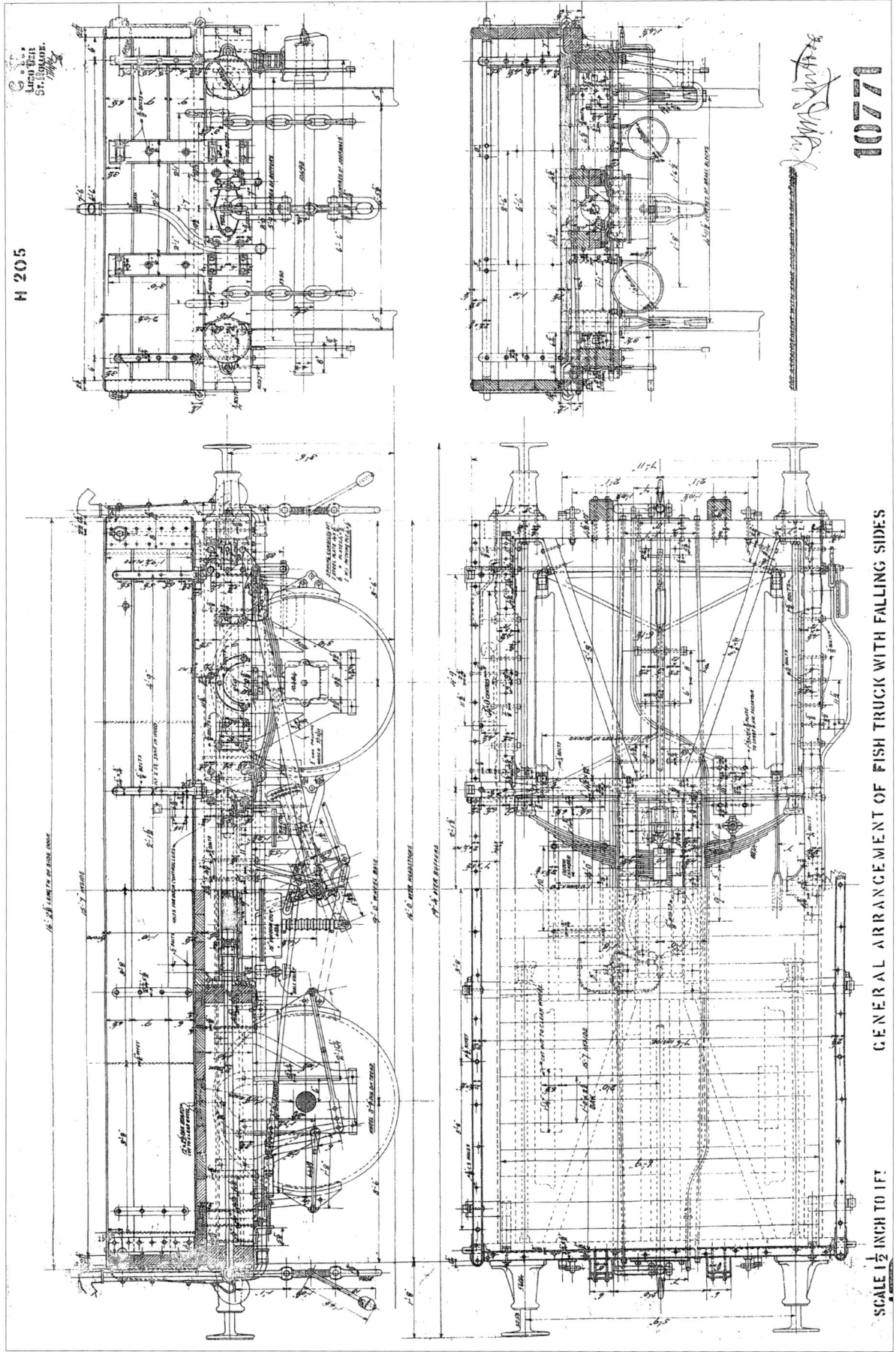

Figure 10.4
The St. Rollox drawing of the Diagram 55 fish trucks, which seem to have escaped photographers' attentions. A single order to H205 was built in 1901. They were numbered 7901-7940 in the ordinary goods wagon series, despite being fitted with continuous brakes and NPCS running gear. They were, however, recorded in the *Carriage Register*. The use of wagon buffers was probably the deciding factor in the allocation of numbers.

Chapter 11
Livestock Wagons

11.1: Cattle

The information in this introduction is adapted from Haldane's book *The Drove Roads of Scotland*. Traditionally, cattle were driven on foot from farms all over Scotland to the great markets in the south, such as the Falkirk Tryst. In the early years of the nineteenth century, improved farming methods allowed cattle to be fattened where they were born. This meant that body weight, and therefore value, was lost during the long drive south. The first solution to this problem was to transport the beasts by sea. This was especially effective from Aberdeen, the Western Isles and ports in Galloway.

The railways began to have an impact on this traffic when they developed from their first purpose of moving minerals over short distances. In 1848 the Scottish Central's line to Perth gave access from the Highlands to the South, and Aberdeen was connected in the same year via the Aberdeen and the Scottish North Eastern railways.

The Scottish Central carried livestock from the outset. Peter Marshall's company history[1] quotes local newspaper reports in 1848 of cattle specials from Perth to London, which took 24 hours at less than the £2 per head which the six to eight weeks' journey by road would have cost.

When the long distance lines opened, buyers went north by train to deal with graziers, and livestock was sent south by rail. Auction marts to serve sellers and buyers were established in population centres such as Oban, Perth and Stirling.

The traffic was intensive. The Callander & Oban annual traffic statistics for 1913 record the departure of 3,825 livestock wagons

Above: Plate 11.1
The picture at Peebles which was used to illustrate the early dual purpose sheep and coke wagon is repeated here because it shows three early cattle wagons with the ends partially open. There is a vertical upright in the centre of the opening, and the bar across the gap can be seen. A drawing of a similar sheep and coke wagon is on p. 190.

Left: Plate 11.2
Here we have the same design of cattle wagon with the ends boarded in. This was achieved by screwing boards behind the existing framing, which is still retained along with the iron rod, as can be seen on the left-hand end. The cupboard doors have been extended upwards compared with the previous wagons and the works drawing. The load is written on the bottom rail of the body, but the tare weight is in a cramped position on the solebar. Ordinary wagon springs are fitted, whereas the drawing in Figure 11.1 showed swing link suspension for the springs.

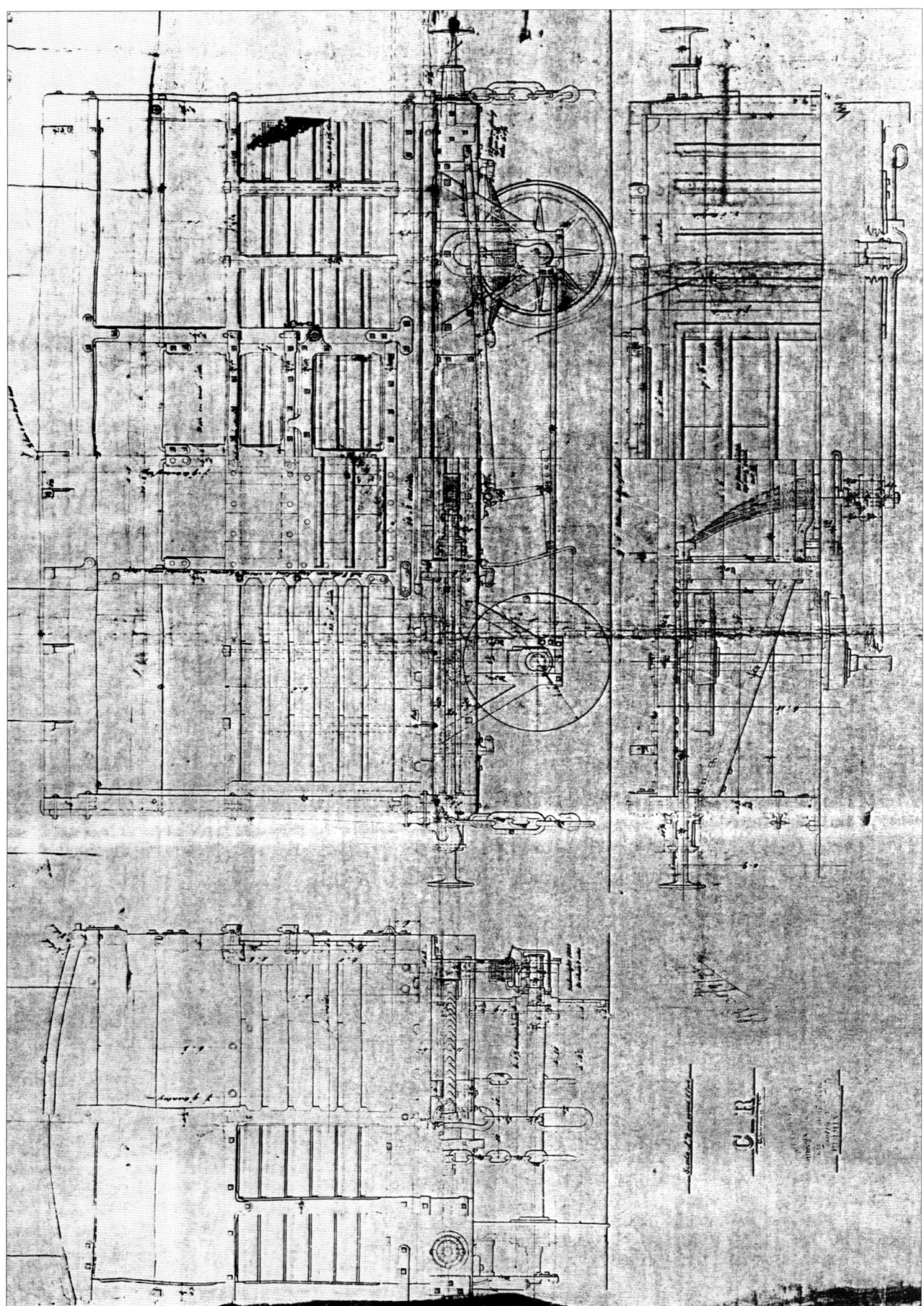

Figure 11.1
The later of the two surviving Metropolitan drawings of cattle trucks, which is dated September 1872. The 1870 drawing was an identical design. The drawing shows a cupboard door that only extends to the height of the body opening. Most wagons photographed show a higher door, as in Plate 11.2. This modification may have coincided with boarding in the ends. These wagons were still in traffic in 1911. A longer version was also built; this is shown in Plate 11.3

from the various stations on the line, plus a further 425 from Callander itself.² It was also seasonal. Over one Monday to Saturday period in August/September 1920, the C&O ran fourteen livestock specials empty from the south, returning loaded from Oban and intermediate stations. Most trains were loaded to the maximum allowed on the line, that is, thirty-five wagons.³

Pre-Diagram Book Designs

It will come as no surprise from the foregoing that the Caledonian transported cattle from an early date. The first reference in the minutes comes in January 1848, when there were insufficient wagons for the traffic and Robert Sinclair was instructed to build stock at a rate not exceeding £300 per week.⁴ This probably equated to four, or possibly five, wagons.

The stock of cattle wagons stood at 152 in 1853 and rose to 255 in 1858. Early drawings of wagons have not survived, but they include both open and covered versions (drawings 196 and 205 respectively), a wagon described as carrying 15 tons (drawing 560) and drawing 630 of 1868, for a wagon 18 feet outside and 7 feet 4 inches inside. Drawings 193 and 194 were for a dual purpose coke and cattle wagon, which must have been roofless.

In 1861, the Board of Directors authorised compliance with a request from the War Office that future cattle wagons should be built so as to admit cavalry horses without the need to remove their saddles.⁵ Similar modifications at the War Office's behest would be made during the First World War.

The early trucks were almost certainly open vehicles. A December 1865 minute specifically refers to a tender for covered cattle trucks.⁶ These wagons were supplied by Ashbury, perhaps to St. Rollox drawing 205.

The first design whose details survive dates from 1870. Two drawings are in the Metropolitan Carriage & Wagon Co. archive in Birmingham City Library.⁷ The earlier drawing was for a tender accepted by the Caledonian in July 1870 for 100 wagons at £88 18s each.⁸

The wagons were 15 feet 8 inches long externally by 8 feet wide. The wheelbase was 9 feet and the springs were suspended on swing links. Photographs of these vans in later years show them with conventional wagon suspension. Buffers with spindles bearing on laminated springs were fitted. A single wood brake block was operated by a pushrod. Originally, the ends were open above the waist, but they were later boarded in. The wagons were still in revenue service in 1910, according to the date attributed to a photograph which included wagon 5579.

A longer version to the same design was built on the standard goods van underframe of the time, with a 9-foot 6-inch wheelbase and a 16-foot 6-inch body. Judging by the price differential, these were probably the wagons in a successful tender from Metropolitan for twenty wagons at £134 7s 6d each.⁹ Wagons at a similar price were ordered in 1873: 100 from Brown & Marshall and fifty from Metropolitan.¹⁰ This suggests that there 170 long cattle wagons in total.

The wagons were presumably the type that was converted to coke traffic sometime in the late 1880s under St. Rollox order G24. One at least (number 2408) survived to be photographed for the *1900 Register of Wagon Plant*.

Another design of medium wagon was introduced in 1876 to St. Rollox drawing 2035.¹¹ It developed the previous design by the addition of diagonal bracing to add strength to the sides. The running gear was also upgraded. The wagons were carried on 3-foot 6-inch springs suspended from swing links. The axle guards were linked by a tie bar. A wood brake block with push rod was fitted. The rolling stock returns record that 498 cattle wagons were built between 1876 and 1883, when the Diagram 10 design was introduced. The only number visible in photographs is 7724 – see Plate 11.4 (p. 187).

The rolling stock renewal records show that 470 wagons to Diagram 10 were built between 1907 and June 1914. It is reasonable to assume that they replaced the earlier types at the end of their accountancy lives and were allocated the same running numbers. Many cattle wagons with numbers in the 5XXX and 7XXX range were recorded by number takers on the Callander & Oban in 1920.¹²

Wagons Inherited from Absorbed Lines

In the six-month period ending January 1866, the Caledonian inherited 126 cattle wagons from the Scottish Central Railway and a further sixty-five from the Scottish North Eastern a year later. Nothing definite is known about the design of these wagons, although they may have been supplied by Joseph Wright, who built carriage stock for the Scottish Central.

Cattle Wagon – Diagram 10

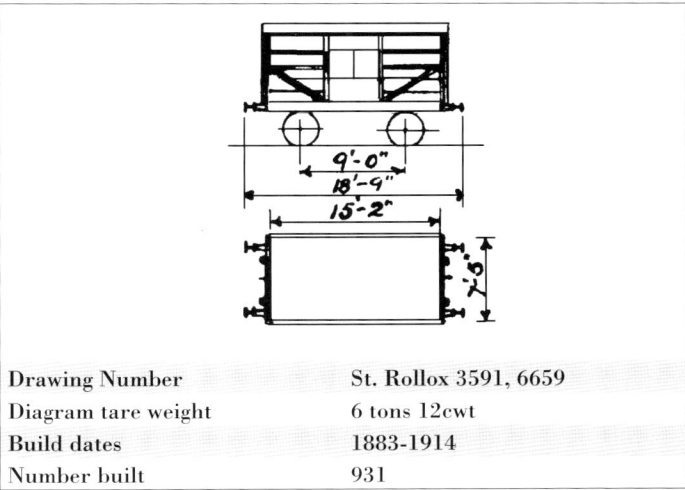

Drawing Number	St. Rollox 3591, 6659
Diagram tare weight	6 tons 12cwt
Build dates	1883-1914
Number built	931

No further cattle wagons were ordered from contractors after the introduction of the Diagram 10 design in 1883. They were fitted with Drummond standard wagon suspension, buffers and the iron

Plate 11.3
This is the large and less common version of the same design of early cattle wagon. It is fitted with heavy duty self-contained buffers, screw couplings and a push rod operated brake. The screw couplings may have been a late addition – the wagon was photographed for the *1900 Register*. There a no bars across the gap between lower body and roof. The door design is unusual; it seems be a one-piece drop door, which, when open, would have created an obstacle for the livestock to step over. There is no visible load lettering. The tare weight is written on the solebar, presumably to avoid being obscured by lime wash from the regular cleaning process. Finally, the wagon rides on one old style wheel set, and a modern version that has very worn tyres.

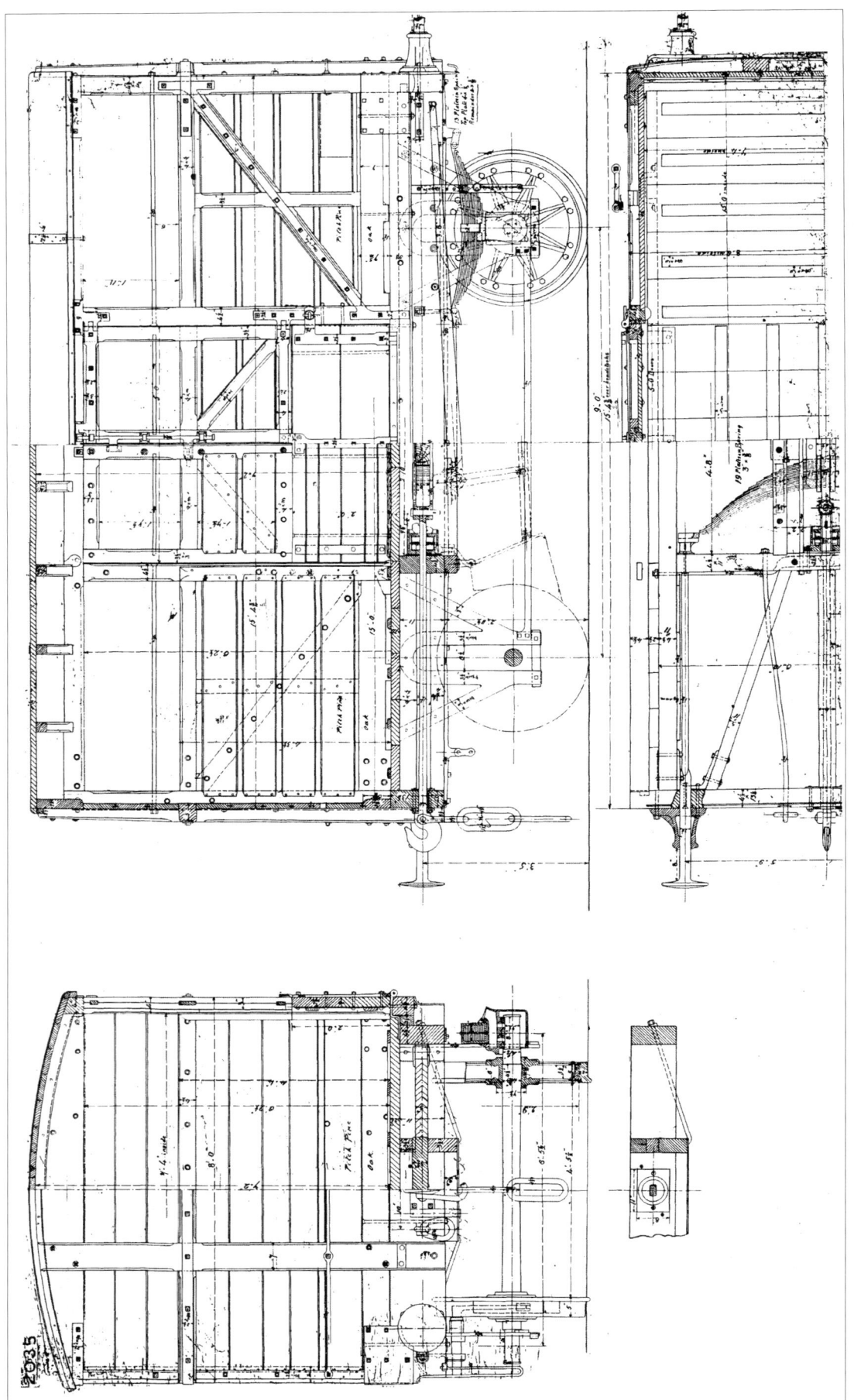

Figure 11.2
St. Rollox drawing 2035 dates from 1876.

Plate 11.4
Behind *Cardean* and a pre-diagram book goods wagon stands a cattle wagon to drawing 2035. The photograph was taken after 1911, because in the original, *Cardean* is superheated. This design can be identified by the heavy framing on the ends, and their greater height compared with other cattle wagons. This example has cupboard doors which extend to full height. In the drawing and other photographs they only extend to the height of the body woodwork. The wagon number, in script style, is repeated on the end. This was not always applied to cattle wagons.

brake block. Until 1891, they were 15 feet 2 inches long inside, to drawing 3591; thereafter they were 15 feet 6 inches, to drawing 6659.[13] The St. Rollox orders show that 141 of the shorter wagons were built.

Orders G209 in 1903 and G257 of 1906 were probably fitted with the McIntosh brake. Wagon 8259 was photographed with the brake, which suggests that it was part of the latter order, authorised as renewals in 1906.[14] Later, the Morton either side brake was fitted. Numbers 73367, 73392, 73411 and 73412 of the 100 authorised to the capital account in 1903 were recorded on the Callander & Oban in 1920.[15]

Starting in 1909 the Board agreed to build fifty cattle wagons each half year for the next ten half years out of the revenue account. The company had fallen foul of the Animal Transit & General Amendment Order 1904 by carrying sheep in improvised trucks during the busy season.[16]

Echoing the intervention by the War Office in 1861, the fifty wagons constructed as renewals in the half year ending January 1912 to order G303 were fitted with 3½ inches higher roofs to suit cavalry horses.[17] Drawing 15811[18] records the modification.

Cattle Box with Louvres – Diagram 40

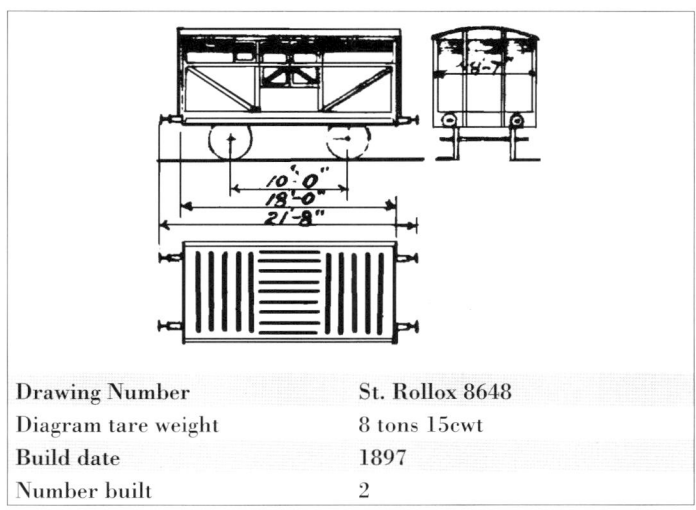

Drawing Number	St. Rollox 8648
Diagram tare weight	8 tons 15cwt
Build date	1897
Number built	2

Like many companies, for example its west coast partner the L&NWR,[19] the Caledonian built a small number of vehicles for valuable animals. These beasts were exhibited at agricultural shows and represented a substantial investment to their owners. As such they merited a better class of transport than that offered to the common herd.

The Caledonian produced two designs to NPCS standards, thus enabling them to be attached to passenger trains. They were treated

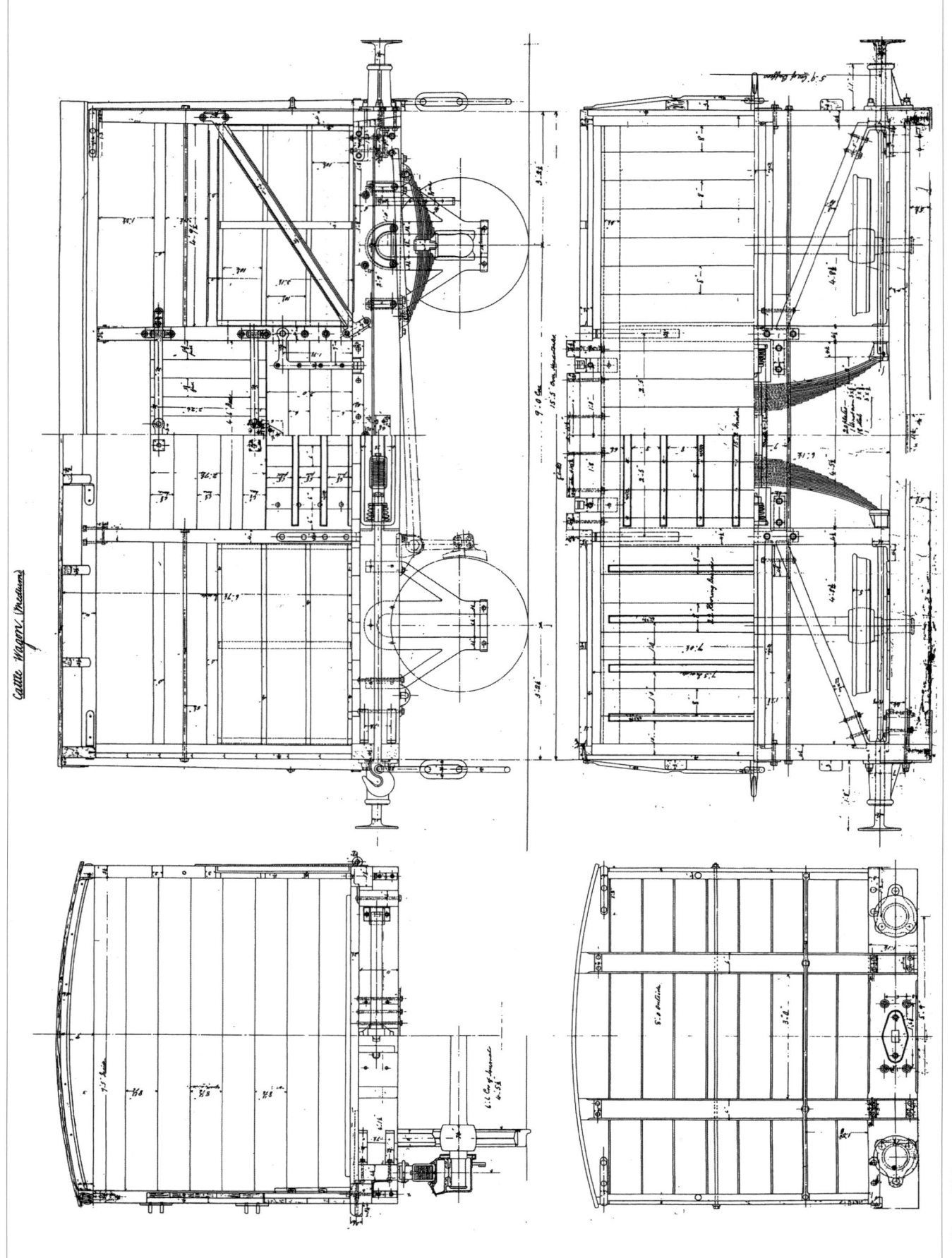

Figure 11.3
St. Rollox drawing 3591 shows the first design of the Diagram 10 wagon, built with standard Drummond running gear. From 1891, the body was lengthened by 2 inches on either side of the doors to give an internal length of 15 feet 6 inches. In this guise, the wagons replaced earlier designs during the first two decades of the twentieth century.

Plate 11.5
The unusual angle for a photograph well illustrates the essentials of a Diagram 10 wagon's construction. At some stage, oil axleboxes have been fitted. The Morton brake working on one side only was a standard fitting to these wagons after about 1911.

as renewals and allocated numbers from withdrawn vehicles in the horse box series.

First to be built was the Diagram 40 design to order H164.[20] Mansell wheels were fitted, wagon buffers and oil axleboxes. The 4-foot 6-inch springs were suspended on swing links. They were dual braked, fitted with safety chains and piped for steam heating. Numbers were 53 and 66, and both received the first LM&SR number. Vehicle 66 lasted long enough to receive a second LM&SR number before withdrawal in 1934. See Plate 11.6 overleaf.

CATTLE BOX WITH GROOM'S COMPARTMENT – DIAGRAM 70

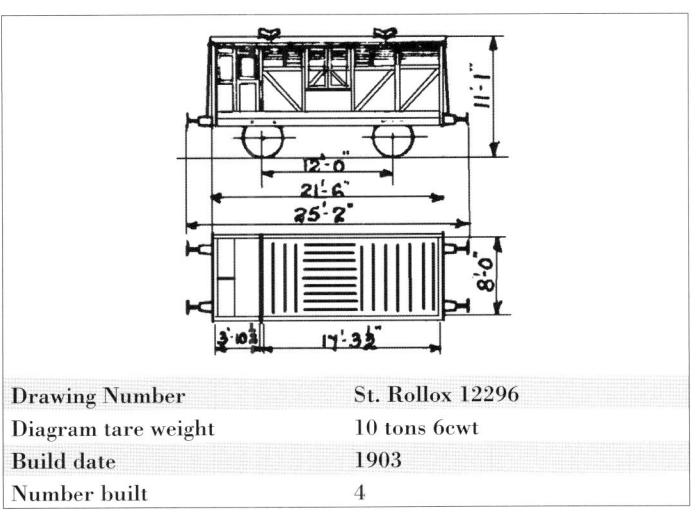

Drawing Number	St. Rollox 12296
Diagram tare weight	10 tons 6cwt
Build date	1903
Number built	4

The Diagram 70 'improved cattle boxes' were similar to the Diagram 40 design with the addition of a groom's compartment and consequently a longer wheelbase. This echoed the development of the standard horse box, where a compartment for tack was added to the Diagram 9 design to form the longer wheelbase Diagram 8. They had trumpet ventilators as well as louvres. The springs were suspended on J-hangers. They were built to order H217.[21] Carriage buffers were fitted and the hand brake was applied by the McIntosh patent system. They were numbered 59, 65, 70 and 71. All survived into the LM&SR era, and the first two received the second LM&SR number.

REFERENCES
1. *The Scottish Central Railway* pp. 94-95
2. Taken from Station Traffic Books, NRS BR/CAL/4/87-90, CRA Archive 3/8/6
3. NRS BR/CAL/5/60
4. NRS BR/CAL/1/8 no entry number
5. NRS BR/CAL/1/12 entry 1647
6. NRS BR/CAL/1/14 entry 1421
7. City Archive refs: 2315 of 1870 and 2286 of 1872
8. NRS BR/CAL/1/18 entry 977
9. NRS BR/CAL/1/20 entry 413
10. NRS BR/CAL/1/20 entry 724, NRS BR/CAL/1/21 entry 465
11. NRM 8044/W RHP 69171
12. NRS BR/CAL/5/60
13. NRM 8064/W RHP 69172
14. NRS BR/CAL/1/53 entry 1151
15. NRS BR/CAL/5/60
16. NRS BR/CAL/1/57 entry 1038
17. Annotation to G order list
18. NRM 11392/W
19. L&NWR Diagram 23 was the equivalent of CR Diagram 40 and L&NWR Diagram 25 was the equivalent of CR Diagram 70 – see *LNWR Wagons Volume 1* pp. 133 and 137 respectively
20. NRS BR/CAL/1/40 entry 1484
21. NRS BR/CAL/1/47 entry 1127

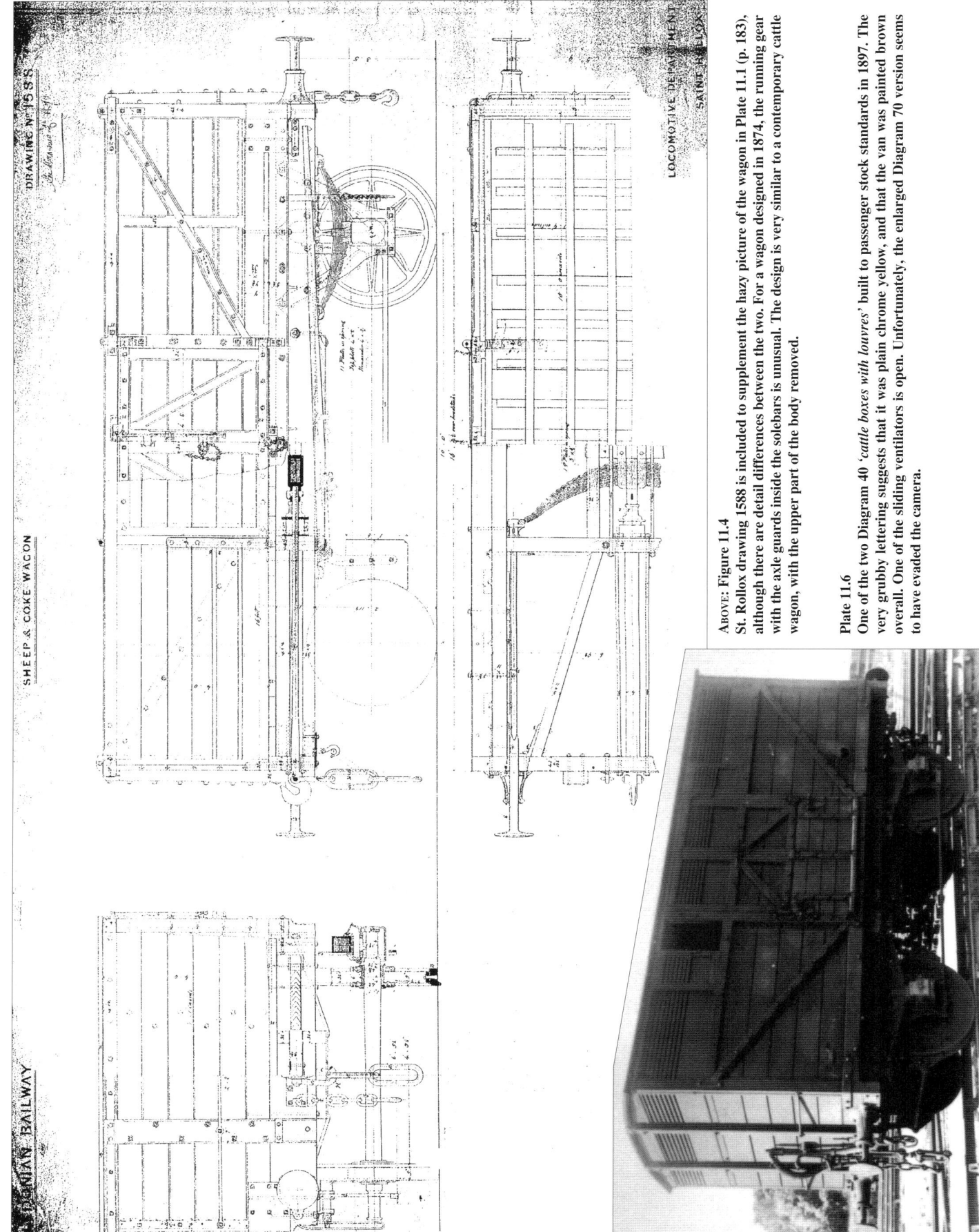

ABOVE: Figure 11.4
St. Rollox drawing 1588 is included to supplement the hazy picture of the wagon in Plate 11.1 (p. 183), although there are detail differences between the two. For a wagon designed in 1874, the running gear with the axle guards inside the solebars is unusual. The design is very similar to a contemporary cattle wagon, with the upper part of the body removed.

Plate 11.6
One of the two Diagram 40 'cattle boxes with louvres' built to passenger stock standards in 1897. The very grubby lettering suggests that it was plain chrome yellow, and that the van was painted brown overall. One of the sliding ventilators is open. Unfortunately, the enlarged Diagram 70 version seems to have evaded the camera.

11.2: Sheep and Other Livestock

As well as being carried in cattle wagons, some specialist or adapted vehicles were provided. The early rolling stock returns recorded sheep wagons separately from cattle (ten in each year from 1853 to 1861), suggesting that they were different types of vehicle. After 1878 the returns show cattle and sheep as a single item.

A very early drawing (St. Rollox 173) for a sheep wagon has not survived. In 1874 drawing 1588 for a sheep and coke wagon had spindle buffers and 4 feet deep sides. It was 16 feet long and had 4-foot 8-inch cupboard doors. For the time, the running gear was unusual, in that the axle guards were inside the solebars. This drawing has survived.[1] Drawing 2223 of 1877 also depicts a sheep and coke truck, but this drawing has not survived.

Sheep were also conveyed in Diagram 24 open goods wagons, fitted with temporary spars to increase their height to prevent animals escaping. The end spars were attached using the corner strapping bolts. The centre pair was attached by one bolt through holes drilled in the second plank from the top. The spars were 4 inches wide by 1⅛ inch thick. The spars and supports were sometimes unpainted, as in the photograph below, but other pictures show them a darker colour than body paint, perhaps tar or creosote.

Plate 11.7
A Diagram 24 wagon fitted for sheep traffic, complete with inspection hole. The spars look to be unpainted. In other photographs they are dark, perhaps tarred or creosoted.

A 5 inches diameter hole was cut into the bottom plank just to the right of the letter 'C' on each side. This was authorised in a 1905 minute

'Drill 2 holes in sides of about 300 Wagons for the Transport of Sheep, to comply with Board of Agriculture & Fisheries (see drawing 14422, 6/12/1907).'[2]

The drawing referred to was described as *'sketch showing observation hole when used for carrying sheep.'*[3]

Outline drawing 14963[4] was dated 29th April 1909. It is reproduced overleaf. It depicts a sheep wagon with the observation holes, battens fixed to the floor and sides extended in height to 4 feet 6 inches. The observation holes seem to have originally (i.e., from 1905) been covered by wrought iron plates that could be pivoted out of the way. This arrangement was apparently removed from 1909 onwards. The two dimensions on the drawing suggest that the modification was applied to pre-diagram book goods wagons with 2 feet high, three-plank sides, and Diagram 24 wagons with 2-foot 2-inch sides. The drawing does not show any details of modification to the drop doors, but after 1912, doors had to conform as follows to the Animals (Transit and General) Order.

'Every falling loading door … shall be fitted with longitudinal battens or other proper footholds.'[5]

Sample numbers of wagons modified for carrying sheep were 1266, 2902, 3432, 3721, 4218, 4773, 5343, 6408, 6595, 6616 and 8275. All these examples were recorded in livestock trains on the C&O during August and September 1920.[6]

Other Livestock

Drawings were made for a pig and sow wagon in the late 1850s and mid 1860s (St. Rollox 193 and 341), but neither has survived. The six-monthly reports on rolling stock changes do not mention these wagons.

In 1907 the working timetable announced that the CR, NBR and G&SWR had agreed to lift the restriction on conveying *'sheep, goats, calves and pigs in the guards vans of passenger trains.'* The note went on to state that, on the Caledonian at least, the restriction still applied to corridor trains.[7]

References
1. Not yet catalogued
2. NRS BR/CAL/1/51 entry 346
3. Not yet catalogued
4. Not yet catalogued
5. *Working Timetable Appendix 1915*, p. 131
6. NRS BR/CAL/5/60
7. *July 1907 Working Timetable*, p. 141

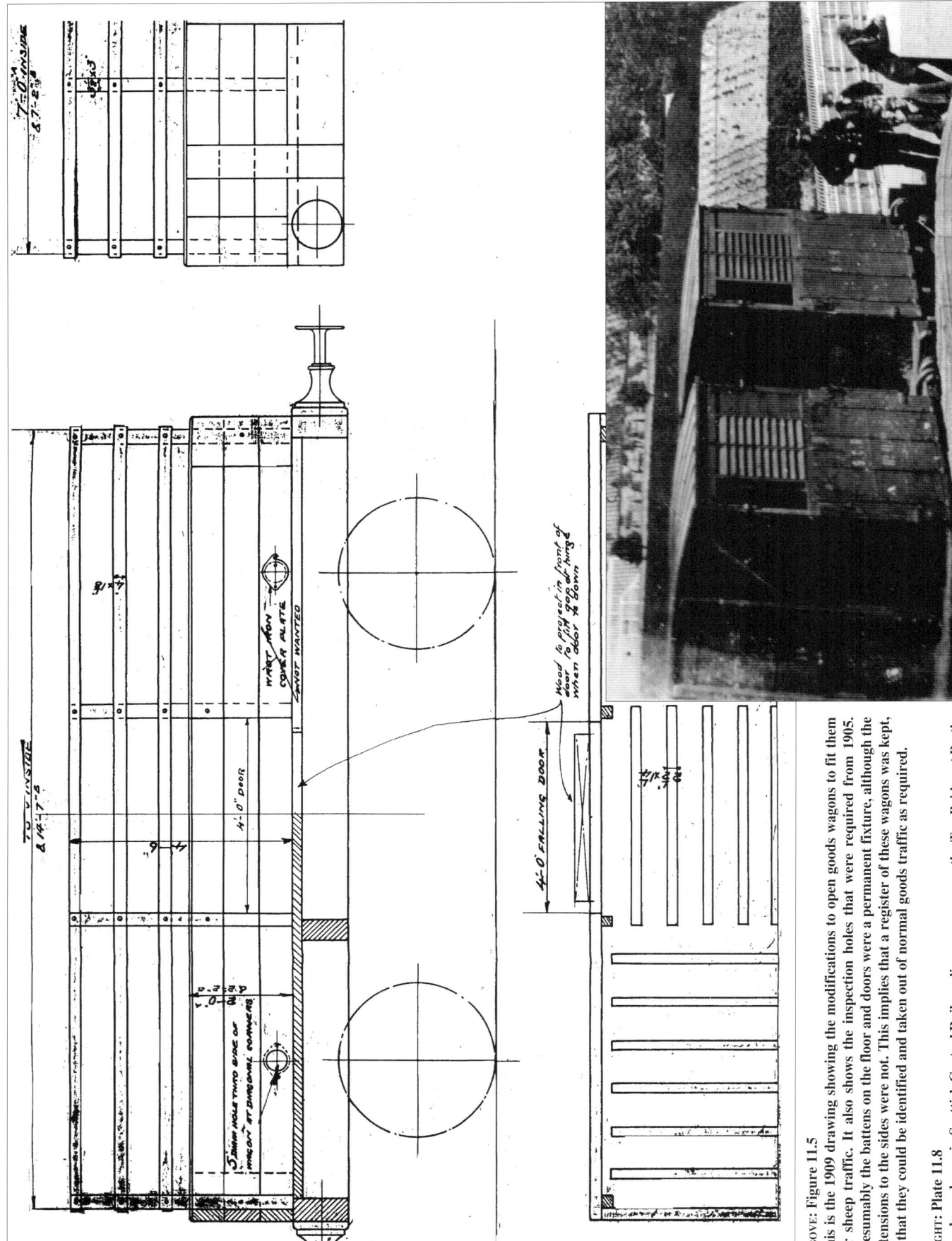

ABOVE: Figure 11.5
This is the 1909 drawing showing the modifications to open goods wagons to fit them for sheep traffic. It also shows the inspection holes that were required from 1905. Presumably the battens on the floor and doors were a permanent fixture, although the extensions to the sides were not. This implies that a register of these wagons was kept, so that they could be identified and taken out of normal goods traffic as required.

RIGHT: Plate 11.8
Two horse boxes in Scottish Central Railway livery are seen on the Tay Bridge at Perth. The nearest one looks to be numbered 41. The Caledonian acquired twenty-one horse boxes when the Scottish Central became part of the system in 1865.

11.3: Horses

Pre-Diagram Book Designs

Horses were carried by the Caledonian from the outset. Ten horse boxes and ten carriage trucks to go with them were ordered from Dunn of Lancaster in July 1846.[1] Another minute on the same day authorised a further twenty of each to be built at the Greenock Works of the Glasgow, Paisley & Greenock Railway. The works were leased by the Caledonian and some construction was undertaken there before the opening of St. Rollox works in 1856.[2]

There were fifteen horse boxes in the rolling stock return of January 1853, rising to thirty-four in the half year ending July 1865. Four each had been built by Brown & Marshall and Ashbury in 1858 and 1860 respectively.[3] The latter order cost £147 each.

The earliest company drawings (St. Rollox 49 and 97, but built at Greenock) have not survived, but 476, dated 1860, for a horse box with a dog box at each end, has been preserved.[4] It shows a vehicle with carriage suspension, but no indication of brakes. It accommodated three horses but there was no space for human attendants.

A later design was ordered from the Metropolitan Carriage & Wagon Co. to drawing 2280 in Birmingham City Archive. It had a central compartment for the horses, flanked on the left by a groom's compartment and on the right by two dog boxes one above the other. Suspension to contemporary coaching stock standards was fitted. The wheelbase was 11 feet and the body was 17 feet 11 inches over headstocks by 7 feet 11 inches wide.

Two horse boxes dating from 1875 and 1884 survived to be taken over by the LM&SR. They were originally numbered 11 and 44 and later renumbered 1813 and 1849 in 1893 and 1898 to make way for two Diagram 8 boxes. The Loco & Stores Committee had agreed to take offers for twelve new horse boxes in May 1875.[5] While there is no record of tenders for either of these years, the description in the Carriage Register of the earlier vehicle matches the Metropolitan design mentioned above.

Horse Boxes Inherited from Absorbed Lines

The Scottish Central Railway contributed twenty-one horse boxes in 1866, with a further seven from the Scottish North Eastern Railway a year later. Fortunately, a photographic record of the Scottish Central vehicles survives. The vans resembled St. Rollox drawing 476, but without the end dog boxes.

Horse Box – Diagram 9

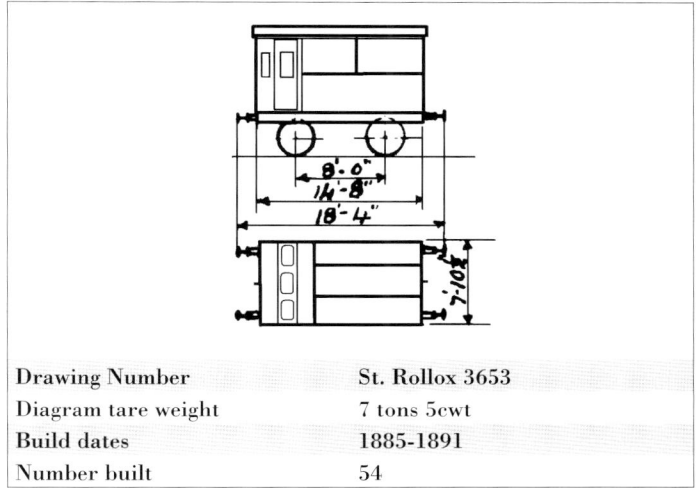

Drawing Number	St. Rollox 3653
Diagram tare weight	7 tons 5cwt
Build dates	1885-1891
Number built	54

The Diagram 9 boxes were built in small batches to H order numbers. They were dual braked and had carriage buffers. Fourteen had steam heating pipes, probably fitted retrospectively in 1914, when a minute authorised the fitting of steam pipes to fifty horse boxes.[6] The axle guards were outside the solebars. The twenty-one built before order H41 in 1890 had bare wood seats.[7]

Plate 11.9
Again taken at Perth, this shows a pair of Diagram 9 horse boxes coupled to one of the earlier Metropolitan vehicles, drawn in Figure 11.6. Number 5 was renumbered in 1896 to make way for a Diagram 8 box. Its second CR number is not known, as it did not survive long enough to be included in the *Carriage Register*.

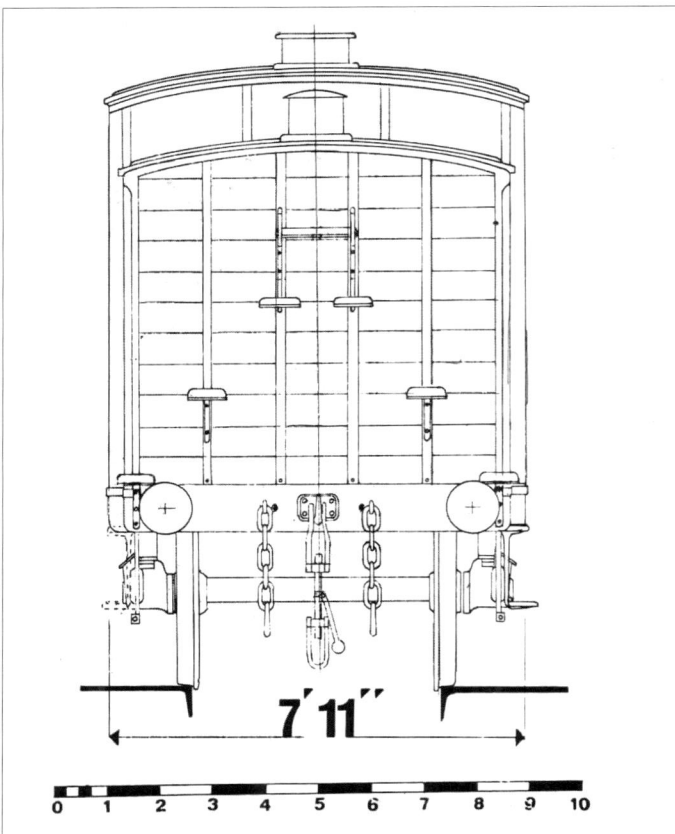

They were originally numbered within the same series as Diagram 8, but thirty-two with numbers that fell within the two blocks later allocated to Diagram 8 were renumbered into a series starting at 1800.

The short wheelbase must have limited their use to slower trains after the appearance of the Diagram 8 vehicles. Despite this drawback, most lasted until the mid 1920s and about half received an LM&SR number, in some cases ciphered by the addition of a zero in front of the number.[8]

Horse Box – Diagram 8

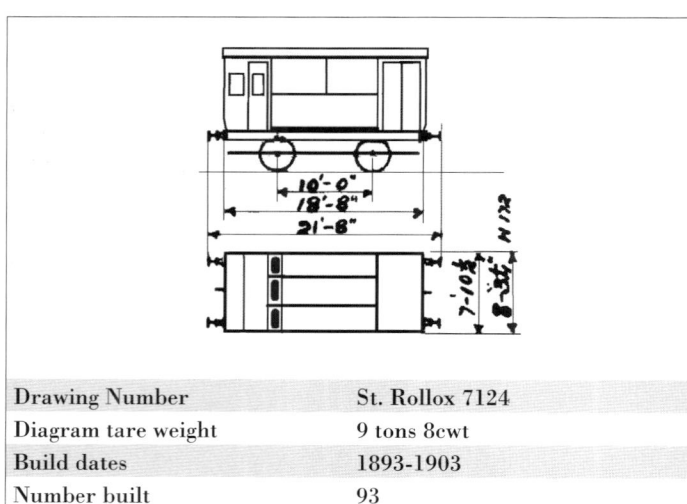

Drawing Number	St. Rollox 7124
Diagram tare weight	9 tons 8cwt
Build dates	1893-1903
Number built	93

There were 93 vehicles to Diagram 8, built in small batches every six months to H-series orders as renewals of older vehicles. The bodies were similar to the Diagram 9 boxes, with the addition of a harness compartment at the right-hand end. Drawing 4601[9] of a Diagram 9 wagon has a pencil sketch addition which shows the proposed modification. The axle guards were inside the solebars, and carriage suspension was fitted.

The early boxes had 3-foot 9-inch Mansell wheels but the final twenty-four to be built, starting with order H172 in 1899, ran on disc wheels. These were the subject of drawing 8975.[10] Carriage buffers were fitted. All were dual braked. Steam heating pipes were fitted from order H204 in 1902. All but six of those built earlier (numbers 109-114 inclusive) were fitted with pipes retrospectively in 1914.[11]

The majority were 7 feet 10½ inches wide like the Diagram 9 boxes. Some were 8 feet 3¼ inches: this width was first used for two out of the five boxes built to H145 in 1897; it applied to all the vehicles built after January 1899, except for the four that were built to order H204 in 1902, which were narrow. A further variation dating from 1899 was the fitting of three trumpet-style ventilators rather than two.

A controller to the drop door was fitted to some of these horse boxes. St. Rollox issued two drawings in 1902 and 1903 (numbers 11223 and 12089). The latter was specifically for order H216. A photograph shows this controller fitted to number 106, which was built in 1894. This suggests that the controller was fitted retrospectively to some horse boxes.

Numbers were in the range 1-117. Most were scrapped in the late 1920s, but some survived into the 1930s. About two thirds received a first LM&SR number, but none received the second.

Horse Box to Carry 6 Horses – Diagram 73

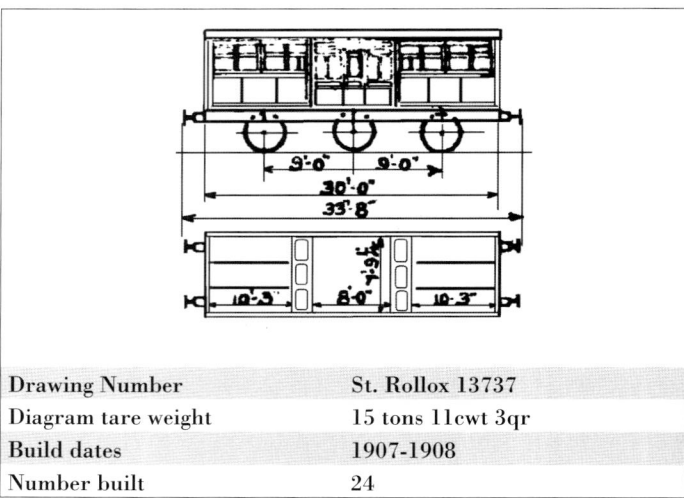

Drawing Number	St. Rollox 13737
Diagram tare weight	15 tons 11cwt 3qr
Build dates	1907-1908
Number built	24

The Diagram 73 horse boxes were based on the Diagram 8 design, with two compartments for three horses separated by a groom's and luggage compartment. They had metal underframes and ran on 3-foot 9-inch disc wheels. The springs were suspended on J-hangers.

Twenty-five horse boxes were authorised as capital expenditure in March 1903.[12] A further minute in August 1905 authorised the construction of twenty-four boxes at a cost of £7,320 (£305 each) to the capital account.[13] They were eventually built two years later to order H250. They were dual fitted, with carriage buffers. All were piped for steam heat from the outset. The hand brake was originally the McIntosh patent; they were probably the last vehicles to be so fitted. CR numbers were 118-141. All except one lasted long enough to receive both LM&SR numbers. The last two survivors were withdrawn in 1935.

Allocation of Horse Boxes

Horse boxes were concentrated at twenty 'stock stations', located at strategic points around the system. All other stations

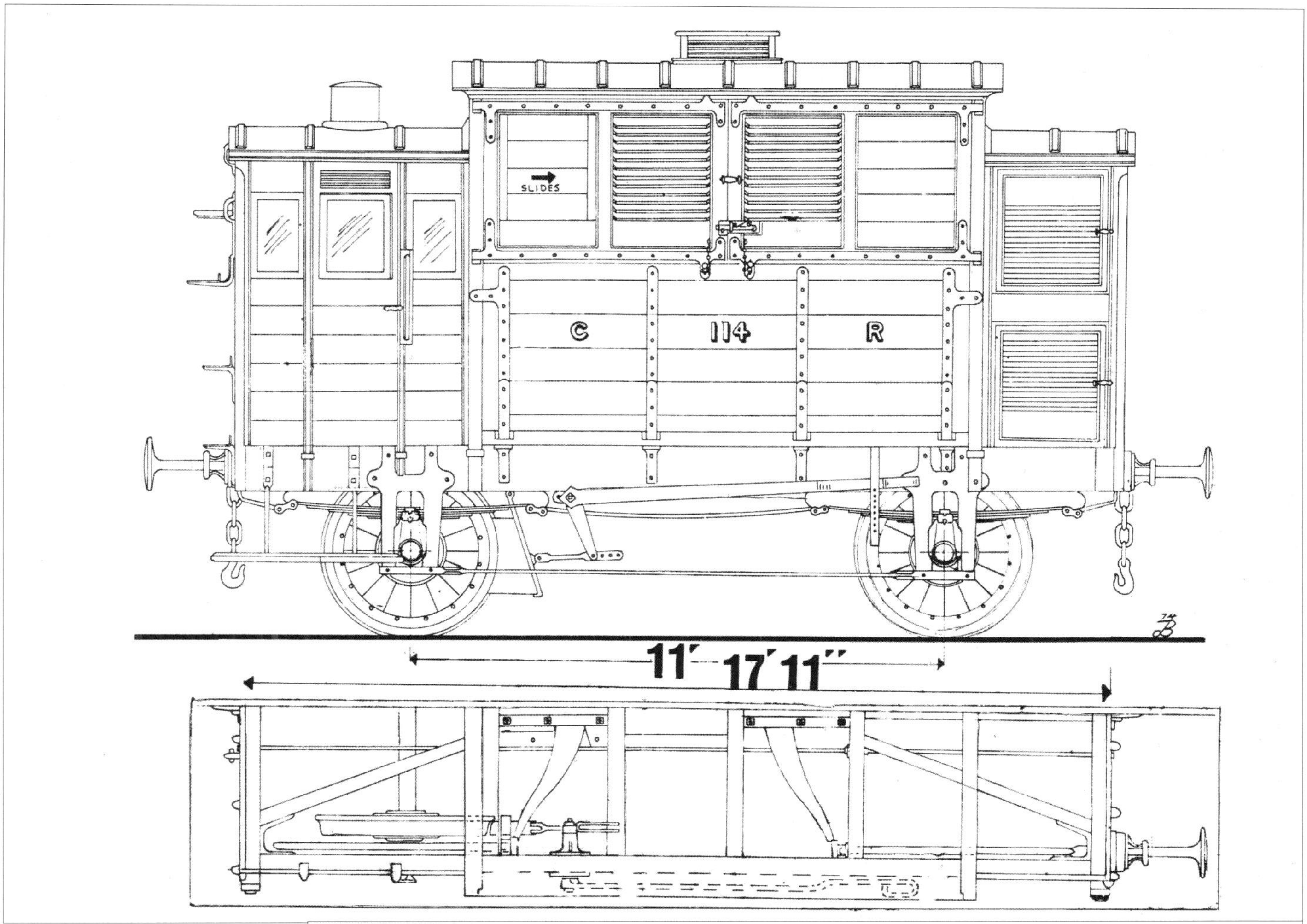

11.3: HORSES

ABOVE AND FACING PAGE: **Figure 11.6** This is a redrawing by CRA member John Boyle of the original Metropolitan general arrangement for the 1870 style of horse box. A copy of the original drawing is in the CRA Archive. The two small compartments one on top of each other at the right-hand end are dog boxes.

Plate 11.10
This was the final version of the four-wheeled horse box to Diagram 8. It is painted in purple brown with shaded lettering, and the panels under the eaves at each end look to be lined. If that is so, the remainder of the panelling on the compartments would also have received straw lining. The van is too travel-stained to be certain either way. The footboards extended an unusual distance beyond the headstocks on these vehicles. Note the lamp bracket about two thirds up the body at the extreme right-hand side. In Caledonian days, this was standard practice for NPCS and was repeated at the diagonally opposite corner. It would only have been used in trains that were completely made up of NPCS, as photographs show that the vehicles were usually coupled behind the locomotive on passenger trains.

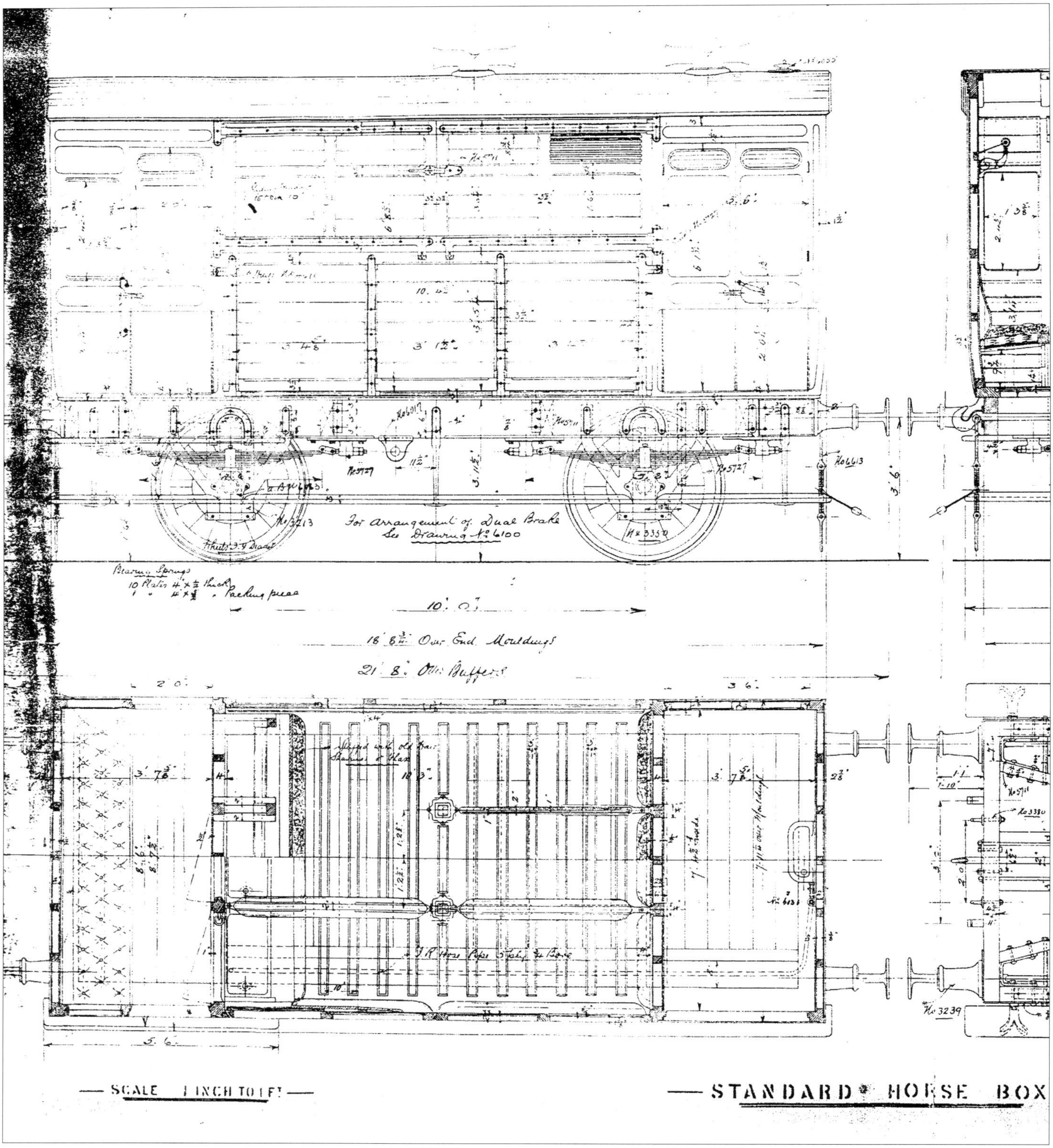

— SCALE 1 INCH TO 1 FT — — STANDARD HORSE BOX

ABOVE AND FACING PAGE: Figure 11.7
St. Rollox drawing 7124 shows the standard Diagram 8 four-wheeled horse box design. It shared many design features with the Diagram 9 horse box that preceded it and the six-wheeled version to Diagram 73.

LEFT: Plate 11.11
The drop door for the horse compartment was very wide (over 10 feet), unwieldy and heavy. The solution was a door controller mounted on the centre line of the body. It has been painted white in this photograph that was taken especially to show the modification. It is not known how many horse boxes were modified, but it does not appear on the photographs in which these vehicles often figure. In the original poor quality photograph from which this is enlarged, the end compartments of horse box 106 were lined in yellow.

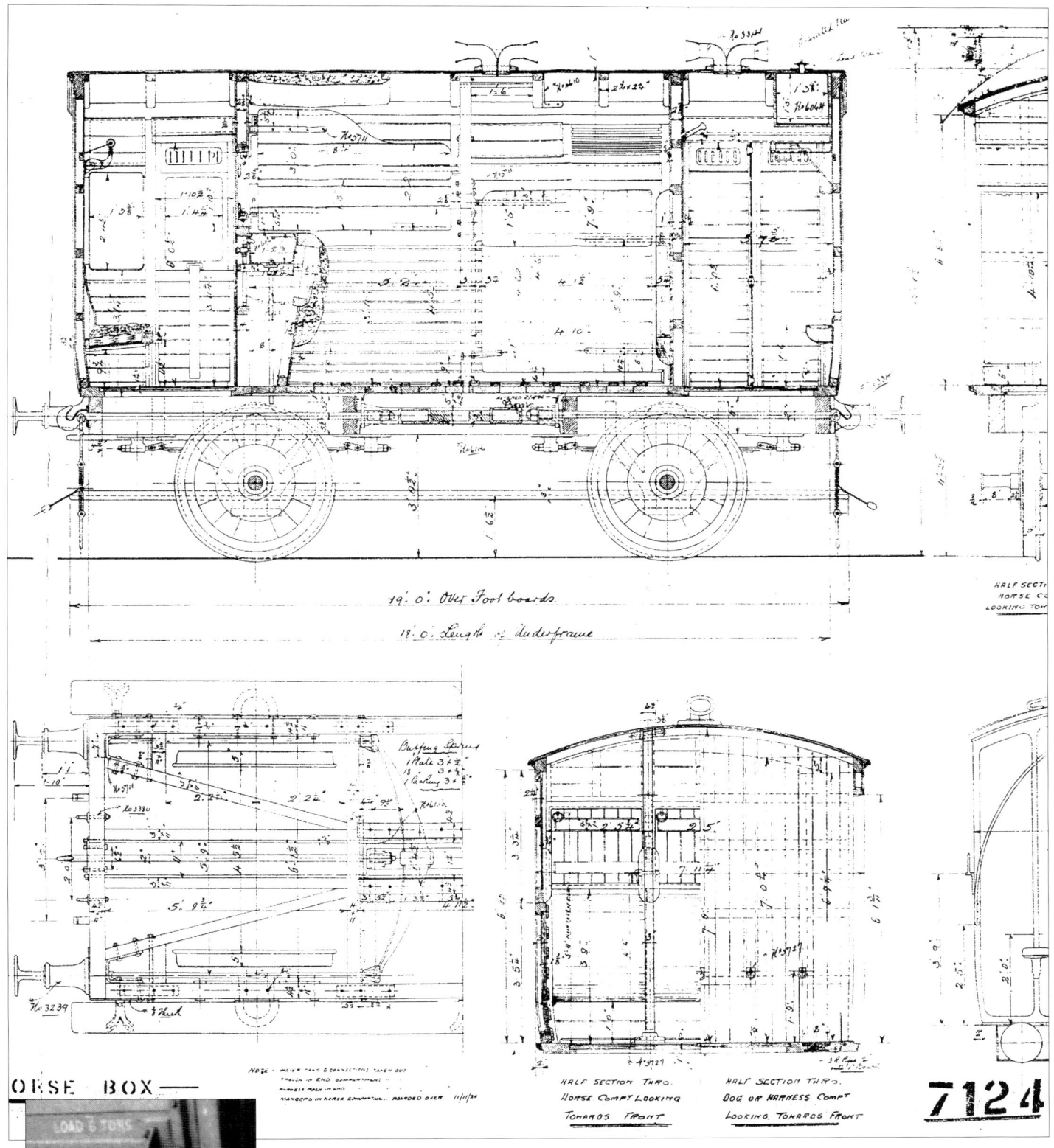

LEFT: **Plate 11.12**
This is a close-up of the door controllers that were fitted at each end of the four drop doors on Diagram 73 horse boxes. This picture was taken of a box in LM&SR livery. The same type of controller may have been fitted to Diagram 55 fish trucks, but this was not specified on the original drawing.

'*must make application direct to the Coaching Plant Superintendent ... stating the number of horses for which the supply is wanted, and the day, place and, if possible, the Train by which the traffic is intended to be forwarded, also if the vehicles require to be fitted with Steam-heating Pipes.*'[14]

The centralised allocation system led to trains of empty horse boxes converging on these points. For instance, in the 1913 working timetable, there was a path for a conditional train of horse boxes to leave Callander at 9.30 am for Stirling. The *1915 Appendix* listed the stock stations as:

Aberdeen	Glasgow (Central)
Ardrossan	Gourock
Carlisle	Hamilton (Central)
Carstairs	Kirtlebridge
Dumfries	Law Junction
Dundee (West)	Lockerbie
Dundee (East)	Larbert
Edinburgh	Oban
Forfar	Perth (General)
Glasgow (Buchanan Street)	Stirling

References

1. NRS BR/CAL/1/7 p. 359
2. NRS BR/CAL/1/7 p. 360
3. NRS BR/CAL/1/11 entry 1814, NRS BR/CAL/1/12 entry 600
4. NRM 8046/W RHP 69164
5. NRS BR/CAL/1/22 entry 826
6. NRS BR/CAL/1/64 entry 950
7. Information extracted from *Carriage Register*
8. Information extracted from *Carriage Register*
9. NRM 11982/C
10. NRM 11991/C, RHP 70120
11. NRS BR/CAL1/64 entry 950
12. NRS BR/CAL/1/47 entry 783
13. NRS BR/CAL/1/51 entry 1007
14. *1915 Working Timetable Appendix*, p. 86

Plate 11.13
A Diagram 73 horse box freshly painted in purple brown, with chrome yellow lining on the central compartment panels. Under magnification, the letters can be seen to be shaded.

Plate 11.14
Glasgow Central was one of the stock stations for horse boxes, and here we see six Diagram 8 boxes in the east bank siding against the loading bank. The loading bank extended beyond platforms 11 and 12. The image is part of an enlargement of SRX 502, courtesy of National Railway Museum / SSPL.

Chapter 12
Carriage and Scenery Trucks

12.1: Open Carriage Trucks

Pre-Diagram Book Designs

As was recounted in the section dealing with horse boxes, ten carriage trucks and ten horse boxes were ordered from Dunn of Lancaster in 1846.[1] Another minute on the same day authorised twenty of each to be built at the Greenock Works of the Glasgow, Paisley & Greenock Railway.[2] The Caledonian's own workshops at St. Rollox were not opened until 1856.[3]

The rolling stock returns did not differentiate between open and covered carriage trucks. The early returns record fifteen trucks from 1853, rising to nineteen in 1865. Fifteen more were acquired on amalgamation of the Scottish Central Railway and a further three from the Scottish North Eastern.

A minute of 14th February 1872 records acceptance of a tender from Metropolitan Carriage & Wagon Co. which included two carriage trucks at £122 10s each.[4] They were treated as renewals in the rolling stock return. A drawing is in Birmingham City Archive.[5] It is described as *'Carriage Truck, or Fish and Game.'* The fixed sides were slatted and 1 foot 1 inch high. The ends folded down. The truck was 15 feet 9 inches over buffers, on a 9-foot 6-inch wheelbase, with 3-foot 6-inch Mansell wheels. Brake gear was the standard Metropolitan arrangement of a single wooden block operated by push rod.

Rolling stock returns first mention furniture van wagons in 1871. They were built to St. Rollox drawing 988, which has not survived. Their purpose was to carry horse-drawn pantechnicons for house or farm removals. Two more were added in 1874 and 1877. The Loco & Stores Committee authorised the former two in 1873.[6] This is the only mention in the minutes of these vehicles. The details of these early wagons are unknown.

In 1878 a new drawing (St. Rollox 2428) was made.[7] Nine wagons were built to this design, authorised to the capital account, judging by their original numbers. The numbering sequences suggest that they were built in small batches over a period of some years. There is no record of them in the minutes or the rolling stock returns. Although they were built in the 1890s, they were not recorded in the diagram book.

The wagons were 18 feet long by 8 feet wide externally, with fixed sides and ends 5 or 5½ inches high. They had small ramps for end loading. The wheelbase was 11 feet 8 inches. Seven-leaf springs were fitted and heavy self-contained buffers. The axle journals were 9 inches by 4 inches.

They were originally numbered as goods wagons, but renumbered into the special class series at some time between the printing of the *1890* and *1894 Working Timetable Appendices* – see the table below.

| 1890 | 35401, 35402 | 35754, 35755 | 36868-36870 | 37333, 37334 |
| 1894 | 26, 27 | 28, 29 | 30-32 | 33, 34 |

Plate 12.1
This furniture van truck was originally numbered 35402 in the goods wagon series. Its sister wagon, numbered 35755 when built, is just behind it. They were first recorded and numbered as special wagons in 1894. Number 27 was withdrawn between July 1908 and 1909. Number 29 was still in traffic in 1915. The wagon is fitted with heavy duty self-contained buffers, with a step cast in the top. The coupling hook is particularly ornate in shape. Just visible is the metal strip on top of the single plank side. It is pierced with a series of holes to take pegs to which ropes were attached to secure the load. The 9-inch company initials cross the sides and the curb rail. Unusually, the load lettering is centred on the curb rail, rather than the right-hand end of the body plank, with the return location immediately above.

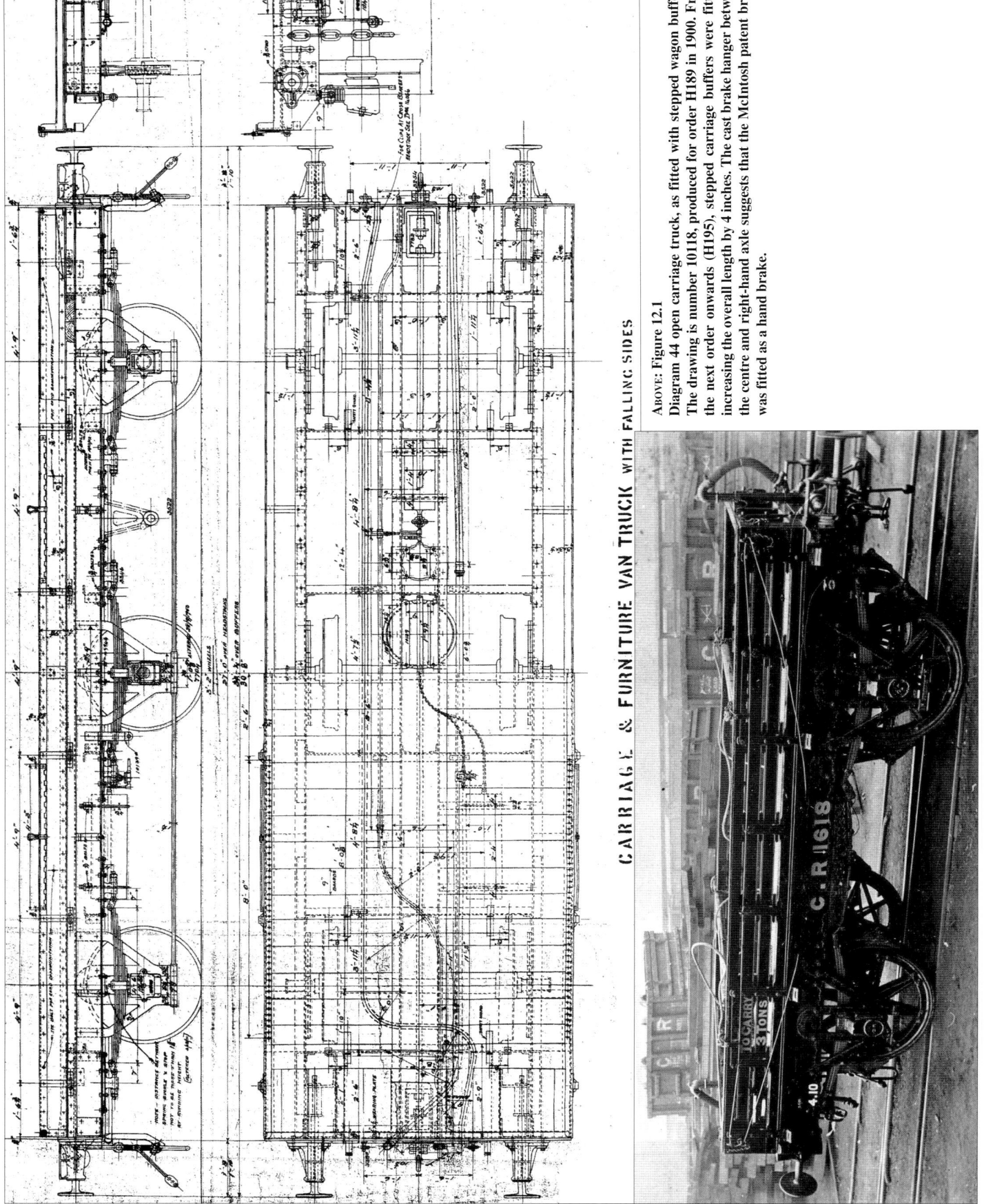

ABOVE: Figure 12.1
Diagram 44 open carriage truck, as fitted with stepped wagon buffers. The drawing is number 10118, produced for order H189 in 1900. From the next order onwards (H195), stepped carriage buffers were fitted, increasing the overall length by 4 inches. The cast brake hanger between the centre and right-hand axle suggests that the McIntosh patent brake was fitted as a hand brake.

In the *1894 Appendix* an extra wagon, built to the same overall design and numbered 35, was included. It was 6 inches longer and 3 inches narrower than its predecessors. Between the returns of July 1908 and July 1909, wagon 27 was withdrawn, leaving nine in stock when the *1915 Appendix* was published. The trucks were allocated to St. Rollox.

10 Ton Carriage & Furniture Van Truck – Diagram 44

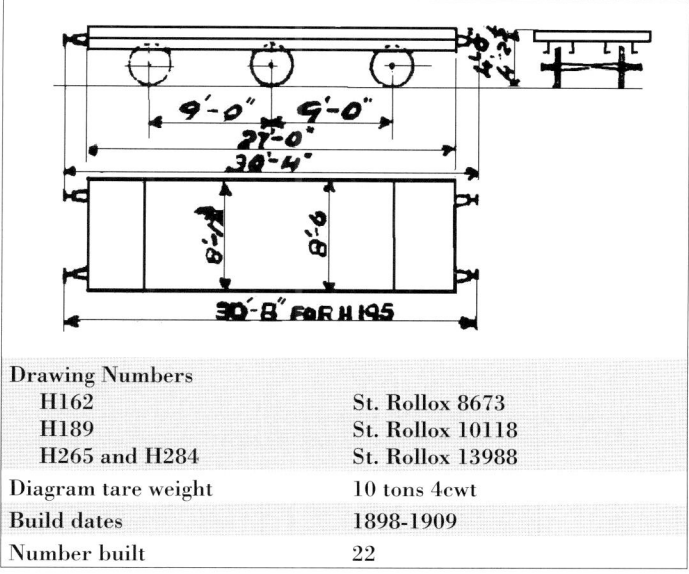

Drawing Numbers	
H162	St. Rollox 8673
H189	St. Rollox 10118
H265 and H284	St. Rollox 13988
Diagram tare weight	10 tons 4cwt
Build dates	1898-1909
Number built	22

The Diagram 44 carriage and furniture van trucks had folding sides and ends made of iron, except for the first batch of five, built in 1898 to H162, which had no ends. They were 27 feet long by 8 feet 6 inches wide and ran on 3-foot 2-inch wheels (type unspecified, but presumably standard open spoke wagon wheels). The 4 feet 6 inches long springs and oil axle boxes were suspended on swing links. They were dual braked with steam heating pipes. The brake and heating pipes were underslung.

Screw couplings, safety chains and stepped buffers were fitted. Drawing 10118, which dates from 1900, shows that the buffers on the original order were the wagon type. An annotation shows that they were changed to the coach type for orders starting with H195, which appeared 1903. This explains the increased overall length of 4 inches, on the drawing, which is repeated in the diagram book sketch above.

The first batch was numbered 72-76. They were designated well trucks, because the floor was only 3 feet 6 inches above rail height. Ramps at each end allowed loading into the well. The remainder, with floors at 3 feet 9 inches from rail level, appeared between 1900 and 1909. Numbers were 31, 34-36, 92, 93 (order H195), 95-97 (order H189), 153-156 (order H265) and 171-174 (order H284). All but two (numbers 36 and 72) received the first LM&SR number.

Open Trucks Built without a Diagram Number

Two orders of carriage trucks were constructed on old carriage underframes without receiving a diagram number. They did not appear in the rolling stock returns. The numbers are shown in the following table.

Order	Date	Qty	Numbers
H27	1889	12	1518, 1520, 1540, 1544, 1547, 1554, 1587-1589, 1594, 1595, 1618
H106	1894	5	32, 33, 42-44

According to the carriage register, the length for the H27 order was 16 feet 6 inches; widths varied from 6 feet 8 inches to 7 feet 2 inches. The sides were fixed and the ends folded down. Open spoke wheels were 3 feet 6 inches in diameter and the axle guards were outside the solebars. All were dual brake fitted, with the pipe standards hinged to fold out of the way of the ends when they were dropped down.

The order was said to be built to St. Rollox drawing 6004,[8] but there are major differences between the drawing (see Figure 12.2 overleaf), the dimensions given in the carriage register and the photograph of 1618 in the *1900 Register*, reproduced opposite as Plate 12.2. The drawing shows a modern, 9-foot underframe with axle guards inside the solebars and a hand brake only. The length agrees at 16 feet 6 inches, but the width on the drawing is 8 feet 1 inch.

It is probable that the trucks were originally to be built to the drawing, but the availability of surplus coach underframes provided the opportunity for an economy measure. In support of this, the carriage register records that the H27 trucks were converted in 1889 from older vehicles dating from the 1870s. Presumably the modification involved the fitting of beams to which carriage wheels were lashed with leather straps.

Four other trucks, numbered 1531, 1540, 1541 and 1591, were survivors from the order of thirty-two fish and game trucks constructed in 1871.[9] Number 1591, fitted with Mansell wheels on a 9-foot wheelbase) was photographed coupled to the bus fitted with wagon wheels which transported road vehicles and their occupants over the Connel bridge on the Ballachulish Branch.[10] A similar truck, number 1541, was also photographed on this service. More information about these trucks is in Chapter 10.2.

References
1. NRS BR/CAL/1/7 p. 359
2. NRS BR/CAL/1/7 p. 360
3. Taken from Appendix 7.5 of *Caledonian Railway Livery*
4. NRS BR/CAL/1/19 entry 1562
5. Ref: 2281
6. NRS BR/CAL/1/21 entry 195
7. Drawing not yet catalogued
8. NRM 11955/C RHP 70045
9. NRS BR/CAL/1/18 no entry number
10. *The True Line*, issue 106, p. 32

FACING PAGE: BOTTOM: Plate 12.2
One of the pre-diagram book open carriage trucks converted to order H27 in 1889 from stock dating from the 1870s. The buffers with fluted stocks, thin rams and a long extension are typical of early coaching stock and NPCS. In this case, steps are welded to the tops to take the ends when folded down. The vacuum pipe was hinged to fold out of the way. The sides folded down on over-centre hinges and rested on the headstock ends. The string running through eyelets is the Harrison cord – the alarm system in use on the West Coast route. Note also the transverse beams and lashing ropes. The beams were fitted into a series of notches to accommodate different lengths of carriage. The truck, freshly painted for the *1900 Register*, is brown with unshaded chrome yellow company initials, number and load information. The company initials and running number characters are 6½ inches high. The board on which the tare writing is located is 3½ inches high, making the letters 3 inches, except for the first letter of each word and the number. The tone of these elements differs from the tare weight, which is written in white.

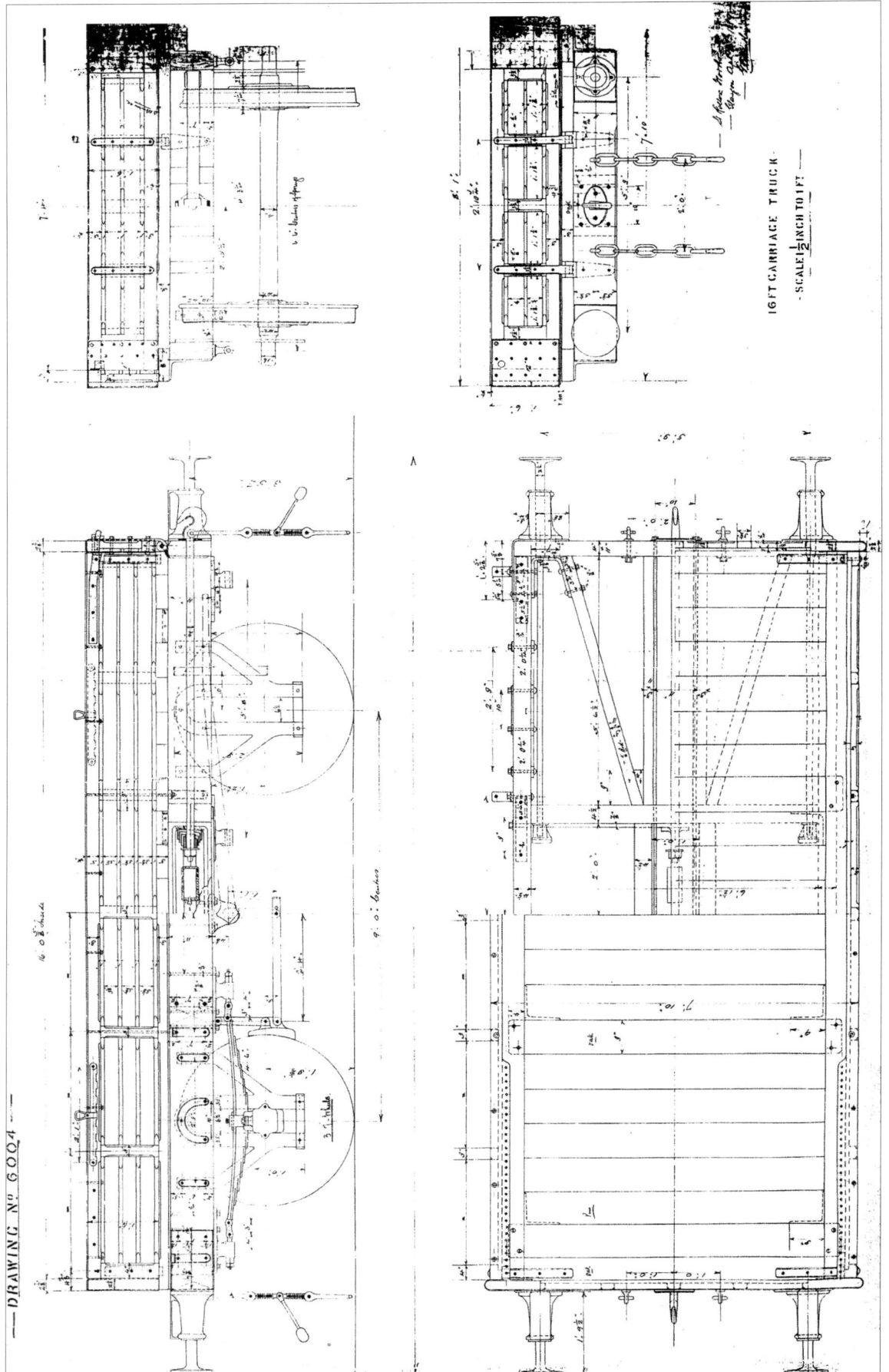

Figure 12.2
The St. Rollox drawing, number 6004, to which open carriage truck 1618 in Plate 12.2 was supposed to have been built.

12.2: Covered Carriage Trucks

Pre-Diagram Book Designs

There are no references to covered carriage trucks in pre-1882 minutes, but there were early St. Rollox drawings – 540 dates from the mid-1860s and 1121 from 1872. The earlier drawing may refer to trucks which were built in twos and threes as replacements, according to the six-monthly stock returns. A similar pattern of replacements took place between 1875 and 1880.

One of these drawings has survived,[1] but the section bearing the drawing number has been torn off. The drawing depicts a truck 15 feet 1 inch long, with an 8-foot 10-inch wheelbase. It had an iron roof and double iron end doors. Iron plates were permanently fixed over the buffers.

Drawing 1092, of a dual purpose covered truck which could also be used to carry fish and game, which also dates from 1872, has not survived.

Plate 12.3
Four-wheeled Diagram 11A covered carriage truck No. 28 was built in 1895 to order H117 and withdrawn in 1924. The vacuum pipe is hinged to swing out of the way when the end doors were opened. Lamp brackets are fitted to the right-hand end of each side, just above the middle door hinge. The truck is painted purple brown with shaded yellow lettering. The louvres are painted yellow. The number is centred in its body panel. The dot of 'C . R' is centred in the opposite panel, with the letters centred below the adjacent louvres. The load lettering is just visible towards the right-hand end. One door on each side has a glass droplight and one is boarded over. This arrangement also applied to the Diagram 91 road vans. The panel below the drop light may be slate. Mansell wheels are fitted. The coach buffers do not have steps welded to the top, as are normally fitted to end-loading vehicles.

Covered Carriage Truck Load 3 Tons – Diagram 11

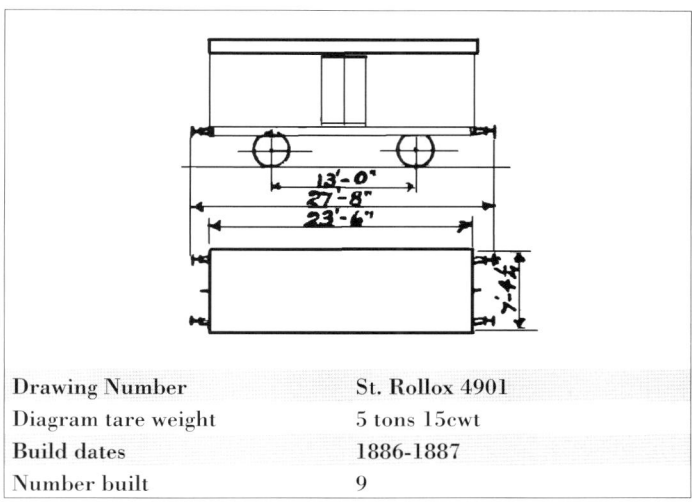

Drawing Number	St. Rollox 4901
Diagram tare weight	5 tons 15cwt
Build dates	1886-1887
Number built	9

The four-wheeled vehicles built to Diagram 11 were 24 feet long and 7 feet 10¼ inches wide. They were all dual fitted, with carriage buffers, and 1636 had a steam heat pipe. The building dates are taken from the carriage register, as there is no reference to these trucks in the minutes. At some point, perhaps when the Diagram 11A trucks were built, they were used as fish vans. Again this information is from the carriage register. Numbers were 1510, 1630, 1635, 1636, 1640, 1641, 1652-1654. All were withdrawn just after the Grouping without being allocated an LM&SR number.

Covered Carriage Truck – Diagram 11A

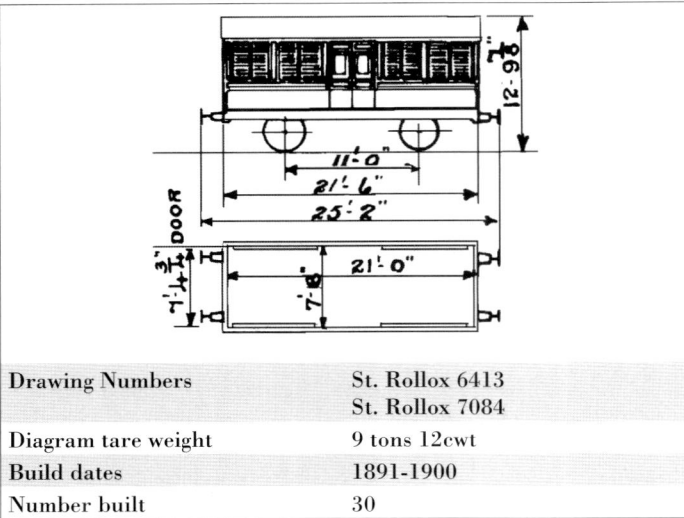

Drawing Numbers	St. Rollox 6413
	St. Rollox 7084
Diagram tare weight	9 tons 12cwt
Build dates	1891-1900
Number built	30

The Diagram 11A trucks were built in small lots between 1891 and 1900. They were 21 feet 6 inches long by 8 feet wide. There were two styles of body. The first, to orders H61 and 74 comprised six trucks. These were built to drawing 6413. The panelling on the sides was similar to the first style of Diagram 3 covered vans.

The later style for the remainder of the trucks was to drawing 7084. They had contemporary coach-style panelling to the sides and vertically boarded end doors. A pair of doors with droplight windows was fitted at the centre of each side. All but five had four pairs of louvre ventilators in the sides. The five exceptions were numbers 10, 94 and 98-100.

Sixteen trucks were built on old carriage underframes and are not mentioned in company minutes.[2] The rest were built new. The upright vacuum pipe seen in photographs must have been hinged to fold away when the end doors were opened. Springs were 5 feet in length, suspended on swing links. The 3-foot 6-inch Mansell wheels ran in oil boxes.

All the trucks were dual fitted and most had steam heat pipes. Safety chains were fitted. Numbers were 6-10, 16-18, 21-30, 45, 94, 98-100, 102, 119-122, 128, 129. Numbers 122 and 128 were successively redesignated as fish and then gunpowder vans. There is no record of any modification to meet the safety requirements for carrying explosives. Nine received the first LM&SR number; the last was withdrawn in 1928.

Five were allocated to coach builders, and presumably marked as such if the practice of the L&NWR was followed.[3] There is no record of special lettering in the St. Rollox drawing register. The numbers were 94 (Kinross & Sons, Stirling), 102 (Wylie & Lochhead, Glasgow), 119 (Liddel & Johnston, Edinburgh), 121 (James Henderson, Glasgow) and 129 (Thompson, Stirling). All these firms were coach builders except one; Wylie & Lochhead were originally coffin makers, outfitted the interiors of luxury ocean liners built on the Clyde, and moved into cabinet making towards the end of the nineteenth century.

Covered Carriage Truck – Diagram 68

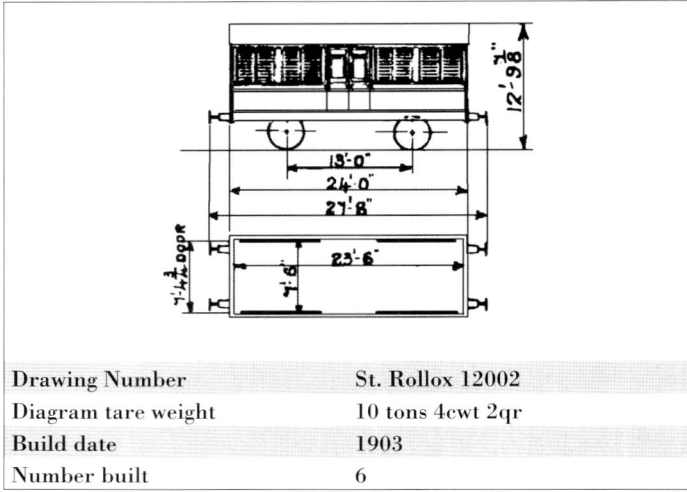

Drawing Number	St. Rollox 12002
Diagram tare weight	10 tons 4cwt 2qr
Build date	1903
Number built	6

The Diagram 68 trucks of 1903 were similar in design to Diagram 11A, but 24 feet long on a 13-foot wheelbase. All were fitted with steam heat pipes. They had the same end profile as Diagram 11A. Construction was to order H213 as part of the renewal programme

Above: Plate 12.4
An enlargement of part of a picture taken at Glasgow Central. The main interest to the photographer was *Cardean* at the head of the 2 pm 'Corridor' in platform 2. On platform 3 is one of the six Diagram 68 covered carriage trucks, dwarfing the Conner 2-4-0 in front of it.

Facing Page: Plate 12.5
The Diagram 83 covered carriage trucks were mounted on the standard 30-foot steel underframe – note the support brackets for the floor. They had coach buffers with steps welded on top to facilitate end loading. For the same reason, the brake and heating pipes were underslung. This example has 3-foot 9-inch spoked wheels. It is fitted with the McIntosh patent brake, although the usual three position instructions are missing. The brackets for the pivot rod across the van are much longer than normal, presumably to ensure that the brake lever did not foul the spring suspension. It is painted purple brown, with yellow lining and shaded yellow lettering. The louvres appear to be body colour, but in a broadside picture of the same van under different lighting conditions, they are clearly light coloured. Slate panels were set into the mouldings on the doors. A picture of 177, built two years later in 1908, also carried the patent brake, but was fitted with 3-hole disc wheels. It did not have the slate panels, and there was no lining around the mouldings. Finally, both examples had lamp brackets fitted to the right-hand end of each side, just above the middle door hinge.

for the period ending July 1903.[4] Numbers were 37-41 and 58. They all received LM&SR numbers and were withdrawn by 1929.

6 Wheel Covered Carriage Truck – Diagram 83

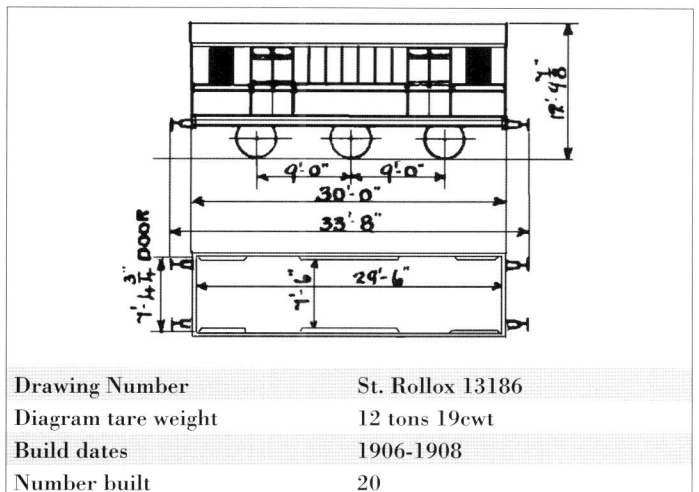

Drawing Number	St. Rollox 13186
Diagram tare weight	12 tons 19cwt
Build dates	1906-1908
Number built	20

All the vehicles described so far in this section were designed to carry a 3-ton load. The Diagram 83 trucks were of 6 tons capacity. The general body design was the same as Diagrams 11A and 68. They were built on the by then standard 30-foot six-wheeled underframe. They were fitted with stepped carriage buffers. They had two doors fitted with drop lights each side and two sets of louvres.

CR numbers were 132, 135-144, 157-160, 175-179. Spoked 3 feet 6 inches diameter wheels were fitted to the first lot (numbers 135-144). The final lot (numbers 175-179) had disc wheels.

The first lot to order H236 was fitted with the McIntosh patent brake, on the evidence of a photograph of 138. This lot was not part of the renewal programme but the remaining two (H270 and H278) were so authorised for the half years ending January and July 1908.[5] All but four received the first LM&SR number. The few withdrawal dates known suggest that they had all been withdrawn by 1929.

Covered Carriage Truck – Diagram 101

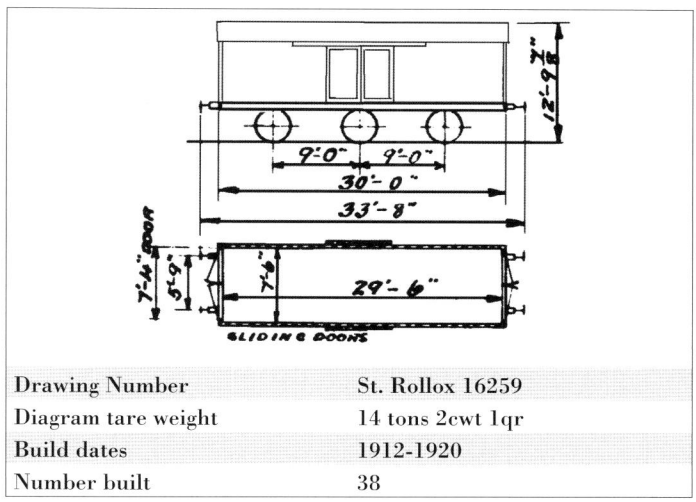

Drawing Number	St. Rollox 16259
Diagram tare weight	14 tons 2cwt 1qr
Build dates	1912-1920
Number built	38

Diagram 101 was the last type of covered truck to be built, again on the 30-foot underframe. They differed from the Diagram 83 trucks in having the bottom portion of the end doors arranged to drop down to form a platform across the stepped buffers. The Diagram 83 trucks had full height folding doors.

The first order for ten trucks was H300 in 1912. The trucks were built on pressed steel underframes provided by Leeds Forge. Numbers were 125, 134, 180-187. Sixteen were built on the capital account to goods orders G324 (numbers 73283-73292) and G346 (73537-73542) in 1913 and 1914.[6] Order G346 was described as 'motor car vans.' Another six were built under the same authorisation as G346 to carriage order H322. Numbers were 123, 133, 191-194. Number 194 was strengthened to carry elephants, to drawing 17374.[7] The final six were built to order H350 in 1920. Their numbers were 11, 14, 89, 152, 170 and 195. The minutes do not record whether they were allocated to the revenue or capital account.

All the trucks had sliding side doors; but, according to the carriage register only the carriage stock orders, with one exception,

had windows. Iracier axleboxes were fitted to the first of the goods and carriage orders. The tare weight of orders H322 and 350 was reduced to 12 tons 19cwt.

All but one of the trucks built to H orders received the second LM&SR number. Withdrawal dates are unknown, apart from 134, which was withdrawn in 1928. The first LM&SR numbers of the G order trucks are not known, but the second LM&SR numbers of the first goods order were recorded in the register.

REFERENCES
1. Not yet catalogued
2. St. Rollox orders H61, 74, 89 and 105
3. See drawings in *LNWR Liveries*, pp. 108-13
4. NRS BR/CAL/1/46 entry 1363
5. NRS BR/CAL/1/54 entry 1090, NRS BR/CAL/1/55 entry 1143
6. NRS BR/CAL/1/62 entry 558, NRS BR/CAL/1/63 entry 1383
7. RHP 68398

ABOVE: Plate 12.6
Diagram 101 carriage truck 123 was built in 1914 to order H322. Like most of its companions, it lasted into the nationalised era. It was also photographed before the end of 1920, when standard RCH oil boxes replaced the Iracier axleboxes seen here. The cast number plate is fixed to the sliding door because the solebar is partially obscured by the channel for the sliding door runner. A slate panel is prominent towards the left-hand end. There are no lamp brackets. The tare weight is written on the solebar, but there is no sign of company ownership or load lettering. The 'RELEASE WAGONS EARLY' label is interesting. The small letters along the bottom of the label may begin with the words 'FOR MOTOR SHOW', but the last word is indecipherable.

BELOW: Plate 12.7
73541 is a Diagram 101 carriage truck numbered in the goods wagon series. Body and underframe details are identical to number 123, including the Iracier axleboxes. Under magnification it is lettered 'DUMFRIES WHEN EMPTY' below the slate panel. The words 'Castle Douglas', written in chalk, partially obscure this. The van was reserved for traffic from the Arrol Johnson motor factory, which was situated a few miles to the north-east of Dumfries. It built cars from 1898 to 1915 and 1918 to 1931. The firm had a private connection with the Caledonian called Heath Hall Siding, with invoices to be sent to Locharbriggs station. The company initials, 'MOTOR' and 'VAN' are centred in the space left when the doors are shut. The word 'CAR' is offset to avoid splitting the middle letter. This van was one of the six to order G346 that were specifically described as Motor Car Vans, and it may be that these were the only ones so lettered. Livery is probably red oxide.

12.3: Scenery Trucks

Pre-Diagram Book Designs

Scenery trucks were not reported separately in the rolling stock returns, nor were they mentioned in minutes up to 1882. There are no minutes after 1882 referring to scenery trucks before the introduction of Diagram 69, but trucks were in fact built in the 1880s and '90s. These are discussed in the final part of this section.

Open Scenery Truck with Falling Ends – Diagram 69

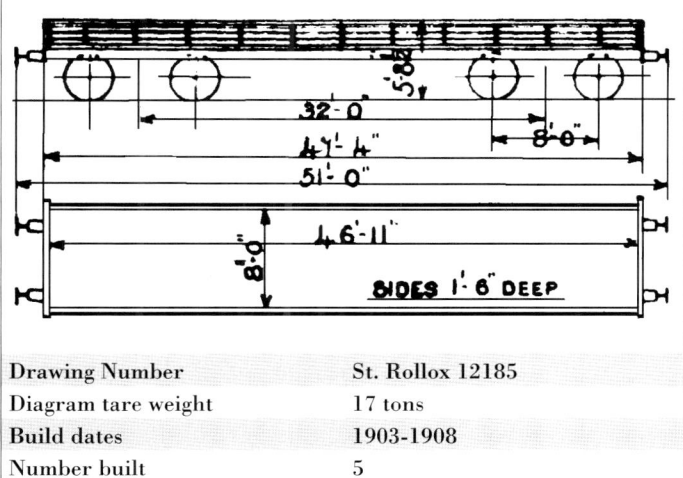

Drawing Number	St. Rollox 12185
Diagram tare weight	17 tons
Build dates	1903-1908
Number built	5

Diagram 69 and 88 bogie scenery trucks shared a common underframe, which was 47 feet 4 inches overall. They were authorised in the wagon renewal programme, but what they replaced is not known.[1] The trucks had falling ends according to the diagram book, and fixed sides 1 foot 6 inches deep and no ends according to the carriage register; the former statement is correct on photographic evidence. The sides were slatted, with outside framing. Stepped carriage buffers were fitted.

Two were built to order H218 and three to H271, numbered 103, 112 and 161-163. The minutes refer to the last order as scenery and caravan trucks.[2] All but number 112 were allocated an LM&SR number, and at least one came into British Railways ownership.

Covered Scenery Truck – Diagram 88

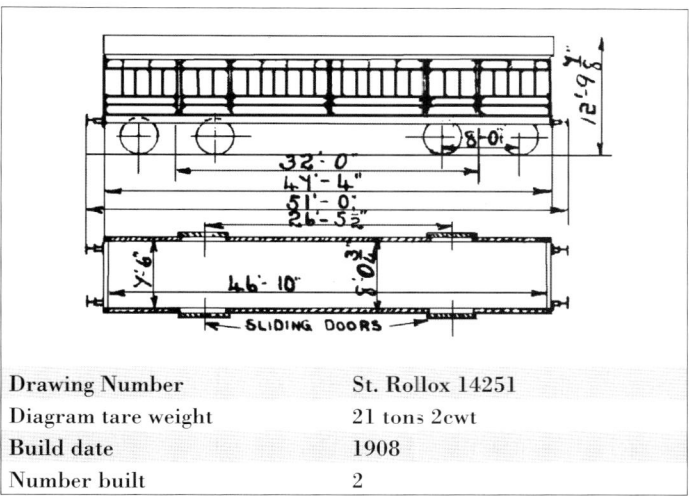

Drawing Number	St. Rollox 14251
Diagram tare weight	21 tons 2cwt
Build date	1908
Number built	2

The covered version of the bogie trucks, built to order H272, was authorised at the same time as the last order for open scenery trucks.[3] They shared an end profile with the Diagram 83 covered carriage trucks and had panelled sides. Two sets of sliding doors were fitted each side. They were numbered 164 and 165. They were allocated LM&SR numbers, but were withdrawn at an unknown date before the second LM&SR renumbering.

Plate 12.8
The Diagram 69 scenery trucks were of similar construction to Diagram 92, and shared an underframe with the covered trucks to Diagram 88. Unfortunately the Diagram 88s managed to dodge the camera. This photograph shows one of the five trucks in British Railways livery. The carriage register incorrectly described the trucks as having no ends.

Open Scenery Truck with Side and End Doors – Diagram 92

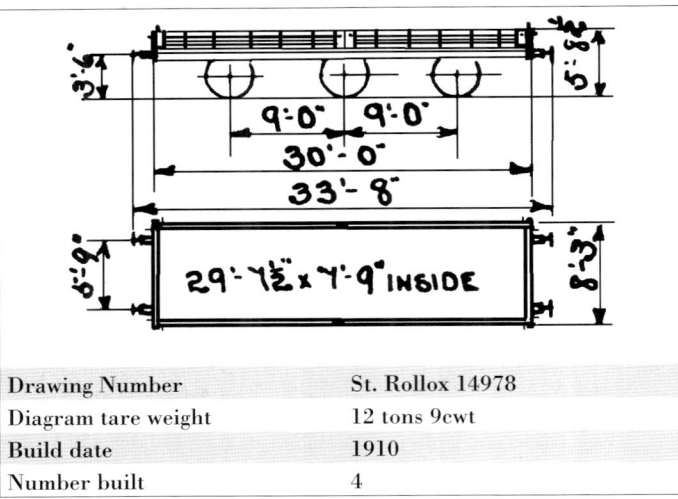

Drawing Number	St. Rollox 14978
Diagram tare weight	12 tons 9cwt
Build date	1910
Number built	4

Four six-wheeled open trucks were built to H292. The minutes described them as *'caravan and scenery open trucks.'*[4] Body construction was the same as the Diagram 69 trucks. The sides were in two parts divided at the centre line and folded down. The 5-foot springs were suspended on J-hangers. They were dual fitted and had steam heat pipes. These were hung rather than upright because the solid ends could be folded down. For the same reason, stepped carriage buffers were fitted. Numbers were 166-169. Three received the first LM&SR number.

Trucks Not Given a Diagram Number

The carriage register records ten other scenery trucks. They did not appear in the order number register, so they were either built on old carriage underframes at St. Rollox or by outside contractors. The latter possibility is less likely, as there is no reference to tenders in the minutes.

The four wheeled vehicles were 24 feet long and 7 feet 3 inches wide, with one exception, number 118, which was 26 feet 2 inches long. They all had fixed 5 inches high sides, with combinations of open or folding ends. Dual brakes were fitted, but only 117 and 1581 had steam heating pipes. The building dates and numbers are:

Date	Numbers
Unknown	1585, 1602, 1612
6/1885	1581
1/1891	117, 118, 1573

The carriage register also records two six-wheeled trucks on an 18-foot wheelbase. They measured 26 feet 10 inches by 7 feet 3 inches and were dual fitted. They had fixed sides, one fixed end and one open end. They were described as twin vehicles in the register. Number 1623 was built in 1886 and 1649 in 1887. None of the non-diagram book trucks survived into LM&SR ownership.

References
1. NRS BR/CAL/1/47 entry 1127
2. NRS BR/CAL/1/54 entry 1090
3. Ibid.
4. NRS BR/CAL/1/57 no entry number

Plate 12.9
One of the four Diagram 92 open scenery trucks in late LM&SR livery. The two pairs of springs to receive the sides when folded down are very noticeable. Originally, the truck would have had the company initials on the two filled in panels, with the number towards the left-hand end and the load lettering to the right. Hutchison stated that the letters were the shaded variety, but this seems unlikely with a plain brown livery. All the brake and heating pipes are underslung because the ends folded down, hence also the steps welded to the buffer stocks. Mansell wheels may have been fitted when built; at the time of the photograph they were three-hole disc. The photograph was taken at Cardington on 27th March 1940.

Chapter 13
Special Class Wagons – The Trollies
13.1: Introduction and Pre-Diagram Book Designs

Steel and iron sections were routinely carried on combinations of four-wheeled swivel and flat wagons coupled together as a semi-rigid unit, as shown in Chapter 2. This was acceptable when the length of the fabrication was the deciding factor, but such arrangements could not be used for loads such as steel plates for the ship building industry, large components or finished goods. Like its competitor the North British Railway, the Caledonian developed a fleet of specialised well wagons to keep such loads within the loading gauge.

The North British used the term 'rulley' to describe these wagons. The Caledonian preferred the word 'trolly'. This spelling was used by the Caledonian in company minutes and the first part of the wagon diagram book, and has been adopted in the text for consistency. The variations in the title descriptions are reproduced from the diagram book. They were the first type of wagon to be allocated special class numbers. Most wagons were lettered to be returned to specific locations when empty.

Pre-Diagram Book Designs

In 1870 St. Rollox produced drawing number 961 for a trolly, capacity unspecified. A design for a 50-ton trolly followed in 1871 (drawing 1225) and for a 40-ton wagon in 1872 (drawing 1308). None of these drawings have survived, and the wagons are not mentioned in minutes or rolling stock returns.

The first two diagrams below describe wagons that were built before Drummond took office. Presumably, their specialised nature warranted recording in the diagram book.

20 Ton Trolly Wagon No. 1 – Diagram 34

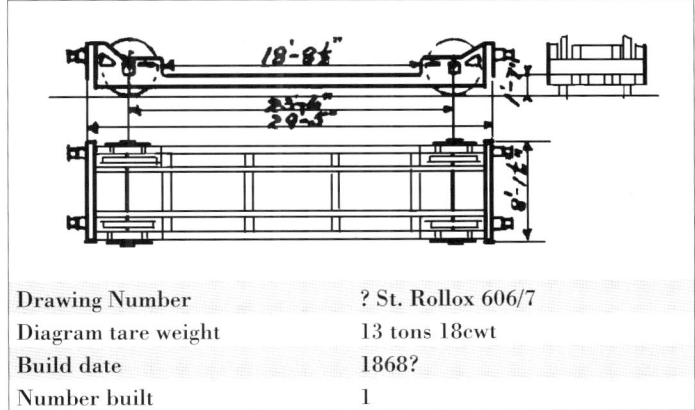

Drawing Number	? St. Rollox 606/7
Diagram tare weight	13 tons 18cwt
Build date	1868?
Number built	1

This was probably the subject of St. Rollox drawings 606 and 607, which were for a boiler wagon. They date from 1868. Drawing 612 was for details of 'boiler wagon, trolly number 1' so it must have entered service. The drawings have not survived. Heavy self-contained buffers were fitted. In comparison with the buffer height, the wheels were probably 4 feet in diameter. Each axle was suspended on two pairs of springs.

There is no mention of the wagon in company minutes or the rolling stock returns. It was the sole four-wheeled trolly. Despite its age, it was only withdrawn in 1917, when it was replaced by the 20-ton trolly to Diagram 123. It was allocated to St. Rollox between 1894 and 1896. By 1902 it had moved to Bridgeton, where it remained.

Trolly Wagon No. 2 – Diagram 33

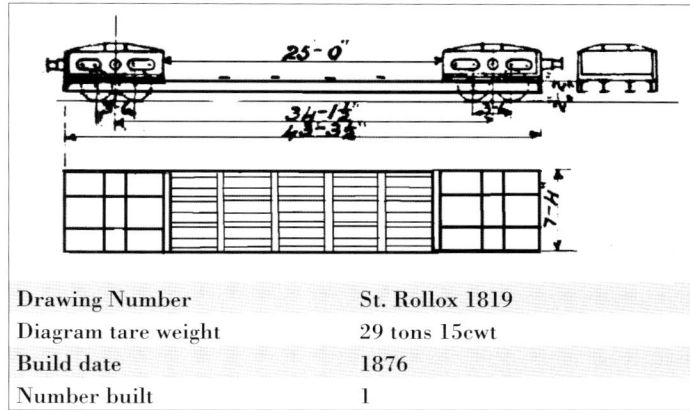

Drawing Number	St. Rollox 1819
Diagram tare weight	29 tons 15cwt
Build date	1876
Number built	1

This wagon was added to the stock list in 1876. It was originally rated at carry 40 tons, but was later down-rated to 35 tons and given diagram number 33. The wheelbase of the bogies was only 3 feet 6 inches and the wheels ran in inside bearings. It was allocated the number 2. It was always based at St. Rollox.

In 1894, chains were fitted inside the bogies. The Working Timetable Appendices from then on note that:

> 'they must be coupled when working on Main Line or ordinary curves, and uncoupled when the Trolly is required to work on curves quicker than 5 chains.'

Modern Designs

No more trolly wagons were built until 1890. The modern trollies were built to thirteen different designs, comprising a total of twenty-four wagons. These wagons are discussed in the following sections. The wagons are described by size of well. There were three sizes: 18/20 feet, 25 feet and 35/40 feet. The latter type was by far the most numerous, accounting for two thirds of the total. The only 40-foot example was to Diagram 53. Within each subsection, the wagons are described in ascending order of capacity. The following table summarises the classification.

Tons	Section 13.2 18/20ft well	Section 13.3 25ft well	Section 13.4 35/40ft well
12			Diagram 53
20	Diagrams 95, 99, 123		Diagrams 42, 56
25		Diagram 20	
30			Diagram 89
35			Diagram 96
40		Diagrams 41, 125	Diagram 100
50		Diagram 118	

13.2: Trollies with 18/20-foot Wells

20 Ton Trolley – Diagram 95

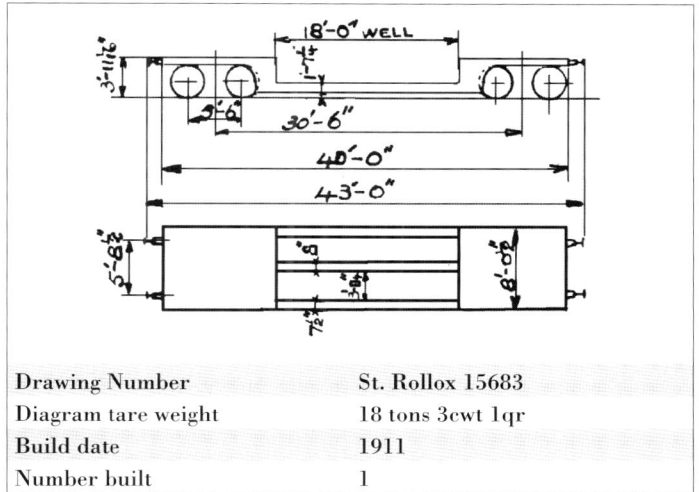

Drawing Number	St. Rollox 15683
Diagram tare weight	18 tons 3cwt 1qr
Build date	1911
Number built	1

Along with the two 35-ton trollies to Diagram 96, this wagon was authorised in the renewal programme for the half year ending July 1911.[1] It was built to order G298 and its purpose was to carry propellers. It was allocated number 27, replacing a furniture van wagon. It was based at St. Rollox.

20 Ton Bogie Well Trolley – Diagram 99

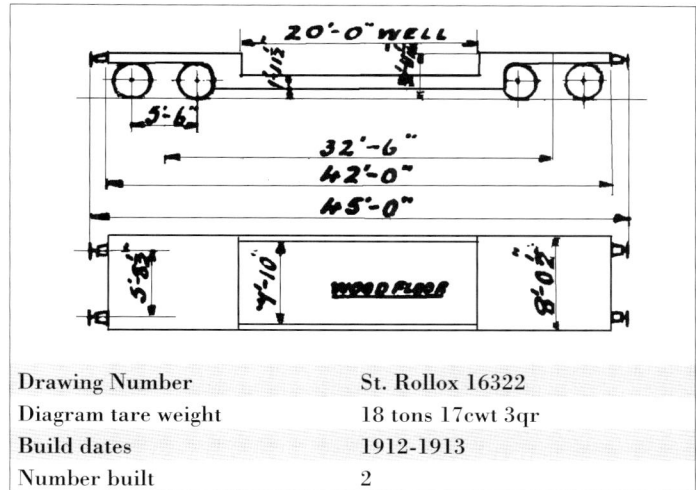

Drawing Number	St. Rollox 16322
Diagram tare weight	18 tons 17cwt 3qr
Build dates	1912-1913
Number built	2

These wagons were a 2 feet longer version of Diagram 95, but with a wooden, rather than an open, floor. They were authorised as renewals for the half years ending July 1912 and 1913, where they were described as '*well wagons*'.[2] Built to orders G313 and G326, they were allocated numbers 224 and 356. They were based at St. Rollox.

20 Ton Trolley – Diagram 123

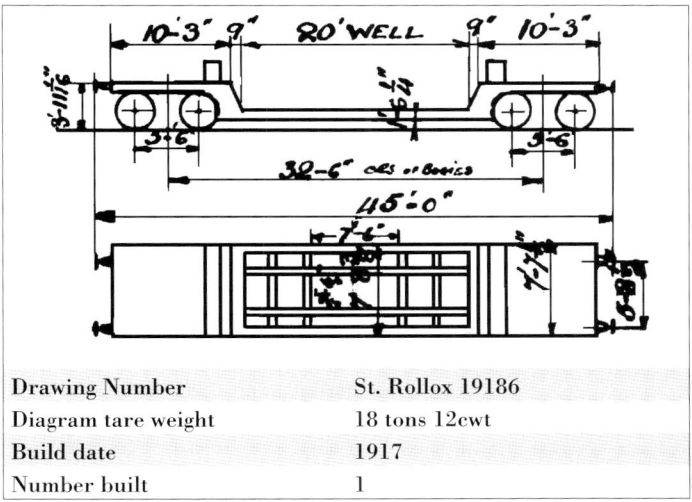

Drawing Number	St. Rollox 19186
Diagram tare weight	18 tons 12cwt
Build date	1917
Number built	1

Special wagon number 1, which dated from the late 1860s, was eventually replaced in 1917 by this wagon, which was built to order G402.[3] Its base is not known.

References
1. NRS BR/CAL/1/58 entry 731
2. NRS BR/CAL/1/61 entry 66, NRS BR/CAL/1/62 entry 558
3. NRS BR/CAL/1/69 entry 605

Facing Page Top: Plate 13.1
The only four-wheeled trolley, probably built in 1868, and surviving until 1917. This was '*Trolly number 1*' assigned diagram number 34 when the diagram book was compiled around 1900. Like special wagon number 2, there does not seem to be a brake.

Facing Page Middle: Plate 13.2
CR 2 is standing outside Clutha Ironworks siding, near Kinning Park. This was one of the rail connections of P & W MacLellan Ltd, who bought thousands of the surplus 'bogies' for scrap. The wagon dates from 1876, but like special wagon number 1, was assigned a diagram number. It was of very heavy box girder construction, with a tare weight of nearly 30 tons. The load lettering is just visible at the right-hand end. It was still in use in 1915.

Facing Page Bottom: Plate 13.3
Diagram 95 wagon number 27 is seen loaded with what looks to be a large commutator at the Beardmore works at Parkhead. It is using the '*cross blocks and holed angles on which can be fitted longitudinal beams for purpose of securing high loads standing on a narrow base*' mentioned in the *1915 Working Timetable Appendix*. Most bogie trollies had these fitments. The number plate is displaced to the left of centre. The bolsters on the platforms over the bogies were not shown in the diagram book, although they were drawn for the later companion wagon to Diagram 123.

Plate 13.4
The last of the special wagons that made up the original series – trolly number 4, built in 1890. The company initials and number are disposed differently from that on trolly number 2. Heavy four-bolt self-contained buffers are fitted, with a square rather than shaped packing piece. The tare weight with four units seems a bit over the top, especially as the last unit is zero.

Plate 13.5
Trolly number 40, built to Diagram 41, was one of five special wagons authorised in 1898. The locomotive style buffers are fitted to the bogies to enable this long vehicle to traverse what the Caledonian called 'quick radius' curves. The bogies have both leaf and coil spring suspension. Another different lettering layout is exhibited, the number positioned on the centre line with the two digits separated by one of the shackles. The letters are equally spaced along the girder from the centre. In the background are 'bogies' carrying large lettering, and pre-diagram book open and covered goods wagons. Nearer the camera is a single Diagram 24 open goods wagon.

13.3: Trollies with 25-foot Wells

Trolly Wagon No. 4 Load 25 Tons – Diagram 20

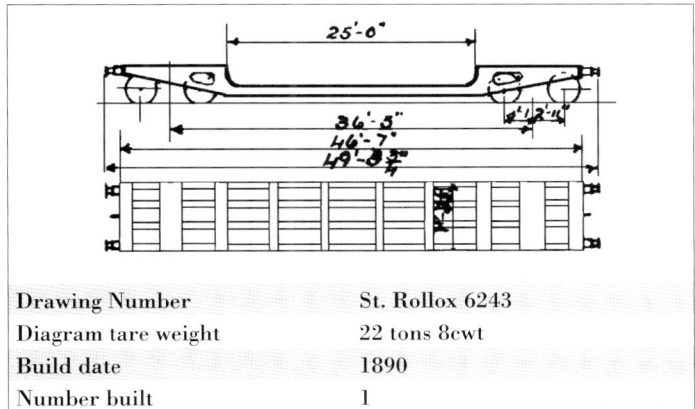

Drawing Number	St. Rollox 6243
Diagram tare weight	22 tons 8cwt
Build date	1890
Number built	1

The drawing for this wagon dates from 1890, but it did not appear in the special wagon listing until 1892. It was built to order G81 and charged to the capital account.[1] The minute authorising construction was in response to a report from Drummond that business was being lost because of *'inability to supply wagons for the conveyance of large articles.'* He recommended construction of two wagons at £550 each. The Traffic Committee agreed to *'get one trolly wagon meantime.'*

It was allocated number 4. The bogie wheelbase was 6 feet, but the pivots were set 1 inch off centre. The wagon was fitted with pre-Drummond heavy self-contained buffers. This was not the anachronism that it seems. It was still the only self-contained sprung buffer available at that time. The wagon was always based at St. Rollox.

40 Ton Trolly – Diagram 41

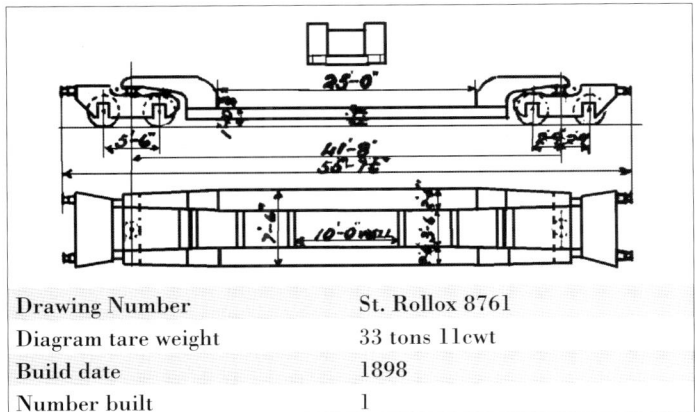

Drawing Number	St. Rollox 8761
Diagram tare weight	33 tons 11cwt
Build date	1898
Number built	1

Authorised in May 1896 as one of five new special wagons,[2] this trolly was charged to the capital account in the half year ending July 1898. It was built to order G141, which suggests that it was built shortly after it was authorised

Like the Diagram 42 wagons described in the next section, which were authorised at the same time, the well body was connected to the bogies by swan necks. The drawgear and the self-contained buffers were mounted on the bogies. It was allocated number 40. In 1902, it had chains fitted to the bogies, with similar restrictions to the Diagram 33 trolly. It was based at St. Rollox.

40 Ton Trolley – Diagram 125

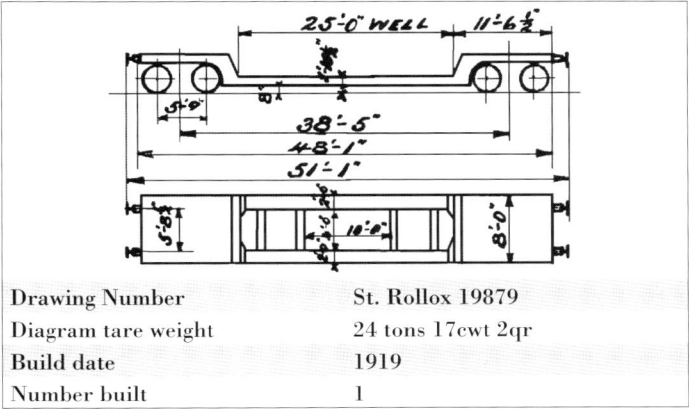

Drawing Number	St. Rollox 19879
Diagram tare weight	24 tons 17cwt 2qr
Build date	1919
Number built	1

The St. Rollox order described this wagon *'new class, 8ft wide No. 40 class'*. It replaced pre-Drummond flat wagon number 15. There is no record of the wagon in the minutes. Its base is not known.

50 Ton Trolley – Diagram 118

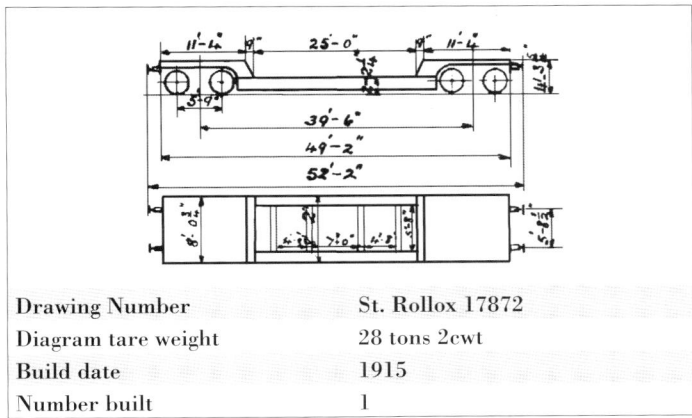

Drawing Number	St. Rollox 17872
Diagram tare weight	28 tons 2cwt
Build date	1915
Number built	1

Although this wagon had the greatest load capacity of all the trollies, it was one of the shorter wagons of the class. It was part of the renewal programme for the half year ending June 1915,[3] but what, if anything, it replaced is unclear. It was built to order G364 and allocated number 371, which suggests that it was an addition to the special wagon fleet rather than a renewal. Its base is not known.

References
1. NRS BR/CAL/1/33 entry 1220
2. NRS BR/CAL/1/39 entry 911
3. NRS BR/CAL/1/65 entry 1041

ABOVE: **Plate 13.6**
Another wagon built as part of the special class expansion programme, this time to Diagram 42. The constructional details and bogies are similar to the Diagram 41 wagon. This photograph shows the triangular brackets which could be used to carry steel plates that would otherwise have fouled the loading gauge. This modification was added in 1902.

Plate 13.7
A close-up of the same wagon carrying Lambie 4-4-0 number 13 after the Coupar Angus accident in 1899. The weight of the engine was well beyond the 20 tons capacity of the wagon, suggesting that it was only used to move it around St. Rollox. The floor of the well is quite seriously deflected.

13.4: Trollies with 35/40-foot Wells

20 Ton Trolly – Diagram 42

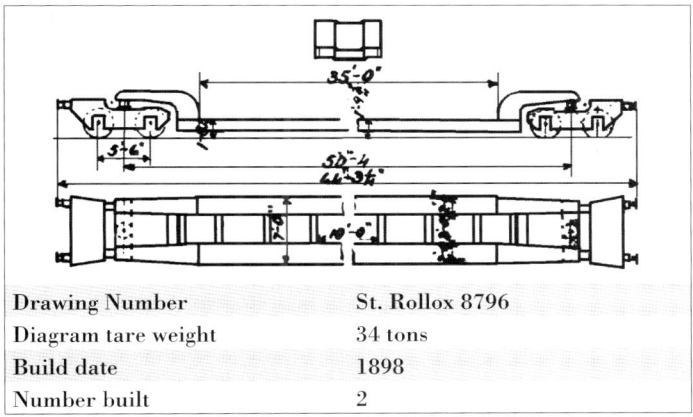

Drawing Number	St. Rollox 8796
Diagram tare weight	34 tons
Build date	1898
Number built	2

The wagons were built to order G142 and like their Diagram 41 companion were charged to the capital account in July 1898.[1] The drawing described them as *'trolly boiler wagons.'* Constructional details were similar to Diagram 41. They received numbers 41 and 42 in the special wagons list. They were allocated to St. Rollox. In the 1902 special wagons list, they were provided with triangular brackets to enable them to carry plates 11 feet 2 inches wide and 5 inches thick, and still remain within the loading gauge.

20 Ton Trolly – Diagram 56

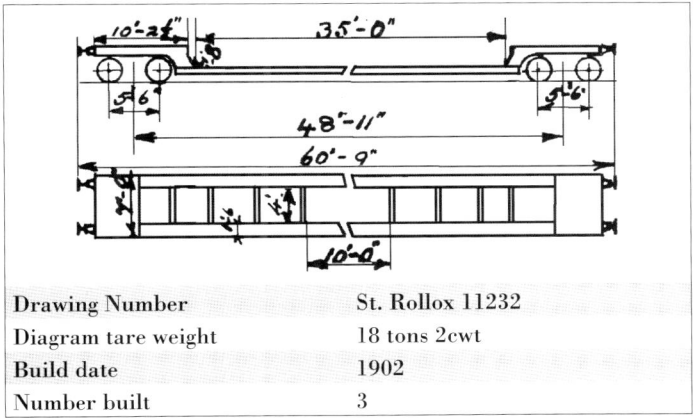

Drawing Number	St. Rollox 11232
Diagram tare weight	18 tons 2cwt
Build date	1902
Number built	3

Authorised in December 1901[2] by the Loco & Stores Committee, *'similar to Nos. 41 and 42'*, these trollies were built on the capital account to order G195 and allocated numbers 79-81. Their dimensions were indeed similar to the Diagram 42 wagons, but the construction was radically different, almost halving the tare weight.

With the exception of trolly number 1, these were the first to have the buffers and drawgear fitted to the body rather than the bogies. This configuration applied to all subsequent designs, except the exceptionally long Diagram 53 trollies.

The length of these particular wagons necessitated non-standard buffers with large rectangular heads. Some time between the 1902 special wagons list and the 1906 list they were modified to accommodate triangular brackets like their Diagram 42 predecessors. They were always based at St. Rollox.

30 Ton Trolley – Diagram 89

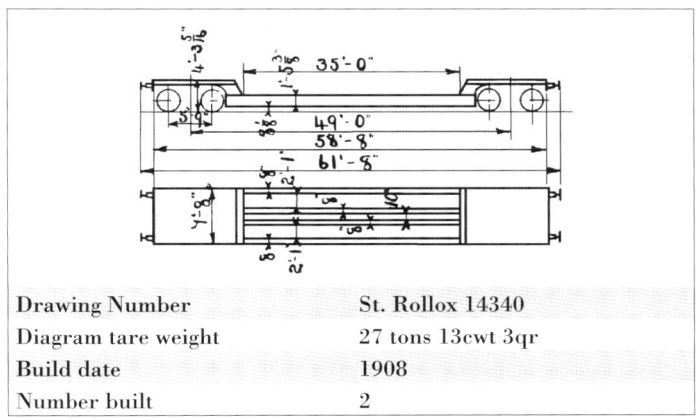

Drawing Number	St. Rollox 14340
Diagram tare weight	27 tons 13cwt 3qr
Build date	1908
Number built	2

The wagons were intended to carry steel plate, according to the Traffic Committee minute authorising their construction in July 1907.[3] According to *The Locomotive* magazine they could

'carry the largest sizes of plates hitherto made, up to 35ft by 12ft 9in, and can thus convey, by any ordinary goods train at usual speed, exceptional loads which could only be otherwise dealt with on Sundays and by blocking the opposite set of rails.'

They were built to order G266 and allocated numbers 217 and 218, following the 30-ton bogie swivel bar wagons. They were based at St. Rollox.

35 Ton Trolley – Diagram 96

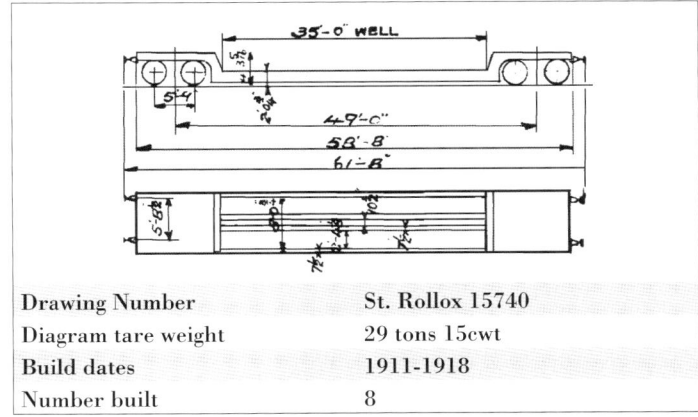

Drawing Number	St. Rollox 15740
Diagram tare weight	29 tons 15cwt
Build dates	1911-1918
Number built	8

Designed to carry steel plates, the wagons were allocated numbers 221 and 222, although they were classed as renewals.[4] Two more, numbered 357 and 358, were built in 1913 to order G334.[5] Three wagons were authorised and built to G357 in 1914[6] and allocated numbers 365-367, although they did not appear in the May 1915 list.

Plate 13.8
This was the modern version of Diagram 42. It is the last of three that were built to Diagram 56 in 1902. They were the first modern bogie trollies to have the buffers mounted on the body. Rectangular-head buffers have been fitted to compensate for the end throw. The tare is given in two units only, and for once agrees with the diagram book. The return instructions on the right-hand end are more verbose than usual. Diamond frame bogies are fitted, similar to those on the bogie coal wagons. There are no brakes. The load plate and builder's plate are separated to the right and left respectively. The former reads 'LOAD 20 TONS DISTRIBUTED.' There is good view of the bracket arrangements and the chains securing the various elements.

Plate 13.9
One of the two Diagram 89 wagons built in 1908. For some reason the number plate is square. Was it just because there was more space on the side girder than a normal oval plate would require? The builder's plate and load information are combined in one plate towards the right-hand end. Brakes were applied by a wheel just visible at the left-hand end.

Finally, one wagon, number 380, was built to order G405 in 1918.[7] The first two wagons were based at St. Rollox; the allocation of the remainder is not known.

40 Ton Trolley – Diagram 100

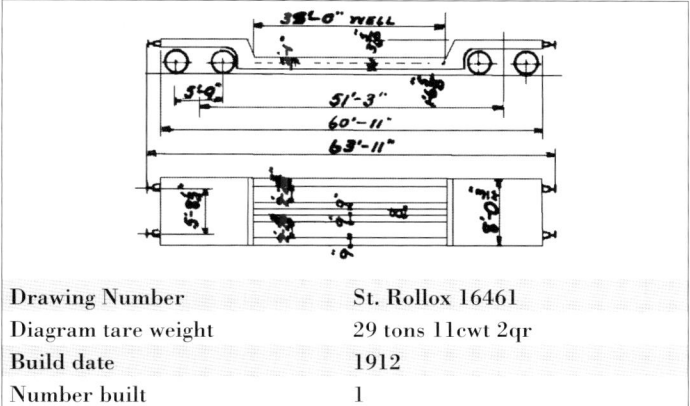

Drawing Number	St. Rollox 16461
Diagram tare weight	29 tons 11cwt 2qr
Build date	1912
Number built	1

As Diagram 99 was a lengthened Diagram 95, so this was a 2 feet longer version of Diagram 96. It was built to order G322 in the next six-month accounting period to the Diagram 96 wagon.[8] It was numbered 355, which suggests that it entered service before the Diagram 99 wagon. It was allocated to St. Rollox.

12 Ton Trolly – Diagram 53

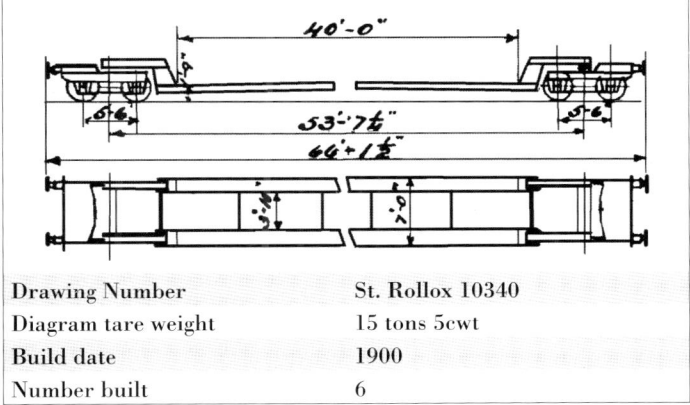

Drawing Number	St. Rollox 10340
Diagram tare weight	15 tons 5cwt
Build date	1900
Number built	6

These trollies were the longest goods wagons on the system, and the only design with a 40-foot well. They were built to carry electric tramcars and other long, but fairly light, loads. They were authorised in August 1900,[9] and built to order G181. The length dictated that buffers and drawgear be fitted to the bogies. They were assigned numbers 70-75 in the special wagons list, where they were described as '*12 ton Trolly (distributed).*' They were allocated to Motherwell. A photograph of all six wagons loaded with tramcars for delivery to the Dundee system is shown in Plate 2.9 (p. 23).

10-Ton Trolley Design

In June 1916, a lightweight trolly with a 35-foot well was designed. It was the subject of drawing 18600.[10] This depicted a wagon 57 feet long over headstocks, with 5 feet 6 inches wheelbase bogies at 47 feet 6 inch centres. The overall width was 8 feet. Along with the Diagram 99 trollies which the design strongly resembled, the floor of the well was covered like an ordinary goods wagon with 7-inch by 2½-inch transverse planks.

There is no reference to such a wagon in company minutes, the St. Rollox order list or the wagon diagram book. It is not known whether any wagons were actually built.

References
1. NRS BR/CAL/1/39 entry 911
2. NRS BR/CAL/1/45 entry 816
3. NRS BR/CAL/1/55 entry 1143
4. NRS BR/CAL/1/59 entry 977
5. NRS BR/CAL/1/63 entry 26
6. NRS BR/CAL/1/64 entry 1149
7. NRS BR/CAL/1/70 entry 335
8. NRS BR/CAL/1/61 entry 921
9. NRS BR/CAL/1/43 entry 2082
10. RHP 68782

Plate 13.10

This was numerically the largest class of trolly. Eight were built between 1911 and 1917. This example was photographed in LM&SR days. The original number was 357. The load capacity of 35 tons is reflected in the heavier construction and heavy duty bogies. For the same reason, the wheels have ten spokes rather than eight.

Plate 13.11

One of six trollies built to carry tramcars in 1902. There is a picture of the whole fleet carrying their load in Plate 2.9 of this book. The bogies have light girder frames. The design has reverted to the swan neck configuration with buffers mounted on the bogies, to compensate for the end throw of the longest goods vehicles on the Caley. Note the bow upwards in the well girder. This was designed so that a load would deflect the girder to the horizontal.

Chapter 14
Other Special Class Bogie Wagons
14.1: Bogie Rail and Swivel Bar Wagons

Although the six-wheeled rail wagons were listed among the special class wagons, they were never fully assimilated. They retained general goods wagon numbering, and, apart from the six wagons up-rated to carry 25 tons, were not allocated to a return depot when empty. On the other hand, the bogie rail wagons were full members of the special class wagon fleet. Longer wagons were needed to transport the 32-foot rail sections which became increasingly common.

All but the last twenty of the bogie rail wagons were built by Leeds Forge to their drawing 15426.[1] The wagons shared a common pressed steel underframe 52 feet long by 8 feet wide. The drawings register mentions type A and type C wagons. Presumably the Diagram 106 version was type B.

With the exception of 333 and 334, they all had fixed sides and ends 1 foot 0½ inch high. Bolsters increased the height from rail level to 5 feet 7½ inches in Diagram 105. The bogies were the Fox patent pressed steel type. When new they were fitted with Iracier axleboxes. The story of these wagons is complicated, not helped when the minutes sometimes describe them as bogie rail wagons and gondola wagons at others.

35 Ton Rail Wagon – Diagram 105

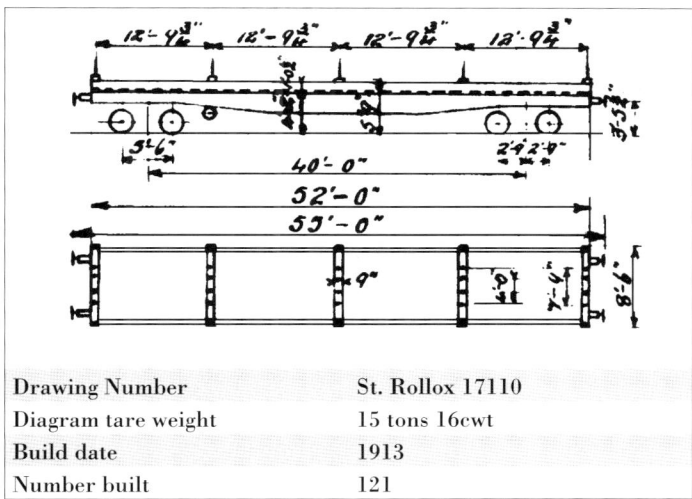

Drawing Number	St. Rollox 17110
Diagram tare weight	15 tons 16cwt
Build date	1913
Number built	121

An initial order for twenty-seven wagons was authorised on 2nd April 1912 as part of the renewal programme for the period ending December 1912.[2] A Loco & Stores minute of 30th April records the *'acceptance of Leeds Forge offer'* for these wagons.[3] A further order for thirty was placed in July 1912 for completion *'by end of October.'*[4] The company maintained the reputation for speedy delivery which they had established with the first bogie coal wagons, because an order for a further forty-three wagons was placed in early September, to be completed by the end of November.[5] This completed the construction of 100 wagons.

The wagon sides and fixed ends were 1 foot deep. One bolster was fitted at each end and was an integral part of the body. Three more removable non-swivelling bolsters were provided equally divided along the wagon body.

On 17th September 1912 the Traffic Committee agreed the construction of ten more wagons as part of the renewals programme for the half year ending 30th June 1913.[6] On the 1st October a minute reported that ten additional wagons had been purchased from Leeds Forge.[7]

The wagons were numbered from 225-325, which means that one of the wagons in the lot of ten was built to Diagram 105, with the remaining nine to Diagrams 106 and 107, whose numbers in the special wagon fleet continued the series from 326-334. See below for details of these designs.

On 29th October 1912 the Board of Directors recommended the purchase of twenty additional wagons,[8] which took the numbers 335-354. There is no record of a tendering process, but photographs of wagons 349 and 354 show that this order was also supplied by Leeds Forge. Two wagons to this diagram are in the SRPS collection.

A minute dated 22nd December 1922[9] stated that 461 wagons had been built for the period ending 31st December 1922. The St. Rollox order lists show that the total included fourteen 35-ton bogie rail wagons. They were the subject of drawing 21377[10] dated 5th December 1921.

35 Ton Rail Wagon with End Doors – Diagram 106

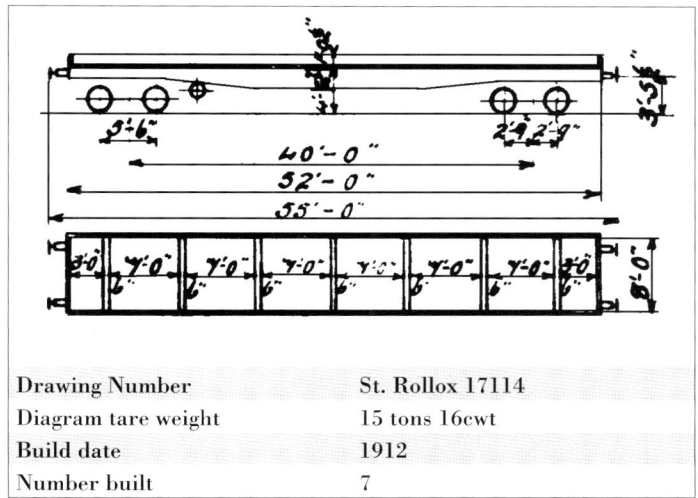

Drawing Number	St. Rollox 17114
Diagram tare weight	15 tons 16cwt
Build date	1912
Number built	7

The seven Diagram 106 wagons did not have bolsters, but were fitted with 6-inch crossbars at 7-foot centres. They had falling ends. According to the *1915 Working Timetable Appendix* they were numbered 326-332. They were recorded as purchased from Leeds Forge on 1st October 1912.

35 Ton Rail Wagon – Diagram 107

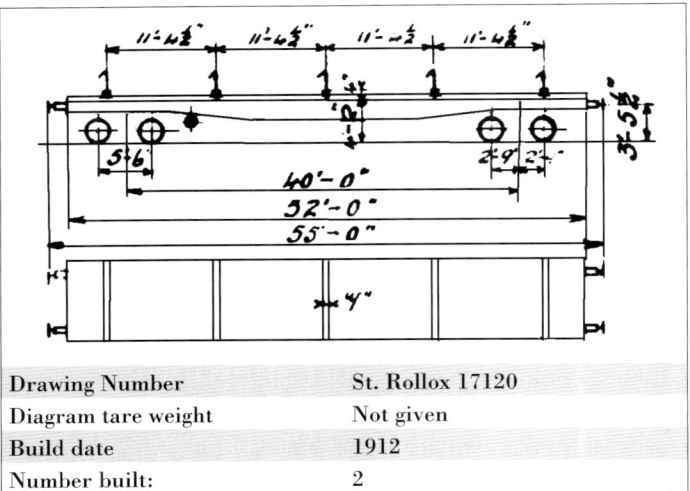

Drawing Number	St. Rollox 17120
Diagram tare weight	Not given
Build date	1912
Number built:	2

The pair of wagons to Diagram 107, numbered 333 and 334, had angle top stanchions for unloading rails, and no ends. There were five crossbars on the floor. According to the *1915 Working Timetable Appendix* they were lettered '*Engineer's Department, Motherwell Shops.*' These were the only bogie rail wagons to be allocated to a specific base.

30 Ton Swivel Wagon – Diagram 81

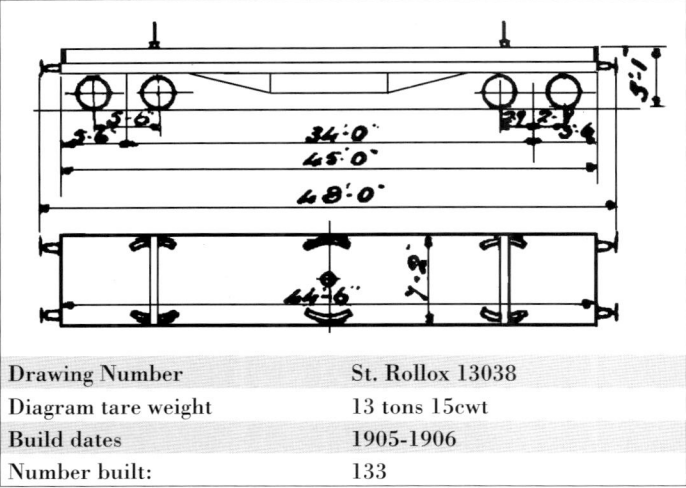

Drawing Number	St. Rollox 13038
Diagram tare weight	13 tons 15cwt
Build dates	1905-1906
Number built:	133

The bogie swivel bar wagons to Diagram 81 were by far the most numerous type in the special wagon number series. They were 45 feet long and 7 feet 8 inches wide externally, with truss rod underframes. The sides and ends were 12 inches high. The ends folded down. They had two pivoting bolsters, with the facility for adding a third in the centre of the wagon.

The initial order was for eight wagons to G230, authorised as part of the renewal programme for the half year ending 31st July 1905.[11] The underframe was the same as the St. Rollox built Diagram 54 bogie coal wagons, with diamond frame bogies. The running numbers of the first order were 84-91. The other St. Rollox order was G242, for fifty wagons. The numbers ran from 167 to 216. The LM&SR renumbering records state that this lot was fitted with pressed steel bogies. This suggests that the bogies were supplied by Leeds Forge, as were many CR carriage bogies.

Leeds Forge contributed a further seventy-five wagons. A Loco & Stores Committee minute authorised fifty for completion by 31st December 1905,[12] and twenty-five additional wagons were ordered on 23rd January 1906.[13] The Leeds Forge wagons had the usual pressed steel underframes and bogies.

The tare weight of 13 tons 15cwt in the diagram book applies to the Leeds Forge wagons. The tare of the St. Rollox order was 15 tons 6cwt according to the LM&SR special wagon book. This vividly illustrates the saving in weight afforded by the patented pressed steel body construction, compared with channel underframes strengthened with truss rods.

The publicity photograph shows wagon number 92. The LM&SR renumbering records confirm that the first lot of Leeds Forge wagons were numbered 92-141 and that the twenty-five of the additional order was numbered 142-166. Although the *1915 Appendix* does not show allocation to a specific base, photographic evidence shows that the first wagon to be built was allocated to Motherwell.

In 1909, seven special wagons were fitted with cradles for carrying large cast iron pipes.[14] While the type of wagon was not specified, the modification detailed in the next paragraph makes this type of wagon a strong candidate for the traffic.

In November 1911 the Traffic Committee resolved that twenty of the wagons used on the Glengarnock Company's traffic should be fitted with centre blocks in order to prevent rails when loaded becoming '*broken-backed.*'[15] The register does not record a drawing for this modification and the running numbers of the wagons involved are not known.

In May 1920 a new drawing, St. Rollox 20754[16] was issued for a wagon to the Leeds Forge design. The minutes do not provide details of the wagons authorised at this period.

References

1. HMRS collection – reference 12735
2. NRS BR/CAL/1/61 entry 921
3. NRS BR/CAL/1/61 entry 1016
4. NRS BR/CAL/1/62 entry 149
5. NRS BR/CAL/1/62 entry 467
6. NRS BR/CAL/1/62 entry 558
7. NRS BR/CAL/1/62 entry 591
8. NRS BR/CAL/1/62 entry 796
9. NRS BR/CAL/1/80 entry 869
10. RHP 69623
11. NRS BR/CAL/1/50 entry 217
12. NRS BR/CAL/1/52 entry 166
13. NRS BR/CAL/1/52 entry 705
14. NRS BR/CAL/1/57 entry 1451
15. NRS BR/CAL/1/61 entry 60
16. NRM 11203/W

Plate 14.1
Number 354 was the last wagon to be built to Diagram 105 in 1914. It is fitted with Iracier axleboxes and the Fox pressed steel bogies have coil springs. The number plate and the Leeds forge plate are disposed on either side of the centre line. A Leeds Forge plate is also fitted to each bogie.

14.2: Glass and Well Wagons

30 Ton Well Wagon – Diagram 82

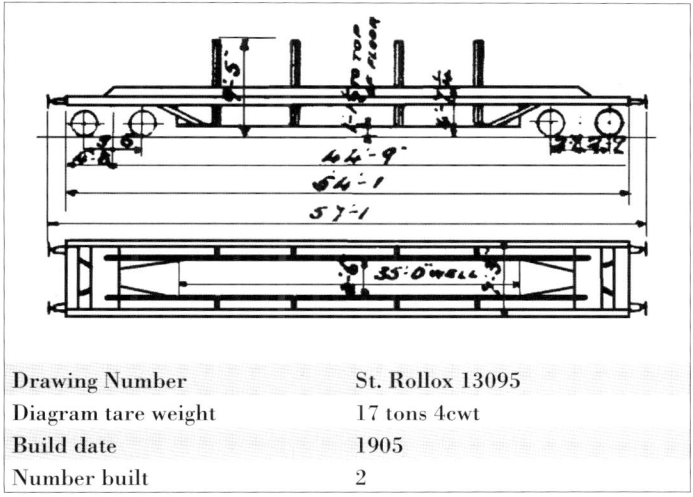

Drawing Number	St. Rollox 13095
Diagram tare weight	17 tons 4cwt
Build date	1905
Number built	2

In April 1905, the Traffic Committee authorised two 30-ton well wagons *'for large plates.'*[1] The plates were plates of glass, not steel. The metal well had a wooden planked floor. They were built to order G241 and numbered 76 and 77. They replaced two of the three Diagram 58 'boat wagons' described in Chapter 15.4, p. 238. They were allocated to St. Rollox.

35 Ton Well Wagon – Diagram 112

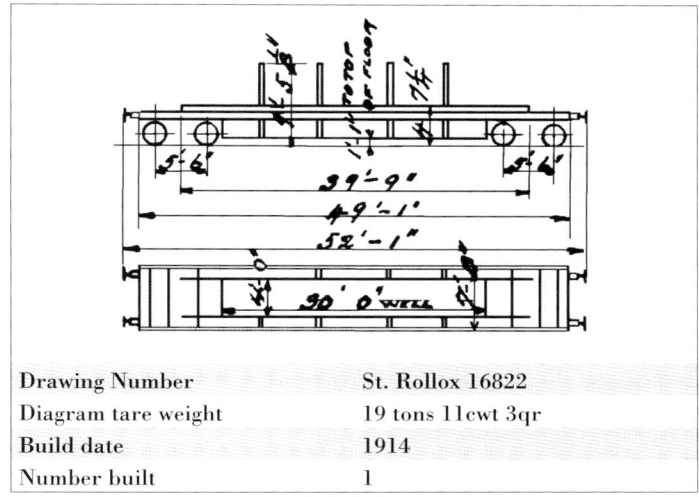

Drawing Number	St. Rollox 16822
Diagram tare weight	19 tons 11cwt 3qr
Build date	1914
Number built	1

Number 359, the sole member of Diagram 112, was a 5 feet shorter and 3 inches wider version of Diagram 82, but with 5 tons greater capacity. It was built to order G335 in the renewal programme for the half year ending December 1914.[2] It was based at St. Rollox.

References
1. NRS BR/CAL/1/51 entry 226
2. NRS BR/CAL/1/63 entry 26

Plate 14.2
The first St. Rollox built Diagram 81 swivel bar wagon, number 84. The underframe is of similar construction to the Diagram 54 bogie coal wagons. The brake hand wheel is on the centre line. In the background are 'bogies' with centre and offset doors and a Diagram 15 goods wagon. One of the Diagram 17 machinery wagons is partially obscured by the lamp post.

Plate 14.3

The first Leeds Forge built Diagram 81 wagon, number 92, although the number and tare weight have not yet been applied. The buffers have tapering casings and large heads. The hand wheel to apply the brake is towards the right-hand end. The company initials divide the wagon side into three equal spaces.

Plate 14.4

The Diagram 112 well wagon was built in 1914 to carry glass in wooden packing cases that were clamped between the four sets of uprights. The earlier Diagram 82 wagons were of similar construction. The number plate is slightly offset to avoid a row of rivets. The combined load and builder's plate is at the left-hand end of the wagons, and the label clip on the right. The lettering over the pivot line of the left-hand bogie reads 'OIL'.

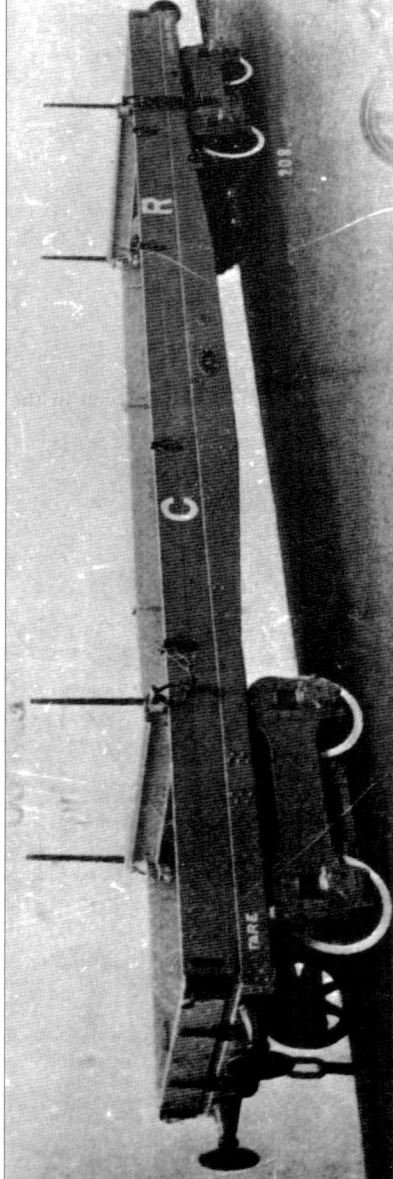

Plate 14.5

The Barnum & Bailey wagon, before it was modified by Pickering and sold to the Caledonian in 1907, when it was assigned to Diagram 103. It was numbered 223 in the CR special wagon series.

14.3: Flat Wagons

30 Ton Flat Wagon – Diagram 77

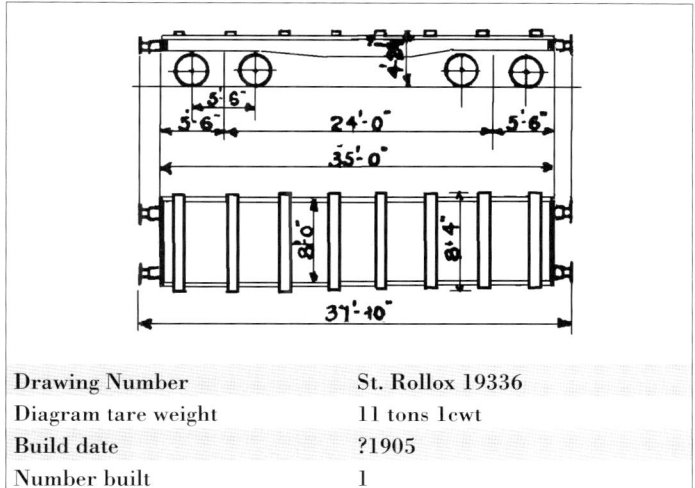

Drawing Number	St. Rollox 19336
Diagram tare weight	11 tons 1cwt
Build date	?1905
Number built	1

The diagram number suggests a construction date of 1905. The dimensions given on the diagram do not correspond with anything in a special wagons list, company minutes or the St. Rollox order list.

The drawing quoted above dates from January 1918. It depicts a modification to number 66022 of the first batch of Leeds Forge bogie mineral wagons. The body has been stripped from the underframe, and transverse battens have been fitted. Perhaps this was a way of prolonging the wagon's life after accident damage to the body had rendered it unsuitable for carrying coal.

Clearly, the simplicity of the modification did not justify a drawing at the time that it was undertaken, but one was made later for record purposes, as was the case for the Diagram 103 wagon described below. The wagon did not survive to be recorded among the wagons in the 1931 LM&SR document on bogie types and their application.

25 Ton Flat Wagon No. 223 – Diagram 103

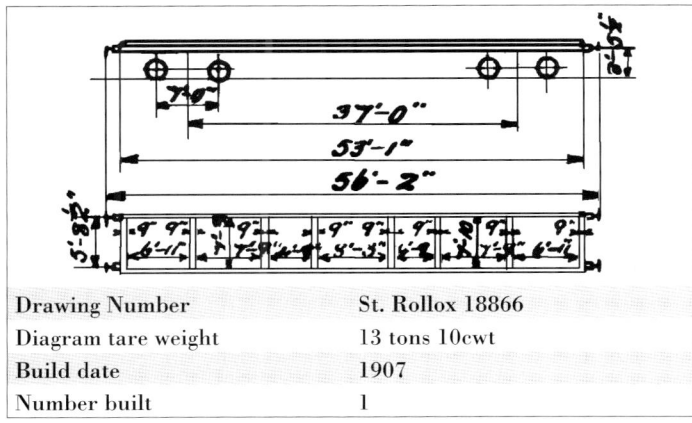

Drawing Number	St. Rollox 18866
Diagram tare weight	13 tons 10cwt
Build date	1907
Number built	1

One wagon was allocated to Diagram 103, numbered 223. It was built for Barnum & Bailey's *'Greatest Show on Earth'*. The sides look to have been made of metal and there were no ends. It had a truss rod underframe, although this is not shown in the diagram book sketch.

In its original state it had no buffers, American style knuckle couplings and a hand brake operated by a vertical hand wheel. It came into the hands of R Y Pickering, where it was rebuilt with British buffing and drawgear, and, presumably modified braking arrangements.

How it came into Pickering's hands in the first place is a mystery. According to the Wikipedia entry, the circus train of the time comprised forty-five flat wagons. Barnum and Bailey had purchased these, after starting in 1872 with Pennsylvania Rail Road vehicles which had proved to be in poor condition. A poster shows the cars in use.[1] The cars have the same livery as the photograph opposite.

The sale took place at the same time that Pickering was trying to offload their two 25-ton bogie mineral wagons. These wagons had been in the service of Thos. Muir Son & Patton. They are described and illustrated in Chapter 5.4 (p. 93). The Barnum & Bailey wagon was offered to the CR for £100. The Traffic Committee minute[2] authorised acceptance *'if the Locomotive Supt. is satisfied as to the condition of the vehicle.'*

The condition was obviously satisfactory, because the Pickering card order stated:

'We have sold the 30 ton sprung buffer flat wagon at present in these works ex Barnum & Bailey stock as and where it stands at Wishaw South station, Caledonian Railway.'[3]

The wagon was allocated to St. Rollox. A drawing, which in the register entry gives its capacity as 20 tons, is dated 17th November 1916. It has not survived. The wagon did not survive to be included in the 1931 LM&SR list of heavy weight wagons

Later Additions

A minute[4] authorised the construction of ten 35-ton and ten 30-ton gondola wagons as part of the renewals programme for the period ending 30th June 1918. Drawing 19190[5] may apply to the 35-ton wagons. This was described on the drawing as a *'flat wagon.'* It shows a wagon identical to the 35-ton Diagram 94 boiler wagon design (see section 14.4 and Plate 14.7 overleaf), without the central well. Neither type of wagon figures in the St. Rollox order list and there is no record of a contractor supplying them. They are not mentioned in Graeme Miller's history. The records of CR rolling stock orders were very confused at this stage in the war. It is possible that, instead of building these wagons, the warflats discussed in section 14.5 (p. 227) served the purpose.

References
1. http://en.wikipedia.org/wiki/File:Barnum_%26_Bailey_greatest_show_on_Earth_poster.jpg
2. NRS BR/CAL/1/60 entry 355
3. Pickering card order 19463
4. NRS BR/CAL/1/70 entry 335
5. RHP 68380

Plate 14.6
Number 53 was the last of five Diagram 43 wagons built in 1898. The Diagrams 94 and 111 wagons were of similar construction. The heavy plate frame bogies are of unusual design, with outside compensating levers between the axleboxes. The buffers seem to be the standard locomotive type. At the far end, the pocket for the coupling spring can be seen. The company initials are directly over the inner axle of each bogie. The number plate is displaced to the right by a shackle. The lettering is the largest that will fit on to the planking and curb rail. In the background are three pre-diagram book swivel wagons. In the further distance a Bannockburn colliery wagon is ahead of a Diagram 21 loco coal wagon modified to carry coke.

Plate 14.7
Although the diagram book described the Diagram 94 wagons as 35-ton boiler wagons, the load plate shows that 219 was rated at 40 tons. This is confirmed by the *1915 Working Timetable Appendix*, which rated companion wagon 220 at 35 tons. Four more were built in 1916 to replace the Diagram 43 wagons requisitioned for coastal defence. The wagons had heavy duty diamond frame bogies. For connoisseurs of variations in company initials, this wagon and the ingot wagons did not have any!

Plate 14.8
The last of the four short, massively constructed ingot wagons to Diagram 113, built in 1915. The heavy duty diamond frame bogies show up very well. Heavy self-contained buffers are fitted. The only evidence of company ownership is the cast number plate. The bottom of the load plate has been filed away to fit into the side frame channel. There are horse hooks at both ends of the wagon.

14.4: Heavy Weight and Ingot Wagons

Pre-Diagram Book Designs

The fleet included a 30-ton wagon from 1858. It was deemed to be worn out in 1876 and renewed the following year. It was described in the rolling stock return as '*15–30 ton special.*' There is no information about the original wagon. The drawing for its replacement, St. Rollox 2083, was for a 30-ton six-wheeled '*rulley wagon*'.[1]

According to Miller, its outside dimensions were 25 feet 3 inches by 8 feet. The folding sides were 7½ inches deep. The wheelbase was 16 feet and the axle box journals were 9 inches by 4½ inches. Braking was applied by a screw arrangement to blocks on the centre and one end wheel. It had self-contained sprung buffers. There is no record of this wagon in the 1890 list of special class wagons and no mention of any special wagon in the rolling stock returns after 1877, so one must assume that it had either been withdrawn or subsumed into the general goods stock.

30 Ton Wagon – Diagram 43

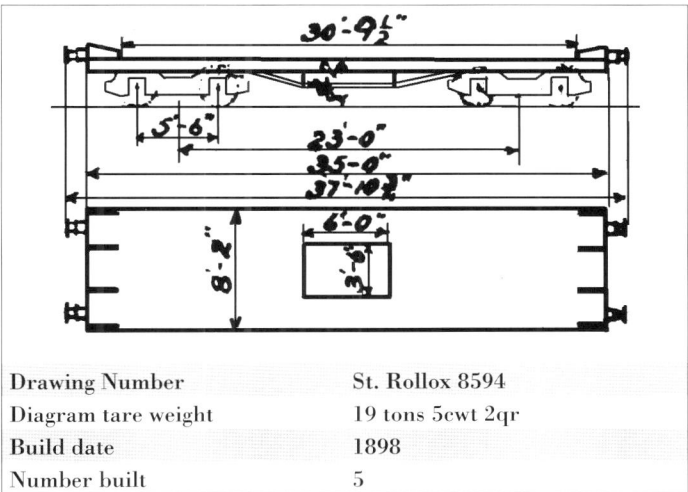

Drawing Number	St. Rollox 8594
Diagram tare weight	19 tons 5cwt 2qr
Build date	1898
Number built	5

Five 30-ton bogie wagons were built to order G163 and numbered 45, 46, 51-53 as part of the renewal programme for the first half of 1898.[2] They were of all-metal construction. Ramped ends were fitted but no sides. They had a 6 feet long by 3 feet 6 inches hole in the floor. They were all based at St. Rollox.

The first four of these wagons were requisitioned to serve in two armoured trains in the First World War. Two went into military service as gun trucks in 1914 and the others followed a year later. One of the trains protected East Anglia and the other the east coast of Scotland. The conversion work was undertaken at Crewe. They were replaced by four wagons to Diagram 94.

An example, original number unknown, is in the Scottish Railway Preservation Society collection. An article on the armoured trains appeared in the Historical Model Railway Society Journal.[3] This included a reproduction of drawing 8594.

35 Ton Boiler Wagon – Diagram 94

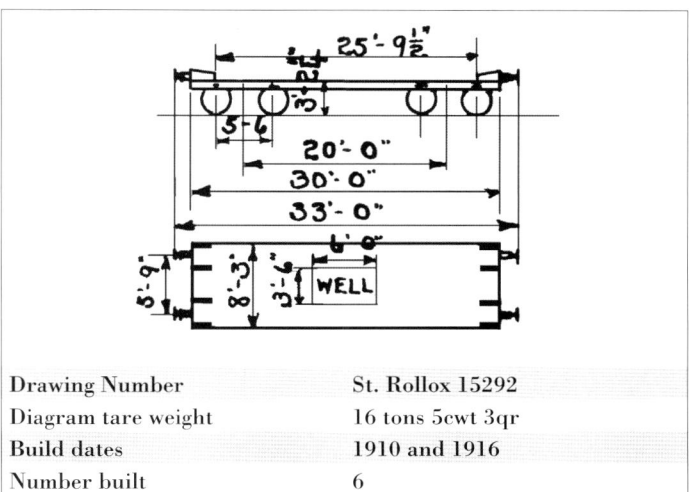

Drawing Number	St. Rollox 15292
Diagram tare weight	16 tons 5cwt 3qr
Build dates	1910 and 1916
Number built	6

Two wagons to order G285 were built in the half year ending July 1910 as renewals.[4] They were similar in construction to Diagram 43, but ran on conventional heavy duty diamond framed bogies. Their numbers were 219 and 220 in the special series, where they were described as heavy weight wagons. Number 219 was based at Bridgeton and 220 at St. Rollox.

Four more wagons were built in 1916 to order G380 to replace the Diagram 43 wagons which were requisitioned for armoured trains.[5] They took the numbers of the wagons that they replaced. Like the Diagram 43 wagons, they were used as part of set of wagons to carry heavy guns when required – see section 14.5.

35 Ton Ingot Wagon – Diagram 113

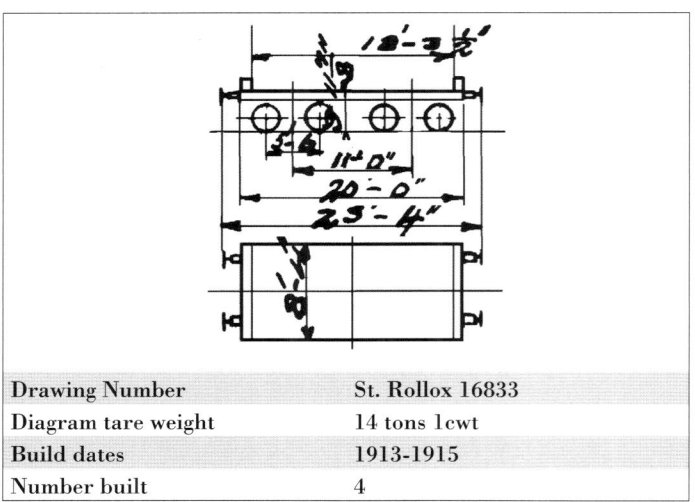

Drawing Number	St. Rollox 16833
Diagram tare weight	14 tons 1cwt
Build dates	1913-1915
Number built	4

The Diagram 113 ingot wagons authorised for construction in the half year ending December 1913[6] and built to order G336 were numbered 360 and 361. They had raised ends, but no sides. They ran on heavy diamond frame bogies. Numbers 373 and 374 were authorised for the half year ending June 1915,[7] but had not been built when the special wagon list for May was issued. The first two wagons were allocated to Bridgeton. The base of the last two is not known.

40 Ton Heavy Weight Wagon – Diagram 111

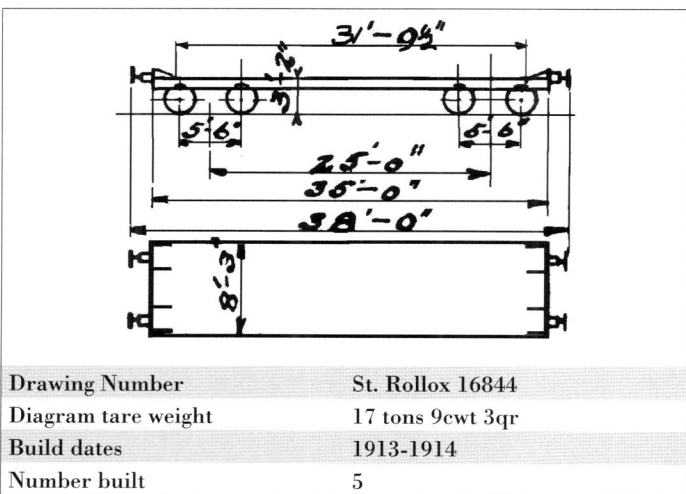

Drawing Number	St. Rollox 16844
Diagram tare weight	17 tons 9cwt 3qr
Build dates	1913-1914
Number built	5

Two wagons, numbered 362 and 363, were built to order G337.[8] Numbers 368-370 were built to order G358 in 1914.[9] Although the wagons were classed as renewals, they were allocated new numbers in the special wagons series. The first two wagons were based at St. Rollox. The allocation of the remainder is not known.

References
1. NRM 8045/W RHP 69182
2. NRS BR/CAL/1/41 entry 44
3. *HMRS Journal Volume 11*, pp. 231-34
4. NRS BR/CAL/1/67 entry 1010
5. NRS BR/CAL/1/58 entry 731
6. NRS BR/CAL/1/63 entry 26
7. NRS BR/CAL/1/65 entry 1041
8. NRS BR/CAL/1/63 entry 26
9. NRS BR/CAL/1/64 entry 1149

Plate 14.9
This is a typical gun set, comprising Diagram 94 wagon 219 and the first two ingot wagons, numbered 360 and 361. The 'INGOT WAGON' lettering is extended, i.e. stretched horizontally. The three wagons are close coupled and special cradles are fitted. The inner buffers of 219 have been removed. A diagram showing the weight distribution of this load is reproduced on p. 228.

14.5: Gun Sets and Warflats

In 1912 Britain began to make contingency plans in case of a war in continental Europe. The Railway Executive Committee (REC) was formed, which would ultimately take over control of the railway system when war broke out. One aspect of preparation for war was a re-armament programme, involving the production of heavy guns for the navy and army.

Transportation of Guns

The material in this section is taken from an article in the Caledonian Railway Association's journal, which used the 1921 publication *'British Railways and the Great War (Organisation, Efforts, Difficulties and Achievements)'* as its source.[1]

The REC took control of gun traffic over 50 tons in weight. Most of these were naval guns. Requests to move guns lighter than this were made direct to the railway companies. Between 1914 and the middle of 1916 the Caledonian carried eighty-four heavy guns. There is no record of how many smaller guns were carried by the company.

Source of Traffic

On the Caledonian system, Beardmore and Co. was a major source of gun traffic. The firm managed various national projectile factories on behalf of HM Government. During the war, their works at Parkhead manufactured approximately 100 guns of various sizes ranging from 6 tons in weight to 100 tons.

Wagons Used

Heavy weight and ingot wagons were used in various configurations to carry guns after the outbreak of hostilities. The Caledonian had produced a series of drawings between 1909 and 1911 showing how their wagons could be combined to carry guns of various sizes. The wagons used were Diagram 43 30-ton flat wagons and the Diagram 94 35-ton boiler wagons either singly or in pairs. The drawing numbers are 15081 and 15176 of 1909. These were for a 70-ton gun and a 12-inch gun respectively. These have not survived. The 1910 drawings 15336A-H have survived, as has 15890 of the following year.[2]

After the introduction of the Diagram 113 ingot wagons in 1913 a typical 100-ton gun was carried on two ingot wagons close coupled and fitted with a cradle to support the gun breech, with Diagram 94 boiler wagon 219 close coupled to them. This was fitted with a cradle to support the barrel. The Diagram 94's buffers were removed from the inner end to facilitate close coupling.

The increasing demand for transporting guns diverted wagons from their intended traffic, which had also increased to support the war effort. Extra wagons were built to Diagram 113 in 1915, but it was eventually found necessary to provide a specialised gun set capable of carrying even larger guns.

The 165 Ton Gun Truck

By 1916, even heavier equipment was envisaged. St. Rollox drawing 18627, dated 19th June 1916 which has not survived, was a diagram for a 160-ton gun truck. Nothing actually transpired until May 1918, when Hurst Nelson delivered a three-wagon gun set of 165 tons capacity to the Caledonian. The firm had recently built a similar set for the L&NWR. The REC obtained the set from the Admiralty who paid for the wagons. They were for the exclusive use of the Caledonian and could not be despatched to any government depot. Between its delivery and the end of the war the gun set carried fifteen guns weighing from 70 to 100 tons.

The gun set consisted of three wagons each with a pair of six-wheeled bogies. Two of the wagons were close coupled and carried between them a bolster to support the breech of a gun. The third wagon, which supported the gun muzzle, was coupled to the other two with a draw bar that could be extended or shortened as required. The wagons could also be used as separate units, each capable of carrying a load of from 55 to 60 tons. The wagons were numbered 377-379 in the special list.

The Warflats

Surplus bogie wagons originally built for the War Department were distributed among the railway companies. Sources suggest that the Caledonian received 192, the G&SWR nine and the Highland four. The majority of the wagons appear to have survived in revenue service until 1959/60. The BR scrapping record also suggests that the wagons were built in 1917 by contractors, rather than railway workshops, and that the War Department disposed of them in 1921.[3] An LM&SR version of the Caledonian diagram book assigned diagram number 126 (the last in the book) to these wagons.

The LM&SR diagram book of special heavy weight wagons,[4] which contains LM&SR Diagram 19 wagons based on the Midland, has the note *'The Northern Division Trucks are included.'* The numbers of the wagons are not listed. Based on a privately owned BR wagon scrapping record a list of possible Caledonian wagons can be extracted based on the principle that ex CR wagons were numbered in the 300XXX series. These numbers suggested the figure of 192 wagons.

In fact, the wagons were not disposed of, but remained within the government pool. This is confirmed by three minutes, two of which refer to 104 wagons, not 192. The minutes[5] are concerned with the timing of the payment of

'an amount of £11,750 received from War Office in respect of the cost of fitting bolsters and chains to 104 40ton Bogie Flat Wagons which the Company has on loan from Ministry of Transport.'

References

1. *The True Line* issue 84, pp. 9-14
2. Not yet catalogued
3. Jim MacIntosh, private correspondence
4. NRM DIAG/LMS/4, TNA: PRO RAIL422/12
5. NRS BR/CAL/1/77 entry 984,
   NRS BR/CAL/1/78 entry 347,
   NRS BR/CAL/1/79 entry 747

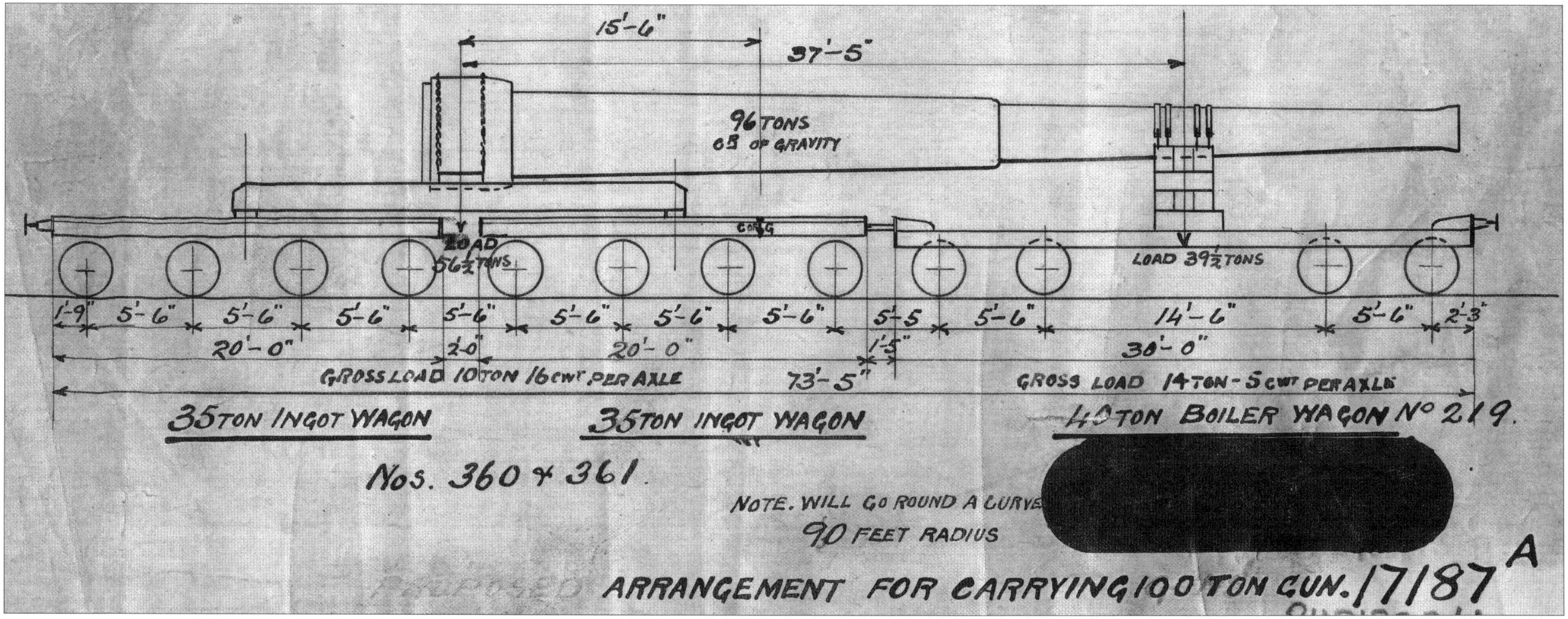

Above: Figure 14.1
This sketch shows how the weight of the 100 ton gun was distributed over the gun set shown in Plate 14.9. The drawing is dated 6th November 1913.

Above: Plate 14.10
Here is the Hurst Nelson-built heavy gun set. It consists of three identical wagons which could be used separately if required.

Right: Plate 14.11
The LM&SR number 335937 suggests that this was one of the Warflats allocated to the Caledonian after the end of the war. The Caledonian added the bolsters at a total cost of £11,750 for 104 wagons. The LM&SR described them as 40-ton bogie bolsters.

Chapter 15
Four- and Six-Wheeled Special Class Wagons
15.1: Glass Well Wagons

15 Ton Glass Wagon – Diagram 38

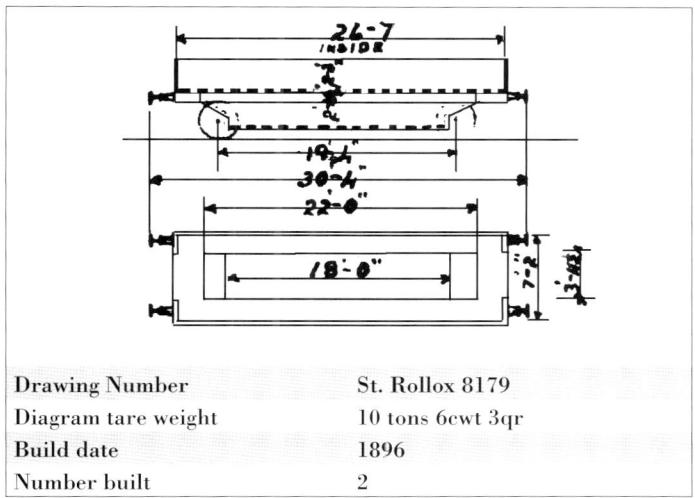

Drawing Number	St. Rollox 8179
Diagram tare weight	10 tons 6cwt 3qr
Build date	1896
Number built	2

Two four-wheeled glass well wagons numbered 43 and 44 were built to this Diagram. They were authorised in May 1896 and built to order G143. They were charged to the capital account in 1897.[1] The floor of the wagon was cut out to form a well which was 3 feet 11½ inches wide. The well was formed of metal, extending down between the wheels to 1 foot 2 inches above track level. The ends of the well sloped to clear the axles, so that the opening in the floor was 4 feet longer than the bottom of the well. The bottom of the well was lined with wood planks. The four-plank sides were 2 feet 3 inches deep. The ends were fixed, but an opening equal to the well width was left.

The underframe and headstocks were made of steel channel. The standard Drummond wagon buffer was used. Heavy duty fifteen-leaf springs, oil axleboxes with 12-inch by 5-inch journals and plate axle guards were fitted. The wagons were allocated to St. Rollox.

Other Glass Wagon

At some time between the compilation of the special wagons lists for 1906 and 1915, Diagram 18 heavy machinery wagon number 83 was redesignated as a glass well wagon. It was fitted with iron straps at a height of 2 feet above rail level for conveying glass in cases and was excluded from carrying heavy loads. There is no mention of this modification in the minutes.

Reference
1. NRS BR/CAL/1/39 entry 911

Plate 15.1
One of the two Diagram 38 glass well wagons, built in 1896, carrying a circular fabrication. Note the heavy duty springs, oil lubricated axleboxes and plate axle guards. The first style of cast number plate is fitted to the centre of the body on the bottom plank, overlapping the curb rail. The four small lettering groups are spaced symmetrically along the side of the wagon, with the company initials filling the vacant areas.

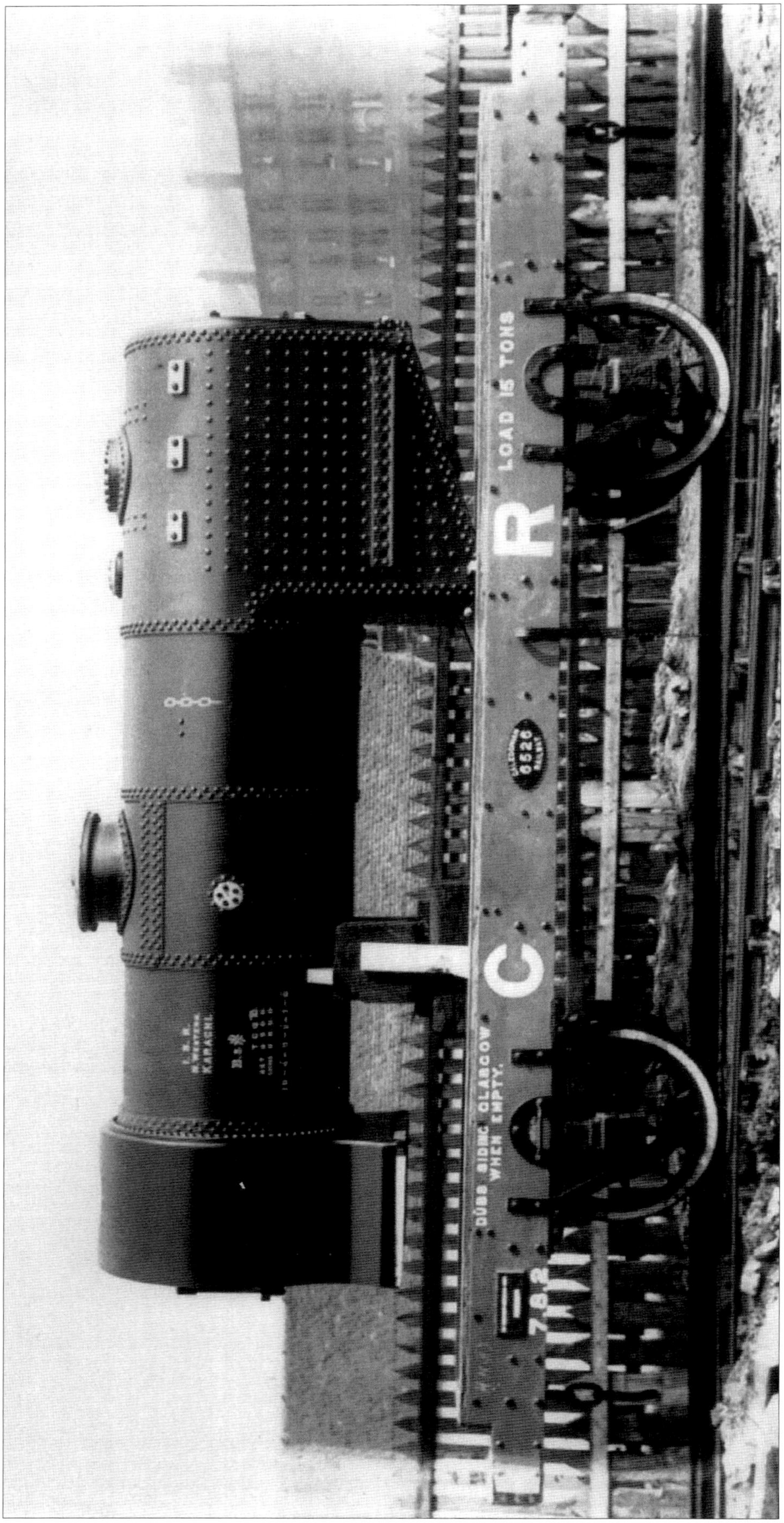
C R
LOAD 15 TONS
DUBS SIDING GLASGOW
WHEN EMPTY.
782

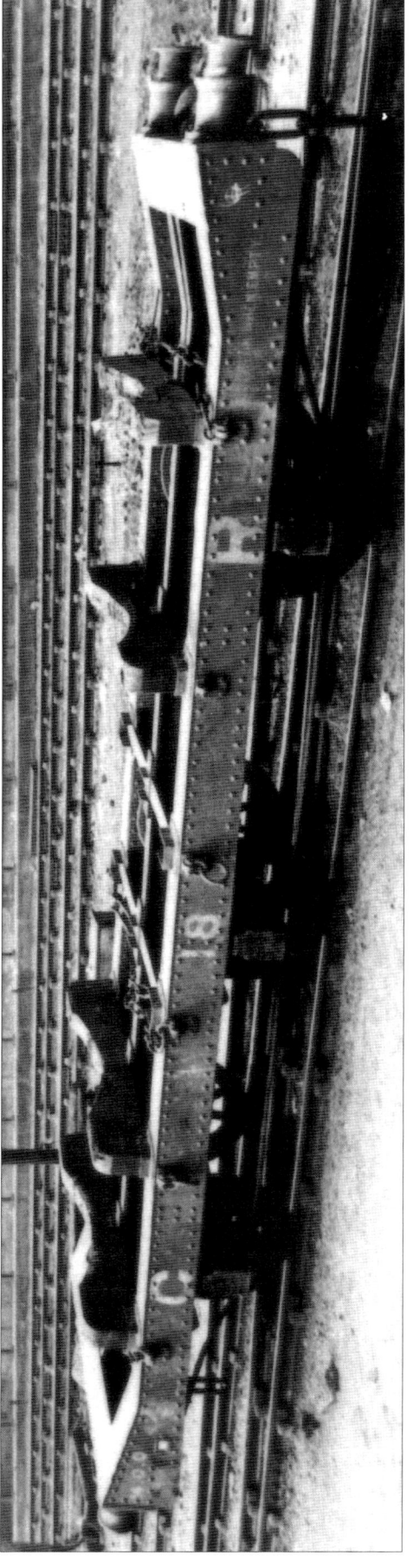

15.2: Locomotive and Boiler Wagons

Locomotive Wagon Load 15 Tons – Diagram 19

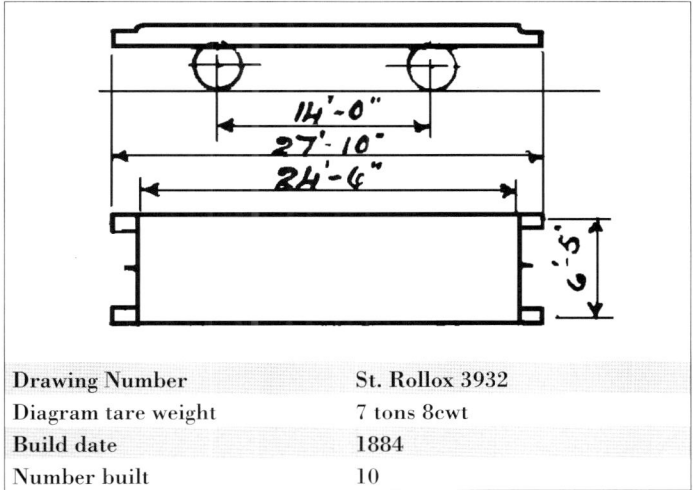

Drawing Number	St. Rollox 3932
Diagram tare weight	7 tons 8cwt
Build date	1884
Number built	10

These wagons, like the rail wagons, were numbered in the ordinary goods wagon series, and were regarded as open goods wagons in the 1910 return. Unlike the rail wagons, they were never listed among the special class wagons in working timetable appendices. They are included here because they carried a specialised load and were probably all assigned to a specific location.

They were fitted with solid buffers. The sides and ends were 6 inches high, as extensions to the solebars and headstocks. The sides and ends tapered from top to bottom and were ¼ inch narrower at the top. Four shallow wrought iron knees attached the sides to the floor of the wagon.

An iron brake block acted on one left-hand wheel. The wheels were 3 feet 6 inches diameter and the ten-leaf springs were 3 feet 9 inches between hangers. Journals were 9 inches by 5 inches. The solebars and sides were 'flitched', i.e. faced with a metal plate, giving a completely smooth appearance to the side view.

The drawing dates from early 1884. There is no reference in the minutes or the rolling stock returns to the construction of these wagons. A photograph of one of these wagons, numbered 6526, is lettered '*Dübs siding when empty.*' It is not known whether this allocation applied to all the wagons.

The wagons were probably sold to the North British Locomotive Co. in 1908, when a November Traffic Committee minute authorised the sale of '*10 15-ton wagons and 10 10-ton wagons.*'[1] The 1907-1910 statement of wagon stock shows that ten 15-ton locomotive wagons were taken out of service in the period ending July 1909.[2] The 10-ton wagons mentioned in the minute have so far resisted identification.

16 Ton Boiler Wagon – Diagram 26

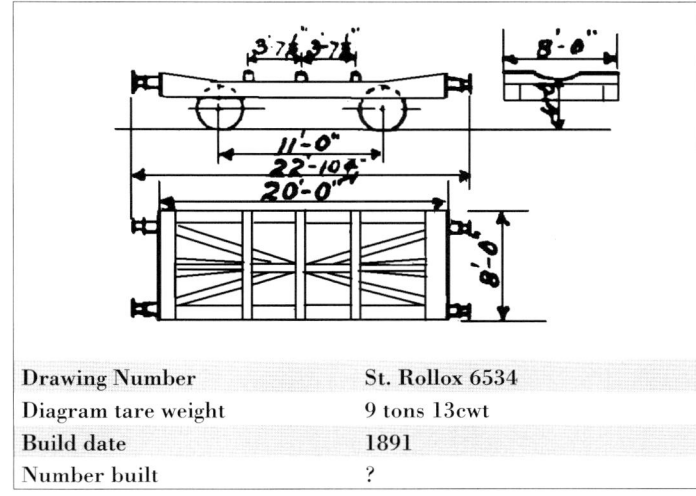

Drawing Number	St. Rollox 6534
Diagram tare weight	9 tons 13cwt
Build date	1891
Number built	?

Diagrams 26 and 28 were built to order G89, along with the machinery wagons to Diagrams 27 and 31. They formed part of the renewal programme for the half year ending July 1891.[3] The programme was for 262 wagons, types not specified. Their inclusion is deduced from the St. Rollox order numbers.

The two designs of boiler wagon had no floors. The side members were riveted metal in an inverted u-shape with the wagon springs inside the channel. 12-inch by 5-inch oil axleboxes were fitted. Tie rods connected the plate axle guards to each other and to the side members. A metal section formed a spine down the middle of the wagon. Shaped wooden cradles fitted into sockets on the top of each side member to support the load.

Wagons to the Diagram 26 specification did not appear in the 1892 or 1894 special wagon lists, but three to the machinery wagon specification *were* listed. It is probable that, although a drawing and a diagram were produced, no wagon was actually built to this design.

Facing Page Top: Plate 15.2
Although the Diagram 19 wagons were not numbered in the special series, they were designed for specialist traffic. Here 6526 carries a locomotive boiler built by Dübs, en route for Karachi. Wagons do not get more basic than this. Although not obvious in the photograph, the wheels were 3 feet 6 inches diameter and the wagon springs longer than usual. Note also the old-style solid-buffer wagon coupling with short centre link. The ten wagons had been taken out of service by 1910.

Facing Page Bottom: Plate 15.3
This is the six-wheeled boiler wagon to Diagram 28, built like its four-wheeled counterpart in 1891. The picture shows the way the cradles fitted into sockets on the sides and cross members. It has the early four-bolt self-contained buffer. Note the tiebars between the axle guards and the wagon body. There does not seem to be a brake. The tare weight is written at the left-hand end, but there is no corresponding load writing on the right. The company initials and number are painted on the axlebox centre lines. The number is slightly smaller than the letters. The letter C is not as wide as it should be, resulting in a small straight portion to the letter.

25 Ton Boiler Wagon – Diagram 28

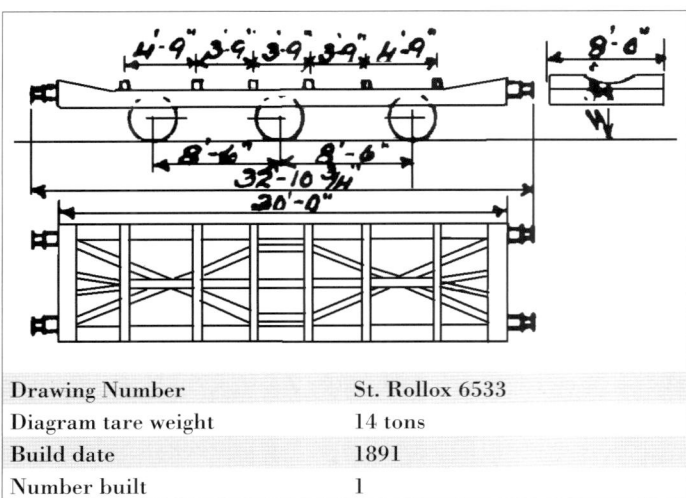

Drawing Number	St. Rollox 6533
Diagram tare weight	14 tons
Build date	1891
Number built	1

References
1. NRS BR/CAL/1/57 entry 257
2. NRS BR/CAL/4/134, p. 5
3. NRS BR/CAL/5/11 entry 121

Left: Plate 15.4a
This enlargement from Plate 15.9 shows the solid ends fitted to wagon number 24.

Diagram 28 was the six-wheeled version of Diagram 26. The drawing is annotated to the effect that one wagon was built with bolsters and two with flooring. Those with flooring were the machinery wagons to Diagram 31. These wagons are described on p. 234. The November 1892 Working Timetable Appendix lists one *'new boiler wagon'* number 38368 with an internal length of 29 feet. The number was 18 in the special series of 1894 with a length of 30 feet, as in the diagram book. It was allocated to Bridgeton.

Below: Plate 15.4
Two 15-ton machinery wagons were probably built in 1887 as rebuilds of earlier wagons. The diagonal lines of bolts on the cupboard doors secured the three middle door planks. These wagons did not have a separate internal lining to the doors with the planks disposed vertically like mineral wagons. The wood packing pieces behind the buffers are the same shape as the buffer casting. The axleboxes are very unusual. Wheels with nine solid spokes are fitted and the springs are heavy duty. The letter C is painted slightly lower than the R. The load is written on the bottom body plank, but the tare has been displaced to the curb rail to accommodate the depot lettering, which is very small. The incised circle mark is visible on the curb rail at the right-hand side.

15.3: Machinery and Agricultural Implement Wagons

Machinery Wagon Load 15 Tons – Diagram 17

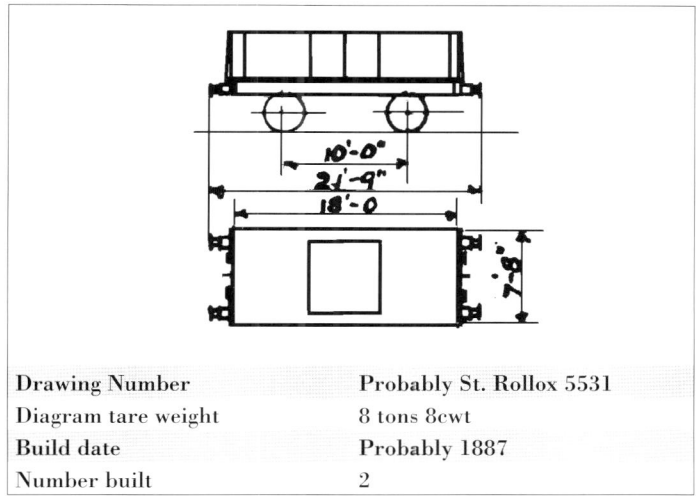

Drawing Number	Probably St. Rollox 5531
Diagram tare weight	8 tons 8cwt
Build date	Probably 1887
Number built	2

The Diagram 17 wagons looked like large goods wagons with a 5-foot 2-inch by 6-foot 1½-inch aperture along the centre line of the floor. The fixed sides and ends had five planks and were 4 feet high. The door opening was the same width as the well, i.e. 5 feet 2 inches. The ends were said in the *1915 Working Timetable Appendix* to have openings 3 feet 3 inches broad by 2 feet 6 inches deep. Photographs of wagon 24 show continuous planks. A photograph with one of these wagons in the background does show the opening, however. The number cannot be seen, but by implication it is 25. The wheels were 3 feet 6 inches diameter and in the photograph of number 24 they have nine solid spokes. Oil axleboxes and heavy self-contained buffers were fitted.

They were probably built to St. Rollox drawing 5531 for a 15-ton well or machinery wagon, dating from 1887. The drawing has not survived. They were originally allocated numbers 2494/5 as general goods wagons, but were renumbered 24 and 25 in the 1894 listing, and allocated to St. Rollox. There is no mention of specific wagon orders in the minutes between 1886 and 1888. The St. Rollox order number was G42, where they were described as rebuilds of 2494 and 2495. Number 25 was replaced by a Diagram 117 implement wagon in 1918.

Well Wagon for Heavy Machinery Load 15 Tons – Diagram 18

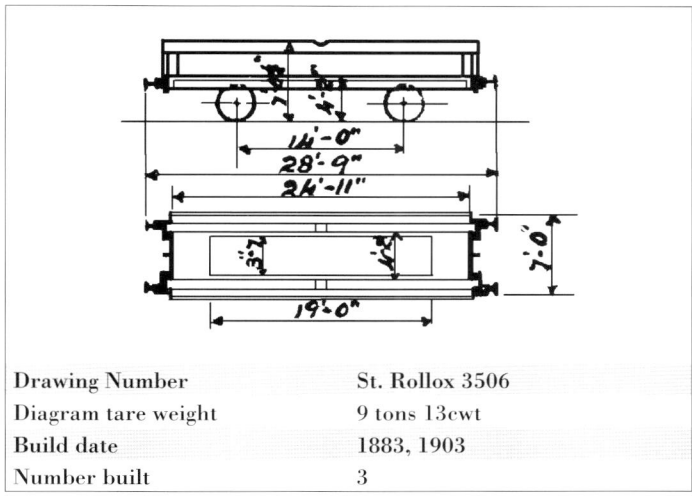

Drawing Number	St. Rollox 3506
Diagram tare weight	9 tons 13cwt
Build date	1883, 1903
Number built	3

The first wagon to this diagram was built to a drawing dated April 1883. The minutes make no mention of this wagon. It was

Plate 15.5
This picture shows the first Diagram 18 machinery wagon, adapted to carry a ship's propeller. It was number 3 in the original four-strong special wagon number series. There are tie bars between the axle guards and, apparently, no brake. The wheels have ten solid spokes. The tare and load lettering are aligned with the bottom of the body plank; the return depot lettering is centred on the same plank, but not in the space available for it. The load lettering is too long to fit in the available space, so it has been centred on the right-hand piece of ironwork. As in Plate 15.1, the company initials are centred in spaces created by the body ironwork.

number 3 of the first three wagons to be allocated a special class number in the 1890 list.

The 3-inch thick three-planked sides and ends were 2 feet 1 inch deep. The fixed ends had a gap in the centre and were surmounted by heavy longitudinal trestles set 4 feet 2 inches apart. A well ran down the centre of the floor. Ten-spoke wheels ran in oil lubricated 9-inch by 6-inch axleboxes. Heavy duty fifteen-leaf springs were fitted. The axle guards were connected by tie rods. There is no sign of brake gear in the photograph, which was taken for the *1900 Register*. In May 1900 an either side brake was fitted, presumably the McIntosh patent variety. This modification was the subject of St. Rollox drawings 10810 and 10811, neither of which has survived.

Two further wagons were built to order G206, annotated '*same as number 3.*' A new drawing, number 11879, was issued.[1] The Traffic Committee authorised them in January 1903 at £125 each.[2] They were allocated numbers 82 and 83 in the special list. All three wagons were allocated to St. Rollox.

They were normally fitted with three-link couplings, but drawings 14041 and 14042 detailed an arrangement of cross beams for carrying propellers, and specified the fitting of screw couplings when carrying such loads. The drawings date from January 1907, but they must have been made to formalise an earlier arrangement, because the *1900 Register* shows the original wagons carrying a propeller. The drawings have not survived.

As mentioned in the section on glass and well wagons, number 83 was later adapted to carry glass and excluded from carrying heavy machinery.

16 Ton Machinery Wagon – Diagram 27

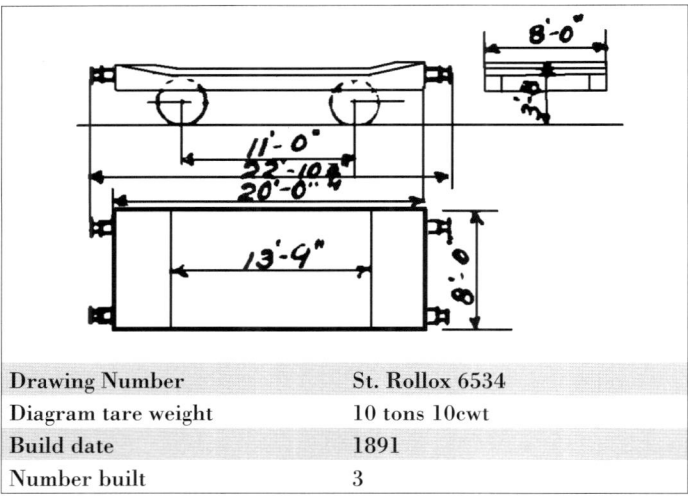

Drawing Number	St. Rollox 6534
Diagram tare weight	10 tons 10cwt
Build date	1891
Number built	3

The 16-ton Diagram 27 and 25-ton Diagram 31 machinery wagons were dimensionally identical to the Diagram 26 and 28 boiler wagons, but with a conventional floor. Both types had 6½-inch metal sides to contain the floorboards. Otherwise, construction was the same as the boiler wagons. The 1892 special wagons list described them as new boiler and machinery wagons, giving their numbers as 35981, 36084 and 36134. The dimensions given vary greatly from those in the diagram book. Subsequent listings give the diagram book dimensions. In the 1894 list they were allocated numbers 19-21 and were based at St. Rollox.

25 Ton Machinery Wagon – Diagram 31

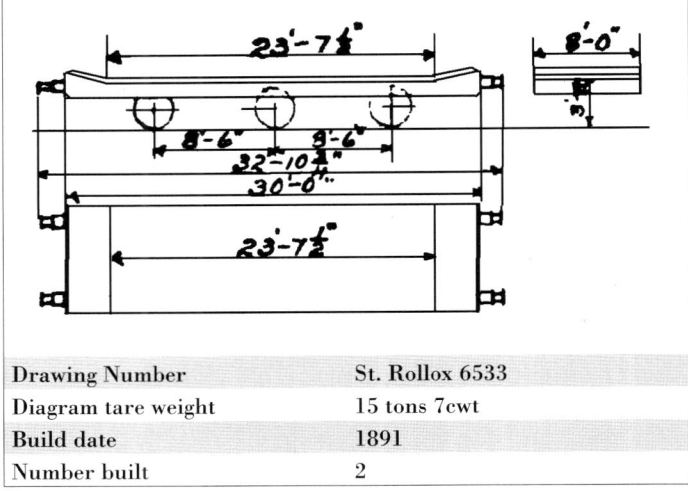

Drawing Number	St. Rollox 6533
Diagram tare weight	15 tons 7cwt
Build date	1891
Number built	2

This design was derived from Diagram 27, with a floor rather than an open construction spanned by cradles. The floorboards seem to have been laid loose as Plate 15.7 on the page opposite shows temporary cradles fitted, like the Diagram 27 wagon. The 1892 list gave their numbers as 38361 and 38387. Their length was given as 24 feet rather than 30 feet. The wagons were allocated special class numbers 22 and 23 in the 1894 listing, and the dimensions given were as the diagram book.

Number 22 was originally based at St. Rollox and number 23 at Bridgeton. At some time between 1906 and 1915 they changed places.

15 Ton Agricultural Implement Wagon – Diagram 93

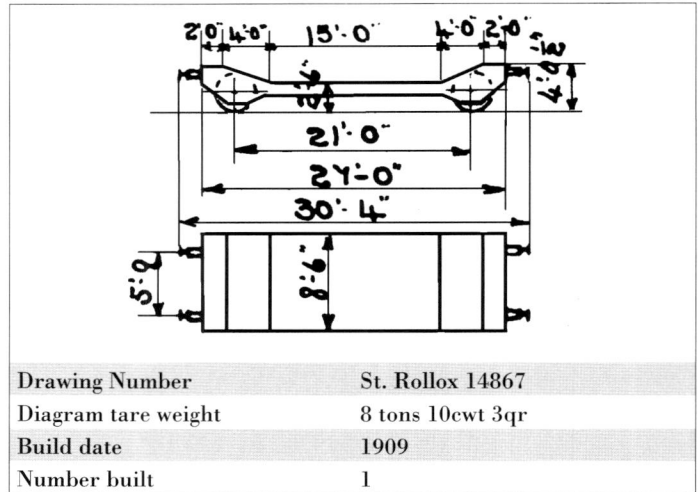

Drawing Number	St. Rollox 14867
Diagram tare weight	8 tons 10cwt 3qr
Build date	1909
Number built	1

Diagrams 93 and 117 on the next page were very similar. The drawing described them as a '*furniture van or implement wagon.*' The single Diagram 93 wagon, to order G281, was numbered 78, which had originally been allocated to the last of the Diagram 58 'boat wagons'. These wagons had disappeared from the special list by 1906. It was authorised in the renewal programme for the half year ending January 1910.[2] It was based at St. Rollox.

15.3: MACHINERY AND AGRICULTURAL IMPLEMENT WAGONS

15 Ton Agricultural Implement Wagon – Diagram 117

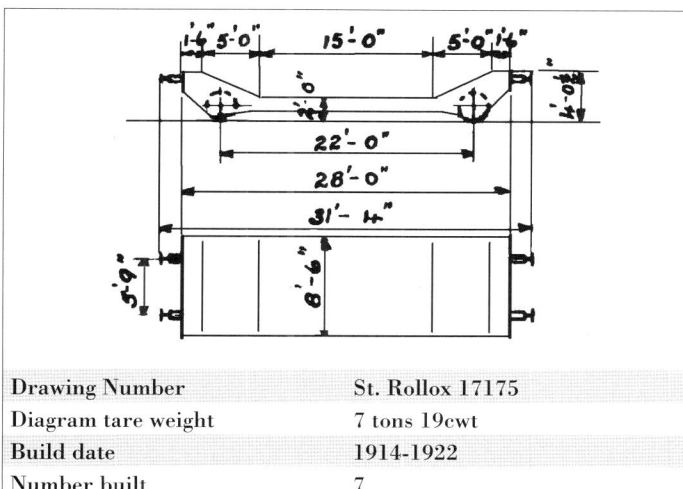

Drawing Number	St. Rollox 17175
Diagram tare weight	7 tons 19cwt
Build date	1914-1922
Number built	7

The first two Diagram 117 wagons were numbered 10 and 13. They had a 1 foot longer wheelbase and body than the Diagram 93 design. The floor was 6 inches lower. The reduction was partly achieved by fitting 2-foot 9-inch diameter wheels rather than the 3-foot diameter of Diagram 93

The wagons were authorised under the renewal programme in 1914 to order G348.[4] They replaced two of the early flat wagons described in the next section. This pair was based at St. Rollox.

A further two were built in 1917 to order G400.[5] These and subsequent orders were 20-ton wagons. The order record states that their numbers were 375 and 376 and that they were *'similar to number 10.'*

Although there is no further reference to these wagons in the minutes, a wagon was built in 1918 to order G411, taking the number 25, which was originally a Diagram 17 machinery wagon. In the same year a wagon was built to order G416. This took number 63, replacing a swivel bar wagon. Finally, at the end of the Caley's existence, one more wagon was built to order G422. The number of this wagon is unknown. The base of the last five wagons is not known.

References
1. NRM 11293/W
2. NRS BR/CAL/1/47 entry 285
3. NRS BR/CAL/1/57 no entry number
4. NRS BR/CAL/1/63 entry 1383
5. NRS BR/CAL/1/69 entry 605

Top Left: Plate 15.6
Diagram 27 machinery wagon number 19, fitted with the wooden floor that distinguished machinery from boiler wagons. The number is smaller than the company initials to accommodate the depot location above it, and has been displaced left by a shackle. The load designation is not painted. Instead, a small cast plate is attached to the side member to the right and below the tare numerals. This reads TO CARRY 8 TONS. The self-contained buffers have square bases. In the far background stands an empty barrel truck.

Bottom Left: Plate 15.7
The special list number 22 of this Diagram 31 machinery wagon is just visible above the centre axlebox. It has temporary cradles fitted like its boiler wagon equivalent and the floorboards are loose fitted, being retained by the 6-inch metal sides. Again there is no load lettering. In the background stands a line of sewage disposal wagons operated by the Glasgow Police Commissioners. The early solid-buffered versions carry an oval ownership plate on the right-hand side. The wagons had fixed sides and ends, which makes one wonder about how they were unloaded. One hopes that a tipping arrangement existed at the depots, which were situated at Dalmarnock, Dalmuir and Shieldhall. In the articles in the HMRS Journal from which this information was taken, the livery was said to be black underframe and red body with white lettering. Wagons 11-30 (Pickering card order 2467 of January 1898) were painted with *'two coats of red lead and one of brown oxide.'* Between 1902 and 1906 240 modern wagons of up to 10 tons capacity were ordered.

Plate 15.8
One of two wagons built to drawing 774 in 1868. The wood brake block is probably actuated by a bell crank. Once again, there seems to be no load designation. The axle guards have curved bridles, in contrast to the six-wheeled version in the next plate, which has straight bridles.

Plate 15.9
This is the six-wheeled version, built to drawing 775. As in the four-wheeled wagon, the headstocks are slightly higher than the solebars. The four-bolt self-contained buffers are on rectangular, rather than shaped, packing pieces. At the right-hand end one of the buffers is stepped, the other is plain. The company initials and number are centred in the spaces between the axle centres. The tare and load lettering are centred over their respective axles, the depot lettering is not. It would be more usual to have the load lettering at the right-hand end, with the depot lettering in the centre. Immediately behind is machinery wagon 24, with solid ends. In the background are two of the ten pre-diagram book furniture van trucks.

Plate 15.10
Special flat wagon 12 was one of two. The brake pivot ironwork looks distinctly home made. The packing behind the four-bolt self-contained buffers extends to the end of the headstock. The company initials are centred over the axles. The 9-inch letters overlap on to the curb rail. The T in St. Rollox is small with a dot below it. Normally it was the same size as the rest of the depot lettering. In the background is an early Banknock Coal Co. wagon which looks to be built to the Diagram 22 mineral wagon design.

Plate 15.11
One of eight pre-diagram book runner wagons, number 39. Note the very thin floor planks, and the low tare weight. There is no room to apply company lettering. Behind are two of the Diagram 14 style swivel bar wagons, special list numbers 47 and 49.

15.4: Flat Wagons and Runners

Pre-Diagram Book Flat Wagons

Two very similar designs of flat wagon dated from 1868. Two 15-ton four-wheeled wagons were built to St.Rollox drawing 774.[1] The inside dimensions were 17 feet 6 inches by 7 feet 6 inches, with fixed 7½-inch sides and ends. A photograph of number 9 in the *1900 Register* shows it without sides or ends. This is confirmed in a note to the *1902 Appendix*, although the dimensions list still mentions the 7½-inch sides.

The wheelbase was 11 feet. Heavy self-contained buffers were fitted. In the *1890 Working Timetable Appendix*, they were numbered 8128 and 8129. In the *January 1895 Appendix*, they had been renumbered 9 and 10. In the *1890 Appendix* they were said to have an open space in the bottom. By 1900, when number 9 was photographed for the *Register of Wagon Plant*, this had been filled in to form a continuous floor. This is confirmed in the *1902 Appendix*, which does not include these wagons among those with an opening in the floor.

The second type had six wheels and was built to drawing 775.[2] It was described as a *'heavy flat wagon.'* Internal dimensions were 20 feet 6 inches by 7 feet 6 inches. Their original numbers were 2139, 2140, 8126 and 8127, later special series numbers 13, 14, 16 and 17. Number 15 (originally 7999) was 4 feet longer. They too had the heavy four-bolt self-contained buffer. The wagon floors had a 4 feet 5 inches wide opening above the centre axle. The length of the opening varied from wagon to wagon between 3 feet 8 inches and 4 feet 9 inches.

Originally, the sides of 2139 and 7999 folded down. By 1902 they had no sides. 2140 had fixed sides and ends in 1890, which had been removed by 1902. The fixed sides of 8126 were altered to fold by 1902; number 8127 continued with fixed sides and ends.

A further type of flat wagon was represented in the special lists. They were originally numbered 936 and 137, but were renumbered 11 and 12 by the time the 1895 list was published. They were originally 15 tons capacity but were down-rated to 12 tons. They were of light construction with the four-bolt heavy duty buffers. The wheelbase was 11 feet. They had ordinary grease axleboxes and the axle guards were inside the solebars. The fixed sides and ends were 6 inches high. The single wood brake block was actuated by push rod. They were allocated to St. Rollox. The drawing for these wagons has not been traced.

Pre-Diagram Book Runner Wagons

In the 1895 listings, four 30cwt runner wagons numbered 5-8 appeared for the first time, followed by a further four numbered 36-39 in the 1902 list. These wagons are discussed here because they were clearly pre-diagram book in origin.

The internal dimensions differed from one listing to another. In the 1906 list, 5 and 8 were 11 feet 6 inches by 6 feet 8 inches. Number 7 was only 10 feet 6 inches long. Number 6 was 12 feet 4 inches long and 6 feet 5½ inches wide. Numbers 36-38 were *'similar to Nos. 5, 7, and 8'*, while number 39 was the same as number 6.

The wheelbase is not recorded, but the underframe looked very similar to that of the early swivel timber wagons. The floor was covered with very thin planks, hence the design load of 30cwt. The tare weight is not given in most of the listings, except for 1906 when wagon 6 tared at 3 tons 7½cwt and number 39 at 3 tons 1cwt. The photograph of 39 places it even lower at 2 tons 18cwt. The solebars were extended as usual to form solid buffers and were built up by a further wooden pad above. A single wooden brake block was fitted. There is no record of a drawing for these wagons. They may well have been rebuilt on old wagon underframes.

Given the very light construction and the nominal load capacity they would only have been used as spacers between wagons carrying overhanging loads. Numbers 5 and 6 were allocated to Bridgeton; 7 and 8 to St. Rollox. The other four wagons had no specific base.

The Diagram 122 wagons replaced them. One redundant wagon was reported as sold to Hardie & Gordon, owners of an iron foundry at Dalreoch, in January 1911.[3]

Another type of flat wagon is represented by number 8006, photographed for the *1900 Register*. This was another flat bed solid buffer wagon, but more modern in design. It had axle guards inside the solebars, heavy duty springs and larger axlebox journals. The wheelbase looks to be 10 feet.

There is no contemporary drawing of these wagons in the St. Rollox records, which might suggest that they were old wagons stripped down for a new purpose. Order G76, which was described as *'runner*

Plate 15.12
Flat wagon number 8006 was photographed for the *1900 Register*, where twelve such wagons were reported in stock. So far, these have not been traced. The writing 'DUBS [illegible, but probably SIDING] GLASGOW WHEN EMPTY' can just be discerned on the edge of the floor, at the left-hand side. The cast number plate has to suffice for company identification, as there is no room for the company initials.

wagons for boiler wagons,' may refer to them. The minutes record authorisation for a total of 308 merchandise stock with no details about wagon type.[4]

In support of this possibility, wagon 8006 is lettered for return to Dübs siding, so could have been built to run in conjunction with the wagons represented by number 6526 which were described in Section 15.2. However, order G76 was recorded as being for six wagons. Another possibility is that they were built to accompany the three boiler wagons which were authorised in the following accounting period. This seems less likely as there is no reference to any runner wagon in the 1892 special wagon list.

8 TON SPECIAL GOODS WAGON WITH FALLING SIDES – DIAGRAM 58

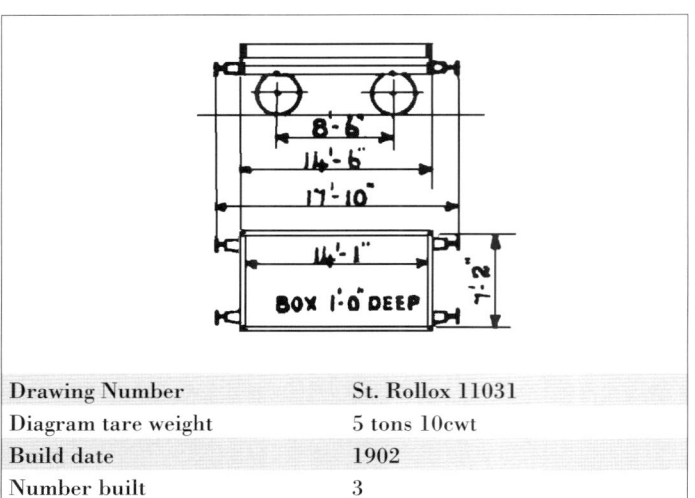

Drawing Number	St. Rollox 11031
Diagram tare weight	5 tons 10cwt
Build date	1902
Number built	3

Built as part of order G189, the wagons were allocated numbers 76-78, according to the May 1902 listing of special class wagons, where they were described as '*boat wagons*'. They were based at Greenock. The single plank sides were 1 foot high and the ends folded down. The standard wagon buffer with the cast step was fitted, and the McIntosh patent brake. The 9-inch by 4-inch axle journals were larger than normal, but the springs only had eight leaves.

Numbers 76 and 77 were replaced by Diagram 82 well wagons in 1905. Number 78 had disappeared from the special class listing by October 1906 and was eventually replaced by the Diagram 93 agricultural implement wagon. Given their robust construction and up-to-date running gear, the wagons would not have been withdrawn after a few years service. Presumably they were renumbered and assigned to general goods traffic.

12 TON RUNNER WAGON – DIAGRAM 122

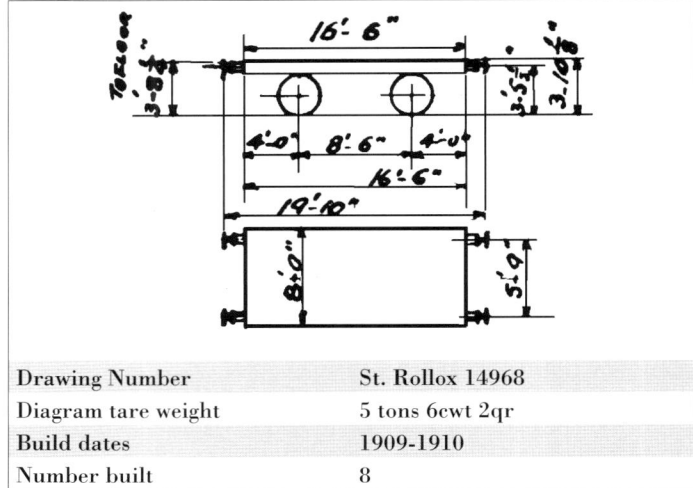

Drawing Number	St. Rollox 14968
Diagram tare weight	5 tons 6cwt 2qr
Build dates	1909-1910
Number built	8

Runner wagons to Diagram 122 were numbered 5-8 and 36-39. They were a flat bed with a 2-inch side. They replaced the pre-diagram book era 30cwt wagons and took their numbers. The first four were authorised in 1909 to order G283.[5] The last four were authorised in 1910 and built to order G292.[6] The diagram number should have been 95 if it had been allocated at the date of building; there is no obvious explanation for this omission and the assignment of the diagram number 122.

Numbers 5 and 6 were allocated to Bridgeton. The remainder were based at St. Rollox.

REFERENCES
1. Not yet catalogued
2. Not yet catalogued
3. NRS BR/CAL/1/59 entry 1319
4. NRS BR/CAL/1/33 entry 1038
5. NRS BR/CAL/1/57 no entry number
6. NRS BR/CAL/1/59 entry 125

Plate 15.13
This is one of the 'boat wagons' that appeared for a brief time in the special wagons lists. The three wagons were built in 1902 and had disappeared from the special wagons list by 1906. It is fitted with the McIntosh patent brake. The cross rod for the either side levers is set back further than usual from the headstock, and is underneath the spring. The horse hook is the non-standard type used on the Diagram 67 covered vans. The letters and writing are centred in their respective spaces. The typeface of the depot lettering has been condensed to fit the space. There is no tare weight writing.

15.5: Swivel Bar and Heavy Weight Wagons

Pre-Diagram Book Designs

The fleet included a 30-ton wagon from 1858. According to the wagon returns it was deemed to be worn out in 1876 and renewed the following year. There is no information about the original wagon. The drawing for the renewal, St. Rollox 2083, dated 1874, was for a 30-ton six-wheeled *'rulley wagon'*.[1]

Its outside dimensions were 25 feet 3 inches by 8 feet. The folding sides were 7½ inches deep. The ends were fixed. There was a 5 feet square hole in the floor at the centre of the wagon. The wheelbase was 16 feet and the axle box journals were 9 inches by 4½ inches. It ran on wheels with ten solid spokes. Brakes were applied by a screw arrangement to blocks on the centre and the right-hand wheel. The screw arrangement terminated in a hand wheel below the headstock at the same end of the wagon as the brake gear. It had heavy self-contained sprung buffers and safety chains. There is no record of this wagon in the 1890 list of special class wagons.

Swivel Bar Wagon – Diagram 14

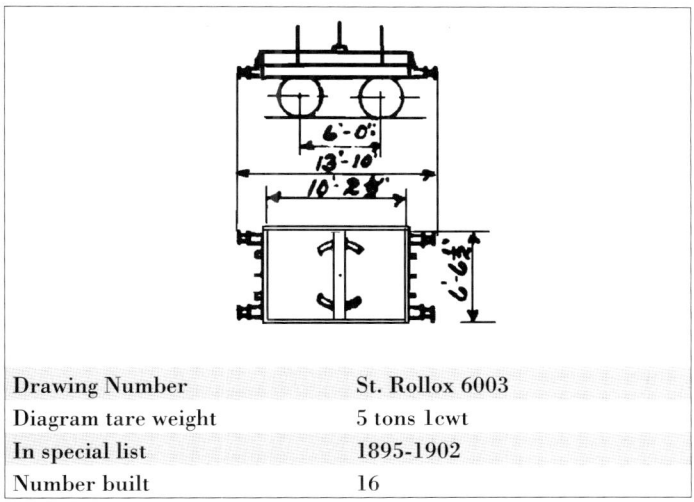

Drawing Number	St. Rollox 6003
Diagram tare weight	5 tons 1cwt
In special list	1895-1902
Number built	16

The swivel timber design to Diagram 14 was modified to carry a 12-ton load. Sixteen wagons were allocated numbers in the special wagon series, where they were described as swivel bar wagons. Four appeared in the special wagons list in 1895, numbered 47-50. A photograph of number 49 appears overleaf. In the 1902 list the remainder were recorded, numbered 58-69.

The wagons had larger axle journals than the general traffic equivalents and fifteen-leaf springs. This allowed the increased capacity. The solebars were not 'flitched' and stanchions were not fitted to the bolsters.

There is no record of their authorisation in company minutes, or in the St. Rollox wagon orders; this leads to the conclusion that they were probably modified general service wagons, which were built in considerable numbers at the time. They were originally allocated to St. Rollox, but the *1915 Appendix* does not list them with a specific base.

Number 63 was replaced by a Diagram 117 implement wagon in 1918.

16 Ton Heavy Weight Wagon – Diagram 49

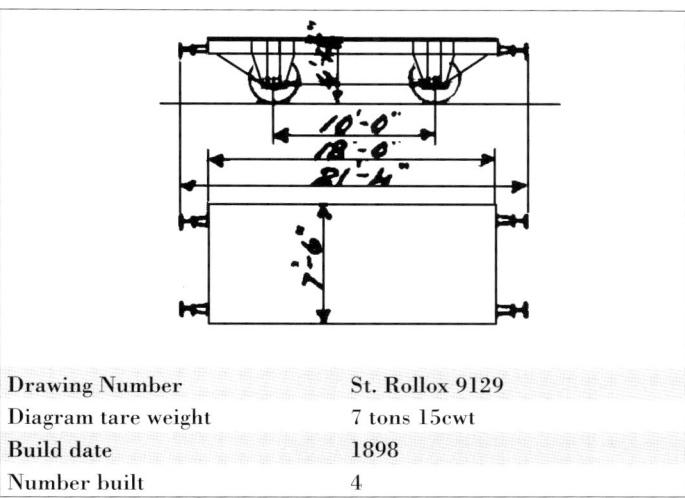

Drawing Number	St. Rollox 9129
Diagram tare weight	7 tons 15cwt
Build date	1898
Number built	4

Diagram 49 comprised wagons numbered 54-57, built to order G168. They were authorised as part of the renewal programme for the half year ending January 1899.[2] They were built on steel channel underframes, surmounted by a wood floor. The McIntosh patent brake was fitted, and standard wagon buffers. The axle box journals were 12 inches by 5 inches with fifteen-leaf heavy duty springs, fitted to plate axle guards. They were based at St. Rollox. A photograph of number 54 appears overleaf.

References
1. NRM 8045/W RHP 69182
2. NRS BR/CAL/5/11 entry 323

Plate 15.14

A Diagram 14 design swivel bar wagon in the special fleet. Compared with the general traffic version (see Plate 8.12) the solebars are not flitched, and the ironwork securing the buffers to the solebars is differently shaped. The running gear is heavier to allow a 50 per cent greater load. The company initials are slightly too large for the body plank and overlap the curb rail. The axle guards show both straight and curved bridles.

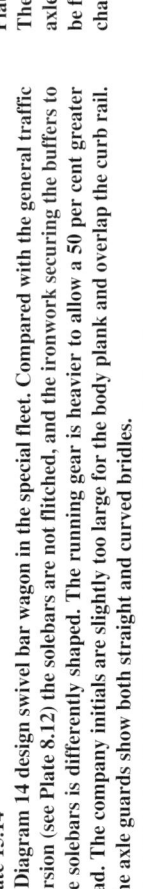

Plate 15.15

The first of four heavy weight wagons built to Diagram 49 in 1898. It has plate axle guards and oil axleboxes. The axle guards are tied to each other and the solebars. It was one of the first wagons to be fitted with the McIntosh patent brake. The V-hanger is bolted through wood packing pieces in the channel solebar. There are no company initials or load lettering.

Plate 15.17

This Diagram 4 van uses the same lettering style as the pre-diagram book vehicles. The word 'VAN' is centred in the space available, not offset to the right.

Plate 15.16

This is the second of the pre-diagram book gunpowder vans. The construction is typical of the 1860s and 1870s. The first style of cast number plate has been added later. The tare and load are written on the edge of the floor. The depot lettering exhibits an early example of grocer's apostrophe. The 'GUNPOWDER VAN' lettering was repeated on the later wooden vans. The G and O are condensed and not based on the shape of the C in the company initials.

15.6: Gunpowder Vans

Pre-Diagram Book Design

The possibility of carrying gunpowder was first considered in 1858, when the General Committee turned down a proposal from the Military Storekeeper in Edinburgh for its conveyance in boxes of from one to two tons each. The minute recorded that

'The Manager recommends this to be declined and that the Government should provide their own powder van for Scotland, to be conveyed at reasonable rates of carriage, say 1s per mile to include the return journey.'[1]

The one shilling rate was agreed at a committee meeting later in 1858, with the note that the government was providing vans,[2] but the Military Storekeeper was not to be denied. In July 1864 a minute records that the Board of Directors, after reading a letter from him, had ordered a powder van.[3] The van was recorded in the 1865 rolling stock return. It was joined by another in 1867. This addition is not mentioned in the minutes.

There are no early drawings in the St. Rollox register, so one must assume that the vans were built by an outside contractor. However, there is no record of a tender process for them. Perhaps the first wagons were taken over from the government. The two vans sufficed for traffic until 1889 when a minute stated that three new vans should be constructed.[4] The estimated cost was £170.

The two original vans were still in use, and number 2 was freshly painted for the occasion, when the *Register of Wagon Plant* was compiled in 1900. Their capacity was five tons. The underframe and floor was made of wood. The body and roof were of riveted metal construction. There was a single door on each side. Each pair of wooden end posts was attached to their opposite numbers by long reinforcing rods. Early Metropolitan Carriage & Wagon Co. style carriage buffers and a push rod-operated wooden brake were fitted.

The vans were not replaced by the early lots of Diagram 78 vans, because they were still in traffic in 1910, described as *'five ton Gunpowder Vans.'*[5] The *1915 Appendix* does not give details of the different gunpowder wagons, although vans with numbers 1 and 2 were still part of the series. Their withdrawal date cannot be ascertained, but it is possible that they survived until the final Diagram 78 vans were built in 1922

Gunpowder Van Load 6 Tons – Diagram 4

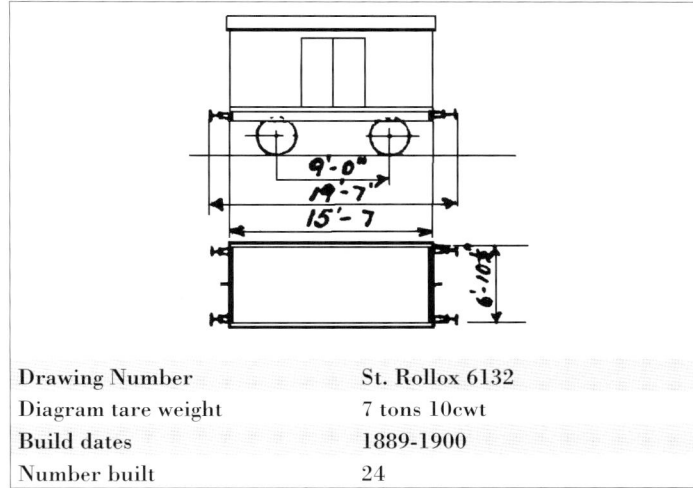

Drawing Number	St. Rollox 6132
Diagram tare weight	7 tons 10cwt
Build dates	1889-1900
Number built	24

As mentioned above, three new vans were built in 1889. The company modified the standard Diagram 3 goods van for the purpose. The body sides and ends were lined internally with lead

Plate 15.18
The final design of gunpowder van to Diagram 78, one of twenty-five built by Hurst Nelson in 1922. The C in the 18-inch company initials is an unusual shape which echoes the extended style used on the bogie coal wagons. The blank space which forms the C is larger than usual and the ends are angled rather than horizontal. The special purpose lettering follows a similar style to previous vans, but the letter strokes are much lighter and the initial letters are larger than the rest. This latter feature also applies to the load and depot lettering.

sheet at 4lbs per square foot. The floor was lined with lead at 6lbs per square foot, fixed with copper nails ¾ inch long.[6] This increased the diagram tare by nearly a ton. The first three vans were classed as additions in the rolling stock returns.

Nine more vans were built in lots of three each between 1892 and the half year ending January 1896. They were treated as renewals.[7] The return of 1895 noted that six covered vans had been transferred to gunpowder traffic. This accounted for the two lots of three built in 1892 and 1894. The three built in 1895 allegedly replaced three gunpowder vans, but in fact they did not, because the two old vans remained in traffic. The 1895 order must have been treated as renewals for ordinary covered vans.

At first gunpowder vans did not have a number series of their own. If they were numbered at all, they must have been included in the general goods and merchandise series. There is no record of them among the special class wagons until the *January 1894 Working Timetable Appendix*. In this listing, the first two vans were numbered 36 and 37 after the furniture van wagons and lettered 'Steps Road when empty.' The first six Diagram 4 vans were numbered 38-43, lettered 'Harburn when empty.'

In the January 1895 Appendix a separate number series for gunpowder vans was introduced. Vans 1 and 2 were lettered 'Steps Road.' Numbers 3-10 were lettered for Harburn, and number 11 was empty to Stevenston. By May 1896 vans 12-14 had been added to the Stevenston allocation.

A further twelve vans were authorised in 1897. The renewal programme for the half year ending January 1898 included six powder wagons and a further six as part of an amended order for covered vans.[8] The original St. Rollox drawing (Figure 9.5, p. 156) was annotated for the horizontally planked style of body, which was applied at the same time to the Diagram 3 vans. The first six were built to G158 and the last formed part of order G159, which was also for 36 Diagram 3 vans built to the new body style. This brought the total of gunpowder vans to twenty-six.

At the start of the twentieth century the records are contradictory. The *1900 Register* has the two iron vans and a further twenty-seven vans described as '*wood lined with lead.*' It illustrates the modern type with a photograph of number 18, which was built to G158. The *May 1902 Working Timetable Appendix* gives the numbers as 1-14 as in 1895, plus 30-35, also lettered for Stevenston. This only accounts for twenty wagons in total. It seems to ignore the vans built to G158, but includes those that were part of the amended order to G159.

Gunpowder Van – Diagram 78

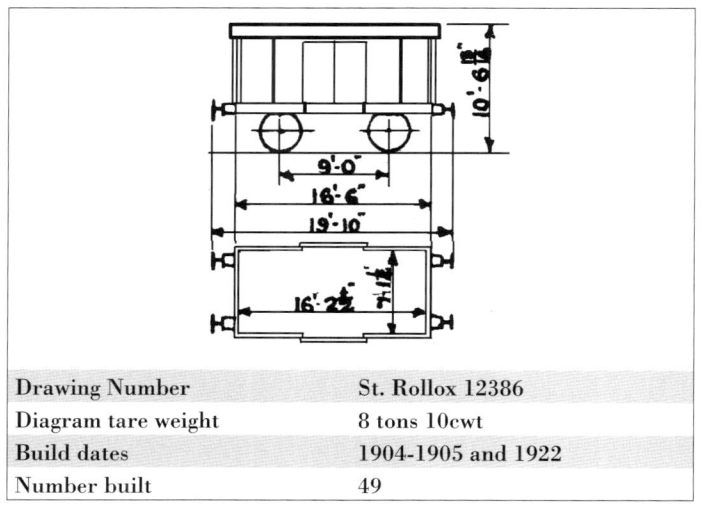

Drawing Number	St. Rollox 12386
Diagram tare weight	8 tons 10cwt
Build dates	1904-1905 and 1922
Number built	49

Diagram 78 vans looked similar to the well-known GWR 'iron mink.' The drawing described the vans as '⅛in plate steel with wooden lining.' They were fitted with oil lubricated 8-inch by 4½-inch axle boxes and Morton either side brakes. The springs with four leaves were unusually light for a Caledonian wagon, and again resembled the GWR running gear. Twelve were authorised in the renewal programme for the half year ending July 1904 to order G216.[9] A further twelve were authorised in the next half year, to order G223.[10]

There is no record of these vans in the rolling stock returns. The *October 1906 Working Timetable Appendix* lists thirty-five vans. It looks as if thirteen of the Diagram 4 vans were withdrawn, or perhaps converted back to goods vans. In 1906 the allocations were as shown in the table below. The only change in the *1915 Appendix* was that numbers 1 and 2 had joined 34 and 35 at Cambuslang.

Van Numbers	Location
1, 2	Steps Road
3-10	Harburn
11-33	Stevenston
34, 35	Cambuslang

The stock remained the same until April 1922, when a minute from the Traffic Committee read:

'*The Chief Goods Manager has recommended that 25 additional Gunpowder Vans should be constructed. The Directors have already authorised the construction of 32 Gunpowder Vans under the renewal programme on the understanding that construction should not begin without special instruction from the Board. The General Manager recommends that 25 of the 32 should be constructed. The Locomotive Superintendent feels that it might be cheaper by an outside firm.*'[11]

A Loco & Stores Committee minute in May[12] recorded that Hurst Nelson was awarded the contract for twenty-five vans. An example is in the Scottish Railway Preservation Society collection, bearing the number 57.

References
3. NRS BR/CAL/1/11 entry 1862
4. NRS BR/CAL/1/11 entry 1987
5. NRS BR/CAL/1/13 entry 1825
6. NRS BR/CAL/1/33 entry 600
7. NRS BR/CAL/4/134 p. 6
8. Annotations on wagon drawing 6132
9. NRS BR/CAL/1/35 entry 827, NRS BR/CAL/1/38 entry 77, NRS BR/CAL/1/38 entry 602
10. NRS BR/CAL/1/40 entry 1484
11. NRS BR/CAL/1/48 entry 691
12. NRS BR/CAL/1/49 entry 769, NRS BR/CAL/1/50 entry 217
13. NRS BR/CAL/1/79 entry 246
14. NRS BR/CAL/1/79 entry 424

Opposite Page: Plate 16.1
Brake van number 268 was built to drawing 1448 or its Metropolitan C & W Co. predecessor. The 12-inch company initials are in the standard position for brake vans – centred in the void left in the body by the verandah opening. The painted number is displaced upwards from the horizontal centre line of the body by the handrail. The allocation, assumed to be Bothwell, is just visible on the bottom framing. If there is a number painted on the end, it must be below the verandah opening.

Chapter 16
Goods and Mineral Brake Vans
16.1: Four-Wheeled Brake Vans and Wagons

Brake vans were classed as service vehicles, because they were not revenue earning rolling stock. They were numbered in a separate series. In the nineteenth century the Caledonian seems to have made a distinction between brake vans for goods and mineral service. Some St. Rollox orders were described as *'goods and mineral'* (G8, 35, 63 and 164). Orders G47, 48, 110, 123 and 135 were *'goods'*. Order G90 was described as *'mineral'* in the order list and in the company minutes concerning its authorisation.[1] A similar distinction between 'goods' and 'mineral' was made with locomotives.

The mineral connotation may have been used specifically for the heavier 14-ton vans to Diagram 5. When the earlier Diagram 6 vans were weighted up to 14 tons, the distinction became redundant. By the time that the wagon diagram book was complied in the early 1900s, all brake vans were simply described as *'goods'*.

Van numbers steadily grew as traffic increased. For instance, in 1851, the minutes reported a

'Deficiency of brake vans for goods trains. 5 additional necessary to ensure 1 per train. Order construction of 5 after due advertisement.'[2]

(Continued on page 246)

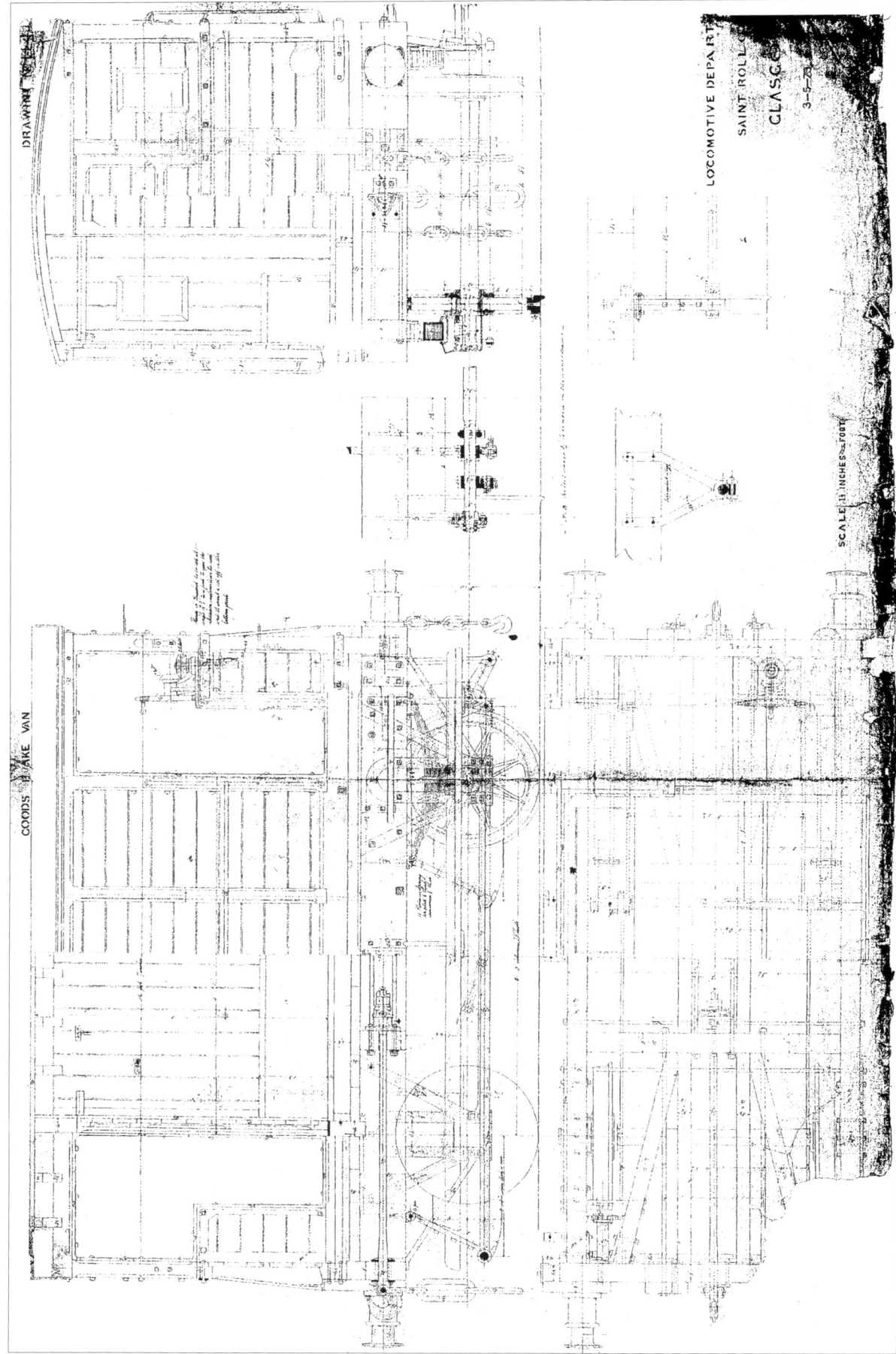

Figure 16.1
St. Rollox drawing 1448 of 1873 is the same as a Metropolitan Cammell drawing issued three years previously. Heavy self-contained buffers are fitted. Note the wooden brake blocks operating on the left-hand side of the wheel in each case.

16.1: FOUR-WHEELED BRAKE VANS AND WAGONS

ABOVE: Plate 16.2
This wonderful picture comes courtesy of CRA member Michael Dunn. Starting with the brake van, it is another example built to drawing 1448. Comparing it with Plate 16.1, the company initials are separated by a dot, although framing intervenes between the letters. The painter has made extra work for himself by positioning the running number on the plank just below the centre of the body, behind the handrail. The number on the end is painted just under the arc of the roof. The two hand cranes effecting the rescue vary in construction. The Forfar crane on the left is on a four-wheeled underframe with heavy duty axleboxes and springs. It is fitted with a wooden brake, actuated by a pushrod. Unusually for this type of brake, the lever is suspended from a V-hanger, causing the pushrod to take up a sharp angle to the brake block. The buffers with the ornate base are the style of locomotive and tender buffers fitted by Benjamin Conner. Under magnification, the cast letters on the counterweight box probably read 'CRAVENS CO. / LIMITED / MANCHESTER' on three lines. The fourth line seems to carry a date. This crane's jib is made of iron, whereas the Perth crane to the right has a wooden octagonal jib, with cast iron fittings at top and bottom. The Perth crane is carried on a six-wheeled underframe with solid buffers. The axle guards are fitted inside the solebars. This underframe also has heavy duty springs and journals. The underframe is reinforced by two transverse I-section girders at each end. It has no brake gear. The counterweight box carries the crane's identification. The company initials are properly separated by a dot. Presumably 'S.C SECTION' stands for South(ern) Central.

RIGHT: Plate 16.3
J Bruce was allocated van number 308, one of the second type of pre-diagram book brake vans, dating from 1875. The number is centred on the bottom framing, avoiding the framing on the body side. The left-hand element of the depot lettering has been compressed and the right-hand extended in a partially successful attempt to produce a symmetrical effect. Three-bolt self-contained buffers are fitted. A rail extends across the verandah opening in the end. Both this and brake van 268 have handrails on the roof.

(Continued from page 243)

The early rolling stock returns show the following progression. In each case, the period ends on 31st January.

Year	1853	1855	1857	1859	1861	1863	1865
Vans	21	32	36	46	70	95	121

The 1865 stock included thirty-two vans taken over with the Scottish Central Railway. The census in November 1867 recorded 204 vans, including thirteen taken over with the Scottish North Eastern. In that year the spelling on the returns changed to '*brake*' although it did not always do so in the minutes.

The picture from 1868 up to 1890 is set out in the table below. A division is made in 1883 as this was when the first Drummond-designed brake van to Diagram 6 was introduced. The early vans had been more or less all replaced, and a large number of new vans were built.

Period	1868-1883		1884-1889	
	Replace	New	Replace	New
Vans	130	166	34	15

From 1890 until the end of the returns in 1912, the picture is of large scale renewal and rather fewer additions. There were 530 vans on the system in 1900, according to the *Register of Wagon Plant*. The stock of vans peaked at 596 in the year ending July 1908, reducing to 578 in July 1910.[3] The stock of vans increased during the First World War and its aftermath. In 1922 a *Railway Gazette* article reported that there were 647 vans.[4]

Period	1890-1899		1900-1912	
	Replace	New	Replace	New
Vans	103	115	214	58

Pre-Diagram Book Designs

Early CR drawings of brake vans have not survived. Numbers include 152 (an open van), 168, 247, and 1015 (for a brake wagon). Drawings 718 and 1448 date from 1872 and 1873 respectively. They were dimensionally identical, according to Miller. The length over buffers was 14 feet 6 inches and width 7 feet 6 inches. Wheels were 3 feet 1½ inches diameter. The axle guards were outside the solebars. They were fitted with the early four-bolt self-contained buffers and safety chains. Wood brake blocks, operated from a single stanchion, acted on all wheels. The axle guards were tied to each other and the van solebars.

The surviving drawing 1448[5] was used for the contract that the North of England Wagon Company won in 1873 to supply twenty-five Goods Break vans at £192 10s each.[6] The design was the same as that from a Metropolitan Carriage & Wagon Co.'s drawing[7] in 1870, when four vans were supplied.

According to the stock returns, ninety-five brake vans were built between July 1870 and July 1874, twenty-seven of which were renewals. If the minutes record all the outside contractors' contributions, fifty-eight vans were built at St. Rollox. It is reasonable to assume that the Caledonian took the Metropolitan design and redrew it for its own and subsequent contractor's use. Known numbers are 8, 248[8] and 268. When photographed after the First World War, 248 had been fitted with Westinghouse pipes and possibly the continuous brake.

The 1870 vans were only rated at 10 tons, which was beginning to be too light for the growing traffic demands. In 1875, an 18-ton van was proposed (St. Rollox drawing 1723), but the design was not implemented, and the drawing has not survived.

The next type of van was to Metropolitan drawing 2313,[9] which was rather larger and heavier (14 tons) at 16 feet over buffers on a 9-foot 6-inch wheelbase. The axle guards were fitted inside the solebar, and the first three-bolt buffer was fitted. The design dated from 1875.

In the years up to the end of 1883, when the first Drummond design appeared, Metropolitan supplied twenty-four vans in 1875[10] and a further thirty the year after.[11] Pickering tendered successfully for fifteen vans to be delivered by March 1878.[12] The returns record the construction of 169 new and renewal vans over the period, suggesting that once again, St. Rollox built the remainder of the vans to the same design. Known numbers are 308 and 339. The latter van was lettered 'EDINBURGH GOODS'.[13]

These two types of van were still in use into the twentieth century, if only on branch line duties. They were superseded by the 15-ton brakes constructed under the wagon renewal programme and other Drummond era brake vans displaced from the heaviest traffic by the six wheeled brakes.

Common Design Aspects of Post-1882 Vans

Like the manufacture of cattle wagons, supplies from outside contractors ceased after Drummond's arrival, with the exception of the Clayton & Shuttleworth contract for Diagram 63 vans in 1920.

All the post 1882 four-wheeled brake vans had similar basic dimensions – 16 feet 3 inches long on a 9-foot wheelbase. The twelve-leaf springs were 5 feet long between suspension points. Originally

Plate 16.4
This is a Diagram 6 van, lettered 'LIVE STOCK ST. ROLLOX' just above the hand rail. Its number on a cast plate is 194, displaced to the right by the running board support. The upper ends of these vans were unique among Caledonian brakes in that they were slightly raked back. The very short upper foot boards were also unique to these vans.

Plate 16.5
The raking of the ends is much more evident in this picture of the other body style of Diagram 6 van. The company initials are separated by a dot because they occupy the same uninterrupted space. This time, the cast number plate is on the vertical centre line; the running board support is displaced to the right. The number on the end is on the first full plank from the top, between the windows. The interior partitions are fully panelled.

grease axleboxes were fitted, but later order numbers had oil boxes. Open spoke wheels were fitted to early vehicles. Vans were 8 feet 7½ inches wide with side lookouts and 7 feet 5½ inches without. Heights varied, but part of the variation was attributable to the difference in wheel diameter.

Goods Brake Van – Diagram 6

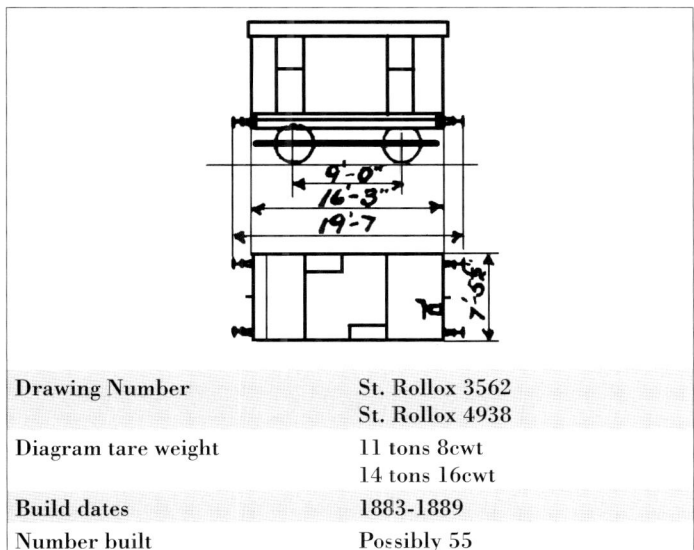

Drawing Number	St. Rollox 3562
	St. Rollox 4938
Diagram tare weight	11 tons 8cwt
	14 tons 16cwt
Build dates	1883-1889
Number built	Possibly 55

The Diagram 6 vans are discussed first because they pre-dated the Diagram 5 design. Diagram 6 vans had panelled bodies. The first style of Diagram 3 goods vans shared the panelled construction and main dimensions of the brake vans when the design was introduced two years later.

The brake vans had enclosed verandahs with windows in the ends. Standard wagon buffers and three-link couplings were fitted. The open spoke wheels were 3 feet 2 inches diameter. The original weight was increased to conform with the weight of the Diagram 5 vans by adding ballast to the underframe.

One school of thought suggests that van number 383 in Plate 16.5 represents a rebuild of the original body. It might also be a parallel body style, as exhibited in the two different bodies of the Diagram 3 goods vans, although the goods vans did not change style until 1897, after construction of the brake vans had ceased.

The information from the rolling stock returns states that fifty-five goods brake vans were built between the periods ending January 1884 and July 1889, forty of them as replacements. This does not entirely reconcile with the St. Rollox order records, particularly order G6, which was for twenty heavy goods brakes. The heavier version of Diagram 6 was introduced in 1886, after this order had been executed and appeared in the January and July 1886 returns. The possible source of order G6 is discussed further in the next paragraphs describing the Diagram 5 vans.

Goods Brake Van – Diagram 5

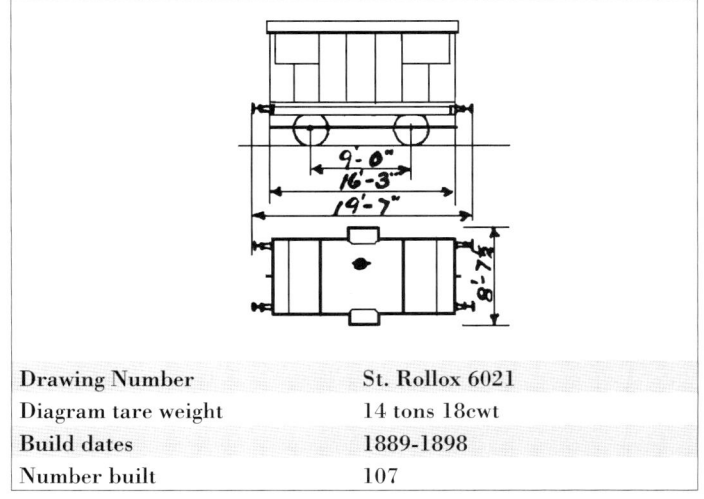

Drawing Number	St. Rollox 6021
Diagram tare weight	14 tons 18cwt
Build dates	1889-1898
Number built	107

Diagram 5 vans were built to a panelled design similar to Diagram 6. They and their Diagram 45 successors were the only CR brakes with side lookouts.

LEFT: Plate 16.6
The number of this Diagram 5 van is indecipherable, although the allocation to Polmadie is clear. The buffer in the foreground belongs to *Cardean*. The oil lamp fitted to the lookout echoes the arrangement in passenger brake vans, and is not shown on the drawing.

BELOW AND FACING PAGE: Figure 16.2
This is the St. Rollox drawing for the Diagram 5 van. The brake arrangement was the same as for Diagram 6. This was the only design of CR van with a horizontal brake wheel.

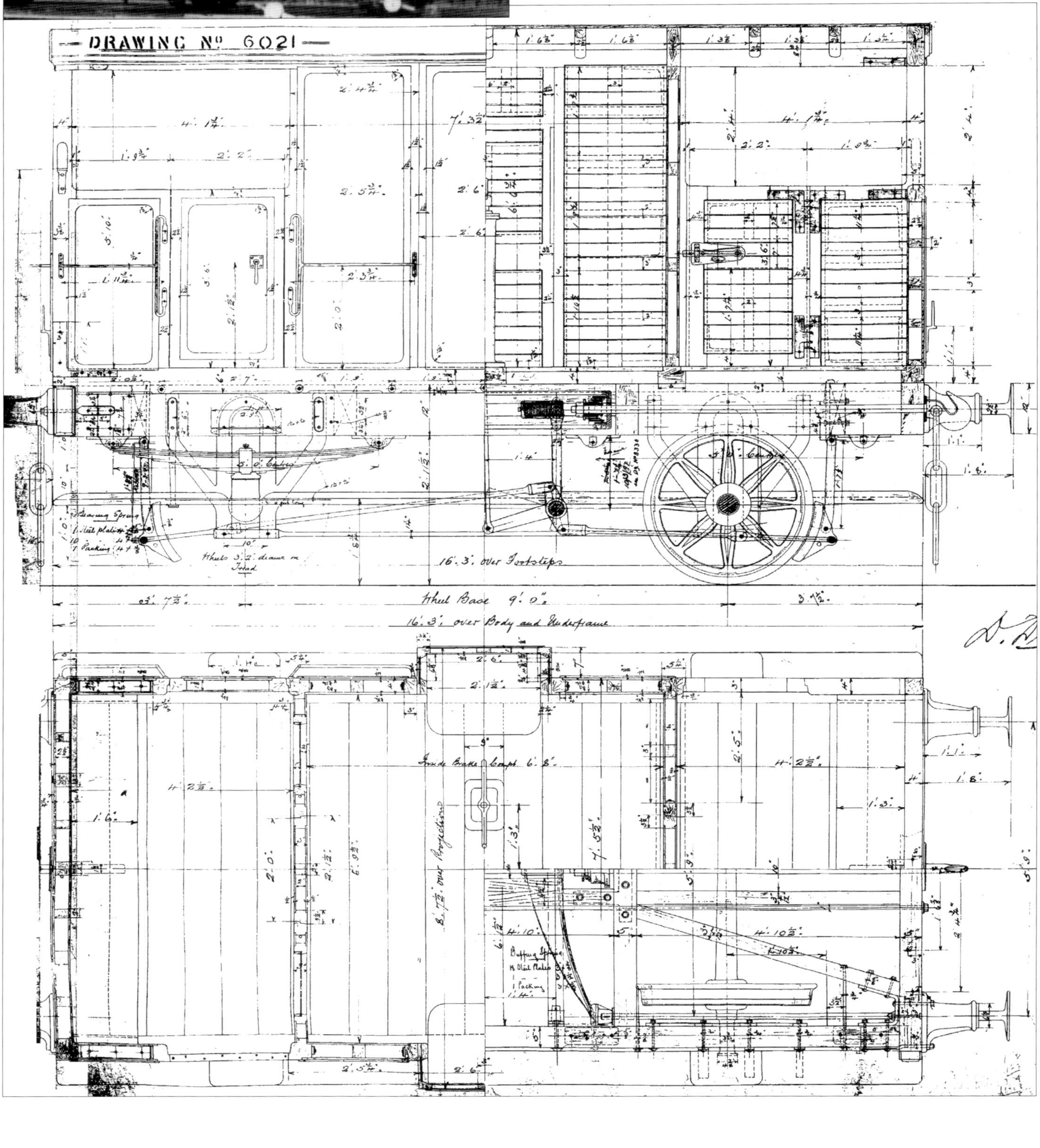

RIGHT: Plate 16.7
Diagram 45 van number 496 was allocated to Buchanan Street and the brakesman was A Simpson. The company initials look heavy and clumsily painted. The number is repeated on the ends above the verandah opening. An oil lamp is incorporated in the lookout. The brake wheels on each verandah are just visible, proving that it is not a van to the predecessor Diagram 5. The two subsequent designs also had this feature.

Orders G90 and G110 were built in 1892/93.[14] The authority for G90 refers to *Mineral Brake Vans as per the 14 ton vans built some years ago by Pickering & Co.*' although there are no such vans in the surviving Pickering building records. It is possible that Pickering fulfilled St. Rollox order G6, which was for twenty heavy goods brake vans, although the minutes do not record a tendering process. The surviving Pickering records start in 1888, several years after order G6 was built.

Whether for the increased weight or other reasons, this design was considered to be an important development. The minute noted General Manager James Thompson's request *'I shall feel obliged by you having one of this class of vans brought down to Buchanan Street for my inspection.'*[15]

Goods Brake Van – Diagram 45

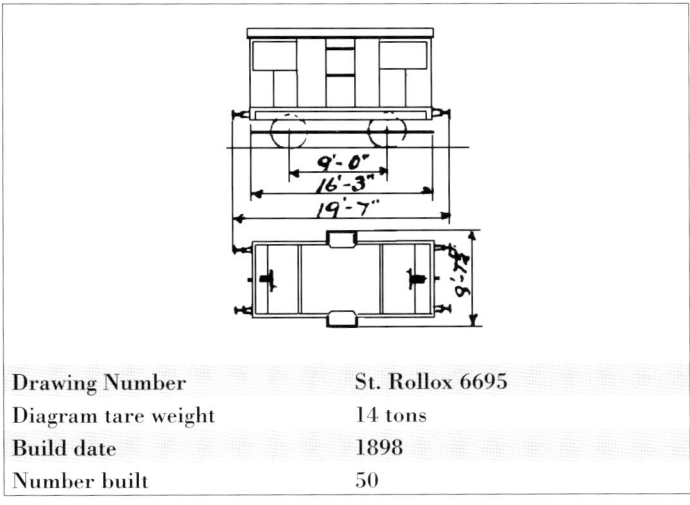

Drawing Number	St. Rollox 6695
Diagram tare weight	14 tons
Build date	1898
Number built	50

In December 1897 the minutes recorded a proposal for fifty goods and mineral brake vans costed for single (price £150) and double brake handles (£155).[16] The result was the Diagram 45 van, built to order G164. The rolling stock returns show that they were charged to the capital account.

The design was a modification of Diagram 5 with brake wheels on each verandah, rather than a single wheel in the centre of the cabin. Length and width were the same as Diagram 5. The modification justified a new diagram number. A Diagram 5 drawing (6695) was annotated for the modification. Drawing 6658, which showed the alterations to the brake gear, has not survived. The vans were horizontally planked, unlike their panelled successors.

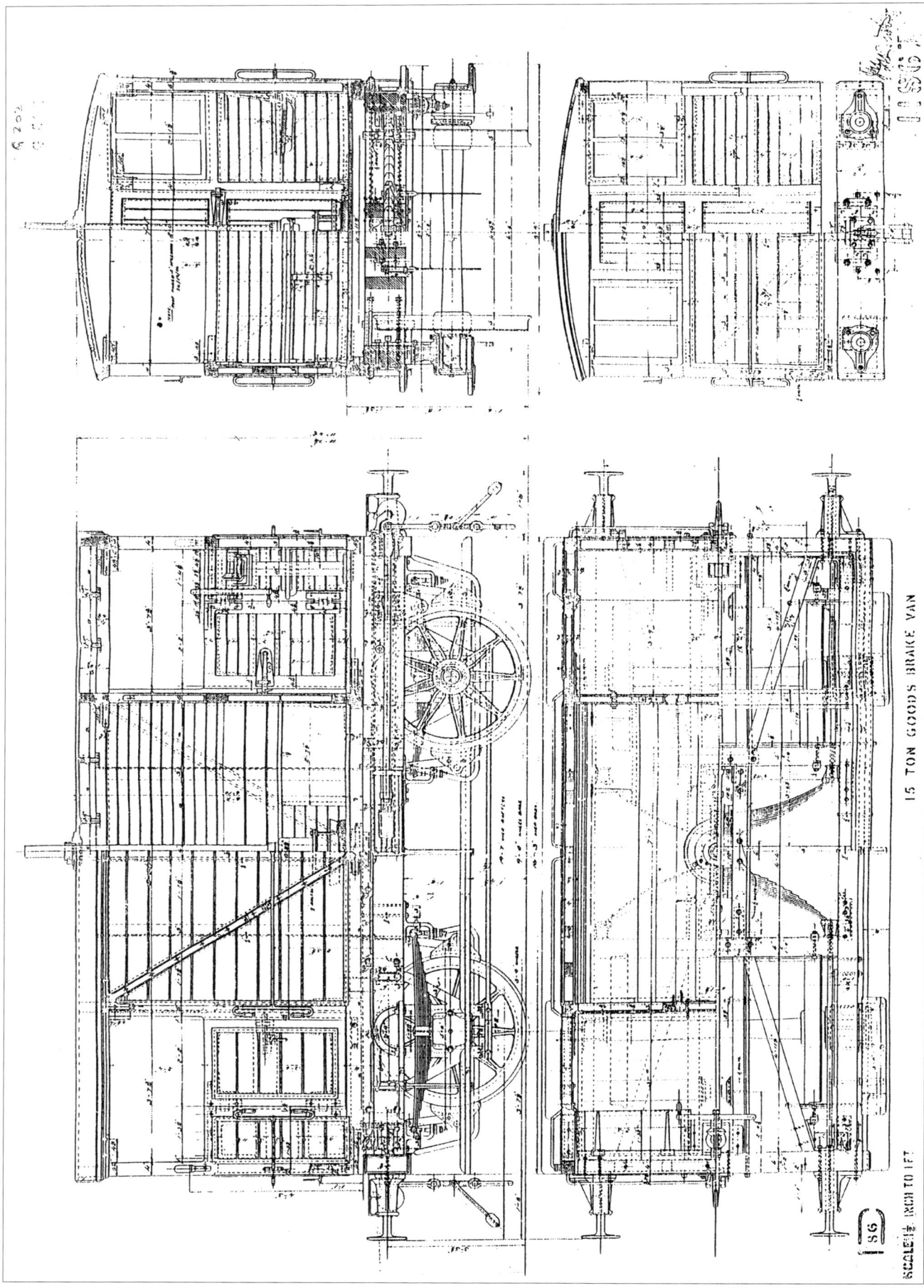

Figure 16.3
The twentieth-century style of brake van was ushered in by Diagram 62. Screw couplings, oil axleboxes and clasp brakes were also introduced with this design. St. Rollox drawing 11867 shows wheels with nine open spokes. Wagon buffers fitted with steps are specified for no apparent reason. The door to the cabin is vertically boarded. A photograph in the January 1938 *Model Railway News* shows a panelled version.

RIGHT: Plate 16.8
Diagram 62 vans were rarely photographed. Here is CR 355 in early LM&SR livery with the running number enclosed by a scalloped panel in Midland Railway style.

15 Ton Goods Brake Van – Diagram 62

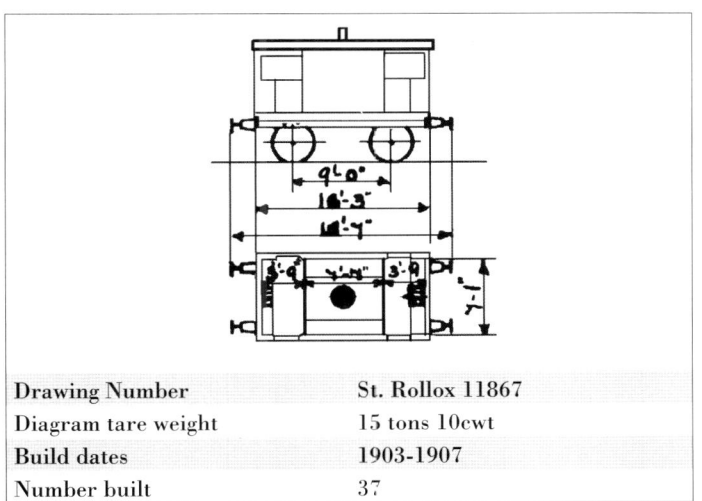

Drawing Number	St. Rollox 11867
Diagram tare weight	15 tons 10cwt
Build dates	1903-1907
Number built	37

The Diagram 62 vans were built in five lots. They were all charged to revenue as renewals, although numbers such as 576 and 578 in the table below suggest otherwise.[17] Wheels were 3 feet 9 inches diameter and had nine open spokes according to the works drawing. Another drawing (St. Rollox 14768,[18] dated 25th November 1908, after the last lot was built) shows three-hole 3-foot 9-inch disc wheels. Oil boxes, screw couplings and the standard wagon buffer with a step cast on top were fitted. The 5-foot springs were suspended on J-hangers.

Some known numbers, allocations and weights are given in the table below. The information originates from various sources – brakesman's journals, accident reports, LM&SR photographs and eyewitness records.

Combination Goods and Brake Van – Diagram 104

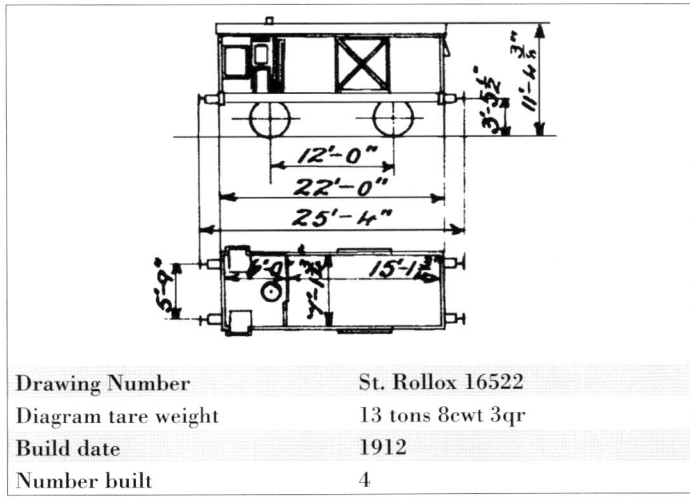

Drawing Number	St. Rollox 16522
Diagram tare weight	13 tons 8cwt 3qr
Build date	1912
Number built	4

The Diagram 104 vans were road vans like Diagram 91, but different in concept and design. They were similar to combined brake and parcels vans used on some branch lines of the London & South Western Railway. Nearer home, the Highland Railway six-wheeled brake vans performed a similar function.

They were said to have been originally designed to work on the Callander & Oban, but this seems unlikely, as the C&O's needs were adequately met by the four vans to Diagram 91. They were later used on services to Crieff. This is substantiated by the only known photograph of one of these vans, which shows it at Lochearnhead, on the line from Balquhidder on the C&O to Crieff and beyond. The photograph was taken at the end of 1922 or not much later, as the van is attached to a very clean Class '191' 4-6-0. This class was built

Number	Home Depot	Tare
37		
105	St. Rollox	16 tons 10cwt
189		
355		
465	Motherwell	14 tons 8cwt
472	Larbert	13 tons 10cwt
473	St. Rollox	
576	St. Rollox	14 tons 18cwt
578	St. Rollox	14 tons 18cwt

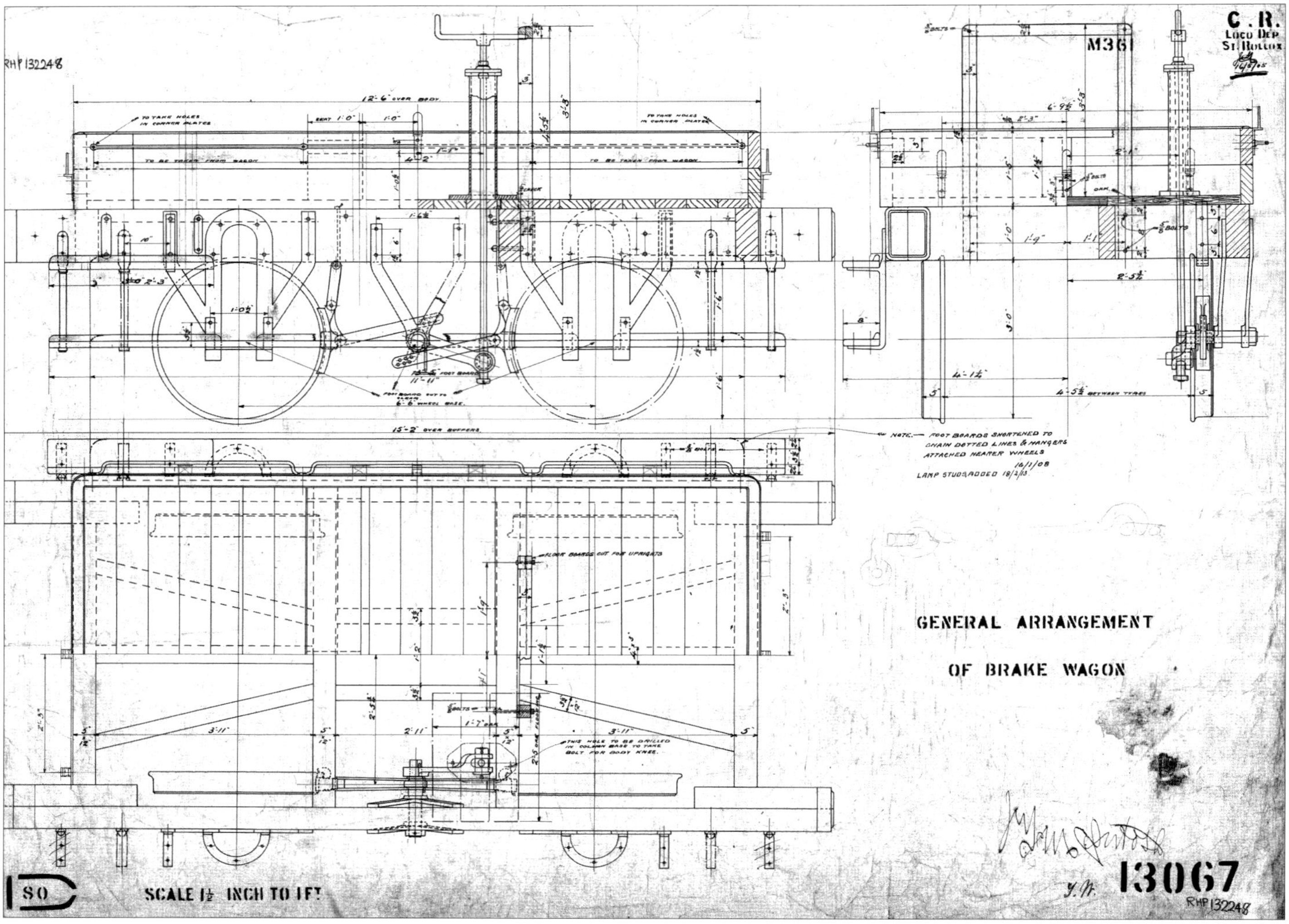

Figures 16.4 (Above) **and 16.5** (Below)
The drawing for the first of two types of open brake wagon dates from 1905. It shows a conversion rather like the 'pug tenders' discussed in Chapter 17. The second drawing, St. Rollox 17113, shows a more refined version with sprung buffers.

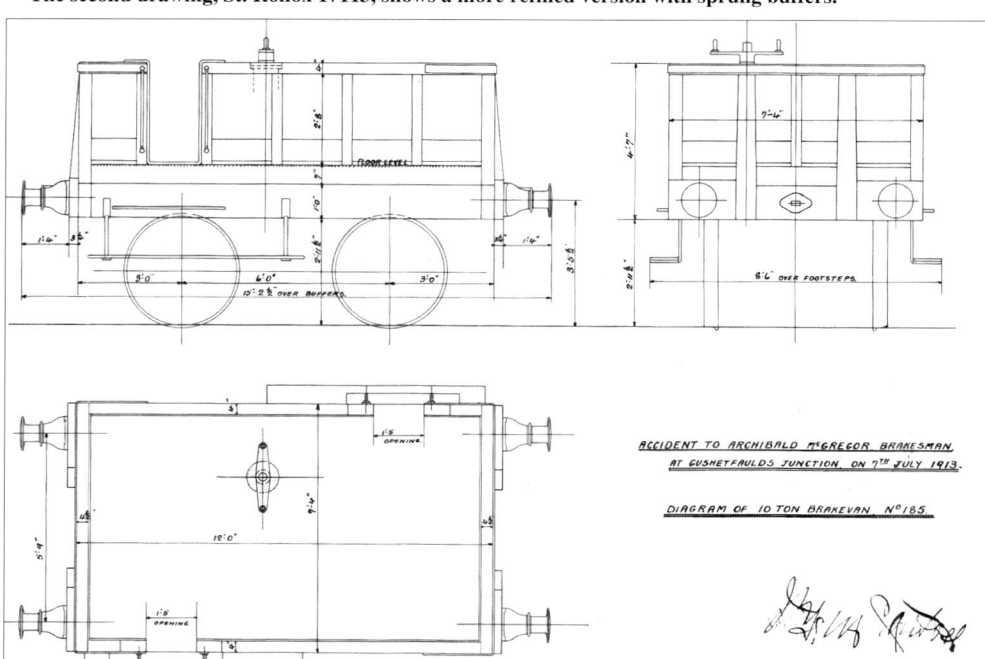

Facing Page: Plate 16.9
The only known picture of one of the four Diagram 104 combination goods and brake vans built in 1912. The tender belongs to a Class '191' 4-6-0. The location is said to be Lochearnhead, on the line linking Balquhidder by way of Crieff with the main line from Perth to Aberdeen. There is no sign of an allocation. The tone of the end strongly suggests that it was painted vermilion, but the lookout end is red oxide.

at the very end of the Caledonian's existence.

The vans looked like the outside framed version of a Diagram 67 van with a guard's compartment added. The compartment had lookouts each side and two end windows. It was fitted with a stove. The wheels were 3-foot 6-inch discs. The 4-foot springs were suspended on J-hangers. Heavy duty wagon buffers and three-link couplings were fitted.

There was one sliding door each side. The non-guard's end had a ventilator and drop flap like the Diagram 67 vans. Illumination in the merchandise section came from an oil lamp, with another over the guard's compartment. There was a continuous footboard at axlebox level, like all brake vans. Access to the roof was by a ladder at the guard's end. The merchandise section was just over half the size of the Diagram 91 vans.

They were not equipped with a continuous brake, but had the usual guards van arrangement for applying two brake blocks to each wheel. Obviously, they travelled at the rear of the train. Livery would have been red oxide. The photograph strongly suggests that the brake end was vermilion, but the merchandise end may have been red oxide. They, like the Diagram 91 road vans, were built as part of the renewal programme.[19] Numbers and scrapping date are not known.

WEST COAST JOINT STOCK BRAKE VANS

Goods traffic between Scotland and England was normally tailed by company brake vans that were exchanged at Carlisle. Six vans were built in 1873 for working one through train each way per day from Perth to London. According to *West Coast Joint Stock*, they were standard 10-ton L&NWR vans. They remained in use until 1895, when the Caledonian deemed their weight insufficient for use on its part of the route.[20]

The stock returns show that two of the vans were absorbed into the Caledonian fleet in the period ending July 1895, but their numbers are unknown. Given the Caley's reservations about them, and the fact that by then CR brake vans weighed 15 tons, they probably did not survive long.

BRAKE WAGONS BUILT FOR SPECIFIC LOCATIONS

While modern vans had a home depot which was painted on the body side, this may not have been the case in the early days of the Caledonian. Some vans were built specifically for certain duties. In the early days, there were drawings for a brake wagon for the Greenock section and a brake van for the Strathaven Branch (St. Rollox 535 and 566). Drawing 1319 in 1872 was for a brake wagon for Wemyss Bay. Finally, in 1885, drawing 4665 was for a brake wagon for Crianlarich quarry. This is the only one of these drawings to have survived, as RHP 68478.

BRAKE WAGONS

As we have seen, open brake wagons were used from an early date. In May 1905, the Traffic Committee ordered the conversion of forty-one low sided wagons into brake wagons to comply with a Board of Trade Order. Apparently, goods trains had been travelling on running lines without a brake van in the rear. This practice contravened the Prevention of Accidents Act.[21]

St. Rollox drawing 13067,[22] dated two weeks after the minute, gives details of the modification. The works order number was M361. The basic dimensions do not accord with any surviving drawing of a flat or low sided wagon. It strongly resembles a 'pug tender' as described in Chapter 17.1.

Brakes were applied to both wheels on one side only, using a conventional brake van stanchion, which was mounted directly above the brake gear. The brakesman stood throughout his journey, with a handrail to grasp for support. An annotation on the drawing concerning the fitting of lamp studs shows that wagons of this type were still in service in 1913.

A different design was also in service in that year, although its date of introduction is not known. St. Rollox drawing 17113[23] depicts brake wagon number 185 which was under the control of Archibald McGregor when he met with an accident at Gushetfaulds Junction on 7th July. This was a more sophisticated wagon, with higher sides and the pre-Drummond four-bolt self-contained sprung buffer.

REFERENCES

1. NRS BR/CAL/5/11 entries 77 and 86
2. NRS BR/CAL/1/10 entry 580
3. NRS BR/CAL/4/134 p. 7
4. *Freight Rolling Stock Distribution on the Caledonian Railway*, reproduced in *The True Line*, issue 73, pp. 8-13
5. Not yet catalogued, currently with The Ballast Trust
6. NRS BR/CAL/1/20 entry 1272
7. Birmingham City Archive ref: 2316
8. *Caledonian Cavalcade* p. 60
9. Birmingham City Archive reference number
10. NRS BR/CAL/1/22 entry 665
11. NRS BR/CAL/1/23 entry 765
12. NRS BR/CAL/1/23 entry 1990
13. *Caledonian Railway Livery*, pp. 288–9.
14. NRS BR/CAL/5/11 entry 77,
    NRS BR/CAL/5/11 entry 107
15. NRS BR/CAL/5/11 entry 86
16. NRS BR/CAL/1/41 entry 133
17. NRS BR/CAL/1/46 entry 1363,
    NRS BR/CAL/1/48 entry 691,
    NRS BR/CAL/1/49 entry 769,
    NRS BR/CAL/1/52 entry 1307,
    NRS BR/CAL/1/53 entry 1151
18. NRM 11937/W
19. NRS BR/CAL/1/61 entry 921
20. *West Coast Joint Stock*, p. 274
21. NRS BR/CAL/1/51 entry 347
22. NRM 11941/W, the NRS plan awaits cataloguing
23. NRM 11940/W, the NRS plan awaits cataloguing

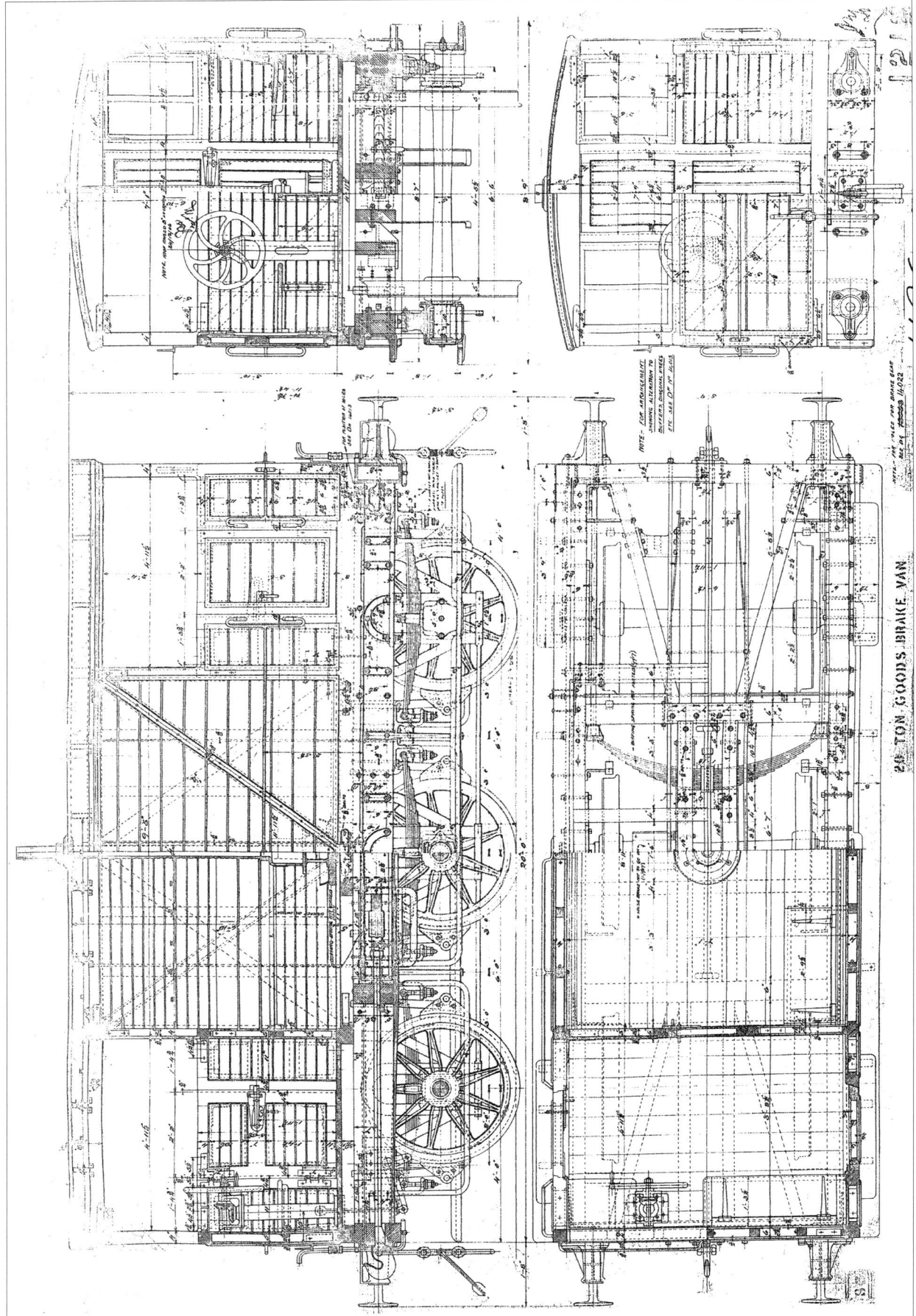

Figure 16.6
The St. Rollox drawing number 12120 of the original style of Diagram 63 van. Nine-spoke wheels and stepped wagon buffers are shown and the van is fitted with the Westinghouse brake, although it was only fitted to the prototype. The brake arrangement was the subject of a separate drawing, number 12063.

16.2: Six-Wheeled Brake Vans

20 Ton Goods Brake Van – Diagram 63

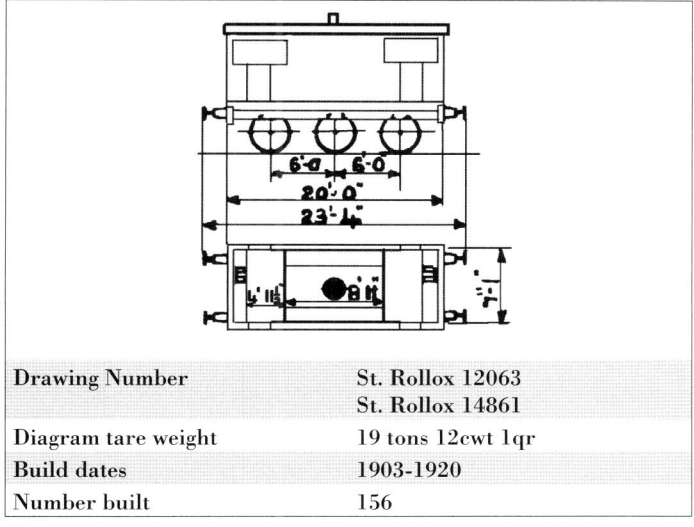

Drawing Number	St. Rollox 12063
	St. Rollox 14861
Diagram tare weight	19 tons 12cwt 1qr
Build dates	1903-1920
Number built	156

Forty six-wheeled vans were authorised to the capital account in the period ending January 1903.[1] They were to be built to lot G210. They were originally to have the Westinghouse brake. The vans were probably intended for use with block trains of 30-ton mineral wagons, but that concept was quickly abandoned, removing the need for vans with continuous brakes. Only the prototype, built in 1904, was Westinghouse fitted. The rest of the order remained unbuilt.

The drawing dated June 1903 (St. Rollox 12063) shows the Westinghouse brake arrangement and is annotated *'for brake arrangement for future [these last two words crossed out] see Drawing 14022 (19/1/07). For vans without w'house brake.'*

On the original drawing, a note dated 24th December 1906 and initialled by McIntosh states that the roof was to be raised 3 inches at the centre. Two other annotations dated 11th January 1907 stated that the Westinghouse brake was not to go on and that alterations were to be made to the buffers and some details of the underframe.

These annotations were in response to a minute of 18th December 1906,[2] when the General Manager asked for authority to proceed with the original order for forty vans, which had been halted with only one built. He received the go-ahead, but only for twenty of the outstanding thirty-nine vans.

The 1903 drawing shows 3-foot 9-inch open spoke wheels like the 15-ton vans, but photographs show three-hole discs. The original body design followed that of the Diagram 62 vans. In effect, Diagram 63 was an enlarged, heavier version of Diagram 62.

After the first batch of twenty-one vans, a further 135 were built as renewals, starting with order G320, authorised in 1912.[3] This order was the first to have the body with heavy outside framing to drawing 14861.[4] This drawing dates from February 1909. The variation in construction echoed the two styles of body built for the Diagram

Left: Plate 16.10
A flush boarded Diagram 63 van, numbered 600. The number suggests that it was one of the twenty built on the capital account in 1907. The company initials are only just visible under the grime. All the other writing is obscured. The number plate is in the more usual location for these vans, but to the left of centre rather than to the right; Plate 16.11 shows another variation in location. Heavy self-contained buffers are fitted in line with the annotation on drawing 12120. Disc wheels are fitted, rather than the spoked type shown on the drawing.

Right: Plate 16.11
This is the publicity photograph of one of the vans built by Clayton & Shuttleworth in 1920, which was published in *The Railway Engineer*. The accompanying text specifically stated that the ends were vermilion, but the photograph shows no variation in tone between end and side. A depot allocation has not yet been assigned, but would be on the bottom horizontal of the outside framing. The number is repeated on the ends immediately below the verandah. The number plate is fitted to the body. The more usual position was on the bottom horizontal frame member to the right of centre, according to eyewitnesses. The sand pipes are prominent.

Plate 16.12
The Diagram 63 van modified for the Callander and Oban line is seen on a southbound train at Connel Ferry. The photograph shows the boarding in of the verandah sides – compare with Plate 16.11. The van is in grubby LM&SR colours, but the class 55 4-6-0 and the 45-foot bogie carriage are still in clean Caledonian livery. All the photographs of this van in traffic show it in this position on passenger trains.

67 merchandise vans. The thirteen vans to order G378 may have been 'replacements of replacements'. They were authorised at the same time as the twenty-five replacement 30-ton coal wagons in 1916.[5] They and the bogie coal wagons may have been sent overseas, according to James McEwan.

The final batch of thirty vans was authorised in 1920[6] and built by Clayton & Shuttleworth. The publicity photograph of number 196 shows that the vans were fitted with sanding gear to the outer wheels. This addition is not documented.

Two photographs of inside framed vans record 600 and 596 – the latter in LM&SR days. The table below lists other known numbers of outside framed 20-ton vans and their home depots.

Number	Home Depot	Tare
193	Carlisle	20 tons 10cwt 1qr
234	Motherwell	
395	Stirling	
400	Perth	19 tons 16cwt
407	Carstairs	19 tons 14cwt
430	Stirling	
432	St. Rollox	19 tons 18cwt 1qr
560	Dundee West	20 tons 1cwt
596	Motherwell	20 tons 7cwt 2qr
659	Grangemouth	
668	Buchanan Street	20 tons 2cwt
671	Hamilton	

Withdrawal dates are unknown; some probably survived into the late 1940s but few if any would have lasted into the 1950s. Clayton-constructed van number 437 is in the Scottish Railway Preservation Society collection after working in colliery service.

Modification for the Callander & Oban Line

By the time that the C&O had reached Tyndrum in 1873, a special 12-ton goods brake van was requested. Heavy braking power was obviously required for Up trains descending Glen Ogle. Approval from the Traffic Committee was recorded,[7] but there are no details of the van in question.

A special design of brake van was again proposed in 1890. St. Rollox drawing 6340, which has not survived, gave the details. Nothing appears to have come of this proposal and there is no reference to it in company minutes. Both this and the previous van would have had four wheels. The decisions to build these vans could, of course, have been taken at officer level.

Later, a Diagram 63 van (one of order number G356, July 1914) had part of the verandahs boarded in and windows fitted to the ends for service on the line. This was the subject of St. Rollox drawing 17431.[8] The reason for enclosing the verandahs is not clear. The drawing, which is of the body only, has the van fitted with a Westinghouse brake pipe.

According to the 1920 C&O number taker's book,[9] brake van 424 was coupled between the locomotive and a 30-ton bogie coal wagon on empty cattle wagon specials. This strongly suggests that it was Westinghouse fitted, making it a candidate for the modified van.

The three photographs of the van in traffic show it coupled between the engine and the first coach of passenger trains. There is no obvious role for it in this position as the need for extra braking power would surely not have been an issue.

References
1. NRS BR/CAL/1/47 entry 464
2. NRS BR/CAL/1/54 entry 209
3. NRS BR/CAL/1/61 entry 921
4. NRM 11938/W
5. NRS BR/CAL/1/67 entry 1010
6. NRS BR/CAL/1/74 entry 876
7. NRS BR/CAL/1/20 entry 1820
8. RHP 68480
9. NRS BR/CAL/5/60

Plate 16.13
This picture of the modified C&O van is included to show the enclosure of the ends. It was taken at Hellifield on the Settle & Carlisle line in the LM&SR era.

Chapter 17
Service Vehicles
17.1: Loco Coal and Ash

Pre-Diagram Book Designs

Originally, loco coal was carried in ordinary mineral wagons. After complaints from the traffic department concerning lack of rolling stock causing insufficient supply, the Traffic Committee decided in December 1871 to provide 500 dedicated loco coal wagons.[1] A 10-ton *'coal wagon for loco dept'* was introduced in 1872, presumably to implement this decision, to St. Rollox drawing 1251.[2] R Y Pickering secured the contract to build the wagons, but delivery was very slow. In July 1872, *'only some had been delivered.'*[3] The situation did not improve much; in March 1873 the Loco & Stores Committee

'Reported that Ms. Pickering & Sons have only delivered 193 wagons to their contract for 500 wagons. Secretary to write complaining of delay in delivery.'[4]

To alleviate the problem, during October and November, 300 ordinary mineral wagons were ordered to be marked as loco coal wagons.[5] Pickering was pursued for the non-delivery of the remaining 105 wagons in January 1874.[6] Later that month it was reported that the delay was caused by a strike in Pickering's smithy.[7] In 1874 St. Rollox issued drawing 1690 for a loco coal wagon.[8]

The January minute was the last record of the Pickering order, but not the end of problems with availability. In February 1875 the Loco & Stores Committee communicated to the Board *'a statement as to the supply of Locomotive Coal and the number of wagons used for that purpose from 18th December 1874 to 30th January 1875.'*[9] In August

'Mr Haig explained the difficulty he had to encounter in getting the necessary supply of coal for locomotive purposes, owing to the very inadequate number of wagons supplied to him for the service. The quantity of coal being received from the pits – in particular those of the Coltness Co. – being not only much short of what might be got but at a higher price than the coal could be given at, were the wagon supply adequate.

'Resolved that Mr Conner be requested to furnish a list of the Company's wagons adopted specially for Locomotive Coal services and that Mr Cook's attention be also at once requested to the subject, so that every effort be made to furnish the requisite number of wagons.'[10]

The minutes do not record any action in response to the problem. There seems to have been a temporary respite, as it was not until October 1877 that the minutes reported:

'Locomotive Coal: Accept S J Claye for 300, 10 ton wagons @ £62 7s 6d. Delivery 15 per week beginning 9th Feb (Strikes excepted)'[11]

Plate 17.1
Many photographs of locomotives show pre-diagram book loco coal wagons in the background. On the coal bench incline here are two loco coal wagons, with the early 6½-inch company initials and numbers. The initials are separated by a square dot. The lettering of wagon 33365 is described in detail on p. 63 (Plate 3.32).

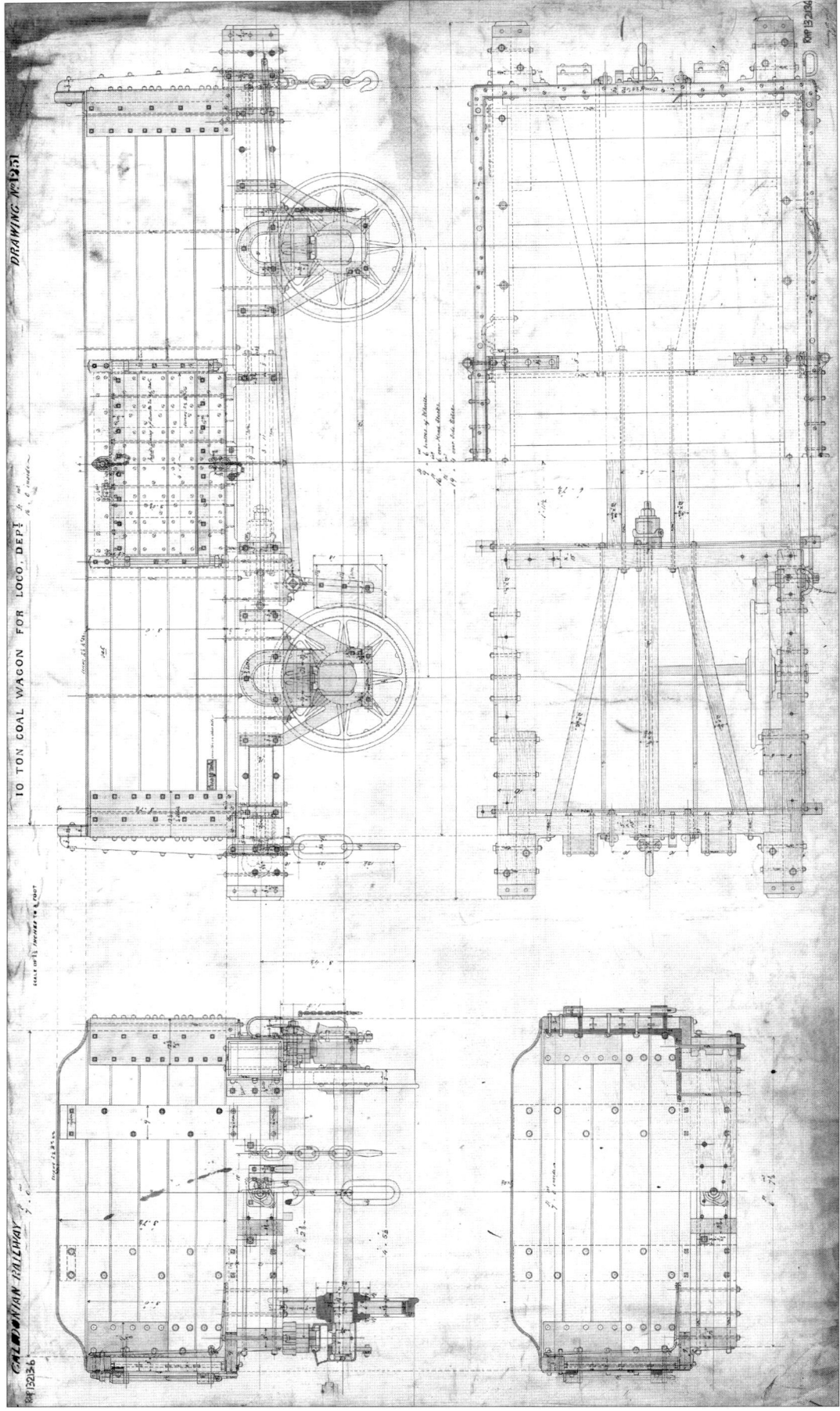

Figure 17.1
This is the earliest type of dedicated loco coal wagon with raised ends, dating from 1872. The contract for 500 wagons was awarded to Pickering, but delivery was very slow. The cast spoke assembly is riveted to the tyre, a practice outlawed by the Railway Clearing House in 1887. The wagon is fitted with the *'patent cushioned bearing spring'* which also appears on a contemporary mineral wagon drawing – see Figure 5.1.

17.1: LOCO COAL AND ASH

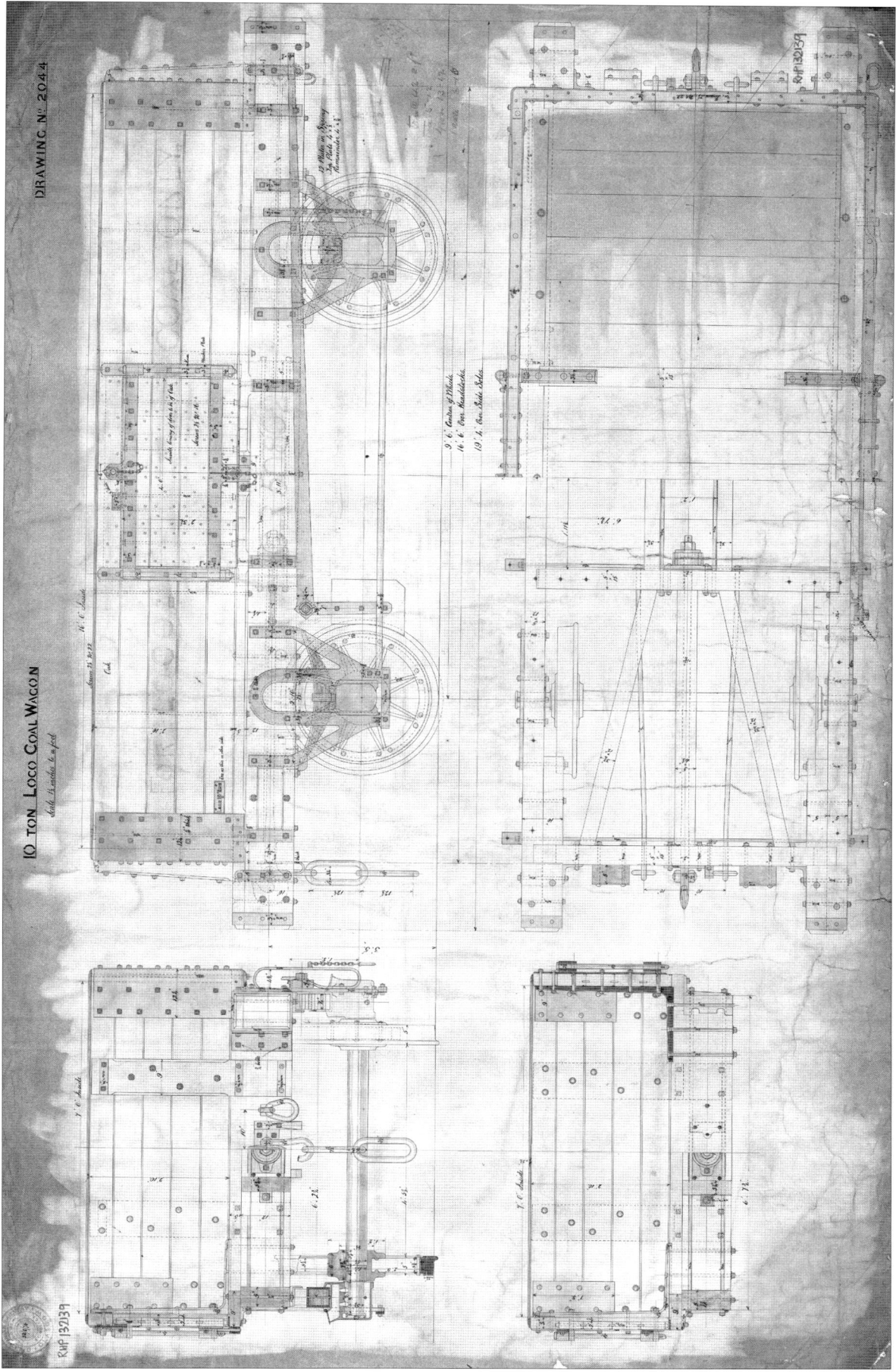

Figure 17.2
Drawing 2044 of 1876 depicts a later style of loco coal wagon. Compared to the wagon in Figure 17.1, the spoke assemblies are welded to the tyre, and reinforced with bolts. Note also the sketched-in lettering on the solebar which reads 'C.R 50802'. This was the early layout for loco coal wagons, but photographs show the word FOR omitted, as in Plate 17.1. This and the previous wagon drawing show small cast capacity plates screwed to the body at the left-hand corner.

ABOVE: Plate 17.2

This photograph, courtesy of John Boyle, shows the new locomotive depot at Arbroath, which, according to *LMS Loco Sheds Volume 5*, was probably opened in 1897. The Caledonian shared this depot with the North British. There was no coaling bench at Arbroath; coal was loaded direct from wagons. Caley locomotives used the track next to the rake of CR wagons. From left to right the rake consists of: a 'bogie' with no side doors, this and the short wheelbase suggest that it might be a ballast wagon built to St. Rollox drawing 1002; next are two Diagram 22 minerals lettered for the Hamilton Section (the second with 6½-inch letters), a Loco Coal wagon to the 1876 design (district lettering indistinguishable), a Diagram 22 lettered for Hamilton, a 'bogie' with offset door (no lettering visible), an 1876 loco coal wagon, followed by a Diagram 21 wagon in loco coal service, and finally two Diagram 22s with indistinguishable branding. Behind the rake of Caley wagons, three Fife Coal Company wagons can be seen. From the height of the sides, they probably carried coke. The first is lettered with the full name, the second and third with F C C only.

RIGHT: Plate 17.3

Sixty Diagram 59 mineral wagons were substituted for an order for twenty-five extra bogie coal wagons during the First World War. Pickering built them on wood underframes, because steel was unobtainable. The original St. Rollox works drawing 11664 was used, but with the later version of end door. The end door variations and their accompanying drawings are described in Chapter 5.5.

The wagons were probably built to St. Rollox drawing 2044 from August 1876 or 2270, produced a year later. Only the former has survived.[12] It shows a 9-foot 6-inch wheelbase wagon, with a sketch of the lettering positions for loco coal and CR 50802 on the solebar. The axle guards were attached to the outside of the solebars and were connected with a tie bar. One wooden brake block was fitted.

Side doors could be vertically or horizontally planked on the outside. Some of the wagons were numbered in a series before the thirled wagons. Sample numbers from photographs are 33365, 33622, 51137, 51289, 51290 (horizontally planked side doors) and 33357, 51022 and 51199 (vertical). There were just under 1,000 10-ton wagons in loco coal service in 1910.[13]

Bogie Coal and Ordinary Mineral Wagons

As mentioned in Chapter 5, 300 of the 30-ton bogie wagons were used for loco coal, but they may not all have been branded as such. Wagons specifically recorded as *'Loco Coal'* on the Callander & Oban in 1920 were 66061, 66297, 66342, 66371 and 66435. Nine others, although on loco coal traffic, were not so identified. Douglas Castle colliery was the most common source of coal. Canderrig, Tulligarth, Greenhill, Bothwell Castle and Dykehead collieries were also recorded.[14] A photograph of part of a St. Rollox-built wagon lettered for loco coal traffic appears in Chapter 5, Plate 14.

Although the diagram book described them as mineral wagons, some wagons to Diagram 21 carried loco coal and were lettered for the traffic – see Plate 5.5 (p. 88). The lettering was in the later style. They are easily distinguished from their predecessors in photographs, because they have end doors, axle guards inside the solebars and the cast iron single brake. The earlier wagons have fixed ends, outside axle guards and the wooden brake. The Diagram 21 wagons also used the first type of cast number plate, rather than a painted number on the solebar.

An order of sixty Diagram 59 mineral wagons was authorised in 1916 for loco coal traffic. The wagons were substitutes for an original order of twenty-five bogie coal 30-ton wagons. As discussed in Chapter 5, the bogie coal wagons may have been authorised as replacements for wagons that were sent overseas The 30-ton wagons were not built because of difficulties in sourcing steel.[15] The four-wheeled wagons themselves were built with oak underframes for this reason.

Pickering constructed them in June/July 1916 to card order 29760. They were fitted with self-contained buffers and the Morton brake working on one side of the wagon only. Random numbers were allocated, as they were part of the renewal programme. Sample numbers were 10067, 34876, 48285, 50583 and 56087.

The order of sixty wagons may have sufficed at the time, but other Diagram 59 wagons were allocated later for loco coal traffic. There is an often published picture of Pickersgill 4-4-0 number 86, with wagon number 30656 behind it on the coal bench.[16] The locomotive was built by Armstrong Whitworth in 1921. The vertical boarding to the side doors of the wagon and the simplified three-hoop end door suggest that it was part of an order of 400 wagons built under the renewal programme by the Motherwell Wagon Company, authorised in April 1920.[17]

An unknown number of re-buffered Diagram 22 wagons seem also to have been used. Drawing 17595,[18] dating from February 1917, was for a *'10-ton loco coal wagon, converted from 8-ton dumb buffer.'* A Drummond single brake was fitted on either side. The body as drawn was 3 inches higher than the original design. Even then, the cubic capacity was nowhere near 10 tons. The drawing has lettering LOCO COAL and LMS added in pencil.

Plate 17.4
A 'pug tender' attached to 0-6-0 mineral tank engine 510A. The wagon probably retains its original number 14207 in the mineral wagon series. The initials and number are two different sizes, for no apparent reason. The small cast plate below the R reads 'TO BE RETURNED TO GLASGOW SOUTH SIDE' on three lines. The handrail and full length footboard to allow wagon shunters to ride with the engine are typical.

Plate 17.5
This enlargement shows two Diagram 22 wagons in departmental use, presumably both lettered 'ASH WAGON ABERDEEN'. The letters are the original 6½ inches height. The right-hand wagon does not carry company initials.

Plate 17.6
An old stone or ballast wagon, looking as if it has been freshly transferred to ash wagon duties at Carlisle. The 12 inches high company initials have displaced the load lettering, which is lettered on the horizontal centre line of the wagon. The 'ASH WAGON CARLISLE' letters are the same size as the load writing.

Pug Tenders

These wagons are included here as an alternative method of carrying loco coal. Early mineral 'bogies' were stripped of their bodies and the underframes used as the basis for carrying coal supplies for shunting engines with limited or no bunker capacity.

Foot boards were fitted to each side and a new low wooden body was added. There is no drawing recording the modification, and no reference in the minutes. They were lettered in a variety of ways. Some, but not all, had numbers and a depot allocation.

Ash Wagons

Three types of wagon ended their days as containers for removing ash from locomotive depots – the 7-ton 'bogies,' stone wagons and the first design of ballast wagon, which is described in the next section. They were lettered as ash wagons and usually with the name of their home shed.

References

1. NRS BR/CAL/1/19 entry 1286, NRS BR/CAL/1/19 entry 1357
2. Not yet catalogued
3. NRS BR/CAL/1/20 entry 253
4. NRS BR/CAL/1/20 entry 1236
5. NRS BR/CAL/1/21 entry 184, NRS BR/CAL/1/21 entry 246
6. NRS BR/CAL/1/21 entry 596
7. NRS BR/CAL/1/21 entry 689
8. Not yet catalogued
9. NRS BR/CAL/1/22 entry 453
10. NRS BR/CAL/1/22 entry 1213
11. NRS BR/CAL/1/23 entry 1989
12. Not yet catalogued
13. NRS BR/CAL/4/134 p. 7
14. NRS BR/CAL/5/60
15. NRS BR/CAL/1/67 entry 1221, NRS BR/CAL/1/67 entry 1268
16. See, for instance *Caledonian Railway Livery*, p. 42
17. NRS BR/CAL/1/74 entry 876
18. NRM 11931/W

Top Left: Plate 17.7
This is a superannuated 'bogie' in use as an ash disposal wagon at Perth depot. On available photographic evidence, only Perth seems to have adopted a private number series for service wagons, which was prefaced by 'No.' The company initials are very small, possibly only 4 inches high. 'FOR ASHES ONLY' is also unusually inconspicuous. Other photographs (for example, *Caledonian Railway Livery*, p. 284) show the words in larger block lettering spread across the wagon body.

Bottom Left: Plate 17.8
17289 is seen in departmental use with chalked writing 'Fitting Shop'. This 6-ton wagon has no side doors and possibly a hopper bottom. It seems in good condition for its age, and bears 15-inch CR condensed initials. The paint date is 16/2/03. The wheel rims were painted white when it was repainted. The number has been painted on the sides because there is no room on the solebar to position it with an unobscured view. The axle guards are the relatively unusual version with one curved and one straight leg. The curved bridles to the axle guards are two different types. The wood brake block is just about worn out. The wagon still has the old solid buffer couplings with the short middle link. Loco coal wagon 33357 in the background has vertically boarded side doors, which were less common than horizontal planking. The obscured wagon to its right is a Diagram 21 mineral wagon lettered for loco coal traffic, evidenced by the end door.

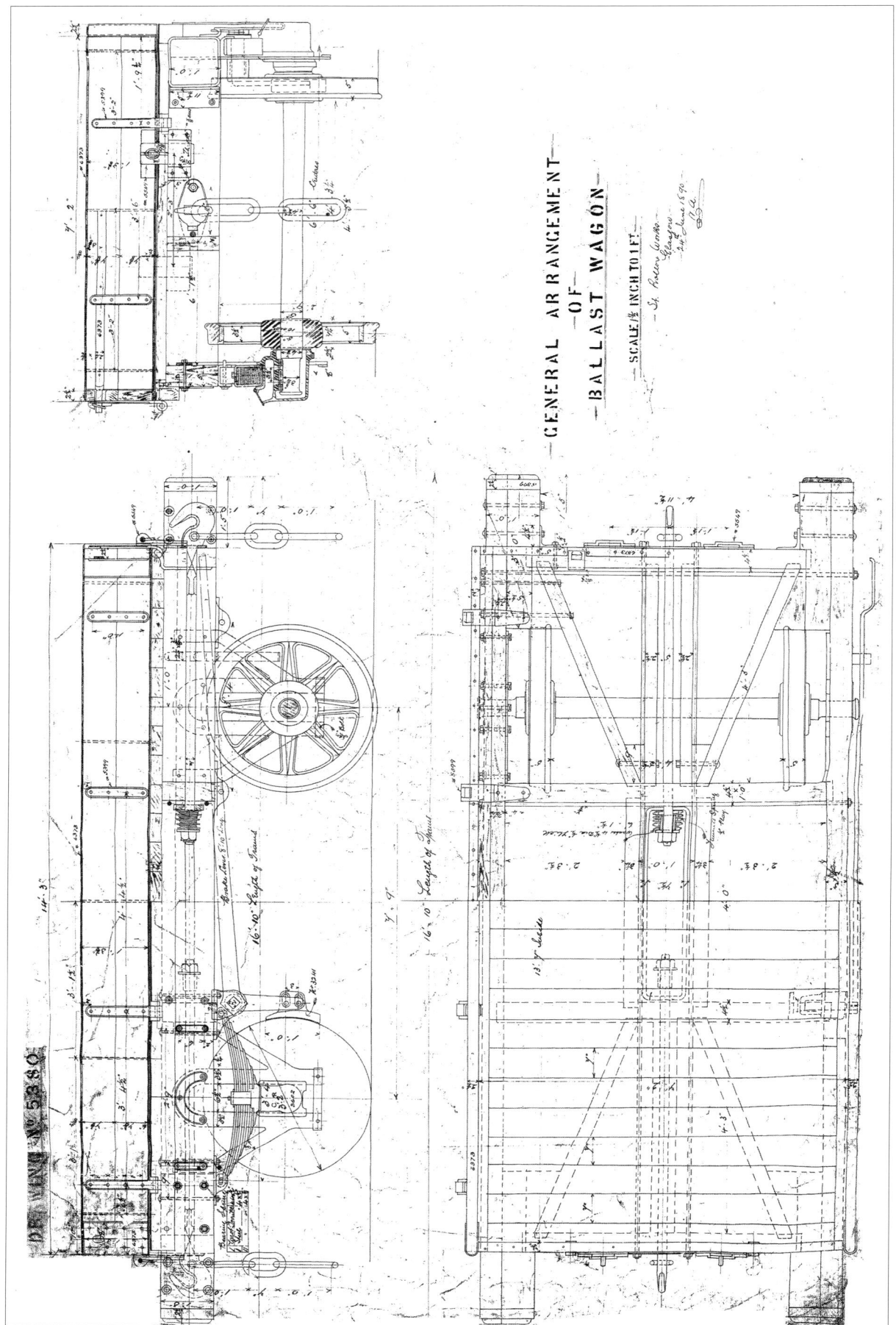

Figure 17.3
St. Rollox drawing 5380 shows the early type of ballast wagon that was still in use in the twentieth century.

17.2: Ballast Wagons

Some of the information in this introduction is adapted from an article by Jim Summers in the Caledonian Railway Association's magazine.[1] The material in the article was drawn from a visit to the USA made by senior managers of the Caledonian and London & North Western railways in 1903.

Railway companies used various materials as ballast. Some used limestone or granite, others beach shingle. For instance, the Caley's west coast partner, the London & North Western, had a large granite quarry at Shap. The quarry is still in use today. The advantage of granite or limestone lies in their shape when crushed. The angular stones lock together when they were compacted and the hard stones are long lasting under the pounding of traffic. The L&NWR originally used furnace slag, but could not ensure sufficient supplies, hence the move to granite.

The Caledonian used slag, which was readily available as a waste product from iron works in Glasgow and Lanarkshire. It was prepared for use at the company's crusher at Chapelhall, just south of Airdrie. The material was toxic and inhibited weed growth. It was also considerably cheaper than crushed stone. Its main disadvantage was that traffic impact and repeated tamping turned it to dust, thus requiring more frequent renewal than granite or limestone.

Pre-Diagram Book Design

Ballast wagons first appeared in 1859, according to the stock returns, when thirty wagons were added to the fleet. In 1858 the Board had

'ordered the cost of these (£1,800) to be charged to Capital, as the Company have never had Ballast Wagons, Goods Wagons having been used hitherto.'[2]

The next year, six ballast wagons were taken over from the Lesmahagow line, according to the stock returns. In 1865 the Board agreed to take tenders for 134 ballast wagons.[3] There is no further mention of this order and no evidence from the rolling stock returns that the wagons were supplied. A further twenty-six wagons came among the stock of the Scottish North Eastern Railway in 1867. The rolling stock census reported that there were 104 wagons in November 1867. There is no documentary evidence for this increase in stock.

In 1870, the minutes record acceptance of tenders from Pickering for 120 flat ballast wagons, and Faulds for thirty wagons *'coal pattern'*.[4] The costs were £53 5s and £51 15s respectively.

The increase was in response to an earlier directive requiring Benjamin Conner to get a specification for new special ballast wagons and the number required. It had come to the notice of the Board of Directors that wagons had been destroyed by hot slag. The Board wanted to know how many wagons had been lost *'and why it had not been reported sooner.'*[5] The design of these wagons is unknown. There were now 254 ballast wagons in the stock return.

In the years between 1872 and 1882, just over half (fifty-five) of the original ballast wagons were declared to be worn out and were replaced. The renewal design was probably to St. Rollox drawing 1002, which was for a ballast wagon with falling ends.[6] This was produced in 1871. The wagon was a standard 'bogie' with no side doors and two end doors. Two earlier drawings, numbers 704 and 993, have not survived.

Above Left: Plate 17.9
Without seeing both ends we cannot be sure, but the spacing of the framing and lack of side doors suggest that this may be an early ballast wagon built to St. Rollox drawing 1002. This would account for the wagon being numbered in the goods, rather than the mineral series. It was still in use in 1896, proved by the paint date on the underframe of the tank wagon in front of it in the original photograph. There is another possible early ballast wagon in Plate 17.2.

Above Right: Plate 17.10
This is a typical pre-diagram book ballast wagon to drawing 5380, with 12-inch lettering. The axleboxes are protected by canvas flaps. The hinges of the ends were so arranged that the ends folded flat onto the top of the buffers, making an extension to the floor. The design was derived from the stone wagon which is shown in Plate 8.17 (p. 141). The tare numbers are painted on the body, but the load letters and numbers cannot be accommodated in a similar position on the right-hand side, so have been displaced to the curb rail. The load lettering is not centred in the space available.

The next design of ballast wagon does not seem to have merited a drawing. It was almost identical to the stone wagons with side doors that were built to drawing 1082,[7] but with folding, rather than fixed, ends. To facilitate this, the buffer pad was not built up in height above solebar level. In this they resembled the early timber wagons. The sides were 3 inches higher than the stone wagon design. The capacity was eight tons. Outside axle guards were fitted and a single wood brake block.

The renewal of wagons on a like for like basis continued throughout the 1880s (seventy-nine wagons) and 1890s (a further sixty-seven wagons). The renewals are not mentioned in the minutes but are recorded in the rolling stock returns. Although supplanted by the Diagram 23 wagons described below, the 1871 design was still in use in 1900, because one was photographed for the *Register of Wagon Plant*. It is reproduced here in Plate 17.10.

Construction continued into the Drummond era and beyond. St. Rollox built twelve more wagons of the drawing 1082 design, to orders G45 and G80. The latter order was part of a blanket authorisation for 308 wagons as renewals in the half year ending July 1890.[8]

BALLAST WAGON LOAD 8 TONS – DIAGRAM 23

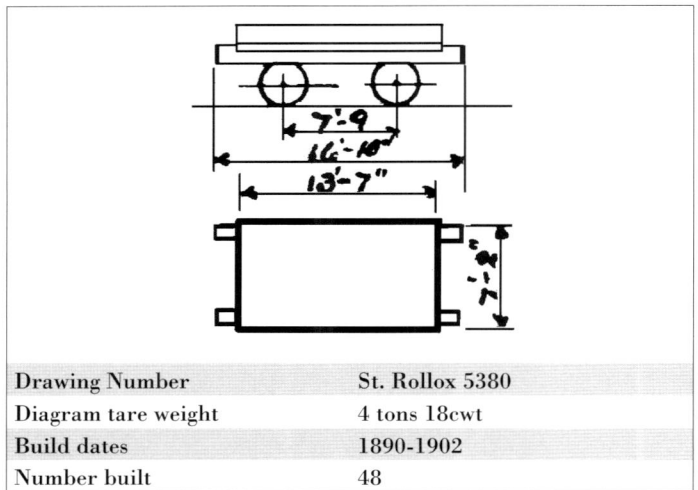

Drawing Number	St. Rollox 5380
Diagram tare weight	4 tons 18cwt
Build dates	1890-1902
Number built	48

The first order to Diagram 23 was authorised in August 1890 among 262 wagons which were treated as renewals.[9] The minute did not specify the types of wagon, but they can be inferred from the St. Rollox orders.

This design used the same underframe, running gear and body dimensions as the Diagram 22 mineral wagons, except for the ends, which were 1 inch thinner, increasing the internal length by 2 inches. The outside dimensions were 14 feet by 7 feet 7 inches. They had drop-down two-plank sides and ends 1 foot 3½ inches deep.

The rolling stock returns record construction of wagons, mostly in multiples of six or twelve up to the accounting period ending in July 1902.[10] All these wagons were renewals; the 1902 return remained at 254 wagons.

8 TON BALLAST WAGON WITH FALLING SIDES AND ENDS – DIAGRAM 57

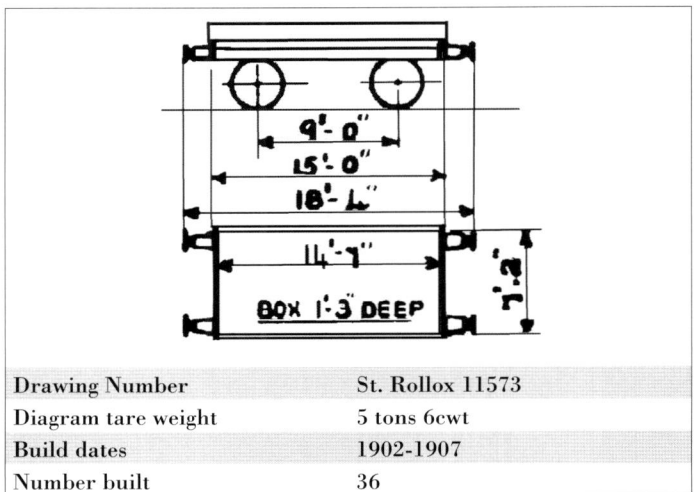

Drawing Number	St. Rollox 11573
Diagram tare weight	5 tons 6cwt
Build dates	1902-1907
Number built	36

The Diagram 57 version to order G199 also had falling sides and ends, 1 foot 3 inches deep. They were 15 feet long over headstocks and 7 feet 7 inches wide externally. They were introduced in 1902.[11] The order number suggests that they were built after the Diagram 64 wagons described in the next paragraph. The wagons appeared in multiples of six or twelve as renewals.[12]

12 TON HOPPER BALLAST WAGON – DIAGRAM 64

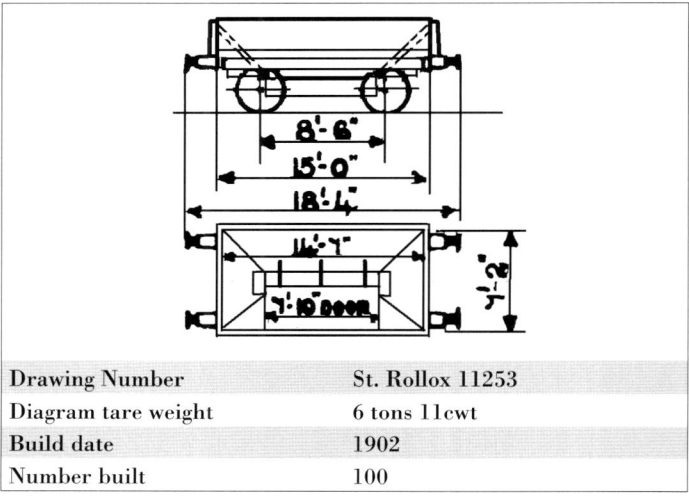

Drawing Number	St. Rollox 11253
Diagram tare weight	6 tons 11cwt
Build date	1902
Number built	100

In October 1901 the Traffic Committee approved the order of twenty-five hopper wagons and a spreading plough brake van for the Blackwood to Darvel and Muirkirk railway.[13] They were later in general use throughout the Western Division, according to the same minute. The combination of bottom discharge wagon and spreading

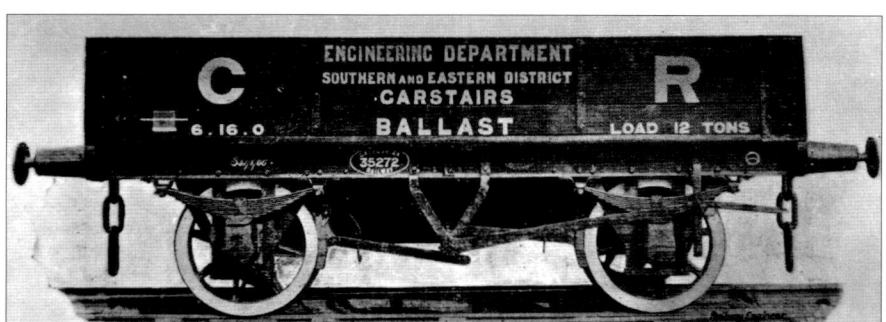

Plate 17.11
The 1906 paint date in the photograph of 35272 suggests that it was one of forty Diagram 86 wagons authorised that year to order G246. The photograph originally appeared in *The Railway Engineer*. The number indicates that it replaced a wagon that was built relatively late, around the mid-1880s. The small oval plate to the right of centre was the Leeds Forge patent plate – these wagons were built on a pressed steel underframe with integral curb rail. The brake safety hangers are cranked.

plough meant that ballasting could be undertaken much more rapidly than the old method of shovelling ballast out of a wagon standing on a parallel track to the one being treated.

The wagons, first built to order G190, had three-planked wooden bodies just over 2 feet deep, with fixed sides and ends. They were 15 feet long by 7 feet 7 inches wide, carried on steel underframes. They had the steel underframe buffer. A double brake was fitted to one side. In August 1902 a further seventy-five wagons were authorised. They were built to order G200.[14] Fifty appeared in the rolling stock returns in 1903, with the remainder in 1904. All these wagons were treated as capital expenditure.

12 Ton Hopper Ballast Wagon – Diagram 86

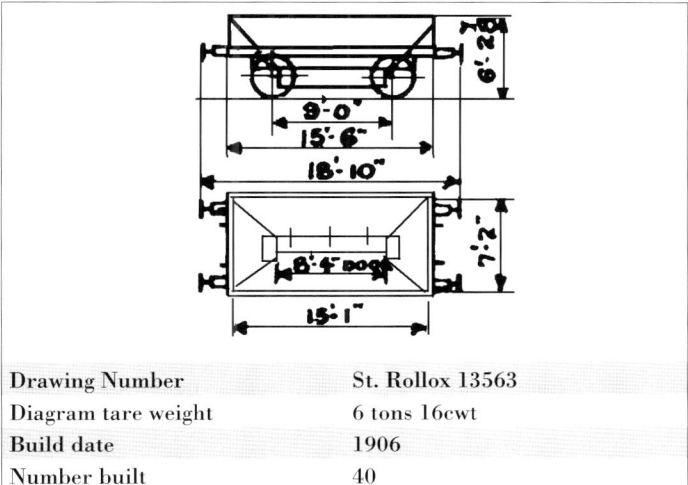

Drawing Number	St. Rollox 13563
Diagram tare weight	6 tons 16cwt
Build date	1906
Number built	40

Forty Diagram 86 wagons were authorised in November 1905 by the Traffic Committee to order G246, along with three more spreading plough brake vans.[15] The wagons were similar to Diagram 64, but with a 6 inches longer wheelbase and body.

The arrival of the modern wagons to Diagrams 64 and 86 allowed the solid-buffered stone and ballast wagons to be cascaded into service use as ash wagons, as described in the previous section.

Old 'Bogies' Used for Ballast Traffic

As noted in Chapter 5, eighty old mineral wagons were repaired, repainted and put into Engineering Department use for carrying permanent way materials. In May 1911 the Traffic Committee agreed the adaptation of forty disused 7-ton wagons, to be set aside for the Engineering Department on the Southern & Eastern Division. The estimated cost of their repair, painting & lettering was £82.[16] In August 1912 the Committee authorised forty to fifty more to be repaired and set aside for *'the Engineering Dept. in the maintenance of the line.'*[17] This time the estimated cost was £75 for fifty wagons. In the event, only forty were transferred, according to the rolling stock return.

Some of these wagons remained in service into the First World War. This is confirmed in the *1915 Working Timetable Appendix* which stated:

> *'For the carriage of slag ashes or other permanent way material for the Engineer's Department, or for contractors, only mineral wagons with solid buffers must be used.'*[18]

The material transported was probably worn out ballast and spoil being removed, prior to new ballast being laid. New ballasting would have been accomplished much more efficiently with falling side or hopper discharge wagons. The old wagons in their new guise appeared as additions in the rolling stock returns for the periods ending July 1911 and December 1912. The additions were balanced by corresponding deductions from the mineral wagon stock.

References

1. *The True Line*, issue 115, p. 17. A copy of the official report of the trip is in the CRA Archive, ref: 2/3/1/16
2. NRS BR/CAL/1/11 entry 1779
3. NRS BR/CAL/1/14 entry 174
4. NRS BR/CAL/1/18 entry 977
5. NRS BR/CAL/1/18 entry 407
6. Not yet catalogued
7. Not yet catalogued
8. NRS BR/CAL/1/33 entry 1038
9. NRS BR/CAL/1/34 entry 22
10. NRS BR/CAL/1/34 entry 1217 (1890),
    NRS BR/CAL/1/35 entry 827 (1892),
    NRS BR/CAL/5/11 entry 221 (1896),
    NRS BR/CAL/5/11 entry 323 (1898),
    NRS BR/CAL/1/46 entry 548 (1902)
11. NRS BR/CAL/1/46 entry 508
12. NRS BR/CAL/1/46 entry 1363 (1903),
    NRS BR/CAL/1/49 entry 769 (1904),
    NRS BR/CAL/1/52 entry 1307 (1906),
    NRS BR/CAL/1/53 entry 1151 (1907)
13. NRS BR/CAL/1/45 entry 453
14. NRS BR/CAL/1/46 entry 744
15. NRS BR/CAL/1/52 entry 233
16. NRS BR/CAL/1/60 entry 442
17. NRS BR/CAL/1/62 entry 432
18. *Working Timetable Appendix*, p. 70

Plate 17.12
On 16th May 1911 the Traffic Committee agreed to *'adapt 40 disused 7 ton wagons, to be set aside for Engineering Dept. on Southern & Eastern Division.'* The total cost of repair, painting and lettering was estimated at £82. 15807 is one such example, still with very fresh looking paint and lettering, engaged in removing spoil during the demolition of the old Carstairs station in 1913. The number is repeated low down on the fixed end.

LEFT: Plate 17.13
This is a partial view of a ballasting brake van to drawing 1747. The number is 306, making it a contemporary of the brake van in Plate 16.3. The top line of lettering reads 'ENGINEERS BRAKE VAN'. The bottom line starts with an indecipherable letter, followed by 'CENTRAL DIVISIONS'.

BELOW: Plate 17.14
This photograph shows a ballast train with Dunblane cathedral in the background. The picture was taken before work started on re-roofing the cathedral nave in 1888. The ballast wagons look to be the pre-diagram book variety, with their axleboxes protected by canvas flaps. Purely on the basis of location, and with no supporting evidence, the open ended brake van might be one of thirty-two inherited from the Scottish Central Railway in 1865, relegated to departmental use. The covered van does not match with any drawing so far discovered. It has the early four-bolt self-contained buffers and is fitted with safety chains. The outside framing on the sides extends over the solebar.

BELOW: Plate 17.15
One of the five *'ballast plough and brake vans'* built to Diagram 65. The glossy appearance suggests that the van was varnished. The company initials are separated by a dot because they occupy a common space. The cast number plate and tare weight writing are transposed from the normal position. The lack of a continuous footboard, the small diameter wheels and the long overhang of the body gave these vans a rather ungainly appearance.

17.3: Ballast Brakes

Pre-Diagram Book Design

A drawing for a brake van specifically for ballast trains appeared in 1874 (St. Rollox 1747).[1] The van was 17 feet 6 inches long and 7 feet 9 inches wide. It was horizontally planked and had two doors each side towards the ends. Between the doors, and separated by heavy vertical framing, were four small fixed windows. Two similar windows were fitted in each end.

One end was partitioned off to form the brake compartment. Wooden brake blocks were applied to each wheel. The rest of the van was fitted out with wooden seats in pairs with a centre aisle. Unfortunately the condition of the drawing is too poor to allow reproduction. The only known number is 306.

Ballast Plough and Brake Van – Diagram 65

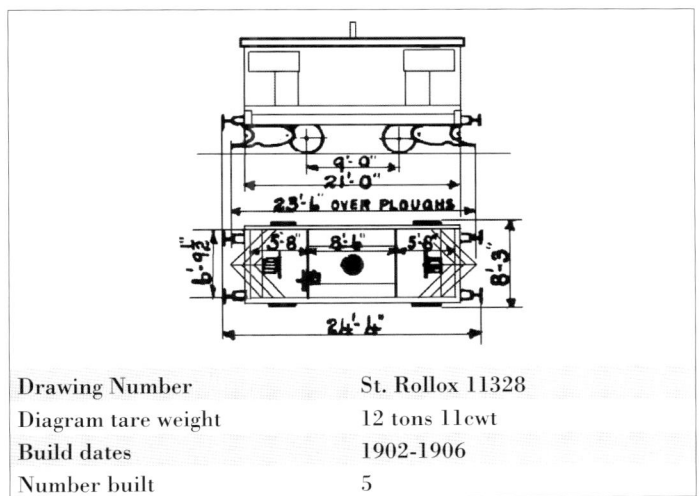

Drawing Number	St. Rollox 11328
Diagram tare weight	12 tons 11cwt
Build dates	1902-1906
Number built	5

Although they were described as ballast brakes in the diagram book, the minutes, order list and lettering all describe the vans as slag spreading ploughs. This recognised the material that was used as ballast by the Caledonian.

The first plough was authorised in October 1901 as part of the ballast train for the Blackwood to Darvel and Muirkirk railway.[2] It was built against order M281 to a drawing dated April 1902. The body design was similar to the contemporary Diagram 62 goods brakes, but wider and longer to accommodate the plough mechanisms at each end.

One was built to order G197, anticipating the construction of seventy-five hopper ballast wagons to order G200, which was authorised in August 1902. This brake van was not recorded in the minutes. A further three were built to G247 in 1906.[3] These vans accompanied forty hopper ballast wagons which were built to order G246 and made up what seems to have been a shortfall in brake van numbers following the hopper wagon construction in 1902.

Oil axleboxes were fitted, and footsteps like those on engine tenders, rather than a continuous lower footboard. The buffers were the standard three-bolt wagon type. Photographs show the vans fitted with 3-foot 1½-inch open spoke wheels. Known numbers are 564 and 583. The paint date of number 583 shows that it was part of the G247 order.

Other Permanent Way Department Brake Vans

In October 1901, St. Rollox issued drawing 11030 for a brake van for the permanent way department.[4] It was probably built in response to a minute in the previous August, when the Traffic Committee authorised construction of such a van for Aberdeen.[5] It did not receive a G order number. It does not correspond to any wagon in the diagram book. There is no record of how many were built, and no photograph.

The drawing is reproduced as Figure 17.6 and is shown alongside Figure 17.5 for comparison purposes (pp. 276). This shows the van to be identical in dimensions and internal layout to the Diagram 7 breakdown van design which was built to drawing 5307 in 1887, and is discussed in section 6 of this chapter. The more modern van differed from the original in having a rigid wheelbase, and in its horizontal planking.

A further drawing was issued in 1913. St. Rollox 17151 showed a van which was of the same general construction as in drawing 11030, but with no side windows.[6] There was a small door 1 foot 6 inches square above the buffer beam at the opposite end from the lookout. There is no order record of this van, or minute authorising its construction.

References
1. Not yet catalogued
2. NRS BR/CAL/1/45 entry 453
3. NRS BR/CAL/1/52 entry 233
4. NRM 11240/W
5. NRS BR/CAL/1/44 entry 1628
6. NRM 11241/W

Plate 17.16
A mystery picture of a van in service use. The only lettering that can be distinguished is 'BRAKE VAN' towards the right. The open end and the body framing are similar to the pre-diagram book brake van design shown in Plates 16.1 and 16.2, and Figure 16.1. The narrow pair of doors in the centre of the side, the overall length and the wheelbase echo the stores van design depicted in St. Rollox drawing 776. Perhaps it was a conversion?

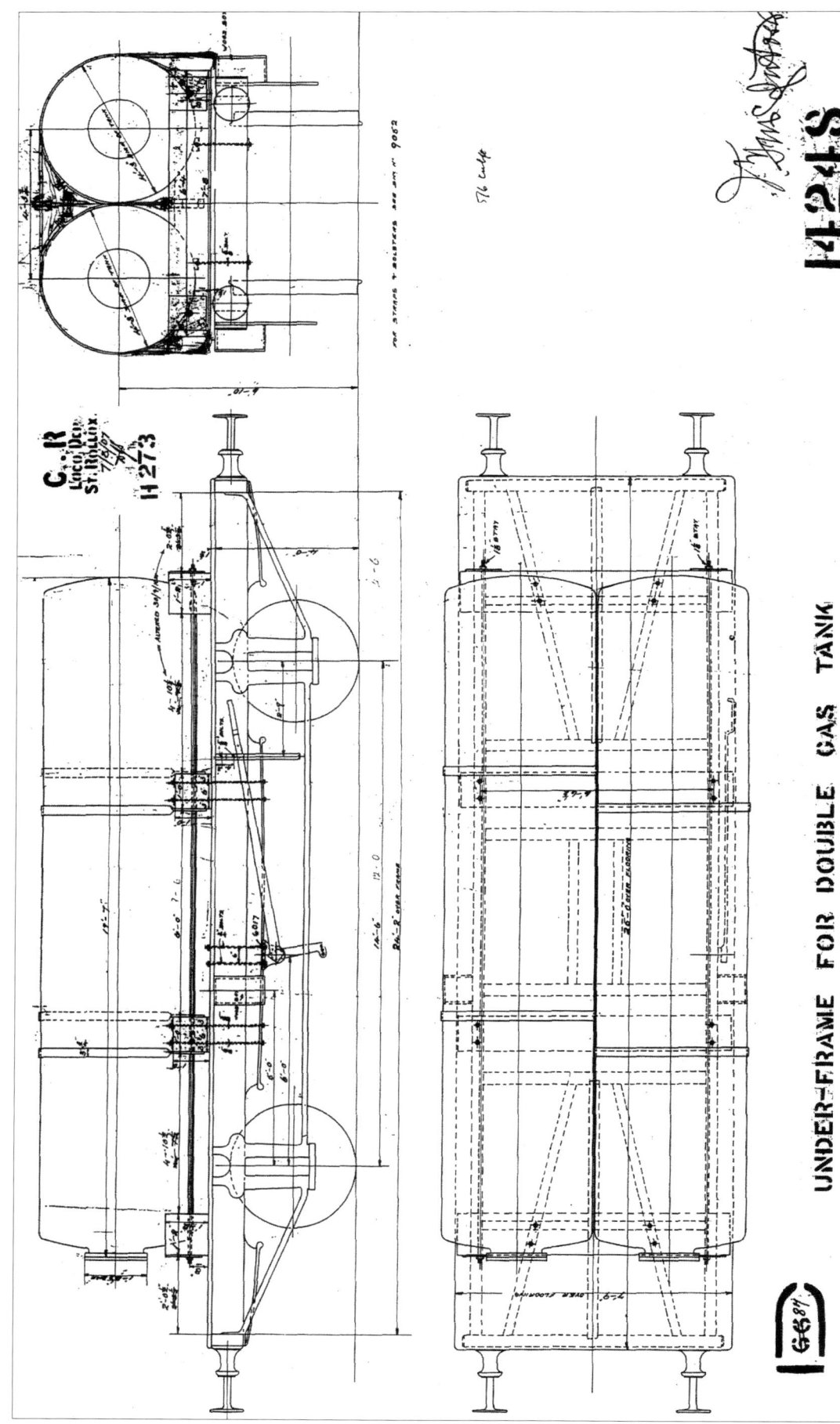

Figure 17.4
The St. Rollox drawing for travelling gas tank number 23, built in 1907. Tank number 24 was similar. The single tanks had the same style underframe, with the same diameter tank fitted on the centre line of the underframe.

17.4: Gas Tanks

Originally the Caledonian used oil lamps to light carriages. In 1870 Benjamin Conner submitted a letter setting out the cost of introducing gas lighting in carriages. The Traffic Committee delayed a decision *'pending further consideration.'*[1]

The matter was not actively considered again until 1877, when the minutes refer to a *'new system of fitting up and lighting carriages with gas'* which had been described in a letter from Pintsch & Co. The Traffic Committee responded to the letter by instructing the General Manager to consider the matter and report further.[2]

Julius Pintsch, who had patented the lighting system in question, was an American. His original system used naphtha, a gas derived from oil, which was compressed into storage tanks under the carriage body. The gas was drawn off through a regulating valve and burnt at a lower pressure. The major advantage of oil gas was that it retained most of its illuminating power when compressed, whereas coal gas lost the greater part of its power.

The General Manager's recommendations are not recorded, but no immediate action was taken on Pintsch's proposal. In late 1881, Pope, a rival oil gas patent holder, tried to get in on the act; the Traffic Committee proposed not to adopt this system.[3] In January 1882 the Loco & Stores Committee decided to countermand the Traffic Committee's decision and gave a *'Remit to the Glasgow Committee to have a trial of Pope's and Pintsch's systems at the expense of the patentees.'*[4] In late March 1882 the Committee

> *'Submitted costs of Pope's and Pintsch's systems. Gas Works of Pintsch's System to supply 500 Carriages will cost £2650 and each Carriage £39 10s. The Committee are of the opinion that we should adopt Pintsch's System and fit up the Gas Works but only fit up 100 Carriages.'*[5]

In April, Pintsch submitted a tender which was accepted *'to see and approve the site of the works and carry out the erection as early as possible.'*[6] In May, Peters (the agents for the Pope system) made a further attempt to secure the contract for gas lighting to the company. The Loco & Stores Committee decided to *'accept subject to the conditions as to quality of fittings being as good as Pintsch's but only to the extent of 50 Carriages, prices 5% below Pintsch's.'*[7]

In September 1882, Peters accepted the order to fit up fifty carriages.[8] In the following month the Committee accepted Pintsch's offer

> *'to supply 6 double necked filling hose heads and 18 couplings, free of charge, to enable Pope's Coaches to be gassed at Pintsch's filling posts and vice versa.'*[9]

Pintsch became the preferred supplier and the company is frequently mentioned in the fitting out of new carriages for gas lighting. The final development in gas lighting occurred early in the twentieth century with the invention of the incandescent burner. This replacement for the flat flame gas mantle more than halved gas consumption and simplified the lighting and extinguishing of the lamps. The Caledonian resolved to install the new system in 1907, equipping all gas lit carriages at the rate of 400-500 in each six-month period at a revenue cost of £800 per period.[10]

The Raw Material for Producing Gas

A ready supply of oil was available in the Central Lowlands. In the early 1850s, the Scottish chemist James 'Paraffin' Young discovered that mineral oil could be extracted from coal mined near Bathgate and even more easily extracted from oil shale deposits underlying much of West Lothian.

One of the fractions produced was what was known as 'gas oil'. The oil was heated in coke-fired retorts until it vaporised. It was then condensed and tar and naphtha were drawn off to leave oil for lighting purposes. Thirteen gallons of oil produced 1,000 cubic feet of gas, 4.7 gallons of tar and 0.8 gallons of lighter hydrocarbon. Finally the gas was filtered and stored. The gas in travelling gas tanks was compressed to about 11 atmospheres (approximately 162psi, similar to a typical locomotive boiler of the period).

The Caledonian was a major customer for the oil, which was converted in the company's oil gas works. As an example, in 1897 the company agreed to purchase *'120,000 gallons Oil for manufacture of Gas for carriages, deliver over 12 months Oakbank Oil Coy.'*[11] Oakbank was a major player in the Scottish oil industry. It was one of the earliest companies, founded in 1869, with a rail connection at Midcalder.[12]

Caledonian Railway Gas Works

Although not explicitly stated in the minutes, the original gas works installed by Pintsch must have been at Dawsholm. A plant at Glasgow Cook Street catered for the gassing points at Larkfield and Smithy Lye. Plans for the Edinburgh works at Lothian Road were submitted in December 1891.[13] The gassing point for the Northern section tanks was Perth. The gas works there was approved in 1887.[14] In 1889 it was agreed that:

> *'to avoid detention to trains, six filling taps to be provided at southern end on the down and six at the north end of the up platform.'*[15]

Fixed Gassing Points

Fixed gassing points were established at strategic locations around the system. In 1906 the charging points for carriages on the Southern, Eastern and Western sections of the system were Glasgow (Central, Smithy Lye and Larkfield), Maryhill, Dawsholm and Edinburgh Princes Street.[16]

Travelling Gas Tanks

Company minutes first refer to a *'gas travelling store'* in September 1883, when the Loco & Stores Committee considered a *'Letter offering to supply a Travelling Store holder, tank and all fittings complete for £320.'*[17] The offer came from Pintsch & Co. A week later, Drummond offered to buy the tank alone for £240.[18] St. Rollox drawing 3686 was for a travelling gas tank, and probably showed the Pintsch tank fitted to an underframe built at St. Rollox. The drawing has not survived.

The surviving Caledonian coaching stock register includes seventeen travelling gas tanks, but the list is far from complete. It

Tank No.	Type	Order	Minute Date	Carriage Register Base	Additional Information
	Single		11/9/83		Pintsch tank mounted on St. Rollox-built underframe
3	Single	M79		Dumfries	Drawings 6600/6642 show date 3/91. The Minute of 19/11/90 probably refers to this tank. No base mentioned in Minutes
1	Single		20/5/91	Aberdeen	
4	Single	M84		Larbert	Drawings 6600/6642 show date 10/91
2	Single		5/9/94	Law Junction	At Aberdeen in 1907
5	Single			Forfar	Build date 1895 in Carriage Register. At Law Junction in 1906
10	Double	M154	23/12/96	Dundee East	
11	Double	M154	23/12/96	Dundee East	
12	Single	M159	3/2/97	Irvine	No mention of base in Minutes. At Holytown in 1906
13	Single	M159	3/2/97	Oban	No mention of base in Minutes. At Rutherglen in 1906
	Double	M181	7/9/98	Dundee East	
	Double	M181	7/9/98	Dundee East	
	Double	M181	7/9/98	Dundee East	
14	Double	M202	11/1/99	Buchanan Street	Existing Single Tank rebuilt as twin
15	Double	M202	11/1/99	Buchanan Street	Existing Single Tank rebuilt as twin
	Double	M207	1/3/99	Lockerbie	
16	Double	M235	10/1/00	Rutherglen	Originally allocated to Hamilton or Law Junction
17	Double	M235	10/1/00	Rutherglen	Originally allocated to Hamilton or Law Junction
22	Double			Law Junction	Build date of 1/04 in Carriage Register. At Oban in 1907
23	Double	H273	23/4/07	Rutherglen	Renewal half year ending Jan 1908. No base mentioned
24	Double			Steps Road	Build date of 1/08 in Carriage Register, as for number 23
27	Triple	H336	16/11/15	Rutherglen	

only records tanks in stock after the First World War. A full list of travelling tanks referred to in company minutes is shown above. The tanks with numbers are those listed in the *Carriage Register*. The tanks do not appear in the rolling stock returns. Those listed in the *Carriage Register* received LM&SR numbers. Withdrawal dates are not known.

Most had the Westinghouse brake, although three are known to have had pipes only. Numbers 1 and 2, although recorded in the register as painted in passenger livery, did not have continuous brakes. Number 23, built to H273, was fitted with a steam heating pipe from the outset. A minute in January 1920[19] authorised the remaining sixteen to be fitted, but only five were so fitted according to the Coaching Stock Register.

None of the tanks received diagram numbers. Dimensions are not available for most of them. The drawing of the tank used for numbers 3 and 4 was St. Rollox 6600. The underframe details were on a separate drawing, St. Rollox 6642. The running gear was adapted from old carriage underframes, in the same manner as the Diagram 12 empty barrel trucks. Two other surviving drawings were also for tanks on old carriage underframes – number 23 and 27 to orders H273 and H336 respectively, the drawing references are St. Rollox 14248 and 18752.[20] Drawing 14100, dated 2nd April 1907, for a double gas tank has not survived.

References
1. NRS BR/CAL/1/18 entry 460
2. NRS BR/CAL/1/23 entry 1002
3. NRS BR/CAL/1/27 entry 113
4. NRS BR/CAL/1/27 entry 202
5. NRS BR/CAL/1/27 entry 465
6. NRS BR/CAL/1/27 entry 645
7. NRS BR/CAL/1/27 entry 742
8. NRS BR/CAL/1/27 entry 1076
9. NRS BR/CAL/1/27 entry 1261
10. NRS BR/CAL/1/55 entry 1332
11. NRS BR/CAL/1/40 entry 909
12. *Oil on the Rails*, published by the HMRS, has a chapter on the shale oil industry, and a section on *'gas oil'*. See also, Harry Knox, *The Scottish Shale Oil Industry & Mineral Railway Lines*, published in 2013 by Lightmoor Press
13. NRS BR/CAL/5/11 entry 92
14. NRS BR/CAL/5/11 entry 34
15. NRS BR/CAL/5/11 entry 47
16. *Local Working of Carriages 1906* p. 25. CRA Archive ref: 3/3/2/1
17. NRS BR/CAL/1/28 entry 855
18. NRS BR/CAL/1/28 entry 876
19. NRS BR/CAL/1/74 entry 317
20. RHP 67536 and 67529 respectively

17.5: Tank Wagons

With a few exceptions, the Caledonian seems to have decided at an early stage not to provide tank wagons for revenue traffic. Instead, it hired out underframes to private traders. The traders mounted tanks to their own specification on the underframes. These wagons and the underframes were discussed in Chapter 7. The tanks covered in this section were classed as service vehicles in the official returns of 1907-10.[1]

As well as their use for carrying gas oil, they also probably carried lubricating oil. A Loco & Stores Committee minute in November 1897 records the *'Adoption of Compound Oil for lubrication of Locomotives, with sketch and estimate of appliances required at St Rollox.'*[2] A further use was probably the carriage of creosote to the sleeper works at Greenhill.

Pre-Diagram Book Designs

A tank wagon first appeared in the rolling stock returns for 1861, along with four vitriol (i.e., sulphuric acid) wagons that were converted from ordinary wagons. They were probably tanks mounted on cradles in the body of a low sided wagon. There were eight vitriol wagons from January 1866.

Another tank was added in 1871. This may have been a water tank. The only reference in the minutes is in June 1870, concerning a tank wagon to supply water for engines at Benhar branch, to carry about 3,000 gallons, at a supposed cost of about £100.[3] The Loco & Stores Committee instructed Benjamin Conner to supply the tank *'at the lowest price he can.'* St. Rollox drawing 987, which has not survived, may be the subject of this wagon.

There are no further references to tank wagons of any description in company minutes or rolling stock returns before Drummond's accession. Between 1877 and 1884 the drawings register refers to acid wagons (drawing numbers 2266, 3290, 3888 and 3939). The last of these was for a private trader; so, presumably, were the others. None of these drawings has survived.

To add to the confusion, the rolling stock returns show that five tanks were replaced between 1885 and 1887 when only two were recorded as having been built in pre-Drummond days. The design of tank cannot be ascertained

Tank Wagon 1,770 Gallons – Diagram 5A

Although this design is not recorded in the Small Diagram Book, there is a reference to it, with diagram number, in the Big Diagram Book. St. Rollox drawing 6141 dating from November 1889 depicts this type.[4] The tank was 5 feet 5½ inches in diameter. Length over headstocks was 17 feet and the width was 6 feet 11½ inches. The wheelbase was 9 feet 6 inches.

The number of tanks built to this design is unclear. There are no contemporary St. Rollox wagon G order numbers that refer to tanks. This is not necessarily significant, as tanks may well have been built to M order numbers that have not been recorded. One tank was added to stock for the half year ending July 1891, just before the drawing for the Diagram 32 tanks discussed below was issued. It is therefore possible that only one wagon was built to this design.

Tank Wagon 2,100 Gallons – Diagram 32

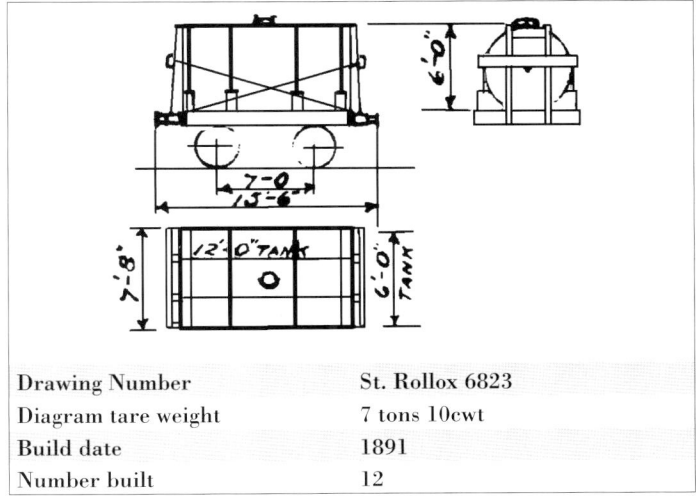

Drawing Number	St. Rollox 6823
Diagram tare weight	7 tons 10cwt
Build date	1891
Number built	12

The design had heavy duty self-contained buffers and fifteen-plate springs. Journals were 9 inches by 4 inches. Originally a conventional floor was intended, but the drawing is annotated that it should be omitted. The omission exposed the underframe members to view. The North British Railway produced an almost identical design in 1887.[5]

Plate 17.17
A partial picture, probably of a 1,800 gallon tank wagon. It shares general constructional details with the Diagram 32 wagon seen in the next plate.

The St. Rollox drawing states that twelve were built to order C93. The rolling stock returns record ten additional tanks and three renewals between 1892 and 1900. The only tank photographed with a visible number is 45063, which appears in the *Register of Wagon Plant*. Company initials are not visible in the photograph but they may have been obscured by the very obvious heavy spillage from the tank filling hatch.

The following table shows orders for gas oil tanks which, with two exceptions, may have involved these tanks.

Order	Minute Date	Additional Information
	7/1/96	Store tank for Cook Street, probably a static tank
	7/1/96	Three travelling tanks for conveying oil for carriage gas lighting
M148	2/9/96	Travelling tank for Dawsholm. Conversion of old tender @ £44
M208	12/4/99	New tank for carrying gas oil – no gas works mentioned
	15/10/01	Additional tank for conveying gas oil to Dawsholm

The Cook Street store tank was probably a static tank, as it was distinguished from the three travelling tanks which were authorised at the same time.[6] Order M148[7] may have involved mounting a tank on a stripped-down tender body. It is also possible that the tender water tank was used, with alterations to the tank filler and the addition of discharge apparatus. M208 was authorised in April 1899.[8] It was probably built to St. Rollox drawing 9676[9] dated May 1899, and recorded as one of two additions in the first half of 1900.

The other addition in that period was a tank built as part of order G179, which was supposedly treated as a renewal.[10] The minute authorised 300 mineral wagons. The St. Rollox orders show that only 291 were built. The remainder of the order consisted of eight hopper wagons, the prototype Diagram 51 ore wagon and a tank wagon. This was probably the other additional tank recorded in the 1900 return.

In late 1904, the Traffic Committee authorised the purchase of five tanks from the Caledonian Mineral Oil Co.[11] The rolling stock returns of July 1905 and July 1906 probably record these wagons as replacements.

According to the 1910 return, there were twenty-five tanks, an increase of three since 1908. One more tank was added in the last rolling stock return, for the period ending December 1912. None of these are referred to in minutes or in the St. Rollox order lists.

Other Tank Wagon Designs

St. Rollox drawing 10299[12] dates from 1900. It depicts a double tank wagon for carrying oil, type of oil not specified. There is no reference to this type of wagon in minutes, or in the St. Rollox order book. As it did not receive a diagram number, one must assume that the design was for a private trader. The rolling stock returns do not record any additions to the company fleet that are not already accounted for.

References
1. NRS BR/CAL/4/134 p. 7
2. NRS BR/CAL/1/40 entry 1853
3. NRS BR/CAL/1/18 entry 811
4. RHP 68429
5. Cowlairs drawing 131W reproduced in *NBR Wagons, Some Design Aspects*
6. NRS BR/CAL 139, entry 276
7. NRS BR/CAL/5/11 entry 249
8. NRS BR/CAL/5/11 entry 371
9. RHP 68423
10. NRS BR/CAL/1/43 entry 449
11. NRS BR/CAL/1/50 entry 296
12. RHP 68422

Plate 17.18
2,100 gallon tank wagon number 40563 to Diagram 32 was photographed for the *1900 Register*. The self-contained buffers, springs and axlebox journals are all heavy duty. The company initials, if they were ever applied, are obscured by spillage.

17.6: Breakdown Cranes and Associated Vehicles

The Breakdown Cranes

The Caledonian owned four steam breakdown cranes. They were not allocated pages in the Small Diagram Book. Numbers 1 and 2 were 15-ton vehicles, built by Cowans Sheldon in 1886. Originally based at Motherwell, they were moved to Carlisle and Perth respectively when the cranes numbers 3 and 4 were added to the fleet.[1] Numbers 3 and 4 were 20-tonners, built by Craven Brothers in 1907 and allocated to Motherwell.

The cranes were part of a breakdown train, which consisted of a runner wagon for the crane, a breakdown van and an emergency van. The full story of these vehicles is in volume 1 of Peter Tatlow's *Railway Cranes*.

Crane Runner Wagons

Photographs show the cranes with a variety of wagons supporting the end of the jib for travelling purposes. One was an early open wagon with sides two planks high. Both cranes were accompanied by these wagons. One was lettered 'STEAM CRANE RUNNER' and bore the number 2 to match its crane. The wagon attached to crane number 1 was not lettered in photographs, apart from the company initials.

The wagons originally had four wheels, but a centre axle was added in 1898. Presumably the weight of the jib was overloading two axles. St. Rollox drawing 8810, which has not survived, was for *'the addition of centre wheels to number 1 crane runner, Motherwell.'*

The press photograph of crane number 3[2] shows it with a pre-diagram book three-plank open wagon number 4746. Other photographs[3] of the same combination show that the wagon had modified running gear including oil-lubricated axle boxes and modern buffers.

The trestle supporting the jib was not on the wagon centre line, which put an unequal load on the axles. The jib also overhung the end of the wagon. For these reasons Diagram 13 rail wagons were substituted as runners for the two 20-ton cranes. One at least of these wagons had a flexible wheelbase. The caption to Plate 17.20 (p. 278) describes some of the modifications to the wagons.

Their replacements in revenue earning stock were authorised for construction in the half year ending July 1908, to order G271.[4] The runner wagon for crane number 3 took the crane number; presumably the same applied to the runner for crane number 4.

Breakdown Van – Diagram 7

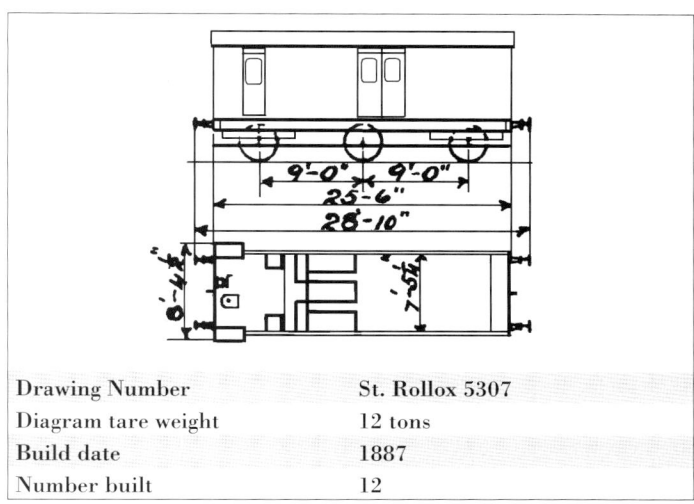

Drawing Number	St. Rollox 5307
Diagram tare weight	12 tons
Build date	1887
Number built	12

In 1887 emergency vans were built to be based at Perth (order G25), Motherwell (G26), Carlisle (G30), Dawsholm (G31) and Hamilton

Plate 17.19
Breakdown crane number 1 is seen here with its runner wagon. This originally had four wheels; the centre axle was added in 1898. The company initials are 12 inches high, and truly circular. The wagon has the heavy variety of early self-contained sprung buffer. The left-hand buffer has a step cast into the top, the right-hand one does not. The headstock nearest to the crane is misaligned, causing the buffers to sag. On the crane, the company initials (properly separated by a dot) and number are rendered in shaded passenger livery lettering. Was the metalwork of the crane purple lake?

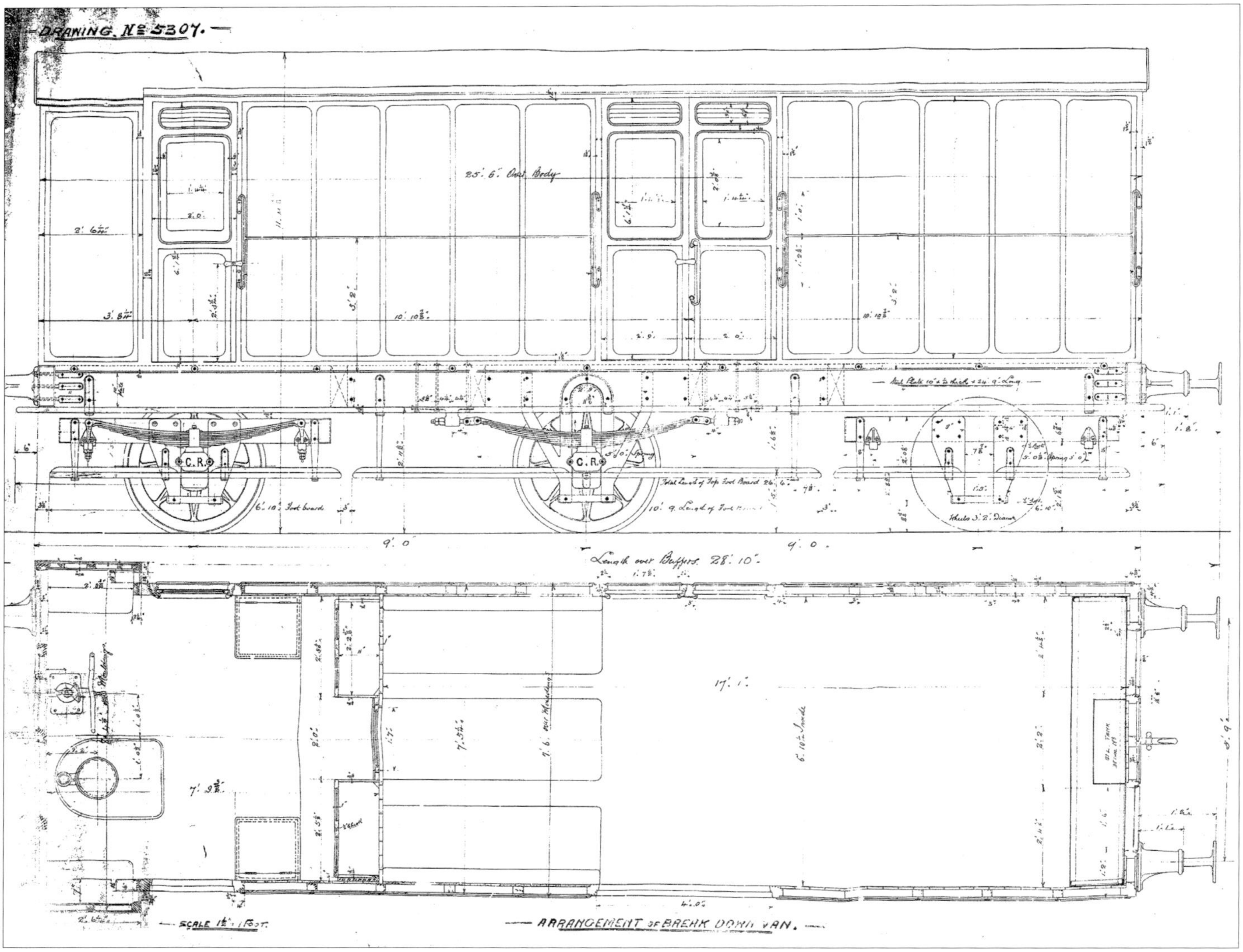

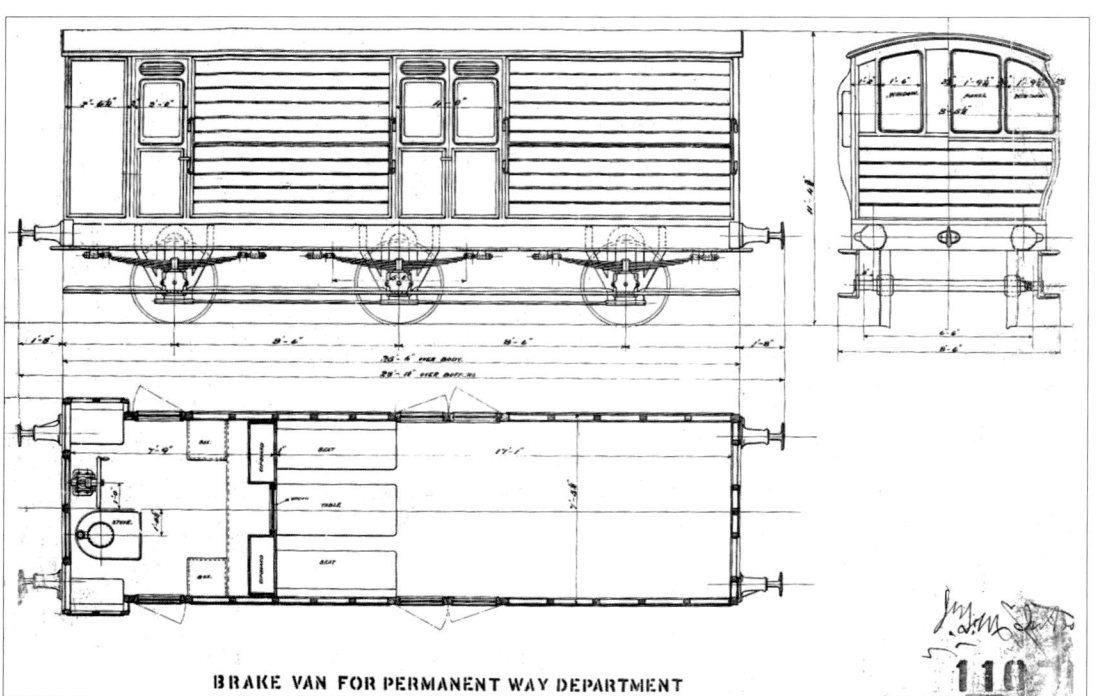

ABOVE AND RIGHT: **Figure 17.5** St. Rollox drawing 5307 was for the Diagram 7 breakdown van. The vans shared an underframe with the first design of Diagram 13 rail wagons, which had a flexible wheelbase. Oil axleboxes, rather than grease, were fitted to allow the vans to travel at higher speeds when responding to an emergency. Twelve of these vans were built and allocated to strategic parts of the CR system.

LEFT: **Figure 17.6** St. Rollox drawing 11030 dates from October 1901 according to the register. Comparison with Figure 17.5 shows how the original design's suspension was modernised in the same way as the later orders of the Diagram 13 rail wagons – see Chapter 8. The body style evolved in the same way as did the covered goods vans to Diagram 3. This change is discussed in Chapter 9.

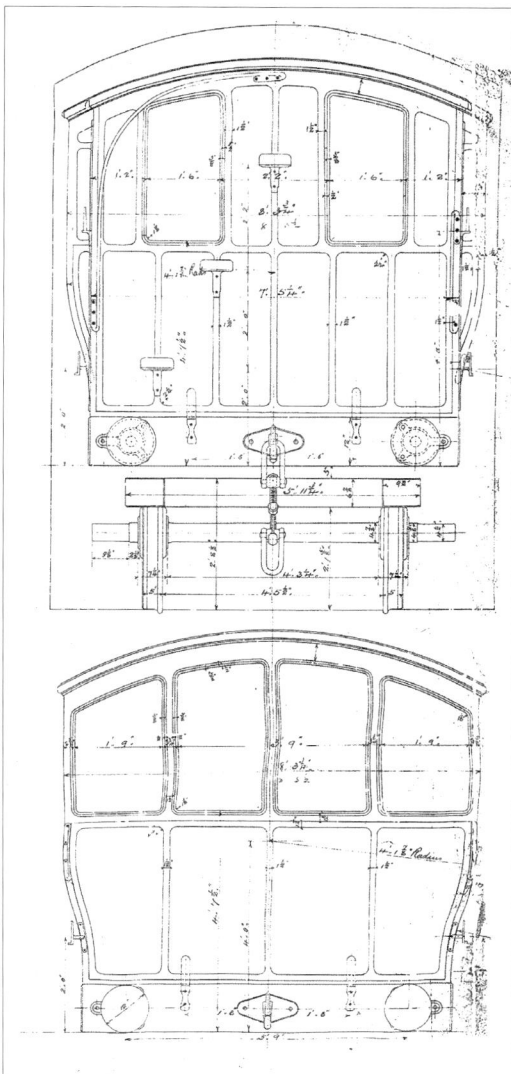

Emergency Van – Diagram 119

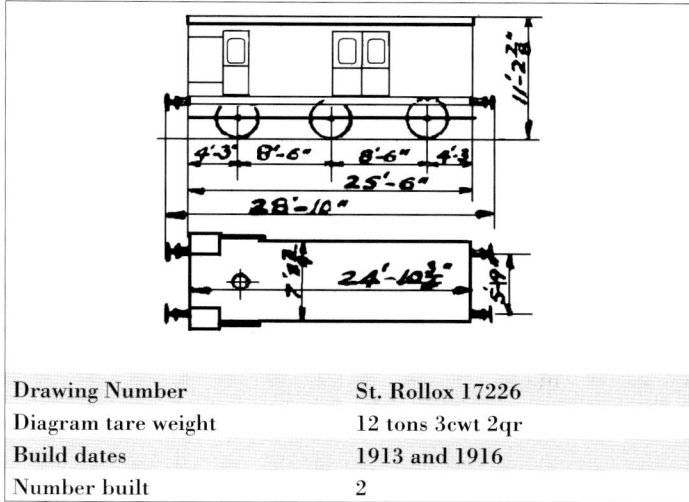

Drawing Number	St. Rollox 17226
Diagram tare weight	12 tons 3cwt 2qr
Build dates	1913 and 1916
Number built	2

Two vans to carry tools and equipment were built to this diagram in 1913 (G352 for Carstairs) and 1916 (G388 for the Northern District).[8] The latter *'equipped with necessary tools and lights'* was probably based at Perth, along with the breakdown crane. They were similar in configuration to the Diagram 7 vans, with seating and a stove at the lookout end. The body had outside framing, in common with the later Diagram 67 variation.

The Carstairs van was number 95 in the brake van series, and the Northern Division van was 279. They may have replaced Diagram 7 vans, which by this time were thirty years old. If that was the case, it is likely that they took the old vans' numbers.

Tool Van Number 156

In 1914, drawing 17490[9] sketched the conversion of brake van 156 into a tool van. Although the dimensions on the drawing are slightly different from those in *West Coast Joint Stock*, the van was almost certainly six-wheeled WCJS brake van 156, built to Diagram P32 in 1877/78. It was acquired along with eight others by the Caledonian in 1898, when the vans were taken out of WCJS service.[10] Examination of numbers in the *Carriage Register* suggests that the WCJS numbers were carried over into the CR luggage van series.

According to *West Coast Joint Stock*, the vans were 30 feet long and 6 feet 10 inches wide. The lookouts projected 10 inches. They were flat sided. When built they were panelled in the Wolverton works style of the time. A photograph which may represent this van (Plate 17.23, p. 280) has different panelling. The original mouldings may have been removed and the original panels boarded over. This would account for the extra width on the St. Rollox sketch compared with the original Wolverton dimension.

Catering and Sleeping Vehicles

Drawing 18183, dating from 1915, was for a kitchen van for breakdown purposes.[11] The drawing has not survived and there is no information on this vehicle.

Although strictly outside the scope of this book, 48-foot by 8-foot 6-inch passenger brake vans to carriage Diagram 47 were converted to kitchen cars for the breakdown trains in 1917. Presumably a van was converted for each of the four trains. The St. Rollox drawing number is missing on the damaged surviving copy,[12] and there is no record of the drawing in the register. There are, however, two drawings for fitments within the kitchen cars.[13]

Equally outside this book's remit is the conversion of saloon 1419 into a *'travelling dormitory for tradesmen.'*[14] This was originally

(G32). Breakdown vans were built at the same time: Perth (G27), Motherwell (G28), Carlisle (G33), Dawsholm (G34) and Hamilton (G35). Two further breakdown vans were built to G41, with no base mentioned.

Company minutes do not mention these vehicles, but they were probably built for use with the first two travelling cranes, which received tender approval in February 1886.[5] The end profile and windows at the lookout end were the same as the contemporary Drummond six-wheeled brake end coach. There was also a pair of windows at the other end.

The body panelling was similar to the first style of Diagram 3 covered van. The vans had radial trucks at either end, which were the subject of drawing 5296. The underframe was the same as the original design of Diagram 13 rail wagons.[6] The wheels were ordinary wagon type. The drawing does not show the braking arrangement, but the plan view includes a brake stanchion at the end fitted with lookouts.

It is not clear whether the emergency and breakdown vans were significantly different. It is possible that only the interiors were fitted out to suit different purposes. Drawing 5375[7] is for the breakdown van interior. A number of other drawings showing constructional details are all for breakdown vans.

Plate 17.20
This photograph (Image SRX270 1B, courtesy of National Railway Museum / SSPL) shows one of the two Diagram 13 rail wagons which were modified for use as runners to go with the 20-ton cranes. It is newly painted, as the wheel rims are still white. The following modifications from the original design are visible: the ends are now fixed, and the original hinges have been replaced by end pillars; the stepped buffers have been retained, although they are no longer necessary; the three folding stanchions have been removed from the sides; the left-hand part of each side has been hinged to fold down, and short footboards are hung from the solebar; oil axleboxes are fitted; the wagon is lettered 'STEAM CRANE RUNNER', and the painted crane number has supplanted the original cast revenue service number plate. The two offset door 'bogies' next to it carry 12-inch company initials. Behind them is a Diagram 22 mineral wagon; the section lettering on the top plank has been painted over in compliance with the Traffic Committee's 1908 directive, as discussed in Chapter 3.3.

17.6: BREAKDOWN CRANES AND ASSOCIATED VEHICLES

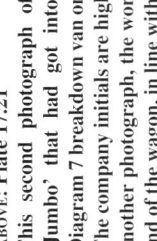

ABOVE: Plate 17.21
This second photograph of the rescue of a 'Jumbo' that had got into trouble shows a Diagram 7 breakdown van on the embankment. The company initials are high up on the side. In another photograph, the words at the left-hand end of the wagon, in line with the visible writing 'BRAKE VAN' were 'STEAM CRANE'. Image SRX270 1C, courtesy of National Railway Museum / SSPL.

LEFT: Plate 17.22
Two emergency vans to Diagram 119 were built in 1913 and 1917. This is the earlier of the two, which was allocated to Carstairs. It is seen in LM&SR days as 353095. It was originally numbered 95 in the brake van series.

the pioneer West Coast Joint Stock 32-foot sleeping saloon number 101 of 1874 which was transferred to the Caledonian in 1885. After thirty-five years of CR service as a third class open saloon, it was converted in 1921, to drawing 21249.[15]

Vans Built after the Diagram Book

In 1920, five Third Class brake carriages returned from war duty. They had been converted into goods and mineral brake vans before being sent overseas. The Traffic Committee agreed that they be made into breakdown vans as they were *'about 42 years old'*, and not worth reconverting to passenger use.[16] The vans may have been part of a contract supplied by Brown & Marshall, authorised in October 1877.[17] Nothing more is known about these vehicles.

In 1921, emergency and tool vans were built for Motherwell and Perth. The emergency vans were to drawing 21192 (orders M25 and 26) and the tool vans to 21111 (orders M27 and 28).[18] Both types of vehicle were built on the standard 30 feet long 18-foot wheelbase steel underframe, as fitted to the Diagram 101 covered carriage trucks, with vertically-planked bodies. Although built to non-passenger coaching stock standards, the vans were not fitted with continuous brakes.

The equipment of the vans as set out by Miller is worth recording. The emergency van was divided into three sections: a kitchen and brake compartment, a central lavatory and a dining compartment. The kitchen had a stretcher press for ambulance appliances as well as the usual cooking equipment. The dining section contained an ambulance box, fog signals and a fire extinguisher.

The tool van was equipped with a work bench and vice at one end, with storage space for bolts and a spanner rack above. Down one side of the van there were hydraulic jacks, pinch bars and clamps. On the other side and the far end there were screw jacks, acetylene tanks and burners. Outside, a box for ramps was fitted to the underframe. The van had roof skylights.

In October 1922, a further drawing (St. Rollox 21981)[19] gave details of altered interiors for breakdown vans for Carlisle (order M33), Dawsholm (M34) and Hamilton (M35). Small bench seats were fitted along the sides of the van at one end. There is no reference to any of these vans in minutes or the St. Rollox order book.

References

1. NRS BR/CAL/5/12 entry 221
2. Published in *The Railway Magazine*, December 1907 issue, pp. 491-92
3. For example in *Caledonian Railway Livery*, p. 324
4. NRS BR/CAL/1/55 entry 1143
5. NRS BR/CAL/1/30 entry 751
6. St. Rollox drawing 4224, NRM 8055/W NRS RHP 69145
7. NRM 11242/W NRS RHP 70032
8. NRS BR/CAL/1/64 entry 159, NRS BR/CAL/1/68 entry 276 respectively
9. Not yet catalogued
10. Details in *West Coast Joint Stock*, pp. 78-79, 90
11. NRS BR/CAL/1/67 entry 221
12. NRM 11237/C
13. St. Rollox 18369 and 18372
14. NRS/BR/CAL/1/76 entry 825
15. NRM 11227/C
16. NRS/BR/CAL/1/74 entry 459
17. NRS/BR/CAL/1/23 entry 1961
18. NRM 11236/C and 11239/C
19. NRM 11238/C

Right: Plate 17.23
The van in the background may be Tool Van 156. The flat sided body configuration compares well with the sketch drawing, with a lookout and door on the centre line, and a pair of doors towards the visible end. The curved grab handle and ring pattern door handles strongly suggest a nineteenth-century Wolverton-built vehicle. The panelling, of course, is unlike anything produced by the L&NWR. It is possible that the original mouldings were removed, the panels boarded over and half-round beading applied. This would account for the 3 inches extra body width on the St. Rollox sketch, compared with the original dimension.

Plates 17.24 (Left) and 17.25 (Right)
These are two of the pairs of emergency and tool vans built in 1921 for Motherwell and Perth, in British Railways livery when they had both gravitated to Dawsholm. The bodies are dimensionally identical and each had windows in the ends, as seen in Plate 17.25. The three toplights in the centre of this tool van were boarded over, according to the drawing. The boxes containing re-railing ramps are prominent between the wheels. The door openings on the emergency van (Plate 17.24) were 2 feet 10½ inches wide. The window openings were 1 foot 4 inches by 2 feet 6 inches.

17.7: Engineer's Department Vehicles

Brake Van For Engineer's Department – Diagram 61

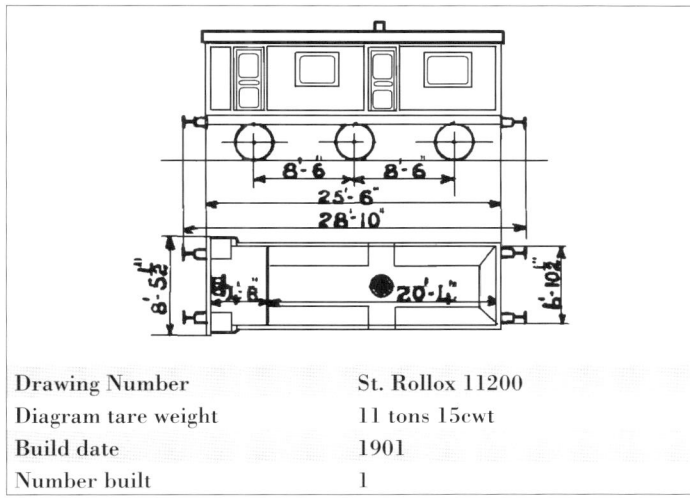

Drawing Number	St. Rollox 11200
Diagram tare weight	11 tons 15cwt
Build date	1901
Number built	1

Diagram 61 was a brake van for the engineer's department, built to order G191. The configuration was similar to the breakdown and emergency vans, but there were only two single doors on each side. It was fitted with an elaborate braking arrangement which applied clasp brake blocks to all six wheels, which anticipated the Diagram 63 six-wheeled brake van design.

Drawing 11213[1] shows the interior sections. The larger part of the van was fitted with seats around the sides and ends, with a stove in the middle of the space. The general arrangement drawing 11200 is shown in Figure 17.7 overleaf. An annotation shows that three oil lamps were fitted along the centre line of the roof over the left-hand door and the side windows.

Non-Diagram Design

In 1905, drawing 12952[2] depicted the body only of a brake van for the engineering department. This was a short vehicle (17 feet 7¾ inches over headstocks) so one assumes that it ran on four wheels. It was 8 feet 6 inches wide. The body was built of horizontal planks. The single entrance doors were offset towards one end. There were two windows on each side and two on each end. Two oil lamps provided illumination. Box seats were fitted around the interior. Nothing more is known of this design.

Stores Vans

The first mention of a stores van was a drawing of 1869 (St. Rollox 776 '*with spindle buffers*'). It was 20 feet long and 7 feet 7 inches wide over its heavy outside framing. The wheelbase was 12 feet. It had

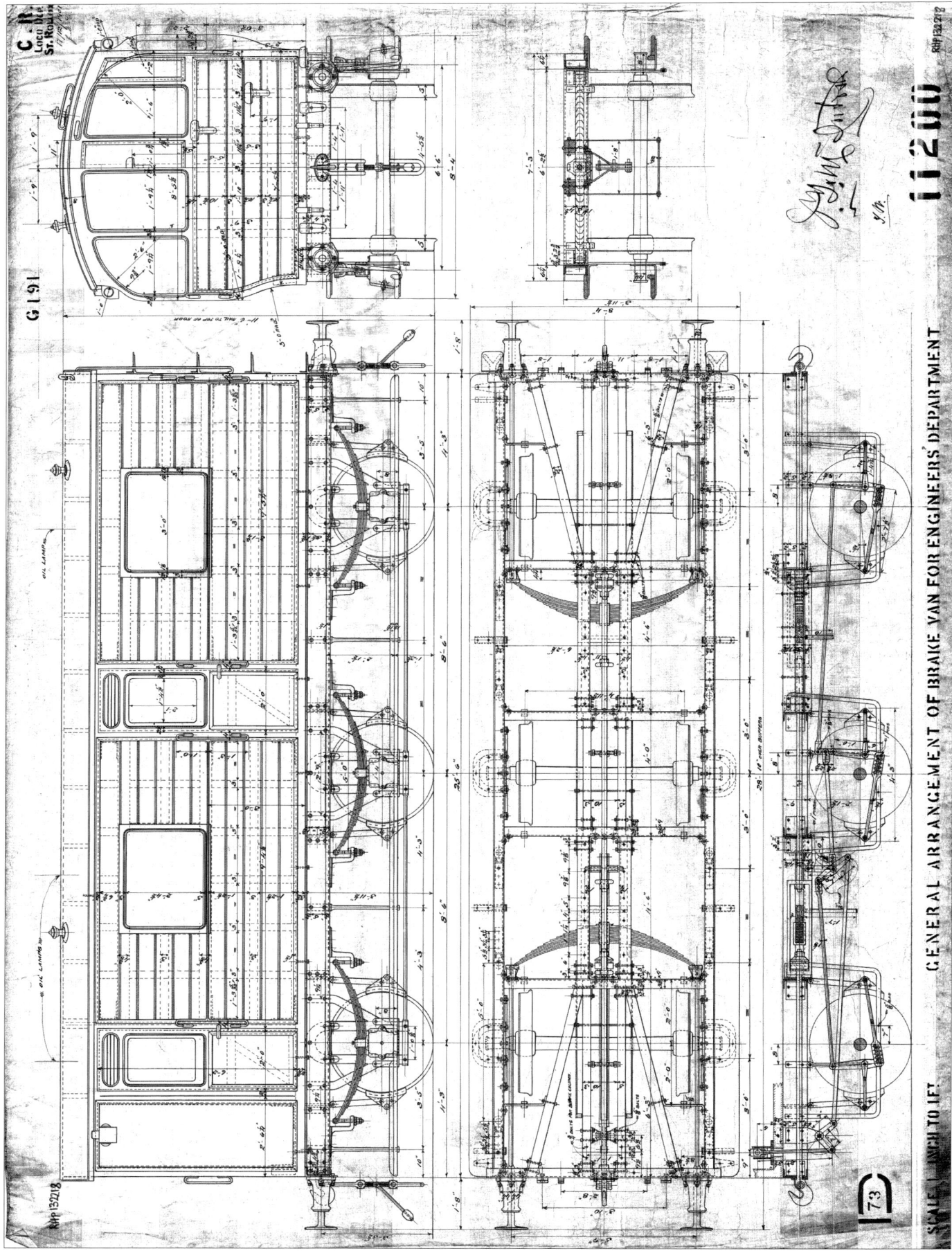

17.7: ENGINEER'S DEPARTMENT VEHICLES

FACING PAGE: Figure 17.7
A general arrangement of the Diagram 61 brake van for the engineer's department. The interior was the subject of a separate drawing. Of particular interest are the braking arrangements and the very light 5 feet long springs.

LEFT: Plate 17.26
This poor quality enlargement may show the large stores van to drawing 1129. The body and running gear look appropriate for the early 1880s and the writing on the waist could easily read 'STORES VAN', plus a word like 'ENGINEER'S'.

BELOW: Figure 17.8
The 1919 three-vehicle stores train. Van number 1, built in 1893, is in the centre, flanked by newly built vans 2 and 3. Readers are invited to speculate on the livery.

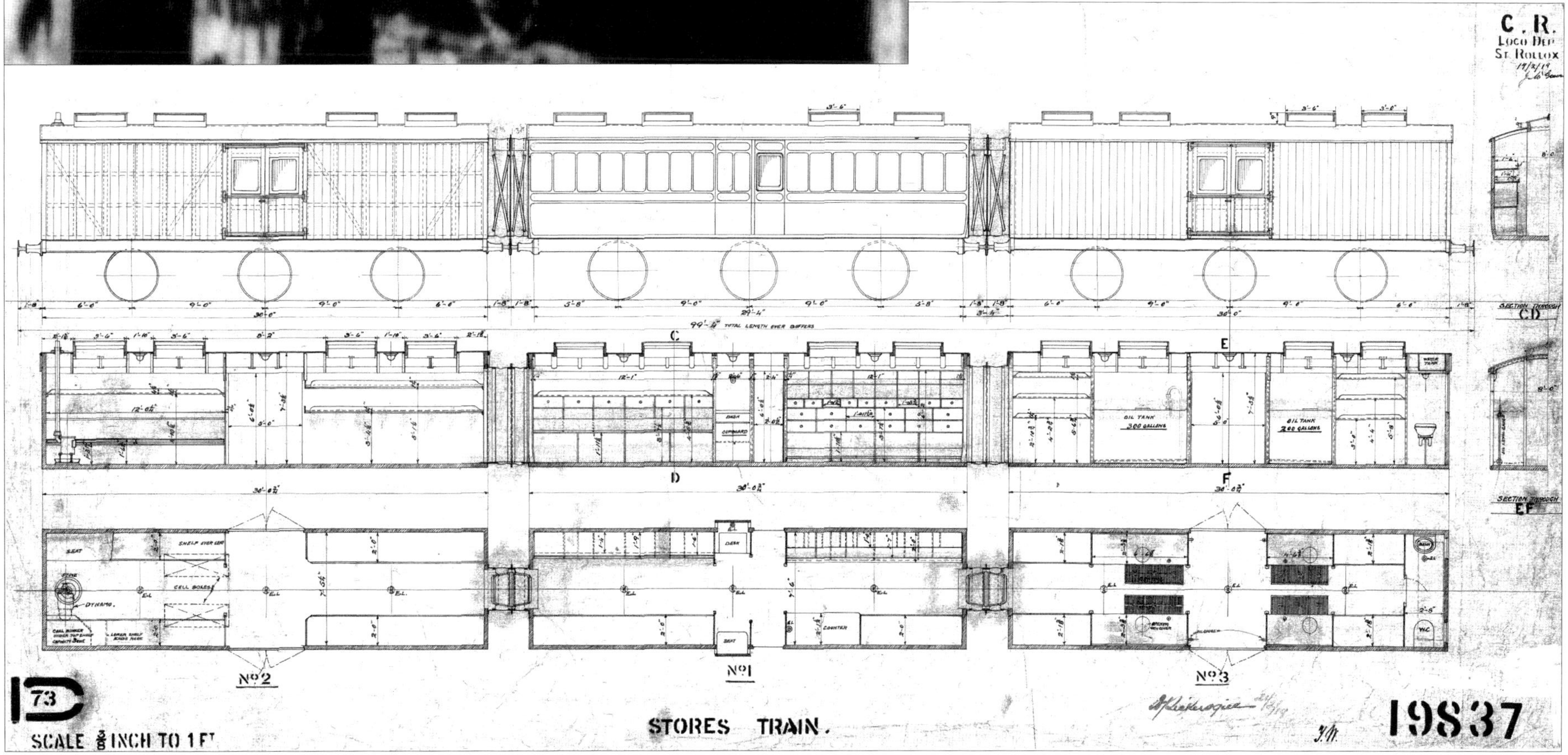

a narrow pair of doors in the centre of each side, with a total opening of only 3 feet 5 inches. The doors had fixed windows. Two oil lamps provided further illumination. The early four-bolt self-contained buffer was fitted. The minutes do not record an authorisation to build any of these vans.

Later drawings which have not survived were 1129 of 1870, for a stores van (large size), and 2739 of 1872. The latter was probably drawn on the authority of a Loco & Stores Committee minute of March 1871.[3]

In 1893 a stores van was built to carriage stock order H99. St. Rollox drawings 7128 and 7192[4] refer, but no diagram was issued, and there is no mention of this van in the minutes. The van was built on a 30-foot passenger brake van underframe. It had gangways at each end, and was fitted internally with shelves, drawers and a desk. It was identified as Stores Van number 1. The month after the stores van drawings, a three-vehicle stores train was proposed, but not proceeded with – the word *'cancelled'* is written alongside the drawing title.[5]

The concept was resurrected in 1919, when drawing 19837[6] showed three vehicles coupled in a 'stores train'. This is shown in Figure 17.8. This time construction went ahead, using van number 1, although there is no authorisation recorded in the minutes and vans 2 and 3 were not built to G or H order numbers. Like stores van 1, the new vans were built on the standard six-wheeled underframe. The bodies of stores vans 2 and 3 were the subject of drawings 19966 and 20009 respectively.[7] The vans had gangways at one end only, so the existing van number 1 was marshalled in the middle of the train. Vans 2 and 3, like van 1, were fitted with electric light.

Weighing Machine Vans

All railways had large numbers of weighing machines. On the Caledonian, there were sixty wagon weighing stations at strategic points around the system, where complete trains were weighed, wagon by wagon.[8] Wayside goods yards had small weighbridges and smaller hand weighing machines. Weighing machines were sited at main stations and all stations had parcel and letter scales.

The machinery required regular maintenance, and rapid repair if they went out of order. This service was provided by the weighing machine manufacturers. The dispersal of the machines around the system necessitated travelling vans to move equipment and personnel.

The Caledonian's contract was with Henry Pooley & Son of Liverpool. A copy of the contract between the CR and Pooley starting in 1913 is in the CRA Archive.[9] It was worth £1,000 per annum. On the railway's side, it agreed to provide six covered vans, to be fitted up at Pooley's expense, and for them to be conveyed by goods train free of charge. Pooley employees were given passes for free travel over the system on company business. Two small repair shops were provided at Glasgow and Dundee.

The only reference in company minutes dates from June 1875, when the Traffic Committee approved construction of *'an extra travelling workshop'* at a cost of £128.[10] This was the subject of St. Rollox drawing 1857.[11] Two copies of this drawing exist, one dated 1881 and the other 12th July 1875. The drawing is not suitable for reproduction.

The drawing depicts a van with horizontally planked sides 16 feet 4¾ inches long by 7 feet 8 inches wide. There were windows towards each end of the sides and one window in the centre of each end. Two oil lamps provided further illumination. The wheelbase was 10 feet, and a wood brake block acted on one wheel.

The only other drawing in the register is St. Rollox 16012 of August 1911.[12] This is for a *'weighing machine road van.'* This was a longer van (17 feet 7½ inches internally). There is no mention of this van in the minutes or the St. Rollox orders, but the company purchased a platform weighing machine from Pooley in April 1911, which may have been part of the equipment for the van.[13]

References
1. NRM 111246/W
2. NRM 11244/W
3. NRS BR/CAL/1/19 entry 329
4. NRS RHP 70079/80
5. St. Rollox drawing 7223, NRM 11235/C, NRS RHP 70081
6. NRM 11234/C
7. NRM 11231/C and NRM 11232/C
8. *1915 List of Goods stations etc.*, p. 79, in the CRA Archive, ref: 3/7/2/9
9. CRA Archive ref: 2/2/1/28
10. NRS BR/CAL/1/22 entry 905
11. NRS RHP 68179, NRM 8052/W
12. NRM 11262/W
13. NRS BR/CAL/1/60 entry 214

Appendix I: Types of Wagon and Numbers in Service

Details of the Wagon Stock in 1874

The information in these tables is taken from a census of rolling stock undertaken in 1874, conducted by independent experts. It amplifies the summary written in Chapter 2.

A further 144 wagons from the 'Portpatrick and Stranraer line' were recorded separately. Most were 6-ton goods (ninety in total). Thirty-nine were recorded as having buffers, for the remaining fifty-one no buffers were mentioned. There were also forty-five cattle trucks, six horse boxes and three carriage trucks from this source. All the wagons and NPCS were four-wheeled. The horseboxes were numbered 21-26 and the carriage trucks 16-20. A photograph of a Portpartrick wagon appears in Plate 9.2 (p. 144).

Opposite Page: Plate 17.27
This early photograph of a lengthy goods train crossing Perth bridge, courtesy of CRA member John Boyle, shows very few vans and an array of goods wagons with their loads mostly covered by tarpaulins. The enlargement of the front of the train on p. 142 reveals that the leading vehicles are early CR goods wagons. In the middle of the train is a CR pre-diagram book 6-ton van. The lettering and running number are painted centrally on the side of the body, and the end carries the additional number. The brake van is a CR pre-diagram book type as shown in Plate 16.1.

Below: Plate App.I.1
A Class '300' 0-6-0 hauls a lengthy goods train in the later years of the Caledonian. Behind the unidentifiable open wagon, there is a Diagram 24 open goods wagon. It is followed by a pig iron wagon with wood underframe, probably to Diagram 16. Next is a Diagram 22 mineral wagon with solid buffers – nearly 4,000 of these wagons remained to be re-buffered in 1918 when the '300' class first appeared. The two wagons in front of the tank wagons are a Diagram 59 mineral, followed by another Diagram 24.

Type of Wagon	In Stock
Ordinary (i.e. goods) with buffers	3,714
Ordinary without buffers	4,152
Cattle	685
Covered vans	989
Coke or sheep	80
Swivel wagons	763
Bar iron or round timber	270
Stone	375
Ballast	216
Beer	50
Furniture van wagons	2
Gunpowder	2
Goods brakes	279
Mineral	21,807
Special 15 ton	6
Special 25 ton	4
Special 30 ton	1
30 ton trolley	1
Total	33,396

NPCS Type	In Stock
Horse box	100
Carriage trucks	35
Fish and game trucks	62
Milk trucks	23
Bullion vans	2
Stores vans	2
Total	224

Details of the Wagon Stock and Changes 1907-1910

For ease of reading, the data has been split into five sections – open goods wagons and vans, other goods wagons, mineral wagons, service vehicles and special class wagons.

Open Goods Wagons and Vans		1907	1910
Empty cask trucks	3 tons	50	46
	6 tons	20	23
Open goods wagons	6 tons	458	438
	7 tons	180	179
	8 tons	12,991	12,764
	10 tons	295	325
	12 tons	36	36
Twin wagons		950	950
Timber wagons		319	319
Lime wagons		40	40
Locomotive wagons		10	
Rail wagons	15 tons	903	903
	25 tons	6	6
Frames carrying tanks		141	137
Goods vans	6 tons	1,601	1,589
	10 tons	206	261
	15 tons	10	14
Meat vans	5 tons	62	60
	6 tons	56	60
Refrigerator		10	10
Total		**18,344**	**18,160**

Other Goods Wagons		1907	1910
Cattle and sheep trucks		997	1,088
Swivel wagons	8 tons	1,954	1,952
	10 tons	198	197
	30 tons	133	133
Gunpowder vans	5 tons	2	2
	7 tons	33	33
Total		**3,317**	**3,405**

Mineral Wagons		1907	1910
Coal wagons	6 tons	4,203	7,576
	7 tons	10,826	
	8 tons	16,802	16,674
	10 tons	1,145	1,142
	14 tons	2,209	2,207
	16 tons	3,415	4,711
	30 tons	100	100
Hopper	40 tons	12	12
Pig iron wagons	6 tons	214	130
	7 tons	8	8
	8 tons	700	681
	10 tons	149	148
	14 tons	750	750
	15 tons	40	40
Total		**40,573**	**34,179**

Service Wagons		1907	1910
Goods and mineral brake vans		591	578
Tank wagons		22	25
Ballast wagons	7 tons	106	91
	8 tons	147	145
	10 tons	1	1
	hopper 12 tons	140	140
Locomotive coal wagons	10 tons	994	992
	30 tons	300	300
Total		**2,301**	**2,272**

Special Class Wagons		1907	1910
Runner wagons	30cwt	8	4
	12 ton		4
Furniture van wagons	8 tons	2	2
	10 tons	8	7
Flat wagons	12 tons	2	2
	15 tons	2	2
	16 tons	4	4
	20 tons	5	5
	30 tons	5	5
Agricultural implement wagons			4
Trolly wagons	12 tons	6	6
	20 tons	6	6
	25 tons	1	1
	30 tons		2
	35 tons	1	1
	40 tons	1	1
Boiler wagons	16 tons	3	3
	25 tons	3	3
	35 tons		2
Machinery wagons		2	2
Well wagons	15 tons	5	5
	30 tons	2	2
Swivel wagons		16	16
Goods wagon	50 tons	1	1
Total		**83**	**90**

Appendix II: St. Rollox Wagon and Service Vehicle Orders

Date DD/MM/YY is the authorisation date, if known, taken from Company minutes, in the series NRS BR/CAL/1/. Stock was usually built within the next six months accountancy period.
C = capital expenditure, R = replacement (charged to the revenue account)
Diagram number refers to the Small Wagon Diagram Book. A blank entry means that the diagram number cannot be ascertained.

Orders Pre-1890

No.	Date	No. Built	C/R	Description	Additional Description	Diag No.
G0		5		Goods Wagons		?15/24
G1		20		Covered Goods Vans		3
G2		15	R	Cattle Wagons	18 recorded as replacements July 1885	10
G3		206	R	Mineral Wagons		21, 22
G4		150		Flexible 6-Wheel Wagons		13
G5		100	C	Swivel Wagons	added in return period ending July 1885	N/D
G6		20		Brake Vans	heavy goods – possibly built by Pickering	?6
G7	17/03/85	30	C	Dead Meat Vans	part of larger request 'reserved for consideration'	2
G8	14/04/85	15	C	Brake Vans	goods & mineral	6
G9	do.	100	C	Rail Wagons	with folding sides	13
G10	do.	400	C	Goods Wagons		15, 24
G11	do.	100	C	Swivel Bar Wagons		N/D
G12	do.	100	C	Round Timber or Iron Wagons		N/D
G13		20	C	Dead Meat Vans	probably rest of order started with G7	2
G14		200		Sets of wheels & axles		N/D
G15		16		Goods Wagons		15, 24
G16		1		Swivel Wagon		N/D
G17		200	R	Mineral Wagons		21, 22
G18		100		Goods Wagons		15, 24
G19		10	R	Cattle Wagons	90 in July 1886 return. See also G23/28	10
G20		6		Swivel Wagons		N/D
G21		10	R	Covered Goods Vans		3
G22		8	R	Empty Barrel Trucks	on old carriage underframes	12
G23		65	R	Cattle Wagons	medium sized, replaced G24 wagons	10
G24		65	R	Coke Wagons	converted from large cattle wagons	N/D
G25		1		Emergency Van	for Perth	?7
G25	1886	10		Lime Wagons		25
G26		1		Emergency Van	for Motherwell	?7
G26		70		Goods Wagons		15, 24
G27		1		Breakdown Van	for Perth	7
G27		100	R	Mineral Wagons		22
G28		1		Breakdown Van	for Motherwell	7
G28		15	R	Cattle Wagons		10
G29		10		Covered Goods Vans		3
G30		2		Brake Vans	goods	6
G30		1		Emergency Van	for Carlisle	?7
G31		1		Emergency Van	for Dawsholm	?7
G31		170		Mineral Wagons		22
G32		1		Emergency Van	for Hamilton	?7
G32		100		Goods Wagons		15, 24
G33		1		Breakdown Van	for Carlisle	7

No.	Date	No. Built	C/R	Description	Additional Description	Diag No.
G33		3		Swivel Wagons		N/D
G34		1		Breakdown Van	for Dawsholm	7
G34		10		Covered Goods Vans		3
G35		5		Brake Vans	goods & mineral	6
G35		1		Breakdown Van	for Hamilton	7
G36		2	R	Empty Barrel Trucks	on old carriage underframes	12
G37		20		Covered Goods Vans		3
G38		100		Goods Wagons		15, 24
G39		180		Mineral Wagons		22
G40		10		Lime Wagons		25
G41		2		Breakdown Vans		7
G42		2	R	Machinery Wagons	rebuild Nos 2494 & 2495	17
G43		50		Goods Wagons		15, 24
G44		6	R	Swivel Wagons		N/D
G45		6		Ballast Wagons		23
G46		160		Mineral Wagons		22
G47		6	R	Brake Vans	goods	6
G48		6		Brake Vans	goods	6
G49	1888/9	76		Goods Wagons for 24-foot boards	Montrose timber traffic	N/D
G50		25		Fresh Meat Vans		1
G51		10	R	Cattle Trucks		10
G52		6	R	Swivel Wagons		N/D
G53		188	R	Mineral Wagons		22
G54		20		Lime Wagons		25
G55		25		Fresh Meat Vans		1
G56		180		Goods Wagons		15, 24
G57		6	R	Swivel Wagons		N/D
G58		40		Rail Wagons	six-wheel	13
G59	08/01/89	200	C	Swivel Bar Wagons	ordered prior to Board approval	14
G60	do.	180		Goods Wagons		15, 24
G61	do.	20		Cattle Trucks		10
G62	do.	100		Mineral Wagons		22
G63	do.	20	C	Brake Vans	goods & mineral	5
G64	do.	300	C	15-ton Rail Wagons		13
G65	do.	500	C	Goods Wagons		15, 24
G66		100		Goods Wagons		15, 24
G67		10	R	Covered Goods Vans	recorded in January 1890 return	3
G68		100		Mineral Wagons		22
G69	02/10/89	3	R	Gunpowder Vans	possibly recorded in July 1890 return	4
G70	05/11/89	250		Pig Iron Wagons		16
G71		6	R	Empty Barrel Trucks	on old carriage underframes	12
G72	04/12/89	1	R	Tanks, Oil, on old wagon underframes	Maxwell, Dundee	N/D
G73	do.	3	C	Tanks, on new underframe	C. Tennant & Coy	N/D
G74	03/12/89	500	C	Goods Wagons	} 750 wagons approved, no details given	15, 24
G75	do.	250	C	Pig Iron Wagons		16

Orders 1890-1894

No.	Date	No. Built	C/R	Description	Additional Description	Diag No.
G76	21/01/90	6	R	Runner Wagons for boiler wagons		N/D
G77	do.	180	R	Goods Wagons		15, 24
G78	do.	100	R	Mineral Wagons	} 308 *'merchandise stock'* approved	22
G79	do.	6	R	Swivel Bar Wagons		14
G80	do.	6	R	Ballast Wagons		23

No.	Date	No. Built	C/R	Description	Additional Description	Diag No.
G81	04/03/90	1	C	25-ton Trolley Wagon		20
G82	19/08/90	150	R	Goods Wagons		15, 24
G83	do.	100	R	Mineral Wagons	262 wagons authorised, no details given	22
G84	do.	6	R	Swivel Bar Wagons		14
G85	do.	6	R	Ballast Wagons		23
G86	26/11/90	150	R	Goods Wagons		15, 24
G87	do.	100	R	Mineral Wagons		22
G88	do.	6	R	Cattle Wagons		10
G89	do.	1	R	25-ton Boiler Wagon	262 wagons authorised, no details given	28
G89	do.	2		16-ton Boiler Wagon		26
G89	do.	2		16-ton Machinery Wagons		27
G89	do.	2		25-ton Machinery Wagons		31
G90	24/02/91	25	C	14-ton Brake Vans	mineral	5
M77	20/05/91	1		Single Gas Tank	to run between Perth and Aberdeen	N/D
G91	22/05/91	1,500	C	8-ton Coal wagons	2,000 authorised. Painted 'to be returned to Lesmahagow Section'	22
G92	do.	200	C	10-ton Loco Coal Wagons	painted as above	N/D
G93	02/06/91	100	R	Goods Wagons	12 for Alum & Ammonia Coy	15, 24
G94	do.	150	R	Mineral Wagons		22
G95	do.	6	R	Ballast Wagons		23
G96	do.	6	R	Cattle Trucks		10
M84	Oct 91	1		Single Gas Tank		N/D
G97	05/01/92	200	R	Swivel Bar Wagons		14
G98	do.	200	R	Twin Wagons		37
G99	19/01/92	1		Tanks, on underframe	C. Tennant & Coy	N/D
G100	16/02/92	4		Tanks	Coltness Iron Coy	N/D
G101		500	R	Goods Wagons	side doors, 400 built to this order, 100 to G102	24
G102	07/06/92	100	R	Goods Wagons		24
G103	do.	200	R	8-ton Mineral Wagons		22
G104	do.	6	R	Ballast Wagons		23
G105	do.	6	R	Cattle Trucks		10
G106	do.	6	R	Covered Goods Vans		3
G107	do.	3	R	Gunpowder Vans		4
G108	22/12/92	6	R	Goods Wagons		15, 24
G109	do.	6	R	Cattle Trucks		10
G110	do.	12	R	Brake Vans	goods	5
G111	23/05/93	4	R	Empty Barrel Trucks		12
G112	do.	50	R	Pig Iron Wagons		16
G113	do.	250	R	Mineral Wagons	341 wagons authorised, no details given	22
G114	do.	12	R	Cattle Trucks		10
G115	do.	25	R	Covered Goods Vans		3
G116	06/12/93	250	R	Mineral Wagons	spindle buffers	46
G117	do.	50	R	Cattle Wagons		10
G118	do.	50	R	Covered Goods Vans	with double doors	3
G119	do.	6	R	Empty Barrel Trucks		12
G120	20/03/94	500	C	Mineral Wagons	spindle buffers	46
G121	do.	500	C	Mineral Wagons	spindle buffers	46
G122	do.	500	C	Mineral Wagons	spindle buffers	46
G123	do.	20	C	14-ton Brake Vans	goods	5
G124	07/08/94	450	R	Mineral Wagons	spindle buffers	46
	05/09/94	1	C	Single Gas Tank	'on Law Junction, Holytown, Hamilton & Coatbridge Circuits'	N/D
G125	21/12/94	300	R	Mineral Wagons	spindle buffers	46

No.	Date	No. Built	C/R	Description	Additional Description	Diag No.
G126	21/12/94	16	R	Covered Goods Vans		3
G126	do.	6	R	Covered Goods Vans	with ventilator for yeast traffic	3
G126	do.	3	R	Gunpowder Vans		4
G127	do.	75	R	Goods Wagons		15, 24

Orders 1895-1899

No.	Date	No. Built	C/R	Description	Additional Description	Diag No.
G128	04/09/95	50	R	Twin Timber Trucks	folding ends & iron standards on sides	37
G129	do.	47	R	Covered Goods Vans		3
G130	do.	3	R	Gunpowder Vans		4
G131	do.	50	R	Cattle Trucks		10
G132	do.	170	R	Goods Wagons		15, 24
G133	do.	100	R	Mineral Wagons	spindle buffers	46
G134	06/11/95	500	C	Mineral Wagons	spindle buffers	46
G135	do.	20	C	Brake Vans	goods	5
G136	do.	750	C	Mineral Wagons	spindle buffers	46
G137	19/11/95	500	R	Goods Wagons	with centre side doors	24
G138	12/02/96	2		Underframes, wagon	United Alkali Co.	N/D
G139	22/04/96	500	R	Goods Wagons	with centre side doors	24
G140	do.	12	R	Ballast Wagons		13
G141	06/05/96	1	C	40-ton Trolley Wagon		41
G142	do.	2	C	20-ton Boiler Wagons		42
G143	do.	2	C	15-ton Glass Wagons	nos 43 & 44	38
G144	19/05/96	2	C	Tanks, on new underframe	Alex Hope Jnr & Co.	N/D
G145	01/09/96	2	R	Empty Barrel Trucks	on old carriage underframes	12
G146	08/07/96	2	C	Tanks, Vitriol, on new wagon underframes	C. Tennant & Coy (Panmure)	N/D
G147		750	C	Mineral Wagons	spindle buffers	46
G148	09/08/96	2		Tanks, Vitriol, on new wagon underframes	C. Tennant & Coy (cancelled, wagons to G146 supplied)	N/D
M148	02/09/96	1	R	Gas Tank for Dawsholm Works	conversion of old tender	N/D
G149	04/11/96	200	R	Goods Wagons	with centre side doors	24
G150	do.	100	R	Swivel Bar Wagons		14
G151	do.	100	R	Twin Wagons		37
G152		100		Mineral Wagons	spindle buffers	46
G153		200	C	Swivel Bar Wagons		14
G154		100		Twin Wagons		37
G155	23/12/96	3	C	Tanks, on new wagon underframes	Robinson & Hunter	N/D
M154	do.	2		Double Gas Tanks	for Dundee and Kirriemuir trains	N/D
G156	06/01/97	2	C	Tanks, on new wagon underframes	Alex Cross & Sons Ltd	N/D
M159	03/02/97	2		Travelling Gas Tanks	single	N/D
G157	01/09/97	2	C	Tanks, on new wagon underframes	George Miller & Coy	N/D
G158	do.	6	R	Gunpowder Vans		4
G159	do.	38	R	Covered Goods Vans	made with horizontal boarding	3
G159	do.	6	R	Gunpowder Vans		4
G160	do.	10	R	Brake Vans	goods	5
G161	17/11/97	200	R	Mineral Wagons	spindle buffers	46
G162	do.	200	R	Goods Wagons	with centre side doors	24
G163	do.	5	R	30-ton Heavy Weight Wagons	flat wagon	43
G164	01/12/97	50	C	Brake Vans	goods & mineral	45
G165	15/03/98	1,000	C	Goods Wagons	with centre side doors	24
G166	do.	500	C	Twin Wagons	folding sides	47
G167	do.	500	C	Swivel Bar Wagons	folding doors	48

No.	Date	No. Built	C/R	Description	Additional Description	Diag No.
G168	21/04/98	4	R	16-ton Heavy Weight Wagons	4-wheel	49
G169	do.	4	R	Empty Cask Wagons	on old carriage underframes	12
G170	do.	300	R	Goods Wagons		15, 24
G171	do.	12	R	Ballast Wagons		23
M181	25/05/98	3		Twin Gas Tanks	for Dundee East	N/D
M202	11/01/99	2	R	Equip 2 Travelling Tank Wagons in use with an additional tank each	gas supply for Buchanan Street	N/D
G172	25/01/99	300	R	Goods Wagons		15, 24
G173	do.	80	R	Covered Goods Vans		3
M207	01/03/99	1		Twin Travelling Gas Tank	for charging at Lockerbie	N/D
G174	24/03/99	1	C	50-ton Iron Ore Bogie Wagon	100 authorised, reduced to 2, only 1 built	50
M208	12/04/99	1		New tank for carrying gas oil		N/D
G175	29/05/99	300	R	8-ton Goods Wagons		24
G176	24/03/99	1,000	C	8-ton Goods Wagons		24
G177	do.	15	R	Empty Cask Wagons	on old carriage underframes	12
G178	15/11/99	1	R	16-ton Ore Wagon	300 mineral wagons authorised. The hopper wagons may not have been built. Eight 'tipping wagons for the Muirkirk section' may have been purchased in May 1900 instead	51
G179	do.	8	R	Hopper Wagons		
G179	do.	291	R	Mineral Wagons		46
G179	do.	1	R	Tank Wagon		32

Orders 1900-1904

No.	Date	No. Built	C/R	Description	Additional Description	Diag No.
M235	10/01/00	2		Travelling Gas Tanks	1 Hamilton, 1 Law Junction	N/D
M237	23/02/00	1		Tank underframe	Robinson & Hunter tar distillers	N/D
G180	11/08/00	87	C	14-ton Mineral Wagons	400 mineral authorised 05/00	52
G180	do.	201	R	16-ton Mineral Wagons		51
G180	do.	12	C	10-ton Mineral Wagons	with hopper bottoms – probably built for United Turkey Red Co. in 1904	75
G181	do.	6	C	12-ton Trolley Wagons		53
G182	19/09/00	1		Tank Underframe	Cross's gas tank 102 (2 authorised)	N/D
G183	10/01/01	2		Tank Underframe	United Alkali Co. Ltd	N/D
G184	18/02/01	87	C	14-ton Mineral Wagons		52
G185	07/03/01	2		Tanks, on underframe	E B Robinson & Coy	N/D
G186	23/03/01	250	R	14-ton Mineral Wagons		52
G187	03/04/01	1		Tanks, on underframe	Glengarnock Chemical Co.	N/D
G188	29/05/01	1		Tanks, on underframe	Cross's Chemical Co.	N/D
	15/10/01	1		Additional Gas Tank	for conveyance of gas oil to Dawsholm	N/D
G189	11/01	3		Boat Wagons	'Special Goods Wagon' in diagram book	58
G189	11/01	122		14-ton Mineral Wagons		52
G190	29/10/01	25		Hopper Wagons	for Blackwood to Darvel & Muirkirk Railways	64
M281	do.	1		Slag Spreading Plough	to go with above	65
G191	do.	1		Brake Van	Engineer's Department	61
G192	03/12/01	1		Tank Underframe	United Alkali Co., new wagon, mounted with tank	N/D
G193	05/12/01	290	R	14-ton Mineral Wagons		52
G194	17/12/01	70	C	30-ton Mineral Wagons	500 authorised 'to be built own workshop.' 300 built by contractors. 12 were built as hopper wagons to G201	54
G195	do.	3	C	Trolley Wagons	'similar to Nos. 41 & 42'	56
G196	14/01/02	1000	C	14-ton Mineral Wagons	spindle buffers	52
G197		1		Brake Van	slag spreading plough	65
G198	08/07/02	250	R	14-ton Mineral Wagons	spindle buffers	52
G199	do.	6	R	Ballast Wagons		57
G200	12/08/02	75	C	Hopper Wagons	ballast	64

No.	Date	No. Built	C/R	Description	Additional Description	Diag No.
G201	21/10/02	12	C	40-ton Hopper Wagons	mineral	66
G202	18/11/02	12	R	15-ton Brake Vans	goods	62
G203	do.	200	R	Pig Iron Wagons		16
G204	do.	70	R	16-ton Mineral Wagons	Fox pressed steel underframes	59
G205	do.	6	R	Ballast Wagons		57
G206	13/01/03	2	R	Well Wagons	same as no. 3	18
G207	27/01/03	1,000	C	16-ton Mineral Wagons		59
G208	do.	300	C	14-ton Pig Iron Wagons		16
G209	do.	100	C	Cattle Trucks		10
G210	do.	40	C	20-ton Brake Vans	annotated *'Goods, 1 built with w/house, the remainder in 1907'*	63
G211		2		Tanks, on new underframe	Alex Cross & Sons Ltd	N/D
G212	19/05/03	250	R	14-ton Pig Iron Wagons		16
G213	do.	20	R	Empty Cask Wagons	4 wheels	74
G214	do.	4		Tanks, on new underframe	Alex Hope Jnr & Co.	N/D
G215	02/06/03	4		Tanks, on new underframe	Alex Hope Jnr & Co.	N/D
G216	03/11/03	12	R	Gunpowder Vans		78
G217	do.	2	R	15-ton Brake Vans	goods	62
G218	do.	50	R	10-ton Goods Wagons		24
G219	do.	200	R	16-ton Mineral Wagons	steel underframe	59
G220	26/01/04	2		Tanks, on wagon frames	for Alex Hope Jnr	N/D
G221	1903	13		16-ton Mineral Wagons	Leeds Forge steel underframe	59
G222	24/05/04	36	R	12-ton Goods Wagons		79
G223	do.	12	R	Gunpowder Vans		78
G224	do.	6	R	Covered Goods Vans		67
G225	do.	5	R	15-ton Brake Vans	goods	62
G226	do.	6	R	Ballast Wagons		57
G227	do.	4		Tank Underframe	new wood, tanks supplied by Alex Hope	N/D
G228	26/01/04	1		Tanks, on underframe	Alex Cross & Sons Ltd	N/D
G229	01/08/04	1		Tank, on underframe	United Alkali Co. Ltd	N/D
G230	04/10/04	8	R	30-ton Bogie Swivel Wagons		81
G231	do.	9	R	Gunpowder Vans		78
G232	do.	50	R	10-ton Goods Wagons		24
G233	do.	40	R	16-ton Coke Wagons	hopper bottom	75
G234	do.	85	R	16-ton Mineral Wagons		59
G235	13/09/04	2		10-ton Tanks, on steel underframes	Messrs Briggs, Arbroath	N/D
G236		1		10-ton Tank Underframe	build new for Alex Hope Jnr & Co.	N/D

Orders 1905-1909

No.	Date	No. Built	C/R	Description	Additional Description	Diag No.
G237	28/03/05	10	R	15-ton Covered Goods Vans		80
G238	do.	10	R	Refrigerator Meat Vans		84
G239	do.	20	R	14-ton Hopper Wagons		75
G240	do.	190	R	16-ton Mineral Wagons	210 mineral wagons authorised	59
G241	11/04/05	2	R	30-ton Well Wagons		82
G242	14/11/05	50	C	Bogie Swivel Wagons	possibly supplied by Leeds Forge	81
G243	04/09/05	210	R	16-ton Mineral Wagons	steel underframe	59
G244	do.	40	R	15-ton Pig Iron Wagons	steel underframe	85
G245	14/11/05	35	R	Hopper Wagons	with steel underframes	75
G246	do.	40	R	Hopper Ballast Wagons	with steel underframes	86
G247	do.	3	R	Brake Vans	slag spreading ploughs	65
G248		2		Tanks, on wagon underframes	Alex Cross & Sons Ltd	N/D
G249		3		Tanks, on 10-ton CR underframes	United Alkali Co. Ltd	N/D

APPENDICES

No.	Date	No. Built	C/R	Description	Additional Description	Diag No.
G250	24/04/06	40	R	10-ton Goods Wagons	steel underframe and centre doors	87
G251	do.	12	R	15-ton Brake Vans	goods	62
G252	do.	6	R	8-ton Ballast Wagons		57
G253	do.	200	R	16-ton Mineral Wagons	steel underframe	59
G254	15/05/06	2		Tanks, on 10-ton CR underframes	Alex Hope Jnr & Co.	N/D
G255		1		Tank Underframe	wood for D McQueen	N/D
G256	02/10/06	20	R	16-ton Mineral Wagons	steel underframe. Leeds Forge offer of 20 underframes accepted on date given	59
G257	23/10/06	20	R	Cattle Wagons		10
G258	23/10/06	6	R	15-ton Brake Vans	goods	62
G259	do.	12	R	8-ton Ballast Wagons		57
G260	do.	157	R	16-ton Mineral Wagons	steel underframe	59
G261	08/01/07	300	R	16-ton Mineral Wagons	steel underframe	59
G262	05/02/07	2		Tank Underframe	Cross Chemical Co.	N/D
G263	do.	2		Tank Underframe	United Alkali Co.	N/D
G264	23/04/07	190	R	16-ton Mineral Wagons	steel underframe	59
G265	do.	300	R	16-ton Mineral Wagons	steel underframe purchase authorised	59
G266	02/07/07	2	R	30-ton Trolley Wagons	for steel plate	89
G267	do.	300	R	16-ton Mineral Wagons	steel underframe	59
G268	26/09/07	100	R	10-ton Goods Wagons	steel underframe and folding sides	87
G269	do.	12	R	10-ton Covered Goods Vans	4-wheel	67
G270	do.	4	R	10-ton Covered Goods Vans	for C&O with Westinghouse brake	91
G271	do.	2	R	15-ton Rail Wagons		60
G272	do.	56	R	16-ton Mineral Wagons	steel underframe	59
G273	do.	4	R	6-ton Meat Vans	4-wheel, dual brake	90
G274	31/03/08	4	R	15-ton Covered Goods Vans		80
G275	do.	181	R	16-ton Mineral Wagons		59
G276	14/04/08	50		16-ton Mineral Wagons	charged to suspense account	59
G277	31/10/08	190	R	16-ton Mineral Wagons		59
G278	29/09/08	1		Tank Underframe	United Alkali Co.	N/D
G279		1		Tank Underframe	Alex Cross & Co.	N/D
G280	30/03/09	20	R	10-ton Covered Goods Vans	Morton brake either side, grease axleboxes	67
G281	do.	1	R	15-ton Agricultural Implement Wagon	No. 78	93
G282	do.	50	R	Cattle Trucks		10
G283	do.	4	R	12-ton Runner Wagons		122
G284	16/11/09	50	R	Cattle Trucks		10
G285	do.	2	R	35-ton Boiler Wagons		94
G286	do.	20	R	10-ton Covered Goods Vans		67
G287	do.	3	R	Empty Cask Wagons		74
G288	14/12/09	2		Tank Underframe	acid tank for United Alkali Co.	N/D

Orders 1910-1914

No.	Date	No. Built	C/R	Description	Additional Description	Diag No.
G289	24/05/10	50	R	Cattle Trucks		10
G290	do.	20	R	10-ton Covered Goods Vans		67
G291	do.	6	R	15-ton Covered Goods Vans		80
G292	do.	4	R	12-ton Runner Wagons		122
G293	do.	110	R	16-ton Mineral Wagons	steel underframe	59
G294	do.	250	R	16-ton Mineral Wagons		59
G295	15/11/10	50	R	Cattle Trucks		10
G296	do.	20	R	10-ton Covered Goods Vans		67
G297	do.	75	R	16-ton Mineral Wagons	110 authorised – see order G300	59
G298	do.	1	R	20-ton Trolley Wagon	for propellers	95

No.	Date	No. Built	C/R	Description	Additional Description	Diag No.
G299	15/11/10	2	R	35-ton Trolley Wagons	for plates	96
G300	do.	20	R	20-ton Hopper Wagons	instead of 35 16-ton minerals to G297	97
G301	10/01/11	3		Tank Underframe	Scottish Oil & Fuel Co.	N/D
G302	24/01/11	4		Tank Underframe	A Hope Jnr & Co.	N/D
G303	21/03/11	500	R	16-ton Mineral Wagons	were to be sub-contracted	59
G304	16/05/11	50	R	Cattle Trucks	higher roofs to suit cavalry horses	10
G305	do.	68	R	10-ton Covered Goods Vans		67
G306	do.	56	R	16-ton Mineral Wagons		59
G307	19/11/11	100	C	10-ton Covered Goods Vans	originally approved 07/03/11, Iracier axleboxes & bushes. 40 to be fitted with dual brake and screw couplings	67
G308		1		Tank Underframe	United Alkali Co.	N/D
G309	14/11/11	50	R	Cattle Trucks	either side brake – Morton	10
G310	do.	25	R	10-ton Covered Goods Vans	either side brake	67
G311	do.	25	R	16-ton Hopper Wagons	either side brake	98
G312	do.	15	R	12-ton Goods Wagons	either side brake	79
G313	do.	1	R	20-ton Trolley Well Wagons	bogie	99
G314	do.	18	R	16-ton Mineral Wagons	either side brake	59
G315	28/11/11	1		Tank Underframe	Alex Cross & Sons	N/D
G316	12/12/11	6		Tank Underframes	2 Steel, 4 Wood, Jas Ross & Co. Camelon	N/D
G317	20/02/12	4		Tank Underframes	Alex Hope Jnr & Co.	N/D
G318	02/04/12	50	R	Cattle Trucks		10
G319	do.	60	R	10-ton Covered Goods Vans		67
G320	do.	10	R	20-ton Goods Brake Vans	outside framed	63
G321	do.	4	R	Combination Brake & Road Vans		104
G322	do.	1	R	40-ton Trolley Wagon		100
G323	17/09/12	50	R	Cattle Trucks		10
G324	do.	10	R	Covered Carriage Trucks	with end doors	101
G325	do.	30	R	10-ton Covered Goods Vans	dual brake	67
G326	do.	1	R	20-ton Trolley Well Wagon		99
G327	do.	140	R	16-ton Mineral Wagons		59
G328		1		Tank Underframe	United Alkali Co.	N/D
G329	29/10/12	250	R	16-ton Pig Iron Wagons	either side brake	110
G330	do.	250	R	16-ton Mineral Wagons	Iracier axle boxes – 750 authorised	59
G331	07/01/13	10	R	20-ton Brake Vans	goods, outside framed	63
G332	04/02/13	50	R	Cattle Trucks		10
G333	do.	50	R	10-ton Covered Goods Vans		67
G334	do.	2	R	35-ton Trolley Wagons		96
G335	do.	1	R	35-ton Well Wagon		112
G336	do.	2	R	30-ton Ingot Wagons		113
G337	do.	2	R	40-ton Heavy Weight Wagons		111
G338	do.	175	R	10-ton Goods Wagons	with falling sides	87
G339	18/03/13	10	C	20-ton Brake Vans	goods, outside framed	63
G340	15/04/13	25	C	16-ton Tube Wagons		114
G341		1		Tank Underframe	Alex Cross & Sons Ltd	N/D
G342	02/09/13	50	R	Cattle Trucks		10
G343	do.	100	R	10-ton Covered Goods Vans		67
G344	do.	20	R	15-ton Covered Goods Vans		115
G345	do.	10	R	20-ton Hopper Wagons		97
G346	do.	6	R	30-foot Motor Car Vans	covered carriage trucks, end doors. Probably built 09/16	101
G347	do.	1	R	20-ton Trolley Wagons		95
G348	do.	2	R	15-ton Agricultural Implement Wagons		117

APPENDICES

No.	Date	No. Built	C/R	Description	Additional Description	Diag No.
G349	02/09/13	12	R	Empty Cask Wagons	either side brake	74
G350	do.	30	R	10-ton Goods Wagons		87
G351	16/09/13	4	R	6-Wheel Fish Vans	with ice tanks, dual brake, steam pipe	116
G352	14/10/13	1	R	Emergency Tool Van	to be stationed at Carstairs	119
G353	10/03/14	40	R	Cattle Trucks		10
G354	do.	35	R	10-ton Goods Wagons		87
G355	do.	25	R	16-ton Tube Wagons		114
G356	do.	8	R	20-ton Brake Vans	goods outside framed	63
G357	do.	3	R	35-ton Trolley Wagons		96
G358	do.	3	R	40-ton Heavy Weight Wagons		111
G359	do.	90	R	16-ton Mineral Wagons		59
G360	do.	40	R	10-ton Covered Goods Vans	dual fitted, new brake arrangement	67
G361	02/06/14	1		Tank Underframe, steel	for Jas Ross & Co. Camelon	N/D
G362	04/10/14	45	R	10-ton Covered Goods Vans		67
G363	do.	12	R	6-ton Empty Cask Wagons	either side brake	74
G364	do.	1	R	50-ton Trolley Wagon		118
G365	do.	1	R	20-ton Trolley Well Wagon		99
G366	do.	2	R	35-ton Ingot Wagons		113
G367	do.	40	R	10-ton Hopper Wagons		98
G368	do.	40	R	10-ton Goods Wagons	falling sides, dual brake, steam heat pipe	87
G369	01/12/14	1		Tank Underframe, wood	for acid, R Smith's Executors	N/D

Orders 1915-1922

No.	Date	No. Built	C/R	Description	Additional Description	Diag No.
G370	09/03/15	80	R	10-ton Covered Goods Vans		67
G371	do.	20	R	10-ton Covered Goods Vans	dual fitted	67
G372	do.	20	R	10-ton Hopper Wagons	16-ton wagons authorised	121
G373	do.	24	R	12-ton Goods Wagons	with centre doors	120
G374	do.	9	R	20-ton Brake Vans	goods outside framed	63
G375	23/05/15	1		Tank Underframe	United Alkali Co.	N/D
G376	27/05/15	1		Tank Underframe, steel	for sulphuric acid, Richard Smith's executors	N/D
G377	11/01/16	60	R	10-ton Covered Goods Vans		67
G378	do.	13	R	20-ton Brake Vans	goods outside framed	63
G379	do.	20	R	16-ton Tube Wagons		114
G380	do.	4	R	35-ton Boiler Wagons		94
G381	do.	1	R	20-ton Trolley Well Wagon		99
G382	do.	70	R	16-ton Pig Iron Wagons	priced as batches of 50 & 20	110
G383	04/04/16	100	R	10-ton Goods Wagons	eventually built by Pickering, CO 30872	87
G384	do.	100	R	16-ton Mineral Wagons	wood underframes, built by Clayton	59
G385	do.	100	R	16-ton Pig Iron Wagons	120 authorised, built by Hurst Nelson	110
G386	07/03/16	2		Tank Underframes, wood	for sulphuric acid, Alex Cross & Sons	N/D
G387	02/05/16	2		Tank Underframes	old wagon, John Miller & Co., Aberdeen	N/D
G388	do.	1		Emergency Tool Van	Northern District	119
G389	13/06/16	1		Tank Underframe	Richard Smith's executors	N/D
G390	05/09/16	45	R	10-ton Covered Goods Vans		67
G391	do.	25	R	10-ton Covered Goods Vans	dual brake	67
G392	do.	80	R	10-ton Goods Wagons	falling sides	87
G393	do.	60	R	16-ton Pig Iron Wagons		110
G394	do.	100	R	16-ton Mineral Wagons	wood underframes	59
G395	do.	60	R	16-ton Loco Coal Wagons	wood underframes. Built by Pickering CO 29760	59
G346	do.	6	R	6-wheel Covered Carriage Trucks	probable re-authorisation of minute dated 02/09/13	101

No.	Date	No. Built	C/R	Description	Additional Description	Diag No.
G396	14/11/16	1		Tank Underframe, wood	for sulphuric acid, United Alkali Co.	N/D
G397	20/03/17	210	R	16-ton Mineral Wagons	wood underframes. Only 60 may have been built	59
G398	do.	30	R	20-ton Brake Vans	goods & mineral. 1 van modified with closed ends and Westinghouse fitted	63
G399	do.	60	R	10-ton Covered Goods Vans		67
G400	do.	2	R	15-ton Agricultural Implement Wagons	Nos 375 & 376 similar to No. 10	117
G401	do.	2	R	20-ton Trolley Wagons	same as CR 224	99
G402	do.	1	R	20-ton Trolley Wagon	to replace No. 1, Diagram 34	123
G403	17/04/17	1		Tank Underframe, wood	for acid, United Alkali Co.	N/D
G404	18/09/17	50	R	20-ton Rail Wagons	cancelled, perhaps built to G419	124
G405	do.	1	R	35-ton Trolley Wagon		96
G406	do.	30	R	20-ton Brake Vans	goods, outside framed	63
G407	do.	105	R	16-ton Mineral Wagons	wood underframes	59
G408	16/04/18	290	R	16-ton Mineral Wagons	wood underframes	59
G409	do.	50	R	10-ton Goods Wagons		87
G410	do.	50	R	20-ton Rail Wagons	cancelled 29/07/19 – See G419	124
G411	do.	1	R	20-ton Implement Wagon	special wagon No. 25	117
G412		50		16-ton Mineral Wagons		59
G413		71		10-ton Goods Wagons		87
G414		1		40-ton Trolley Wagon	'new class, 8ft wide No. 40 class'	125
G415		1		20-ton Trolley Wagon	same as G313 & No. 224 class	99
G416		1		20-ton Implement Wagon	No. 63	117
G417		15		20-ton Brake Vans	cancelled 29/07/19	63
G417		66		16-ton Mineral Wagons		59
G418		300		16-ton Mineral Wagons	cancelled 29/07/19	59
G418		25		10-ton Goods Wagons		87
G419		66		10-ton Goods Wagons	cancelled 29/07/19	87
G419		50		20-ton Rail Wagons		124
G420		15		20-ton Brake Vans	cancelled 29/07/19	63
G420	1922	15	R	20-ton Brake Vans		63
G421	do.	12	R	6-ton Gunpowder Vans		78
G422	do.	1	R	20-ton Implement Wagon	a minute dated 22nd December 1922 stated that 461 wagons were authorised for the period ending 31st December 1922, so these wagons must have been built during that year	117
G423	do.	30	R	16-ton Tube Wagons		114
G424	do.	50	R	12-ton Goods Wagons		120
G425	do.	260	R	16-ton Mineral Wagons		59
G426	do.	14	R	35-ton Bogie Rail Wagons		
G427	do.	50	R	10-ton Goods Wagons		87
G428	do.	29	R	16-ton Mineral Wagons		59

Appendix III: St. Rollox Non-Passenger Coaching Stock Orders

Dates are usually the 6 month accountancy period during which the vehicles were built. Dates are taken from the reprint of the Coaching and NPCS Register, CRA Archive ref: 3/4/1/14. The reprint is available for sale from the Association.
Diagram numbers refer to the Wagon Diagram Book
C = capital, R = replacement (charged to the revenue account)

Orders Pre-1890

No.	Date	No. Built	C/R	Description	Additional Description	Diag No.
H8	11/85	10	R	Horse Boxes		9
H18	1/87	10	R	Covered Carriage Trucks		11
H22	do.	6	R	Horse Boxes		9
H25	do.	4	R	Covered Carriage Trucks		11
H27	04/89	12	R	Open Carriage Trucks	on old carriage underframes	N/D
H35	07/89	7	R	Horse Boxes		9
H36	do.	8	R	Fish & Milk Trucks	on old carriage underframes	N/D
H38	1889	9	R	Empty Barrel Trucks	on old carriage underframes	N/D

Orders 1890-1894

No.	Date	No. Built	C/R	Description	Additional Description	Diag No.
H41	01/90	25	R	Horse Boxes		9
H45	07/90	17	R	Fish & Milk Trucks	from old carriage underframes	N/D
H51	1891	10	R	Open Fish Trucks	on old carriage underframes	N/D
H60	1891	2	R	Covered Milk Trucks		29
H61	01/91	4	R	Covered Carriage Trucks	old underframes	11A
H68	do.	3	R	Horse Boxes		9
H69	do.	2	R	Milk Trucks		29
H74	01/92	2	R	Covered Carriage Trucks	on old underframes	11A
H75	do.	5	R	Fish, Fruit & Milk Vans	2 built for carriage of live fish	30
H76	do.	5	R	Horse Boxes		9
H88	01/93	5	R	Horse Boxes		8
H89	do.	5	R	Covered Carriage Trucks	on old underframes	11A
H93	07/93	5	R	Horse Boxes		8
H94	do.	5	R	Covered Carriage Trucks		11A
H95	do.	5	R	Covered Milk Trucks	3 on old coach underframes	29
H99	1893	1		Stores Van	became part of 3-vehicle stores train in 1919	N/D
H104	01/94	5	R	Horse Boxes		8
H105	do.	5	R	Covered Carriage Trucks	on old underframes	11A
H106	do.	5	R	Open Carriage Trucks	on old underframes	N/D
H112	07/94	5	R	Horse Boxes		8
H113	do.	5	R	Covered Milk Trucks		29

Orders 1895-1899

No.	Date	No. Built	C/R	Description	Additional Description	Diag No.
H116	01/95	5	R	Horse Boxes		8
H117	do.	4	R	Covered Carriage Trucks		11A
H122	07/95	5	R	Horse Boxes		8
H123	do.	5	R	Fish Vans 6-wheel	dual brake. 3 branded for Waddell's sausage traffic	30
H127	01/96	10	R	Horse Boxes		8
H128	do.	5	R	Fish Vans 6-wheel	dual brake	30
H134	07/96	5	R	Horse Boxes		8
H135	do.	5	R	Fish Vans 6-wheel	dual brake	39
H140	01/97	5	R	Horse Boxes		8
H141	do.	5	R	Fish Vans 6-wheel	dual brake	39
H145	do.	5	R	Horse Boxes		8
H146	do.	5	R	Fish Vans 6-wheel		39

No.	Date	No. Built	C/R	Description	Additional Description	Diag No.
H150	1897	8	R	Luggage Vans 6-wheel	3 were dedicated Tobacco Vans, 1 branded for Lipton's sausage traffic	39
H162	01/98	5	R	Open Carriage Trucks		44
H163	do.	4	R	Horse Boxes		8
H164	do.	2	R	Cattle Boxes		40
H168	07/98	10	R	Fish Vans 6-wheel		39
H172	01/99	5	R	Horse Boxes		8
H173	do.	5	R	Fish Vans 6-wheel		39
H178	07/99	5	R	Horse Boxes		8
H181	01/00	14	R	Luggage Vans 6-wheel	3 for Lipton's sausage traffic, 1 Linen Van	39

Orders 1900-1904

No.	Date	No. Built	C/R	Description	Additional Description	Diag No.
H188	07/00	5	R	Horse Boxes	3-foot 9-inch coach disc wheels	8
H189	do.	3	R	Open Carriage Trucks		44
H190	do.	5	R	Covered Carriage Trucks		11A
H191	do.	6	R	Luggage Vans	2 for Lipton's sausage traffic, 1 Linen Van	39
H195	01/03	6	R	Open carriage Trucks	folding sides, dual brake	44
H204	01/02	5	R	Horse Boxes	steam heated	8
H205	01/01	40	R	Fish Trucks	dual brake	55
H208	01/03	8	R	Horse Boxes	steam heat pipe, 3-foot 9-inch disc wheels	8
H210	do.	8	R	Fish Vans with sliding doors		71
H210	do.	4	R	Sealed Fish Vans		72
H212	do.	8	R	Luggage Vans		71
H213	07/03	6	R	Covered Carriage Trucks		68
H216	01/04	19	C	Horse Boxes	1 built to H216. Rest of order cancelled and built as H250, authorised 15/8/05	8
H217	do.	4	R	Cattle Vans	dual brake, steam heat pipe	70
H218	do.	2	R	45-foot Scenery Trucks	dual brake, steam heat pipe	69
H221	1904	6	C	Horse Boxes		73
H224	07/04	8	R	Fish Vans	dual brake, steam heat, roof lamps	76
H225	do.	4	R	Fish Vans lined with zinc	for Southampton traffic	76

Orders 1905-1909

No.	Date	No. Built	C/R	Description	Additional Description	Diag No.
H236	01/06	10	C	Covered Carriage Trucks		83
H250	01/07	24	C	6-wheel Horse Boxes	see entry for H216	73
H254	do.	4	R	Fish, Fruit or Milk Vans	dual brake, steam heat pipe	39
H258	07/06	4	R	Fruit or Milk Vans	used for meat traffic	39
H265	07/07	4	R	Furniture Van Trucks		44
H270	01/08	5	R	6-wheel Covered Carriage Trucks	dual brake, steam heat pipe	83
H271	do.	3	R	45-foot Open Scenery & Caravan Trucks	dual brake, steam heat pipe	69
H272	do.	2	R	45-foot Covered Scenery Trucks	dual brake, steam heat pipe	88
H273	do.	1	R	Double Gas Tank	on old underframe	N/D
H278	07/08	5	R	6-wheel Covered Carriage Trucks	dual brake, steam heat pipe	83
H284	01/09	4	R	Carriage or Furniture Van Trucks	dual brake, steam heat pipe	44

Orders 1910-1914

No.	Date	No. Built	C/R	Description	Additional Description	Diag No.
H292	01/10	4	R	Caravan & Scenery Trucks	6 wheels, dual brake, steam heat	92
H300	07/12	10	R	Covered Carriage Trucks	6 wheels	101
H301	1912	3	R	Meat Vans	6 wheels	102
H322	06/14	6	R	Covered Carriage Trucks	dual brake. 1 to carry elephants	101

Orders 1915-1919

No.	Date	No. Built	C/R	Description	Additional Description	Diag No.
H336	09/16	1	C	Triple Gas Tank	on old underframe, for Lanarkshire & Dumbartonshire line	N/D
H350	06/20	6		Covered Carriage Trucks	steam heating pipes	101

Appendix IV: Known Orders Placed with Contractors

Diagram Book numbers do not apply to wagons built before 1883
Up to and including 1883, the tender acceptance date is taken from minutes in the series NRS BR/CAL/1/. From 1895 onwards, the date is that of the minute authorising construction. Wagons went into traffic up to nine months afterwards.
C = capital, R = replacement (paid out of revenue) In many cases this has been deduced from the Half Yearly Returns

Orders Pre-1849

Date	No. Built	C/R	Description	Contractor
14/07/46	10	C	Horse Boxes	Dunn of Lancaster
	10	C	Carriage Trucks	Dunn of Lancaster
	200	C	Wagons	John Stephenson, Glasgow
	200	C	Wagons	Fox Henderson, Birmingham
	100	C	Wagons	Davidson, Greenock
	100	C	Wagons	Rowan, Glasgow
20/11/46	200	C	Wagons	Johnathan Dunn & Co.
	200	C	Coal Wagons for Garnkirk Rly	'to be contracted for'
18/09/47	50	C	Coal Wagons	'to be ordered immediately'
20/07/49	5		Brake Vans	'or to convert wagons into such'

Orders 1855-1859

Date	No. Built	C/R	Description	Contractor
17/12/56	20	R	Bar Iron Wagons	Law
	20	R		R Faulds
21/01/57	250	R	Mineral Wagons	Ashbury
	84		Goods Wagons	R Faulds
02/09/57	137		Mineral Wagons	Ashbury
	20		Goods Wagons	Joseph Wright
	10		Cattle Wagons	Joseph Wright
	100		Pig Iron Wagons	Ashbury
	20	C	Bar Iron Wagons	Ashbury
28/10/57	38		Timber Wagons (19 pairs)	Ashbury
24/03/58	2	R	Covered Vans complete	R Faulds
	2		Covered Vans without iron brake	R Faulds
	1		Round End Goods Wagon without iron brake	R Faulds
	1		Lancaster & Carlisle Covered Van without iron brake	R Faulds
11/08/58	4	R	Horse Boxes	Brown & Marshall
25/08/58	49	R	Goods Wagons	Ashbury
	251	R	Mineral Wagons	Ashbury
30/08/59	210	R	Mineral Wagons	Ashbury
	50	R	Covered Goods Vans	Ashbury
	10	R	Horse Boxes	Ashbury

Orders 1860-1864

Date	No. Built	C/R	Description	Contractor
14/02/60	4	R	Horse Boxes	Ashbury
12/02/61	100		Deep Sided Wagons	Ashbury
	100		Deep Sided Round End Wagons	Ashbury
	40	R	Swivel Wagons	Ashbury
	20		10-ton Wagons	Ashbury
	100		Ordinary Wagons	J Faulds
	120	R	Covered Vans	J Faulds
	21	C	Goods Brakes	J Faulds

Date	No. Built	C/R	Description	Contractor
09/12/62	60	R	Timber and Iron Wagons	Ashbury
03/02/63	1000	C	Goods Wagons Covered Vans Breaks	Ashbury
19/07/64	20		Cattle Wagons with solid iron wheels	Ashbury

Orders 1865-1869

Date	No. Built	C/R	Description	Contractor
19/12/65	88		Pig Iron Wagons	Ashbury
	125		Goods Wagons	
	62	C	Goods Wagons (Round End)	
	50	C	Swivel Timber Trucks	
	62		Covered Cattle Trucks	
	15		Goods Break Vans	
	400	C	Covered Goods Vans	
24/11/68	2	R	Horse Boxes	Metropolitan
	40		6-ton Coal Wagons	Pickering
	57		6-ton Goods Wagons	
09/12/68	300	C	Wagons	Ashbury
19/01/69	149		Platform Wagons	Pickering
	15	C	Break Vans – one charged as replacement	Lancaster Wagon Co.
17/08/69	4	C	Milk Trucks	Metropolitan
07/12/69	2	C	Horse Boxes	Metropolitan
	20	C	Goods Break Vans	
	12	R	Pig Iron Wagons	Faulds
	5	R	Swivel Wagons	
	12	R	Cattle Trucks	Lancaster Wagon Co.
07/12/69	34	R	Coal Wagons	Lancaster Wagon Co.
	30	R	Coal Wagons	Ashbury
	44	R	Box Goods Wagons	

Orders 1870-1874

Date	No. Built	C/R	Description	Contractor
08/02/70	50	C	Swivel Wagons	Pickering
	50	C		Ashbury
01/03/70	400		Mineral Wagons (Benhar branch)	Faulds
24/05/70	136	C	Mineral Wagons	North of England Wagon Co.
	68	R	Open Goods Wagons	Ashbury
	5		Covered Cattle Wagons	
	4		Horse Boxes	Brown & Marshall
23/06/70	300		Round End Wagons	Ashbury
	150		Ordinary Wagons	
	50	C	Beer Wagons	
	3	C	Break Vans	Metropolitan
20/07/70	100	C	Cattle Wagons – 96 charged to capital	Metropolitan
	120	C	Ballast Wagons (flat)	Pickering
	30	C	Ballast Wagons (coal type)	Faulds
25/10/70	50		Wagons offered for sale	North of England Wagon Co.
22/11/70	2	R	Horse Boxes	Ashbury
	150	C	Covered Wagons	Lancaster Wagon Co.
	100		8-ton Open Wagons	
	60		6-ton Open Wagons	
	250		Round End Wagons	Ashbury
	60		Mineral Wagons	

Date	No. Built	C/R	Description	Contractor
13/12/70	350		Deep Sided Wagons	Ashbury
	350		Flat Wagons	
	100	C	Swivel Wagons	
	200	C	Stone Wagons	
21/12/70	350		Flat Wagons	Lancaster Wagon Co.
10/01/71	32	C	Game Trucks	Metropolitan
	10	R	Horse Boxes	Brown & Marshall
11/04/71	50		Mineral Wagons	Pickering
03/08/71	9		Horse Boxes	Faulds
	13		Goods Brake Vans	
	5	C	Covered Goods Vans	
19/09/71	4	C	Break Vans (mineral traffic)	Faulds
24/10/71	300		Wagons	Pickering
24/10/71	700		Wagons	Faulds
03/11/71	300		Wagons	Pickering
11/71	250		Pig Iron Wagons	Ashbury
27/12/71	300		Loco Coal Wagons	Pickering – contract amended to 499
06/02/72	100	R	7-ton Goods Wagons	North of England Wagon Co.
14/02/72	12	C	Covered Fish and Game Trucks	Metropolitan
	2	R	Open Carriage Trucks	
09/04/72	500		6-ton Mineral Wagons	North of England Wagon Co.
17/04/72	600	C	Wagons (rolling stock returns suggest that these were minerals)	Lancaster Wagon Co.
	400	C		Faulds
21/05/72		R	Goods Brake Vans (no quantity stated. Return has 2 replacements in 2nd half year 1872)	Lancaster Wagon Co.
09/07/72	100	R	7-ton Goods Wagons	Ashbury
05/09/72	20		Cattle Wagons	Metropolitan
19/11/72	100	C	Swivel Wagons *'with iron tyres'*	Brown & Marshall
	100	C	Cattle Wagons – 62 charged to capital	
26/11/72	500	C	Mineral Wagons	North of England Wagon Co.
10/12/72	100	C	Swivel Wagons	Oldbury
24/12/72	120		8-ton Goods Wagons	Midland Wagon Co.
	300		10-ton Mineral Wagons	Ashbury
25/03/73	25	C	Horse Boxes	Brown & Marshall
	25	C	Goods Break Vans	North of England Wagon Co.
08/04/73	1000	C	Wagons with Bessemer Steel tyres	Faulds
	500	C	Wagons. Type of wagon not specified, but over 3,000 mineral wagons were acquired in 1873	North of England Wagon Co.
09/04/73	100	C	Mineral Wagons (200 offered)	Pickering
24/07/73	700	C	Mineral Wagons	Ashbury
	300	C		Lancaster Wagon Co.
29/07/73	1000	C	Wagons (mineral assumed)	North of England Wagon Co.
27/08/73	225		Open Goods Wagons	Ashbury
14/10/73	200		Wagons (mineral assumed)	Lancaster Wagon Co.
16/12/73	50		Cattle Wagons	Metropolitan
	18	R	Covered Goods	
30/12/73	25	C	Goods Break Vans – 21 charged to capital account	Lancaster Wagon Co.
14/01/74	60		7-ton Mineral Wagons	Lancaster Wagon Co.
	170		8-ton Goods Wagons	North of England Wagon Co.
17/11/74	4	C	Brake Vans	Brown & Marshall

Orders 1875-1879

Date	No. Built	C/R	Description	Contractor
05/05/75	100		Coal Wagons	Faulds
10/08/75	500		Mineral Wagons	Ashbury
17/11/75	200		Goods Wagons	Union Carriage Co.
	200			Ashbury
	200			Lancaster Wagon Co.
21/12/75	24		Goods Brake Vans	Metropolitan
13/01/76	300	C	Mineral Wagons	Faulds
	200	C		Ashbury
	400	C		Lancaster Wagon Co.
	100	C		North of England Wagon Co.
24/10/76	200		Goods Wagons	Union Carriage Co.
24/10/76	50		Cattle Wagons	Midland Co.
07/12/76	700	C	Mineral Wagons	North of England Wagon Co.
	800	C		Ashbury
	500	C		Cravens
19/12/76	30	C	Goods Brake Vans	Metropolitan
	300	C	Goods Vans	Oldbury
02/03/77	250	C	Mineral Wagons	Lancaster Wagon Co.
	250	C		Ashbury
	750	C		Purchased from Merry & Cunningham
07/03/77	500		8-ton Goods Wagons	S J Claye
	50		Cattle Wagons	
07/05/77	1000	C	7-ton Mineral Wagons	Ashbury
13/06/77	500	C	Mineral Wagons	Union Carriage Co.
	300	C		Lancaster Wagon Co.
	250	C		Olive & Co.
	200	C		Pickering
	750	C		Ashbury
30/10/77	300		10-ton Locomotive Coal Wagons	S J Claye
	15	C	Goods Brake Vans – 14 charged to capital	Pickering
19/02/79	10		Dead Meat Vans	Oldbury
	10			Ashbury
	20			Brown & Marshall
10/06/79	100	R	Goods Wagons	Ashbury
	80	R	Cattle Wagons	
26/11/79	10	R	Roadside Covered Goods Vans	Brown & Marshall
26/11/79	18	R	Fresh Meat Vans (4-wheel)	Brown & Marshall
	10	R	Fresh Meat Vans (6-wheel)	

Orders 1880-1882

Date	No. Built	C/R	Description	Contractor
23/02/80	100		Timber Wagons	Brown & Marshall
	125		Ordinary Wagons	Lancaster Wagon Co.
14/05/80	60	R	Cattle Wagons	Oldbury
06/07/80	200	R	Mineral Wagons	Olive & Co.
	40	R	Covered Goods Vans	Ashbury
16/11/80	19		15-ton Wagons	Olive & Co.
	260		8-ton Wagons	
	50		Round Timber Wagons	
	250		7-ton Wagons	
	50	R	Cattle Wagons	S J Claye
	12	R	Covered Goods Vans	Oldbury
	12		Roadside Goods Vans	Craven Bros

Date	No. Built	C/R	Description	Contractor
30/11/80	200		Locomotive Coal Wagons	S J Claye
18/01/81	100		15-ton Rail Wagons	Craven Bros
	200		8-ton Wagons	Brown & Marshall
	200		8-ton Wagons	Oldbury
14/02/82	100	R	Ordinary Goods	
	30	R	Covered Goods Vans	
	30	R	Cattle Trucks	S J Claye
	70	R	Round Timber Wagons	
	10	R	Roadside Parcels Vans	
25/07/82	80	C	8-ton Goods Wagons	S J Claye
	80	C		Ashbury
	70	C	7-ton Mineral Wagons	S J Claye
	70	C		Ashbury
	30	C	Covered Wagons	S J Claye
	30	C	Cattle Trucks	S J Claye

Orders 1883-1899

Date	No. Built	C/R	Description	Contractor	Diag No.
03/07/83	125	C	8-ton Coal Wagons	Harrison & Camm	22
	350	C		Craven Bros	
	125	C		S J Claye	
	400	C	10-ton Coal wagons	Craven Bros	N/D
23/09/95	500	C	Mineral, solid buffers		22
	150	C	Covered Goods Vans	Hurst Nelson	3
	50	C	Rail Wagons, fixed wheelbase, falling ends		13
	100	C	Swivel Timber Wagons		14
06/11/95	1,000	C	Mineral, solid buffers, 'Hamilton Section'	Pickering Card Orders 1687, 1702, 1730	22
	500	C	Mineral, solid buffers, 'Carfin & Cleland Section'	Hurst Nelson	22
01/06/97	100	C	Mineral Wagons, to Diagram 22 dimensions, but with spindle	Hurst Nelson	
	300	R	buffers. Taken over from Messrs Dunn Bros		
27/12/98	1,000	C	8-ton Goods Wagons	Pickering CO 3352	24
	1,000	C	8-ton Mineral Wagons	Hurst Nelson	46

Orders 1900-1904

Date	No. Built	C/R	Description	Contractor	Diag No.
25/02/01	30	C	30-ton Bogie Mineral Wagons	Leeds Forge	54
27/01/03	100	C	30-ton Bogie Mineral Wagons	Leeds Forge	54
17/02/03	100	C	30-ton Bogie Mineral Wagons	Metropolitan C&W	54
	30	C		Pickering CO 6638	
	30	C		Hurst Nelson	
	30	C		Birmingham RC&W	
	10	C		J Renshaw	
17/02/03	300	C	15-ton Rail Wagons	Hurst Nelson	60
03/03/03	150	R	10-ton Covered Goods Vans	Pickering CO 6673	67
	25	R		Motherwell Wagon	
	25	R		J Renshaw	
17/03/03	300	R	16-ton Mineral Wagons	Darlington Wagon	59
	500			Metropolitan C&W	
	30			Motherwell Wagon	
	70			Pickering CO 6708	
	30			J Renshaw	
	70			Hurst Nelson	

Orders 1905-1909

Date	No. Built	C/R	Description	Contractor	Diag No.
23/01/06	50		Bogie Swivel Wagons	Leeds Forge	81
15/05/06	400	R	16-ton Mineral Wagons, steel underframe	Metropolitan C&W	59
	300			Pickering CO 10164	
	100			Hurst Nelson	
	100			Motherwell Wagon	
	100			S J Claye	

Orders 1910-1914

Date	No. Built	C/R	Description	Contractor	Diag No.
21/03/11	250	R	16-ton Mineral Wagons, steel underframe	Pickering CO 19105	59
16/05/11	1		30-ton Flat Wagon ex Barnum and Bailey	Pickering CO 19463	103
30/04/12	27		35-ton Bogie Rail Wagons	Leeds Forge	105
09/07/12	30		35-ton Bogie Rail Wagons	Leeds Forge	105
23/07/12	150	R	16-ton Pig Iron Wagons	Pickering CO 21679	110
	150	R		Hurst Nelson	
03/09/12	45		35-ton Bogie Rail Wagons	Leeds Forge	105
	50	R	16-ton Pig Iron Wagons	Pickering CO 21679	110
	50	R		Hurst Nelson	
01/10/12	20		35-ton Bogie Rail Wagons	Leeds Forge	105
10/12/12	50	C	20-ton Rail Wagons	Cravens	108
	50	C		Motherwell W&RS	
	100	C	15-ton Twin Wagons, steel underframe (50 pairs) Iracier axleboxes	Pickering CO 22691	109
	100	C	15-ton Twin Wagons, steel underframe (50 pairs) Iracier axleboxes. Underframes provided by Leeds Forge	Pickering CO 22699	109

Orders 1915-1919

Date	No. Built	C/R	Description	Contractor	Diag No.
19/10/15	20		10-ton Hopper Wagons	Hurst Nelson	121
08/02/16	60	R	16-ton Mineral Wagons for Loco Coal, oak frames	Pickering CO 29760	59
22/08/16	100	R	10-ton Goods Wagons, St. Rollox order G383	Pickering CO 30872	87
	100	R	16-ton Mineral wagons	Clayton & Shuttleworth	59
	120	R	16-ton Pig Iron Wagons, St. Rollox order G385	Hurst Nelson	110
23/01/17	150	C	Covered Goods vans for the conveyance of explosives	Pickering CO 31321	67
	150	C		Clayton & Shuttleworth	
7/19	500	R	16-ton Mineral Wagons, oak frames	Pickering CO 36083	59

Orders 1920-1922

Date	No. Built	C/R	Description	Contractor	Diag No.
06/04/20	400	R	16-ton Mineral Wagons	Motherwell W&RS	59
	70	R	20-ton Iron and Steel Carrying Wagons	Cravens	?108
	30	R	20-ton Goods Brake Vans	Clayton & Shuttleworth	63
16/05/22	25	C	Gunpowder Vans	Hurst Nelson	78
27/06/22	250	R	16-ton Mineral Wagons	Hamilton Wagon Co.	59
1922	500	R	16-ton Mineral Wagons	Hurst Nelson	59

Appendix V: St. Rollox and Contractors' Wagon and NPCS Drawings

Where no archive reference is given, the drawing is awaiting an RHP number following cataloguing by The Ballast Trust

SRX No.	Date	Description	Diag No.	Archive Ref NRM	RHP
476	1868	Horse box with dog boxes at both ends	N/D	8046W	69164
718	1868	Brake van	N/D		
757	1868	1520 gallon welded acid tank – Kye Chemical Co., Irvine	N/D		68373
774	1868	15-ton flat wagon, heavy self contained buffers	N/D		
775	1868	6-wheel heavy weight flat wagon, heavy self contained buffers	N/D		
776	1868	Stores van, spindle buffers	N/D		
984	1871	8-ton goods wagon, solid buffers, 1-foot 6-inch sides 15 feet 6 inches over body	N/D		
994	1871	Beer wagon, spindle buffers, 1-foot 9-inch sides, centre doors, 15 feet inside	N/D		
1002	1871	Ballast wagon, falling ends	N/D		
1082	1871	10-ton stone wagon, solid buffers	N/D		
1104	1871	6-ton mineral wagon, solid buffers	N/D		
1244	1872	10-ton coal wagon	N/D		
1251	1872	10-ton loco coal wagon, solid buffers	N/D		
1293	1872	6-ton mineral wagon, solid buffers	N/D		
1359	1872	10-ton swivel wagon	N/D		
1396	1872	10-ton pig iron wagon	N/D		
1397	1872	8-ton goods wagon	N/D		
1424	1873	7-ton mineral wagon	N/D		
1448	1873	Goods brake van, single brake column	N/D		
1502	1873	8-ton goods wagon side doors	N/D		
1522	1873	8-ton goods wagon without doors	N/D		
1540	1873	7-ton mineral wagon	N/D	13747W	
1588	1874	Sheep or coke wagon spindle buffers, 4 feet deep, 16 feet inside	N/D		
1659	1874	8-ton goods wagon side doors, 10-foot wheelbase	N/D		
1690	1874	10-ton loco coal wagon, solid buffers	N/D		
1747	1874	Brake van, ballasting	N/D		
1751	1874	6-wheel 30-ton heavy weight wagon drop ends	N/D		
1819	1875	40-ton trolley (later rated at 35-tons and given a diagram number)	33		70051
1857	1875	Pooley's tool van	N/D	8052W	69179
2035	1876	Cattle wagon	N/D	8044W	69171
2044	1876	10-ton loco coal wagon, solid buffer, 9-foot 6-inch wheelbase. LOCO COAL lettering and running number C.R 50802 sketched in pencil	N/D		
2083	1876	30-ton 6-wheel Rulley wagon	N/D	8045W	69182
2209	1877	13-ton rail wagon	N/D		
2209A	1877	13-ton rail wagon. Pencil note *'altered to 9in x 5in Journal & heavier Springs for Special Wagons'*	N/D		
2273	1877	6-wheel underframe for acid wagon	N/D		
2428	1878	Furniture wagon	N/D		
2558	1879	7-ton mineral wagon	N/D	8059W	69151
2913	1881	Service wagon, Perth Motive Power Depot	N/D		68372
3141	1882	New 7-ton mineral wagon	N/D		69139
3141	1882	New 7-ton mineral wagon, as above. *'250 wagons only'* hand written note	N/D	8050W	
3235	1917	8-ton open goods wagon. Redrawing of original on next page	15	12003W	70008

SRX No.	Date	Description	Diag No.	NRM	RHP
3235	1882	8-ton open goods wagon (falling sides) 4-plank	15	12004W	70009
3242	1882	Timber wagon, single bolster, one of twin	N/D	8048W	69163
3248	1882	10-ton mineral wagon with doors at sides and at one end	21	8043W	69183
3368	1917	8-ton mineral wagon redrawing of original below	22	11921W	70004
3368	1882	8-ton mineral wagon	22	8042W	69181
3496	1883	Covered goods van, iron body, spindle buffers	N/D		
3504	1883	8-ton goods wagon 4-plank, centre door	24	8060W	69143
3506	1883	15-ton well or machinery wagon	18		67295
3562	1883	15-ton goods brake van (single brake stanchion)	6	8058W	69140
3589	1883	Covered goods van	3	8061W	69142
3589	1883	Covered goods van – previous drawing with amendments	3		69175
3589	1883	Covered goods van	3	8063W	
3591	1883	Cattle wagon 15 feet 2 inches inside – see 6659 for 4 inches longer wagons built after 1891	10		70003
3602	1883	Standard wagon axlebox	N/A		
3653	1883	Horse box	9		70001
3667	1883	Bearing springs for horsebox	9		70013
3808	1883	10-ton brake van, diagram of brake arrangement	?6	11944W	70017
3932	1884	15-ton flat wagon for locomotives	19	8054W	69185
4224	1884	15-ton 6-wheel rail wagon, flexible wheelbase	13	8055W	69145
4389	1885	Meat van, fully panelled sides and ends, single round roof vent	1	11981C	70023
4410	1885	2 plank round timber wagon, solid buffer	N/D	8057W	69180
4484	1885	5-ton hopper wagon – altered from 7-ton mineral	N/D		68457
4601	1885	Short horse box 8-foot wheelbase – sketched extension for Diagram 8	9	11982C	
4665	1885	Brake wagon for Crianlarich Quarry	N/D		68478
4901	1886	24-foot covered carriage truck on old carriage underframe	11	11978C	70026
4938	1886	15-ton goods brake van – wider body panels than drawing 3562	6	11942W	
5307	1887	6-wheel breakdown van	7	11226W	70031
5375	1887	6-wheel breakdown van – interior of drawing 5307	7	11242W	70032
5380	1887	Ballast wagon	23	11204W	70033
5514	1887	8-ton mineral wagon	22		
5581	1887	Timber wagon for Montrose to carry 24-foot boards	N/D		69141
5688	1888	Meat van, 2 vents	1	11952W	70037
5721	1888	8-ton mineral wagon, solid buffers, bottom door arrangement	22	11918W	70038
6003	1889	Timber or swivel bar wagon	14	8047W	69178
6004	1889	16-foot open carriage truck on old carriage underframe	N/D	11955C	70045
6007	1889	Carriage truck details	N/D		68407
6014	1889	Carriage truck details	N/D		68406
6016	1889	Carriage truck details	N/D		68405
6017	1889	Carriage truck details	N/D		68385
6021	1889	Brake van, goods	5	7695W	
6132	1889	Gunpowder van, adapted from Diagram 3 van	4	8062W	69174
6141	1889	Tank wagon, oil 1,770 gallons	5A		68429
6145	1889	Interior of horse box order H216	8		70048
6170	1889	Tank wagon, oil	5A		68428
6180	1890	Pig iron wagon 1 plank	16	11900W	70050
6234	1890	15-ton 6-wheel rail wagon (flexible wheelbase)	13	11894W	70052
6243	1890	8-wheel 25-ton trolley number 4 (2 sheets in NRM copy)	20	11290W	70053
6413	1890	22-foot covered carriage truck, on old underframes	11A	11979C	70055
6419	1890	Details of carriage truck	11A		67544

SRX No.	Date	Description	Diag No.	Archive Ref NRM	RHP
6460	1890	Details of carriage truck	11A		67542
6533	1891	6-wheel 25-ton Boiler wagon. 1 wagon with bolsters, 2 with flooring	28, 31	11209W	70060
6534	1891	16-ton boiler wagon	26	11196W	70061
6600	1891	Gas tank – see also drawing 6642	N/D		68377
6642	1891	Underframe for single gas tank – see drawing 6600	N/D		67532
6659	1891	Cattle wagon medium 15 feet 6 inches inside	10	8064W	69172
6695	1891	14-ton goods brake van, single brake column, annotated with alterations to form Diagram 45 in 1898	5	11945W	70067
6745	1891	6-wheel covered milk van (slatted sides)	29	11266C	70068
6750	1891	Details for milk truck	29		68411
6751	1891	Details for milk truck	29		68410
6786	1891	Details for milk truck	29		68412
6788	1891	6-wheel fish, fruit & milk van. 2 to be built with sliding shutters & glass in panels each side. 3 to have wooden panels instead of glass	30	11948C	70069
6823	1891	2,100 gallon tank wagon	32		67547
6823	1891	2,100 gallon tank wagon, order C94	32		68425
6945	1892	Swivel bar or timber wagon. List of 4 modifications to order G152	14	11263W	70073
6973	1892	Single bolster timber wagon fold down ends between twins	37	11273W	70074
7059	1892	8-ton open wagon, side doors	24	12009W	70075
7059	1892	Duplicate of 12009W/70075	24	8041W	69170
7084	1892	Covered carriage truck louvred sides, on old carriage underframe	11A	11946C	70076
7124	1892	Horse box	8	11973C	70078
7128	1892	Proposed 30-foot 6-wheel stores van – see also drawing 7192	N/D		70079
7192	1893	6-wheel stores van (inside & out) 1 off to order H99	N/D	11229C	70080
7233	1893	3 vehicle stores train – annotated *'cancelled'* against title	N/D	11235C	70081
7312	1893	8-ton mineral wagon	46		
7352	1893	3-ton open carriage truck on old underframes, various lengths	N/D	11199W	70083
7391	1893	Barrel truck on old carriage underframes, various lengths	12	11903W	70084
7621	1894	21-foot covered carriage truck to H117, details altered for H190, 1900	11A	11202C	70090
8004	1896	6-wheel fish, fruit & milk van	39	11950C	70096
8121	1896	Underframe for vitriol tank. C Tennant & Co.	N/D		67546
8179	1896	15-ton glass well wagon	38	11291W	70098
8341	1897	Alteration to horse box and general arrangement	8	11976C	70100
8357	1897	6-wheel luggage van	39		70101
8594	1897	8-wheel 30-ton flat wagon	43	11286W	70104
8648	1897	Prize cattle box	40	11984C	70106
8673	1897	6-wheel carriage or furniture van truck	44	11270C	70108
8703	1897	Standard covered goods van	3	8049W	69177
8703	1909	Standard covered goods van. Insulating of ends side & door for vans for meat traffic, roof double skinned for insulated vans	3	11902W	70109
8731	1897	Underframe for 8-wheel 30-ton flat wagon – see 8594	43	11284W	70110
8761	1897	8-wheel 40-ton trolley	41		67550
8796	1898	8-wheel 20-ton trolley (low girder bed)	42	11279W	70112
8886	1899	Twin wagon with hinged sides	47	11264W	70116
8896	1898	Single bolster timber and ore wagon	48	11272W	70117
8909	1898	8-ton mineral wagon	46	11920W	70119
8975	1898	Horse box, 3-foot 9-inch disc wheels	8	11991C	70120
9129	1898	16-ton heavy weight wagon	49	11287W	70124
9432	1898	Patent brake on heavy weight wagon	49		68375
9462	1899	8-wheel 50-ton ore wagon wood body, steel frame	50	11905W	70127

SRX No.	Date	Description	Diag No.	Archive Ref NRM	RHP
9676	1899	2,000 gallon oil tank for stores	32		68423
9852	1899	16-ton wooden ore wagon 2 door hinges	51	11926W	70132
10026	1899	Arrangement of either side brake for barrel trucks (G177)	12		68463
10118	1900	10-ton 6-wheel carriage & furniture truck (falling sides)	44	11268C	70136
10184	1900	Mineral wagon to carry 14-ton of ore	52	11929W	70139
10299	1900	Tank wagon, double oil	N/D		68422
10340	1900	12-ton trolley. Load plate is SRX 10479, RHP 68379	53		67548
	1901	30-ton bogie coal wagon. Not a CR drawing although catalogued as such. Leeds Forge drawing 4761. Marked in pencil 'not adopted.'	54	11907W	
10648	1901	10-ton sulphuric acid tank wagon for United Alkali Co.	N/D		68427
10771	1901	Fish truck with falling sides – see also 10898	55	11911W	70148
10851	1901	Meat van, 3 roof vents, on old underframe	?2	11980W	70149
10898	1901	Diagram of spar ends & sides for fish trucks – see 10771	55	11965W	70150
11016	1901	15-ton 6-wheel rail wagon	13	11895W	
11030	1901	6-wheel brake van for Permanent Way Dept	N/D	11240W	
11031	1901	8-ton special goods wagon 1-plank, with end doors	58	12008W	
11200	1901	6-wheel brake van for Engineers Dept - see also 11213	61	11245W	
11213	1901	Interior sections of 6-wheel brake van for Engineers Dept	61	11246W	
11232	1902	20-ton trolley	56		
11247	1902	Wagon number plate	N/A		69655
11253	1902	12-ton hopper ballast wagon (3-plank)	64	11212W	
11264	1902	8-wheel 20-ton trolley	56	11278W	
11281	1902	8-wheel steel coal wagon 30-ton	54	11208W	
11328	1902	Brake van with ballast plough	65	11225W	
11438	1902	8-wheel 40-ton hopper wagon	66	8027W	69156
11439	1902	End elevation of above wagon	66	8028W	69138
11467	1902	Builder's plate for wagons	N/A		
11573	1902	8-ton ballast wagon	57	11265W	
11576	1902	Fish van	71	11935W	
11664	1902	16-ton ore wagon, wood or steel underframe	59	11898W	
11706	1902	Body of sealed fish van	72	11934W	
11732	1902	14-ton pig iron wagon	16	11932W	
11818	1903	15-ton 6-wheel rail wagon	60	12007W	
11819	1903	10-ton covered goods van	67	11966W	
11861	1903	Cattle wagon (short)	10	11987W	
11867	1903	15-ton goods brake van	62	11968W	
11879	1903	Well wagon for heavy machinery	18	11293W	
11897	1903	Underframe for mineral wagon	59	11925W	
11950	1903	12-ton coal wagon on Fox pressed steel frames	59	11901W	
12002	1903	Covered carriage truck 24 feet long	68	11993C	
12007	1903	24-foot Carriage truck	68		68391
12014	1903	16-ton mineral wagon, steel frame, 2 end door hinges	59	11909W	
12049	1904	Interior arrangement of 4-wheel horse box – see also 12068, 12340	8	11975C	
12063	1903	Westinghouse brake on 6-wheel 20-ton goods brake	63	11943W	
12067	1903	Underframe for 16-ton mineral wagon	59	11924W	
12068	1903	Alterations to side doors on horse box – see 12049	8	11972C	
12098	1903	Barrel truck, order G213, annotated with alterations for order G349	74	11904W	
12113	1903	Goods van lettering	67		68573
12120	1903	6-wheel 20-tons goods brake van	63	11967W	
12120	1903	Suffixed A - Diagram only of 20-tons brake van	63	11936W	

APPENDICES

SRX No.	Date	Description	Diag No.	Archive Ref NRM	RHP
12185	1903	8-wheel scenery truck (open)	69	11247C	
12296	1903	Cattle box with groom's compartment	70	11954C	
12305	1903	Solid buffer wagon, altered to suit spring buffers	22		69653
12340	1903	Alterations to partitions in horse box – see 12049	8	11971W	
12386	1903	Gunpowder van ⅛-inch plate steel with wooden lining	78	11963W	
12434	1904	6-wheel sealed fish van	76	11949C	
12453	1904	10-ton open goods wagon, wooden underframe. Changed dimensions and Morton brake for new wagons 4/8/1916	24	11995W	
12471	1904	10-ton hopper wagon (5-plank)	75	11213W	
12500	1904	16-ton mineral wagon with steel frame	59	11910W	
12611	1904	Underframe for 10-ton tanks	N/D		67538
12648	1904	12-ton open goods wagon	79	11994W	
12649	1904	Oil tank A Hope & Sons, Provanmill, no underframe details	N/D		
12668	1904	12-ton hopper wagon, timber frame	N/D		
12686	1904	10-ton covered goods van	67	11960W	
12725	1904	Proposed 10-ton sulphuric acid tank wagon for United Alkali Co.	N/D		67537
12789	1904	Underframe for tank for Wm Briggs & Sons, Arbroath	N/D		67535
12952	1905	Body of 4-wheel brake van for Engineers Dept	N/D	11244W	
12972	1905	8-ton mineral wagon altered to spring buffers, double brake on opposite side to existing brake	22	11923W	
12980	1905	10-ton mineral wagon altered to spring buffers	21		
13005	1905	14-ton hopper ore wagon	75	11216W	
13038	1905	8-wheel 30-ton bolster swivel wagon	81	11292W	
13067	1905	Brake wagon (open) 12 feet 6 inches over body M361	N/D	11941W	
13070	1905	Steel underframe for mineral wagon G240	59	11912W	
13077	1905	6-wheel 15-ton covered goods van	80	11961W	
13082	1905	16-ton mineral wagon, steel frame, 3 end door hinges order G240	59	11914W	
13095	1905	30-ton well wagon	82		67549
13137	1905	Refrigerator van	84	11395W	
13186	1905	6-wheel covered carriage truck – see also 13213 and 13222	83	11977C	
13213	1905	Body details for 6-wheel covered carriage truck	83		68388
13222	1905	Covered carriage truck	83		68387
13359	1905	12-ton hopper wagon (steel frame)	86	11214W	
13407	1905	15-ton pig iron wagon (steel frame) Incomplete version NRM 11916	85	11917W	
13563	1906	12-ton hopper ballast wagon (wooden, 3-plank)	64	11211W	
13737	1906	6-wheel horse box	73	11974C	
13821	1906	10-ton open goods wagon, centre door, steel frame	87	12000W	
13887	1906	Arrangement of underframe for tank for David M'Queen	N/D		68443
13938	1906	Pre-diagram book 8-ton goods wagon, centre door, reconstructed. 'Old iron work to be re-used if in good condition.'	N/D	12006W	
13952	1906	4-wheel covered carriage truck	68		68389
13962	1906	Alterations to 24-foot covered carriage truck	68	11957W	
13972	1906	Addition to sides & ends of pig iron wagon	?85	11930W	
13988	1906	6-wheel carriage and furniture van truck (open)	44	11269C	
14119	1907	Arrangement of tank wagon. Alex Cross & Sons	N/D		68424
14248	1907	Underframe for double gas tank	N/D		67536
14251	1907	Body of 8-wheel scenery truck	88	11248C	
14340	1907	8-wheel 30-ton trolley	89		
14373	1907	General arrangement: 6-wheel rail wagon	?60		69612
14422	1907	Sketch showing observation holes on open goods wagon when used to carry sheep	24		

SRX No.	Date	Description	Diag No.	Archive Ref NRM	RHP
14439	1907	10-ton goods wagon, steel framed, falling sides	87	11996W	
14457	1908	10-ton covered goods van	67	11959W	
14496	1908	6-wheel 10-ton goods van (Callander & Oban)	91	7516W	
14523	1908	6-ton meat van	90	11953W	
14653	1908	6-wheel 15-ton goods van	80	11970W	
14768	1908	15-ton goods brake van	62	11937W	
14789	1909	10-ton goods van, Morton brake either side, grease axleboxes	67	11969W	
14833	1909	15-ton agricultural implement wagon	93		68781
14861	1909	20-ton 6-wheel goods brake van	63	11938W	
14867	1909	15-ton Implement wagon	93	11280W	
14963	1909	Sheep wagon	24		
14968	1909	12-ton flat or runner wagon	122	11897W	
14978	1909	6-wheel 30-foot open scenery truck	92	11249C	
14991	1909	Horse box interior and sections	8	11267C	
15057	1909	Cattle wagon	10	11985W	
15080	1909	4-wheel underframe for 5-ton hand crane	N/D	11271W	
15292	1910	8-wheel 35-ton boiler wagon	94	11207W	
15643	1910	Underframe for cylindrical tank	N/D		67534
15663	1910	Six sketches of ordnance on various wagons, suffixed C-F, J and K	43, 94		
15683	1911	20-ton trolley	95		
15685	1911	10-ton coke, top frame on old wagon	21		
15697	1911	Tank for Scottish Oil and Fuel Co.	N/D		68442
15740	1911	35-ton trolley	96		
15748	1911	20-ton hopper wagon (wooden)	97	11218W	
15811	1911	Cattle wagon – higher roof to suit cavalry horses	10	11392W	
15869	1911	16-ton hopper ore wagon	98	11215W	
15890	1911	Two sketches of ordnance on two 35-foot boiler wagons	94		
16012	1911	Weighing machine road van, traced from Messrs Pooley's drawing	N/D	11262W	
16167	1911	30-foot steel underframe, 6-wheel carriage truck to H300	101	8072/C	
16215	1911	10-ton covered goods van, underframe for van with 3-foot 9-inch wheels	67	11964W	
16259	1912	6-wheel covered carriage truck, Iracier axleboxes for G324, 1913	101	11951W	
16262	1912	16-ton wooden hopper wagon on steel underframe	98	11219W	
16322	1912	20-ton trolley	99		
16390	1912	10-ton 6-wheel meat van	102	11992W	
16461	1912	40-ton trolley	100		
16489	1912	16-ton pig iron wagon	110	11927W	
16522	1912	Combination goods van & brake van (2 sheets)	104	11990W	
16668	1912	15-ton twin wagon with stanchions, bar coupling between wagons	109	11908W	
16669	1912	20-ton 6-wheel rail wagon 2-plank	108	11933W	
16708	1912	20-ton rail wagon lettering	108		69651
16710	1912	Lettering on 15-ton twin wagons	109		
16782	1913	16-ton mineral wagon, steel underframe, grease axleboxes. G314	59	11928W	
16822	1913	35-ton well wagon	112		
16833	1913	8-wheel ingot wagon 35 tons	113	11282W	
16844	1913	8-wheel 40-ton flat wagon – see also 17243	111	11285W	
16938	1913	16-ton tube wagon	114	12005W	
16964	1913	10-ton open goods wagon, steel chassis, falling sides	87	11998W	
17110	1913	35-ton Bolster Wagon	105		
17113	1913	10-ton open brake wagon No. 185 (Gushetfaulds accident 1913)	N/D	11940W	
17114	1913	35-ton rail wagon	106		

SRX No.	Date	Description	Diag No.	Archive Ref NRM	RHP
17120	1913	35-ton rail wagon, Engineer's Dept	107		
17146	1913	6-wheel underframe for 15-ton covered goods van G344	115	8074W	69147
17149	1913	6-wheel underframe for 30-foot carriage and fish trucks H322, G346/51	101	8068C	69137
17151	1913	Emergency van for tools and materials – Carstairs	119	11241W	
17175	1913	15-foot flat bed, G348, G411 & G416 are the 20-ton Implement Wagon version. Drawing date of 1918 reflects the alteration	117	11281W	
17202	1913	6-wheel 15-ton 30-foot covered goods van	115	11962W	
17226	1913	6-wheel emergency van for Engineer's Dept	119	11228C	
17243	1914	40-ton flat wagon annotated '362/3' – see also 16844	111		69628
17248	1914	15-ton agricultural implement wagon	117		69627
17254	1914	6-wheel fish van	116	11956W	
17374	1914	Details for carriage truck for elephants	101		68398
17431	1914	End of brake van for Oban line. One van thus to G351	63		68480
17490	1914	Tool Van, No. 156 (ex West Coast Joint Stock brake van with same number)	N/D		
17595	1914	10-ton loco coal wagon, converted from 8-ton solid buffer	22	11931W	
17724	1914	Acid tank for Richard Smith's executors	N/D		68426
17741	1914	10-ton open goods wagon, falling sides, dual braked	87	11997W	
17872	1915	8-wheel 50-ton trolley	118		
17899	1915	10-ton tank wagon. United Alkali Co. Ltd	N/D		68421
17925	1915	Tank for J Ross & Co.	N/D		67530
18159	1915	Body of 10-ton steel hopper wagon	121	11223W	
18186	1915	10-ton steel hopper wagon	121	11217W	
18216	1916	12-ton open goods wagon	120	12002W	
18547	1916	Arrangement of tank wagon for Messrs Richard Smith's executors	N/D		67531
18600	1916	10-ton trolley – no evidence that this design was ever built	N/D		68782
18630	1916	Name plate, munitions wagon	N/D		69654
18645	1916	Arrangement of ingot wagons with girder frame	94		68369
18698	1916	16-ton mineral wagon, wood underframe, 3 end door hinges G397 Duplicate copy	59	11899W 11933W	
18733	1916	16-ton pig iron wagon (1-plank, wooden underframe)	110	11915W	
18740	1916	Lettering on 10-ton goods wagon	87		
18741	1916	'Pig iron' lettering on wagon – see 18733 for general arrangement drawing	110		
18752	1916	Triple gas tank on old carriage underframe	N/D		67529
18851	1916	10-ton open, centre door, all wood	87	12001W	
18856	1916	Old 8-ton swivel wagon with sides added, solid buffers	N/D	8056W	69144
18882	1916	10-ton open goods wagon with falling sides	87	11999W	
19141	1917	20-ton rail wagon (1-plank)	124	11251W	
19186	1917	20-ton trolley	123		
19190	1917	35-ton flat wagon	N/D		68380
19284	1917	20-ton rail wagon	124	11289W	
19336	1918	8-wheel bolster wagon No. 66022	77	11906W	
19471	1918	6-ton covered van (redrawing of GA dated 1876, probably SRX 2090)	N/D	8053W	69162
19700	1918	Proposed standard goods wagons (metal bodied) 10 wagons one 1 drawing	N/D		
19837	1919	3 vehicle Stores train	N/D	11234C	
19928	1919	Underframe for 30-foot Stores van	N/D	11233C	
19966	1919	Body of Stores van No. 2	N/D	11231C	
20009	1919	Body of Stores van No. 3	N/D	11232C	
20062	1919	8-ton mineral wagon, wooden trap door arrangement	22	11919W	
20514	1920	Bolster wagons 9-foot and 6-foot wheelbase	N/D		68371
20708	1920	30-foot pressed steel chassis for 6-wheel vehicles	N/A	8070C	69135

SRX No.	Date	Description	Diag No.	Archive Ref NRM	RHP
20754	1920	8-wheel 30-ton bolster swivel wagon. Fox pressed steel underframe	81	11203W	
20838	1920	Standard wagons, diagrams for 20 feet by 9 feet inside and outside (10 wagons)	N/D		
21111	1921	Body of tool van Perth & Motherwell	N/D	11239C	
21192	1921	Body of emergency van Perth & Motherwell	N/D	11236C	
21377	1921	35-ton rail wagon, bogie	105		69623
21861	1922	4-wheel old frames with new fish bodies	71	11958W	
21981	1922	Interior for breakdown van Carlisle & Dawsholm	N/D	11238C	
21991	1922	General arrangement: timber wagon with altered bolster	N/D		69635
21995	1922	Cylindrical tank, 3485 gallons	N/D		68370

Metropolitan C&W Co. Drawings – Birmingham City Council Archive

Date	Description	Ref
1/1/1869	Horse box, 4-wheel 11-foot wheelbase, 17 feet 11 inches over buffers	2280
4/9/1869	Milk truck (open), 4-wheel 8-foot wheelbase, 14 feet over buffers	2260
6/1/1870	Goods break van, 4-wheel 8-foot wheelbase, 14 feet 6 inches over buffers. One brake stanchion	2316
17/8/1870	Cattle waggon, 4-wheel 9-foot wheelbase, open spoke wheels, 15 feet 8 inches over buffers	2315
16/2/1871	Carriage truck or fish & game, open, 4-wheel 9-foot 6-inch wheelbase, 15 feet 9 inches over buffers	2281
25/4/1871	Covered fish & game truck, 4-wheel 10-foot wheelbase, 16 feet 6 inches over buffers	2265
28/9/1872	Cattle truck, 4-wheel 9-foot wheelbase, open spoke wheels	2286
30/2/1875	Goods break van, 4-wheel 9-foot 3-inch wheelbase, 16 feet over buffers	2313
2/5/1877	Dummy van, 4-wheel, 16 feet 6 inches over buffers	2307

R Y Pickering Drawings – Historical Model Railway Society Collection

Date	Description	Ref
17/8/1899	8-ton 4-plank open, special brake, CR Diagram 24. RYP 1295, SRX 7059 had single brake block	17
7/1/1901	30-ton bogie mineral wagon CR Diagram 54. RYP 1693	8
undated	16-ton 5-plank open, steel underframe, CR Diagram 59. RYP 2344	7
26/8/1903	Goods van CR Diagram 67. RYP 2475, SRX 11819	11
25/8/1903	16-ton open wagon, steel underframe, CR Diagram 59. RYP 2512, SRX 11664	18
25/3/1903	30-ton bogie steel open wagon CR Diagram 54. RYP 2605, SRX 11281	2
21/4/1911	16-ton mineral wagon, CR Diagram 59. RYP 6836, SRX 13082	12
20/1/1913	15-ton twin wagon, CR Diagram 109. RYP 7840, SRX 16668	9
2/10/1916	10-ton 4-plank open wagon, CR Diagram 24. RYP 9138, SRX 12453	16
15/3/1916	16-ton mineral wagon, CR Diagram 59. RYP 8981, SRX 11664	10
1919	16-ton mineral wagon, CR Diagram 59. RYP 9941, SRX 18698	19

Leeds Forge Drawings – Historical Model Railway Society Collection

Date	Description	Ref
13/3/1907	30-ton bogie coal wagon, CR Diagram 54. Leeds Forge 4895	10369
undated	30-ton bogie coal wagon, CR Diagram 54. Leeds Forge 6060	10370
undated	35-ton bogie rail wagon, CR Diagram 105. Fox pressed steel underframe. Leeds Forge 15426	12735
29/1/1913	15-ton twin wagon, CR Diagram 109. Pressed steel underframe; Leeds Forge 16024	12736
21/11/1916	10-ton goods wagon, CR Diagram 87. Pressed steel underframe with combined solebar and side rail. Leeds Forge 20467	12745
21/11/1916	16-ton pig iron wagon, CR Diagram 110. Pressed steel underframe with combined solebar and side rail. Leeds Forge 20566	12746
19/12/1919	10-ton goods wagon, CR Diagram 87. Fox pressed steel underframe; Leeds Forge 22175	12747

Appendix VI: Photographs in the 1900 Register of Wagon Plant

In the TOTAL STOCK column, numbers marked with an asterisk include all types of wagons covered by the general description, not only the type illustrated in the photograph.
The entry in the PLATE column refers to Plate numbers in this book.

Photo No.	Wagon No.	Load	Description	Diag. No.	Total Stock	Plate
01	9818	8-ton	Goods Wagon, side doors, improved McIntosh brake	24	* 16,249	
02	50677	7-ton	Mineral Wagon, solid buffers	N/D	* 41,281	
03	63951	8-ton	Mineral Wagon, sprung buffers, McIntosh brake	46	* 41,281	5.8
04	21519	10-ton	Loco Coal Wagon	21	1,476	5.5
05	64872	16-ton	Iron Ore Wagon	51	1	5.17
06	72000	50-ton	Iron Ore Wagon	50	1	5.9
07	49	12-ton	Swivel Wagon, special class	14	16	15.14
08	25	15-ton	Machinery Wagon	17	2	15.4
09	23473	7-ton	Hopper Bottom Mineral Wagon	N/D	20	6.1
10	12853	6-ton	Pig Iron Wagon	N/D	1,412	6.9
11	58993	8-ton	Coke Wagon, adaptation to standard mineral wagon	46	150	6.5
12	38613	8-ton	Lime Wagon	25	40	9.26
13	3386	8-ton	Timber Wagon	N/D	335	8.11
14	35399	10-ton	Stone Wagon	N/D	171	8.17
15	9367	8-ton	Ballast Wagon	N/D	254	17.10
16	8006	10-ton	Flat Wagon	N/D	12	15.12
17	12	12-ton	Flat Wagon	N/D	2	15.10
18	9	15-ton	Flat Wagon	N/D	2	15.8
19	15	20-ton	Flat Wagon	N/D	5	15.9
20	54	16-ton	Heavy Weight Wagon	49	4	15.15
21	27	10-ton	Furniture Van Wagon	31	10	12.1
22	39	30 cwt	Runner	N/D	8	15.11
23	??	25-ton	Rail Wagon – special class	13	6	8.2
24	37414	15-ton	Rail Wagon	N/D	610	8.1
25	40677	8-ton	Swivel Wagon, coupled to 37663, 37639 (no diagram)	14	2,167	8.10
26	43640/1	16-ton	Twin Wagons, McIntosh brake	47	950	8.15
27	6526	15-ton	Locomotive Wagon	19	10	15.2
28	3	15-ton	Well Wagon, loaded with propeller	18	1	15.5
29	43	15-ton	Glass Well Wagon	38	2	15.1
30	40563	N/A	2,100 gallon Tank Wagon	32	* 83	17.18
31	2	35-ton	Trolley	33	1	13.2
32	4	25-ton	Trolley	20	1	13.4
34	18	25-ton	Boiler Wagon	28	1	15.3
35	22	25-ton	Boiler and Machinery Wagon	31	2	15.7
36	1	20-ton	Trolley	34	1	13.1
37	41	20-ton	Trolley	42	2	13.6/7
38	19	16-ton	Boiler and Machinery Wagon	27	3	15.6
39	53	30-ton	Heavy Weight Wagon	43	5	14.6
40	1704	3-ton	Empty Barrel Wagon	12	55	
41	2408		Large Cattle Wagon	N/D	* 890	11.3
42	4507	8-ton	Fish Truck	15	159	4.7
43	1614		Open Fish or Milk Truck	N/D	129	10.17
44	5126	6-ton	Covered Goods Van	N/D	* 1,733	9.16
45	3046	6-ton	Covered Goods Van, modified for meat traffic	3	* 1,733	10.8

Photo No.	Wagon No.	Load	Description	Diag. No.	Total Stock	Plate
46	798(?4)		Dead Meat Van	N/D	121	10.1
47	8		Horse Box	8	160	11.10
48	53 or 66		Special Cattle Box	40	2	11.6
49	1618	3-ton	Open Carriage Truck	N/D	31	12.2
50	28		Covered Carriage Truck	11A	40	12.3
51	13		Covered Milk Truck	29	66	10.10
52	2	5-ton	Powder Van	N/D	2	15.16
53	18	6-ton	Powder Van	4	27	
54	383	14-ton	Goods or Mineral Brake Van 'Bonnybridge Branch'	6	* 530	16.5
55	308	14-ton	Goods or Mineral Brake Van 'Buchanan St. Goods'	N/D	* 530	16.3

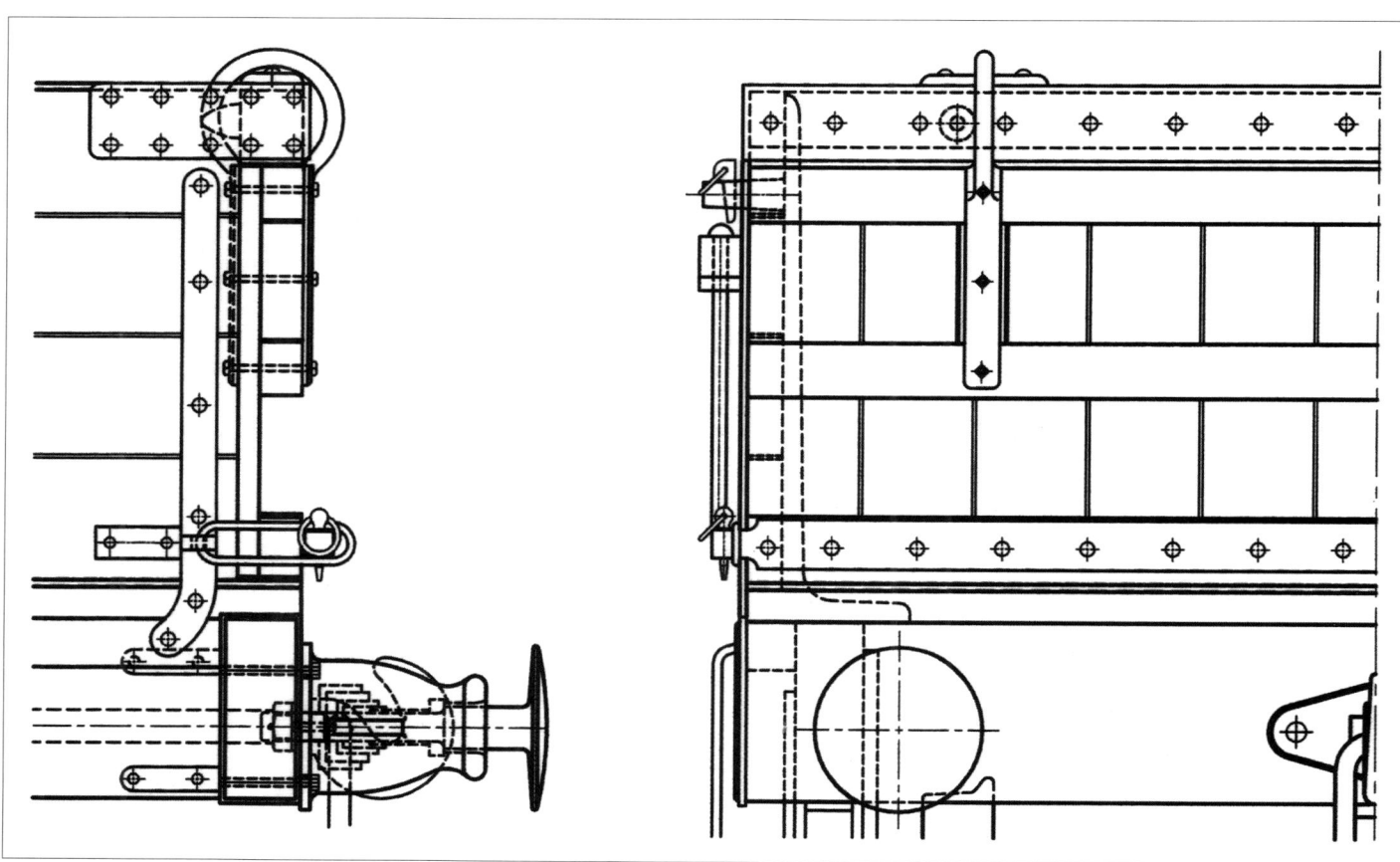

Mineral Wagon End Doors
Figure App.VII.1
Heavily framed end doors hinged on iron hoops were typical of Caledonian and North British Railway mineral wagons from the early days through to the first version of the 16-ton wagons built in the early 1900s. The crossbeam over which the hinges turned strengthened the body at a vulnerable point. The drawing alongside shows the arrangement on a Diagram 22 wagon which had been upgraded with sprung buffers. The sides of 8-ton wagons were cut back to accommodate the door which was the full width of the body, and the end of the floor was visible on top of the headstock.

Appendix VII: Information for the Modeller

A series of drawings has been produced for the Caledonian Railway Association by John Boyle and Ronnie Cockburn. They are at 7mm to 1ft, copied from original drawings and/or photographs and supplied as an aid to modellers. Copies can be purchased from CRA Sales Officer, CRA Archive ref: 3/4/1/23. There are other drawings in the series, but they are not of Caledonian Railway rolling stock. The full list is to be found at the Archive reference.

The date is that when the design was first built. The right-hand column gives the corresponding St. Rollox drawing number. An asterisk indicates a Metropolitan C&W Co. drawing reference number in the Birmingham City Archive.

Archive No.	Title/Description/Notes	Diag. No.	Date	SRX Drg
33	Agricultural Implement Wagon, 15-ton	117	1914	17175
48	Agricultural Implement Wagon, 15-ton	93	1909	14867
27	Boiler Wagon, 16-ton	26	1891	6534
29	Boiler Wagon, 25-ton, 6-wheel	28	1891	6533
10	Brake Van, 13-ton Drummond, boarded version 'Bonnybridge Branch'	6	1883	4938
21	Brake Van, 13-ton Drummond, panelled version 'Livestock St. Rollox'	6	1883	4938
12	Brake Van, 14-ton	45	1898	6695
11	Brake Van, originally to Metropolitan C&W Co. drawing 2313 (1870)	N/D	1873	1448
22	Brake Van, outside frame	N/D	1875	2313*
20	C&O Road Van, 4-wheel	104	1912	16522
9	C&O Road Van, 6-wheel	91	1908	14496
14	Cattle Van	N/D	1870	2315*
3	Cattle Van, 9-foot wheelbase	N/D	1876	2035
5	Coke Wagon, adapted from sprung buffered mineral wagon – the St. Rollox drawing number is for the similar modification to a Diagram 21 loco coal wagon	46	Pre 1900	15685
34	Covered Fish and Fowl Truck, 3-ton on old carriage underframe	29	1891	6745
49	Covered Goods Van, 15-ton, 6-wheel, sliding doors	115	1914	17202
35	Covered Milk Truck, 6-ton, 6-wheel	29	1894	6745
7	Dummy Van, 10-foot wheelbase	N/D	1877	2307*
31	Empty Barrel Truck, 3-ton, 13-foot wheelbase, old carriage underframe	12	1885	7391
32	Empty Barrel Truck, 3-ton, 14-foot wheelbase, old carriage underframe	12	1885	7391
18	Goods Van, 6-ton, panelled body	3	1885	3589
8	Gunpowder Van, 9-foot wheelbase	4	1889	6132
2	Horse Box, 8-foot wheelbase	9	1885	3653
13	Horse Box, 9-foot wheelbase. Early design with two dog boxes	N/D	1860	476
23	Horse Box, dual braked	8	1893	7124
4	Lime Wagon, dumb buffer	25	1886	4760
37	Machinery Wagon, 15-ton	17	1887	5531
28	Machinery Wagon, 16-ton	27	1891	6534
30	Machinery Wagon, 25-ton, 6-wheel	31	1891	6533
47	Mineral Wagon, 8-ton, 7-foot 9-inch wheelbase, fitted with self-contained buffers	22	1903	12972
50	Mineral Wagon, 8-ton, 8-foot 6-inch wheelbase	46	1894	8909
15	Mineral Wagon, 8-ton, solid buffer 'Hamilton Section'	22	1895	3368
17	Mineral Wagon, 8-ton, solid buffer 'Carfin & Cleland Section'	22	1896	3368
25	Steam Breakdown Crane, 20-ton built by Craven Bros	N/D	1907	none
26	Tank Wagon, 2100 gallons	32	1891	6823
51	Tender for 'Pug' Engines, converted from mineral wagon	N/D		none
36	Tube Wagon, 16-ton	114	1913	16938
38	Well Wagon, 15-ton	18	1883	3506

'Caley Coaches' Drawings

The drawings below are by Caledonian Railway Association member Jim Smellie, who markets kits and components for locomotives, coaches, NPCS and wagons under the name *'Caley Coaches.'* The drawings, which are derived from the St. Rollox general arrangements, form part of the kit instructions and may be downloaded from the website www.caleycoaches.co.uk

Kit No.	Title/Description/Notes	Diag. No.	Date	SRX Drg
CC17	6-wheel Covered Carriage Truck	101	1912	16259
CC18	6-wheel Fish Van	116	1914	17254
CC19	28-foot 6-wheel Meat van	102	1912	16390
CC20	15-ton 4-wheel Goods Brake Van	62	1903	11867
CC25	20-ton 6-wheel Goods Brake Van – one prototype built in 1903	63	1907	12063

Drawings and Illustrations of Components

The drawings in this Appendix, prepared from official sources by CRA member Angus McIntosh, supplement those in Chapter 2. They depict aspects of CR wagon practice and variations from the usual, and along with the accompanying enlargements from photographs are included as examples of the 'Caledonian signature' on rolling stock.

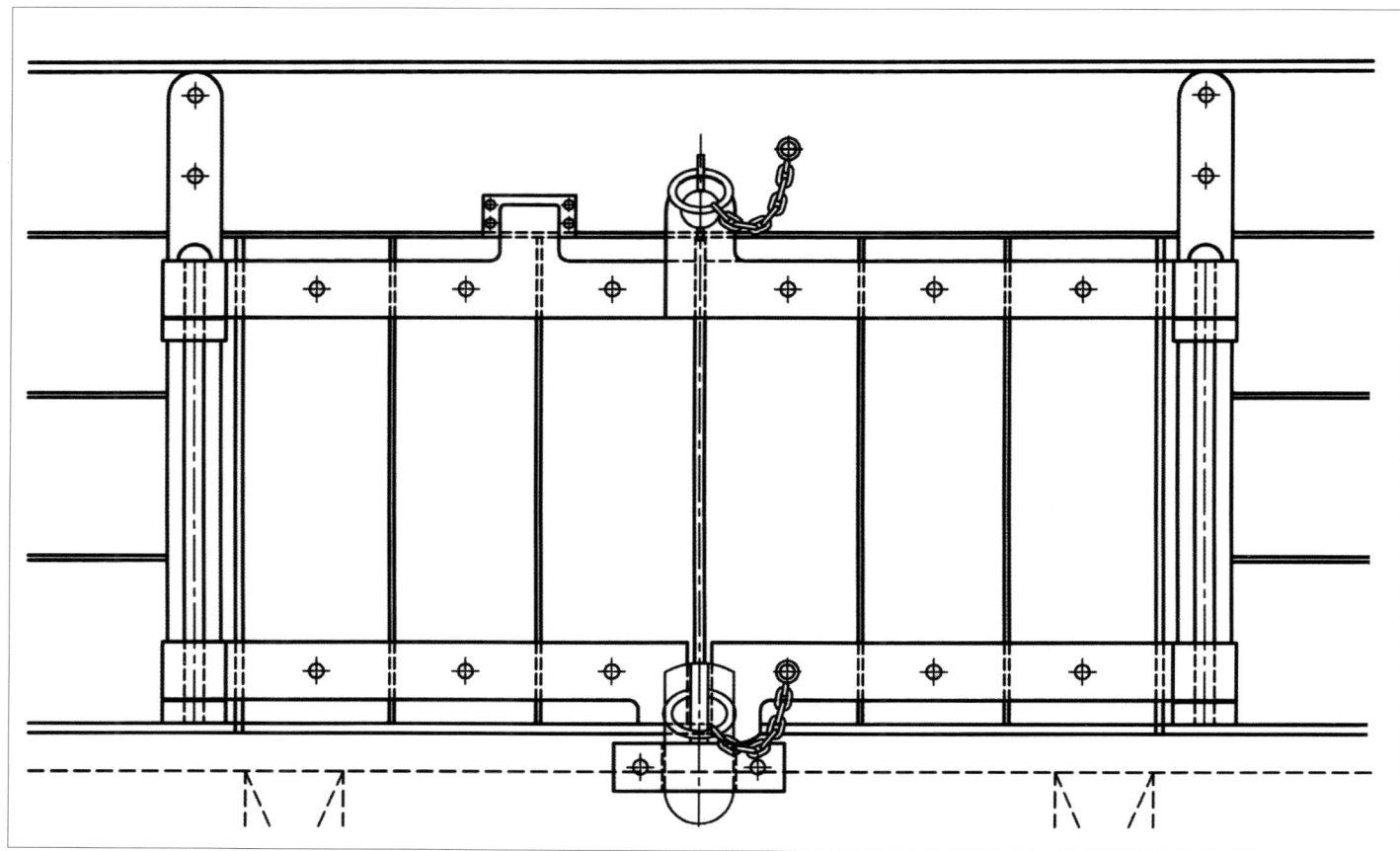

Mineral Wagon Side Doors
Above: Figure App.VII.2
The Caley used 'cupboard' i.e. side-opening doors on mineral wagons. The width of the door opening was established with the Diagram 22 wagons at 4 feet 1 inch wide. The Diagram 46 wagons and their successors retained this measurement. The height of the opening was governed by the space available between the floor and the continuous top plank of the body. The exception to this rule was the Diagram 52 design, which retained the Diagram 46 opening even though the sides were extended in height by one plank. This example shows vertically planked doors, which were common on private traders' wagons. On the Caley, the door planks usually followed the main body planking, so that, on the face of it, the middle plank was unsupported. In fact, the doors were double-skinned. The inside skin was made of vertical planks of oak 1 inch thick, screwed to the outside horizontal boards.

EARLY AXLE GUARDS
ABOVE: Plates App.VII.1, App.VII.2 and App.VII.3:
Originally the axle guards were bolted to the outer face of the solebar, with the spring behind the w-iron. There were three patterns, as seen here. The bridle retaining the axlebox could be either straight or curved.

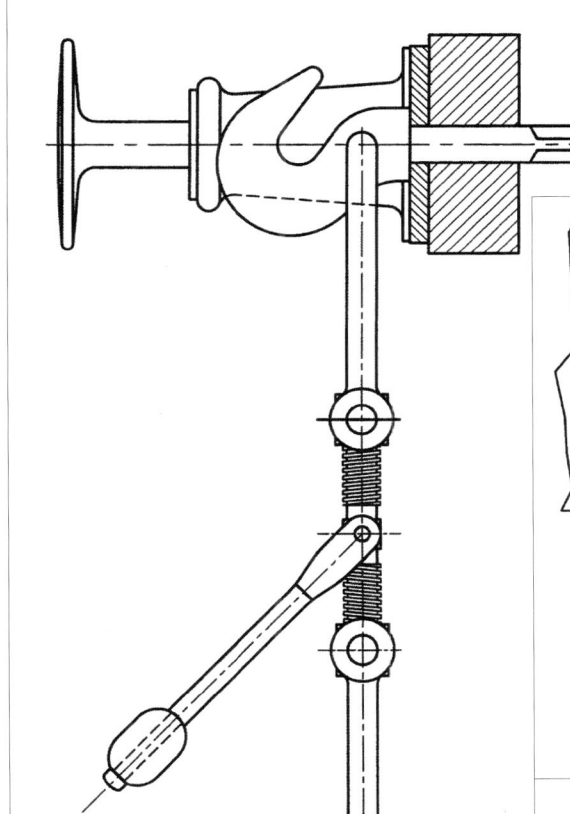

DRAWGEAR
Left: Figure App.VII.3
Some types of wagon were fitted with screw couplings. The tommy bar was hinged. The bob weight on the end of the tommy bar was normally elongated; other railway companies' were usually circular. Apart from continuous brake-fitted vehicles, where they were the norm, these couplings were fitted to cattle wagons and empty barrel trucks to reduce jolting. Swivel wagons and runners used them to create rigid units when carrying long loads.

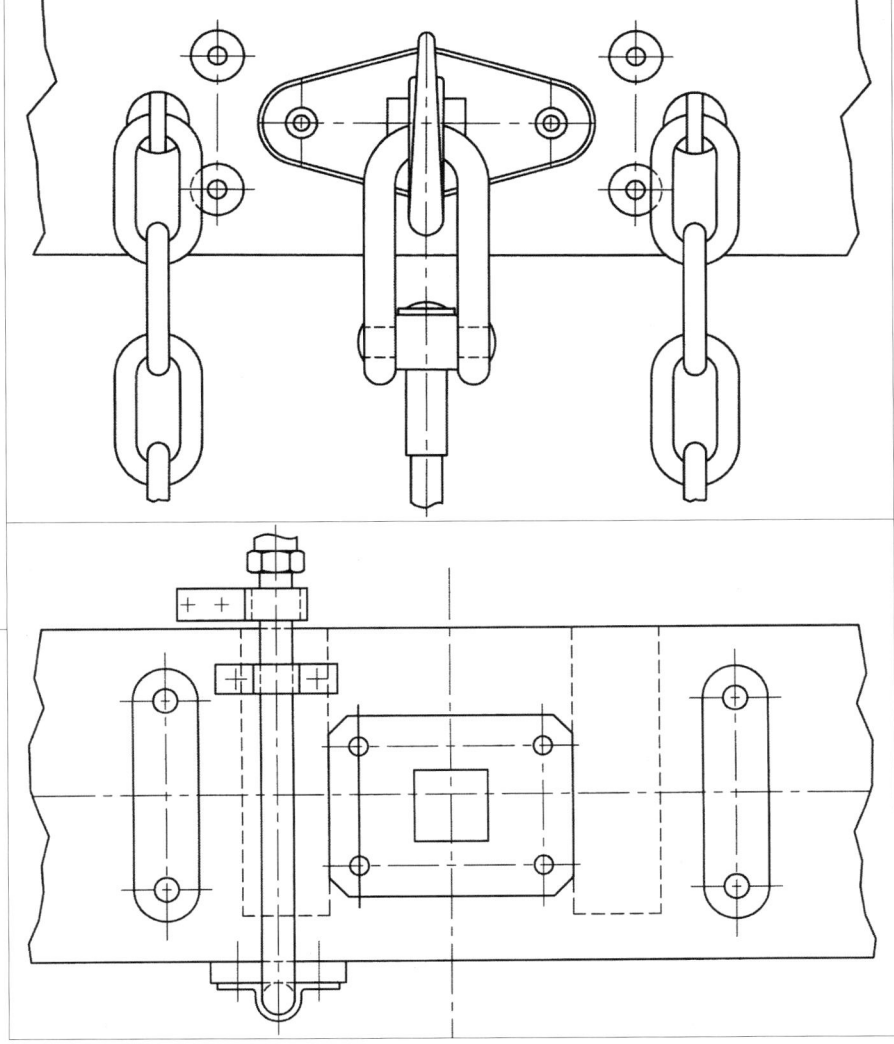

RIGHT: Figures App.VII.4 and App.VII.5
Side chains were fitted to some passenger-rated rolling stock, such as fish and game trucks. This practice continued into the early years of the twentieth century. Their position is shown in this drawing, which also shows the early pattern drawbar plate. On wooden framed wagons this was originally lozenge shaped and fixed by two bolts. Some time around 1900 this was changed to a rectangular plate 10 inches by 7½ inches with corners cut at 45° and a 4-bolt fixing, as in Figure App.VII.5 (*bottom*). Metal underframe wagons seem to have had the rectangular plate from the outset.

Brake Safety Hangers
Right: Plate App.VII.4
When brakes operating both wheels were introduced, safety loops were fitted to prevent the push rods from fouling the track in the event of breakage. Starting with the McIntosh patent brake, the loop used by the Caley consisted of a flat metal bar in the shape of a reversed letter 'J'. It was also fitted for a number of years to wagons fitted with Morton double brake gear, until superseded by the hanger made of flat bar that was used by most other companies.

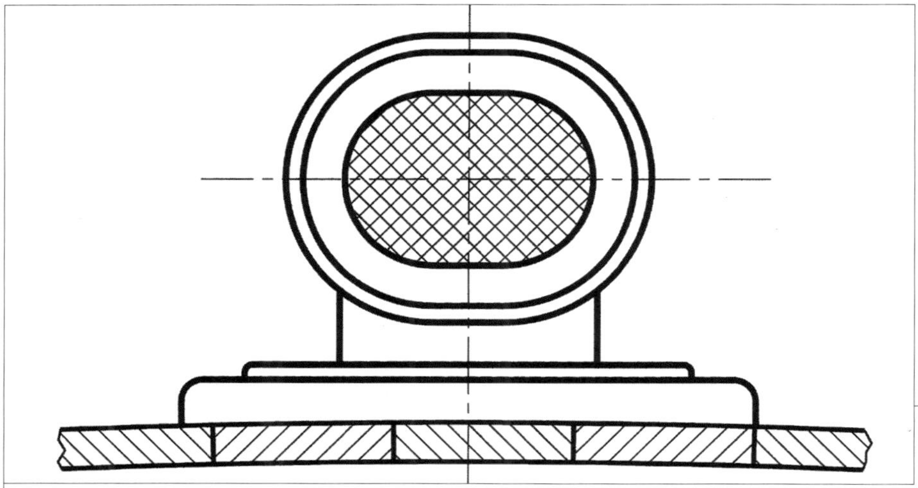

Roof Ventilator
Left and Below: Figures App.VII.6 and App.VII.6A
The ventilator fitted to vans and horse boxes was unique to the Caledonian. It consisted of two trumpet-shaped castings facing fore and aft, on a circular base. The overall length was 2 feet and the base was 1 foot in diameter.

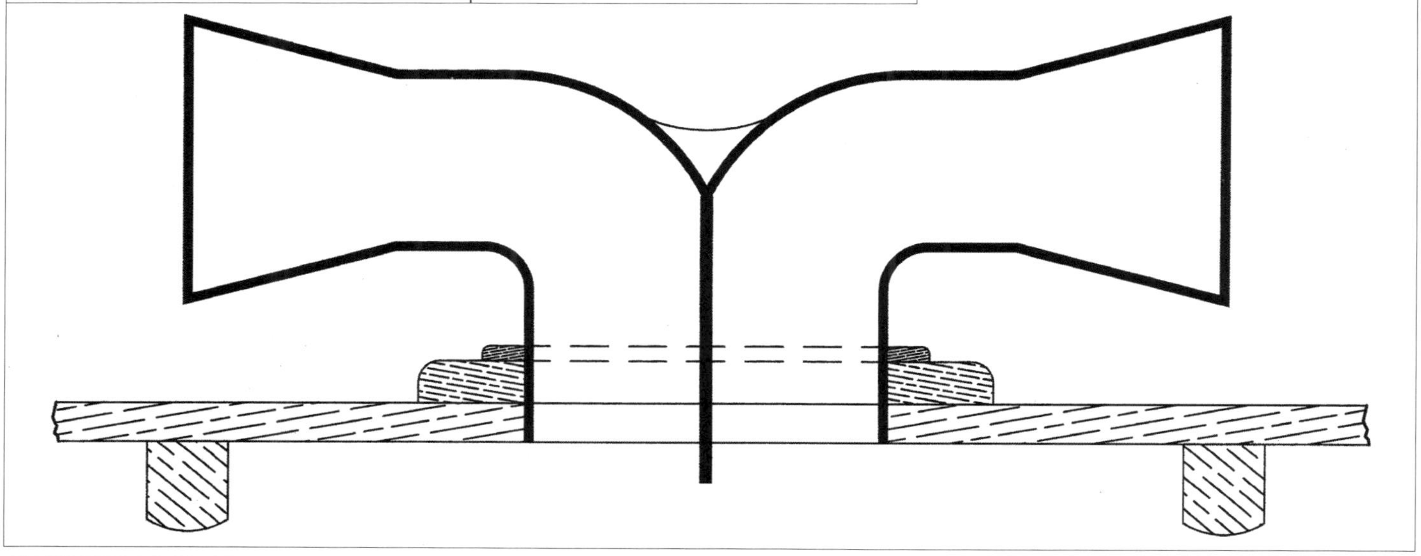

Horse Hook
Plates App.VII.5, App.VII.6 and App.VII.7
A 'horse-hook' was fitted to sprung buffered goods wagons for rope shunting. Most hard-buffered wagons seem not to have had one fitted. Those that did were fitted with the type shown in Plate App.VII.5 (*left*). The most common pattern for sprung buffered wagons consisted of a round section metal staple with flattened ends, attached to the bottom two bolts that held the left-hand crown plate on either side of the wagon – see Plate App.VII.6 (*centre*). Mineral and goods wagons with wood underframes were fitted with the hook, but many photographs show wagons built on steel underframes without them. Diagram 67 vans and some open wagons were fitted with a hook which was the same as that fitted to many wagons on the North British Railway; its flattened centre was attached to the solebar and a hook was formed at either end. It can be seen in Plate App.VII.7 (*right*).

INDEX

brake vans
   ballast/permanent way, 268-9, 276
   breakdown, 275-277, 279
   Callander & Oban, 256
   combination goods, 251, 253
   Engineer's Department, 281-282
   four-wheeled, 243-251, 253
   open brake wagons, 252-253
   six-wheeled, 254-256
builder/capacity plates (CR), 68, 70
builder's plates (contractor), 12

Caledonian Railway wagon types
   agricultural implement, 234-235
   ballast, 264-268
   bogie coal and iron ore, 92-99, 150-151, 261
   brake van, ballast, 268-269
   brake van, goods and mineral, 243-256
   breakdown catering and dormitory vehicles, 277, 280
   breakdown, emergency and tool van, 275-277, 279-281
   breakdown train, 283-284
   carriage truck, open, 199-202
   carriage truck, covered, 203-206
   cattle, 183-190
   coke, 110-112, 183-184, 190
   empty barrel truck, 163-164
   fish, fruit and milk, 78, 173-182
   flat wagon, bogie, 222-223
   flat wagon, four-wheeled, 236-238
   gas tank, 270-272
   glass and well, bogie, 221-222
   glass well, four-wheeled, 229
   goods, covered, 151-162
   goods, open, 142-151
   gun set, 226-228
   gunpowder, 64-65, 240-242
   heavy weight and ingot, bogie, 224-226
   heavy weight, four-wheeled, 239-240
   hopper, bogie, 112
   hopper, four-wheeled, 106-109
   horse box, 192-198
   lime, 161-162
   loco coal and ash, 88, 257-261
   locomotive and boiler, 230-232
   machinery, 232-235
   meat van, 166-173
   mineral, four-wheeled, 82, 84-91, 99-105
   pig iron, 63, 113-116
   rail, bogie, 219-220
   rail, four- and six-wheeled, 124-129
   road van, 164-165
   runner, breakdown crane, 275, 278
   runner, special class, 236-238
   scenery truck, 207-208
   sheep and other livestock, 190-192
   stone, 141
   stores van, 281, 283, 284
   swivel bar, bogie, 220-221
   swivel bar, four-wheeled, 239-240
   swivel timber, 130-136
   tank wagon, 273-274
   trolly, 209-217
   tube, 129-130
   twin, 137-140
   warflat, 227-228
   weighing machine van, 284
Callander & Oban Railway
   brake van designs, 256
cast number plates on wagons
   location, 68-69
   styles, 67-68, 69
commercial influences, 16-26
continuous brakes, 40

depreciation policy, 31-32
   attempt to change policy, 31
   dispute with government, 31-32
   fixed replacement fund, 31-32
   wartime difficulties, 31

goods and marshalling yards, 20-25

Lanarkshire & Dumbartonshire Railway, 20, 24-26
letters and numbers, goods
   additional numbers, 54-55, 64-66
   brake vans, 50, 64
   changes in location, 59-61
   evolution of letter shape, 55-58
   for specific sections, 61-62
   for specific traffic, 62-63
   gunpowder vans, 64-65
   loco coal, 63, 88, 99
   relationship with loco and coach lettering, 52-53
   script style, 51-53
   size and shape variation, 53-57, 66
   specification on drawings, 53-55, 58
   tare and load letters, 58
letters and numbers, NPCS
   location, 79
   other markings, 79
   special lettering on vans, 79-81
   styles, plain and shaded, 79
livery, goods, general
   all-metal wagons, 48-49
   buffers, 46-49
   contemporary references, 47
   official specifications, 47-48
   open goods interiors, 49
   red oxide composition, 48
   wooden wagons, 47-48

This photograph of Carnwath goods yard shows mineral wagons being unloaded. Nobody seems to mind the extra labour involved in emptying coal onto the ground before loading it into carts. Perhaps the fear of being charged demurrage was the incentive. The loads are of different grades of coal, which was cause for complaint by the CR and other railways, as discussed on p. 118.

   The first wagon visible is to Diagram 59, to the original design with two hoop hinges to the end door. The side cupboard doors are open. There is an extra number over the side doors, which is larger than specified in drawing 11938 (p. 54). The number on the fixed end is obscured by the wagon in front of it. Next come two Diagram 46 minerals. The smaller dimensions of these wagons compared with the twentieth-century Diagram 59 is very apparent.

   Further back is a 7-ton 'bogie' and two more Diagram 46 wagons, with a Diagram 59 between them. This wagon has the later end door arrangement with three hooped hinges. The brake van cannot be positively identified, but it looks like one of the pre-diagram book vans illustrated on p. 243.

livery, goods, specific vehicles
  ballast brakes, 50
  'bogies' in Engineer's Dept. service, 267
  brake vans, 50
  continuous brake fitted, 49
  gunpowder vans, 49
  meat vans, 49
  wagons sold out of service, 99
livery, NPCS, general
  Carriage Register descriptions, 74
  early, 73
  full passenger, 77-78
  interiors, 75
  ironwork and underframes, 74
  later (post 1900) livery, 74
  lining, 73-74
  L&NWR practice changes, 74
  louvres and ventilators, 73-74
  roofs, 74
  standard (to 1900) livery, 73
livery, NPCS, specific vehicles
  carriage and scenery trucks, 76
  livestock, 75
  fish, fruit and milk vans, 76
  meat vans, 75-76

mineral wagons
  description and capacities, 83-84
mineral wagons – four-wheeled
  'bogies' post 1900, 99-100, 112, 262-263, 267
  coke traffic modifications, 110-112
  development 1883-1899, 88-91
  development post 1900, 99-105
  Diagram 22 upgrade, 100-101
  early 'bogies', 82-87
  hopper wagons, 106-109
  pig iron, 113-116
mineral wagons – high capacity
  1899-1901 experiments, 92-95
  1902/3 designs, 95-97, 99

30-ton wagon advantages, 98
50-ton iron ore wagon, 92-93
eventual use on CR, 97, 150-151, 261
infrastructure constraints, 21, 97-98
other railways' designs, 98
payload considerations, 93, 98

numbering, NPCS
  1874 census numbers, 81
  carriage, fish & milk, 81
  gas tank, 81, 272
  horse box, 81
  in goods wagon series, 178, 180, 205-6
  luggage and brake van, 81
  renumbering by LM&SR, 81
numbering, wagon
  allocation within series, 69
  anomalies in allocation, 14, 71
  brake vans, 72
  departmental stock, 72, 263
  ordinary service stock, 69-70
  renumbering by LM&SR, 71-72
  revenue and capital, 71-72
  service vehicles, 72
  special class series, 71-72
  thirled wagons, 121-122

patent brakes, 38-41
Portpatrick Railway
  open wagon, 144
  wagons absorbed 1865, 285
private traders' wagons
  attempts to eliminate, 118-120
  CR recommended designs, 120-121
  disadvantages for CR, 117-118
  number on the CR system, 119-120
  RCH specifications, 117
  registration plates, 117, 120
  tank wagons and frames, 122-124
  thirling agreements, 121-122
  thirled wagon numbers, 121-122

'pug tenders', 261, 263

St. Rollox works
  diagram book, 7, 10
  drawing registers, 10-11
  inadequate capacity, 33
  order numbers, 10, 287-298
  surviving drawings, 11, 305-312
Scottish Central Railway
  cattle traffic, 183
  horse box, 192
  wagons absorbed 1866, 29
Scottish North Eastern Railway
  wagons absorbed 1867, 29
sources of information
  archives, 8, 13
  Caledonian Railway, 6, 9-12
  contractors, 12-14
  technical and enthusiast's press, 15-16
steam heating pipes, 40

wagon renewal programme, 31, 34
wagon technical development
  brakes, 38-41
  buffers and drawgear, 41-45, 139, 317
  Drummond revolution, 33
  early stagnation, 33
  modernisation from 1900, 33-34
  running gear, 34-38, 317
wagons, numbers in service
  1870-1905, trends, 29-30
  1874, census, 29, 285
  1900, fleet size, 30, 313-314
  1907-1910, changes, 30-31, 286
  1922, 32
  handed over to LM&SR, 32
West Coast Joint Stock
  conversions of old stock, 277, 280
  goods brake van, 253
  fish van, 181
  meat van, 172

Loaded mineral wagons passing through Almondbank. Despite the evidence on the painted panel, the village name was all one word, as it was in the CR *1907 Working Timetable*. From left to right the wagons are as follows: a Diagram 22 solid buffer mineral, a 'bogie' with no side doors, a Diagram 22 rebuilt with sprung buffers, a solid buffer Diagram 22, and a 'bogie' with offset doors. The next wagon is a Diagram 46 mineral, followed by four 'bogies,' three with centrally located doors and one offset. Another Diagram 46 completes the picture. All the wagons have 12-inch letters, some freshly painted.

In the goods yard nearest the camera is a Diagram 24 open goods wagon with centre door and a falling side Diagram 15 wagon behind it. The trader's wagon in the background belongs to David McEwen who was based at Almondbank, according to *Leslie's 1911/12 Perthshire Directory*. McEwen does not appear among the traders listed in the CR *1904 Mineral Timetable*.

Finally, by the scotch derrick, is a timber carrier, as seen in the picture of Buchanan Street on p. 28. In this case the two parts of the carrier, which were adjustable to suit the load, have been disassembled.